매일

고**2**

3 단계로 푸는

영어독해

전국연합
학력평가 **기출**

시간은 없고 과목은 많은 통합 수능! 절대평가인 영어부터 끝내는 것이 최적의 전략입니다.

수능 기본 단어부터 필수 구문과 유형별 독해 Tip까지, <매3영 고2>로 단 2주에 완벽 정리하세요!

• 수능 영어에 대한 근거 있는 자신감을 키워주는 책

• 수능+내신 필수 단어/구문을 끝내주는 책

• 친절한 해설로 독학 영어의 길잡이가 되어주는 책

고등 영어 마스터, <매3영>이라면 가능합니다!

KB082397

체계적인 **3단계** 학습으로
내신·학력평가 동시대비

구성과 특징

 **STEP 1**

모든 영어 공부의 시작은 단어!
수능 필수 단어 & 어구 익히기

❶ 수능 필수 단어 LIST

문제 풀이에 앞서 지문 속 필수 어휘를
완벽하게 정리할 수 있습니다.

❸ 단어 SELF-TEST

암기한 단어를 확인해 보고, 놓친 단어는
그 자리에서 바로 정리할 수 있습니다.

DAY 01

주제 추론

A

STEP 1 • 수능에 진짜 나오는 단어

✓ 문제에 나오는 단어들을 확인하세요.

시간이 없다면 색으로 표시된 단어만이라도 꼭 외우고 넘어가세요!

01	trunk	n. (나무의) 줄기	the (✓ trunk) of a tree / 나무의 줄기
02	reveal	v. 밝혀내다, 드러내다	( ) the secrets / 비밀을 밝혀내다
03	emerge	v. 나오다, 생겨나다, 출현하다	( ) from a common core / 공통의 핵심에서 나오다
04	stem from	~에서 비롯되다	challenges that ( ) ( ) adversity / 역경에서 비롯되는 도전 과제들
05	practitioner	n. 실무자	( )s in different fields / 다양한 분야의 실무자
06	discover	v. 발견하다	( ) links between their activities / 활동 간의 연결고리를 발견하다
07	term	n. 용어	employ the same ( )s across the curriculum / 교육과정 전반에 걸쳐 같은 용어를 사용하다
08	abstract	v. 추상화하다, 요약하다	work on ( )ing in drawing class / 그림 그리기 수업에서 추상을 연습하다
09	disciplinary	a. 학문의	( ) boundaries / 학문의 경계
10	transform	v. 바꾸다, 변모시키다	( ) their thoughts positively / 그들의 생각을 긍정적으로 바꾸다
11	universal	a. 보편적인	as part of a ( ) imagination / 보편적 상상력의 일부로

❂ 본문 문장 속에서 단어들을 확인해 보세요.

Education must focus on the trunk of the tree of knowledge. / revealing the ways / in which the branches, twigs, and leaves all emerge from a common core.

교육은 지식의 나무 줄기 / 에 초점을 맞추면서 / 방식을 밝혀야 한다 / 나뭇가지, 잔가지, 잎이 모두 공통의 핵심에서 나오는

9

단어 다시보기 문제를 풀기 전에 단어들을 **30초** 동안 다시 확인하세요.

01	trunk	✎ (나무의) 줄기	the trunk of a tree	나무의 줄기
02	reveal		reveal the secrets	비밀을 밝혀내다
03	emerge		emerge from a common core	공통의 핵심에서 나오다
04	stem from		challenges that stem from adversity	역경에서 비롯되는 도전 과제들
05	practitioner		practitioners in different fields	다양한 분야의 실무자
06	discover		discover links between their activities	활동 간의 연결고리를 발견하다
07	term		employ the same terms across the curriculum	교육과정 전반에 걸쳐 같은 용어를 사용하다
08	abstract		work on abstracting in drawing class	그림 그리기 수업에서 추상을 연습하다
09	disciplinary		disciplinary boundaries	학문의 경계
10	transform		transform their thoughts positively	그들의 생각을 긍정적으로 바꾸다
11	universal		as part of a universal imagination	보편적 상상력의 일부로

❂ 본문 문장 속에서 단어의 의미를 우리말로 해석해 보세요.

Education must focus on the trunk of the tree of knowledge. / revealing the ways / in which the branches, twigs, and leaves all emerge from a common core.

➜ 교육은 _____에 초점을 맞추면서 / _____ / 나뭇가지, 잔가지, 잎이 모두 _____

10

---

❷ 예문 확인 & 빈칸 채우기

지문에 실제로 쓰인 표현에서 단어의 용법을
확인하며 쉽게 암기할 수 있습니다.

❹ 문장 속 단어 CHECK

외운 단어를 문장 속에서 직접 해석해 보며
단어의 응용력을 기를 수 있습니다.

STEP 2

좋은 기출 문제도 풀어야 내 것!

문제 풀이 실전 훈련

❶ 시간 & 난이도 확인

유형 및 난이도에 따른 문제 풀이 제한 시간을 확인하고, 실전처럼 시간 안배를 연습할 수 있습니다.

❸ 종합 성적표 REVIEW

3일마다 종합 성적표를 작성해 보면서 나의 문제 풀이 습관을 돌아볼 수 있습니다.

❷ 매일 실전 훈련 연습

매일 유형별 문제풀이로 실전 감각을 기를 수 있습니다.

❹ 맞춤 솔루션 찾기

나의 문제 풀이 상황에 따라 맞춤 솔루션을 찾고, 앞으로의 학습 방향을 설계할 수 있습니다.

체계적인 **3단계** 학습으로
내신·학력평가 동시대비

구성과 특징

STEP 3
작은 단어, 구문도 놓치지 않는다!
첨삭 해설로 지문 복습하기

❶ 전 문장 직독직해

끊어읽기로 모든 문장을 직독직해 해보고
정확한 해석 능력을 기를 수 있습니다.

❸ 지문 속 단어 복습

STEP 1에서 외웠던 단어가 지문 속에
어떻게 활용되었는지 최종 확인하고,
암기 여부를 재점검할 수 있습니다.

❷ 구문 첨삭 해설

실제 수능에 자주 나오는 구문을 꼼꼼히
학습하고, 다음 문제 풀이에 적용할 수
있습니다.

❹ 구문 CHECK-UP

첨삭 해설로 학습한 구문 포인트를
어법 변형 문제로 한 번 더 정리할 수
있습니다.

기본기를 독해력으로 끌어올린다!

정답 및 해설

❶ 해석

직독직해로 읽은 의미를
매끄러운 말로 확인할 수 있습니다.

❸ 상세 오답 풀이

선택지 함정과 오답의 근거를
자세히 설명해주는 오답 풀이를 통해
나의 약점을 보완할 수 있습니다.

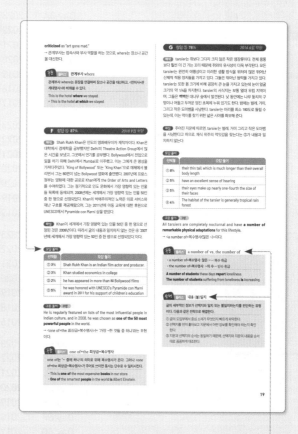

❷ 해설

근거 중심의 자세한 해설로
정답 도출의 과정을 확인할 수 있습니다.

❹ 구문플러스 & 유형플러스

필수 구문/어법 사항, 유형별 주의 사항을
추가로 확인하며 실전력을 기를 수 있습니다.

Contents

14일 만에 완성하는 내신과 학력평가 등급 **up** 프로그램
좋은 기출 문제와 기본기가 튼튼해지는 영어 공부법의 만남

최신 7개년 고2 전국연합 학력평가 기출문제
● 독해 유형별 훈련 시스템 ● 모든 지문 문장별 첨삭 해설

공부한 날	단원			페이지	학습일
Day 8	빈칸 추론 Ⅰ	Day 8A Day 8B Day 8C Day 8D Day 8E Day 8F Day 8G	2023년 학평 2022년 학평 2021년 학평 2020년 학평 2019년 학평 2018년 학평 2017년 학평	p.209	___월 ___일
Day 9	빈칸 추론 Ⅱ	Day 9A Day 9B Day 9C Day 9D Day 9E Day 9F Day 9G	2023년 학평 2022년 학평 2021년 학평 2020년 학평 2019년 학평 2018년 학평 2017년 학평	p.237	___월 ___일
Day 10	무관한 문장 찾기	Day 10A Day 10B Day 10C Day 10D Day 10E Day 10F Day 10G	2023년 학평 2022년 학평 2021년 학평 2020년 학평 2019년 학평 2018년 학평 2017년 학평	p.267	___월 ___일
Day 11	주어진 문장 넣기	Day 11A Day 11B Day 11C Day 11D Day 11E Day 11F Day 11G	2023년 학평 2022년 학평 2021년 학평 2020년 학평 2019년 학평 2017년 학평 2016년 학평	p.295	___월 ___일
Day 12	글의 순서 배열	Day 12A Day 12B Day 12C Day 12D Day 12E Day 12F Day 12G	2023년 학평 2022년 학평 2021년 학평 2020년 학평 2019년 학평 2018년 학평 2016년 학평	p.323	___월 ___일
Day 13	요약문 완성	Day 13A Day 13B Day 13C Day 13D Day 13E Day 13F Day 13G	2023년 학평 2022년 학평 2021년 학평 2020년 학평 2019년 학평 2018년 학평 2017년 학평	p.353	___월 ___일
Day 14	장문의 이해	Day 14A Day 14B Day 14C Day 14D Day 14E Day 14F Day 14G	2023년 학평 2022년 학평 2021년 학평 2020년 학평 2019년 학평 2018년 학평 2017년 학평	p.381	___월 ___일

<매3영>이 제시하는 3단계로

유형 3일 훈련

DAY

01~03

공부한 날			출처	페이지
DAY 1	월	일	학력평가 기출 2023년 학력평가 기출 2022년 학력평가 기출 2021년 학력평가 기출 2020년 학력평가 기출 2019년 학력평가 기출 2018년 학력평가 기출 2017년	9
DAY 2	월	일	학력평가 기출 2023년 학력평가 기출 2022년 학력평가 기출 2021년 학력평가 기출 2020년 학력평가 기출 2019년 학력평가 기출 2018년 학력평가 기출 2017년	37
DAY 3	월	일	학력평가 기출 2023년 학력평가 기출 2022년 학력평가 기출 2021년 학력평가 기출 2020년 학력평가 기출 2019년 학력평가 기출 2018년 학력평가 기출 2017년	65

STEP 1 • 수능에 *진짜* 나오는 *단어*

✔ 문제에 나오는 단어들을 확인하세요.

시간이 없다면 색으로 표시된 단어만이라도 꼭 외우고 넘어가세요!

01	trunk	*n.* (나무의) 줄기	the (✔ trunk) of a tree	나무의 줄기
02	reveal	*v.* 밝히다, 드러내다	( ) the secrets	비밀을 밝히다
03	emerge	*v.* 나오다, 생겨나다, 출현하다	( ) from a common core	공통의 핵심에서 나오다
04	stem from	~에서 비롯되다	challenges that ( ) ( ) adversity	역경에서 비롯되는 도전 과제들
05	practitioner	*n.* 실무자	( )s in different fields	다양한 분야의 실무자
06	discover	*v.* 발견하다	( ) links between their activities	활동 간의 연결고리를 발견하다
07	term	*n.* 용어	employ the same ( )s across the curriculum	교육과정 전반에 걸쳐 같은 용어를 사용하다
08	abstract	*v.* 추상화하다, 요약하다	work on ( )ing in drawing class	그림 그리기 수업에서 추상을 연습하다
09	disciplinary	*a.* 학문의	( ) boundaries	학문의 경계
10	transform	*v.* 바꾸다, 변모시키다	( ) their thoughts positively	그들의 생각을 긍정적으로 바꾸다
11	universal	*a.* 보편적인	as part of a ( ) imagination	보편적 상상력의 일부로

⊕ 본문 문장 속에서 단어들을 확인해 보세요.

Education must focus on the trunk of the tree of knowledge, / revealing the ways / in which the branches, twigs, and leaves all emerge from a common core.

교육은 지식의 나무 줄기에 초점을 맞추면서, / 방식을 밝혀야 한다 / 나뭇가지, 잔가지, 잎이 모두 공통의 핵심에서 나오는.

01	trunk	✏️ (나무의) 줄기	the trunk of a tree	나무의 줄기
02	reveal		reveal the secrets	비밀을 밝히다
03	emerge		emerge from a common core	공통의 핵심에서 나오다
04	stem from		challenges that stem from adversity	역경에서 비롯되는 도전 과제들
05	practitioner		practitioners in different fields	다양한 분야의 실무자
06	discover		discover links between their activities	활동 간의 연결고리를 발견하다
07	term		employ the same terms across the curriculum	교육과정 전반에 걸쳐 같은 용어를 사용하다
08	abstract		work on abstracting in drawing class	그림 그리기 수업에서 추상을 연습하다
09	disciplinary		disciplinary boundaries	학문의 경계
10	transform		transform their thoughts positively	그들의 생각을 긍정적으로 바꾸다
11	universal		as part of a universal imagination	보편적 상상력의 일부로

➕ 본문 문장 속에서 단어의 의미를 우리말로 해석해 보세요.

Education must focus on the trunk of the tree of knowledge, / revealing the ways / in which the branches, twigs, and leaves all emerge from a common core.

➡️ 교육은 ＿＿＿＿＿＿＿＿＿＿에 초점을 맞추면서, / ＿＿＿＿＿＿＿＿＿＿＿＿＿＿ / 나뭇가지, 잔가지, 잎이 모두 ＿＿＿＿＿＿＿＿＿＿ ＿＿＿＿＿＿＿＿＿＿.

STEP 2 • 수능 기출 제대로 풀기

A 다음 글의 주제로 가장 적절한 것은?

Education must focus on the trunk of the tree of knowledge, revealing the ways in which the branches, twigs, and leaves all emerge from a common core. Tools for thinking stem from this core, providing a common language with which practitioners in different fields may share their experience of the process of innovation and discover links between their creative activities. When the same terms are employed across the curriculum, students begin to link different subjects and classes. If they practice abstracting in writing class, if they work on abstracting in painting or drawing class, and if, in all cases, they call it abstracting, they begin to understand how to think beyond disciplinary boundaries. They see how to transform their thoughts from one mode of conception and expression to another. Linking the disciplines comes naturally when the terms and tools are presented as part of a universal imagination.

① difficulties in finding meaningful links between disciplines

② drawbacks of applying a common language to various fields

③ effects of diversifying the curriculum on students' creativity

④ necessity of using a common language to integrate the curriculum

⑤ usefulness of turning abstract thoughts into concrete expressions

정답과 해설 p.2

STEP 3 • 수능 지문 제대로 복습하기

01 Education must focus on the trunk of the tree of knowledge, / revealing the ways / in which the branches, twigs, and leaves all emerge from a common core.
분사구문 | 선행사 | 전치사+관계대명사절

02 Tools for thinking stem from this core, / providing a common language / with which practitioners in different fields may share their experience of the process of innovation / and (may) discover links between their creative activities.
분사구문 | 선행사 | 전치사+관계대명사절 | 동사1 | 동사2

03 When the same terms are employed across the curriculum, / students begin to link different subjects and classes. // If they practice abstracting in writing class, / if they work on abstracting in painting or drawing class, / and if, in all cases, they call it abstracting, / they begin to understand / how to think beyond disciplinary boundaries. // They see how to transform their thoughts / from one mode of conception and expression to another.
practice+동명사: ~하는 것을 연습하다 | call A B: A를 B라고 부르다 | how+to부정사: ~할 방법 | from A to B: A부터 B로

04 Linking the disciplines comes naturally / when the terms and tools are presented / as part of a universal imagination.
주어(동명사구) | 동사(단수) | ~의 일부로

---

01 교육은 지식의 나무 줄기trunk에 초점을 맞추면서, / 방식을 밝혀야reveal 한다 / 나뭇가지, 잔가지, 잎이 모두 공통의 핵심에서 나오는emerge.

02 사고를 위한 도구는 이 핵심에서 비롯되어stem from, / 공통 언어를 제공한다 / 다양한 분야의 실무자practitioner들이 혁신 과정에 대한 경험을 공유하고 / 창의적 활동 사이의 연결 고리를 발견할discover 수 있는.

03 교육과정 전반에 걸쳐 동일한 용어term가 사용될 때, / 학생들은 서로 다른 과목들과 수업들을 연결하기 시작한다. // 그들이 글쓰기 수업에서 추상abstracting을 연습하고, / 회화나 그림 그리기 수업에서 추상을 연습하고, / 그리고 모든 경우에 그들이 이를 추상으로 일컫는다면, / 그들은 이해하기 시작한다 / 학문의disciplinary 경계를 넘어 사고하는 법을. // 그들은 자기 생각을 바꾸는transform 법을 알게 된다 / 하나의 개념과 표현 방식에서 다른 방식으로.

04 학문들을 연결하는 것은 자연스럽게 이루어진다 / 용어들과 도구들이 제시될 때 / 보편적universal 상상력의 일부로.

구문 Check up

① Education must focus on the trunk of the tree of knowledge, revealing the ways which / in which the branches, twigs, and leaves all emerge from a common core.

the ways를 수식하는 'the branches ~ emerge ~'가 완전한 절이므로, <전치사+관계대명사> 형태의 in which를 써야 한다.

② Linking the disciplines come / comes naturally when the terms and tools are presented as part of a universal imagination.

동명사구가 주어이므로 단수동사 comes를 써야 한다.

정답 ① in which ② comes

B

STEP 1 • 수능에 *진짜* 나오는 *단어*

✔ **문제에 나오는 단어들을 확인하세요.**

시간이 없다면 색으로 표시된 단어만이라도 꼭 외우고 넘어가세요!

01	well-meaning	a. 좋은 뜻에서(선의에서) 하는	the most (✔ well-meaning) advice	가장 좋은 뜻에서 하는 조언
02	match	v. 맞붙게 하다, 맞추다	( ) oneself with a new habit	새로운 습관에 자신을 맞추다
03	practice	n. 습관, 관행	the right ( ) for you	당신에게 맞는 습관
04	swear	v. 맹세하다, 확언하다	( ) that it is useful	이것이 유용하다고 확언하다
05	doubt	v. 의심하다	( ) his success	그의 성공을 의심하다
06	cautious	a. 주의하는	Be ( ).	주의하라.
07	work	v. 효과가 있다, 잘 되어가다	It ( )ed for him.	이것은 그에게 효과가 있었다.
08	beat up	두들겨 패다	Don't ( ) yourself ( ).	스스로를 자책하지 (때리지) 말라.
09	approach	n. 접근(법)	all of these ( )es	이 모든 접근법은
10	involve	v. 포함하다	The test ( )s difficult questions.	이 시험은 어려운 질문들을 포함한다.
11	guess	v. 추측하다	( ) the next step	다음 단계를 추측하다
12	chance	n. 우연, 운	guessing and ( )	추측과 우연
13	strive for	~를 위해 노력하다	( ) ( ) changes	변화를 위해 노력하다

⊕ **본문 문장 속에서 단어들을 확인해 보세요.**

All of these approaches involve guessing and chance.

이 모든 접근법은 추측과 우연을 포함한다.

01	well-meaning	✏️ 좋은 뜻에서 하는	the most well-meaning advice	가장 좋은 뜻에서 하는 조언
02	match		match oneself with a new habit	새로운 습관에 자신을 맞추다
03	practice		the right practice for you	당신에게 맞는 습관
04	swear		swear that it is useful	이것이 유용하다고 확언하다
05	doubt		doubt his success	그의 성공을 의심하다
06	cautious		Be cautious.	주의하라.
07	work		It worked for him.	이것은 그에게 효과가 있었다.
08	beat up		Don't beat yourself up.	스스로를 자책하지(때리지) 말라.
09	approach		all of these approaches	이 모든 접근법은
10	involve		The test involves difficult questions.	이 시험은 어려운 질문들을 포함한다.
11	guess		guess the next step	다음 단계를 추측하다
12	chance		guessing and chance	추측과 우연
13	strive for		strive for changes	변화를 위해 노력하다

➕ 본문 문장 속에서 단어의 의미를 우리말로 해석해 보세요.

All of these approaches involve guessing and chance.

➡️ 이 모든 ▢▢▢▢▢은 ▢▢▢▢과 ▢▢▢▢을 ▢▢▢▢▢.

STEP **2** · 수능 기출 제대로 풀기

B 다음 글의 요지로 가장 적절한 것은?

Advice from a friend or family member is the most well-meaning of all, but it's not the best way to match yourself with a new habit. While hot yoga may have changed your friend's life, does that mean it's the right practice for you? We all have friends who *swear* their new habit of getting up at 4:30 a.m. changed their lives and that we have to do it. I don't doubt that getting up super early changes people's lives, sometimes in good ways and sometimes not. But be cautious: You don't know if this habit will actually make your life better, especially if it means you get less sleep. So yes, you can try what worked for your friend, but don't beat yourself up if your friend's answer doesn't change you in the same way. All of these approaches involve guessing and chance. And that's not a good way to strive for change in your life.

① 한번 잘못 들인 습관은 바로잡기가 어렵다.
② 꾸준한 반복을 통해 올바른 습관을 들일 수 있다.
③ 친구나 가족의 조언은 항상 귀담아들을 필요가 있다.
④ 사소하더라도 좋은 습관을 들이면 인생이 바뀔 수 있다.
⑤ 타인에게 유익했던 습관이 자신에게는 효과가 없을 수 있다.

정답과 해설 **p.2**

15

01 Advice from a friend or family member / is the most well-meaning of all, / but it's not
= advice
the best way / to match yourself with a new habit.
↑·········┘ to부정사의 형용사적 용법
명사절 접속사 that 생략

02 While hot yoga may have changed your friend's life, / does that mean / it's the right
may have p.p.: ~했을지도 모른다   대명사(앞 절 전체를 의미)
practice for you?
명사절 접속사 that 생략

03 We all have friends / [who *swear* / their new habit of getting up at 4:30 a.m. changed
↑·········· 주격 관계대명사절
their lives / and that we have to do it].
└··········· 병렬연결 (swear의 목적어절 연결) ··········┘

04 I don't doubt / [that getting up super early changes people's lives, / sometimes in good
명사절 접속사   동명사 주어   동사(단수)
ways and sometimes not].

05 But be cautious: / You don't know / [if this habit will actually make your life better, /
명사절 접속사(~인지 아닌지)
especially if it means / you get less sleep].
부사절 접속사(~라면)

06 So yes, / you can try / what worked for your friend, / but don't beat yourself up / if your
관계대명사 what절(try의 목적어)   부사절 접속사(~라고 해도: 양보)
friend's answer doesn't change you in the same way.

07 All of these approaches involve guessing and chance. // And that's not a good way / to
↑·········┘
strive for change in your life.
to부정사의 형용사적 용법

01 친구나 가족의 조언은 / 모든 것 중에서 가장 좋은 뜻에서 하는well-meaning 말이지만, / 그것이 최선의 방법은 아니다 /
새로운 습관에 자신을 맞추는match.

02 핫 요가가 여러분 친구의 삶을 바꿔 놓았을지 모르지만, / 그것이 의미할까 / 핫 요가가 여러분에게 맞는
운동(습관)practice임을?

03 우리 모두에게는 친구들이 있다 / '확언하는swear' / 새벽 4시 30분에 일어나는 새로운 습관이 자신의 삶을 바꿨다고 /
그리고 우리도 그렇게 해야 한다고.

04 나는 의심하지doubt 않는다 / 엄청 일찍 일어나는 것이 사람들의 삶을 바꾼다는 것을 / 때로는 좋은 방식으로 때로는
그렇지 않게.

05 그러나 주의하라cautious: / 여러분은 알 수 없다 / 이 습관이 실제로 여러분의 삶을 더 낫게 만들지 / 특히 그것이
의미한다면 / 잠을 더 적게 자는 것을.

06 그러니 맞다, / 여러분은 시도해 볼 수 있다 / 친구에게 효과가 있었던work 것을, / 그러나 스스로를 자책하지beat up 말라
/ 친구의 해결책이 여러분을 똑같은 방식으로 바꾸지 않는다고 해도.

07 이 모든 접근법approach은 추측과 우연을 포함한다involve guessing and chance. // 그리고 그것은 좋은 방법은 아니다
/ 여러분의 삶의 변화를 위해 노력하는strive for.

구문 Check up

① We all have friends who *swear* their new habit of getting up at 4:30 a.m. changed their lives and that / which we have to do it.

동사 swear의 두 번째 목적어절(명사절)을 이끌어야 하고, 뒤따르는 절이 완전하므로, 명사절 접속사 that이 적절하다. 참고로 swear의 첫 번째 목적어절은 (that) their new habit ~ changed their lives이다.

② So yes, you can try what / that worked for your friend.

선행사가 없고 뒤에 불완전한 절이 나오므로 관계대명사 what이 적절하다.

정답 ① that ② what

C

STEP 1 • 수능에 *진짜* 나오는 *단어*

✔ **문제에 나오는 단어들을 확인하세요.**

시간이 없다면 색으로 표시된 단어만이라도 꼭 외우고 넘어가세요!

01	ecosystem	n. 생태계	damage (✔ ecosystem)s	생태계를 손상시키다
02	sound	a. 건전한, 믿을 만한	the ( ) principle	건전한 원칙
03	conservationist	n. 보호주의자	the ( ) principle	보호주의자 원칙
04	suppose	v. 전제로 하다	( ) a perfect order	완벽한 질서를 전제로 하다
05	order	n. 질서, 규칙	life in ( )	질서가 있는 삶
06	notion	n. 개념, 생각	a romantic ( )	낭만적인 개념
07	misleading	a. 잘못된 인식을 주는	deeply ( )	매우 잘못된 인식을 주는
08	static	a. 고정된	a ( ) condition	정적인 상태
09	apparently	ad. 겉보기에	( ) unchanged	겉보기에 변치 않은
10	alter	v. 바꾸다, 달라지다	( )ed circumstances	달라진 상황들
11	examine	v. 검토하다	( )d in fine detail	미세하게 자세히 검토되는
12	consequent	a. 결과적인	such adaptation and ( ) change	그런 적응과 결과적인 변화
13	constantly	ad. 항상, 끊임없이	take place ( )	항상 발생하다
14	arrangement	n. 배열, 배치 (방식)	The ( )s are dynamic.	사는 방식이 역동적이다.
15	inhabitant	n. 서식자	the planet's ( )s	지구의 서식자들

⊕ **본문 문장 속에서 단어들을 확인해 보세요.**

It is a romantic, not to say idyllic, notion, / but deeply misleading / because it supposes a static condition.

그것은 목가적인 것은 물론 낭만적인 개념이지만 / 매우 잘못된 인식을 준다 / 그것이 정적인 상태를 전제로 하기 때문에.

문제를 풀기 전에 단어들을 30초 동안 다시 확인하세요.

01	ecosystem	🖉 생태계	damage ecosystems	생태계를 손상시키다
02	sound		the sound principle	건전한 원칙
03	conservationist		the conservationist principle	보호주의자 원칙
04	suppose		suppose a perfect order	완벽한 질서를 전제로 하다
05	order		life in order	질서가 있는 삶
06	notion		a romantic notion	낭만적인 개념
07	misleading		deeply misleading	매우 잘못된 인식을 주는
08	static		a static condition	정적인 상태
09	apparently		apparently unchanged	겉보기에 변치 않은
10	alter		altered circumstances	달라진 상황들
11	examine		examined in fine detail	미세하게 자세히 검토되는
12	consequent		such adaptation and consequent change	그런 적응과 결과적인 변화
13	constantly		take place constantly	항상 발생하다
14	arrangement		The arrangements are dynamic.	사는 방식이 역동적이다.
15	inhabitant		the planet's inhabitants	지구의 서식자들

➕ 본문 문장 속에서 단어의 의미를 우리말로 해석해 보세요.

It is a romantic, not to say idyllic, notion, / but deeply misleading / because it supposes a static condition.

→ 그것은 목가적인 것은 물론 낭만적인 _____이지만 / 매우 _____ / 그것이 _____ 상태를 _____ 때문에.

STEP **2** • 수능 기출 제대로 풀기

C   다음 글의 요지로 가장 적절한 것은?

Fears of damaging ecosystems are based on the sound conservationist principle that we should aim to minimize the disruption we cause, but there is a risk that this principle may be confused with the old idea of a 'balance of nature.' This supposes a perfect order of nature that will seek to maintain itself and that we should not change. It is a romantic, not to say idyllic, notion, but deeply misleading because it supposes a static condition. Ecosystems are dynamic, and although some may endure, apparently unchanged, for periods that are long in comparison with the human lifespan, they must and do change eventually. Species come and go, climates change, plant and animal communities adapt to altered circumstances, and when examined in fine detail such adaptation and consequent change can be seen to be taking place constantly. The 'balance of nature' is a myth. Our planet is dynamic, and so are the arrangements by which its inhabitants live together.

*idyllic: 목가적인

① 생물 다양성이 높은 생태계가 기후 변화에 더 잘 적응한다.

② 인간의 부적절한 개입은 자연의 균형을 깨뜨린다.

③ 자연은 정적이지 않고 역동적으로 계속 변한다.

④ 모든 생물은 적자생존의 원칙에 순응하기 마련이다.

⑤ 동식물은 상호 경쟁을 통해 생태계의 균형을 이룬다.

정답과 해설 p.2

01 Fears of damaging ecosystems / are based on the sound conservationist principle /
~를 바탕으로 하다
that we should aim to minimize the disruption / we cause, / but there is a risk / that
동격의 that(=the sound conservationist principle)　　　목적격 관계대명사 생략　　　동격의 that(a risk)
this principle may be confused / with the old idea of a 'balance of nature.'

02 This supposes a perfect order of nature / that will seek to maintain itself / and that we
선행사　　　　　주격 관계대명사절　　　　　목적격 관계대명사절
should not change.
　　　　　　　　　　　　　　　　병렬연결

03 It is a romantic, not to say idyllic, notion, / but deeply misleading / because it supposes
~은 물론, 그리고 심지어
a static condition.

04 Ecosystems are dynamic, / and although some may endure, / apparently unchanged, /
삽입구(분사구문)
for periods that are long / in comparison with the human lifespan, / they must and do
주격 관계대명사절
change eventually.
동사 강조(do+동사원형)

05 Species come and go, / climates change, / plant and animal communities adapt to
altered circumstances, / and when examined in fine detail / such adaptation and
과거분사　　　　　　　접속사가 남아있는 분사구문
consequent change can be seen / to be taking place constantly.
5형식의 수동태: be+p.p.+목적격 보어(원형부정사 보어가 to부정사로 바뀜)

06 The 'balance of nature' is a myth. // Our planet is dynamic, / and so are the
긍정 동의(so+대동사+주어)
arrangements / by which its inhabitants live together.
전치사+관계대명사절(the arrangements 수식)

01 생태계ecosystem에 해를 끼치는 것에 대한 두려움은 / 건전한 환경 보호주의자 원칙the sound conservationist principle을 바탕으로 한다 / (환경) 파괴를 최소화하는 것을 목표로 해야 한다는 / 우리가 초래하는 (파괴) / 하지만 위험이 있다 / 이 원칙이 혼동될지도 모른다는 / '자연의 균형'이라는 오래된 생각과.

02 이것은 자연의 완벽한 질서a perfect order를 전제로 한다suppose / 그 자체를 유지하려고 노력하는 / 그리고 우리가 바꾸어서는 안 되는.

03 그것은 목가적인 것은 물론 낭만적인 개념notion이지만 / 매우 잘못된 인식을 준다deeply misleading / 그것이 정적인 상태a static condition를 전제로 하기 때문에.

04 생태계는 역동적이고, / 일부는 지속될지 모르지만, / 겉보기에는apparently 변하지 않는 채로 / 오랜 기간 동안 / 인간의 수명과 비교해 보면, / 그것은 결국 변할 것임에 틀림없고 정말 변한다.

05 생물 종(種)들은 생겼다 사라지고 / 기후는 변하며 / 동식물 군집은 달라진 환경altered circumstances에 적응한다 / 그리고 미세하게 자세히 검토되면examine / 그런 적응과 결과적인consequent 변화는 보일 수 있다 / 항상constantly 일어나고 있는 것으로.

06 '자연의 균형'은 잘못된 통념이다. // 지구는 역동적이고 / 모습[생활 방식]arrangement도 그러하다 / 지구의 서식자들inhabitant이 함께 사는 (모습).

구문 Check up

① When examining / examined in fine detail such adaptation and consequent change can be seen to be taking place constantly.

접속사가 남아있는 분사구문으로, 생략된 주어인 such adaptation and consequent change가 검토된다는 수동의 의미이므로 과거분사 examined로 쓴다.

② Our planet is dynamic, and so are the arrangements which / by which its inhabitants live together.

뒤따르는 절이 완전하므로 관계대명사 단독으로는 쓸 수 없고, <전치사+관계대명사> by which를 쓴다.

정답 ① examined ② by which

STEP 1 • 수능에 진짜 나오는 단어

✔️ **문제에 나오는 단어들을 확인하세요.**

시간이 없다면 색으로 표시된 단어만이라도 꼭 외우고 넘어가세요!

01	capacity	n. 능력	the (✔️ capacity) for laughter	웃음의 능력
02	characteristic	n. 특징	a peculiarly human ( )	인간의 독특한 특징
03	distinguish	v. 구별하다	( ) a man from a donkey	인간을 당나귀와 구별하다
04	mold	v. 형성하다	a ( )ing force of social groups	사회적 그룹들을 형성하는 힘
05	reinforce	v. 강화하다	( ) their norms	규범을 강화하다
06	regulate	v. 규제하다	( ) behavior	행동을 규제하다
07	preoccupation	n. (뇌리를 사로잡은) 사고, 생각	because of the major ( )s	주요한 사고 때문에
08	prevailing	a. 널리 퍼져있는	the mode ( ) at the time	그 당시에 널리 퍼져있는 방식
09	ultimate	a. 궁극적인	the ( ) goal	궁극적인 목표
10	aptly	ad. 적절히	( ) observe	적절하게 언급하다
11	assimilation	n. 동화	cultural ( )	문화 동화
12	intercultural	a. 문화 간의	( ) competence	문화 간의 역량

➕ **본문 문장 속에서 단어들을 확인해 보세요.**

It has long been held / that the capacity for laughter is a peculiarly human characteristic.

오랫동안 여겨져 왔다 / 웃음의 능력은 인간의 독특한 특징이라고.

01	capacity	능력	the capacity for laughter	웃음의 능력
02	characteristic		a peculiarly human characteristic	인간의 독특한 특징
03	distinguish		distinguish a man from a donkey	인간을 당나귀와 구별하다
04	mold		a molding force of social groups	사회적 그룹들을 형성하는 힘
05	reinforce		reinforce their norms	규범을 강화하다
06	regulate		regulate behavior	행동을 규제하다
07	preoccupation		because of the major preoccupations	주요한 사고 때문에
08	prevailing		the mode prevailing at the time	그 당시에 널리 퍼져있는 방식
09	ultimate		the ultimate goal	궁극적인 목표
10	aptly		aptly observe	적절하게 언급하다
11	assimilation		cultural assimilation	문화 동화
12	intercultural		intercultural competence	문화 간의 역량

➕ 본문 문장 속에서 단어의 의미를 우리말로 해석해 보세요.

It has long been held / that the capacity for laughter is a peculiarly human characteristic.

➡ 오랫동안 여겨져 왔다 / 웃음의 ＿＿＿＿＿＿＿은 인간의 독특한 ＿＿＿＿＿＿＿이라고.

STEP 2 • 수능 기출 제대로 풀기

D 다음 글의 주제로 가장 적절한 것은?

It has long been held that the capacity for laughter is a peculiarly human characteristic. The witty Lucian of Samosata (2nd century A.D.) noted that the way to distinguish a man from a donkey is that one laughs and the other does not. In all societies humor is important not only in individual communication but also as a molding force of social groups, reinforcing their norms and regulating behavior. "Each particular time, each era, in fact each moment, has its own condition and themes for laughter . . . because of the major preoccupations, concerns, interests, activities, relations, and mode prevailing at the time." The ultimate goal of anyone who studies another culture, such as ancient Greece, is to understand the people themselves who were more than the sum total of monuments, historical incidents, or social groupings. One way to approach this goal directly is to study the culture's humor. As Goethe aptly observed: "Men show their characters in nothing more clearly than in what they think laughable."

① typical process of cultural assimilation

② function of laughter in building friendship

③ educational need for intercultural competence

④ roles of humor in criticizing social problems

⑤ humor as a tool for understanding a culture

정답과 해설 **p.3**

01 It has long been held / that the capacity for laughter is a peculiarly human characteristic.
   가주어   진주어(that절)
// The witty Lucian of Samosata (2nd century A.D.) noted / [that the way to distinguish a
                                              목적절   to부정사의 형용사적 용법
man from a donkey / is that one laughs and the other does not].
                     명사절 접속사(보어절 연결)

02 In all societies / humor is important / not only in individual communication / but also
                                          not only A but also B: A뿐만 아니라 B도
as a molding force of social groups, / reinforcing their norms and regulating behavior.
                                                      분사구문 병렬연결

03 "Each particular time, each era, in fact each moment, / has its own condition and
   주어(each+단수명사)   동사(단수)
themes for laughter . . . / because of the major preoccupations, concerns, interests,
                            전치사(~ 때문에)   명사구
activities, relations, and mode / prevailing at the time."
                                   현재분사

04 The ultimate goal of anyone / who studies another culture, such as ancient Greece,
                                  주격 관계대명사절
/ is to understand the people themselves / who were more than the sum total of
  주격보어(명사적 용법)   주격 관계대명사절
monuments, historical incidents, or social groupings.

05 One way to approach this goal directly / is to study the culture's humor. // As Goethe
          to부정사의 형용사적 용법
aptly observed: / "Men show their characters in nothing more clearly / than in
                                              nothing+비교급+than: ~보다 …한 것도 없다(최상급 의미)
what they think laughable."
관계대명사절(전치사 in의 목적어)

01 오랫동안 여겨져 왔다 / 웃음의 능력capacity은 인간의 독특한 특징characteristic이라고. // (기원후 2세기) Samosata의
   재치 있는 Lucian은 지적했다 / 인간을 당나귀와 구별하는distinguish 방법은 / 한쪽은 웃고 다른 한쪽은 그렇지 않다는
   것임을.

02 모든 사회에서 / 유머는 중요하다 / 개인적인 의사소통에서뿐만 아니라 / 사회적 그룹들을 형성하는 힘a molding
   force으로서도 / 규범을 강화하고reinforce their norms 행동을 규제하면서regulate behavior.

03 "각각 특정한 시간, 각각의 시대, 사실상 각각의 순간은 / 웃음에 대한 그 자체의 조건과 주제를 가지고 있다 / 주된 사고the
   major preoccupation, 관심사, 흥미, 활동, 관계, 그리고 방식 때문에 / 그 당시에 널리 퍼져있는prevailing."

04 누군가의 궁극적인 목표the ultimate goal는 / 고대 그리스와 같은 다른 문화를 연구하는 (누군가) / 사람들 그 자체를
   이해하는 것이다 / 유물들, 역사적 사건들, 혹은 사회적 집단화의 총합계 이상이었던.

05 이 목표에 직접적으로 접근하는 한 가지 방법은 / 그 문화의 유머를 연구하는 것이다. // Goethe가 적절하게aptly 언급한
   대로 / "사람들의 특성을 명확히 보여주는 것도 없다 / 그들이 무엇을 웃기다고 생각하는지만큼."

구문 Check up

① In all societies humor is important not only in individual communication but also as a molding force of social groups, reinforces / reinforcing their norms and regulating behavior.

콤마 앞의 완전한 주절 뒤로 접속사 없이 보충 설명이 이어지는 문맥이므로 분사구문인 reinforcing을 쓴다.

② As Goethe aptly observed: "Men show their characters in nothing more clearly than in that / what they think laughable."

전치사 in의 목적어 자리에 명사가 와야 하고, 뒤에 불완전한 문장이 오므로, 선행사를 포함하는 관계대명사 what을 써서 명사절을 만든다.

정답 ① reinforcing ② what

E

STEP 1 • 수능에 *진짜* 나오는 *단어*

✔ 문제에 나오는 단어들을 확인하세요.

시간이 없다면 색으로 표시된 단어만이라도 꼭 외우고 넘어가세요!

01	competent	a. 능력 있는, 경쟁력 있는	being smart or (✓ competent)	똑똑하거나 능력 있는 것
02	recognize	v. 알아차리다, 알다	( ) talent	재능을 알아차리다
03	impression	n. 인상	the first ( )	첫인상
04	present	v. 보여주다	( ) oneself	자신을 보여주다
05	cultivate	v. (재능, 능력을) 연마하다, 기르다, (작물을) 경작하다	actively ( ) your talent	당신의 재능을 적극적으로 연마하다
06	bring to the table	제시하다, (이익에) 기여하다	( ) ( ) ( ) ( )	제시하다
07	cross off	(~에 줄을 그어) 지우다	( ) ( ) the list	목록에서 지우다
08	opportunity	n. 기회	the ( ) to show others	남에게 보여줄 기회
09	appropriate	a. 적절한, 온당한	( ) things	적절한 것들
10	appeal	v. 호소하다, 간청하다	( ) to other people	다른 사람에게 호소하다
11	public	n. 대중	in ( )	대중 앞에서
12	risk	n. 위험	a fire ( )	화재 위험
13	factor	n. 요인	economic ( )s	경제적인 요인들
14	strategy	n. 전략	a great ( )	훌륭한 전략

➕ 본문 문장 속에서 단어들을 확인해 보세요.

Nobody likes to be crossed off the list / before being given the opportunity / to show others who they are.

어느 누구도 목록에서 지워지는 것을 좋아하지 않는다 / 기회를 제공받기 전에 / 다른 사람들에게 그들(자신)이 누구인지를 보여줄.

문제를 풀기 전에 단어들을 **30초** 동안 다시 확인하세요.

01	competent	✎ 능력 있는, 경쟁력 있는	being smart or competent	똑똑하거나 능력 있는 것
02	recognize		recognize talent	재능을 알아차리다
03	impression		the first impression	첫인상
04	present		present oneself	자신을 보여주다
05	cultivate		actively cultivate your talent	당신의 재능을 적극적으로 연마하다
06	bring to the table		bring to the table	제시하다
07	cross off		cross off the list	목록에서 지우다
08	opportunity		the opportunity to show others	남에게 보여줄 기회
09	appropriate		appropriate things	적절한 것들
10	appeal		appeal to other people	다른 사람에게 호소하다
11	public		in public	대중 앞에서
12	risk		a fire risk	화재 위험
13	factor		economic factors	경제적인 요인들
14	strategy		a great strategy	훌륭한 전략

➕ 본문 문장 속에서 단어의 의미를 우리말로 해석해 보세요.

Nobody likes to be crossed off the list / before being given the opportunity / to show others who they are.

➡️ 어느 누구도 목록에서 ⬛⬛⬛⬛⬛ 것을 좋아하지 않는다 / ⬛⬛⬛⬛⬛ 를 제공받기 전에 / 다른 사람들에게 그들(자신)이 누구인지를 보여줄.

STEP **2** • 수능 기출 제대로 풀기

E

다음 글의 주제로 가장 적절한 것은?

In this world, being smart or competent isn't enough. People sometimes don't recognize talent when they see it. Their vision is clouded by the first impression we give and that can lose us the job we want, or the relationship we want. The way we present ourselves can speak more eloquently of the skills we bring to the table, if we actively cultivate that presentation. Nobody likes to be crossed off the list before being given the opportunity to show others who they are. Being able to tell your story from the moment you meet other people is a skill that must be actively cultivated, in order to send the message that you're someone to be considered and the right person for the position. For that reason, it's important that we all learn how to say the appropriate things in the right way and to present ourselves in a way that appeals to other people — tailoring a great first impression.

*eloquently: 설득력 있게

① difficulty of presenting yourself in public

② risks of judging others based on first impressions

③ factors keeping you from making great impressions

④ strategies that help improve your presentation skills

⑤ necessity of developing the way you show yourself

정답과 해설 p.3

01 In this world, / being smart or competent isn't enough. // People sometimes don't
   동명사(주어)   동사(단수)
recognize talent / when they see it.

02 Their vision is clouded / by the first impression we give / and that can lose us /
                                                                    대명사(and 앞 내용)
                                                목적격 관계대명사절
the job we want, or the relationship we want.
       목적격 관계대명사절   목적격 관계대명사절

03 The way we present ourselves / can speak more eloquently of the skills / we bring to
   in which 생략   목적격 관계대명사절
the table, / if we actively cultivate that presentation.
                                          지시형용사(그런)

04 Nobody likes to be crossed off the list / before being given the opportunity / [to show
                                              동명사구(being p.p.: 수동)   to부정사의
                                                                                  형용사적 용법
others who they are].
간접목적어   직접목적어(의문사절)

05 [Being able to tell your story / from the moment you meet other people] / is a
   동명사(주어)   관계부사 when 생략   동사(단수)
skill that must be actively cultivated, / in order to send the message / that you're
     주격 관계대명사절   동격절(=the message)
someone to be considered / and the right person for the position.

06 For that reason, / it's important / [that we all learn / how to say the appropriate things
                      가주어   진주어(that절)   how+to부정사: ~할 방법
in the right way / and to present ourselves in a way that appeals to other people / —
                                                        주격 관계대명사절
tailoring a great first impression].

01 이 세상에서 / 똑똑하거나 능력 있는competent 것만으로는 충분하지 않다. // 사람들은 때때로 재능을 알아차리지
   recognize talent 못한다 / 그들이 그것을 볼 때.

02 그들의 시야는 가려진다 / 우리가 주는 첫인상the first impression에 의해 / 그리고 그것은 우리로 하여금 잃게 할 수
   있다 / 우리가 원하는 일 또는 우리가 원하는 관계를.

03 우리가 우리 스스로를 보여주는present oneself 방식은 / 기술들에 대해 더 설득력 있게 말해줄 수 있다 / 우리가
   제시할bring to the table / 만약 우리가 그러한 보여주기를 적극적으로 계발한다면actively cultivate.

04 어느 누구도 목록에서 지워지는be crossed off the list 것을 좋아하지 않는다 / 기회opportunity를 제공받기 전에 / 다른
   사람들에게 그들(자신)이 누구인지를 보여줄.

05 당신의 이야기를 말할 수 있는 것은 / 당신이 다른 사람을 만나는 그 순간부터 / 적극적으로 계발되어야만 하는 기술이다 /
   메시지를 전달하기 위해서 / 당신이 고려되어야 할 누군가이고 / 그 자리에 적합한 사람이라는 (메시지).

06 그러한 이유로, / 중요하다 / 우리 모두 배우는 것이 / 올바른 방식으로 적절한appropriate 것들을 말하는 방법과 / 다른
   사람에게 호소하는appeal to other people 방식으로 우리 스스로를 보여주는 방법을 / 곧, 훌륭한 첫인상을 재단하는 것.

구문 Check up

① Being able to tell your story from the moment you meet other people is / are a skill that must be actively cultivated.

주어가 동명사이므로 단수로 수 일치하여 is를 쓴다.

② It's important that we all learn how to say the appropriate things in the right way and to present ourselves in a way that appeal / appeals to other people.

that은 주격 관계대명사로, 이어지는 동사는 선행사(a way)의 수에 일치해야 하므로 appeals로 쓴다.

STEP **1** • 수능에 *진짜* 나오는 *단어*

 문제에 나오는 단어들을 확인하세요.

시간이 없다면 색으로 표시된 단어만이라도 꼭 외우고 넘어가세요!

01	neurological	a. 신경학적인	the full (✓ neurological) effects	모든 신경학적인 영향
02	development	n. 발달	young children's ( )	아이들의 발달
03	screen time	스크린 타임 (전자 기기 사용 시간)	the amount of ( ) ( )	스크린 타임의 양
04	passive	a. 수동적인	( ) screen time	수동적인 스크린 타임
05	concern	v. 걱정시키다	( ) many parents	많은 부모를 걱정시키다
06	interact	v. 상호작용하다	( ) with screens	스크린과 상호작용하다
07	educator	n. 교육자	parents and ( )s	부모와 교육자
08	experience	n. 경험	talk about their ( )s	그들의 경험에 대해 말하다
09	tempt	v. 유혹하다	be ( )ed to hand	건네고 싶은 유혹을 받다
10	guide	v. 안내하다	( ) experiences	경험을 안내해주다
11	build	v. 짓다, 발달시키다	( ) important skills	핵심 역량을 발달시키다
12	critical	a. 비판적인	( ) thinking	비판적 사고력
13	literacy	n. 읽고 쓰는 능력, 독해력	media ( )	미디어 정보 독해력

➕ 본문 문장 속에서 단어들을 확인해 보세요.

Although we don't know the full neurological effects of digital technologies / on young children's development, / we do know / that all screen time is not created equal.

비록 우리가 디지털 기술의 모든 신경학적인 영향을 알지 못하지만 / 아이들의 발달에 미치는, / 우리는 분명히 알고 있다 / 모든 스크린 타임이 동등하게 만들어지지 않는다는 사실을.

문제를 풀기 전에 단어들을 **30초** 동안 다시 확인하세요.

01	neurological	🖊 신경학적인	the full neurological effects	모든 신경학적인 영향
02	development		young children's development	아이들의 발달
03	screen time		the amount of screen time	스크린 타임의 양
04	passive		passive screen time	수동적인 스크린 타임
05	concern		concern many parents	많은 부모를 걱정시키다
06	interact		interact with screens	스크린과 상호작용하다
07	educator		parents and educators	부모와 교육자
08	experience		talk about their experiences	그들의 경험에 대해 말하다
09	tempt		be tempted to hand	건네고 싶은 유혹을 받다
10	guide		guide experiences	경험을 안내해주다
11	build		build important skills	핵심 역량을 발달시키다
12	critical		critical thinking	비판적 사고력
13	literacy		media literacy	미디어 정보 독해력

➕ 본문 문장 속에서 단어의 의미를 우리말로 해석해 보세요.

Although we don't know the full neurological effects of digital technologies / on young children's development, / we do know / that all screen time is not created equal.

➜ 비록 우리가 디지털 기술의 _____을 알지 못하지만 / 아이들의 발달에 미치는, / 우리는 분명히 알고 있다 / _____이 동등하게 만들어지지 않는다는 사실을.

STEP 2 • 수능 기출 제대로 풀기

F

다음 글의 주제로 가장 적절한 것은?

Although we don't know the full neurological effects of digital technologies on young children's development, we do know that all screen time is not created equal. For example, reading an e-book, videoconferencing with grandma, or showing your child a picture you just took of them is not the same as the passive, television-watching screen time that concerns many parents and educators. So, rather than focusing on *how much* children are interacting with screens, parents and educators are turning their focus instead to *what* children are interacting with and *who* is talking with them about their experiences. Though parents may be tempted to hand a child a screen and walk away, guiding children's media experiences helps them build important 21st Century skills, such as critical thinking and media literacy.

① the predictors of children's screen media addiction

② reasons for children's preference for screen media

③ importance of what experiences kids have with screens

④ effects of the amount of screen time on kids' social skills

⑤ necessity of parental control on children's physical activities

정답과 해설 p.4

01 **Although** we don't know the full neurological effects of digital technologies / on young
비록 ~에도 불구하고(양보 부사절)
children's development, / **we do know** / that all screen time is not created equal.
동사(know)를 강조   명사절 접속사 that(목적어)

02 For example, / reading an e-book, / videoconferencing with grandma, / **or** showing
└───── 등위접속사 or로 연결된 병렬구조(동명사구 연결) ─────┘
your child a picture / you just took of them / **is** not the same as the passive, television-
                        ↑────── 목적격 관계대명사 that 생략   수 일치(단수)
watching screen time / that **concerns** many parents and educators.
선행사(불가산)   ↑────── 주격 관계대명사절(동사는 선행사에 수 일치)

03 So, / **rather than** focusing on how much children are interacting with screens, / parents
~보다는 차라리   의문사절(간접의문문 어순: 의문사+주어+동사)
and educators are turning their focus instead / **to** what children are interacting with
                        전치사   의문사절1
and who is talking with them / about their experiences.
의문사절2

04 Though parents **may be tempted** / to hand a child a screen and walk away, / **guiding**
5형식의 수동태: be+p.p.+목적격 보어(to부정사)   동명사(주어)
children's media experiences / **helps them build** important 21st Century skills, / **such as**
                        준사역동사(help)+목적어+목적격 보어(동사원형)   ~와 같은
critical thinking and media literacy.

01 비록 우리가 디지털 기술의 모든 신경학적인neurological 영향을 알지 못하지만 / 아이들의 발달development에 미치는,
/ 우리는 분명히 알고 있다 / 모든 스크린 타임screen time이 동등하게 만들어지지 않는다는 사실을.

02 예를 들어, / 전자책을 읽는 것, / 할머니와 화상 통화를 하는 것, / 혹은 사진을 아이에게 보여주는 것은 / 당신이 방금 찍은
아이의 (사진) / TV를 시청하는 수동적인passive 스크린 타임과 같지 않다 / 많은 부모와 교육자를 걱정시키는concern.

03 그래서 / 아이들이 얼마나 많이 스크린과 상호작용하는가interact에 집중하기보다는, / 부모와 교육자educator는 그
대신에 초점을 돌리고 있다 / 아이들이 무엇과 상호작용하고 있는가와 / 누가 그들과 이야기하고 있는가로 / 그들의
경험experience에 대해.

04 비록 부모가 유혹을 받을be tempted 수 있으나 / 아이에게 스크린을 건네주고 떠나도록, / 아이들에게 미디어에 대한
경험을 안내해 주는guide 것은 / 그들이 중요한 21세기 핵심 역량을 발달시키는build 데 도움을 준다 / 비판적critical
사고력과 미디어 정보 독해력literacy과 같은.

구문 Check up

① Although we don't know the full neurological effects of digital technologies on young children's development, we do know that / which all screen time is not created equal.

뒤에 수동태 동사가 포함된 완전한 절이 나오고 있으므로 명사절 접속사 that이 적절하다.

② For example, reading an e-book, videoconferencing with grandma, or showing your child a picture you just took of them is not the same as the passive screen time that concern / concerns many parents and educators.

선행사가 불가산명사인 the passive screen time이므로 주격 관계대명사 that이 이끄는 관계절의 동사 또한 단수(concerns)로 수일치한다.

정답 ① that ② concerns

STEP 1 · 수능에 진짜 나오는 단어

✔ 문제에 나오는 단어들을 확인하세요.

시간이 없다면 색으로 표시된 단어만이라도 꼭 외우고 넘어가세요!

01	hardship	n. 고난	personal (✔ hardship)	개인적인 고난
02	desire	v. 바라다, 욕망하다	( ) a better life	더 나은 삶을 바라다
03	spare	v. (불쾌한 경험을) 겪지 않게 하다	( ) kids from bullying	아이들이 괴롭힘을 당하지 않게 하다
04	aim	n. 목적, 목표	a noble ( )	고귀한 목적
05	stem from	~에서(로부터) 일어나다, 생기다	( ) ( ) a car accident	차 사고로 생기다
06	concern	n. 걱정, 염려	love and ( ) for the child	아이에 대한 사랑과 염려
07	realize	v. 알게 되다	( ) one's error	오류를 알게 되다
08	term	n. 기간	in the short ( )	짧은 기간에
09	acquire	v. 얻다, 취득하다	( ) rights	권리를 얻다
10	self-confidence	n. 자신감	acquire ( )	자신감을 얻다
11	interpersonal	a. 대인 관계의	( ) skills	대인 기술
12	curse	n. 저주	a heavy ( )	심한 저주
13	struggle	v. 분투하다, 애쓰다 n. 분투, 노력	( ) for power	권력을 위해 애쓰다
14	emotion	n. 감정	some painful ( )s	고통스러운 감정

⊕ 본문 문장 속에서 단어들을 확인해 보세요.

To want to spare children from having to go through unpleasant experiences / is a noble aim, / and it naturally stems from love and concern / for the child.

자녀가 불쾌한 경험을 겪지 않도록 해주고자 하는 것은 / 고귀한 목적이고, / 그것은 당연히 사랑과 염려로부터 나오는 것이다 / 자녀에 대한.

01	hardship	🖉 고난	personal hardship	개인적인 고난
02	desire		desire a better life	더 나은 삶을 바라다
03	spare		spare kids from bullying	아이들이 괴롭힘을 당하지 않게 하다
04	aim		a noble aim	고귀한 목적
05	stem from		stem from a car accident	차 사고로 생기다
06	concern		love and concern for the child	아이에 대한 사랑과 염려
07	realize		realize one's error	오류를 알게 되다
08	term		in the short term	짧은 기간에
09	acquire		acquire rights	권리를 얻다
10	self-confidence		acquire self-confidence	자신감을 얻다
11	interpersonal		interpersonal skills	대인 기술
12	curse		a heavy curse	심한 저주
13	struggle		struggle for power	권력을 위해 애쓰다
14	emotion		some painful emotions	고통스러운 감정

➕ **본문 문장 속에서 단어의 의미를 우리말로 해석해 보세요.**

To want to spare children from having to go through unpleasant experiences / is a noble aim, / and it naturally stems from love and concern / for the child.

→ 자녀가 불쾌한 경험을   해주고자 하는 것은 / 고귀한   이고, / 그것은 당연히   것이다 / 자녀에 대한.

제한시간 70초

난이도 ★★★☆☆

STEP 2 · 수능 기출 제대로 풀기

G 다음 글의 주제로 가장 적절한 것은?

Many parents who have experienced personal hardship desire a better life for their children. To want to spare children from having to go through unpleasant experiences is a noble aim, and it naturally stems from love and concern for the child. What these parents don't realize, however, is that while in the short term they may be making the lives of their children more pleasant, in the long term they may be preventing their children from acquiring self-confidence, mental strength, and important interpersonal skills. Samuel Smiles, a nineteenth-century English author, wrote, "It is doubtful whether any heavier curse could be forced on man than the complete gratification of all his wishes without effort on his part, leaving nothing for his hopes, desires, or struggles." For healthy development, the child needs to deal with some failure, struggle through some difficult periods, and experience some painful emotions.

*gratification: 만족(감), 희열

① benefits of traditional child-rearing practices

② critical factors in children's physical development

③ importance of parental emotional support for children

④ necessity of parents letting their child experience difficulties

⑤ differences between the parents' and child's points of view

정답과 해설 p.4

01 Many parents who have experienced personal hardship / desire a better life for their
　　주어　　　　　주격 관계대명사절　　　　　　　　　　　동사
children.

02 [To want to spare children from having to go through unpleasant experiences] / is a
　　주어　　　spare A from ~: A가 ~하지 못하게 하다　　　　　　　　　　　　동사(단수)
noble aim, / and it naturally stems from love and concern / for the child.

03 What these parents don't realize, however, is / that while in the short term they may
　　주어　　　　　　　　　　　　　　　　　　명사절 접속사　동사　　~에 반하여
be making the lives of their children more pleasant, / in the long term they may be
　　make+목적어(A)+목적격 보어: A가 ~하게 만들다
preventing their children / from acquiring self-confidence, mental strength, and
prevent A from ~: A가 ~하지 못하게 하다
important interpersonal skills.

04 Samuel Smiles, a nineteenth-century English author, wrote, / "It is doubtful / [whether
　　　　　　　　　　　동격　　　　　　　　　　　　　　　　　　　가주어　　진주어
any heavier curse could be forced on man / than the complete gratification of all　　~인지 아닌지
his wishes / without effort on his part, / leaving nothing for his hopes, desires, or
　　　　　　　　　　　　　　　　　　　분사구문: ~한 채
struggles]."

05 For healthy development, / the child needs to deal with some failure, / struggle through
some difficult periods, / and experience some painful emotions.
　　　　　　　　　　　　needs to에 병렬연결

01 개인적인 고난hardship을 경험한 많은 부모들은 / 그들의 자녀가 더 나은 삶을 살기를 바란다desire.

02 자녀가 불쾌한 경험을 겪지 않도록spare 해주고자 하는 것은 / 고귀한 목적a noble aim이고, / 그것은 당연히 사랑과
염려로부터 나오는stem from love and concern 것이다 / 자녀에 대한.

03 그러나 이러한 부모들이 깨닫지realize 못하는 것은 / 그들이 단기적으로는in the short term 자녀의 삶을 좀 더 즐겁게
만들어 주고 있을지 모르지만, / 장기적으로는 그들이 자녀를 막고 있을지도 모른다는 것이다 / 자신감self-confidence,
정신력, 그리고 중요한 대인 기술interpersonal skills을 습득하지acquire 못하게.

04 19세기의 영국 작가인 Samuel Smiles는 썼다 / "의문이 든다 / 인간에게 가해지는 더 심한 저주curse가 과연 있을까 /
그의 모든 소망에 대한 완전한 만족보다 / 자신의 노력 없이 (이루어진 만족) / 희망, 욕망, 그리고 분투struggle의 여지를
남기지 않은 채."라고.

05 건전한 발달을 위해 / 아이는 실패를 다루고 / 어려운 시기를 거쳐 발버둥 치며 / 고통스러운 감정emotion을 경험할
필요가 있다.

구문 Check up

① What / That these parents don't realize, however, is that while in the short term they may be making the lives of their children more pleasant.

문장의 주어 역할과 realize의 목적어 역할을 동시에 할 수 있는 것은 관계대명사 What이다.

② For healthy development, the child needs to deal with some failure, struggle / struggles through some difficult periods, and experience some painful emotions.

동사 needs의 목적어(to부정사)에서 to에 연결되는 단어들이 and로 병렬 연결되는 구조이기 때문에 동사원형인 struggle을 쓴다.

정답 ① What ② struggle

STEP 1 • 수능에 *진짜* 나오는 *단어*

✔ 문제에 나오는 단어들을 확인하세요.

시간이 없다면 색으로 표시된 단어만이라도 꼭 외우고 넘어가세요!

01	self-conscious	*a.* 남을 의식하는, 자의식이 강한	a (✔ self-conscious) adolescent	남을 의식하는 청소년
02	awareness	*n.* 의식, 인식	raise ( )	의식을 높이다
03	pay attention	주의를 기울이다	( ) ( ) to others	다른 사람들에게 주의를 기울이다
04	mess up	망치다	( ) ( ) the party	파티를 망치다
05	rough	*a.* 거친, 난폭한	( ) weather	거친 날씨(악천후)
06	observe	*v.* 관찰하다	( ) everything others do	다른 사람들이 하는 모든 것을 관찰하다
07	flaw	*n.* 실수, 결점	discover your ( )s and weaknesses	여러분의 실수와 약점을 발견하다
08	personality	*n.* 성격, 개성	hide your true ( )	진짜 성격을 감추다
09	at the expense of	~을 희생하여	( ) ( ) ( ) ( ) being who you really are	진정한 자기 자신이 되기를 희생하여
10	permanently	*ad.* 영원히	stop growing ( )	영원히 성장을 멈추다

⊕ 본문 문장 속에서 단어들을 확인해 보세요.

You can mess up and be rough and get dirty / because no one even knows you're there.

여러분은 일을 망치고 난폭해지고 비열해져도 되는데, / 아무도 여러분이 거기 있음을 알지조차 못하기 때문이다.

01	self-conscious	남을 의식하는, 자의식이 강한	a self-conscious adolescent	남을 의식하는 청소년
02	awareness		raise awareness	의식을 높이다
03	pay attention		pay attention to others	다른 사람들에게 주의를 기울이다
04	mess up		mess up the party	파티를 망치다
05	rough		rough weather	거친 날씨(악천후)
06	observe		observe everything others do	다른 사람들이 하는 모든 것을 관찰하다
07	flaw		discover your flaws and weaknesses	여러분의 실수와 약점을 발견하다
08	personality		hide your true personality	진짜 성격을 감추다
09	at the expense of		at the expense of being who you really are	진정한 자기 자신이 되기를 희생하여
10	permanently		stop growing permanently	영원히 성장을 멈추다

➕ **본문 문장 속에서 단어의 의미를 우리말로 해석해 보세요.**

You can mess up and be rough and get dirty / because no one even knows you're there.

→ 여러분은 〔   〕 비열해져도 되는데, / 아무도 여러분이 거기 있음을 알지조차 못하기 때문이다.

제한시간 70초

난이도 ★★★☆☆

STEP 2 · 수능 기출 제대로 풀기

A 다음 글의 제목으로 가장 적절한 것은?

Winning turns on a self-conscious awareness that others are watching. It's a lot easier to move under the radar when no one knows you and no one is paying attention. You can mess up and be rough and get dirty because no one even knows you're there. But as soon as you start to win, and others start to notice, you're suddenly aware that you're being observed. You're being judged. You worry that others will discover your flaws and weaknesses, and you start hiding your true personality, so you can be a good role model and good citizen and a leader that others can respect. There is nothing wrong with that. But if you do it at the expense of being who you really are, making decisions that please others instead of pleasing yourself, you're not going to be in that position very long. When you start apologizing for who you are, you stop growing and you stop winning. Permanently.

① Stop Judging Others to Win the Race of Life

② Why Disappointment Hurts More than Criticism

③ Winning vs. Losing: A Dangerously Misleading Mindset

④ Winners in a Trap: Too Self-conscious to Be Themselves

⑤ Is Honesty the Best Policy to Turn Enemies into Friends?

정답과 해설 p.6

01 Winning turns on a self-conscious awareness / that others are watching.
　　　　　　　　　　　　　　　　　　　　　　　동격

02 It's a lot easier to move under the radar / when no one knows you and no one is paying
　　가주어　　　　진주어
attention. // You can mess up and be rough and get dirty / because no one even knows
　　　　　　　　　　　　　　　　　　　　　　　　　　　　　접속사(~ 때문에)
you're there.

03 But as soon as you start to win, / and others start to notice, / you're suddenly aware /
　　　접속사(~하자마자)
that you're being observed. // You're being judged.
접속사(~것)

04 You worry that others will discover your flaws and weaknesses, / and you start hiding
　　　　　목적절(~것)
your true personality, / so (that) you can be a good role model and good citizen / and a
　　　　　　　　　　접속사(~하도록)　　　　　　　주격보어1　　　　　　　　　　　　　　　　　주격보어2
leader that others can respect.
　　　　목적격 관계대명사절

05 There is nothing wrong with that. // But if you do it / at the expense of [being who you
　　　　　　　　　　　　　　　주격 관계대명사　　　　　　　　　　　　　전치사　　동명사구
really are], / making decisions [that please others] instead of pleasing yourself, / you're
　　　　　　분사구문　　　　　　　　　　　　　　　~ 대신에
not going to be in that position very long.

06 When you start apologizing for who you are, / you stop growing and you stop winning.
　　　　　　　　　　　　　　　　　　　　　　　　stop+동명사: ~하기를 멈추다
// Permanently.

01 승리는 남을 의식하는 인식a self-conscious awareness을 촉발한다 / 다른 사람이 보고 있다는.

02 눈에 띄지 않게 움직이기가 훨씬 더 쉽다 / 아무도 여러분을 모르고 주의를 기울이고pay attention 있지 않다면. // 여러분은 일을 망치고mess up 난폭해지고rough 비열해져도 되는데, / 아무도 여러분이 거기 있음을 알지조차 못하기 때문이다.

03 하지만 여러분이 이기기 시작하거나, / 다른 사람이 알아차리기 시작하는 순간부터, / 여러분은 갑자기 인식한다 / 여러분이 관찰되고observe 있다는 것을. // 여러분은 평가받고 있다.

04 여러분은 다른 사람이 여러분의 실수flaw와 약점을 발견할 것이라고 걱정하고 / 여러분 본래의 성격personality을 숨기기 시작한다 / 여러분이 좋은 본보기이자 훌륭한 시민이 될 수 있도록 / 그리고 다른 사람이 존경할 수 있는 지도자가.

05 그것에 문제는 없다. // 하지만 여러분이 그렇게 한다면 / 진정한 자신이 되는 것을 희생하고at the expense of, / 자기 자신을 기쁘게 하는 대신 타인을 기쁘게 하는 결정을 내리면서 / 여러분은 그 지위에 그리 오래 머물지 못할 것이다.

06 여러분이 자신의 모습에 관해 사과하기 시작하는 순간, / 여러분은 성장을 멈추고 승리를 멈추게 된다. // 영원히permanently.

구문 Check up

① Winning turns on a self-conscious awareness which / that others are watching.

문맥상 that절은 인식(awareness)의 내용을 보충 설명하는 것이다. 따라서 동격의 that이 적절하다.

② When you start apologizing for who you are, you stop to grow / growing .

문맥상 '성장하기를 멈춘다'는 의미이므로 'stop+동명사'의 growing을 써야 한다.

정답 ① that ② growing

B

STEP 1 • 수능에 진짜 나오는 단어

✔ 문제에 나오는 단어들을 확인하세요.

시간이 없다면 색으로 표시된 단어만이라도 꼭 외우고 넘어가세요!

01	march	v. 나아가다	(✔ march) toward a more global society	더 글로벌한 사회로 나아가다
02	ethnic	a. 민족의	various ( ) groups	다양한 민족 집단들
03	traditionally	ad. 전통적으로	( ) do things	전통적으로 일을 하다
04	quite	ad. 상당히, 꽤	( ) differently	상당히 다르게
05	perspective	n. 관점	a fresh ( )	새로운 관점
06	valuable	a. 가치 있는, 귀중한	( ) in education	교육에 있어 가치 있는
07	extensive	a. 광범위한	( ) experience	광범위한 경험
08	multicultural	a. 다문화의	( ) experience	다문화 경험
09	measure	v. 측정하다	( ) the length	길이를 측정하다
10	come up with	떠올리다	( ) ( ) ( ) many ideas	많은 생각을 떠올리다
11	association	n. 연상, 관련	( ) skills	연상 능력
12	capture	v. 포착하다	( ) ideas	생각을 포착하다
13	unconventional	a. 관습에 얽매이지 않는	( ) ideas	관습에 얽매이지 않는 생각
14	expose	v. 노출시키다, 접하게 하다	( ) your children to other cultures	자녀가 다른 문화를 접하게 하다

⊕ 본문 문장 속에서 단어들을 확인해 보세요.

Extensive multicultural experience / makes kids more creative / and allows them to capture unconventional ideas / from other cultures / to expand on their own ideas.

광범위한 다문화 경험은 / 아이들을 더 창의적으로 만들고 / 아이들이 관습에 얽매이지 않는 생각을 포착할 수 있게 한다 / 다른 문화로부터 / 자신의 생각을 확장하기 위해.

01	march	나아가다	march toward a more global society	더 글로벌한 사회로 나아가다
02	ethnic		various ethnic groups	다양한 민족 집단들
03	traditionally		traditionally do things	전통적으로 일을 하다
04	quite		quite differently	상당히 다르게
05	perspective		a fresh perspective	새로운 관점
06	valuable		valuable in education	교육에 있어 가치 있는
07	extensive		extensive experience	광범위한 경험
08	multicultural		multicultural experience	다문화 경험
09	measure		measure the length	길이를 측정하다
10	come up with		come up with many ideas	많은 생각을 떠올리다
11	association		association skills	연상 능력
12	capture		capture ideas	생각을 포착하다
13	unconventional		unconventional ideas	관습에 얽매이지 않는 생각
14	expose		expose your children to other cultures	자녀가 다른 문화를 접하게 하다

➕ 본문 문장 속에서 단어의 의미를 우리말로 해석해 보세요.

Extensive multicultural experience / makes kids more creative / and allows them to capture unconventional ideas / from other cultures / to expand on their own ideas.

➔ 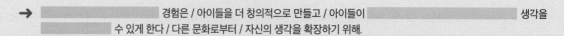 경험은 / 아이들을 더 창의적으로 만들고 / 아이들이   생각을
                         수 있게 한다 / 다른 문화로부터 / 자신의 생각을 확장하기 위해.

STEP 2 · 수능 기출 제대로 풀기

B 다음 글에서 필자가 주장하는 바로 가장 적절한 것은?

Though we are marching toward a more global society, various ethnic groups traditionally do things quite differently, and a fresh perspective is valuable in creating an open-minded child. Extensive multicultural experience makes kids more creative (measured by how many ideas they can come up with and by association skills) and allows them to capture unconventional ideas from other cultures to expand on their own ideas. As a parent, you should expose your children to other cultures as often as possible. If you can, travel with your child to other countries; live there if possible. If neither is possible, there are lots of things you can do at home, such as exploring local festivals, borrowing library books about other cultures, and cooking foods from different cultures at your house.

① 자녀가 전통문화를 자랑스럽게 여기게 해야 한다.
② 자녀가 주어진 문제를 깊이 있게 탐구하도록 이끌어야 한다.
③ 자녀가 다른 문화를 가능한 한 자주 접할 수 있게 해야 한다.
④ 창의성 발달을 위해 자녀의 실수에 대해 너그러워야 한다.
⑤ 경험한 것을 돌이켜 볼 시간을 자녀에게 주어야 한다.

정답과 해설 p.6

01 Though we are marching toward a more global society, / various ethnic groups
   양보절 접속사(비록 ~지만)
traditionally do things quite differently, / and a fresh perspective is valuable / in

creating an open-minded child.
~할 때, ~하는 데 있어

02 Extensive multicultural experience / [makes kids more creative] / (measured by how
                                        5형식 동사+목적어+목적격 보어(형용사)
many ideas they can come up with and by association skills) / and [allows them to
의문사절(전치사 by의 목적어)   5형식 동사+목적어+목적격 보어(to부정사)
capture unconventional ideas / from other cultures / to expand on their own ideas].
                                                      to부정사의 부사적 용법(~하기 위해서)

03 As a parent, / you should expose your children to other cultures / as often as possible.

04 If you can, / travel with your child to other countries; / live there if possible.
                                                        it is 생략

05 If neither is possible, / there are lots of things you can do at home, / such as exploring
                                    목적격 관계대명사 that 생략
                                              관계대명사절   ~와 같이
local festivals, / borrowing library books about other cultures, / and cooking foods from
동명사구1   동명사구2   동명사구3
different cultures at your house.

01 우리는 더 글로벌한 사회로 나아가고march 있지만, / 다양한 민족ethnic 집단들은 전통적으로traditionally 상당히quite
   다르게 일을 하고 있다 / 그리고 새로운 관점perspective이 가치가 있다valuable / 개방적인 아이를 만드는 데 있어서.

02 광범위한extensive 다문화multicultural 경험은 / 아이들을 더 창의적으로 만들고 / (얼마나 많은 생각을 떠올릴 수
   있는지come up with와 연상association 능력으로 측정measure됨) / 아이들이 관습에 얽매이지 않는unconventional
   생각을 포착할capture 수 있게 한다 / 다른 문화로부터 / 자신의 생각을 확장하기 위해.

03 부모로서, / 자녀가 다른 문화를 접하게 해야expose 한다 / 가능한 한 자주.

04 할 수 있다면, / 자녀와 다른 나라로 여행하고, / 가능하면 거기서 살라.

05 둘 다 가능하지 않다면, / 국내에서 할 수 있는 일이 많다 / 지역 축제 탐방하기, / 다른 문화에 대한 도서관 책 빌리기, /
   집에서 다른 문화의 음식 요리하기와 같이.

구문 Check up

① Despite / Though we are marching toward a more global society, various ethnic groups traditionally do things quite differently, and a fresh perspective is valuable in creating an open-minded child.

명사구가 아니라 절을 이끌고 있으므로 접속사 Though를 쓴다.

② Extensive multicultural experience makes kids more creative / creatively (measured by how many ideas they can come up with and by association skills).

5형식 동사 make의 목적격 보어 자리이므로 형용사 creative가 적절하다.

STEP 1 • 수능에 *진짜* 나오는 *단어*

✔️ 문제에 나오는 단어들을 확인하세요.

시간이 없다면 색으로 표시된 단어만이라도 꼭 외우고 넘어가세요!

01	high-rise	n. 고층 건물	the fancy (✓ high-rise)s	화려한 고층 건물들
02	headquarters	n. 본부	financial ( )	금융 본부
03	peddler	n. 행상인	souvenir ( )s	기념품 행상인들
04	make a way	나아가다	( ) ( ) ( ) to a city	도시로 나아가다
05	gross	a. 혐오스러운, 역겨운	a ( ) landfill	혐오스러운 매립지
06	landfill	n. (쓰레기) 매립지	a giant ( )	거대한 매립지
07	temporarily	ad. 잠시	return it back ( )	그것을 잠시 되돌리다
08	commission	v. 의뢰하다	be ( )ed by the fund	펀드로부터 의뢰받다
09	installation	n. 설치(물)	a living ( )	살아 있는 설치 조형물
10	wheat	n. 밀	a golden ( ) field	황금빛 밀밭
11	gleaming	a. 반짝이는	the ( ) Twin Towers	반짝이는 쌍둥이 빌딩
12	amber	a. 호박색의	( ) waves	호박색 물결
13	irrigation	n. 관개, 물을 끌어들임	farming and ( )	농사와 관개
14	thrive	v. 번성하다, 무성하다	The wheat field was ( )ing.	밀밭이 무성했다.
15	nourish	v. 영양분을 주다	( ) the minds and bodies	마음과 몸에 영양분을 주다

➕ 본문 문장 속에서 단어들을 확인해 보세요.

Before the fancy high-rises, financial headquarters, tourist centers, and souvenir peddlers / made their way to Battery Park City, / the area behind the World Trade Center / was a giant, gross landfill.

화려한 고층 건물, 금융 본부, 관광 센터, 기념품 행상인들이 / Battery Park City로 나아가기 전에, / 세계 무역 센터 뒤편의 지역은 / 거대하고 혐오스러운 쓰레기 매립지였다.

문제를 풀기 전에 단어들을 30초 동안 다시 확인하세요.

01	high-rise	🖉 고층 건물	the fancy high-rises	화려한 고층 건물들
02	headquarters		financial headquarters	금융 본부
03	peddler		souvenir peddlers	기념품 행상인들
04	make a way		make a way to a city	도시로 나아가다
05	gross		a gross landfill	혐오스러운 매립지
06	landfill		a giant landfill	거대한 매립지
07	temporarily		return it back temporarily	그것을 잠시 되돌리다
08	commission		be commissioned by the fund	펀드로부터 의뢰받다
09	installation		a living installation	살아 있는 설치 조형물
10	wheat		a golden wheat field	황금빛 밀밭
11	gleaming		the gleaming Twin Towers	반짝이는 쌍둥이 빌딩
12	amber		amber waves	호박색 물결
13	irrigation		farming and irrigation	농사와 관개
14	thrive		The wheat field was thriving.	밀밭이 무성했다.
15	nourish		nourish the minds and bodies	마음과 몸에 영양분을 주다

➕ **본문 문장 속에서 단어의 의미를 우리말로 해석해 보세요.**

Before the fancy high-rises, financial headquarters, tourist centers, and souvenir peddlers / made their way to Battery Park City, / the area behind the World Trade Center / was a giant, gross landfill.

➔ 화려한 _____, 금융 _____, 관광 센터, 기념품 _____이 / Battery Park City로 _____ 전에, / 세계 무역 센터 뒤편의 지역은 / 거대하고 _____였다.

STEP **2** • 수능 기출 제대로 풀기

C 다음 글의 제목으로 가장 적절한 것은?

Before the fancy high-rises, financial headquarters, tourist centers, and souvenir peddlers made their way to Battery Park City, the area behind the World Trade Center was a giant, gross landfill. In 1982, artist Agnes Denes decided to return that landfill back to its roots, although temporarily. Denes was commissioned by the Public Art Fund to create one of the most significant and fantastical pieces of public work Manhattan has ever seen. Her concept was not a traditional sculpture, but a living installation that changed the way the public looked at art. In the name of art, Denes put a beautiful golden wheat field right in the shadow of the gleaming Twin Towers. For *Wheatfield—A Confrontation*, Denes and volunteers removed trash from four acres of land, then planted amber waves of grain atop the area. After months of farming and irrigation, the wheat field was thriving and ready. The artist and her volunteers harvested thousands of pounds of wheat to give to food banks in the city, nourishing both the minds and bodies of New Yorkers.

① Living Public Art Grows from a Landfill

② Why Does Art Fade Away in Urban Areas?

③ New York: Skyscraper Capital of the World

④ Art Narrows the Gap Between the Old and Young

⑤ How City Expansion Could Affect Food Production

정답과 해설 **p.6**

01 Before the fancy high-rises, financial headquarters, tourist centers, and souvenir peddlers / made their way to Battery Park City, / the area behind the World Trade Center / was a giant, gross landfill.
~로 나아가다, 진출하다

02 In 1982, / artist Agnes Denes decided / to return that landfill back to its roots, / although temporarily.
return ~ back to...: ~를 …로 되돌리다

03 Denes was commissioned by the Public Art Fund / to create one of the most significant and fantastical pieces of public work / Manhattan has ever seen.
one of the+최상급+복수명사: 가장 ~한 …들 중 하나
목적격 관계대명사 생략

04 Her concept was not a traditional sculpture, / but a living installation / [that changed the way / the public looked at art].
not A but B: A가 아니라 B
주격 관계대명사절
관계부사절(the way가 있으므로 how 생략)

05 In the name of art, / Denes put a beautiful golden wheat field / right in the shadow of the gleaming Twin Towers. // For *Wheatfield—A Confrontation*, / Denes and volunteers removed trash / from four acres of land, / then planted amber waves of grain / atop the area.
(and) then으로 동사 병렬연결

06 After months of farming and irrigation, / the wheat field was thriving and ready. // The artist and her volunteers harvested thousands of pounds of wheat / to give to food banks in the city, / nourishing both the minds and bodies of New Yorkers.
to부정사 부사적 용법(결과)
분사구문: ~하면서

01 화려한 고층 건물high-rise, 금융 본부headquarters, 관광 센터, 기념품 행상인들peddler이 / Battery Park City로 나아가기make a way 전에, / 세계 무역 센터 뒤편의 지역은 / 거대하고 혐오스러운 쓰레기 매립지a giant, gross landfill였다.

02 1982년, / 예술가 Agnes Denes는 결정했다 / 그 매립지를 다시 원래의 뿌리로 되돌리기로 / 비록 일시적으로temporarily 라도.

03 Denes는 Public Art Fund로부터 의뢰받았다was commissioned / 가장 의미심장하며 환상적인 공공사업 작품 중 하나를 만들어 달라고 / Manhattan에서 지금까지 본.

04 그녀의 콘셉트는 전통적인 조형물이 아니라 / 살아있는 설치 조형물a living installation이었다 / 방식을 바꾼 (조형물) / 대중이 미술을 보는 (방식).

05 예술의 이름으로, / Denes는 아름다운 황금 밀밭wheat field을 만들었다 / 반짝이는gleaming 쌍둥이 빌딩의 그림자에. // 〈Wheatfield—A Confrontation〉을 위해, / Denes와 자원 봉사자들은 쓰레기를 치우고 / 4에이커의 땅에서 / 그 후 황색 빛깔의 너울거리는 곡물amber waves of grain을 심었다 / 그 지역 위에.

06 수개월의 농사와 관개irrigation 후에 / 밀밭은 무성해져thrive 있었고 준비가 되었다. // 그 예술가와 그녀의 자원 봉사자들은 수천 파운드의 밀을 수확하여 / 뉴욕의 푸드 뱅크에 기부하였고, / 뉴욕 사람들의 마음과 몸에 모두 영양분을 주었다nourish.

구문 Check up

① Her concept was not a traditional sculpture, but a living installation that changing / changed the way the public looked at art.

② The artist and her volunteers harvested thousands of pounds of wheat to give to food banks in the city, nourish / nourishing both the minds and bodies of New Yorkers.

관계대명사절의 동사 자리이므로, 시제를 맞추어 changed로 써야 한다.

앞에 접속사가 없기 때문에 동사원형은 올 수 없고, 분사의 형태로 분사 구문을 만든다. 따라서 nourishing이 적절하다.

정답 ① changed ② nourishing

문제에 나오는 단어들을 확인하세요.

시간이 없다면 색으로 표시된 단어만이라도 꼭 외우고 넘어가세요!

01	origin	n. 기원	know their (✓ origin)s	그것들의 기원을 알다
02	exact	a. 정확한	need an (　　　) description	정확한 묘사를 필요로 하다
03	accurately	ad. 정확하게	tell (　　　　　)	정확하게 말하다
04	possibility	n. 가능성	There is always the (　　　　　).	가능성은 항상 있다.
05	ancient	a. 고대의	(　　　　) inventions	고대의 발명품들
06	pottery	n. 도자기	the invention of (　　　　)	도자기 발명품
07	archaeologist	n. 고고학자	(　　　　　　)s believed	고고학자들은 믿었다
08	pot	n. 항아리	find (　　　)s	항아리를 발견하다
09	date back	(날짜를) 거슬러 올라가다	(　　　) (　　　　) to 9,000 B.C.	기원전 9,000년으로 거슬러 올라가다
10	tell A from B	A와 B를 구별하다	(　　　) original (　　　) fake	진짜와 가짜를 구별하다
11	explore	v. 연구하다, 탐색하다	(　　　　) the materials	물질을 연구하다
12	past	n. 과거	learn from the (　　　　)	과거로부터 배우다

⊕ 본문 문장 속에서 단어들을 확인해 보세요.

Many inventions were invented / thousands of years ago / so it can be difficult / to know their exact origins.

많은 발명품들은 발명이 되었다 / 수천 년 전에 / 그래서 어려울 수 있다 / 그것들의 정확한 기원을 아는 것은.

01	origin	🖊 기원	know their origins	그것들의 기원을 알다
02	exact		need an exact description	정확한 묘사를 필요로 하다
03	accurately		tell accurately	정확하게 말하다
04	possibility		There is always the possibility.	가능성은 항상 있다.
05	ancient		ancient inventions	고대의 발명품들
06	pottery		the invention of pottery	도자기 발명품
07	archaeologist		archaeologists believed	고고학자들은 믿었다
08	pot		find pots	항아리를 발견하다
09	date back		date back to 9,000 B.C.	기원전 9,000년으로 거슬러 올라가다
10	tell A from B		tell original from fake	진짜와 가짜를 구별하다
11	explore		explore the materials	물질을 연구하다
12	past		learn from the past	과거로부터 배우다

➕ **본문 문장 속에서 단어의 의미를 우리말로 해석해 보세요.**

Many inventions were invented / thousands of years ago / so it can be difficult / to know their exact origins.

➡ 많은 발명품들은 발명이 되었다 / 수천 년 전에 / 그래서 어려울 수 있다 / 그것들의   을 아는 것은.

STEP 2 • 수능 기출 제대로 풀기

D 다음 글의 제목으로 가장 적절한 것은?

Many inventions were invented thousands of years ago so it can be difficult to know their exact origins. Sometimes scientists discover a model of an early invention and from this model they can accurately tell us how old it is and where it came from. However, there is always the possibility that in the future other scientists will discover an even older model of the same invention in a different part of the world. In fact, we are forever discovering the history of ancient inventions. An example of this is the invention of pottery. For many years archaeologists believed that pottery was first invented in the Near East (around modern Iran) where they had found pots dating back to 9,000 B.C. In the 1960s, however, older pots from 10,000 B.C. were found on Honshu Island, Japan. There is always a possibility that in the future archaeologists will find even older pots somewhere else.

① How Can You Tell Original from Fake?

② Exploring the Materials of Ancient Pottery

③ Origin of Inventions: Never-Ending Journey

④ Learn from the Past, Change for the Better

⑤ Science as a Driving Force for Human Civilization

정답과 해설 p.7

01 Many inventions were invented / thousands of years ago / so it can be difficult /
동사(과거)   시간 부사구(ago: 과거)   가주어
to know their exact origins.
진주어(to부정사)

02 Sometimes scientists discover a model of an early invention / and from this model /
they can accurately tell us / how old it is and where it came from.
tell+간접목적어+직접목적어(의문사절)

03 However, / there is always the possibility / [that in the future other scientists will
동격의 that절(=the possibility)
discover an even older model of the same invention / in a different part of the world].
비교급 강조

04 In fact, / we are forever discovering the history of ancient inventions. // An example of
this is the invention of pottery.

05 For many years / archaeologists believed / that pottery was first invented in the Near
장소 선행사
East (around modern Iran) / [where they had found pots dating back to 9,000 B.C].
명사절 접속사 that
관계부사절   현재분사구

06 In the 1960s, however, / older pots from 10,000 B.C. were found / on Honshu Island,
Japan. // There is always a possibility / [that in the future archaeologists will find even
동격의 that절(=a possibility)
older pots / somewhere else].

01 많은 발명품들은 발명이 되었다 / 수천 년 전에 / 그래서 어려울 수 있다 / 그것들의 정확한exact 기원을 아는 것은.

02 때때로 과학자들은 초기 발명품의 모형을 발견하고 / 이 모형으로부터 / 정확하게accurately 우리에게 말해 줄 수 있다 /
그것이 얼마나 오래되었고 어디에서 왔는지를.

03 그러나 / 가능성possibility이 항상 존재한다 / 미래에 다른 과학자들이 똑같은 발명의 훨씬 더 오래된 모형을 발견할 /
세계의 다른 곳에서.

04 사실 / 우리는 계속해서 고대 발명품들ancient invention의 역사를 발견하고 있다. // 이것의 한 예는 도자기pottery라는
발명품이다.

05 수 년 동안 / 고고학자archaeologist들은 믿었다 / 도자기가 근동지역(현대의 이란 근처)에서 처음 발명되었다고 / 그들이
기원전 9,000년으로 거슬러 올라가는date back 항아리pot를 발견한.

06 그러나, 1960년대에 / 기원전 10,000년의 더 오래된 항아리가 발견되었다 / 일본의 혼슈섬에서. // 가능성은 언제나 존재한다
/ 미래에 고고학자들이 훨씬 더 오래된 항아리를 발견할 / 다른 어딘가에서.

구문 Check up

① Archaeologists believed that pottery was first invented
in the Near East (around modern Iran) when / where
they had found pots dating back to 9,000 B.C.

② There is always a possibility that / which in the future
archaeologists will find even older pots somewhere
else.

the Near East라는 장소를 대신하면서 뒤에 완전한 문장을 수반하므로
관계부사 where를 쓴다.

명사 a possibility를 추가로 설명하는 뒷문장이 완전하므로 동격 접속사
that을 쓴다.

정답 ① where ② that

52

E

STEP 1 • 수능에 *진짜* 나오는 *단어*

✔ 문제에 나오는 단어들을 확인하세요.

시간이 없다면 색으로 표시된 단어만이라도 꼭 외우고 넘어가세요!

01	staple	n. 주요 산물(상품)	a campus (✔ staple)	캠퍼스의 주요한 것	
02	rapid	a. 빠른, 급한	the ( ) rise	빠른 상승	
03	popularity	n. 인기	gain ( )	인기를 얻다	
04	thanks to	~ 덕분에	( ) ( ) him	그 덕분에	
05	convenience	n. 편리함	thanks to the ( )	편리함 덕분에	
06	regulation	n. 규정	a safety ( )	안전 규정	
07	reckless	a. 무모한, 난폭한	a ( ) child	무모한 아이	
08	motorized	a. 전동기가 달린	( ) modes of transportation	전동 방식의 교통수단	
09	restrict	v. 제한하다, 통제하다	( ) the use of mobile phones	핸드폰 사용을 제한하다	
10	target	v. 목표로 삼다, 겨냥하다	( ) motorized scooters	전동 스쿠터를 겨냥하다	
11	reinforce	v. 강화하다	( ) stricter regulations	더 강력한 규정으로 강화하다	
12	flag down	~에게 정지 신호를 하다	( ) ( ) students	학생들에게 정지 신호를 하다	
13	violate	v. 어기다	( ) the regulations	규정을 어기다	

➕ 본문 문장 속에서 단어들을 확인해 보세요.

Their rapid rise to popularity / is thanks to the convenience / they bring, / but it isn't without problems.

그들의 빠른 인기 상승은 / 편리함 덕분이다 / 그들이 가져다주는 / 하지만 그것이 문제가 없는 것은 아니다.

문제를 풀기 전에 단어들을 30초 동안 다시 확인하세요.

01	staple	✎ 주요 산물(상품)	a campus staple	캠퍼스의 주요한 것
02	rapid		the rapid rise	빠른 상승
03	popularity		gain popularity	인기를 얻다
04	thanks to		thanks to him	그 덕분에
05	convenience		thanks to the convenience	편리함 덕분에
06	regulation		a safety regulation	안전 규정
07	reckless		a reckless child	무모한 아이
08	motorized		motorized modes of transportation	전동 방식의 교통수단
09	restrict		restrict the use of mobile phones	핸드폰 사용을 제한하다
10	target		target motorized scooters	전동 스쿠터를 겨냥하다
11	reinforce		reinforce stricter regulations	더 강력한 규정으로 강화하다
12	flag down		flag down students	학생들에게 정지 신호를 하다
13	violate		violate the regulations	규정을 어기다

➕ **본문 문장 속에서 단어의 의미를 우리말로 해석해 보세요.**

Their rapid rise to popularity / is thanks to the convenience / they bring, / but it isn't without problems.

➡️ 그들의   은 /   이다 / 그들이 가져다주는 / 하지만 그것이 문제가 없는 것은 아니다.

STEP 2 · 수능 기출 제대로 풀기

E 다음 글에서 필자가 주장하는 바로 가장 적절한 것은?

These days, electric scooters have quickly become a campus staple. Their rapid rise to popularity is thanks to the convenience they bring, but it isn't without problems. Scooter companies provide safety regulations, but the regulations aren't always followed by the riders. Students can be reckless while they ride, some even having two people on one scooter at a time. Universities already have certain regulations, such as walk-only zones, to restrict motorized modes of transportation. However, they need to do more to target motorized scooters specifically. To ensure the safety of students who use electric scooters, as well as those around them, officials should look into reinforcing stricter regulations, such as having traffic guards flagging down students and giving them warning when they violate the regulations.

① 미성년자의 전동 스쿠터 사용을 금지해야 한다.
② 전동 스쿠터 충전 시설을 더 많이 설치해야 한다.
③ 학생을 위한 대중교통 할인 제도를 정비해야 한다.
④ 캠퍼스 간 이동을 위한 셔틀버스 서비스를 도입해야 한다.
⑤ 대학 내 전동 스쿠터 이용에 대한 규정 강화를 검토해야 한다.

정답과 해설 p.7

01 These days, / electric scooters have quickly become a campus staple.
현재완료(have+p.p.)

02 Their rapid rise to popularity / is thanks to the convenience / they bring, / but it isn't
~ 덕분에   that 생략   목적격 관계대명사절
without problems.

03 Scooter companies provide safety regulations, / but the regulations aren't always
부분 부정:
항상 ~하는 것은 아니다
followed by the riders.

04 Students can be reckless / while they ride, / [some even having two people on one
독립분사구문(=and some even have two ~)
scooter at a time].

05 Universities already have certain regulations, / such as walk-only zones, / to restrict
to부정사의
motorized modes of transportation.
부사적 용법(목적)

06 However, / they need to do more / to target motorized scooters specifically.

07 To ensure the safety of students / who use electric scooters, / as well as those
주격 관계대명사절   ~뿐만 아니라
around them, / officials should look into reinforcing stricter regulations, / such as
동명사(사역동사)
having traffic guards / flagging down students and giving them warning / when
목적어   목적격보어(현재분사)
they violate the regulations.

01 요즘 들어 / 전동 스쿠터가 빠르게 캠퍼스의 주요한 것campus staple이 되고 있다.

02 그들의 빠른 인기 상승their rapid rise to popularity은 / 편리함 덕분thanks to the convenience이다 / 스쿠터가
가져다주는 / 하지만 그것이 문제가 없는 것은 아니다.

03 스쿠터 회사는 안전 규정safety regulations을 제공하고 있지만 / 이 규정들이 탑승자들에게 항상 지켜지는 것은 아니다.

04 학생들은 무모할reckless 수 있다 / 탑승하는 동안, / 일부는 한 대의 스쿠터에 두 명이 한꺼번에 탑승하기도 한다.

05 대학들은 이미 특정한 규정들을 두고 있다 / 보행자 전용 구역과 같은 / 전동 교통수단을 제한하기restrict motorized
modes of transportation 위해.

06 그러나 / 그들은 더 많은 것을 해야 한다 / 특히 전동 스쿠터를 대상으로target motorized scooters 하여.

07 학생들의 안전을 지키기 위하여 / 전동 스쿠터를 이용하는 / 그들 주변의 사람들뿐만 아니라 / 관계자들은 더 엄격한
규정을 강화할reinforce stricter regulations 것을 검토해야 한다 / 교통정리원에게 시키는 등의 (규정) / 학생들에게
정지신호를 주고flag down 경고를 주도록 / 학생들이 규정을 위반했을 때violate the regulations.

구문 Check up

① Students can be reckless while they ride, some even have / having two people on one scooter at a time.

콤마 다음에 다시 문장이 오려면 접속사가 있어야 하지만 없기 때문에 접속사가 생략된 분사구문으로 써야 한다. 따라서 having이 적절하다.

② Officials should look into reinforcing stricter regulations, such as having traffic guards flagging down students and given / giving them warning.

<have+목적어+현재분사>의 5형식 구조에서 현재분사가 <A and B> 형태로 병렬 연결되는 문맥이다. 따라서 giving이 적절하다.

정답 ① having ② giving

제목 추론 ➕

STEP 1 • 수능에 진짜 나오는 단어

✔️ 문제에 나오는 단어들을 확인하세요.

시간이 없다면 색으로 표시된 단어만이라도 꼭 외우고 넘어가세요!

01	transport	v. 이동하다, 실어 나르다	be (✔️ transport)ed into a new life	새로운 삶 속으로 들어가보다
02	type	n. 유형, 형태	one ( ) of library	한 형태의 도서관
03	unique	a. 독특한, 특별한	people with ( ) life stories	특별한 인생 이야기를 가진 사람들
04	volunteer	v. 자원하다	( ) to be the "books"	자원해서 "책"이 되다
05	fascinating	a. 매력적인	( ) stories	매력적인 이야기
06	inspiring	a. 영감을 주는, 감동적인	an ( ) book	감동적인 책
07	stereotype	n. 고정관념	some kind of ( )	일종의 고정관념
08	refugee	n. 피난민	speak with a ( )	피난민과 이야기하다
09	suffer	v. 고통을 겪다	a soldier ( )ing from PTSD	외상 후 스트레스 장애로 고통받는 군인
10	homeless	a. 집이 없는	a ( ) person	노숙자
11	encourage	v. 격려하다, 독려하다	( ) people to challenge	사람들이 도전하도록 격려하다
12	notion	n. 관념, 개념	existing ( )s	기존의 관념
13	judgment	n. 판단	quick ( )s	섣부른 판단

➕ 본문 문장 속에서 단어들을 확인해 보세요.

At a Human Library, / people with unique life stories / volunteer to be the "books."

Human Library에서는 / 특별한 인생 이야기를 가진 사람들은 / 자원해서 "책"이 된다.

문제를 풀기 전에 단어들을 **30초** 동안 다시 확인하세요.

01	transport	✎ 이동하다, 실어 나르다	be transported into a new life	새로운 삶 속으로 들어가보다
02	type		one type of library	한 형태의 도서관
03	unique		people with unique life stories	특별한 인생 이야기를 가진 사람들
04	volunteer		volunteer to be the "books"	자원해서 "책"이 되다
05	fascinating		fascinating stories	매력적인 이야기
06	inspiring		an inspiring book	감동적인 책
07	stereotype		some kind of stereotype	일종의 고정관념
08	refugee		speak with a refugee	피난민과 이야기하다
09	suffer		a soldier suffering from PTSD	외상 후 스트레스 장애로 고통받는 군인
10	homeless		a homeless person	노숙자
11	encourage		encourage people to challenge	사람들이 도전하도록 격려하다
12	notion		existing notions	기존의 관념
13	judgment		quick judgments	섣부른 판단

➕ 본문 문장 속에서 단어의 의미를 우리말로 해석해 보세요.

At a Human Library, / people with unique life stories / volunteer to be the "books."

➡ Human Library에서는, / ▭▭▭▭▭ 인생 이야기를 가진 사람들은 / ▭▭▭▭▭ "책"이 된다.

STEP **2** • 수능 기출 제대로 풀기

F

다음 글의 제목으로 가장 적절한 것은?

Why do you go to the library? For books, yes — and you like books because they tell stories. You hope to get lost in a story or be transported into someone else's life. At one type of library, you can do just that — even though there's not a single book. At a Human Library, people with unique life stories volunteer to be the "books." For a certain amount of time, you can ask them questions and listen to their stories, which are as fascinating and inspiring as any you can find in a book. Many of the stories have to do with some kind of stereotype. You can speak with a refugee, a soldier suffering from PTSD, and a homeless person. The Human Library encourages people to challenge their own existing notions — to truly get to know, and learn from, someone they might otherwise make quick judgements about.

*PTSD(Post Traumatic Stress Disorder): 외상 후 스트레스 장애

① Useful Books for Learning Languages

② The Place Where People Are the Books

③ Library: Starting Point for Your Academic Research

④ How to Choose People in the Human Library

⑤ What a Touching Story of a Booklover!

정답과 해설 p.8

01 Why do you go to the library? // For books, yes / — and you like books / because they tell stories. // You hope to get lost in a story / or be transported into someone else's life.
병렬연결(to에 연결)

02 At one type of library, / you can do just that / — even though there's not a single book.

03 At a Human Library, / people with unique life stories / volunteer to be the "books."
전치사구   volunteer to-V: 자원해서 ~하다

04 For a certain amount of time, / you can ask them questions / and listen to their stories, / which are as fascinating and inspiring / as any you can find in a book.
주격 관계대명사   as 원급 as: …만큼 ~한   목적격 관계대명사 that 생략
(계속적 용법)

05 Many of the stories / have to do with some kind of stereotype.
~와 관련이 있다

06 You can speak with a refugee, / a soldier suffering from PTSD, / and a homeless person.
현재분사

07 The Human Library encourages people to challenge their own existing notions / —
encourage+목적어+목적격 보어(to부정사)   현재분사
to truly get to know, and learn from, someone they might otherwise make quick judgements about.
목적격 관계대명사 who(m) 생략

01 당신은 왜 도서관에 가는가? // 그렇다, 책 때문이다 / 그리고 당신은 책을 좋아한다 / 그 책들이 이야기를 들려주기 때문에. // 당신은 이야기에 몰입하기를 바란다 / 다른 사람의 삶 속으로 들어가 보거나be transported.

02 한 형태type의 도서관에서는, / 당신은 그렇게 할 수 있다 / 비록 그곳에는 책이 한 권도 없지만.

03 Human Library에서는, / 특별한unique 인생 이야기를 가진 사람들이 / 자원해서volunteer "책"이 된다.

04 정해진 시간 동안, / 당신은 그들에게 질문할 수 있고 / 그들의 이야기를 들을 수 있는데, / 이것은 매력적이고fascinating 감동적이다inspiring / 당신이 책에서 발견할 수 있는 그 어떤 것만큼이나.

05 그 이야기들 중 많은 것들은 / 일종의 고정관념stereotype과 관련이 있다.

06 당신은 피난민refugee과 이야기할 수 있다, / 외상 후 스트레스 장애로 고통받는suffer 군인 / 그리고 노숙자 a homeless person와.

07 Human Library는 사람들이 기존의 관념notion에 도전하도록 격려하는데encourage, / 즉, 누군가에 대해 진정으로 알고, 그 사람(누군가)으로부터 배울 수 있도록 해준다 / 그렇지 않았다면 그들이 섣부른 판단judgment을 내렸을 (누군가).

① You hope to get lost in a story or be / are transported into someone else's life.

② You can speak with a refugee, a soldier suffered / suffering from PTSD, and a homeless person.

문맥상 '바라고 옮겨간다'는 의미보다 '이야기에 몰입해 다른 삶으로 들어가보기를' 바란다는 의미이다. 즉 to get에 병렬 연결되는 두 번째 목적어가 필요하므로 (to) be가 적절하다.

꾸밈을 받는 명사(a soldier)와의 관계가 능동이므로 현재분사인 suffering이 적절하다.

정답 ① be ② suffering

STEP 1 • 수능에 *진짜* 나오는 *단어*

✔ **문제에 나오는 단어들을 확인하세요.**

시간이 없다면 색으로 표시된 단어만이라도 꼭 외우고 넘어가세요!

01	archaeologist	n. 고고학자	(✔ archaeologist)s in China	중국에서의 고고학자들
02	extra	a. 추가의, 여분의	an ( ) fee	추가금
03	tear apart	갈가리 찢다	( ) paper ( )	종이를 갈가리 찢다
04	reward	n. 보상, 포상금	increase ( )	포상금을 늘리다
05	similarly	ad. 마찬가지로	( ) = likewise	마찬가지로
06	incentive	n. 장려금	offer an ( )	장려금을 제공하다
07	locate	v. ~의 위치를 알아내다	( ) the missing one	분실한 것을 찾다
08	lower	v. 낮추다	( ) the price	가격을 낮추다
09	noteworthy	a. 주목할 만한	something ( )	주목할 만한 어떤 것
10	radically	ad. 급격하게	( ) change	급격하게 변하다
11	intention	n. 의도	read one's ( )	의도를 읽어내다

➕ **본문 문장 속에서 단어들을 확인해 보세요.**

Instead of lots of extra scrolls being found, / they were simply torn apart / to increase the reward.

다량의 추가 두루마리가 발견되는 대신에 / 그것들은 그저 갈가리 찢겼다 / 포상금을 늘리기 위해.

문제를 풀기 전에 단어들을 30초 동안 다시 확인하세요.

01	archaeologist	고고학자	archaeologists in China	중국에서의 고고학자들
02	extra		an extra fee	추가금
03	tear apart		tear paper apart	종이를 갈가리 찢다
04	reward		increase reward	포상금을 늘리다
05	similarly		similarly = likewise	마찬가지로
06	incentive		offer an incentive	장려금을 제공하다
07	locate		locate the missing one	분실한 것을 찾다
08	lower		lower the price	가격을 낮추다
09	noteworthy		something noteworthy	주목할 만한 어떤 것
10	radically		radically change	급격하게 변하다
11	intention		read one's intention	의도를 읽어내다

➕ 본문 문장 속에서 단어의 의미를 우리말로 해석해 보세요.

Instead of lots of extra scrolls being found, / they were simply torn apart / to increase the reward.

➡ 다량의 〔   〕 두루마리가 발견되는 대신에 / 그것들은 그저 〔   〕 / 〔   〕을 늘리기 위해.

STEP **2** • 수능 기출 제대로 풀기

G 다음 글의 제목으로 가장 적절한 것은?

In 1947, when the Dead Sea Scrolls were discovered, archaeologists set a finder's fee for each new document. Instead of lots of extra scrolls being found, they were simply torn apart to increase the reward. Similarly, in China in the nineteenth century, an incentive was offered for finding dinosaur bones. Farmers located a few on their land, broke them into pieces, and made a lot of money. Modern incentives are no better: Company boards promise bonuses for achieved targets. And what happens? Managers invest more energy in trying to lower the targets than in growing the business. People respond to incentives by doing what is in their best interests. What is noteworthy is, first, how quickly and radically people's behavior changes when incentives come into play, and second, the fact that people respond to the incentives themselves, and not the higher intentions behind them.

*scroll: 두루마리

① Relieve the Glory of the Golden Past

② How Selfishness Weakens Teamwork

③ Rewards Work Against Original Purposes

④ Nonmaterial Incentives: Superior Motivators

⑤ Cultural Heritage Becomes Tourism Booster!

정답과 해설 p.8

01 In 1947, / when the Dead Sea Scrolls <u>were discovered</u>, / archaeologists set a finder's fee
/ for each new document.
수동태: 발견되다

02 Instead of <u>lots of extra scrolls</u> <u>being found</u>, / <u>they</u> were simply torn apart / <u>to increase</u>
동명사의 의미상 주어   동명사   =scrolls   to부정사의
the reward.   부사적 용법(목적)

03 Similarly, / in China in the nineteenth century, / an incentive was offered / for
finding dinosaur bones.

병렬 연결(A, B, and C)

04 Farmers located a few on their land, / broke them into pieces, / and made a lot of
money. // Modern incentives are no better: / Company boards promise bonuses for
achieved targets.
과거분사   콜론(:) 추가 설명

invest A in B: A를 B에 투자하다

05 And what happens? // Managers invest more energy / in trying to lower the targets /
than in growing the business. // People respond to incentives / by doing what is in their
best interests.
관계대명사 what절
(do의 목적어)

06 What is noteworthy is, first, / how quickly and radically people's behavior changes
주어(관계대명사 what절)   동사(수 일치)   주격보어1(how+부사+주어+동사: 얼마나 ~한지)
/ when incentives come into play, / and second, the fact that people respond to the
주격보어2   동격의 that절(=the fact)
incentives themselves, / and not the higher intentions behind them.

01 1947년 / 사해 사본이 발견되었을 때 / 고고학자archaeologist들은 포상금을 걸었다 / 새롭게 발견되는 각각의 문서마다.

02 다량의 추가extra 두루마리가 발견되는 대신에 / 그것들은 그저 갈가리 찢겼다be torn apart / 포상금을 늘리기increase the
reward 위해.

03 이와 유사하게similarly / 19세기 중국에서는 / 포상금incentive이 주어졌다 / 공룡의 뼈를 발견하는 것에 대해.

04 농부들은 그들의 토지에서 몇 개를 찾아내어locate / 그것들을 조각으로 부수고 / 많은 돈을 벌었다. // 현대의 장려금 또한, 더
나을 것이 없다. / 회사의 이사회는 달성된 목표에 대해 보너스를 주겠다고 약속한다.

05 그리고 무슨 일이 일어나는가? // 관리자들은 더 많은 에너지를 투자한다 / 목표치를 낮추는lower the target 것에 / 사업을
키우는 것보다. // 사람들은 장려금에 반응한다 / 그들에게 가장 이익이 되는 것을 행하는 방식으로.

06 주목할 만한noteworthy 것은 첫째로 / 얼마나 빠르게, 그리고 급격하게radically 사람들의 행동이 변화하는가이다 /
장려금이 시행될 때, / 두 번째로는 사람들이 장려금 그 자체에 반응한다는 사실이다 / 장려금의 이면에 있는 높은 차원의
의도intention가 아니라.

구문 Check up

① Instead of lots of extra scrolls finding / being found ,
they were simply torn apart to increase the reward.

② Farmers located / were located a few on their land,
broke them into pieces, and made a lot of money.

두루마기가 '발견되다'라는 의미이기 때문에 수동 형태의 <being+p.p.>
를 써야 한다. 따라서 being found가 적절하다.

농부들이 '찾았다'는 능동의 의미이므로 located를 쓴다. be located는
'~에 위치하다'라는 뜻이다.

정답 ① being found ② located

심경 파악 ✚

STEP 1 • 수능에 *진짜* 나오는 *단어*

✔ 문제에 나오는 단어들을 확인하세요.

시간이 없다면 색으로 표시된 단어만이라도 꼭 외우고 넘어가세요!

01	anticipation	n. 기대	nervous (✔ anticipation)	초조한 기대
02	shake off	~을 떨쳐내다	( ) ( ) an uneasy feeling	불안한 감정을 떨쳐내다
03	missing	a. 빠진, 실종된	Something is ( ).	뭔가 빠졌다.
04	doubt	n. 의심	without a ( )	의심 없이
05	come to mind	떠오르다	Nothing ( )s ( ) ( ).	아무것도 떠오르지 않는다.
06	burst	n. 폭발	a sudden ( ) of emotion	감정의 갑작스런 폭발
07	inspiration	n. 영감	a flash of ( )	번뜩이는 영감
08	grab	v. 쥐다, 잡다	( ) a brush	붓을 쥐다
09	fade	v. 사라지다, 옅어지다	Her smile ( )s.	그녀의 미소가 옅어진다.

✚ 본문 문장 속에서 단어들을 확인해 보세요.

She looks around the cafe, / but she can't shake off the feeling / that something is missing.

그녀는 카페를 둘러보지만, / 그녀는 느낌을 떨쳐낼 수 없다 / 무엇인가 빠졌다는.

문제를 풀기 전에 단어들을 **30초** 동안 다시 확인하세요.

01	anticipation	기대	nervous anticipation	초조한 기대
02	shake off		shake off an uneasy feeling	불안한 감정을 떨쳐내다
03	missing		Something is missing.	뭔가 빠졌다.
04	doubt		without a doubt	의심 없이
05	come to mind		Nothing comes to mind.	아무것도 떠오르지 않는다.
06	burst		a sudden burst of emotion	감정의 갑작스런 폭발
07	inspiration		a flash of inspiration	번뜩이는 영감
08	grab		grab a brush	붓을 쥐다
09	fade		Her smile fades.	그녀의 미소가 옅어진다.

➕ 본문 문장 속에서 단어의 의미를 우리말로 해석해 보세요.

She looks around the cafe, / but she can't shake off the feeling / that something is missing.

→ 그녀는 카페를 둘러보지만, / 그녀는   수 없다 / 무엇인가   는.

2023 3월 학평 19번 문제

STEP **2** • 수능 기출 제대로 풀기

A 다음 글에 드러난 Isabel의 심경 변화로 가장 적절한 것은?

On opening day, Isabel arrives at the cafe very early with nervous anticipation. She looks around the cafe, but she can't shake off the feeling that something is missing. As she sets out cups, spoons, and plates, Isabel's doubts grow. She looks around, trying to imagine what else she could do to make the cafe perfect, but nothing comes to mind. Then, in a sudden burst of inspiration, Isabel grabs her paintbrush and transforms the blank walls into landscapes, adding flowers and trees. As she paints, her doubts begin to fade. Looking at her handiwork, which is beautifully done, she is certain that the cafe will be a success. 'Now, success is not exactly guaranteed,' she thinks to herself, 'but I'll definitely get there.'

① calm → surprised

② doubtful → confident

③ envious → delighted

④ grateful → frightened

⑤ indifferent → uneasy

정답과 해설 **p.10**

01 On opening day, / Isabel arrives at the cafe very early / with nervous anticipation. //
She looks around the cafe, / but she can't shake off the feeling / that something is
missing.
　　　　　　　　　　　　　　　　　　　　　　　　동격의 that(=the feeling)

02 As she sets out cups, spoons, and plates, / Isabel's doubts grow. // She looks around,
　접속사(~할 때)　　　　　　　간접의문문
/ trying to imagine [what else she could do / to make the cafe perfect], / but nothing
　분사구문　　　　　　　　　　　　　　　　부사적 용법(~하기 위해)
comes to mind.

03 Then, / in a sudden burst of inspiration, / Isabel grabs her paintbrush / and transforms
　　　　　　　　　　　　　　　　　　　　　동사1　　　　　　　　　　　　동사2
the blank walls into landscapes, / adding flowers and trees.
　　　　　　　　　　　　　　　분사구문

04 As she paints, / her doubts begin to fade.
　　　　　　　　　　　　begin+to부정사: ~하기 시작하다

05 Looking at her handiwork, / which is beautifully done, / she is certain that the cafe will
　분사구문　　　　　　　handiwork 보충 설명(계속적 용법)
be a success.

06 'Now, success is not exactly guaranteed,' / she thinks to herself, / 'but I'll definitely get
there.'

01 개업식날, / Isabel은 카페에 매우 일찍 도착한다 / 초조한 기대anticipation와 함께. // 그녀는 카페를 둘러보지만, /
그녀는 느낌을 떨쳐낼shake off 수 없다 / 무엇인가 빠졌다missing는.

02 컵과 숟가락, 접시를 차려 놓으며 / Isabel의 의심doubt은 커진다. // 그녀는 주변을 둘러보지만 / 자신이 무엇을 더 할 수
있을지를 상상하기 위해 애쓰면서 / 카페를 완벽하게 만들기 위해 / 아무것도 머릿속에 떠오르지 않는다come to mind.

03 그때 / 갑작스러운 영감의 폭발burst of inspiration과 함께 / Isabel은 그녀의 붓을 쥐고grab / 텅 빈 벽을 풍경화로
변화시킨다 / 꽃과 나무를 더해서.

04 그림을 그리면서, / 그녀의 불안도 서서히 사라지기fade 시작한다.

05 그녀의 작품을 보며, / 아름답게 완성된 / 그녀는 카페가 성공할 거라고 확신한다.

06 '자, 성공이 확실히 보장된 것은 아니지,' / 그녀는 혼자 생각한다. / '하지만 나는 분명 이룰 거야.'

구문 Check up

① She looks around the cafe, but she can't shake off the
feeling that / which something is missing.

뒤에 완전한 절이 나오는 것으로 보아 the feeling을 보충 설명하는 동격
절이다. 따라서 명사절 접속사 that이 적절하다.

② Looking at her handiwork, that / which is beautifully
done, she is certain that the cafe will be a success.

관계대명사 that은 콤마 뒤에서 계속적 용법으로 쓰일 수 없으므로, 관계
대명사 which를 써야 한다.

정답 ① that ② which

B

STEP 1 • 수능에 *진짜* 나오는 *단어*

✔ **문제에 나오는 단어들을 확인하세요.**

시간이 없다면 색으로 표시된 단어만이라도 꼭 외우고 넘어가세요!

01	distribution	n. 분포, 분배	show the (✔ distribution)	분포를 보여 주다
02	demand	n. 수요	oil ( )	원유 수요
03	sector	n. 부문	the distribution by ( )	부문별 분포
04	transportation	n. 교통	road ( )	도로 교통
05	petrochemical	a. 석유화학의 n. (석유화학) 제품	the ( ) industry	석유화학 공업
06	residential	a. 주거의	a ( ) area	주거 지역
07	commercial	a. 상업의	a ( ) success	상업적 성공
08	agricultural	a. 농업의	( ) production	농업 생산
09	aviation	n. 항공, 비행	( ) technology	항공 기술
10	bunker	n. 벙커	marine ( )s	해상 벙커
11	generation	n. (에너지) 발전, 생산	electricity ( )	전기 발전
12	domestic	a. 국내의	( ) politics	국내 정세
13	take up	차지하다	It ( )s ( ) 50%.	그것이 50퍼센트를 차지한다.

⊕ **본문 문장 속에서 단어들을 확인해 보세요.**

The above graph shows / the distribution of oil demand by sector / in the OECD in 2020.

위 그래프는 보여준다 / 원유 수요의 부문별 분포를 / 2020년 OECD에서의.

01	distribution	✎ 분포, 분배	show the distribution	분포를 보여 주다
02	demand		oil demand	원유 수요
03	sector		the distribution by sector	부문별 분포
04	transportation		road transportation	도로 교통
05	petrochemical		the petrochemical industry	석유화학 공업
06	residential		a residential area	주거 지역
07	commercial		a commercial success	상업적 성공
08	agricultural		agricultural production	농업 생산
09	aviation		aviation technology	항공 기술
10	bunker		marine bunkers	해상 벙커
11	generation		electricity generation	전기 발전
12	domestic		domestic politics	국내 정세
13	take up		It takes up 50%.	그것이 50퍼센트를 차지한다.

➕ **본문 문장 속에서 단어의 의미를 우리말로 해석해 보세요.**

The above graph shows / the distribution of oil demand by sector / in the OECD in 2020.

➔ 위 그래프는 보여준다 / 원유   의   별   를 / 2020년 OECD에서의.

STEP **2** · 수능 기출 제대로 풀기

B

다음 도표의 내용과 일치하지 <u>않는</u> 것은?

Distribution of oil demand in the OECD in 2020, by sector

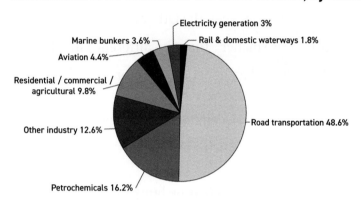

The above graph shows the distribution of oil demand by sector in the OECD in 2020. ① The Road transportation sector, which took up 48.6%, was the greatest oil demanding sector in the OECD member states. ② The percentage of oil demand in the Petrochemicals sector was one-third that of the Road transportation sector. ③ The difference in oil demand between the Other industry sector and the Petrochemicals sector was smaller than the difference in oil demand between the Aviation sector and the Electricity generation sector. ④ The oil demand in the Residential, commercial and agricultural sector took up 9.8% of all oil demand in the OECD, which was the fourth largest among all the sectors. ⑤ The percentage of oil demand in the Marine bunkers sector was twice that of the oil demand in the Rail & domestic waterways sector.

정답과 해설 **p.10**

01 The above graph shows / the distribution of oil demand by sector / in the OECD in 2020.

02 The Road transportation sector, / which took up 48.6%, / was the greatest oil
주어(선행사)　　　　　　　　계속적 용법의 관계대명사절　　　　　the+최상급(가장 ~한)
demanding sector in the OECD member states.

03 　　　　　　　　　　　　　　　　　　　　　　　　　　　　　분수 표현(분자-분모: 기수-서수)
The percentage of oil demand in the Petrochemicals sector / was one-third that of the
　　　　　　　　　　　　　　　　　　　　　　　　　　　　　　　= the percentage of oil demand
Road transportation sector.

04 The difference in oil demand between the Other industry sector and the
주어(단수)　　　　　　　전치사구1　　　전치사구2
Petrochemicals sector / was smaller / than the difference in oil demand between the
　　　　　　　　　　　　동사
Aviation sector and the Electricity generation sector.

05 The oil demand in the Residential, commercial and agricultural sector / took up 9.8%
　　　　　　　　　　　　　　　　　　　　　　　　　　　　　　　　　　　　선행사
of all oil demand in the OECD, / which was the fourth largest among all the sectors.
　　　　　　　　　　　　계속적 용법의 관계대명사절

06 　　　　　　　　　　　　　　　　　　　　　　　　　　　　　　배수사(2배인)
The percentage of oil demand in the Marine bunkers sector / was twice that of the oil
　　　　　　　　　　　　　　　　　　　　　　　　　　　　　　　= the percentage
demand in the Rail & domestic waterways sector.

01 위 그래프는 보여 준다 / 원유 수요demand의 부문sector별 분포distribution를 / 2020년 OECD에서의.

02 도로 교통transportation 부문은 / 48.6%를 차지했는데take up / OECD 회원국들 중 가장 큰 원유 수요 부문이었다.

03 석유화학petrochemical 부문의 원유 수요 비율은 / 도로 교통 부문의 원유 수요 비율의 삼 분의 일이었다.

04 기타 산업 부문과 석유화학 부문 사이의 원유 수요 차이는 / 작았다(→컸다) / 항공aviation 부문과 전기 발전generation
부문 사이의 원유 수요 차이보다.

05 주거, 상업, 그리고 농업 부문residential, commercial, and agricultural sector의 원유 수요는 / OECD의 총 원유
수요의 9.8%를 차지했는데, / 이는 전체 부문 중 네 번째로 컸다.

06 해상 벙커marine bunker 부문의 원유 수요 비율은 / 철도와 국내domestic 수로 부문의 원유 수요 비율의 두 배였다.

구문 Check up	① The percentage of oil demand in the Petrochemicals sector was one-third that / those of the Road transportation sector.	② The oil demand in the Residential, commercial and agricultural sector took up 9.8% of all oil demand in the OECD, that / which was the fourth largest among all the sectors.
	단수인 the percentage를 대신하는 대명사이므로 that을 쓴다.	콤마 뒤의 계속적 용법의 관계대명사로 that은 쓸 수 없으므로 which를 쓴다.

정답 ① that ② which

STEP 1 • 수능에 진짜 나오는 단어

✔️ 문제에 나오는 단어들을 확인하세요.

시간이 없다면 색으로 표시된 단어만이라도 꼭 외우고 넘어가세요!

01	natural gas	천연가스	(✔ natural) (gas) producing countries	천연가스 생산국
02	billion	n. 십억	400 ( )s	4천억
03	cubic meter	세제곱미터	400 billion ( ) ( )s	4천억 세제곱미터
04	respectively	ad. 각각	in 2014 and 2018 ( )	2014년과 2018년 각각
05	gap	n. 차이	the ( ) between Russia and Iran	러시아와 이란 사이의 차이
06	rank	v. (순위에) 오르다	( ) seventh	7위에 오르다
07	three times	세 배	more than ( ) ( )	세 배 이상
08	include	v. 포함시키다	( )d among the top countries	상위 국가에 포함된

➕ 본문 문장 속에서 단어들을 확인해 보세요.

In 2014 and 2018 respectively, / the gap of the amount of natural gas production between Russia and Iran / was larger than 400 billion cubic meters.

2014년과 2018년 각각, / 러시아와 이란 간의 천연가스 생산량 차이는 / 4천억 세제곱미터보다 더 컸다.

01	natural gas	🖉 천연가스	natural gas producing countries	천연가스 생산국
02	billion		400 billions	4천억
03	cubic meter		400 billion cubic meters	4천억 세제곱미터
04	respectively		in 2014 and 2018 respectively	2014년과 2018년 각각
05	gap		the gap between Russia and Iran	러시아와 이란 사이의 차이
06	rank		rank seventh	7위에 오르다
07	three times		more than three times	세 배 이상
08	include		included among the top countries	상위 국가에 포함된

⊕ **본문 문장 속에서 단어의 의미를 우리말로 해석해 보세요.**

In 2014 and 2018 respectively, / the gap of the amount of natural gas production between Russia and Iran / was larger than 400 billion cubic meters.

→ 2014년과 2018년   , / 러시아와 이란 간의 천연가스 생산량   는 /   보다 더 컸다.

2021 6월 학평 25번 문제

제한시간 50초
난이도 ★☆☆☆☆

STEP **2** · 수능 기출 제대로 풀기

C 다음 표의 내용과 일치하지 <u>않는</u> 것은?

Top Seven Natural Gas Producing Countries Worldwide

(unit: billion cubic meters)

2014

Rank	Country	Amount
1	The United States	729
2	Russia	610
3	Iran	172
4	Canada	161
5	Qatar	160
6	China	132
7	Norway	108

2018

Rank	Country	Amount
1	The United States	863
2	Russia	725
3	Iran	248
4	Qatar	181
5	China	176
6	Canada	172
7	Australia	131

The table above shows the top seven natural gas producing countries worldwide in 2014 and 2018. ① The United States, Russia, and Iran were the top three natural gas producing countries in both 2014 and 2018. ② In 2014 and 2018 respectively, the gap of the amount of natural gas production between Russia and Iran was larger than 400 billion cubic meters. ③ Canada ranked lower in 2018 than in 2014 even though the amount of natural gas produced in Canada increased. ④ Between 2014 and 2018, the increase in natural gas production in China was more than three times that in Qatar. ⑤ Australia, which was not included among the top seven natural gas producing countries in 2014, ranked seventh in 2018.

정답과 해설 p.10

75

01 The table above / shows the top seven natural gas producing countries worldwide / in 2014 and 2018.

02 The United States, Russia, and Iran / were the top three natural gas producing countries / in both 2014 and 2018.

03 In 2014 and 2018 respectively, / the gap of the amount of natural gas production
  ⌐----- 수 일치 -----¬
between Russia and Iran / was larger than 400 billion cubic meters.
  비교급+than: ~보다 더 …한

04 Canada ranked lower in 2018 than in 2014 / even though the amount of natural gas
  접속사: ~이긴 하지만(양보)   주어
produced in Canada / increased.
과거분사(natural gas 수식)   동사

05 Between 2014 and 2018, / the increase in natural gas production in China / was more than three times / that in Qatar.
  =the increase in natural gas production

06 Australia, / [which was not included among the top seven natural gas producing
  관계대명사의 계속적 용법 (Australia에 대한 보충설명)
countries in 2014], / ranked seventh in 2018.
  rank+서수: ~위에 오르다

01 위의 표는 / 전 세계의 천연가스natural gas 생산 상위 7개 국가들을 보여준다 / 2014년과 2018년에.

02 미국, 러시아, 이란은 / 상위 3개 천연가스 생산 국가였다 / 2014년과 2018년 모두.

03 2014년과 2018년 각각respectively, / 러시아와 이란 간의 천연가스 생산량 차이gap는 / 4천억 세제곱미터400 billion cubic meters보다 더 컸다.

04 캐나다는 2014년보다 2018년에 더 낮은 순위에 올랐다rank / 비록 캐나다에서 생산된 천연가스 양은 / 증가했지만.

05 2014년과 2018년 사이, / 중국의 천연가스 생산 증가량은 / 3배 이상(→미만)이었다more than three times / 카타르의 그것이.

06 호주는 / 2014년 상위 7개 천연가스 생산 국가에 포함되지be included 않았는데 / 2018년에 7위에 올랐다.

구문 Check up

① Canada ranked lower in 2018 than in 2014 even though the amount of natural gas produced in Canada increasing / increased .

접속사 even though로 시작되는 양보 부사절에 동사가 없으므로, 주절과 시제 일치하여 과거형인 increased를 쓴다.

② Between 2014 and 2018, the increase in natural gas production in China was more than three times that / those in Qatar.

앞에 나온 명사구 the increase ~ gas production을 지칭하므로, 단수인 that이 적절하다.

정답 ① increased ② that

D

STEP 1 • 수능에 진짜 나오는 단어

심경 파악 +

✔ 문제에 나오는 단어들을 확인하세요.

시간이 없다면 색으로 표시된 단어만이라도 꼭 외우고 넘어가세요!

01	summer break	여름 방학	(✔ Summer) (break) started!	여름 방학이 시작되었다!
02	refrigerator	n. 냉장고	in front of the ( )	냉장고 앞에
03	pack	v. (짐을) 싸다	( ) the bag	가방을 싸다
04	soar	v. 치솟다, 날아오르다	( ) like a balloon	풍선처럼 날아오르다
05	beam	v. 반짝거리다, 활짝 웃다	His eyes ( )ed.	그의 눈이 반짝거렸다.
06	groan	v. 신음하다	( ) with pain	고통으로 신음하다
07	anticipation	n. 기대	the feeling of ( )	기대의 감정
08	disappear	v. 사라지다	( ) in a minute	즉시 사라지다
09	in a flash	순식간에	come ( ) ( ) ( )	순식간에 오다
10	miserable	a. 비참한, 우울하게 만드는	( ) conditions	비참한 환경

⊕ 본문 문장 속에서 단어들을 확인해 보세요.

The anticipation he had felt / disappeared in a flash.

그가 느꼈던 기대가 / 순식간에 사라졌다.

01	summer break	🖊 여름 방학	Summer break started!	여름 방학이 시작되었다!
02	refrigerator		in front of the refrigerator	냉장고 앞에
03	pack		pack the bag	가방을 싸다
04	soar		soar like a balloon	풍선처럼 날아오르다
05	beam		His eyes beamed.	그의 눈이 반짝거렸다.
06	groan		groan with pain	고통으로 신음하다
07	anticipation		the feeling of anticipation	기대의 감정
08	disappear		disappear in a minute	즉시 사라지다
09	in a flash		come in a flash	순식간에 오다
10	miserable		miserable conditions	비참한 환경

➕ **본문 문장 속에서 단어의 의미를 우리말로 해석해 보세요.**

The anticipation he had felt / disappeared in a flash.

→ 그가 느꼈던 ▭▭▭▭▭가 / ▭▭▭▭▭▭▭▭▭.

STEP **2** • 수능 기출 제대로 **풀기**

 다음 글에 드러난 Ryan의 심경 변화로 가장 적절한 것은?

Ryan, an eleven-year-old boy, ran home as fast as he could. Finally, summer break had started! When he entered the house, his mom was standing in front of the refrigerator, waiting for him. She told him to pack his bags. Ryan's heart soared like a balloon. *Pack for what? Are we going to Disneyland?* He couldn't remember the last time his parents had taken him on a vacation. His eyes beamed. "You're spending the summer with uncle Tim and aunt Gina." Ryan groaned. "The whole summer?" "Yes, the whole summer." The anticipation he had felt disappeared in a flash. For three whole miserable weeks, he would be on his aunt and uncle's farm. He sighed.

① excited → disappointed

② furious → regretful

③ irritated → satisfied

④ nervous → relaxed

⑤ pleased → jealous

정답과 해설 p.11

01 Ryan, an eleven-year-old boy, / ran home as fast as he could. // Finally, summer break
　복합형용사(수사+명사)　　　　　　　　　　as+원급+as ~ can[could]: 최대한 ~한/하게
had started!

02 When he entered the house, / his mom was standing in front of the refrigerator, /
waiting for him. // She told him to pack his bags.
분사구문　　　　　　　　tell+목적어+to부정사: ~에게 …하라고 말하다

03 Ryan's heart soared like a balloon. // *Pack for what?* / *Are we going to Disneyland?*
　　　　　　　　　　전치사(~처럼)

　　　　　　　　　　　　　　　　관계부사 when 생략
04 He couldn't remember the last time / his parents had taken him on a vacation. // His
eyes beamed.

05 "You're spending the summer with uncle Tim and aunt Gina."
　　현재진행(비교적 확실한 미래)

06 Ryan groaned. // "The whole summer?" // "Yes, the whole summer."

　　　　　　　　　　　　　　자동사
07 The anticipation he had felt / disappeared in a flash.
주어　　　　　　목적격 관계대명사절

08 For three whole miserable weeks, / he would be on his aunt and uncle's farm. // He
for+(숫자) 기간: ~ 동안
sighed.

---

01 11살 소년 Ryan은 / 최대한 빨리 집으로 달려갔다. // 마침내, 여름 방학summer break이 시작되었다!

02 그가 집으로 들어갔을 때 / 그의 엄마는 냉장고refrigerator 앞에 서 있었다 / 그를 기다리면서. // 그녀는 그에게 가방을
싸라pack고 말했다.

03 Ryan의 심장이 풍선처럼 날아올랐다soar. // '왜 가방을 싸지? / 우리 디즈니랜드라도 가나?'

04 그는 마지막으로 ~한 때가 기억나지 않았다 / 부모님이 자신을 데리고 휴가를 갔던. // 그의 두 눈이 반짝거렸다beam.

05 "너는 Tim 삼촌과 Gina 숙모와 함께 여름을 보내게 될 거야."

06 Ryan은 신음을 냈다groan. // "여름 내내요?" // "그래. 여름 내내."

07 그가 느꼈던 기대anticipation가 / 순식간에 사라졌다disappear in a flash.

08 끔찍한miserable 3주 내내, / 그는 삼촌과 숙모의 농장에서 지내게 될 것이었다. // 그는 한숨을 쉬었다.

구문 Check up

① When he entered the house, his mom was standing in front of the refrigerator, waited / waiting for him.

was standing 이후로 접속사가 없으므로 새로운 동사를 추가하는 것은 불가능하다. 따라서 분사인 waiting을 써야 한다.

② The anticipation he had felt disappeared / was disappeared in a flash.

disappear는 수동태로 쓸 수 없는 자동사이다. 따라서 disappeared가 적절하다.

정답 ① waiting ② disappeared

E

STEP 1 • 수능에 *진짜* 나오는 *단어*

✔ 문제에 나오는 단어들을 확인하세요.

시간이 없다면 색으로 표시된 단어만이라도 꼭 외우고 넘어가세요!

01	disaster	n. 재난, 재해	a natural (✔ disaster)	자연재해
02	region	n. 지역	natural disasters by ( )	지역별 자연재해
03	amount	n. 양, 액수	a large ( ) of information	많은 양의 정보
04	damage	n. 피해	the amount of ( )	피해액
05	account for	~을 차지하다	( ) ( ) 36 percent	36%를 차지하다
06	a third	3분의 1	( ) ( ) = one third	3분의 1
07	combined	a. 합쳐진	the ( ) amount	합쳐진 금액
08	rank	v. (순위를) 차지하다	( ) third	3위를 차지하다

⊕ 본문 문장 속에서 단어들을 확인해 보세요.

The amount of damage in Asia / was the largest / and more than the combined amount of Americas and Europe.

아시아의 피해액이 / 가장 많았으며 / 아메리카와 유럽의 합쳐진 액수보다 더 많았다.

01	disaster	재난, 재해	a natural disaster	자연재해
02	region		natural disasters by region	지역별 자연재해
03	amount		a large amount of information	많은 양의 정보
04	damage		the amount of damage	피해액
05	account for		account for 36 percent	36%를 차지하다
06	a third		a third = one third	3분의 1
07	combined		the combined amount	합쳐진 금액
08	rank		rank third	3위를 차지하다

⊕ 본문 문장 속에서 단어의 의미를 우리말로 해석해 보세요.

The amount of damage in Asia / was the largest / and more than the combined amount of Americas and Europe.

→ 아시아의   이 / 가장 많았으며 / 아메리카와 유럽의   액수보다 더 많았다.

STEP **2** · 수능 기출 제대로 풀기

E

다음 도표의 내용과 일치하지 <u>않는</u> 것은?

Natural Disasters by Region, 2014

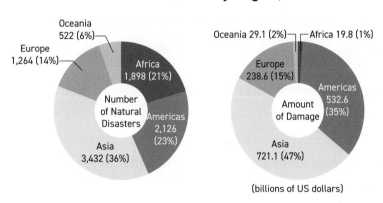

(billions of US dollars)

The two pie charts above show the number of natural disasters and the amount of damage by region in 2014. ① The number of natural disasters in Asia was the largest of all five regions and accounted for 36 percent, which was more than twice the percentage of Europe. ② Americas had the second largest number of natural disasters, taking up 23 percent. ③ The number of natural disasters in Oceania was the smallest and less than a third of that in Africa. ④ The amount of damage in Asia was the largest and more than the combined amount of Americas and Europe. ⑤ Africa had the least amount of damage even though it ranked third in the number of natural disasters.

정답과 해설 p.11

01 The two pie charts above show / the number of natural disasters / and the amount of damage / by region in 2014.

02 The number of natural disasters in Asia / was the largest of all five regions / and
   주어(the number of+복수명사: 단수 취급)   동사1
accounted for 36 percent, / which was more than twice the percentage of Europe.
동사2   선행사   관계대명사 계속적 용법(=and it was~)

03 Americas had the second largest number of natural disasters, / taking up 23 percent.
                                                              분사구문

04 The number of natural disasters in Oceania / was the smallest / and less than a third of
that in Africa.
=the number of natural disasters

05 The amount of damage in Asia / was the largest / and more than the combined amount
                                                              과거분사
of Americas and Europe.

06 Africa had the least amount of damage / even though it ranked third / in the number of
                                      양보 부사절 접속사: 비록 ~이지만
natural disasters.

---

01 위의 두 원그래프는 보여 준다 / 자연재해natural disaster 횟수와 / 피해액the amount of damage을 / 2014년의
   지역region별.

02 아시아의 자연재해 횟수가 / 다섯 지역region 중 가장 많았으며, / 36%를 차지했다account for / 그것은 유럽의 비율의
   2배가 넘는다.

03 아메리카가 자연재해 횟수가 두 번째로 많았다 / 23%를 차지하면서.

04 오세아니아의 자연재해 횟수가 / 가장 적었으며 / 아프리카의 자연재해 횟수의 3분의 1a third도 안 되었다.

05 아시아의 피해액이 / 가장 많았으며 / 아메리카와 유럽을 합친 액수the combined amount보다 더 많았다(→더 적었다).

06 아프리카가 피해액은 가장 적었다 / 비록 3위를 차지했지만rank third / 자연재해 횟수에서는.

Check up

① The number of natural disasters in Oceania was the smallest and less than a third of it / that in Africa.

비교급에서 앞의 단수 명사를 받을 때는 that을 쓰는데, 여기서도 the number of natural disasters를 받기 때문에 that을 쓴다.

② The amount of damage in Asia was the largest and more than the combining / combined amount of Americas and Europe.

amount가 '합쳐지는' 대상이므로 과거분사 combined를 써서 꾸민다.

정답 ① that ② combined

F

STEP 1 • 수능에 *진짜* 나오는 *단어*

✔ 문제에 나오는 단어들을 확인하세요.

시간이 없다면 색으로 표시된 단어만이라도 꼭 외우고 넘어가세요!

01	momentous	a. 중요한	a (✔ momentous) event	중요한 사건
02	reunion	n. 동창회, 재결합	a ( ) of the class of 1960	1960년 졸업생들의 동창회
03	regretfully	ad. 안타깝게도, 애석한 듯	( ), life is not so simple.	안타깝게도, 인생은 그렇게 간단하지 않다.
04	afford	v. (~을) 살[감당할] 여유가 있다	( ) the trip	여행을 갈 여유가 있다
05	envelope	n. 봉투	hand me an ( )	내게 봉투를 건네주다
06	lecture	v. 잔소리하다, 설교하다, 강연하다	( ) me about friendship	내게 우정에 관해 잔소리하다
07	roughly	ad. 약, 대략	( ) $200 cash	약 200달러
08	sibling	n. 형제자매	competition between ( )s	형제자매들 간의 경쟁
09	pool	v. (공동으로 쓸 자금을) 모으다	( ) their money	그들의 돈을 모으다
10	payback	n. 보상, 회수, 되갚음	Don't even think about ( )!	되갚는 것은 생각도 하지 마세요!
11	stunned	a. (놀라거나 기뻐서) 어안이 벙벙한	She was ( ).	그녀는 어안이 벙벙했다.

✚ 본문 문장 속에서 단어들을 확인해 보세요.

The letter stated / that all four siblings had met / and agreed to pool their money / to get me to the reunion.

그 편지에는 쓰여 있었다 / 사 남매 모두가 만났고 / 자신들의 돈을 모으는 데 동의했다고 / 나를 동창회에 보내기 위해.

문제를 풀기 전에 단어들을 30초 동안 다시 확인하세요.

01	momentous	🖉 중요한	a momentous event	중요한 사건
02	reunion		a reunion of the class of 1960	1960년 졸업생들의 동창회
03	regretfully		Regretfully, life is not so simple.	안타깝게도, 인생은 그렇게 간단하지 않다.
04	afford		afford the trip	여행을 갈 여유가 있다
05	envelope		hand me an envelope	내게 봉투를 건네주다
06	lecture		lecture me about friendship	내게 우정에 관해 잔소리하다
07	roughly		roughly $200 cash	약 200달러
08	sibling		competition between siblings	형제자매들 간의 경쟁
09	pool		pool their money	그들의 돈을 모으다
10	payback		Don't even think about payback!	되갚는 것은 생각도 하지 마세요!
11	stunned		She was stunned.	그녀는 어안이 벙벙했다.

➕ 본문 문장 속에서 단어의 의미를 우리말로 해석해 보세요.

The letter stated / that all four siblings had met / and agreed to pool their money / to get me to the reunion.

→ 그 편지에는 쓰여 있었다 / 사 남매 모두가 만났고 / 　　　　　　　데 동의했다고 / 　　　　　　　.

86

STEP **2** · 수능 기출 제대로 풀기

F

다음 글에 드러난 'I'의 심경 변화로 가장 적절한 것은?

Our class of 1960 was going to be returning for our momentous 50th reunion, but I had sadly stated to one of my four kids that regretfully, I was going to miss the reunion because I just couldn't afford the trip. Then one evening my youngest daughter, Kelly, handed me an envelope and said, "Read this later." A letter inside the envelope lectured me all about how important old friendships are at all ages and that I absolutely "must attend my 50th reunion since it is a once in a lifetime event." Included within was a round-trip airline ticket to and from Syracuse and roughly $200 cash. The letter stated that all four siblings had met and agreed to pool their money to get me to the reunion. "And don't even think about payback!" I sat there in stunned silence. And I wept.

① jealous → satisfied

② panicked → relieved

③ sorrowful → touched

④ excited → disappointed

⑤ frightened → indifferent

정답과 해설 p.12

STEP 3 • 수능 지문 제대로 복습하기

01 Our class of 1960 was going to be returning for our momentous 50th reunion, / but
I had sadly stated to one of my four kids / that regretfully, I was going to miss the
reunion / because I just couldn't afford the trip.
과거완료(was going to보다 이전)　　접속사(~것)

02 Then one evening / my youngest daughter, Kelly, / handed me an envelope and said, /
"Read this later."
　　　　　　동격

03 A letter inside the envelope / lectured me all about how important old friendships are
at all ages / and that I absolutely "must attend my 50th reunion / since it is a once in a
lifetime event."
how+형/부+주어+동사: 얼마나/어떻게 ~한지　　접속사(이유)

04 Included within was / a round-trip airline ticket to and from Syracuse / and roughly
$200 cash.
보어(도치 구문)　동사　　　　　　　　　　주어

05 The letter stated / that all four siblings had met / and agreed to pool their money / to
get me to the reunion. // "And don't even think about payback!"
동사1　목적절　　　　　　동사2
부사적 용법(~하기 위해)

06 I sat there in stunned silence. // And I wept.
　　　　과거분사

---

01 우리 1960년 졸업생들은 중요한momentous 50주년 동창회reunion를 맞아 다시 모일 것이었지만, / 나는 나의 네 아이 중 한 명에게 슬프게 얘기했었다 / 안타깝게도regretfully 내가 동창회에 가지 못할 거라고 / 왜냐면 나는 오고 가는 여비를 감당할afford 수 없어서.

02 그러던 어느 날 / 저녁에 막내딸인 Kelly가 / 내게 봉투envelope 하나를 건네며 말했다 / "이거 이따 읽어보세요."라고.

03 그 봉투 속 편지는 / 내게 모든 연령대에서 오래된 우정이 얼마나 중요한지에 관해 내내 잔소리하고lecture 있었다 / 그리고 내가 꼭 "내 50주년 동창회에 참석해야 한다고 / 그것이 내 인생 단 한 번뿐인 행사이므로".

04 안에는 있었다 / Syracuse 왕복 항공권과 / 약roughly 200달러의 현금이.

05 그 편지에는 쓰여 있었다 / 사 남매sibling 모두가 만났고 / 자신들의 돈을 모으는pool 데 동의했다고 / 나를 동창회에 보내기 위해. // "그리고 돈을 갚을payback 생각조차 하지 마세요!"

06 나는 어안이 벙벙해진 채stunned 할 말을 잃고 거기 앉아 있었다. // 그리고 나는 눈물을 흘렸다.

구문 Check up

① A letter inside the envelope lectured me all about how **important / importantly** old friendships are at all ages.

'how+형/부+주어+동사'의 동사가 are인 것으로 보아 how 뒤는 보어 자리이다. 따라서 형용사인 important가 적절하다.

② Included within **was / being** a round-trip airline ticket to and from Syracuse and roughly $200 cash.

'보어(수동태의 과거분사)+동사+주어' 어순의 도치 구문이므로, 주어인 명사구 앞에 동사 was가 적절하다.

정답 ① important ② was

STEP 1 • 수능에 진짜 나오는 단어

✔ 문제에 나오는 단어들을 확인하세요.

시간이 없다면 색으로 표시된 단어만이라도 꼭 외우고 넘어가세요!

01	distribution	n. 분배, 분포	(✓ distribution) of music listeners	음악 청취자의 분포
02	format	n. 형태, 형식	traditional ( ) music	고전적인 형식의 음악
03	download	v. 내려받다	( ) music	음악을 내려받다
04	consume	v. 소비하다	( ) music	음악을 소비하다
05	take up	차지하다	( ) ( ) more than 60 percent	60% 이상을 차지하다
06	gap	n. 격차	the percentage point ( )	퍼센트 포인트 격차
07	outnumber	v. ~보다 수가 많다	tourists ( ) the locals	여행객이 현지인보다 수가 더 많다

⊕ 본문 문장 속에서 단어들을 확인해 보세요.

In ages 45 to 54, / those who only listened to traditional formats / outnumbered music listeners of the other types, / taking up more than 60 percent.

45~54세 집단에서 / 전통적인 형식만을 들은 사람들이 / 나머지 유형의 음악을 들은 사람들보다 수가 더 많았다 / 60퍼센트 이상을 차지하며.

문제를 풀기 전에 단어들을 **30초** 동안 다시 확인하세요.

01	distribution	✏ 분배, 분포	distribution of music listeners	음악 청취자의 분포
02	format		traditional format music	고전적인 형식의 음악
03	download		download music	음악을 내려받다
04	consume		consume music	음악을 소비하다
05	take up		take up more than 60 percent	60% 이상을 차지하다
06	gap		the percentage point gap	퍼센트 포인트 격차
07	outnumber		tourists outnumber the locals	여행객이 현지인보다 수가 더 많다

⊕ **본문 문장 속에서 단어의 의미를 우리말로 해석해 보세요.**

In ages 45 to 54, / those who only listened to traditional formats / outnumbered music listeners of the other types, / taking up more than 60 percent.

➜ 45~54세 집단에서 / 전통적인 _____ 만을 들은 사람들이 / 나머지 유형의 음악을 들은 사람들보다 _____ / 60퍼센트 이상을 _____.

90

STEP 2 • 수능 기출 제대로 풀기

G 다음 도표의 내용과 일치하지 않는 것은?

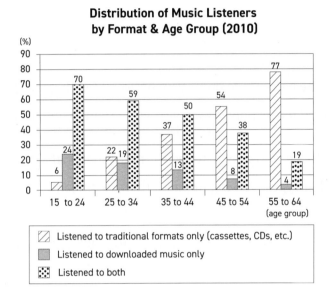

**Distribution of Music Listeners
by Format & Age Group (2010)**

Listened to traditional formats only (cassettes, CDs, etc.)
Listened to downloaded music only
Listened to both

The graph above shows the percentage of music listeners from different age groups who consumed only traditional format music, only downloaded music, or both formats of music in 2010. ① In each age group, except for in ages 15 to 24, those who only listened to downloaded music took up the lowest percentage. ② The older the age group was, the lower the percentage of those who listened to both was. ③ In ages 25 to 34, the percentage point gap between listeners of traditional formats only and downloaded music only was narrower than in any other age group. ④ In ages 45 to 54, those who only listened to traditional formats outnumbered music listeners of the other types, taking up more than 60 percent. ⑤ More than 70 percent of the 55 to 64 age group listened to traditional formats only.

정답과 해설 p.12

STEP 3 • 수능 지문 제대로 복습하기

01 The graph above shows / the percentage of music listeners from different age groups / who consumed only traditional format music, only downloaded music, or both
주격 관계대명사절
formats of music / in 2010.

02 In each age group, / except for in ages 15 to 24, / those who only listened to
주어   주격 관계대명사절
downloaded music / took up the lowest percentage.
동사

03 The older the age group was, / the lower the percentage of those who listened to both
the 비교급 ~, the 비교급 …: ~할수록 더 …하다   주격 관계대명사절
was.

04 In ages 25 to 34, / the percentage point gap [between listeners of traditional formats
주어   전치사구
only and downloaded music only] / was narrower / than in any other age group.
동사(단수)

05 In ages 45 to 54, / those who only listened to traditional formats / outnumbered music
주어   주격 관계대명사절   동사
listeners of the other types, / taking up more than 60 percent.
분사구문: ~하면서

06 More than 70 percent of the 55 to 64 age group / listened to traditional formats only.
~ 이상인

---

01 위 그래프는 보여준다 / 다른 연령 집단의 음악 청취자들의 비율을 / 전통적인 형식traditional format music만을, 또는 다운로드 음악만을, 또는 둘 다 소비한consume, / 2010년에.

02 각 연령 집단에서 / 15~24세 집단을 제외한 / 다운로드 음악download music만을 들었던 사람들이 / 최저 비율을 차지했다take up.

03 연령 집단의 나이가 많을수록, / 두 형식을 모두 들은 사람들의 비율은 점차 낮아졌다.

04 25~34세 집단에는 / 전통적인 형식만을 들은 사람들과 다운로드 음악만을 들은 사람들 간의 퍼센트포인트 격차gap가 / 더 좁았다 / 다른 연령 집단보다.

05 45~54세 집단에서 / 전통적인 형식만을 들은 사람들이 / 나머지 유형의 음악을 들은 사람들보다 수가 더 많았다outnumber / 60퍼센트 이상(→미만)을 차지하며.

06 55~64세 연령 집단의 70퍼센트 이상이 / 전통적인 형식만 들었다.

구문 Check up

① The older the age group was, the lower the percentage of those who listened to both was / were .

주어가 the percentage로 단수이기 때문에 수 일치하여 was를 써야 한다.

② In ages 45 to 54, those who only listened to traditional formats outnumbered music listeners of the other types, took / taking up more than 60 percent.

이 문장의 동사는 outnumbered이고 접속사가 없기 때문에, 바로 동사 took이 연결될 수 없고 분사구문인 taking으로 써야 한다.

정답 ① was ② taking

92

☑ 종합 성적표

구분	공부한 날 ❶	결과 분석			틀린 이유 ❸
		출처	풀이 시간 ❷	채점 결과 (O, X)	
Day 1	월 일	학력평가 기출 2023년	분 초		
		학력평가 기출 2022년	분 초		
		학력평가 기출 2021년	분 초		
		학력평가 기출 2020년	분 초		
		학력평가 기출 2019년	분 초		
		학력평가 기출 2018년	분 초		
		학력평가 기출 2017년	분 초		
Day 2	월 일	학력평가 기출 2023년	분 초		
		학력평가 기출 2022년	분 초		
		학력평가 기출 2021년	분 초		
		학력평가 기출 2020년	분 초		
		학력평가 기출 2019년	분 초		
		학력평가 기출 2018년	분 초		
		학력평가 기출 2017년	분 초		
Day 3	월 일	학력평가 기출 2023년	분 초		
		학력평가 기출 2022년	분 초		
		학력평가 기출 2021년	분 초		
		학력평가 기출 2020년	분 초		
		학력평가 기출 2019년	분 초		
		학력평가 기출 2018년	분 초		
		학력평가 기출 2017년	분 초		

3일간
공부한 내용을
다시 보니,
……

❶ 매일 지문을 하루 계획에 맞춰 풀었다. vs. 내가 한 약속을 못 지켰다.

<매3영 고2 기출>은 단순 문제풀이를 위한 책이 아니라, 매일 규칙적으로 영어를 공부하는 습관을 잡는 책입니다. 따라서 푸는 문제 개수는 상황에 따라 다르더라도 '매일' 학습하는 것이 중요합니다.

❷ 주어진 시간을 자꾸 넘긴다?

풀이 시간이 계속해서 권장 시간을 넘긴다면 실전 훈련이 부족하다는 신호입니다. 아직 조급함을 가질 필요는 없지만, 매일의 문제 풀이에 더 긴장감 있게 임해보세요.

❸ 틀린 이유 맞춤 솔루션: 오답 이유에 따라 다음 해결책을 참고하세요.

(1) 단어를 많이 몰라서

▶ <STEP 1 단어>에 제시된 필수 어휘를 매일 챙겨보고, SELF-TEST까지 꼼꼼히 진행합니다.

(2) 문장 해석이 잘 안 돼서

▶ <STEP 3 지문 복습>의 구문 첨삭과 끊어읽기 해설을 정독하며 문장구조를 보는 눈을 길러보세요.

(3) 해석은 되지만 내용이 이해가 안 되거나, 선택지로 연결을 못 해서

▶ <정답과 해설>의 해설과 오답풀이를 참고해 틀린 이유를 깊이 고민하고 정리해 보세요.

! 결론적으로, 내가 **취약한 부분**은 [   ] 이다. **취약점을 보완하기 위해서** 나는
[   ] 을/를 해야겠다.

3일 뒤 다시 봐야 할 문항과, 꼭 다시 외워야 할 사항·구문 등이 있는 페이지는 지금 바로 접어 두세요.

<매3영>이 제시하는 3단계로

유형 3일 훈련

DAY

04~06

함축적 의미 추론 +

STEP 1 • 수능에 진짜 나오는 단어

✔ 문제에 나오는 단어들을 확인하세요.

시간이 없다면 색으로 표시된 단어만이라도 꼭 외우고 넘어가세요!

01	get over	~을 극복하다	(✔ get) (over) a breakup	이별을 극복하다
02	obstacle	n. 장애물	a major ( )	중대한 장애물
03	all-or-nothing	a. 전부 아니면 전무의, 양자택일의	have an ( ) mentality	전부 아니면 전무 식의 사고방식
04	alter	v. 바꾸다, 고치다	( ) your idea	당신의 생각을 바꾸다
05	emerge	v. 나타나다, 떠오르다, 부상하다	Problems began to ( ).	문제가 나타나기 시작했다.
06	well-funded	a. 투자를 많이 받은	a ( ) company	투자를 많이 받은 회사
07	conceive	v. 고안하다, (생각을) 품다	( ) an idea	아이디어를 고안하다
08	bill	n. 법안	approve a ( )	법안을 승인하다
09	troubled	a. 힘든, 문제가 많은	kids in ( ) areas	힘든 지역의 아이들

➕ 본문 문장 속에서 단어들을 확인해 보세요.

You have to be willing / to alter your idea / and let others influence its outcome.

여러분은 기꺼이 ~해야 한다 / 아이디어를 바꾸고 / 다른 사람들이 그 결과에 영향을 미치게.

문제를 풀기 전에 단어들을 30초 동안 다시 확인하세요.

01	get over	✎ ~을 극복하다	get over a breakup	이별을 극복하다
02	obstacle		a major obstacle	중대한 장애물
03	all-or-nothing		have an all-or-nothing mentality	전부 아니면 전무 식의 사고방식
04	alter		alter your idea	당신의 생각을 바꾸다
05	emerge		Problems began to emerge.	문제가 나타나기 시작했다.
06	well-funded		a well-funded company	투자를 많이 받은 회사
07	conceive		conceive an idea	아이디어를 고안하다
08	bill		approve a bill	법안을 승인하다
09	troubled		kids in troubled areas	힘든 지역의 아이들

➕ 본문 문장 속에서 단어의 의미를 우리말로 해석해 보세요.

You have to be willing / to alter your idea / and let others influence its outcome.

→ 여러분은 기꺼이 ~해야 한다 /   / 다른 사람들이 그 결과에 영향을 미치게.

A 밑줄 친 helping move the needle forward가 다음 글에서 의미하는 바로 가장 적절한 것은?

Everyone's heard the expression *don't let the perfect become the enemy of the good.* If you want to get over an obstacle so that your idea can become the solution-based policy you've long dreamed of, you can't have an all-or-nothing mentality. You have to be willing to alter your idea and let others influence its outcome. You have to be okay with the outcome being a little different, even a little *less*, than you wanted. Say you're pushing for a clean water act. Even if what emerges isn't as well-funded as you wished, or doesn't match how you originally conceived the bill, you'll have still succeeded in ensuring that kids in troubled areas have access to clean water. That's what counts, that *they* will be safer because of your idea and your effort. Is it perfect? No. Is there more work to be done? Absolutely. But in almost every case, helping move the needle forward is vastly better than not helping at all.

① spending time and money on celebrating perfection

② suggesting cost-saving strategies for a good cause

③ making a difference as best as the situation allows

④ checking your resources before altering the original goal

⑤ collecting donations to help the education of poor children

정답과 해설 p.13

01 Everyone's heard the expression / *don't let the perfect become the enemy of the good*.
　　　　　　　　　　　　　 └──── 동격 ────┘

02 If you want to get over an obstacle / so that your idea can become the solution-based
　　　　　　　　　　　　　　　　　　　접속사(~하기 위해)
policy / you've long dreamed of, / you can't have an all-or-nothing mentality.
　　　 목적격 관계대명사절

03 You have to be willing / to alter your idea / and let others influence its outcome. // You
　　　　　 be willing to+동사원형: 기꺼이 ~하다
have to be okay / with the outcome being a little different, even a little *less*, / than you
　　　　　　　 전치사　　의미상 주어　　동명사구
wanted.

04　　　　　　　　　　　　　　　　 접속사(설령 ~하더라도)
Say you're pushing for a clean water act. // Even if what emerges isn't as well-funded
명령문(~하라)　　　　　　　　　　　　 주어　　　 동사1 as+원급+as: ~만큼 …한
/ as you wished, / or doesn't match how you originally conceived the bill, / you'll have
　 　　　　　　 동사2
still succeeded in ensuring / that kids in troubled areas have access to clean water.
　　　　　　　　　　　 명사절 접속사(~것)

05 That's what counts, / that *they* will be safer / because of your idea and your effort.
　　　　　　　　　　　　　　　　　　　　　 전치사(~ 때문에)

06 Is it perfect? // No. // Is there more work to be done? // Absolutely.
　　　　　　　　　　　　　　　 └┄┄┄ 형용사적 용법

07 But in almost every case, / helping move the needle forward / is vastly better than not
　　　　　　　　　　　　　 주어(동명사)　　　　　　　　　　 동사 비교급+than: ~보다 더 …한
helping at all.

---

01 표현을 누구나 들어 본 적이 있다 / '완벽함이 좋음의 적이 되게 두지 말라'는.

02 여러분이 장애물을 극복하기get over an obstacle를 원한다면 / 여러분의 아이디어가 해결을 기반으로 한 방책이 될 수 있게 하려고 / 여러분이 오랫동안 꿈꿔 왔던 / 전부 아니면 전무all-or-nothing라고 여기는 사고방식을 가져서는 안 된다.

03 여러분은 기꺼이 ~해야 한다 / 아이디어를 바꾸고alter / 다른 사람들이 그 결과에 영향을 미치게. // 여러분은 괜찮아야 한다 / 결과가 조금 다르거나, 심지어 조금 '못해도' / 여러분이 원했던 것과는.

04 여러분이 수질 오염 방지법을 추진하고 있다고 가정해 보자. // 설령 나타난emerge 것이 자금을 충분히 지원받지well-funded 못했거나 / 여러분이 원했던 만큼 / 여러분이 처음에 이 법안을 고안한conceive the bill 방식과 일치하지 않더라도, / 여러분은 확실히 하는 데 여전히 성공하는 것이다 / 힘든troubled 지역의 아이들이 깨끗한 물을 이용할 수 있게.

05 그게 중요한 것이다 / 바로 '그들'이 더 안전하리라는 것 / 여러분의 아이디어와 노력 덕분에.

06 완벽한가? // 아니다. // 더 해야 할 일이 있는가? // 당연하다.

07 하지만 거의 모든 경우에, / 바늘이 앞으로 가게 돕는 것이 / 전혀 돕지 않는 것보다 훨씬 더 낫다.

구문 Check up

① You have to be okay with the outcome is / being a little different, even a little *less*, than you wanted.

전치사 with의 목적어 자리이므로 동명사 being이 적절하다. the outcome은 being의 의미상 주어이다.

② But in almost every case, helping / help move the needle forward is vastly better than not helping at all.

동사 is 앞에 주어가 필요하므로 동명사 helping이 적절하다.

정답 ① being ② helping

STEP 1 • 수능에 *진짜* 나오는 *단어*

✔ 문제에 나오는 단어들을 확인하세요.

시간이 없다면 색으로 표시된 단어만이라도 꼭 외우고 넘어가세요!

01	delight	v. 즐겁게 하다	(✓ delight) customers	고객들을 즐겁게 하다
02	exceptional	a. 뛰어난	( ) value and service	뛰어난 가치와 서비스
03	overall	a. 전체적인, 전반적인	the ( ) company culture	기업 문화 전반
04	hospitality industry	(호텔, 식당 등의) 서비스업	rank at the top of the ( ) ( )	서비스업 중 최상위권을 차지하다
05	in terms of	~의 측면에서	( ) ( ) ( ) importance	중요성이라는 측면에서
06	satisfaction	n. 만족	in terms of customer ( )	고객 만족이라는 측면에서
07	sum up	요약하다	( ) ( ) the case	사건을 요약하다
08	memorable	a. 기억될만한	a truly ( ) experience	진정으로 기억될만한 경험
09	relative to	~에 비해, ~ 대비	deliver high satisfaction ( ) ( ) competitors	경쟁사 대비 높은 만족을 제공하다
10	maximize	v. 최대화하다	( ) customer satisfaction	고객 만족을 최대화하다
11	profit	n. 이윤	result in lower ( )s	더 낮은 이윤으로 이어지다
12	generate	v. 창출하다	( ) customer value	고객 가치를 창출하다
13	delicate	a. 미묘한	a very ( ) balance	매우 미묘한 균형

⊕ 본문 문장 속에서 단어들을 확인해 보세요.

For example, / year after year, / Pazano ranks at or near the top of the hospitality industry / in terms of customer satisfaction.

예를 들어, / 해마다, / Pazano는 서비스업 중 최상위 또는 상위권을 차지한다 / 고객 만족이라는 측면에서.

01	delight	✎ 즐겁게 하다	delight customers	고객들을 즐겁게 하다
02	exceptional		exceptional value and service	뛰어난 가치와 서비스
03	overall		the overall company culture	기업 문화 전반
04	hospitality industry		rank at the top of the hospitality industry	서비스업 중 최상위권을 차지하다
05	in terms of		in terms of importance	중요성이라는 측면에서
06	satisfaction		in terms of customer satisfaction	고객 만족이라는 측면에서
07	sum up		sum up the case	사건을 요약하다
08	memorable		a truly memorable experience	진정으로 기억될만한 경험
09	relative to		deliver high satisfaction relative to competitors	경쟁사 대비 높은 만족을 제공하다
10	maximize		maximize customer satisfaction	고객 만족을 최대화하다
11	profit		result in lower profits	더 낮은 이윤으로 이어지다
12	generate		generate customer value	고객 가치를 창출하다
13	delicate		a very delicate balance	매우 미묘한 균형

➕ **본문 문장 속에서 단어의 의미를 우리말로 해석해 보세요.**

For example, / year after year, / Pazano ranks at or near the top of the hospitality industry / in terms of customer satisfaction.

→ 예를 들어, / 해마다, / Pazano는 _____ 중 최상위 또는 상위권을 차지한다 / _____.

제한시간 80초
난이도 ★★★★☆

STEP **2** • 수능 기출 제대로 풀기

B 밑줄 친 'give away the house'가 다음 글에서 의미하는 바로 가장 적절한 것은?

For companies interested in delighting customers, exceptional value and service become part of the overall company culture. For example, year after year, Pazano ranks at or near the top of the hospitality industry in terms of customer satisfaction. The company's passion for satisfying customers is summed up in its credo, which promises that its luxury hotels will deliver a truly memorable experience. Although a customer-centered firm seeks to deliver high customer satisfaction relative to competitors, it does not attempt to *maximize* customer satisfaction. A company can always increase customer satisfaction by lowering its price or increasing its services. But this may result in lower profits. Thus, the purpose of marketing is to generate customer value profitably. This requires a very delicate balance: the marketer must continue to generate more customer value and satisfaction but not 'give away the house'.

*credo: 신조

① risk the company's profitability

② overlook a competitor's strengths

③ hurt the reputation of the company

④ generate more customer complaints

⑤ abandon customer-oriented marketing

정답과 해설 **p.13**

01 For companies <u>interested in delighting customers</u>, / exceptional value and service /
　　　　　　　　　 과거분사
become part of the overall company culture.

02 For example, / year after year, / Pazano ranks <u>at or near</u> the top of the hospitality
industry / in terms of customer satisfaction. or로 두 전치사가 병렬연결(전치사의 목적어 the top ~ industry 공유)

03 The company's passion for satisfying customers / is summed up in <u>its credo</u>, / <u>which</u>
주어　　　　　　　　　　　　　　　　　　　　　　 동사(단수)　　 선행사　　　　　계속적 용법의 관계대명사
promises / that its luxury hotels will deliver a truly memorable experience.
　　　　 명사절 접속사

04 Although a customer-centered firm <u>seeks to deliver</u> high customer satisfaction /
　　　　　　　　　　　　　　　　　　 ~하려 하다
relative to competitors, / it does not attempt to *maximize* customer satisfaction.

05 A company can always increase customer satisfaction / by <u>lowering its price</u> or
<u>increasing its services</u>. // But this may result in lower profits.
　　　　　　　　　　　병렬구조(by+동명사: ~함으로써)

06 Thus, / the purpose of marketing / is to generate customer value profitably.
　　　　　　　　　　　　　　　　　 주격보어(~것)

07 This requires a very delicate balance: / [the marketer must <u>continue to generate more</u>
　　　　　　　　　　　　　　　　　　　 balance 보충 설명
<u>customer value and satisfaction</u> / but <u>not 'give away the house'</u>].
　　　　　　　　 병렬구조(must에 연결)

01 고객들을 즐겁게 하는delight 데 관심이 있는 기업들에게, / 뛰어난exceptional 가치와 서비스는 / 기업 문화
전반overall의 일부가 된다.

02 예를 들어, / 해마다, / Pazano는 서비스업hospitality industry 중 최상위 또는 상위권을 차지한다 / 고객
만족satisfaction이라는 측면에서in terms of.

03 고객을 만족시키기 위한 그 기업의 열정은 / 그것의 신조에 요약sum up되어 있고, / 이는 약속한다 / 그 기업의 고급
호텔이 진정으로 기억될만한memorable 경험을 제공할 것을.

04 고객 중심 기업은 높은 고객 만족을 제공하고자 하지만 / 경쟁사 대비relative to, / 그것은 고객 만족을
'최대화'하려고maximize 하지는 않는다.

05 기업은 고객 만족을 항상 높일 수 있다 / 가격을 낮추거나 서비스를 증진시킴으로써. // 하지만 이것은 더 낮은
이윤profit으로 이어질지도 모른다.

06 따라서, / 마케팅의 목적은 / 수익을 내면서 고객 가치를 창출하는generate 것이다.

07 이것은 매우 미묘한delicate 균형을 필요로 한다: / 마케팅 담당자는 계속해서 더 많은 고객 가치와 만족을 창출해야 한다 /
하지만 '집을 거저나 다름없이 팔아서는' 안 된다.

구문 Check up

① For companies interesting / interested in delighting
customers, exceptional value and service become part
of the overall company culture.

수식을 받는 명사(companies)와 분사의 관계가 수동이므로 과거분사
interested가 적절하다.

② The company's passion for satisfying customers
is summed up in its credo, which promises that /
what its luxury hotels will deliver a truly memorable
experience.

동사 promise의 목적어 자리에 명사절이 와야 하고, 뒤따르는 절이 완전
하므로 명사절 접속사 that을 쓴다.

정답 ① interested ② that

함축적 의미 추론 ⊕

STEP 1 • 수능에 진짜 나오는 단어

✔ 문제에 나오는 단어들을 확인하세요.

시간이 없다면 색으로 표시된 단어만이라도 꼭 외우고 넘어가세요!

01	exhibit	v. 보이다, 전시하다	(✔ exhibit) characteristics	특징들을 보이다
02	paradoxical	a. 역설적인	( ) characteristics	역설적인 특징들
03	mutually exclusive	상호 배타적인	be ( ) ( )	상호 배타적이다
04	contradictory	a. 모순적인	( ) action	모순적인 행동
05	relevant	a. 관련된	( ) to the problem	문제와 관련된
06	involve	v. 수반하다, 포함하다	the processes ( )d	수반되는 과정들
07	prevail	v. 널리 퍼지다	the ( )ing wisdom	널리 퍼진 지혜
08	establish	v. 입증하다, 확립하다	( )ed ways	입증된 방식들
09	newcomer	n. 신참	the ( )s' perspective	신참의 시각
10	naive	a. 순진한	no matter how ( ) the question may seem	질문이 아무리 순진해 보이더라도
11	accelerate	v. 가속화하다	( ) the process	과정을 가속화하다

⊕ 본문 문장 속에서 단어들을 확인해 보세요.

It shows tendencies of thought and action / that we'd assume to be mutually exclusive or contradictory.

그것은 생각과 행동의 경향을 보여준다 / 우리가 상호 배타적이거나 모순된다고 가정할 법한.

문제를 풀기 전에 단어들을 30초 동안 다시 확인하세요.

01	exhibit	보이다, 전시하다	exhibit characteristics	특징들을 보이다
02	paradoxical		paradoxical characteristics	역설적인 특징들
03	mutually exclusive		be mutually exclusive	상호 배타적이다
04	contradictory		contradictory action	모순적인 행동
05	relevant		relevant to the problem	문제와 관련된
06	involve		the processes involved	수반되는 과정들
07	prevail		the prevailing wisdom	널리 퍼진 지혜
08	establish		established ways	입증된 방식들
09	newcomer		the newcomers' perspective	신참의 시각
10	naive		no matter how naive the question may seem	질문이 아무리 순진해 보이더라도
11	accelerate		accelerate the process	과정을 가속화하다

➕ 본문 문장 속에서 단어의 의미를 우리말로 해석해 보세요.

It shows tendencies of thought and action / that we'd assume to be mutually exclusive or contradictory.

➡ 그것은 생각과 행동의 경향을 보여준다 / 우리가   이거나   고 가정할 법한.

제한시간 80초
난이도 ★★★★☆

STEP **2** • 수능 기출 제대로 풀기

C 밑줄 친 bringing together contradictory characteristics가 다음 글에서 의미하는 바로 가장 적절한 것은?

The creative team exhibits paradoxical characteristics. It shows tendencies of thought and action that we'd assume to be mutually exclusive or contradictory. For example, to do its best work, a team needs deep knowledge of subjects relevant to the problem it's trying to solve, and a mastery of the processes involved. But at the same time, the team needs fresh perspectives that are unencumbered by the prevailing wisdom or established ways of doing things. Often called a "beginner's mind," this is the newcomers' perspective: people who are curious, even playful, and willing to ask anything — no matter how naive the question may seem — because they don't know what they don't know. Thus, bringing together contradictory characteristics can accelerate the process of new ideas.

*unencumbered: 방해 없는

① establishing short-term and long-term goals

② performing both challenging and easy tasks

③ adopting temporary and permanent solutions

④ utilizing aspects of both experts and rookies

⑤ considering processes and results simultaneously

정답과 해설 p.13

01 The creative team exhibits paradoxical characteristics. // It shows tendencies of
thought and action / [that we'd assume to be mutually exclusive or contradictory].
목적격 관계대명사절 / 목적어 생략

02 For example, / to do its best work, / a team needs deep knowledge of subjects / [relevant
to the problem it's trying to solve], / and a mastery of the processes involved.
to부정사 부사적 용법(목적) / 형용사구 수식 / 목적어1 / 목적격 관계대명사절 / 목적어2

03 But at the same time, / the team needs fresh perspectives / [that are unencumbered /
by the prevailing wisdom or established ways of doing things].
주격 관계대명사절 / 현재분사 / 과거분사

04 Often called a "beginner's mind," / this is the newcomers' perspective: / people / [who
are curious, even playful, and willing to ask anything / — no matter how naive the
question may seem — / because they don't know what they don't know].
분사구문 / 콜론(:) 보충 설명 / 주격 관계대명사절 / no matter how+형용사: 아무리 ~한다 해도(=however+형용사) / 의문사 what절

05 Thus, / bringing together contradictory characteristics / can accelerate the process of
new ideas.
동명사 주어

01 창의적인 팀은 역설적인 특징을 보인다exhibit paradoxical characteristics. // 그것은 생각과 행동의 경향을 보여준다 / 우리가 상호 배타적이거나mutually exclusive 모순된다고contradictory 가정할 법한.

02 예를 들어, / 최고의 작업을 수행하기 위해서는 / 팀은 주제들에 대한 깊은 지식이 필요하다 / 팀이 해결하려는 문제와 관련된relevant / 그리고 수반되는involved 과정의 숙달도.

03 그러나 동시에, / 팀에게는 신선한 관점이 필요하다 / 구애받지 않는 / 널리 퍼져 있는 지혜prevailing wisdom나 일을 하는 입증된 방법established ways에.

04 종종 '초심자의 마음'이라고 불리는데, / 이것은 신참newcomer의 관점이다. / 즉, 사람들 / 호기심 많고, 심지어 장난기 넘치고, 무엇이든 기꺼이 물어보는 / — 질문이 아무리 순진해naive 보이더라도 — / 자신이 무엇을 모르는지 모르기 때문에.

05 따라서 / 모순되는 특징들을 한데 모으는 것이 / 새로운 아이디어의 과정을 가속화할accelerate 수 있다.

구문 Check up

① For example, to do its best work, a team needs deep knowledge of subjects relevant / relevantly to the problem it's trying to solve, and a mastery of the processes involved.

선행사 subjects를 설명하는 형용사가 필요하다. 따라서 relevant가 적절하다.

② Often calling / called a "beginner's mind," this is the newcomers' perspective: people who are curious, even playful, and willing to ask anything.

분사구문의 의미상 주어인 this가 '불리는' 대상이므로, 수동의 의미인 과거분사 called를 쓴다.

정답 ① relevant ② called

D

STEP 1 • 수능에 *진짜* 나오는 *단어*

✔ 문제에 나오는 단어들을 확인하세요.

시간이 없다면 색으로 표시된 단어만이라도 꼭 외우고 넘어가세요!

01	curriculum	n. 교육 과정	a (✔ curriculum)	교육 과정
02	formula	n. 공식	one right ( )	하나의 올바른 공식
03	standardize	v. 표준화하다	a ( )d test	표준화된 시험
04	authority	n. 권위, 권한	an ( ) figure	권위자
05	alternate	a. 다른, 번갈아 나오는	many ( ) paths	많은 다른 경로들
06	wander	v. 헤매다	( ) down the paths	길을 헤매다
07	misconception	n. 오해	have many ( )s	많은 오해를 하다
08	divine	a. 신의, 신성한	a ( ) visitation	신의 방문
09	revise	v. 수정하다	( ) the laws	법칙을 수정하다
10	notably	ad. 특히, 눈에 띄게	most ( )	무엇보다도 특히
11	alchemy	n. 연금술	experiments in ( )	연금술 실험
12	lead	n. 납	from ( ) to gold	납에서 금으로
13	make the cut	최종 명단에 들다, 목표를 달성하다	( ) ( ) ( ) as the part of story	이야기의 일부로 들어가다
14	one-dimensional	a. 일차원적인	the ( ) story	일차원적인 이야기

⊕ 본문 문장 속에서 단어들을 확인해 보세요.

In school, / there's one curriculum, one right way to study science, and one right formula / that spits out the correct answer on a standardized test.

학교에는, / 하나의 교육과정, 과학을 공부하는 하나의 올바른 방식, 그리고 하나의 올바른 공식이 있다 / 표준화된 시험의 정답을 내어놓는.

01	curriculum	✎ 교육 과정	a curriculum	교육 과정
02	formula		one right formula	하나의 올바른 공식
03	standardize		a standardized test	표준화된 시험
04	authority		an authority figure	권위자
05	alternate		many alternate paths	많은 다른 경로들
06	wander		wander down the paths	길을 헤매다
07	misconception		have many misconceptions	많은 오해를 하다
08	divine		a divine visitation	신의 방문
09	revise		revise the laws	법칙을 수정하다
10	notably		most notably	무엇보다도 특히
11	alchemy		experiments in alchemy	연금술 실험
12	lead		from lead to gold	납에서 금으로
13	make the cut		make the cut as the part of story	이야기의 일부로 들어가다
14	one-dimensional		the one-dimensional story	일차원적인 이야기

➕ **본문 문장 속에서 단어의 의미를 우리말로 해석해 보세요.**

In school, / there's one curriculum, one right way to study science, and one right formula / that spits out the correct answer on a standardized test.

➜ 학교에는, / 하나의   , 과학을 공부하는 하나의 올바른 방식, 그리고 하나의 올바른   이 있다 /   시험의 정답을 내어놓는.

STEP **2** • 수능 기출 제대로 풀기

D 밑줄 친 turns the life stories of these scientists from lead to gold가 다음 글에서 의미하는 바로 가장 적절한 것은?

In school, there's one curriculum, one right way to study science, and one right formula that spits out the correct answer on a standardized test. Textbooks with grand titles like *The Principles of Physics* magically reveal "the principles" in three hundred pages. An authority figure then steps up to the lectern to feed us "the truth." As theoretical physicist David Gross explained in his Nobel lecture, textbooks often ignore the many alternate paths that people wandered down, the many false clues they followed, the many misconceptions they had. We learn about Newton's "laws" — as if they arrived by a grand divine visitation or a stroke of genius — but not the years he spent exploring, revising, and changing them. The laws that Newton failed to establish — most notably his experiments in alchemy, which attempted, and spectacularly failed, to turn lead into gold — don't make the cut as part of the one-dimensional story told in physics classrooms. Instead, our education system turns the life stories of these scientists from lead to gold.

*lectern: 강의대
**alchemy: 연금술

① discovers the valuable relationships between scientists

② emphasizes difficulties in establishing new scientific theories

③ mixes the various stories of great scientists across the world

④ focuses more on the scientists' work than their personal lives

⑤ reveals only the scientists' success ignoring their processes and errors

정답과 해설 **p.14**

01 In school, / there's one curriculum, one right way to study science, and one right formula / that spits out the correct answer on a standardized test.
　　　　　　　　　　　　　　　　　　　　　　　형용사적 용법
　주격 관계대명사　　　　　　　　　　　　　과거분사

02 Textbooks with grand titles / like *The Principles of Physics* / magically reveal "the principles" / in three hundred pages. // An authority figure then steps up to the lectern / to feed us "the truth."
주어　　　　　　　~와 같은 (전치사)　　　　　　동사
to부정사 부사적 용법(feed+간접목적어+직접목적어)

03 As theoretical physicist David Gross explained / in his Nobel lecture, / textbooks often ignore / the many alternate paths that people wandered down, / the many false clues they followed, / the many misconceptions they had.
목적어1　　　　　　　　　　　　　　　　　목적어2
목적어3

04 We learn about Newton's "laws" / — as if they arrived / by a grand divine visitation or a stroke of genius — / but not the years he spent exploring, revising, and changing them.
대시(—): 부연설명　마치 ~인 것처럼
목적격 관계대명사 생략　spend+시간+ -ing: ~하는 데 (시간)을 보내다

05 The laws that Newton failed to establish / — most notably his experiments in alchemy, / which attempted, and spectacularly failed, to turn lead into gold — / don't make the cut as part of the one-dimensional story / told in physics classrooms.
주어　　목적격 관계대명사절　　　대시(—): 예시 연결
계속적 용법: 삽입 형태이므로 수식하여 해석　attempted, failed의 목적어　동사
(which is)

06 Instead, / our education system / turns the life stories of these scientists / from lead to gold.
turn ~ from A to B : ~를 A에서 B로 바꾸다

01 학교에는, / 하나의 교육과정curriculum, 과학을 공부하는 하나의 올바른 방식, 그리고 하나의 올바른 공식formula이 있다 / 표준화된standardized 시험의 정답을 내어놓는.

02 대단한 제목을 가진 교과서들은 / 〈물리학의 원리〉와 같은 / '그 원리들'을 마법처럼 보여준다 / 300페이지에 걸쳐. // 그러고나서 권위authority자가 강의대로 다가간다 / 우리에게 '진실'을 알려 주기 위해서.

03 이론 물리학자 David Gross가 설명했듯이 / 자신의 노벨상 수상자 강연에서, / 교과서들은 종종 묵살한다 / 사람들이 헤매고 다닌wander 그 많은 다른 alternate 경로들과 / 그들이 따랐던 그 많은 잘못된 단서들과 / 그들이 가졌던 그 많은 오해misconception들을.

04 우리는 마치 뉴턴의 '법칙들'에 대해 배우지만 / 마치 그것들이 도래하는 것처럼 / 대단한 신의 방문divine visitation이나 한 번의 천재성에 의해 / 그가 그것들을 탐구하고 수정하고revise 변경하는 데 들인 여러 해에 대해서는 배우지 않는다.

05 뉴턴이 확립하는 데 실패한 법칙들은 / 무엇보다도 특히notably 연금술alchemy 실험 / 납lead을 금으로 바꾸기 위해 시도했다가 엄청나게 실패했던 / 일차원적인one-dimensional 이야기의 일부로 들어가지make the cut 못한다 / 물리학 수업에서 언급되는 (이야기).

06 대신에, / 우리의 교육 시스템은 / 이런 과학자들의 인생 이야기들을 바꿔 버린다/ 납에서 금으로.

① As theoretical physicist David Gross explained in his Nobel lecture, textbooks often ignore / ignoring the many alternate paths that people wandered down, the many false clues they followed, the many misconceptions they had.

주절의 동사에 해당하므로 ignore를 쓴다. 주절의 주어는 textbooks로, 앞에 오는 부사절(As ~ lecture)과 혼동하지 않도록 주의한다.

② The laws that Newton failed to establish don't make the cut as part of the one-dimensional story tell / told in physics classrooms.

문장에 이미 동사(don't make)가 있으며, 앞에 접속사가 없기 때문에 다른 동사는 올 수 없다. 따라서 the one-dimensional story를 수식하기 위한 과거분사 told를 쓴다.

정답 ① ignore ② told

E

함축적 의미 추론 +

STEP 1 • 수능에 진짜 나오는 단어

✔ 문제에 나오는 단어들을 확인하세요.

시간이 없다면 색으로 표시된 단어만이라도 꼭 외우고 넘어가세요!

01	fashion	v. (특히 손으로) 만들다	(✔ fashion) a theory	이론을 만들다
02	masterpiece	n. 걸작	Cindy's last ( )	Cindy의 마지막 걸작
03	progress	v. 전진하다, 나아가다	( ) only forward	앞으로만 나아가다
04	halt	v. 중단하다	( ) the production	생산을 중단하다
05	strike gold	금을 캐다, 큰 성공을 거두다	( ) ( ) with my latest novel	내 최신 소설로 큰 성공을 거두다
06	discard	v. 버리다, 폐기하다	( ) newspapers	신문을 버리다
07	inadequate	a. 부족한	feel ( ) as a parent	부모로서 부족하다고 느끼다
08	scrap	v. 버리다, 폐기하다	( ) a plan	계획을 폐기하다
09	extraordinary	a. 비범한	distinguish an ( ) from an ordinary work	비범한 작품과 평범한 작품을 구별하다
10	composition	n. 작품, 구성	accept his ( ) as a hit	그의 작품을 성공으로 받아들이다
11	in protest of	~에 저항하여	( ) ( ) ( ) fascism	파시즘에 저항하여
12	consistently	ad. 일관되게	get ( ) warmer	일관되게 더 뜨거워지다

⊕ 본문 문장 속에서 단어들을 확인해 보세요.

If creators knew when they were on their way to fashioning a masterpiece, / their work would progress only forward.

만약 창작자가 자신이 언제 걸작을 만들어내고 있는지 안다면, / 그들의 작품은 앞으로만 나아갈 것이다.

문제를 풀기 전에 단어들을 **30초** 동안 다시 확인하세요.

01	fashion	✎ (특히 손으로) 만들다	fashion a theory	이론을 만들다
02	masterpiece		Cindy's last masterpiece	Cindy의 마지막 걸작
03	progress		progress only forward	앞으로만 나아가다
04	halt		halt the production	생산을 중단하다
05	strike gold		strike gold with my latest novel	내 최신 소설로 큰 성공을 거두다
06	discard		discard newspapers	신문을 버리다
07	inadequate		feel inadequate as a parent	부모로서 부족하다고 느끼다
08	scrap		scrap a plan	계획을 폐기하다
09	extraordinary		distinguish an extraordinary from an ordinary work	비범한 작품과 평범한 작품을 구별하다
10	composition		accept his composition as a hit	그의 작품을 성공으로 받아들이다
11	in protest of		in protest of fascism	파시즘에 저항하여
12	consistently		get consistently warmer	일관되게 더 뜨거워지다

➕ **본문 문장 속에서 단어의 의미를 우리말로 해석해 보세요.**

If creators knew when they were on their way to fashioning a masterpiece, / their work would progress only forward.

→ 만약 창작자가 자신이 언제   있는지 안다면, / 그들의 작품은   것이다.

STEP **2** • 수능 기출 제대로 풀기

E 밑줄 친 got "colder"가 다음 글에서 의미하는 바로 가장 적절한 것은?

If creators knew when they were on their way to fashioning a masterpiece, their work would progress only forward: they would halt their idea-generation efforts as they struck gold. But in fact, they backtrack, returning to versions that they had earlier discarded as inadequate. In Beethoven's most celebrated work, the Fifth Symphony, he scrapped the conclusion of the first movement because it felt too short, only to come back to it later. Had Beethoven been able to distinguish an extraordinary from an ordinary work, he would have accepted his composition immediately as a hit. When Picasso was painting his famous *Guernica* in protest of fascism, he produced 79 different drawings. Many of the images in the painting were based on his early sketches, not the later variations. If Picasso could judge his creations as he produced them, he would get consistently "warmer" and use the later drawings. But in reality, it was just as common that he got "colder."

① moved away from the desired outcome

② lost his reputation due to public criticism

③ became unwilling to follow new art trends

④ appreciated others' artwork with less enthusiasm

⑤ imitated masters' styles rather than creating his own

정답과 해설 p.14

01 If creators knew when they were on their way to fashioning a masterpiece, / their work
가정법 과거(현재와 반대 사실 가정)
would progress only forward: / they would halt their idea-generation efforts / as they
struck gold.

02 But in fact, / they backtrack, / returning to versions / that they had earlier discarded as
분사구문　　　　　　목적격 관계대명사절(versions 수식)
inadequate.

03
동격
In Beethoven's most celebrated work, the Fifth Symphony, / he scrapped the conclusion
of the first movement / because it felt too short, / only to come back to it later. // Had
부사적 용법(결국 ~하다)
Beethoven been able to distinguish an extraordinary from an ordinary work, / he would
가정법 과거완료 종속절 도치(=If Beethoven had been ~)　　　　　　　　　　　　가정법 과거완료 주절
have accepted his composition immediately as a hit.

04 When Picasso was painting his famous *Guernica* in protest of fascism, / he produced
~에 저항하여
79 different drawings. // Many of the images in the painting / were based on his early
주어(부분+of+전체)　　　　　　　동사(복수)
sketches, / not the later variations.

05 If Picasso could judge his creations / as he produced them, / he would get consistently
접속사(~할 때)
"warmer" and use the later drawings. // But in reality, / it was just as common that he
가주어　　　　　　　　　진주어
got "colder."

---

01 만약 창작자가 자신이 언제 걸작을 만들어내고fashion a masterpiece 있는지 안다면, / 그들의 작품은 앞으로만
나아갈progress 것이다. / 즉 그들은 아이디어를 만들어내는 노력을 멈출halt 것이다 / 그들이 큰 성공을 거뒀을strike
gold 때.

02 그러나 사실, / 그들은 역추적해서 / 버전으로 돌아간다 / 이전에 그들이 부적절하다고inadequate 폐기했던discard.

03 베토벤의 가장 유명한 작품인 5번 교향곡에서, / 그는 1악장의 결론부를 폐기했다가scrap / 그것이 너무 짧다고 느껴서 /
결국 나중에 그것으로 돌아왔다. // 베토벤이 비범한extraordinary 작품과 평범한 작품을 구분할 수 있었다면 / 그는 자기
작품composition을 바로 성공으로 받아들였을 것이다.

04 피카소가 파시즘에 저항하고자in protest of 그 유명한 <Guernica>를 그릴 당시에, / 그는 79점의 각기 다른 스케치들을
그렸다. // 이 그림의 많은 이미지들은 / 그의 초기 스케치에 바탕을 두었다 / 나중에 나온 변주작이 아닌.

05 만약 피카소가 자기 작품을 판단할 수 있었다면 / 그가 만들던 때에 / 그는 일관되게consistently '더 뜨거워져서' 나중에
그린 스케치를 사용했을 것이다. // 하지만 실제로는 / 그가 '더 차가워진' 것은 그만큼 흔한 일이었다.

구문 Check up

① If creators knew when they were on their way to fashioning a masterpiece, their work will / would progress only forward.

가정법 과거는 <if+주어+과거시제 동사 ~, 주어+조동사 과거형+동사원형 …>으로 쓴다. 따라서 would가 적절하다.

② Beethoven had / Had Beethoven been able to distinguish an extraordinary from an ordinary work, he would have accepted his composition immediately as a hit.

<if+주어+had p.p. ~> 형태의 가정법 과거완료 종속절에서, if를 생략하면 주어와 had의 위치가 바뀐다. 따라서 Had Beethoven이 적절하다.

정답 ① would ② Had Beethoven

STEP 1 • 수능에 *진짜* 나오는 *단어*

✔ 문제에 나오는 단어들을 확인하세요.

시간이 없다면 색으로 표시된 단어만이라도 꼭 외우고 넘어가세요!

01	collaborative	a. 협력적인, 공동의	a (✔ collaborative) project	협력 프로젝트
02	secure	v. 확보하다 a. 안정적인	(　　　) funding for the project	프로젝트 자금을 확보하다
03	cause	n. 대의명분	for a worthy (　　　)	가치 있는 대의명분을 위해
04	fusion	n. 융합	a perfect (　　　) of image and sound	이미지와 사운드의 완벽한 융합
05	capitalism	n. 자본주의	the rise of (　　　)	자본주의의 부상
06	conventional	a. 전통적인, 관습적인	(　　　) rules	전통적 규칙
07	variation	n. 변형	many (　　　)s of a style	한 가지 스타일의 다양한 변형
08	be viewed as	~로 여겨지다	Achieving one's goal can (　　　) (　　　) (　　　) a success.	목표를 성취한 것은 성공으로 여겨질 수 있다.
09	democratization	n. 민주화	fight for (　　　)	민주화를 위해 싸우다
10	allocation	n. 할당, 배분	(　　　) of resources	자원의 배분
11	relatively	ad. 비교적, 상대적으로	(　　　) small	비교적 작은
12	fixed	a. 고정된	a (　　　) minority	고정된 소수
13	empower	v. 권한을 주다, (힘을 주어) ~할 수 있게 하다	(　　　) everyone to access the collective wisdom	모두가 집단 지혜를 이용할 권한을 주다

⊕ 본문 문장 속에서 단어들을 확인해 보세요.

Crowdfunding is a new and more collaborative way / to secure funding for projects.

크라우드 펀딩은 새롭고 더 협력적인 방법이다 / 프로젝트를 위한 자금을 확보하는.

문제를 풀기 전에 단어들을 **30초** 동안 다시 확인하세요.

01	collaborative	🖊 협력적인, 공동의	a collaborative project	협력 프로젝트
02	secure		secure funding for the project	프로젝트 자금을 확보하다
03	cause		for a worthy cause	가치 있는 대의명분을 위해
04	fusion		a perfect fusion of image and sound	이미지와 사운드의 완벽한 융합
05	capitalism		the rise of capitalism	자본주의의 부상
06	conventional		conventional rules	전통적 규칙
07	variation		many variations of a style	한 가지 스타일의 다양한 변형
08	be viewed as		Achieving one's goal can be viewed as a success.	목표를 성취한 것은 성공으로 여겨질 수 있다.
09	democratization		fight for democratization	민주화를 위해 싸우다
10	allocation		allocation of resources	자원의 배분
11	relatively		relatively small	비교적 작은
12	fixed		a fixed minority	고정된 소수
13	empower		empower everyone to access the collective wisdom	모두가 집단 지혜를 이용할 권한을 주다

➕ **본문 문장 속에서 단어의 의미를 우리말로 해석해 보세요.**

Crowdfunding is a new and more collaborative way / to secure funding for projects.

→ 크라우드 펀딩은 새롭고   방법이다 / 프로젝트를 위한   .

STEP 2 • 수능 기출 제대로 풀기

F 밑줄 친 the democratization of business financing이 다음 글에서 의미 하는 바로 가장 적절한 것은?

Crowdfunding is a new and more collaborative way to secure funding for projects. It can be used in different ways such as requesting donations for a worthy cause anywhere in the world and generating funding for a project with the contributors then becoming partners in the project. In essence, crowdfunding is the fusion of social networking and venture capitalism. In just the same way as social networks have rewritten the conventional rules about how people communicate and interact with each other, crowdfunding in all its variations has the potential to rewrite the rules on how businesses and other projects get funded in the future. Crowdfunding can be viewed as the democratization of business financing. Instead of restricting capital sourcing and allocation to a relatively small and fixed minority, crowdfunding empowers everyone connected to the Internet to access both the collective wisdom and the pocket money of everyone else who connects to the Internet.

① More people can be involved in funding a business.

② More people will participate in developing new products.

③ Crowdfunding can reinforce the conventional way of financing.

④ Crowdfunding keeps social networking from facilitating funding.

⑤ The Internet helps employees of a company interact with each other.

정답과 해설 p.15

01 Crowdfunding is a new and more collaborative way / to secure funding for projects.
형용사적 용법

02 It can be used in different ways / such as requesting donations for a worthy cause
~와 같이(예시) 동명사구1
anywhere in the world / and generating funding for a project with the contributors /
동명사구2(A ~ then B … 구조)
then becoming partners in the project.

03 In essence, / crowdfunding is the fusion of social networking and venture capitalism.
전치사구

04 In just the same way as social networks have rewritten the conventional rules /
~와 정확히 마찬가지로
about how people communicate and interact with each other, / crowdfunding in all
명사절(about의 목적어) 주어
its variations / has the potential to rewrite the rules / on how businesses and other
수일치(단수) 형용사적 용법
projects get funded in the future.

05 Crowdfunding can be viewed / as the democratization of business financing.

06 Instead of restricting capital sourcing and allocation / to a relatively small and fixed
empower+목적어+to부정사: ~이 …할 권한을 주다
minority, / crowdfunding empowers everyone connected to the Internet / to access
과거분사구
both the collective wisdom and the pocket money of everyone else / who connects to
주격 관계대명사절
the Internet.

01 크라우드 펀딩은 새롭고 더 협력적인collaborative 방법이다 / 프로젝트 자금을 확보하는secure.

02 그것은 다양한 방법으로 이용될 수 있다 / 세계 어디서든 가치 있는 대의명분cause을 위한 기부를 요청하는 것과 같이 /
그리고 기부자들과 프로젝트 펀딩을 만들고 / 이후 프로젝트 파트너가 되는 것.

03 본질적으로, / 크라우드 펀딩은 소셜 네트워킹과 벤처 자본주의capitalism의 융합fusion이다.

04 소셜 네트워킹이 사람들이 전통적인conventional 규칙을 다시 쓴 것과 정확히 마찬가지로 / 서로 의사소통하고
상호작용하는 방식에 관한 / 온갖 다양한 변형variation의 크라우드 펀딩은 / 규칙을 다시 쓸 잠재력을 가진다 / 미래에
기업과 다른 프로젝트가 자금을 얻는 방식에 관한.

05 크라우드 펀딩은 여겨질 수 있다be viewed as / 기업 자금 조달의 민주화democratization로.

06 자본 조달과 할당allocation을 한정하는 대신에 / 비교적relatively 소규모의 고정된fixed 소수에 / 크라우드 펀딩은
인터넷에 연결된 모든 사람이 ~할 수 있는 권한을 준다empower / 다른 모든 사람의 집단 지혜와 쌈짓돈에 접근할 /
인터넷에 접속하는.

구문 Check up

① Crowdfunding is a new and more collaborative way secures / to secure funding for projects.

② Crowdfunding empowers everyone connected to the Internet accessed / to access both the collective wisdom and the pocket money of everyone else who connects to the Internet.

way는 to부정사의 수식을 받는 명사이다. 따라서 to secure가 적절하다.

empower는 to부정사를 목적격보어로 취한다. 따라서 to access가 적절하다.

STEP 1 · 수능에 *진짜* 나오는 *단어*

✔ **문제에 나오는 단어들을 확인하세요.**

시간이 없다면 색으로 표시된 단어만이라도 꼭 외우고 넘어가세요!

01	seemingly	ad. 겉보기에	(✔ seemingly) minor	겉보기에 사소한
02	imbalance	n. 불균형	subtle ( )	미묘한 불균형
03	trigger	v. 유발하다	( ) a response	반응을 유발하다
04	symptom	n. 증상	get a ( )	증상을 갖게 되다
05	line up	~을 한 줄로 세우다	( ) ( ) a series of dominoes	일련의 도미노를 한 줄로 세우다
06	knock down	~을 쓰러뜨리다	( ) ( ) the first one	첫 번째 것을 쓰러뜨리다
07	initial	a. 처음의, 최초의	an ( ) problem	최초의 문제
08	unnoticed	a. 눈에 띄지 않는	be often ( )	종종 눈에 띄지 않다
09	depression	n. 우울(증), 부진, 침체	fatigue or ( )	피로 또는 우울(증)
10	address	v. 해결하다, 처리하다	The problem isn't ( )ed.	그 문제는 해결되지 않는다.
11	primary	a. 가장 중요한, 첫 번째의	a ( ) problem	가장 중요한 문제

⊕ **본문 문장 속에서 단어들을 확인해 보세요.**

This problem causes another subtle imbalance, / which triggers another, then several more.

이 문제는 또 다른 미묘한 불균형을 유발하고, / 그것이 또 다른 불균형을, 그다음 몇 개의 더 많은 불균형을 유발한다.

01	seemingly	겉보기에	seemingly minor	겉보기에 사소한
02	imbalance		subtle imbalance	미묘한 불균형
03	trigger		trigger a response	반응을 유발하다
04	symptom		get a symptom	증상을 갖게 되다
05	line up		line up a series of dominoes	일련의 도미노를 한 줄로 세우다
06	knock down		knock down the first one	첫 번째 것을 쓰러뜨리다
07	initial		an initial problem	최초의 문제
08	unnoticed		be often unnoticed	종종 눈에 띄지 않다
09	depression		fatigue or depression	피로 또는 우울(증)
10	address		The problem isn't addressed.	그 문제는 해결되지 않는다.
11	primary		a primary problem	가장 중요한 문제

➕ **본문 문장 속에서 단어의 의미를 우리말로 해석해 보세요.**

This problem causes another subtle imbalance, / which triggers another, then several more.

➔ 이 문제는 또 다른   을 유발하고, / 그것이 또 다른 불균형을, 그다음 몇 개의 더 많은 불균형을

STEP **2** • 수능 기출 제대로 풀기

G 밑줄 친 'The body works the same way.'가 다음 글에서 의미하는 바로 가장 적절한 것은?

The body tends to accumulate problems, often beginning with one small, seemingly minor imbalance. This problem causes another subtle imbalance, which triggers another, then several more. In the end, you get a symptom. It's like lining up a series of dominoes. All you need to do is knock down the first one and many others will fall too. What caused the last one to fall? Obviously it wasn't the one before it, or the one before that, but the first one. The body works the same way. The initial problem is often unnoticed. It's not until some of the later "dominoes" fall that more obvious clues and symptoms appear. In the end, you get a headache, fatigue or depression — or even disease. When you try to treat the last domino — treat just the end-result symptom — the cause of the problem isn't addressed. The first domino is the cause, or primary problem.

*accumulate: 축적하다

① There is no definite order in treating an illness.

② Minor health problems are solved by themselves.

③ You get more and more inactive as you get older.

④ It'll never be too late to cure the end-result symptom.

⑤ The final symptom stems from the first minor problem.

정답과 해설 **p.15**

STEP 3 · 수능 지문 제대로 복습하기

01 The body tends to accumulate problems, / often beginning with one small, seemingly
분사구문(=and it often begins ~)
minor imbalance. // This problem causes another subtle imbalance, / which triggers
　　　　　　　　　　　　　　　선행사　　　　　　　　　　　관계대명사 계속적 용법
another, then several more. // In the end, you get a symptom.
　　　　　　　　　　　　　　　　　　　　　　　　(=and it triggers ~)

02 It's like lining up a series of dominoes. // All you need to do / is knock down the first
　　　　　　　　　　　　　　　　　　　that 생략　　　주어　　　　　　동사　보어(to부정사의 to가 생략된 형태)
one / and many others will fall too.

03 What caused the last one to fall? // Obviously / it wasn't the one before it, / or the one
　　　cause+목적어+to부정사: ~이 …하게 야기하다　　　　　　　　not A but B: A가 아니라 B
before that, / but the first one.

04 The body works the same way. // The initial problem is often unnoticed. // It's not until
　　　　　　　　　　　　　　　　　　　　　It's not until ~ that …: ~하고 나서야 비로소 …하다
some of the later "dominoes" fall / that more obvious clues and symptoms appear.

05 In the end, / you get a headache, fatigue or depression / — or even disease.
결국

06 When you try to treat the last domino / — treat just the end-result symptom — / the
　　　　　　　　　　　　　　　　　　　　동격
cause of the problem isn't addressed. // The first domino is the cause, or primary
　　　　　　　　　　　　　　　　　　　　　　　　　　　　　　즉
problem.

01 신체는 문제를 축적하는 경향이 있으며, / 그것은 흔히 하나의 작고 사소해 보이는 불균형seemingly minor imbalance에서 시작한다. // 이 문제는 또 다른 미묘한 불균형을 유발하고, / 그것이 또 다른 불균형을, 그다음 몇 개의 더 많은 불균형을 유발한다trigger. // 결국 여러분은 어떤 증상을 갖게 된다get a symptom.

02 그것은 마치 일련의 도미노를 한 줄로 세워 놓는line up a series of dominoes 것과 같다. // 여러분이 해야 할 모든 것은 / 첫 번째 도미노를 쓰러뜨리는knock down 것이고, / 그러면 많은 다른 것들도 또한 쓰러질 것이다.

03 마지막 도미노를 쓰러뜨린 것은 무엇인가? // 분명히, / 그것은 그것의 바로 앞에 있던 것이 아니라 / 또는 그 앞에 있던 것 / 첫 번째 도미노이다.

04 신체도 같은 방식으로 작동한다. // 최초의initial 문제는 흔히 눈에 띄지 않는다unnoticed. // 뒤쪽의 '도미노' 중 몇 개가 쓰러지고 나서야 / 비로소 좀 더 분명한 단서와 증상이 나타난다.

05 결국 / 여러분은 두통, 피로, 또는 우울증depression을 얻게 된다 / 심지어 질병까지도.

06 여러분이 마지막 도미노를 처리한다면 / 즉 최종 결과인 증상만을 치료하려 한다면, / 그 문제의 원인은 해결되지address 않는다. // 최초의 도미노가 원인, 즉 가장 중요한primary 문제이다.

구문 Check up

① The body tends to accumulate problems, often begin / beginning with one small, seemingly minor imbalance.

두 문장을 연결하는 접속사가 없기 때문에 뒤에 오는 동사는 분사구문으로 쓴다. 따라서 beginning이 적절하다.

② What cause the last one fall / to fall ?

5형식 동사 cause는 목적격 보어로 to부정사를 취한다. 따라서 to fall이 적절하다.

정답 ① beginning ② to fall

122

STEP 1 • 수능에 *진짜* 나오는 *단어*

✔️ **문제에 나오는 단어들을 확인하세요.**

시간이 없다면 색으로 표시된 단어만이라도 꼭 외우고 넘어가세요!

01	blacksmith	*n.* 대장장이	the village (✔️ blacksmith)	마을 대장장이
02	lecture	*v.* 강의하다 *n.* 강의	(　　　　) on a variety of topics	다양한 주제에 관해 강의하다
03	priesthood	*n.* 성직, 사제직	join the (　　　　)	성직에 합류하다 (사제가 되다)
04	recover from	~에서 회복하다	(　　　) (　　　) an illness	병에서 회복하다
05	botany	*n.* 식물학	an interest in (　　　)	식물학에 대한 관심
06	accompany	*v.* ~을 동반하다	(　　　　) an adult	어른을 동반하다
07	wealthy	*a.* 부유한	his (　　　) student and supporter	그의 부유한 학생이자 후원자
08	assemble	*v.* 모아 정리하다, 수집하다	(　　　) plant and animal catalogues	동식물 목록을 모아 정리하다
09	A as well as B	B뿐만 아니라 A도	sell newsapapers (　) (　　) (　　) magazines	잡지뿐만 아니라 신문도 팔다

➕ **본문 문장 속에서 단어들을 확인해 보세요.**

Born in 1627 in Black Notley, Essex, England, / John Ray was the son of the village blacksmith.

1627년 잉글랜드 Essex주 Black Notley에서 태어난 / John Ray는 마을 대장장이의 아들이었다.

01	blacksmith	🖊 대장장이	the village blacksmith	마을 대장장이
02	lecture		lecture on a variety of topics	다양한 주제에 관해 강의하다
03	priesthood		join the priesthood	성직에 합류하다(사제가 되다)
04	recover from		recover from an illness	병에서 회복하다
05	botany		an interest in botany	식물학에 대한 관심
06	accompany		accompany an adult	어른을 동반하다
07	wealthy		his wealthy student and supporter	그의 부유한 학생이자 후원자
08	assemble		assemble plant and animal catalogues	동식물 목록을 모아 정리하다
09	A as well as B		sell newsapapers as well as magazines	잡지뿐만 아니라 신문도 팔다

➕ 본문 문장 속에서 단어의 의미를 우리말로 해석해 보세요.

Born in 1627 in Black Notley, Essex, England, / John Ray was the son of the village blacksmith.

→ 1627년 잉글랜드 Essex주 Black Notley에서 태어난 / John Ray는　　　　　　　　　　이었다.

2023 6월 학평 26번 문제

제한시간 70초
난이도 ★★★☆☆

STEP **2** • 수능 기출 제대로 풀기

A John Ray에 관한 다음 글의 내용과 일치하지 <u>않는</u> 것은?

Born in 1627 in Black Notley, Essex, England, John Ray was the son of the village blacksmith. At 16, he went to Cambridge University, where he studied widely and lectured on topics from Greek to mathematics, before joining the priesthood in 1660. To recover from an illness in 1650, he had taken to nature walks and developed an interest in botany. Accompanied by his wealthy student and supporter Francis Willughby, Ray toured Britain and Europe in the 1660s, studying and collecting plants and animals. He married Margaret Oakley in 1673 and, after leaving Willughby's household, lived quietly in Black Notley to the age of 77. He spent his later years studying samples in order to assemble plant and animal catalogues. He wrote more than twenty works on theology and his travels, as well as on plants and their form and function.

*theology: 신학

① 마을 대장장이의 아들이었다.

② 성직자의 길로 들어서기 전 Cambridge 대학에 다녔다.

③ 병에서 회복하기 위해 자연을 산책하기 시작했다.

④ Francis Willughby에게 후원받아 홀로 유럽을 여행하였다.

⑤ 동식물의 목록을 만들기 위해 표본을 연구하며 말년을 보냈다.

정답과 해설 p.17

01 Born in 1627 in Black Notley, Essex, England, / John Ray was the son of the village
분사구문
blacksmith.

02 At 16, / he went to Cambridge University, / where he studied widely and lectured on
선행사   계속적 용법(거기서 ~)
topics from Greek to mathematics, / before joining the priesthood in 1660.
분사구문(= before he joined ~)

03 To recover from an illness in 1650, / he had taken to nature walks / and developed an
부사적 용법(~하기 위해)
interest in botany.

04 Accompanied by his wealthy student and supporter Francis Willughby, / Ray toured
분사구문(의미상 주어 Ray가 '동반을 받은' 대상)
Britain and Europe in the 1660s, / studying and collecting plants and animals.
분사구문(Ray가 '공부하고 수집한' 주체)

05 He married Margaret Oakley in 1673 / and, (after leaving Willughby's household),
동사1   삽입구
/ lived quietly in Black Notley to the age of 77. // He spent his later years studying
동사2   spend+시간+동명사: ~하는 데 시간을 보내다
samples / in order to assemble plant and animal catalogues.
부사적 용법(~하기 위해)

06 He wrote more than twenty works on theology and his travels, / as well as on plants
-------- A as well as B: B뿐만 아니라 A도(on+명사 병렬) --------
and their form and function.

---

01 1627년 잉글랜드 Essex주 Black Notley에서 태어난 / John Ray는 마을 대장장이blacksmith의 아들이었다.

02 16세에 / 그는 Cambridge 대학교에 들어갔다 / 거기서 그는 폭넓게 공부하고 그리스어부터 수학까지 강의를 했다lecture / 1660년에 성직자의 길priesthood로 들어서기 전까지.

03 1650년 병에서 회복하고자recover from / 그는 자연을 산책하기 시작했고, / 식물학botany에 대한 관심을 키웠다.

04 부유한wealthy 학생이자 후원자였던 Francis Willughby를 동반한accompany 상태로 / Ray는 1660년대에 영국과 유럽을 여행하며 / 식물과 동물을 연구하고 수집했다.

05 그는 1673년 Margaret Oakley와 결혼했고, / Willughby 집안을 떠난 뒤에는 / 77세까지 Black Notley에서 조용히 살았다. // 그는 표본을 연구하면서 말년을 보냈다 / 동식물 목록을 모아 정리하기assemble 위해.

06 그는 신학과 자기 여행에 관한 20편 이상의 저서를 썼다 / 식물과 그 형태, 기능에 관해서뿐만 아니라as well as.

구문 Check up

① At 16, he went to Cambridge University, where he studied widely and lectured on topics from Greek to mathematics, before joined / joining the priesthood in 1660.

before 다음에 주어가 없으므로 동사가 이어질 수 없고, 분사구문을 써야 한다. 따라서 joining이 적절하다.

② Accompanying / Accompanied by his wealthy student and supporter Francis Willughby, Ray toured Britain and Europe in the 1660s, studying and collecting plants and animals.

뒤에 <by+목적격>이 오는 것으로 보아 수동을 나타내는 Accompanied가 적절하다. accompany는 타동사이므로, 능동태/현재분사로 쓰려면 뒤에 목적어가 있어야 한다.

정답 ① joining ② Accompanied

DAY 05

B

STEP 1 · 수능에 *진짜* 나오는 *단어*

내용 불일치 ➕

✔ 문제에 나오는 단어들을 확인하세요.

시간이 없다면 색으로 표시된 단어만이라도 꼭 외우고 넘어가세요!

01	notable	a. 저명한	a group of (✔ notable) Scandinavian researchers	저명한 스칸디나비아 연구자들
02	meteorologist	n. 기상학자	a Norwegian (　　　　　)	노르웨이 기상학자
03	traditional	a. 전통적인	receive a (　　　　) education	전통적인 교육을 받다
04	degree	n. 학위	earn a (　　　　)	학위를 받다
05	physics	n. 물리학	mathematical (　　　　)	수리 물리학
06	apparently	ad. 겉으로 보기에, 보아하니	(　　　　) bored with Stockholm	짐작하기로는 스톡홀름에 지겨워진
07	establish	v. 설립하다	the newly (　　　　)ed institute	새로 설립된 연구소
08	scholarship	n. 장학금	receive a (　　　　)	장학금을 받다
09	practical	a. 실질적인	(　　　　) experience	실질적인 경험
10	circulation	n. 순환	explain the cyclonic (　　　　)	사이클론 순환을 설명하다
11	boundary	n. 경계	develop at the (　　　　)	경계에서 발생하다
12	air mass	n. [기상학] 기단	warm and cold (　　) (　　)es	고온 기단과 저온 기단
13	chair	n. 기관(장), 의장(직)	accept the (　　　) of the institute	연구소장 자리를 받아들이다

➕ 본문 문장 속에서 단어들을 확인해 보세요.

Based in part on his practical experience in weather forecasting, / Rossby had become a supporter of the "polar front theory," / which explains the cyclonic circulation / that develops at the boundary between warm and cold air masses.

일기 예보에 대한 그의 실질적인 경험을 일부 바탕으로 하여, / Rossby는 "polar front theory"의 지지자가 되었다 / 사이클론 순환을 설명하는 / 고온, 저온 기단 사이의 경계에서 발생하는.

01	notable	저명한	a group of notable Scandinavian researchers	저명한 스칸디나비아 연구자들
02	meteorologist		a Norwegian meteorologist	노르웨이 기상학자
03	traditional		receive a traditional education	전통적인 교육을 받다
04	degree		earn a degree	학위를 받다
05	physics		mathematical physics	수리 물리학
06	apparently		apparently bored with Stockholm	짐작하기로는 스톡홀름에 지겨워진
07	establish		the newly established institute	새로 설립된 연구소
08	scholarship		receive a scholarship	장학금을 받다
09	practical		practical experience	실질적인 경험
10	circulation		explain the cyclonic circulation	사이클론 순환을 설명하다
11	boundary		develop at the boundary	경계에서 발생하다
12	air mass		warm and cold air masses	고온 기단과 저온 기단
13	chair		accept the chair of the institute	연구소장 자리를 받아들이다

⊕ 본문 문장 속에서 단어의 의미를 우리말로 해석해 보세요.

Based in part on his practical experience in weather forecasting, / Rossby had become a supporter of the "polar front theory," / which explains the cyclonic circulation / that develops at the boundary between warm and cold air masses.

→ 일기 예보에 대한 그의 _____ 경험을 일부 바탕으로 하여, / Rossby는 "polar front theory"의 지지자가 되었다 / 사이클론 _____ 을 설명하는 / 고온, 저온 _____ 사이의 _____ 에서 발생하는.

STEP 2 · 수능 기출 제대로 풀기

B

Carl-Gustaf Rossby에 관한 다음 글의 내용과 일치하지 <u>않는</u> 것은?

Carl-Gustaf Rossby was one of a group of notable Scandinavian researchers who worked with the Norwegian meteorologist Vilhelm Bjerknes at the University of Bergen. While growing up in Stockholm, Rossby received a traditional education. He earned a degree in mathematical physics at the University of Stockholm in 1918, but after hearing a lecture by Bjerknes, and apparently bored with Stockholm, he moved to the newly established Geophysical Institute in Bergen. In 1925, Rossby received a scholarship from the Sweden-America Foundation to go to the United States, where he joined the United States Weather Bureau. Based in part on his practical experience in weather forecasting, Rossby had become a supporter of the "polar front theory," which explains the cyclonic circulation that develops at the boundary between warm and cold air masses. In 1947, Rossby accepted the chair of the Institute of Meteorology, which had been set up for him at the University of Stockholm, where he remained until his death ten years later.

① Stockholm에서 성장하면서 전통적인 교육을 받았다.

② University of Stockholm에서 수리 물리학 학위를 받았다.

③ 1925년에 장학금을 받았다.

④ polar front theory를 지지했다.

⑤ University of Stockholm에 마련된 직책을 거절했다.

정답과 해설 p.17

01 Carl-Gustaf Rossby was one of a group of notable Scandinavian researchers / [who worked with the Norwegian meteorologist Vilhelm Bjerknes / at the University of Bergen].

주격 관계대명사절

02 While growing up in Stockholm, / Rossby received a traditional education.

접속사가 남아있는 분사구문

03 He earned a degree in mathematical physics at the University of Stockholm in 1918, / but after hearing a lecture by Bjerknes, / and apparently bored with Stockholm, / he moved to the newly established Geophysical Institute in Bergen.

분사구문 병렬구조
과거분사구

04 In 1925, / Rossby received a scholarship from the Sweden-America Foundation / to go to the United States, / where he joined the United States Weather Bureau.

to부정사의 부사적 용법(결과)
계속적 용법의 관계부사(=and there)

05 Based in part on his practical experience in weather forecasting, / Rossby had become a supporter of the "polar front theory," / which explains the cyclonic circulation / that develops at the boundary between warm and cold air masses.

삽입구
선행사
계속적 용법의 관계대명사(=and it)
주격 관계대명사절

06 In 1947, / Rossby accepted the chair of the Institute of Meteorology, / which had been set up for him at the University of Stockholm, / where he remained until his death ten years later.

선행사
계속적 용법의 관계대명사
선행사
계속적 용법의 관계부사

01 Carl-Gustaf Rossby는 저명한notable 스칸디나비아 연구자들 중 한 명이었다 / 노르웨이 기상학자meteorologist인 Vilhelm Bjerknes와 함께 일했던 / Bergen 대학에서.

02 Stockholm에서 성장하면서, / Rossby는 전통적인traditional 교육을 받았다.

03 그는 1918년에 University of Stockholm에서 수리 물리학physics 학위degree를 받았지만, / Bjerknes의 강의를 듣고 나서, / 그리고 짐작하건대apparently Stockholm에 지루함을 느껴서, / Bergen에 새로 설립된established 지구 물리학 연구소로 옮겼다.

04 1925년에 / Rossby는 스웨덴-미국 재단으로부터 장학금scholarship을 받아 / 미국으로 갔고, / 그곳에서 미국 기상국에 합류했다.

05 일기 예보에 대한 그의 실질적인practical 경험을 일부 바탕으로 하여, / Rossby는 "polar front theory"의 지지자가 되었다 / 사이클론 순환circulation을 설명하는 / 고온, 저온 기단air mass 사이의 경계boundary에서 발생하는.

06 1947년에 / Rossby는 기상 연구소장chair 자리를 받아들였다 / University of Stockholm에 그를 위해 마련된 / 그리고 그는 10년 후 생을 마감할 때까지 그곳에서 재직했다.

구문 Check up

① After hearing a lecture by Bjerknes, and apparently boring / bored with Stockholm, he moved to the newly established Geophysical Institute in Bergen.

분사구문의 주어가 주절의 주어와 같은 he이고, 그가 지루함을 느낀 것이므로 과거분사 bored를 쓴다.

② In 1925, Rossby received a scholarship from the Sweden-America Foundation to go to the United States, which / where he joined the United States Weather Bureau.

뒤따르는 절이 완전하므로 관계부사 where을 쓴다.

정답 ① bored ② where

C　STEP 1 • 수능에 진짜 나오는 단어

✔ 문제에 나오는 단어들을 확인하세요.

시간이 없다면 색으로 표시된 단어만이라도 꼭 외우고 넘어가세요!

01	pass away	돌아가시다, 죽다	Her father (✔ pass)ed (away).	그녀의 아버지가 돌아가셨다.
02	bring up	기르다	be (　　　) (　　) by her uncle	삼촌에 의해 길러지다
03	attend	v. ~에 다니다, 출석하다	(　　　　) a school	학교를 다니다
04	debut	n. 데뷔	make a (　　　　)	데뷔하다
05	status	n. 지위	star (　　　　)	스타의 지위
06	tremendous	a. 굉장한	(　　　　　　) acting talent	굉장한 연기 재능
07	angelic	a. 천사 같은	an (　　　　) beauty	천사 같은 미모
08	willingness to	기꺼이 ~하는 태도	(　　　　) (　　) work hard	기꺼이 열심히 일하려는 태도
09	fluent	a. 유창한	(　　　) in five languages	다섯 언어에 유창한
10	a range of	다양한	(　) (　　　) (　　) films	다양한 영화

⊕ 본문 문장 속에서 단어들을 확인해 보세요.

Bergman was considered / to have tremendous acting talent, / an angelic natural beauty / and the willingness to work hard to get the best out of films.

Bergman은 여겨졌다 / 굉장한 연기 재능을 가진 것으로 / 그리고 천사 같은 자연미를 (가진 것으로) / 그리고 영화에서 최상의 것을 얻으려고 기꺼이 열심히 일하려는 태도를 (가진 것으로).

01	pass away	돌아가시다, 죽다	Her father passed away.	그녀의 아버지가 돌아가셨다.
02	bring up		be brought up by her uncle	삼촌에 의해 길러지다
03	attend		attend a school	학교를 다니다
04	debut		make a debut	데뷔하다
05	status		star status	스타의 지위
06	tremendous		tremendous acting talent	굉장한 연기 재능
07	angelic		an angelic beauty	천사 같은 미모
08	willingness to		willingness to work hard	기꺼이 열심히 일하려는 태도
09	fluent		fluent in five languages	다섯 언어에 유창한
10	a range of		a range of films	다양한 영화

➕ 본문 문장 속에서 단어의 의미를 우리말로 해석해 보세요.

Bergman was considered / to have tremendous acting talent, / an angelic natural beauty / and the willingness to work hard to get the best out of films.

→ Bergman은 여겨졌다 / _____ 연기 재능을 가진 것으로 / 그리고 _____ 자연미를 (가진 것으로) / 그리고 영화에서 최상의 것을 얻으려고 _____ 를 (가진 것으로).

제한시간 50초

난이도 ★☆☆☆☆

STEP 2 · 수능 기출 제대로 풀기

C Ingrid Bergman에 관한 다음 글의 내용과 일치하지 <u>않는</u> 것은?

Ingrid Bergman was born in Stockholm, Sweden on August 29, 1915. Her mother was German and her father Swedish. Her mother died when she was three, and her father passed away when she was 12. Eventually she was brought up by her Uncle Otto and Aunt Hulda. She was interested in acting from an early age. When she was 17, she attended the Royal Dramatic Theater School in Stockholm. She made her debut on the stage but was more interested in working in films. In the early 1940s, she gained star status in Hollywood, playing many roles as the heroine of the film. Bergman was considered to have tremendous acting talent, an angelic natural beauty and the willingness to work hard to get the best out of films. She was fluent in five languages and appeared in a range of films, plays and TV productions.

① 어머니는 독일인이었고 아버지는 스웨덴인이었다.

② 17세에 Royal Dramatic Theater School에 다녔다.

③ 영화를 통해 데뷔했으나 연극에 더 관심이 있었다.

④ 1940년대 초에 할리우드에서 스타의 지위를 얻었다.

⑤ 다섯 개의 언어에 유창했다.

정답과 해설 p.17

01 Ingrid Bergman was born / in Stockholm, Sweden on August 29, 1915. // Her mother
    was born: 태어나다
was German / and her father Swedish.
        등위접속사   was 생략

02 Her mother died when she was three, / and her father passed away when she was 12. //
Eventually she was brought up / by her Uncle Otto and Aunt Hulda.
            구동사 수동태(be+p.p.+by)

03 She was interested in acting / from an early age. // When she was 17, / she attended the
    be interested in+(동)명사: ~에 관심이 있다
Royal Dramatic Theater School in Stockholm.

04 She made her debut on the stage / but was more interested in working in films.
        └---------- 동사구 병렬 연결 ----------┘

05 In the early 1940s, / she gained star status in Hollywood, / playing many roles as the
                                                    분사구문
heroine of the film.

06 Bergman was considered / to have tremendous acting talent, / an angelic natural
    5형식 문장의 수동태: be+p.p.+목적격 보어(to부정사)
beauty / and the willingness [to work hard to get the best out of films].
                        └-------- to부정사 형용사적 용법

07 She was fluent in five languages / and appeared in a range of films, plays and TV
        └-------- 동사구 병렬 연결 --------┘
productions.

01 Ingrid Bergman은 태어났다 / 1915년 8월 29일에 스웨덴의 스톡홀름에서. // 그녀의 어머니는 독일인이었고 / 아버지는
스웨덴인이었다.

02 그녀의 어머니는 그녀가 세 살 때 돌아가셨고, / 아버지는 그녀가 열두 살 때 돌아가셨다pass away. // 결국 그녀는
키워졌다be brought up / Uncle Otto와 Aunt Hulda에 의해.

03 그녀는 연기에 관심이 있었다 / 어릴 때부터. // 그녀가 열일곱 살 때 / 스톡홀름에 있는 Royal Dramatic Theater
School에 다녔다attend.

04 그녀는 연극으로 데뷔했지만made her debut / 영화계에서 일하는 데 더 관심이 있었다.

05 1940년대 초에 / 그녀는 할리우드에서 스타의 지위를star status 얻었고 / 영화의 여주인공으로 많은 역할을 맡았다.

06 Bergman은 여겨졌다 / 굉장한 연기 재능tremendous acting talent을 가진 것으로 / 그리고 천사 같은 자연미an
angelic natural beauty를 (가진 것으로) / 그리고 영화에서 최상의 것을 얻으려고 기꺼이 열심히 일하려는 태도the
willingness to work hard를 (가진 것으로).

07 그녀는 다섯 개의 언어에 유창했고fluent / 다양한a range of 영화, 연극, 그리고 TV 작품에 출연했다.

D STEP 1 • 수능에 *진짜* 나오는 *단어*

✔ 문제에 나오는 단어들을 확인하세요.

시간이 없다면 색으로 표시된 단어만이라도 꼭 외우고 넘어가세요!

01	Dutch	a. 네덜란드의	a (✔ Dutch) mathematician	네덜란드의 수학자
02	astronomer	n. 천문학자	a passionate ( )	열정적인 천문학자
03	devote	v. 바치다, 전념하다	( ) time to his research	자신의 연구에 시간을 바치다
04	initially	ad. 처음에는	( ) in mathematics	처음에는 수학에서
05	optics	n. 광학	in ( )	광학에서
06	telescope	n. 망원경	work on ( )s	망원경에 대한 작업을 하다
07	grind	v. 갈다, 연마하다	( ) his own lenses	자신의 렌즈를 갈다
08	motion	n. 운동	forces and ( )	힘과 운동
09	gravitation	n. 중력, 인력	Newton's law of universal ( )	뉴턴의 만유인력의 법칙
10	achievement	n. 업적	wide-ranging ( )s	광범위한 업적
11	astronomical	a. 천문학적인	( ) work	천문학적인 연구
12	moon	n. 위성	Saturn's ( )s	토성의 위성들
13	description	n. 기술, 설명	the ( ) of Saturn's rings	토성의 고리에 대한 기술

⊕ 본문 문장 속에서 단어들을 확인해 보세요.

In addition to his work on light, / Huygens had studied forces and motion, / but he did not accept / Newton's law of universal gravitation.

빛에 관한 연구 외에도 / Huygens는 힘과 운동을 연구했으나, / 그는 받아들이지 않았다 / 뉴턴의 만유인력 법칙을.

01	Dutch	네덜란드의	a Dutch mathematician	네덜란드의 수학자
02	astronomer		a passionate astronomer	열정적인 천문학자
03	devote		devote time to his research	자신의 연구에 시간을 바치다
04	initially		initially in mathematics	처음에는 수학에서
05	optics		in optics	광학에서
06	telescope		work on telescopes	망원경에 대한 작업을 하다
07	grind		grind his own lenses	자신의 렌즈를 갈다
08	motion		forces and motion	힘과 운동
09	gravitation		Newton's law of universal gravitation	뉴턴의 만유인력의 법칙
10	achievement		wide-ranging achievements	광범위한 업적
11	astronomical		astronomical work	천문학적인 연구
12	moon		Saturn's moons	토성의 위성들
13	description		the description of Saturn's rings	토성의 고리에 대한 기술

⊕ 본문 문장 속에서 단어의 의미를 우리말로 해석해 보세요.

In addition to his work on light, / Huygens had studied forces and motion, / but he did not accept / Newton's law of universal gravitation.

→ 빛에 관한 연구 외에도 / Huygens는 힘과   을 연구했으나, / 그는 받아들이지 않았다 / 뉴턴의   을.

STEP 2 • 수능 기출 제대로 풀기

 Christiaan Huygens에 관한 다음 글의 내용과 일치하지 <u>않는</u> 것은?

Dutch mathematician and astronomer Christiaan Huygens was born in The Hague in 1629. He studied law and mathematics at his university, and then devoted some time to his own research, initially in mathematics but then also in optics, working on telescopes and grinding his own lenses. Huygens visited England several times, and met Isaac Newton in 1689. In addition to his work on light, Huygens had studied forces and motion, but he did not accept Newton's law of universal gravitation. Huygens' wide-ranging achievements included some of the most accurate clocks of his time, the result of his work on pendulums. His astronomical work, carried out using his own telescopes, included the discovery of Titan, the largest of Saturn's moons, and the first correct description of Saturn's rings.

*pendulum: 시계추

① 대학에서 법과 수학을 공부했다.
② 1689년에 뉴턴을 만났다.
③ 뉴턴의 만유인력 법칙을 받아들였다.
④ 당대의 가장 정확한 시계 중 몇몇이 업적에 포함되었다.
⑤ 자신의 망원경을 사용하여 천문학 연구를 수행했다.

정답과 해설 p.18

01 Dutch mathematician and astronomer Christiaan Huygens / was born / in The Hague in
주어 동격(지위 설명)   주어
1629.

02 He studied law and mathematics at his university, / and then devoted some time to his
devote A to B: A를 B에 바치다
own research, / initially in mathematics but then also in optics, / working on telescopes
부대상황의 분사구문: ~하면서
and grinding his own lenses.

03 Huygens visited England several times, / and met Isaac Newton in 1689.

04 In addition to his work on light, / Huygens had studied forces and motion, / but he did
~ 외에도   과거완료
not accept Newton's law of universal gravitation.

05 Huygens' wide-ranging achievements / included some of the most accurate clocks of
his time, / the result of his work on pendulums.
동격

06 His astronomical work, / carried out using his own telescopes, / included the discovery
과거분사
of Titan, the largest of Saturn's moons, / and the first correct description of Saturn's
동격
rings.

01 네덜란드의 수학자이자 천문학자인Dutch mathematician and astronomer Christiaan Huygens는 / 태어났다 /
1629년 헤이그에서.

02 그는 대학에서 법과 수학을 공부했고, / 그런 후에 상당 기간을 자기 연구에 헌신했다devote some time to his research
/ 처음에는initially 수학에서, 그다음 광학optics에서도 / 망원경telescope을 연구하고 본인만의 렌즈를 갈면서grind his
own lenses.

03 Huygens는 영국을 몇 차례 방문했고, / 1689년에 아이작 뉴턴을 만났다.

04 빛에 관한 연구 외에도 / Huygens는 힘과 운동forces and motion을 연구했으나, / 그는 뉴턴의 만유인력 법칙Newton's
law of universal gravitation을 받아들이지 않았다.

05 Huygens의 광범위한 업적wide-ranging achievement은 / 당대의 가장 정확한 시계 중 몇몇을 포함했다 / 시계추에
대한 그의 연구의 결과물인.

06 그의 천문학 연구astronomical work는 / 자신의 망원경을 사용하여 수행된 / 토성의 위성Saturn's moons 중 가장 큰
타이탄의 발견을 포함했다 / 그리고 토성의 고리에 대한 최초의 정확한 기술description도.

구문 Check up

① He studied law and mathematics at his university, and
then devoted some time to his own research, worked
/ working on telescopes and grinding his own lenses.

콤마 앞에 'studied ~ and then devoted ~'라는 2개의 동사가 제시되고,
콤마 뒤로 He의 행동을 설명하는 분사구문이 이어진다. grinding과 and
앞뒤로 병렬 연결되도록 working을 써야 한다.

② His astronomical work, carrying / carried out using
his own telescopes, included the discovery of Titan.

연구가 '수행되는'이라는 수동의 의미가 적절하기 때문에 carried로 쓴다.

정답 ① working ② carried

138

E

STEP 1 • 수능에 *진짜* 나오는 *단어*

✔ 문제에 나오는 단어들을 확인하세요.

시간이 없다면 색으로 표시된 단어만이라도 꼭 외우고 넘어가세요!

01	abandon	v. 버리다	(✔ abandon) a family	가족을 버리다
02	support	v. 부양하다	( ) his brothers	그의 형제를 부양하다
03	print shop	인쇄소	work in a ( ) ( )	인쇄소에서 일하다
04	landscape	n. 풍경화, 풍경	paint ( )s	풍경화를 그리다
05	put together	한데 모으다	( ) the result ( )	결과를 한데 모으다
06	art show	미술 전시회	create an ( ) ( )	미술 전시회를 열다
07	severely	ad. 심하게	( ) criticize	심하게 비판하다
08	criticize	v. 비판하다	be severely ( )d	심하게 지탄받다
09	exhibit	v. 전시하다	keep ( )ing	계속 전시를 하다
10	acknowledge	v. 인정하다	( ) him as a genius	그를 천재로 인정하다
11	pioneer	n. 개척자, 선구자	a ( ) of modern landscape art	현대 풍경화의 개척자

✚ 본문 문장 속에서 단어들을 확인해 보세요.

The "Group of Seven," / as they called themselves, / put the results of the tour together / to create an art show / in Toronto in 1920.

'Group of Seven'은 / 그들이 스스로를 불렀던 대로 / 여행의 결과물들을 한데 모아 / 미술 전시회를 열었다 / 1920년에 Toronto에서.

문제를 풀기 전에 단어들을 30초 동안 다시 확인하세요.

01	abandon	버리다	abandon a family	가족을 버리다
02	support		support his brothers	그의 형제를 부양하다
03	print shop		work in a print shop	인쇄소에서 일하다
04	landscape		paint landscapes	풍경화를 그리다
05	put together		put the result together	결과를 한데 모으다
06	art show		create an art show	미술 전시회를 열다
07	severely		severely criticize	심하게 비판하다
08	criticize		be severely criticized	심하게 지탄받다
09	exhibit		keep exhibiting	계속 전시를 하다
10	acknowledge		acknowledge him as a genius	그를 천재로 인정하다
11	pioneer		a pioneer of modern landscape art	현대 풍경화의 개척자

➕ 본문 문장 속에서 단어의 의미를 우리말로 해석해 보세요.

The "Group of Seven," / as they called themselves, / put the results of the tour together / to create an art show / in Toronto in 1920.

➡ 'Group of Seven'은 / 그들이 스스로를 불렀던 대로 / 여행의 결과물들을 ▭▭▭▭▭ / ▭▭▭▭▭ 를 열었다 / 1920년에 Toronto에서.

제한시간 60초
난이도 ★★☆☆☆

STEP 2 • 수능 기출 제대로 풀기

E Alexander Young Jackson에 관한 다음 글의 내용과 일치하지 <u>않는</u> 것은?

Alexander Young Jackson (everyone called him A. Y.) was born to a poor family in Montreal in 1882. His father abandoned them when he was young, and A. Y. had to go to work at age twelve to help support his brothers and sisters. Working in a print shop, he became interested in art, and he began to paint landscapes in a fresh new style. Traveling by train across northern Ontario, A. Y. and several other artists painted everything they saw. The "Group of Seven," as they called themselves, put the results of the tour together to create an art show in Toronto in 1920. That was the show where their paintings were severely criticized as "art gone mad." But he kept painting, traveling, and exhibiting, and by the time he died in 1974 at the age of eighty-two, A. Y. Jackson was acknowledged as a painting genius and a pioneer of modern landscape art.

① Montreal의 한 가난한 가정에서 태어났다.
② 인쇄소에서 일을 하며 미술에 관심을 갖게 되었다.
③ Ontario 북부를 횡단하는 기차 여행을 했다.
④ Toronto 전시회에서 비평가들로부터 좋은 평가를 받았다.
⑤ 사망할 무렵에는 현대 풍경화의 개척자로 인정받았다.

정답과 해설 p.18

01 Alexander Young Jackson (everyone called him A. Y.) / was born to a poor family / in
Montreal in 1882. // His father abandoned them / when he was young, / and A. Y. had to
go to work / at age twelve / <u>to help support his brothers and sisters.</u>
to부정사의 부사적 용법(목적)

02 <u>Working in a print shop,</u> / he became interested in art, / and he began to paint
분사구문(=While he worked ~)
landscapes / in a fresh new style.

03 <u>Traveling by train across northern Ontario,</u> / A. Y. and several other artists painted
분사구문
everything they saw.
관계대명사 that 생략

04 The "Group of Seven," / <u>as they called themselves,</u> / put the results of the tour together
삽입절(주어 보충 설명)
/ to create an art show / in Toronto in 1920. // <u>That</u> was the show / <u>where</u> their
지시대명사(그것)   관계부사절
paintings were severely criticized / as "art gone mad."

05 But he <u>kept painting, traveling, and exhibiting,</u> / and <u>by the time</u> he died in 1974 at
~ 할 무렵
keep+-ing: 계속 ~하다
the age of eighty-two, / A. Y. Jackson was acknowledged / <u>as</u> a painting genius and a
~로서
pioneer of modern landscape art.

---

01 Alexander Young Jackson(모든 사람들이 그를 A. Y.라고 불렀다)은 / 한 가난한 가정에서 태어났다 / 1882년에
Montreal의. // 그의 아버지는 그들을 저버렸고abandon / 그가 어렸을 때, / A. Y.는 일을 해야만 했다 / 12살 때 / 그의
형제와 자매를 부양하는support 것을 돕기 위해.

02 인쇄소에서 일을 하면서work in a print shop / 그는 미술에 관심을 가지게 되었고, / 풍경화를 그리기paint landscapes
시작했다 / 신선하고 새로운 방식으로.

03 기차로 Ontario 북부를 횡단하는 여행을 하면서, / A. Y.와 몇 명의 다른 화가들은 그들이 보는 모든 것을 그렸다.

04 'Group of Seven'은 / 그들이 스스로를 불렀던 대로 / 여행의 결과물들을 한데 모아put the result together / 미술
전시회art show를 열었다 / 1920년에 Toronto에서. // 그것은 전시회였다 / 그들의 그림이 호되게 비판을 받았던be
severely criticized / '미쳐버린 예술'이라고.

05 그러나 그는 계속 그림을 그리고, 여행을 하고, 전시를 했고exhibit, / 1974년 82세의 나이로 사망할 무렵에 / A. Y.
Jackson은 인정받았다be acknowledged / 천재 화가이자 현대 풍경화의 개척자a pioneer of modern landscape art로.

---

① Traveled / Traveling by train across northern Ontario,
A. Y. and several other artists painted everything they
saw.

주어인 A. Y. and several other artists가 '여행하는' 주체이므로 분사구문
자리에 현재분사 Traveling을 쓴다.

② That was the show which / where their paintings
were severely criticized as "art gone mad."

선행사 the show가 공간을 나타내고, 'their paintings ~ gone mad'가 완
전한 수동태 문장이므로 관계부사 where를 쓴다.

STEP 1 • 수능에 *진짜* 나오는 *단어*

 문제에 나오는 단어들을 확인하세요.

01	producer	n. 제작자	an Indian (✓ producer)	인도의 제작자
02	economics	n. 경제학	study ( )	경제학을 공부하다
03	pursue	v. 추구하다, (일에) 종사하다	( ) a full-time career	전업으로 일을 하다
04	fame	n. 명성	great ( )	큰 명성
05	media	n. 매체, 언론	in the ( )	매체에서
06	appear	v. 나타나다, 출연하다	( ) in more than 80 films	80편이 넘는 영화에 출연하다
07	government	n. 정부	the French ( )	프랑스 정부
08	contribution	n. 공헌, 기여, 공로	his ( ) to cinema	영화에 대한 공로
09	feature	v. 특별히 포함하다, 등재하다	be ( )d on lists	목록에 등재되다
10	influential	a. 영향력 있는	the most ( ) people	가장 영향력 있는 인물들
11	endeavor	n. 노력	philanthropic ( )s	박애주의적인 노력
12	disaster	n. 재난	( ) relief	재난 구호
13	honor	v. 수여하다, 영광을 주다	be ( )ed with UNESCO's award	UNESCO에서 상을 받다

➕ 본문 문장 속에서 단어들을 확인해 보세요.

He moved from Delhi to Mumbai / to pursue a full-time career in Bollywood, / which led him to great fame.

그는 Delhi에서 Mumbai로 이주했고 / Bollywood에서 전업으로 일을 하기 위해, / 이는 그에게 큰 명성을 가져다주었다.

01	producer	✎ 제작자	an Indian producer	인도의 제작자
02	economics		study economics	경제학을 공부하다
03	pursue		pursue a full-time career	전업으로 일을 하다
04	fame		great fame	큰 명성
05	media		in the media	매체에서
06	appear		appear in more than 80 films	80편이 넘는 영화에 출연하다
07	government		the French government	프랑스 정부
08	contribution		his contribution to cinema	영화에 대한 공로
09	feature		be featured on lists	목록에 등재되다
10	influential		the most influential people	가장 영향력 있는 인물들
11	endeavor		philanthropic endeavors	박애주의적인 노력
12	disaster		disaster relief	재난 구호
13	honor		be honored with UNESCO's award	UNESCO에서 상을 받다

➕ **본문 문장 속에서 단어의 의미를 우리말로 해석해 보세요.**

He moved from Delhi to Mumbai / to pursue a full-time career in Bollywood, / which led him to great fame.

→ 그는 Delhi에서 Mumbai로 이주했고 / Bollywood에서 [   ] 위해, / 이는 그에게 [   ]을 가져다주었다.

제한시간 60초
난이도 ★★☆☆☆

STEP **2** • 수능 기출 제대로 풀기

F Shah Rukh Khan에 관한 다음 글의 내용과 일치하지 <u>않는</u> 것은?

Shah Rukh Khan is an Indian film actor and producer. Khan studied economics in college but spent much of his time at Delhi's Theatre Action Group, where he studied acting. He moved from Delhi to Mumbai to pursue a full-time career in Bollywood, which led him to great fame. Referred to in the media as the "King of Bollywood" or "King Khan," he has appeared in more than 80 Bollywood films. In 2007, the French government awarded Khan the Order of Arts and Letters for his contribution to cinema. He is regularly featured on lists of the most influential people in Indian culture, and in 2008, he was chosen as one of the 50 most powerful people in the world. Khan's philanthropic endeavors have provided health care and disaster relief, and he was honored with UNESCO's Pyramide con Marni award in 2011 for his support of children's education.

① 인도의 영화배우이자 제작자이다.

② 대학에서 경제학을 공부했다.

③ 80편이 넘는 Bollywood 영화에 출연했다.

④ 2007년에 세계에서 가장 영향력 있는 50인 중 한 명으로 선정되었다.

⑤ 아동 교육에 대한 후원으로 2011년에 UNESCO에서 상을 받았다.

정답과 해설 p.19

01 Shah Rukh Khan is an Indian film actor and producer. // Khan studied economics in college / but spent much of his time / at Delhi's Theatre Action Group, / <u>where he studied acting.</u>
관계부사절(Theatre Action Group 보충 설명)

02 He moved from Delhi to Mumbai / <u>to pursue a full-time career in Bollywood,</u> / which led him to great fame.
to부정사의 부사적 용법(목적)   주격 관계대명사 (계속적 용법)

03 <u>Referred to in the media as the "King of Bollywood" or "King Khan,"</u> / <u>he has appeared</u> / in more than 80 Bollywood films.
분사구문(refer to A as B: A를 B라고 부르다)   현재완료

04 In 2007, / the French government <u>awarded Khan the Order of Arts and Letters</u> / for his contribution to cinema.
수여동사(award)+간접목적어+직접목적어

05 He is regularly featured / on lists of the most influential people / in Indian culture, / and in 2008, / he was chosen / <u>as</u> <u>one of the 50 most powerful people</u> / in the world.
~로서   one of+the 최상급+복수 명사: 가장 ~한 것 중 하나

06 Khan's philanthropic endeavors have provided health care and disaster relief, / and he was honored with UNESCO's Pyramide con Marni award in 2011 / for his support of children's education.

01 Shah Rukh Khan은 인도의 영화배우이자 제작자producer이다. // Khan은 대학에서 경제학economics을 공부했지만 / 많은 시간을 보냈고 / Delhi의 Theatre Action Group에서, / 그곳에서 연기를 공부했다.

02 그는 Delhi에서 Mumbai로 이주했고 / Bollywood에서 전업으로 일을 하기pursue a full-time career 위해, / 이는 그에게 큰 명성fame을 가져다주었다.

03 "King of Bollywood" 또는 "King Khan"으로 매체media에서 불리면서, / 그는 출연했다appear / 80편이 넘는 Bollywood 영화에.

04 2007년에 / 프랑스 정부government는 Khan에게 the Order of Arts and Letters를 수여하였다 / 영화에 대한 공로contribution로.

05 그는 정기적으로 등재되며be featured / 가장 영향력 있는influential 인물들 목록에 / 인도 문화에서, / 2008년에는 / 선정되었다 / 가장 영향력 있는 인물 50인 중 한 명으로 / 세계에서.

06 Khan의 박애주의적인 노력endeavor은 의료 서비스와 재난disaster 구호를 제공해왔으며 / 그는 2011년에 UNESCO에서 Pyramide con Marni 상을 받았다be honored / 아동 교육에 대한 후원으로.

구문 Check up

① He moved from Delhi to Mumbai to pursue a full-time career in Bollywood, which / that led him to great fame.

관계대명사의 계속적 용법으로는 that을 쓸 수 없으므로 which가 적절하다.

② Referred / Referring to in the media as the "King of Bollywood" or "King Khan," he has appeared in more than 80 Bollywood films.

주절의 주어(he)가 '~라고 불렸다'라는 의미가 적절하므로, 수동의 의미를 나타내는 과거분사 Referred를 써서 분사구문을 만든다.

정답 ① which ② Referred

내용 불일치 ➕

✔ 문제에 나오는 단어들을 확인하세요.

시간이 없다면 색으로 표시된 단어만이라도 꼭 외우고 넘어가세요!

01	primate	n. 영장류	little (✓ primate)s	작은 영장류
02	resemblance	n. 유사성	( ) to the rat	쥐와의 유사성
03	exaggerate	v. 과장하다, 부각하다	( ) a story	이야기를 과장하다
04	length	n. 길이	overall body ( )	전체 몸 길이
05	nocturnal	a. 야행성의	( ) animals	야행성 동물
06	adaptation	n. 적응, 적응력	( )s for this lifestyle	이런 생활방식을 위한 적응력
07	enormous	a. 굉장히 큰, 거대한	an ( ) amount of money	엄청난 양의 돈
08	in comparison with	~에 비해	( ) ( ) ( ) its size	그것의 크기에 비해
09	habitat	n. 서식지	a wildlife ( )	야생 동식물의 서식지
10	rain forest	열대 우림 지역	adaptations for ( ) ( )	열대 우림 지역에 대한 적응력
11	dense	a. 빽빽한	( ) rain forest	빽빽한 열대 우림 지역
12	thicket	n. 덤불, 숲	a bamboo ( )	대나무 숲
13	trunk	n. 나무 둥치	holes in tree ( )s	나무 둥치의 구멍
14	vegetation	n. 초목(식물)	in dark ( )	어두운 초목에
15	tangle	v. 엉키게 하다	( )d vegetation	엉킨 초목
16	rotate	v. 회전시키다, 돌리다	( ) heads	머리를 돌리다
17	spot	v. 발견하다, 찾다	vision for ( )ting prey	먹이를 찾기 위한 시야

➕ 본문 문장 속에서 단어들을 확인해 보세요.

The habitat of the tarsier is generally tropical rain forest / and they are found in dense bamboo thickets.

Tarsier의 서식지는 대개 열대 우림 지역이며 / 그것들은 빽빽한 대나무 숲에서 발견된다.

01	primate	✎ 영장류	little primates	작은 영장류
02	resemblance		resemblance to the rat	쥐와의 유사성
03	exaggerate		exaggerate a story	이야기를 과장하다
04	length		overall body length	전체 몸 길이
05	nocturnal		nocturnal animals	야행성 동물
06	adaptation		adaptations for this lifestyle	이런 생활방식을 위한 적응력
07	enormous		an enormous amount of money	엄청난 양의 돈
08	in comparison with		in comparison with its size	그것의 크기에 비해
09	habitat		a wildlife habitat	야생 동식물의 서식지
10	rain forest		adaptations for rain forest	열대 우림 지역에 대한 적응력
11	dense		dense rain forest	빽빽한 열대 우림 지역
12	thicket		a bamboo thicket	대나무 숲
13	trunk		holes in tree trunks	나무 둥치의 구멍
14	vegetation		in dark vegetation	어두운 초목에
15	tangle		tangled vegetation	엉킨 초목
16	rotate		rotate heads	머리를 돌리다
17	spot		vision for spotting prey	먹이를 찾기 위한 시야

⊕ 본문 문장 속에서 단어의 의미를 우리말로 해석해 보세요.

The habitat of the tarsier is generally tropical rain forest / and they are found in dense bamboo thickets.

→ Tarsier의   는 대개   이며 / 그것들은   에서 발견된다.

STEP **2** • 수능 기출 제대로 풀기

G tarsier에 관한 다음 글의 내용과 일치하지 <u>않는</u> 것은?

Tarsiers are little primates not much bigger than rats. Their resemblance to the rat is exaggerated by their thin tail, which is much longer than their overall body length. All tarsiers are completely nocturnal and have a number of remarkable physical adaptations for this lifestyle. They have an excellent sense of hearing. Tarsiers also have enormous eyes in comparison with their body size; their eyes make up nearly one-fourth the size of their faces. The habitat of the tarsier is generally tropical rain forest and they are found in dense bamboo thickets. During the day, they lie in holes in tree trunks and in dark, thickly tangled vegetation. At night, they hunt for insects, spiders, and small lizards. Tarsiers can rotate their heads at least 180 degrees, which gives them a wide field of vision for spotting prey.

① 몸통보다 긴 꼬리를 지니고 있다.

② 뛰어난 청력을 가지고 있다.

③ 눈이 얼굴 크기의 약 4분의 1을 차지한다.

④ 열대 우림 지역에 주로 서식한다.

⑤ 채식 위주의 먹잇감을 찾아 다닌다.

정답과 해설 **p.19**

01 Tarsiers are little primates / not much bigger than rats. // Their resemblance to the rat
　　　　　　　　　　　　　　주격관계대명사+be동사(which are) 생략
is exaggerated / by their thin tail, / which is much longer than their overall body length.
　수동태　　　　　　　　　선행사　　　주격 관계대명사(계속적 용법)

02 All tarsiers are completely nocturnal / and have a number of remarkable physical
　　　　　　　　　　　　　　　　　　　　　　　　a number of+복수 명사: 많은 (명사)
adaptations / for this lifestyle. // They have an excellent sense of hearing.

03 Tarsiers also have enormous eyes / in comparison with their body size; / their eyes
make up nearly one-fourth the size of their faces.　　　　　세미콜론: 두 문장을 연결
　　　　　　분수 표현(분자: 기수, 분모: 서수)

04 The habitat of the tarsier is generally tropical rain forest / and they are found in dense
　　　　　　　　　　　　　　　　　　　　　　　　　　　　　　　　　수동태
bamboo thickets.

05 During the day, / they lie in holes in tree trunks / and in dark thickly tangled
　　　　　　　　　　　　　　　　　동위접속사로 연결된 병렬구조(전치사구 연결)
vegetation. // At night, / they hunt for insects, spiders, and small lizards.

　　　　　　　선행사 문장
06 Tarsiers can rotate their heads / at least 180 degrees, / which gives them a wide field of
　　　　　　　　　　　　　　　　　　　　　　　　　　　(=and it) 앞 문장 전체를 받는 주격 관계대명사
vision / for spotting prey.
　　　　　전치사　동명사구

01 tarsier는 작은 영장류primate이다 / 쥐보다 그다지 크지 않은. // 쥐와의 유사성resemblance이 더욱 부각된다be exaggerated / 가는 꼬리 때문에 / 전체 몸통body length보다 훨씬 더 긴 (가는 꼬리).

02 모든 tarsier는 완전히 야행성nocturnal이고 / 많은 뛰어난 신체적 적응 장치들adaptation이 있다 / 이러한 생활 방식을 위하여. // 그들은 뛰어난 청력을 가지고 있다.

03 tarsier는 또한 굉장히 큰enormous 눈을 가지고 있는데 / 몸 크기에 비해in comparison with / 눈이 얼굴 크기의 약 1/4을 차지한다.

04 tarsier의 서식지habitat는 보통 열대 우림 지역rain forest이며 / 그들은 빽빽한dense 대나무 숲bamboo thicket에서 발견된다.

05 낮 동안에는 / 나무 둥치trunk의 구멍에 누워 있기도 하고 / 어둡고 두꺼운 엉킨thickly tangled 초목vegetation에 (누워 있기도 한다.) // 밤에는 / 벌레, 거미, 그리고 작은 도마뱀을 사냥한다.

06 tarsier는 그들의 머리를 돌릴rotate 수 있다 / 최소 180도로 / 이는 넓은 시야를 확보해 준다 / 먹이를 찾기 위한for spotting prey.

---

① Their resemblance to the rat is exaggerated by their thin tail, which / what is much longer than their overall body length.

사물 선행사 their thin tail을 받을 수 있는 which를 써야 한다. what은 계속적 용법으로 사용될 수 없으며, 선행사도 필요로 하지 않는다.

② Tarsiers can rotate their heads at least 180 degrees, which gives them a wide field of vision for spot / spotting prey.

전치사 for 뒤에 목적어로 동명사 spotting을 쓴다.

DAY 06

STEP 1 • 수능에 *진짜* 나오는 *단어*

✔️ **문제에 나오는 단어들을 확인하세요.**

시간이 없다면 색으로 표시된 단어만이라도 꼭 외우고 넘어가세요!

01	note	v. 주목하다	(✔️ note) that something has changed	뭔가 변했다는 것에 주목하다
02	consistency	n. 일관성	with great ( )	매우 일관성 있게
03	detect	v. 감지하다	( ) change	변화를 감지하다
04	advantageous	a. 유리한	( ) to us	우리에게 유리한
05	statistical	a. 통계적인	a ( ) model	통계 모형
06	examine	v. 조사하다, 검토하다	( ) the possibility	가능성을 조사하다
07	average	v. 평균을 내다 n. 평균	( ) the numbers	숫자의 평균을 내다
08	deny	v. 부인하다	( ) a rumor	소문을 부인하다
09	stable	a. 안정적인, 변동 없는	( ) conditions	변동 없는 상황
10	account for	~을 설명하다	( ) ( ) the effects	그 효과들을 설명하다
11	novel	a. 새로운, 신기한	( ) events	새로운 사건
12	incorporate	v. 통합하다, 포함시키다	( ) his suggestions in the plan	그의 제안을 계획에 포함시키다
13	accurate	a. 정확한	( ) data	정확한 데이터

➕ **본문 문장 속에서 단어들을 확인해 보세요.**

Thus, in changing environments, / it might be advantageous / to combine human judgment and statistical models.

따라서 변화하는 환경에서는 / 유리할 수 있다 / 인간의 판단과 통계 모형을 결합하는 것이.

문제를 풀기 전에 단어들을 **30초** 동안 다시 확인하세요.

01	note	🖊 주목하다	note that something has changed	뭔가 변했다는 것에 주목하다
02	consistency		with great consistency	매우 일관성 있게
03	detect		detect change	변화를 감지하다
04	advantageous		advantageous to us	우리에게 유리한
05	statistical		a statistical model	통계 모형
06	examine		examine the possibility	가능성을 조사하다
07	average		average the numbers	숫자의 평균을 내다
08	deny		deny a rumor	소문을 부인하다
09	stable		stable conditions	변동 없는 상황
10	account for		account for the effects	그 효과들을 설명하다
11	novel		novel events	새로운 사건
12	incorporate		incorporate his suggestions in the plan	그의 제안을 계획에 포함시키다
13	accurate		accurate data	정확한 데이터

➕ **본문 문장 속에서 단어의 의미를 우리말로 해석해 보세요.**

Thus, in changing environments, / it might be advantageous / to combine human judgment and statistical models.

→ 따라서 변화하는 환경에서는 /   수 있다 / 인간의 판단과   을 결합하는 것이.

STEP 2 • 수능 기출 제대로 풀기

A 다음 글의 밑줄 친 부분 중, 문맥상 낱말의 쓰임이 적절하지 <u>않은</u> 것은?

Robert Blattberg and Steven Hoch noted that, in a changing environment, it is not clear that consistency is always a virtue and that one of the advantages of human judgment is the ability to detect change. Thus, in changing environments, it might be ① <u>advantageous</u> to combine human judgment and statistical models. Blattberg and Hoch examined this possibility by having supermarket managers forecast demand for certain products and then creating a composite forecast by averaging these judgments with the forecasts of statistical models based on ② <u>past</u> data. The logic was that statistical models ③ <u>deny</u> stable conditions and therefore cannot account for the effects on demand of novel events such as actions taken by competitors or the introduction of new products. Humans, however, can ④ <u>incorporate</u> these novel factors in their judgments. The composite — or average of human judgments and statistical models — proved to be more ⑤ <u>accurate</u> than either the statistical models or the managers working alone.

*composite: 종합적인; 종합된 것

정답과 해설 p.20

01 Robert Blattberg and Steven Hoch noted / that, in a changing environment, / it is not clear that consistency is always a virtue / and that one of the advantages of human judgment is the ability to detect change.
진주어1 (진주어2) (가주어)

02 Thus, in changing environments, / it might be advantageous / to combine human judgment and statistical models.
(가주어) (진주어)

03 Blattberg and Hoch examined this possibility / by having supermarket managers forecast demand for certain products / and then creating a composite forecast / by averaging these judgments / with the forecasts of statistical models based on past data.
by+동명사1 ~ / and then 동명사2 ~: ~하고 그다음 ~함으로써

04 The logic was / that statistical models deny stable conditions / and therefore cannot account for the effects on demand of novel events / such as actions taken by competitors or the introduction of new products. // Humans, however, can incorporate these novel factors in their judgments.
접속사(~것) / ~와 같이 명사1 ┄┄ 과거분사구 / 명사구2

05 The composite / — or average of human judgments and statistical models — / proved to be more accurate / than either the statistical models or the managers working alone.
주어 / 주어 동격 / prove (to be)+형용사: ~하다고 판명되다 / either A or B: A 또는 B 둘 중 하나

01 Robert Blattberg와 Steven Hoch는 주목했다note / 변화하는 환경에서 / 일관성consistency이 항상 장점인지가 분명하지 않다는 것과 / 인간이 판단하는 것의 이점 중 하나가 변화를 감지하는detect 능력이라는 것에.

02 따라서 변화하는 환경에서는 / 유리할advantageous 수 있다 / 인간의 판단과 통계statistical 모형을 결합하는 것이.

03 Blattberg와 Hoch는 이러한 가능성을 조사했다examine / 슈퍼마켓 관리자들에게 특정한 제품에 대한 수요를 예측하게 함으로써 / 그런 다음 종합적인 예측을 생성해 봄으로써 / 이 판단을 평균을 내어average / 지난 데이터에 근거한 통계 모형의 예측과.

04 그 논리는 ~였다 / 통계 모형들은 변동 없는stable 조건을 부정한다deny(→ 가정한다)는 것 / 그러므로 새로운 사건이 수요에 미치는 영향을 설명할account for 수 없다는 것 / 경쟁자들이 취한 행동이나 신제품의 도입과 같은. // 그러나 인간은 이러한 새로운novel 요인들을 자신들의 판단에 통합할incorporate 수 있다.

05 종합된 것이 / 즉 인간의 판단과 통계 모형의 평균 / 더 정확하다accurate는 것이 증명되었다 / 통계 모형이나 관리자들이 단독으로 처리하는 것보다.

구문 Check up

① One of the advantages of human judgment is / are the ability to detect change.

② The composite — or average of human judgments and statistical models — proved to be more accurate / accurately than either the statistical models or the managers working alone.

<one of the+복수명사> 주어는 단수 취급한다. 따라서 is가 적절하다.

to be 뒤에 보어가 필요하므로 형용사인 accurate가 적절하다.

정답 ① is ② accurate

✔ 문제에 나오는 단어들을 확인하세요.

시간이 없다면 색으로 표시된 단어만이라도 꼭 외우고 넘어가세요!

01	involve	v. 포함하다	What does it (✔ involve)?	그것은 무엇을 포함하는가?
02	primarily	ad. 주로	It is ( ) a matter of puzzle-solving.	그것은 주로 '문제 해결하기'의 문제이다.
03	paradigm	n. 패러다임, 인식의 체계	a successful ( )	성공적인 패러다임
04	encounter	v. ~에 부딪히다	( ) certain problems	특정한 문제들에 부딪히다
05	phenomenon (pl. phenomena)	n. 현상	a strange ( )	이상한 현상
06	accommodate	v. 수용하다	( ) phenomena	현상들을 수용하다
07	eliminate	v. 제거하다	( ) minor puzzles	사소한 문제들을 제거하다
08	conservative	a. 보수적인	a ( ) activity	보수적인 활동
09	earth-shattering	a. 극히 중대한, 근본을 뒤흔드는	( ) discoveries	극히 중대한 발견들
10	novelty	n. 참신함	aim at ( )ies	참신함을 목표로 하다
11	stress	v. 강조하다	( ) the point	그 포인트를 강조하다
12	unquestioningly	ad. 의심하지 않고	accept the paradigm ( )	패러다임을 의심하지 않고 받아들이다
13	conduct	v. 수행하다	( ) the research	연구를 수행하다
14	correspond with	~에 부합하다, 일치하다	( ) ( ) the paradigm	패러다임에 부합하다
15	faulty	a. 결함이 있는	the experimental technique is ( )	실험 기술에 결함이 있다

⊕ 본문 문장 속에서 단어들을 확인해 보세요.

On the contrary, / they accept the paradigm unquestioningly, / and conduct their research / within the limits it sets.

오히려 / 그들은 패러다임을 의심하지 않고 받아들이고, / 자신의 연구를 수행한다 / 그것이 설정한 한계 안에서.

01	involve	포함하다	What does it involve?	그것은 무엇을 포함하는가?
02	primarily		It is primarily a matter of puzzle-solving.	그것은 주로 '문제 해결하기'의 문제이다.
03	paradigm		a successful paradigm	성공적인 패러다임
04	encounter		encounter certain problems	특정한 문제들에 부딪히다
05	phenomenon		a strange phenomenon	이상한 현상
06	accommodate		accommodate phenomena	현상들을 수용하다
07	eliminate		eliminate minor puzzles	사소한 문제들을 제거하다
08	conservative		a conservative activity	보수적인 활동
09	earth-shattering		earth-shattering discoveries	극히 중대한 발견들
10	novelty		aim at novelties	참신함을 목표로 하다
11	stress		stress the point	그 포인트를 강조하다
12	unquestioningly		accept the paradigm unquestioningly	패러다임을 의심하지 않고 받아들이다
13	conduct		conduct the research	연구를 수행하다
14	correspond with		correspond with the paradigm	패러다임에 부합하다
15	faulty		the experimental technique is faulty	실험 기술에 결함이 있다

⊕ **본문 문장 속에서 단어의 의미를 우리말로 해석해 보세요.**

On the contrary, / they accept the paradigm unquestioningly, / and conduct their research / within the limits it sets.

→ 오히려 / 그들은 ▢▢▢▢▢▢ 을 ▢▢▢▢▢▢ 받아들이고, / 자신의 연구를 ▢▢▢▢▢▢ / 그것이 설정한 한계 안에서.

STEP **2** • 수능 기출 제대로 풀기

B 다음 글의 밑줄 친 부분 중, 문맥상 낱말의 쓰임이 적절하지 <u>않은</u> 것은?

What exactly does normal science involve? According to Thomas Kuhn it is primarily a matter of *puzzle-solving*. However successful a paradigm is, it will always ① <u>encounter</u> certain problems — phenomena which it cannot easily accommodate, or mismatches between the theory's predictions and the experimental facts. The job of the normal scientist is to try to ② <u>eliminate</u> these minor puzzles while making as few changes as possible to the paradigm. So normal science is a ③ <u>conservative</u> activity — its practitioners are not trying to make any earth-shattering discoveries, but rather just to develop and extend the existing paradigm. In Kuhn's words, 'normal science does not aim at novelties of fact or theory, and when successful finds none'. Above all, Kuhn stressed that normal scientists are not trying to *test* the paradigm. On the contrary, they accept the paradigm ④ <u>unquestioningly</u>, and conduct their research within the limits it sets. If a normal scientist gets an experimental result which ⑤ <u>corresponds</u> with the paradigm, they will usually assume that their experimental technique is faulty, not that the paradigm is wrong.

*practitioner: (어떤 일을) 실행하는 사람

정답과 해설 **p.20**

01 What exactly does normal science involve? // According to Thomas Kuhn / it is primarily a matter of *puzzle-solving*.

02 However successful a paradigm is, / it will always encounter certain problems / —
복합관계부사(얼마나 ~하든 간에)
phenomena which it cannot easily accommodate, / or mismatches between the theory's
目적격 관계대명사절   between A and B (A, B 사이의)
predictions and the experimental facts.

03 The job of the normal scientist / is to try to eliminate these minor puzzles / [while
접속사가 남아있는 분사구문
making as few changes as possible / to the paradigm].
as+원급+as possible: 가급적 ~한/하게

04 So normal science is a conservative activity / — its practitioners are not trying to make
not A but (rather) B: A가 아니라 (오히려) B인
any earth-shattering discoveries, / but rather just to develop and extend the existing
paradigm.

05 In Kuhn's words, / 'normal science does not aim at novelties of fact or theory, / and
it is 생략
[when successful] finds none'. // Above all, / Kuhn stressed / that normal scientists are
삽입구문(부사절)   and로 병렬연결(동사구)   명사절 접속사
not trying to *test* the paradigm.

06 On the contrary, / they accept the paradigm unquestioningly, / and conduct their
目적격 관계대명사 생략
research / within the limits it sets.

07 If a normal scientist gets an experimental result / which corresponds with the
조건 접속사   현재시제   목적격 관계대명사절
paradigm, / they will usually assume / that their experimental technique is faulty, / not
미래시제
that the paradigm is wrong.

01 정상 과학은 정확히 무엇을 포함하는가involve? // Thomas Kuhn에 따르면, / 그것은 주로primarily '문제 해결하기'의 문제이다.

02 패러다임paradigm이 아무리 성공적이더라도, / 그것은 항상 특정한 문제들에 부딪힐encounter 것이다 / 그것이 쉽게 수용할accommodate 수 없는 현상phenomenon / 또는 이론의 예측과 실험적 사실 사이의 불일치.

03 정상 과학자들의 일은 / 이러한 사소한 문제들을 제거하려고eliminate 노력하는 것이다 / 가능한 한 변화를 거의 주지 않으면서 / 패러다임에.

04 그래서 정상 과학은 보수적인conservative 활동이다 / 그것을 실행하는 사람은 극히 중대한earth-shattering 발견을 하고자 노력하고 있지 않고, / 오히려 단지 현존하는 패러다임을 발전시키고 확장하려는 것이다.

05 Kuhn의 말로 하자면, / '정상 과학은 사실이나 이론의 참신함novelty을 목표로 하지 않으며, / 성공적일 때에는 찾아내는 것이 없다.' // 무엇보다도 / Kuhn은 강조했다stress / 정상 과학자들이 패러다임을 '시험'하려 노력하지 않는다는 것을.

06 오히려 / 그들은 패러다임을 의심하지 않고unquestioningly 받아들이고, / 자신의 연구를 수행한다conduct / 그것이 설정한 한계 안에서.

07 만약 정상 과학자가 실험 결과를 얻는다면 / 패러다임에 부합하는correspond with(→ 상충하는), / 그들은 보통 여길 것이다 / 자신의 실험 기술에 결함이 있는faulty 것이라고 / 패러다임이 틀린 것이 아니라.

구문 Check up

① How / However successful a paradigm is, it will always encounter certain problems.

'얼마나 성공적이든지 상관없이'의 의미이므로 복합관계부사 However가 적절하다.

② In Kuhn's words, 'normal science does not aim at novelties of fact or theory, and when successful find / finds none'.

주어가 normal science이므로 3인칭 단수에 수 일치 하여 finds를 쓴다.

✔ 문제에 나오는 단어들을 확인하세요.

시간이 없다면 색으로 표시된 단어만이라도 꼭 외우고 넘어가세요!

01	refer to A as B	A를 B라고 부르다	(✔ refer) (to) them (as) "photographs"	그것들을 "사진"이라고 부르다
02	unnecessary	a. 불필요한	It was ( ).	그건 불필요했다.
03	adjective	n. 형용사	insert the ( )	형용사를 넣다
04	existence	n. 존재	the ( ) of color photography	컬러 사진의 존재
05	phrase	n. 어구	include the ( )	어구를 포함시키다
06	highlight	v. 강조하다	( ) the reality	현실을 강조하다
07	conscious	a. 의식하는	become ( )	의식하게 되다
08	limitation	n. 한계	current ( )s	현재의 한계들
09	potential	a. 잠재적인	( ) opportunities	잠재적 기회들
10	embattle	v. (전쟁에) 휘말리게 하다	We were ( )d in World War II.	우리는 제2차 세계대전에 휘말렸다.
11	horrific	a. 끔찍한	the ( ) period	끔찍한 시기
12	explicitly	ad. 명시적으로	( ) identify them	명시적으로 그것들을 인지하다
13	identify	v. 인식하다, 확인하다	( ) issues	문제들을 확인하다

⊕ 본문 문장 속에서 단어들을 확인해 보세요.

By highlighting that reality, / we become conscious of current limitations / and thus open our minds / to new possibilities and potential opportunities.

그 현실을 강조함으로써, / 우리는 현재의 한계를 의식하게 되고, / 따라서 마음을 연다 / 새로운 가능성과 잠재적 기회에.

01	refer to A as B	✏️ A를 B라고 부르다	refer to them as "photographs"	그것들을 "사진"이라고 부르다
02	unnecessary		It was unnecessary.	그건 불필요했다.
03	adjective		insert the adjective	형용사를 넣다
04	existence		the existence of color photography	컬러 사진의 존재
05	phrase		include the phrase	어구를 포함시키다
06	highlight		highlight the reality	현실을 강조하다
07	conscious		become conscious	의식하게 되다
08	limitation		current limitations	현재의 한계들
09	potential		potential opportunities	잠재적 기회들
10	embattle		We were embattled in World War II.	우리는 제2차 세계대전에 휘말렸다.
11	horrific		the horrific period	끔찍한 시기
12	explicitly		explicitly identify them	명시적으로 그것들을 인지하다
13	identify		identify issues	문제들을 확인하다

➕ **본문 문장 속에서 단어의 의미를 우리말로 해석해 보세요.**

By highlighting that reality, / we become conscious of current limitations / and thus open our minds / to new possibilities and potential opportunities.

➡️ 그 현실을 _____ 으로써, / 우리는 현재의 _____ 를 _____ 되고, / 따라서 마음을 연다 / 새로운 가능성과 _____ 기회에.

STEP **2** • 수능 기출 제대로 풀기

C 다음 글의 밑줄 친 부분 중, 문맥상 낱말의 쓰임이 적절하지 <u>않은</u> 것은?

Let's return to a time in which photographs were not in living color. During that period, people referred to pictures as "photographs" rather than "black-and-white photographs" as we do today. The possibility of color did not exist, so it was ① <u>unnecessary</u> to insert the adjective "black-and-white." However, suppose we did include the phrase "black-and-white" before the existence of color photography. By ② <u>highlighting</u> that reality, we become conscious of current limitations and thus open our minds to new possibilities and potential opportunities. World War I was given that name only ③ <u>after</u> we were deeply embattled in World War II. Before that horrific period of the 1940s, World War I was simply called "The Great War" or, even worse, "The War to End All Wars." What if we had called it "World War I" back in 1918? Such a label might have made the possibility of a second worldwide conflict an ④ <u>unpredictable</u> reality for governments and individuals. We become conscious of issues when we explicitly ⑤ <u>identify</u> them.

정답과 해설 p.20

01 Let's return to a time / in which photographs were not in living color. // During that
period, / people referred to pictures as "photographs" / rather than "black-and-white
photographs" / as we do today.

전치사+관계대명사절
refer to A as B: A를 B라고 부르다
~하는 것처럼   =refer to pictures

02 The possibility of color did not exist, / so it was unnecessary / to insert the adjective
"black-and-white. // However, / suppose we did include the phrase "black-and-white"
/ before the existence of color photography.

가주어
진주어(to부정사의 명사적 용법)
명사절 접속사 that 생략   동사 강조

03 By highlighting that reality, / we become conscious of current limitations / and thus open
our minds / to new possibilities and potential opportunities.

동사구 병렬 연결
전치사 to(~에)

04 World War I was given that name / only after we were deeply embattled in World War II.

오로지 ~한 후에야
4형식 동사의 수동태(be+p.p.+직접목적어)

05 Before that horrific period of the 1940s, / World War I was simply called "The Great
War" / or, even worse, "The War to End All Wars."

5형식 동사의 수동태(be+p.p.+목적격 보어)
to부정사의 형용사적 용법

06 What if we had called it "World War I" / back in 1918? // Such a label [might have
made / the possibility of a second worldwide conflict / an unpredictable reality / for
governments and individuals].

~라면 어떨까?   가정법 과거완료
might have p.p.(~했을지도 모른다)
[ ]: 5형식 문장(make+목적어+목적격 보어: ~를 …로 만들다)

07 We become conscious of issues / when we explicitly identify them.

01 시기로 돌아가 보자 / 사진이 생생한 색으로 되어 있지 않았던. // 그 기간 동안, / 사람들은 사진을 "사진"이라고
불렀다refer to pictures as "photographs" / "흑백 사진"이라기보다는 / 오늘날 우리가 부르는 것처럼.

02 색의 가능성은 존재하지 않았고, / 따라서 불필요했다unnecessary / "흑백"이라는 형용사adjective를 삽입하는 것은. //
하지만, / 가정해 보자 / 우리가 "흑백"이라는 어구phrase를 포함시켰다고 / 컬러 사진의 존재existence 전에.

03 그 현실을 강조함highlight으로써, / 우리는 현재의 한계를 의식하게 되고conscious of current limitations, / 따라서
마음을 연다 / 새로운 가능성과 잠재적 기회potential opportunity에.

04 제1차 세계대전은 그 이름이 붙여졌다 / 우리가 제2차 세계대전에 깊이 휘말린be deeply embattled 후에야.

05 1940년대의 끔찍한horrific 시기 이전에, / 제1차 세계대전은 단순히 "대전쟁"이라고 불렸다 / 또는, 더 나쁘게는, "모든
전쟁을 끝내는 전쟁"이라고.

06 만약 우리가 그것을 "제1차 세계대전"이라고 불렀더라면 어땠을까 / 1918년으로 돌아가서? // 그러한 명칭은
만들었을지도 모른다 / 두 번째 세계적 충돌의 가능성을 / 예측할 수 없는(→ 더 큰) 현실로 / 정부와 개인에게.

07 우리는 문제들을 의식하게 된다 / 우리가 그것들을 명시적으로 인지했을explicitly identify 때.

구문 Check up

① During that period, people referred to pictures
as "photographs" rather than "black-and-white
photographs" as we **do / are** today.

앞의 "referred to pictures" 부분의 의미를 대신하는 대동사가 적절하므
로, 일반동사 현재형을 대신하는 do를 쓴다.

② What if we **have called / had called** it "World War I"
back in 1918?

가정법 과거완료의 의미로 쓰인 문장이므로 과거완료 시제 had called를
쓴다.

정답 ① do ② had called

D

STEP 1 • 수능에 *진짜* 나오는 *단어*

✔ **문제에 나오는 단어들을 확인하세요.**

시간이 없다면 색으로 표시된 단어만이라도 꼭 외우고 넘어가세요!

01	neurologically	ad. 신경학적으로	(✔ neurologically) designed		신경학적으로 설계된
02	chemical	n. 화학물질	( )s are released.		화학물질이 분비된다.
03	burst	n. 분출	a ( ) of energy		에너지의 분출
04	excitement	n. 흥분	a burst of ( )		흥분의 분출
05	desire	n. 욕구, 갈망	the ( ) to repeat this experience		이런 경험을 반복하려는 욕구
06	addiction	n. 중독	a kind of ( )		어떤 종류의 중독
07	manic	a. 광적인	( ) behavior		광적인 행동
08	take into account	고려하다	( ) ( ) ( ) the role		그 역할을 고려하다
09	recapture	v. ~을 되찾다	( ) that high		그 황홀감을 되찾다
10	superiority	n. 우월	feelings of ( )		우월감
11	resistant	a. 저항하는	become ( )		저항하다
12	sustain	v. 유지하다, 지속하다	This cannot be ( )ed.		그것은 지속될 수 없다.
13	inevitable	a. 필연적인	experience an ( ) fall		필연적인 추락을 경험하다
14	depression	n. 침체, 우울	the ( ) part		침체기
15	be prone to	~하기 쉽다	( ) ( ) ( ) this		이렇게 되기 쉽다

➕ **본문 문장 속에서 단어들을 확인해 보세요.**

Neurologically, / chemicals are released in the brain / that give a powerful burst of excitement and energy, / leading to the desire to repeat this experience.

신경학적으로 / 화학물질들이 뇌에서 분비되며 / 흥분과 에너지의 강력한 분출을 유발하는, / 이 경험을 반복하고자 하는 욕구로 이어진다.

문제를 풀기 전에 단어들을 **30초** 동안 다시 확인하세요.

#	단어	뜻	예시	예시 뜻
01	neurologically	신경학적으로	neurologically designed	신경학적으로 설계된
02	chemical		Chemicals are released.	화학물질이 분비된다.
03	burst		a burst of energy	에너지의 분출
04	excitement		a burst of excitement	흥분의 분출
05	desire		the desire to repeat this experience	이런 경험을 반복하려는 욕구
06	addiction		a kind of addiction	어떤 종류의 중독
07	manic		manic behavior	광적인 행동
08	take into account		take into account the role	그 역할을 고려하다
09	recapture		recapture that high	그 황홀감을 되찾다
10	superiority		feelings of superiority	우월감
11	resistant		become resistant	저항하다
12	sustain		This cannot be sustained.	그것은 지속될 수 없다.
13	inevitable		experience an inevitable fall	필연적인 추락을 경험하다
14	depression		the depression part	침체기
15	be prone to		be prone to this	이렇게 되기 쉽다

➕ 본문 문장 속에서 단어의 의미를 우리말로 해석해 보세요.

Neurologically, / chemicals are released in the brain / that give a powerful burst of excitement and energy, / leading to the desire to repeat this experience.

➡ _____ / _____ 이 뇌에서 분비되며 / _____ 과 에너지의 강력한 _____ 을 유발하는, / 이 경험을 반복하고자 하는 _____ 로 이어진다.

제한시간 80초

난이도 ★★★★☆

STEP **2** • 수능 기출 제대로 풀기

D 다음 글의 밑줄 친 부분 중, 문맥상 낱말의 쓰임이 적절하지 <u>않은</u> 것은?

Sudden success or winnings can be very dangerous. Neurologically, chemicals are released in the brain that give a powerful burst of excitement and energy, leading to the desire to ① <u>repeat</u> this experience. It can be the start of any kind of addiction or manic behavior. Also, when gains come quickly we tend to ② <u>lose</u> sight of the basic wisdom that true success, to really last, must come through hard work. We do not take into account the role that luck plays in such ③ <u>hard-earned</u> gains. We try again and again to recapture that high from winning so much money or attention. We acquire feelings of superiority. We become especially ④ <u>resistant</u> to anyone who tries to warn us — they don't understand, we tell ourselves. Because this cannot be sustained, we experience an inevitable ⑤ <u>fall</u>, which is all the more painful, leading to the depression part of the cycle. Although gamblers are the most prone to this, it equally applies to businesspeople during bubbles and to people who gain sudden attention from the public.

정답과 해설 **p.21**

01 Sudden success or winnings can be very dangerous. // Neurologically, / chemicals are released in the brain / that give a powerful burst of excitement and energy, / leading to
주격 관계대명사절
the desire to repeat this experience.
분사구문(=and they lead ~)

02 It can be the start of any kind of addiction or manic behavior. // Also, when gains come quickly / we tend to lose sight of the basic wisdom / that true success, (to really last), / must come through hard work.
동격의 that(=the basic wisdom)   삽입구

03 We do not take into account the role / that luck plays in such hard-earned gains. // We
목적격 관계대명사절
try again and again to recapture that high / from winning so much money or attention.
전치사구

04 We acquire feelings of superiority. // We become especially resistant to anyone / who tries to warn us / — they don't understand, / we tell ourselves.
주격 관계대명사절

05 Because this cannot be sustained, / we experience an inevitable fall, / which is all the
선행사   관계대명사 계속적 용법
more painful, / leading to the depression part of the cycle.
분사구문(=and it leads ~)

06 Although gamblers are the most prone to this, / it equally applies to businesspeople during bubbles / and to people who gain sudden attention from the public.
주격 관계대명사절

01 갑작스러운 성공이나 상금은 아주 위험할 수 있다. // 신경학적으로neurologically / 화학물질들chemical이 뇌에서 분비되며 / 흥분excitement과 에너지의 강력한 분출burst을 유발하는 (화학물질들) / 이 경험을 반복하고자 하는 욕구desire로 이어진다.

02 그것이 어떤 종류의 중독addiction 또는 광적 행동manic behavior의 출발점일 수 있다. // 또한, 이익이 빨리 얻어질 때, / 우리는 기본적인 지혜를 보지 못하는 경향이 있다 / 진정한 성공이 정말 지속되기 위해서는 노력을 통해야 한다는.

03 우리는 역할을 고려하지take into account 않는다 / 그처럼 어렵게 얻은(→갑작스러운) 이익에 있어 운이 수행하는. // 우리는 그 황홀감을 되찾기recapture 위해 계속해서 시도한다 / 그만큼의 돈이나 관심을 얻는 것으로부터 느끼는.

04 우리는 우월감feelings of superiority의 감정을 느낀다. // 우리는 특히 사람에게 저항한다resistant / 우리에게 경고를 하려고 하는 / — 그들은 이해하지 못한다고 / 우리는 스스로에게 이야기한다.

05 이것은 지속될be sustained 수 없기 때문에 / 우리는 필연적인 추락을 경험하고experience an inevitable fall / 그것은 더욱 큰 고통이 되며 / 사이클의 침체기depression로 이어진다.

06 도박꾼들이 가장 이러기 쉽지만be prone to, / 이것은 거품 경제일 때의 사업가에게 똑같이 적용된다 / 그리고 대중으로부터 갑작스러운 관심을 얻은 사람들에게도 (똑같이 적용된다).

구문 Check up

① Neurologically, chemicals are released in the brain that give / gives a powerful burst of excitement and energy.

관계대명사 that절의 선행사는 주어 chemicals인데, 주어가 너무 길어지지 않도록 관계대명사절을 뒤로 이동시킨 문장이다. 따라서 동사는 선행사 chemicals에 수일치하여 복수형인 give로 쓴다.

② Because this cannot be sustained, we experience an inevitable fall, which is all the more painful, leads / leading to the depression part of the cycle.

which절의 동사는 is이고 접속사가 없으므로 바로 동사 leads가 병렬연결될 수 없다. 따라서 leading을 써서 분사구문으로 만든다.

정답 ① give ② leading

166

E

STEP 1 • 수능에 *진짜* 나오는 *단어*

✔ 문제에 나오는 단어들을 확인하세요.

시간이 없다면 색으로 표시된 단어만이라도 꼭 외우고 넘어가세요!

01	champion	n. 투사, 옹호자, 챔피언	a (✔ champion) of free speech	언론의 자유에 대한 옹호자
02	toleration	n. 관용	religious ( )	종교적 관용
03	controversial	a. 논쟁적인, 논란이 많은	a ( ) figure	논란이 많은 인물
04	defense	n. 변론	a powerful ( )	강력한 변론
05	deserve	v. (마땅히) ~할 만하다	( ) to be heard	들어볼 만하다
06	despise	v. 경멸하다	( ) the view	의견을 경멸하다
07	strictly	ad. 엄격하게	( ) control	엄격하게 통제하다
08	censor	v. 검열하다	His books were ( )ed.	그의 책들이 검열당했다.
09	imprison	v. 감금하다	( ) Voltaire	볼테르를 감금하다
10	insult	v. 모욕하다	( ) a powerful aristocrat	세력가인 귀족을 모욕하다
11	prejudice	n. 편견	challenge the ( )s	편견에 도전하다
12	pretension	n. 가식	( )s around him	그 주변의 가식
13	optimism	n. 낙관주의	religious ( )	종교적 낙관주의
14	contemporary	a. 동시대의, 당대의, 현대의	other ( ) thinkers	당대의 다른 사상가들
15	entertaining	a. 재미있는	in such an ( ) way	그런 재미있는 방법으로

⊕ 본문 문장 속에서 단어들을 확인해 보세요.

A champion of free speech and religious toleration, / Voltaire was a controversial figure.

언론의 자유와 종교적 관용의 옹호자였던 / Voltaire는 논란이 많았던 인물이었다.

01	champion	투사, 옹호자, 챔피언	a champion of free speech	언론의 자유에 대한 옹호자
02	toleration		religious toleration	종교적 관용
03	controversial		a controversial figure	논란이 많은 인물
04	defense		a powerful defense	강력한 변론
05	deserve		deserve to be heard	들어볼 만하다
06	despise		despise the view	의견을 경멸하다
07	strictly		strictly control	엄격하게 통제하다
08	censor		His books were censored.	그의 책들이 검열당했다.
09	imprison		imprison Voltaire	볼테르를 감금하다
10	insult		insult a powerful aristocrat	세력가인 귀족을 모욕하다
11	prejudice		challenge the prejudices	편견에 도전하다
12	pretension		pretensions around him	그 주변의 가식
13	optimism		religious optimism	종교적 낙관주의
14	contemporary		other contemporary thinkers	당대의 다른 사상가들
15	entertaining		in such an entertaining way	그런 재미있는 방법으로

⊕ 본문 문장 속에서 단어의 의미를 우리말로 해석해 보세요.

A champion of free speech and religious toleration, / Voltaire was a controversial figure.

→ 언론의 자유와 종교적   의   였던 / Voltaire는   인물이었다.

E

다음 글의 밑줄 친 부분 중, 문맥상 낱말의 쓰임이 적절하지 <u>않은</u> 것은?

A champion of free speech and religious toleration, Voltaire was a controversial figure. He is, for instance, supposed to have declared, "I hate what you say, but will defend to the death your right to say it," a powerful ① defense of the idea that even views that you despise deserve to be heard. In eighteenth-century Europe, however, the Catholic Church strictly ② controlled what could be published. Many of Voltaire's plays and books were censored and burned in public, and he was even imprisoned in the Bastille in Paris because he had ③ insulted a powerful aristocrat. But none of this stopped him challenging the prejudices and pretensions of those around him. In his short philosophical novel, *Candide*, he completely ④ supported the kind of religious optimism about humanity and the universe that other contemporary thinkers had expressed, and he did it in such an entertaining way that the book became an instant bestseller. Wisely, Voltaire left his name ⑤ off the title page, otherwise its publication would have landed him in prison again for making fun of religious beliefs.

정답과 해설 p.21

01 A champion of free speech and religious toleration, / Voltaire was a controversial figure.

02 He is, for instance, supposed to have declared, / "I hate what you say, / but will defend to the death / your right to say it," / a powerful defense of the idea / that even views that you despise deserve to be heard.
관계대명사 what절(목적어)
동격의 that(=the idea)
목적격 관계대명사절
부정사의 수동태(to be p.p.)

03 In eighteenth-century Europe, however, / the Catholic Church strictly controlled / what could be published.
의문사절(목적어)

04 Many of Voltaire's plays and books / were censored and burned in public, / and he was even imprisoned / in the Bastille in Paris / because he had insulted a powerful aristocrat. // But none of this stopped him / challenging the prejudices and pretension of those around him.
수 일치(복수)
주어(부분+of+전체)
동명사의 의미상 주어
동명사(stopped의 목적어)

05 In his short philosophical novel, *Candide*, / he completely supported the kind of religious optimism about humanity and the universe / that other contemporary thinkers had expressed, / and he did it in such an entertaining way / that the book became an instant bestseller.
선행사
목적격 관계대명사절
such+a(n)+형용사+명사+that ~: 너무 (형용사)한 (명사)라서 ~하다

06 Wisely, Voltaire left his name off the title page, / otherwise its publication would have landed him in prison again / for making fun of religious beliefs.
= if he had not left his name off the title page
가정법 과거완료 주절

01 언론의 자유와 종교적 관용religious toleration의 옹호자champion였던 / Voltaire는 논란이 많았던 인물a controversial figure이었다.

02 예를 들어 그는 선언했다고 여겨진다 / "나는 여러분이 하는 말을 싫어한다 / 하지만 사력을 다해 옹호할 것이다 / 그것을 말할 여러분의 권리를"이라고 / 그리고 이는 생각에 대한 강력한 변론defense이었다 / 여러분이 경멸하는despise 의견조차도 들어볼 만하다deserve to be heard는 (생각).

03 하지만 18세기 유럽에서는 / 가톨릭 교회가 엄격히 통제하였다strictly control / 무엇이 출판될 수 있는지를.

04 Voltaire의 많은 희곡과 책이 / 검열을 받았고be censored 공개적으로 불태워졌으며, / 그는 수감되기be imprisoned까지 하였다 / 파리의 Bastille 감옥에 / 세력이 있는 귀족을 모욕했기insult 때문에. // 하지만 이 중 어떤 것도 그를 멈추게 하지 못했다 / 그의 주변 사람들의 편견prejudice과 가식pretension에 도전하는 것을.

05 그의 철학 단편 소설인 〈Candide〉에서, / 그는 인류와 우주에 대한 종교적인 낙관론religious optimism을 완전히 지지했고(→훼손했고) / 당대의 다른 사상가들other contemporary thinkers이 표명했던, / 이를 매우 재미있는 방식an entertaining way으로 하여 / 그 책은 즉시 베스트셀러가 되었다.

06 현명하게도, Voltaire는 속표지에서 자신의 이름을 지웠는데, / 만약 그렇지 않았다면 그 책의 출판은 다시 그를 감옥에 갇히게 했을지도 모른다 / 종교적 신념을 조롱한 이유로.

구문 Check up

① He did it in so / such an entertaining way that the book became an instant bestseller.

'너무 ~해서 …하다'는 <such+a(n)+형+명+that …>, <so+형/부+that …> 을 이용해 나타낸다. 여기서는 뒤에 <an+형+명>이 오므로 such를 써야 한다.

② Wisely, Voltaire left his name off the title page, otherwise its publication would land / would have landed him in prison again.

과거 사실(left ~ off)에 반대(otherwise)되는 가정이기 때문에 가정법 과거완료 동사인 would have landed가 적절하다.

F

STEP 1 • 수능에 *진짜* 나오는 *단어*

✔ 문제에 나오는 단어들을 확인하세요.

시간이 없다면 색으로 표시된 단어만이라도 꼭 외우고 넘어가세요!

01	phenomenon	n. 현상	a (✔ phenomenon) in social psychology	사회 심리학의 한 현상
02	perceive	v. 인지하다, 인식하다	(　　　　)d attractiveness	인지된 매력도
03	competence	n. 능력	perceived (　　　　)	인지된 능력
04	flawless	a. 흠이 없는, 결함 없는	(　　　　) or perfect	흠이 없거나 완벽한
05	aspect	n. 국면, 측면	in certain (　　　)s	특정한 측면에서
06	commit	v. 저지르다	(　　　) blunders	실수를 저지르다
07	occasional	a. 간헐적인, 이따금의	(　　　　) mistakes	이따금의 실수
08	attribution	n. 귀속, 귀착	the (　　　　) of that quality	그 자질을 귀속하는 것
09	distance	n. 거리, 먼 거리	a perceived (　　　)	인지된 거리감
10	attractive	a. 매력적인	less (　　　)	덜 매력적인
11	public	n. 일반 사람들, 대중	the general (　　　)	일반 대중
12	opposite	a. 반대의	the (　　　) effect	정반대의 효과
13	average	a. 평균의	less than (　　　)	평균 이하의

➕ 본문 문장 속에서 단어들을 확인해 보세요.

Perfection, / or the attribution of that quality to individuals, / creates a perceived distance / that the general public cannot relate to.

완벽성, / 혹은 개인들에게 그 자질을 귀속하는 것은 / 인지된 거리감을 만든다 / 일반 대중들이 (자신과) 관련지을 수 없는.

01	phenomenon	✎ 현상	a phenomenon in social psychology	사회 심리학의 한 현상
02	perceive		perceived attractiveness	인지된 매력도
03	competence		perceived competence	인지된 능력
04	flawless		flawless or perfect	흠이 없거나 완벽한
05	aspect		in certain aspects	특정한 측면에서
06	commit		commit blunders	실수를 저지르다
07	occasional		occasional mistakes	이따금의 실수
08	attribution		the attribution of that quality	그 자질을 귀속하는 것
09	distance		a perceived distance	인지된 거리감
10	attractive		less attractive	덜 매력적인
11	public		the general public	일반 대중
12	opposite		the opposite effect	정반대의 효과
13	average		less than average	평균 이하의

➕ 본문 문장 속에서 단어의 의미를 우리말로 해석해 보세요.

Perfection, / or the attribution of that quality to individuals, / creates a perceived distance / that the general public cannot relate to.

→ 완벽성, / 혹은 개인들에게   은 /   을 만든다 / 일반 대중들이 (자신과) 관련지을 수 없는.

STEP **2** • 수능 기출 제대로 풀기

F

(A), (B), (C)의 각 네모 안에서 문맥에 맞는 낱말로 가장 적절한 것은?

A phenomenon in social psychology, the Pratfall Effect states that an individual's perceived attractiveness increases or decreases after he or she makes a mistake — depending on the individual's (A) perceived / hidden competence. As celebrities are generally considered to be competent individuals, and often even presented as flawless or perfect in certain aspects, committing blunders will make one's humanness endearing to others. Basically, those who never make mistakes are perceived as being less attractive and "likable" than those who make occasional mistakes. Perfection, or the attribution of that quality to individuals, (B) creates / narrows a perceived distance that the general public cannot relate to — making those who never make mistakes perceived as being less attractive or likable. However, this can also have the opposite effect — if a perceived average or less than average competent person makes a mistake, he or she will be (C) more / less attractive and likable to others.

*blunder: 부주의하거나 어리석은 실수

	(A)		(B)		(C)
①	perceived	······	creates	······	less
②	perceived	······	narrows	······	more
③	perceived	······	creates	······	more
④	hidden	······	creates	······	less
⑤	hidden	······	narrows	······	less

정답과 해설 **p.22**

01 A phenomenon in social psychology, / the Pratfall Effect states / that an individual's
명사절 접속사(states의 목적어)
perceived attractiveness increases or decreases / after he or she makes a mistake / —
과거분사
depending on the individual's perceived competence.
~에 따라   과거분사

02 As celebrities are generally considered to be competent individuals, / and often even
병렬연결
presented as flawless or perfect / in certain aspects, / committing blunders will make
동명사(주어)
one's humanness endearing to others.
make+목적어+목적격 보어(형용사구)

03 Basically, / those who never make mistakes / are perceived as being less attractive and
주격 관계대명사절   less+원급+than: 덜 ~한
"likable" / than those who make occasional mistakes.
주격 관계대명사절

04 Perfection, / or the attribution of that quality to individuals, / creates a perceived
=perfection   주격 관계대명사절
distance / that the general public cannot relate to / — [making those who never make
목적격 관계대명사   make+목적어+목적격 보어(과거분사)
mistakes perceived / as being less attractive or likable].

05 However, / this can also have the opposite effect / — if a perceived average or less
than average competent person makes a mistake, / he or she will be less attractive and
if절의 동사(현재시제로 미래 표현)
likable to others.

01 사회 심리학의 한 현상phenomenon인 / Pratfall Effect는 말한다 / 한 개인의 인지된perceived 매력도가 증가 또는 감소한다고 / 그 또는 그녀가 실수를 한 후에 / 그 사람의 인지된 능력competence에 따라.

02 유명 인사들은 일반적으로 능력 있는 사람으로 여겨지고 / 종종 흠이 없고flawless 완벽하다고도 보이기 때문에 / 특정한 측면aspect에서, / 실수를 저지르는commit 것은 그 사람의 인간미를 다른 사람들에게 사랑스럽게 만들 것이다.

03 기본적으로 / 실수를 전혀 저지르지 않는 사람들은 / 덜 매력적이거나 덜 호감을 주는 것으로 인지된다 / 이따금occasional 실수를 저지르는 사람들에 비해.

04 완벽성, 혹은 그 자질을 개인들에게 귀속하는 것attribution은 / 인지된 거리감distance을 만들며 / 일반 대중들public이 (자신과) 관련지을 수 없는 (거리감) / 실수를 전혀 저지르지 않는 사람들을 인지되게 만든다 / 덜 매력적이고attractive 덜 호감이 가는 것으로.

05 하지만 / 이것은 또한 정반대의opposite 효과도 가지는데, / 인지된 평균average 혹은 그 이하의 능력을 가진 사람이 실수를 저지른다면, / 그 또는 그녀는 다른 사람들에게 덜 매력적이고 호감일 것이다.

구문 Check up

① As celebrities are generally considered to be competent individuals, and often even presented as flawless or perfect in certain aspects, commit / committing blunders will make one's humanness endearing to others.

주절의 주어 자리이므로 동사원형이 아닌 동명사를 써야 한다. 따라서 committing이 적절하다.

② Basically, those who never make mistakes perceive / are perceived as being less attractive and "likable" than those who make occasional mistakes.

내용상 '인지된다'는 뜻이므로 수동태인 are perceived가 적절하다.

STEP **1** • 수능에 *진짜* 나오는 *단어*

✔️ 문제에 나오는 단어들을 확인하세요.

시간이 없다면 색으로 표시된 단어만이라도 꼭 외우고 넘어가세요!

No	단어	뜻	예문	뜻
01	argument	n. 주장, 논쟁	a classic (✔️ argument)	고전적 주장
02	equality	n. 평등	( ) of opportunity	기회의 평등
03	fate	n. 운명	the ( ) of the universe	우주의 운명
04	circumstance	n. 환경	( )s lying outside of control	통제 밖에 있는 환경
05	unjust	a. 불공정한	( ) = unfair	불공정한
06	inequality	n. 불평등	eliminate ( )	불평등을 제거하다
07	acceptable	a. 받아들여지는, 허용 가능한	( ) choices	허용 가능한 선택
08	intolerable	a. 견딜 수 없는	( ) pain	견딜 수 없는 고통
09	seek to	~하려고 하다, 노력하다	( ) ( ) make many changes	많은 변화를 만들려고 노력하다
10	eliminate	v. 제거하다	( ) inequality of wellbeing	행복의 불평등을 제거하다
11	value	v. 중시하다	( ) friendship	우정을 중시하다
12	ensure	v. 확실하게 하다, 보증하다	( ) safety	안정을 확실하게 하다
13	neglect	v. 무시하다	( ) safety	안정을 무시하다
14	access	n. 접근	( ) to resources	자원에의 접근
15	fundamental	a. 기본적인	( ) resources	기본적인 자원

➕ 본문 문장 속에서 단어들을 확인해 보세요.

We do so / by ensuring equality of opportunity / or equality of access to fundamental resources.

우리는 그렇게 한다 / 기회의 평등을 보장함으로써 / 또는 기본적인 자원에의 접근의 평등을.

01	argument	✎ 주장, 논쟁	a classic argument	고전적 주장
02	equality		equality of opportunity	기회의 평등
03	fate		the fate of the universe	우주의 운명
04	circumstance		circumstances lying outside of control	통제 밖에 있는 환경
05	unjust		unjust = unfair	불공정한
06	inequality		eliminate inequality	불평등을 제거하다
07	acceptable		acceptable choices	허용 가능한 선택
08	intolerable		intolerable pain	견딜 수 없는 고통
09	seek to		seek to make many changes	많은 변화를 만들려고 노력하다
10	eliminate		eliminate inequality of wellbeing	행복의 불평등을 제거하다
11	value		value friendship	우정을 중시하다
12	ensure		ensure safety	안정을 확실하게 하다
13	neglect		neglect safety	안정을 무시하다
14	access		access to resources	자원에의 접근
15	fundamental		fundamental resources	기본적인 자원

➕ **본문 문장 속에서 단어의 의미를 우리말로 해석해 보세요.**

We do so / by ensuring equality of opportunity / or equality of access to fundamental resources.

→ 우리는 그렇게 한다 / 기회의   을   으로써 / 또는   자원에의   의   을.

STEP **2** · 수능 기출 제대로 풀기

G   (A), (B), (C)의 각 네모 안에서 문맥에 맞는 낱말로 가장 적절한 것은?

Dworkin suggests a classic argument for a certain kind of equality of opportunity. From Dworkin's view, justice requires that a person's fate be determined by things that are within that person's control, not by luck. If differences in wellbeing are determined by circumstances lying outside of an individual's control, they are (A) fair / unjust . According to this argument, inequality of wellbeing that is driven by differences in individual choices or tastes is (B) acceptable / intolerable . But we should seek to eliminate inequality of wellbeing that is driven by factors that are not an individual's responsibility and which prevent an individual from achieving what he or she values. We do so by (C) ensuring / neglecting equality of opportunity or equality of access to fundamental resources.

	(A)		(B)		(C)
①	fair	……	acceptable	……	neglecting
②	unjust	……	acceptable	……	ensuring
③	unjust	……	intolerable	……	ensuring
④	fair	……	intolerable	……	neglecting
⑤	unjust	……	acceptable	……	neglecting

정답과 해설 p.22

01 Dworkin suggests a classic argument / for a certain kind of equality of opportunity.

02 From Dworkin's view, / justice requires / that a person's fate be determined by
   should 생략
   require 다음에 '~해야 한다'라는 의미의 that절이 오면 should가 생략됨
   things / that are within that person's control, / not by luck.
   주격 관계대명사절

03 If differences in wellbeing are determined by circumstances / lying outside of an
   조건의 부사절   현재분사(명사 수식)
   individual's control, / they are unjust.

04 According to this argument, / inequality of wellbeing that is driven by differences
                                 주어   주격 관계대명사절
   in individual choices or tastes / is acceptable.
                                     동사(단수)

05 But we should seek to eliminate inequality of wellbeing / [that is driven by factors
                                                              주격 관계대명사절
   / that are not an individual's responsibility / and which prevent an individual from
   관계대명사 that, which절이 동시에 선행사 factors 수식
   achieving what he or she values].
   관계대명사 what절(achieving의 목적어)

06 We do so / by ensuring equality of opportunity / or equality of access to fundamental
   =seek to eliminate inequality
   resources.

01 Dworkin은 고전적 주장a classic argument을 제시한다 / 어떤 한 종류의 기회의 평등equality에 관한.

02 Dworkin의 관점에서 / 정의는 요구한다 / 한 사람의 운명fate이 어떤 것들에 의해 결정되는 것을 / 그 사람의 통제 내에 있는 (어떤 것들) / 운에 의해서가 아니라.

03 행복에 있어서의 차이가 환경circumstance에 의해 결정된다면 / 개인의 통제 밖에 있는, / 그 차이는 불공평unjust하다.

04 이 주장에 따르면, / 개인의 선택이나 취향의 차이에 의해 만들어진 행복의 불평등inequality은 / 허용 가능acceptable하다.

05 그러나 우리는 행복의 불평등을 제거하기eliminate inequality of wellbeing 위해 노력해야seek to 한다 / 요소에 의해 만들어지는 (행복의 불평등) / 개인의 책임이 아니면서 / 개인이 자신이 중요하게 여기는value 것을 성취하지 못하게 막는 (요소).

06 우리는 그렇게 한다 / 기회의 평등을 보장함ensure으로써 / 또는 기본적인 자원에의 접근access to fundamental resources의 평등을 (보장함으로써).

구문 Check up	① If differences in wellbeing determine / are determined by circumstances lying outside of an individual's control, they are unjust.	② We should seek to eliminate inequality of wellbeing that is / are driven by factors that are not an individual's responsibility.
	'차이가 결정되다'는 수동의 의미이고 뒤에 <by+목적격>이 나오기 때문에 수동태인 are determined를 쓴다.	주격 관계대명사 that 뒤의 동사는 선행사에 수 일치하므로, 불가산명사 주어인 inequality에 맞춰 is를 쓴다.

정답 ① are determined ② is

☑ 종합 성적표

구분	공부한 날 ❶	결과 분석			틀린 이유 ❸
		출처	풀이 시간 ❷	채점 결과 (O, ×)	
Day 4	월 일	학력평가 기출 2023년	분 초		
		학력평가 기출 2022년	분 초		
		학력평가 기출 2021년	분 초		
		학력평가 기출 2020년	분 초		
		학력평가 기출 2020년	분 초		
		학력평가 기출 2019년	분 초		
		학력평가 기출 2019년	분 초		
Day 5	월 일	학력평가 기출 2023년	분 초		
		학력평가 기출 2022년	분 초		
		학력평가 기출 2021년	분 초		
		학력평가 기출 2020년	분 초		
		학력평가 기출 2019년	분 초		
		학력평가 기출 2018년	분 초		
		학력평가 기출 2016년	분 초		
Day 6	월 일	학력평가 기출 2023년	분 초		
		학력평가 기출 2022년	분 초		
		학력평가 기출 2021년	분 초		
		학력평가 기출 2020년	분 초		
		학력평가 기출 2019년	분 초		
		학력평가 기출 2018년	분 초		
		학력평가 기출 2017년	분 초		

3일간
공부한 내용을
다시 보니,
……

❶ **매일 지문을 하루 계획에 맞춰 풀었다. vs. 내가 한 약속을 못 지켰다.**

<매3영 고2 기출>은 단순 문제풀이를 위한 책이 아니라, 매일 규칙적으로 영어를 공부하는 습관을 잡는 책입니다. 따라서 푸는 문제 개수는 상황에 따라 다르더라도 '매일' 학습하는 것이 중요합니다.

❷ **주어진 시간을 자꾸 넘긴다?**

풀이 시간이 계속해서 권장 시간을 넘긴다면 실전 훈련이 부족하다는 신호입니다. 아직 조급함을 가질 필요는 없지만, 매일의 문제 풀이에 더 긴장감 있게 임해보세요.

❸ **틀린 이유 맞춤 솔루션:** 오답 이유에 따라 다음 해결책을 참고하세요.

(1) 단어를 많이 몰라서

▶ <STEP 1 단어>에 제시된 필수 어휘를 매일 챙겨보고, SELF-TEST까지 꼼꼼히 진행합니다.

(2) 문장 해석이 잘 안 돼서

▶ <STEP 3 지문 복습>의 구문 첨삭과 끊어읽기 해설을 정독하며 문장구조를 보는 눈을 길러보세요.

(3) 해석은 되지만 내용이 이해가 안 되거나, 선택지로 연결을 못 해서

▶ <정답과 해설>의 해설과 오답풀이를 참고해 틀린 이유를 깊이 고민하고 정리해 보세요.

! 결론적으로, 내가 **취약한 부분**은 [　　　　　　　] 이다. **취약점을 보완하기 위해서** 나는
[　　　　　　　] 을/를 해야겠다.

3일 뒤 다시 봐야 할 문항과, 꼭 다시 외워야 할 사항·구문 등이 있는 페이지는 지금 바로 접어 두세요.

<매3영>이 제시하는 3단계로

유형 3일 훈련

DAY

07~09

공부한 날			출처	페이지
DAY 7	월	일	학력평가 기출 2023년 학력평가 기출 2022년 학력평가 기출 2021년 학력평가 기출 2020년 학력평가 기출 2019년 학력평가 기출 2018년 학력평가 기출 2017년	181
DAY 8	월	일	학력평가 기출 2023년 학력평가 기출 2022년 학력평가 기출 2021년 학력평가 기출 2020년 학력평가 기출 2019년 학력평가 기출 2018년 학력평가 기출 2017년	209
DAY 9	월	일	학력평가 기출 2023년 학력평가 기출 2022년 학력평가 기출 2021년 학력평가 기출 2020년 학력평가 기출 2019년 학력평가 기출 2018년 학력평가 기출 2017년	237

A

STEP 1 • 수능에 *진짜* 나오는 *단어*

✔ **문제에 나오는 단어들을 확인하세요.**

시간이 없다면 색으로 표시된 단어만이라도 꼭 외우고 넘어가세요!

01	made up of	~로 구성된	a survey (✔ made) (up) (of) questions about oneself	자기 자신에 관한 질문으로 구성된 설문 조사
02	account	n. 설명	verbal ( )s of their behavior	그들의 행동에 관한 구두 설명
03	questionnaire	n. 설문지	a personality ( )	성격 설문지
04	measure	v. 측정하다	the best way to ( ) a variable	변수를 측정하는 최고의 방법
05	take advantage of	~을 (유리하게) 이용하다	( ) ( ) ( ) an opportunity	기회를 이용하다
06	plague	v. 오염시키다, 괴롭히다 n. 전염병	( )d by several kinds of distortion	몇 가지 종류의 왜곡으로 오염된
07	problematic	a. 문제가 되는	a ( ) situation	문제가 되는 상황
08	bias	n. 편향	a personal ( )	개인적 편향
09	approve	v. 용인하다, 승인하다	socially ( )d answers	사회적으로 용인되는 답
10	charity	n. 자선 (단체)	give to a ( )	자선 단체에 기부하다

➕ **본문 문장 속에서 단어들을 확인해 보세요.**

Research psychologists often work with *self-report data*, / made up of participants' verbal accounts of their behavior.

연구 심리학자들은 종종 '자기 보고 데이터'로 작업을 하는데, / 이는 자신의 행동에 대한 참가자들의 구두 설명으로 구성되어 있다.

문제를 풀기 전에 단어들을 30초 동안 다시 확인하세요.

01	made up of	✎ ~로 구성된	a survey made up of questions about oneself	자기 자신에 관한 질문으로 구성된 설문 조사
02	account		verbal accounts of their behavior	그들의 행동에 관한 구두 설명
03	questionnaire		a personality questionnaire	성격 설문지
04	measure		the best way to measure a variable	변수를 측정하는 최고의 방법
05	take advantage of		take advantage of an opportunity	기회를 이용하다
06	plague		plagued by several kinds of distortion	몇 가지 종류의 왜곡으로 오염된
07	problematic		a problematic situation	문제가 되는 상황
08	bias		a personal bias	개인적 편향
09	approve		socially approved answers	사회적으로 용인되는 답
10	charity		give to a charity	자선 단체에 기부하다

➕ 본문 문장 속에서 단어의 의미를 우리말로 해석해 보세요.

Research psychologists often work with *self-report data*, / made up of participants' verbal accounts of their behavior.

→ 연구 심리학자들은 종종 '자기 보고 데이터'로 작업을 하는데, / 이는 █████████████████████████████ 있다.

STEP **2** • 수능 기출 제대로 풀기

A

다음 글의 밑줄 친 부분 중, 어법상 틀린 것은?

Research psychologists often work with *self-report data*, made up of participants' verbal accounts of their behavior. This is the case ① whenever questionnaires, interviews, or personality inventories are used to measure variables. Self-report methods can be quite useful. They take advantage of the fact that people have a unique opportunity to observe ② themselves full-time. However, self-reports can be plagued by several kinds of distortion. One of the most problematic of these distortions is the social desirability bias, which is a tendency to give ③ socially approved answers to questions about oneself. Subjects who are influenced by this bias work overtime trying to create a favorable impression, especially when subjects ④ ask about sensitive issues. For example, many survey respondents will report that they voted in an election or ⑤ gave to a charity when in fact it is possible to determine that they did not.

정답과 해설 p.24

01
Research psychologists often work with *self-report data*, made up of participants'
선행사　　　　　　　　　　　　　　　　　　which is 생략
과거분사구
verbal accounts of their behavior. // This is the case / whenever questionnaires,
복합관계부사(~할 때마다)
interviews, or personality inventories are used / to measure variables.
be used to+동사원형: ~하기 위해 사용되다

02
Self-report methods can be quite useful. // They take advantage of the fact / that
동격
people have a unique opportunity to observe themselves full-time.
형용사적 용법

03
However, / self-reports can be plagued by several kinds of distortion. // One of the most
one of the+최상급+복수명사(가장 ~한 것들 중 하나)
problematic of these distortions / is the social desirability bias, / which is a tendency /
동사(단수)　　　　　　　　　　　　　　　　　　　계속적 용법
to give socially approved answers to questions about oneself.

04
Subjects who are influenced by this bias / work overtime / trying to create a favorable
주격 관계대명사절　　　　　　　　　　　　　　분사구문
impression, / especially when subjects are asked about sensitive issues. // For example,
/ many survey respondents will report / that they voted in an election or gave to a
목적절
charity / when in fact it is possible to determine that they did not.
가주어　　　　　　　진주어　　　　　　　　　　대동사(= did not vote ~ or give to a charity)

---

01 연구 심리학자들은 종종 '자기 보고 데이터'로 작업을 하는데, / 이는 자신의 행동에 대한 참가자들의 구두
설명account으로 구성되어 있다made up of. // 여기 해당한다 / 설문지questionnaire, 면접 또는 성격 목록이 사용될
때마다 / 변인을 측정하기measure 위해.

02 자기 보고 방법은 꽤 유용할 수 있다. // 이것은 사실을 이용한다take advantage of / 사람들이 자신을 풀타임으로 관찰할
수 있는 독특한 기회를 갖는다는.

03 그러나, / 자기 보고는 몇 가지 종류의 왜곡으로 오염될plague 수 있다. // 이러한 왜곡 중 가장 문제가 되는problematic
하나는 / 사회적 바람직성 편향bias인데, / 이것은 경향이다 / 자신에 관한 질문에 사회적으로 용인되는socially approved
답을 제공하는.

04 이러한 편향에 영향을 받은 피실험자들은 / 추가로 노력한다 / 호의적인 인상을 만들기 위해 / 특히 피실험자들이 민감한
문제에 관해 질문받을 때. // 예를 들어 / 설문 조사 응답자들 중 많은 수가 보고할 것이다 / 그들이 선거에서 투표했다거나
자선 단체charity에 기부했다고 / 사실은 그들이 하지 않았다고 밝히는 것이 가능할 때.

---

① One of the most problematic of these distortions are /
is the social desirability bias.

<one of the+최상급+복수명사>가 주어이면 동사는 단수형(is)으로 쓴다.

② Many survey respondents will report that they voted
in an election or gave to a charity when in fact it is
possible to determine that they was not / did not .

앞에 나온 일반동사구 'voted ~ or gave ~'를 부정하는 의미의 대동사로
did not을 써야 한다.

정답 ① is ② did not

B

어법의 이해 ⊕

STEP 1 • 수능에 진짜 나오는 단어

✔ 문제에 나오는 단어들을 확인하세요.

시간이 없다면 색으로 표시된 단어만이라도 꼭 외우고 넘어가세요!

01	institution	n. 기관	(✔ institution)s like the World Bank	World Bank같은 기관들
02	differentiate	v. 구별하다	( ) between the two diseases	두 질병을 구별하다
03	developed	a. 선진(국)의	( ) countries	선진국들
04	developing	a. 개발도상(국)의	( ) countries	개발도상국들
05	accompany	v. 수반하다	( ) economic growth	경제 성장을 수반하다
06	awareness	n. 인식	( ) has grown	인식이 커졌다
07	address	v. (문제를) 다루다	the question needs to be ( )ed	문제가 다루어질 필요가 있다
08	suffering	n. 고통	cause much less ( )	훨씬 적은 고통을 야기하다
09	imperfect	a. 불완전한	It is always ( ).	그것은 항상 불완전하다.
10	indicate	v. 나타내다, 의미하다	( ) a greater understanding	더 큰 이해를 나타내다
11	moral	a. 도덕적인, 도덕의	( ) issues	도덕적 쟁점들
12	concern	n. 관심, 우려	moral ( )	도덕적 관심
13	previous	a. 이전의	the ( ) attitude	이전의 태도
14	widespread	a. 널리 퍼진	the ( ) attitude	널리 퍼진 태도

⊕ 본문 문장 속에서 단어들을 확인해 보세요.

Even though institutions like the World Bank use wealth / to differentiate between "developed" and "developing" countries, / they also agree / that development is more than economic growth.

비록 World Bank와 같은 기관들은 부를 사용하지만 / "선진" 국가와 "개발도상" 국가를 구별하기 위해, / 그들은 또한 동의한다 / 발전이 경제 성장 그 이상이라는 것에.

01	institution	🖉 기관	institutions like the World Bank	World Bank같은 기관들
02	differentiate		differentiate between the two diseases	두 질병을 구별하다
03	developed		developed countries	선진국들
04	developing		developing countries	개발도상국들
05	accompany		accompany economic growth	경제 성장을 수반하다
06	awareness		awareness has grown	인식이 커졌다
07	address		the question needs to be addressed	문제가 다루어질 필요가 있다
08	suffering		cause much less suffering	훨씬 적은 고통을 야기하다
09	imperfect		It is always imperfect.	그것은 항상 불완전하다.
10	indicate		indicate a greater understanding	더 큰 이해를 나타내다
11	moral		moral issues	도덕적 쟁점들
12	concern		moral concern	도덕적 관심
13	previous		the previous attitude	이전의 태도
14	widespread		the widespread attitude	널리 퍼진 태도

➕ 본문 문장 속에서 단어의 의미를 우리말로 해석해 보세요.

Even though institutions like the World Bank use wealth / to differentiate between "developed" and "developing" countries, / they also agree / that development is more than economic growth.

→ 비록 World Bank와 같은 ＿＿＿＿＿＿은 부를 사용하지만 / "＿＿＿＿＿" 국가와 "＿＿＿＿＿" 국가를 ＿＿＿＿＿＿＿ 위해, / 그들은 또한 동의한다 / 발전이 경제 성장 그 이상이라는 것에.

2022 6월 학평 29번 문제

제한시간 80초
난이도 ★★★★★

STEP **2** • 수능 기출 제대로 풀기

B 다음 글의 밑줄 친 부분 중, 어법상 틀린 것은?

Even though institutions like the World Bank use wealth ① to differentiate between "developed" and "developing" countries, they also agree that development is more than economic growth. "Development" can also include the social and environmental changes that are caused by or accompany economic growth, some of ② which are positive and thus may be negative. Awareness has grown — and continues to grow — that the question of how economic growth is affecting people and the planet ③ needs to be addressed. Countries are slowly learning that it is cheaper and causes ④ much less suffering to try to reduce the harmful effects of an economic activity or project at the beginning, when it is planned, than after the damage appears. To do this is not easy and is always imperfect. But an awareness of the need for such an effort indicates a greater understanding and moral concern than ⑤ was the previous widespread attitude that focused only on creating new products and services.

정답과 해설 **p.24**

STEP 3 · 수능 지문 제대로 복습하기

01 Even though institutions like the World Bank use wealth / to differentiate between
to부정사의 부사적 용법(~하기 위해서)
"developed" and "developing" countries, / they also agree / that development is more
명사절 접속사
than economic growth.

02 "Development" can also include the social and environmental changes / [that are
주격 관계대명사절
caused by or accompany economic growth], / [some of which are positive and thus may
병렬구조(접속사 or로 연결되어 목적어 ───── *계속적 용법의 관계대명사절*
be negative]. *economic growth를 공유함)* *(선행사: the social and environmental changes)*

03 Awareness has grown / — and continues to grow — / that the question of how economic
전치사
동격의 that(=Awareness) *의문사절*
growth is affecting people and the planet / needs to be addressed.

04 Countries are slowly learning / that it is cheaper and causes much less suffering /
명사절 접속사 *가주어*
[to try to reduce the harmful effects of an economic activity or project / at the
진주어(to부정사)
beginning, when it is planned], / than after the damage appears.
──── *시점의 비교* ────

05 To do this / is not easy and is always imperfect.
주어(to부정사의 명사적 용법)

06 But / an awareness of the need for such an effort / indicates a greater understanding
주어 *비교급+than: ~보다 더 …한*
and moral concern / than did the previous widespread attitude / [that focused only on
동사
도치(대동사+주어) *주격 관계대명사절*
creating new products and services]. *(the ~ attitude 수식)*

01 비록 World Bank와 같은 기관institution들은 부를 사용하지만 / "선진developed" 국가와 "개발도상developing" 국가를 구별하기differentiate 위해, / 그들은 또한 동의한다 / 발전이 경제 성장 그 이상이라는 것에.

02 "발전"은 또한 사회적이고 환경적인 변화도 포함할 수 있다 / 경제 성장에 의해 야기되거나 경제 성장을 수반하는accompany, / 그리고 그 (변화 중) 일부는 긍정적이고 따라서 부정적일지도 모른다.

03 인식awareness이 커졌고 / 계속해서 커지고 있다 / 경제 성장이 인간과 지구에 어떻게 영향을 미치고 있는지에 대한 문제가 / 다루어질be addressed 필요가 있다는 (인식).

04 국가들은 서서히 깨닫고 있다 / 비용이 덜 들고 훨씬 적은 고통suffering을 야기한다는 것을 / 경제 활동이나 프로젝트의 해로운 영향을 줄이려고 노력하는 것이 / 초기에, 즉 그것이 계획되는 때에 / 해당 피해가 나타난 이후보다.

05 이것을 하는 것은 / 쉽지 않고 항상 불완전하다imperfect.

06 그러나 / 그러한 노력의 필요성에 대한 인식은 / 더 큰 이해와 도덕적 관심moral concern을 나타낸다indicate / 이전의 previous 널리 퍼진widespread 태도가 했던(나타냈던) 것보다 / 새로운 제품과 서비스를 만드는 데만 집중했던 (태도).

구문 Check up

① "Development" can also include the social and environmental changes that are caused by or accompany / accompanies economic growth.

관계대명사 that절의 선행사가 복수명사인 the social and environmental changes이므로, 복수인 accompany로 수일치한다.

② Awareness has grown — and continues to grow — what / that the question of how economic growth is affecting people and the planet needs to be addressed.

뒤따르는 절이 완전하므로 접속사 that을 쓴다. 여기서 that절은 주어 awareness를 부가 설명하는 동격절이다.

정답 ① accompany ② that

✔ 문제에 나오는 단어들을 확인하세요.

01	reflect on	~을 곰곰이 생각하다	(✔ reflect) (on) the needs	요구를 곰곰이 생각하다
02	inclusivity	n. 포용성	(　　　　　) supports collaboration.	포용성은 협력을 뒷받침한다.
03	ultimately	ad. 궁극적으로	what everyone (　　　　) wants	모두가 궁극적으로 원하는 것
04	collaboration	n. 협력	their (　　　　　)	그들의 협력
05	paradigm	n. 패러다임, 이론 체계	the old (　　　)	낡은 패러다임
06	educated	a. 교육을 받은	the most (　　　)	가장 교육을 많이 받은 사람
07	exclusivity	n. 배타성	result in (　　　)	배타성을 초래하다
08	inadequate	a. 부적절한	be considered (　　　　)	부적절한 것으로 여겨지다
09	solution	n. 해결책	A (　　　　) is developed.	해결책이 발전된다.

➕ 본문 문장 속에서 단어들을 확인해 보세요.

Because inclusivity supports / what everyone ultimately wants from their relationships: / collaboration.

포용성은 뒷받침하기 때문이다 / 모든 사람이 자신의 관계에서 궁극적으로 원하는 것을 / 즉 협력을.

문제를 풀기 전에 단어들을 30초 동안 다시 확인하세요.

01	reflect on	~을 곰곰이 생각하다	reflect on the needs	요구를 곰곰이 생각하다
02	inclusivity		Inclusivity supports collaboration.	포용성은 협력을 뒷받침한다.
03	ultimately		what everyone ultimately wants	모두가 궁극적으로 원하는 것
04	collaboration		their collaboration	그들의 협력
05	paradigm		the old paradigm	낡은 패러다임
06	educated		the most educated	가장 교육을 많이 받은 사람
07	exclusivity		result in exclusivity	배타성을 초래하다
08	inadequate		be considered inadequate	부적절한 것으로 여겨지다
09	solution		A solution is developed.	해결책이 발전된다.

➕ 본문 문장 속에서 단어의 의미를 우리말로 해석해 보세요.

Because inclusivity supports / what everyone ultimately wants from their relationships: / collaboration.

➔ _____ 은 뒷받침하기 때문이다 / 모든 사람이 자신의 관계에서 _____ 원하는 것을 / 즉 _____ 을.

STEP **2** • 수능 기출 제대로 풀기

C 다음 글의 밑줄 친 부분 중, 어법상 틀린 것은?

While reflecting on the needs of organizations, leaders, and families today, we realize that one of the unique characteristics ① is inclusivity. Why? Because inclusivity supports ② what everyone ultimately wants from their relationships: collaboration. Yet the majority of leaders, organizations, and families are still using the language of the old paradigm in which one person — typically the oldest, most educated, and/or wealthiest — makes all the decisions, and their decisions rule with little discussion or inclusion of others, ③ resulting in exclusivity. Today, this person could be a director, CEO, or other senior leader of an organization. There is no need for others to present their ideas because they are considered ④ inadequate. Yet research shows that exclusivity in problem solving, even with a genius, is not as effective as inclusivity, ⑤ which everyone's ideas are heard and a solution is developed through collaboration.

정답과 해설 **p.24**

STEP **3** • 수능 **지문** 제대로 **복습하기**

01 While reflecting on the needs / of organizations, leaders, and families today, / we
접속사가 남아있는 분사구문
realize / that one of the unique characteristics is inclusivity.
명사절 접속사

02 Why? // Because inclusivity supports / what everyone ultimately wants from their
relationships: / collaboration.
동격

03 Yet / the majority of leaders, organizations, and families / are still using the language
주어(the majority of+복수명사)　　　　　　　　　　동사(복수형 수일치)
of the old paradigm / [in which one person — typically the oldest, most educated,
　　　　　　　　　　　　　　　　　주어1　　　대시(—): 부연설명
and/or wealthiest — makes all the decisions, / and their decisions rule / with little
　　　　　　　　　동사1　　　　　　　　　　주어2　　　　동사2
discussion or inclusion of others, / resulting in exclusivity].
분사구문

04 Today, / this person could be a director, CEO, or other senior leader of an organization.

05 There is no need / for others to present their ideas / because they are considered
　　　　　　　　의미상 주어+to부정사의 형용사적 용법
inadequate.
be considered+형용사: 5형식 수동태(~하다고 여겨지다)

06 Yet / research shows / that exclusivity in problem solving, / even with a genius, / is
　　　　　　　　　명사절 접속사
not as effective as inclusivity, / [where everyone's ideas are heard / and a solution is
원급비교 부정 not as ~ as(…만큼 ~하지 않다)　　　관계부사절(뒤에 완전한 수동태 문장)
developed through collaboration].

01 요구에 관해 곰곰이 생각할reflect on the needs 때 / 오늘날 조직, 지도자, 그리고 가족의, / 우리는 깨닫는다 / 독특한 특성 중 하나가 포용성inclusivity이라는 것을.

02 왜 그런가? // 포용성은 뒷받침하기 때문이다 / 모든 사람이 자신의 관계에서 궁극적으로ultimately 원하는 것을 / 즉 협력collaboration을.

03 그러나 / 대다수의 지도자, 조직, 그리고 가족은 / 여전히 오래된 패러다임paradigm의 언어를 사용하고 있고, / 거기서는 한 사람이 — 보통 가장 연장자, 가장 교육을 많이 받은 사람the most educated, 그리고/또는 가장 부유한 사람이 — 모든 결정을 내린다 / 그리고 그들의 결정이 지배한다 / 토론이나 다른 사람을 포함시키는 것이 거의 없이 / 결과적으로 배타성exclusivity을 초래하면서.

04 오늘날 / 이 사람은 어떤 조직의 이사, 최고 경영자, 또는 다른 상급 지도자일 수 있다.

05 필요가 없는데 / 다른 사람들이 자신의 생각을 제시할 (필요가) / 왜냐하면 그것은 부적절한inadequate 것으로 여겨지기 때문이다.

06 그러나 / 연구는 보여준다 / 문제 해결에 있어서 배타성은, / 심지어 천재와 함께하는 것이더라도, / 포용성만큼 효과적이지 않다는 것을, / (포용성이 있는 경우에는) 모든 사람의 생각을 듣게 되고 / 해결책solution은 협력을 통해 발전된다.

① While reflect / reflecting on the needs of organizations, leaders, and families today, we realize that one of the unique characteristics is inclusivity.

접속사 While 뒤에 주어가 없으므로 접속사가 남아 있는 분사구문임을 알 수 있다. 따라서 reflecting이 적절하다.

② There is no need of / for others to present their ideas because they are considered inadequate.

to부정사의 의미상 주어는 일반적으로 <for+명사>로 쓰므로 for가 적절하다.

정답 ① reflecting ② for

192

D

STEP 1 • 수능에 진짜 나오는 단어

✔ 문제에 나오는 단어들을 확인하세요.

시간이 없다면 색으로 표시된 단어만이라도 꼭 외우고 넘어가세요!

01	commercial	a. 민간의, 상업적인	(✔ commercial) airplanes	민간 항공기
02	airway	n. 항공로	travel ( )s	항공로로 운항하다
03	structure	n. 구조(물)	physical ( )s	물리적 구조물
04	fixed	a. 고정된	( ) price	고정된 가격
05	width	n. 폭	fixed ( )s	고정된 폭
06	define	v. 규정하다	( )d altitudes	규정된 고도
07	vertical	a. 상하의, 수직의	( ) separation	상하 간격
08	intense	a. 고강도의, 강렬한	( ) pilot activity	고강도 조종사 활동
09	takeoff	n. 이륙	at ( ) and landing	이륙과 착륙시
10	assess	v. 평가하다	( ) aircraft status	항공기 상태를 평가하다
11	collision	n. 충돌	( )s between aircraft	항공기 간의 충돌
12	crash	n. (비행기의) 추락	( )es occur during flight.	추락은 비행 중 일어난다.
13	malfunction	n. 오작동, 고장	aircraft ( )	항공기 오작동

✚ 본문 문장 속에서 단어들을 확인해 보세요.

Commercial airplanes generally travel airways / similar to roads, / although they are not physical structures.

일반적으로 민간 항공기는 항공로로 운항한다 / 도로와 유사한 / 그 항공로들이 물리적 구조물은 아니지만.

문제를 풀기 전에 단어들을 **30초** 동안 다시 확인하세요.

01	commercial	🖊 민간의, 상업적인	commercial airplanes	민간 항공기
02	airway		travel airways	항공로로 운항하다
03	structure		physical structures	물리적 구조물
04	fixed		fixed price	고정된 가격
05	width		fixed widths	고정된 폭
06	define		defined altitudes	규정된 고도
07	vertical		vertical separation	상하 간격
08	intense		intense pilot activity	고강도 조종사 활동
09	takeoff		at takeoff and landing	이륙과 착륙시
10	assess		assess aircraft status	항공기 상태를 평가하다
11	collision		collisions between aircraft	항공기 간의 충돌
12	crash		Crashes occur during flight.	추락은 비행 중 일어난다.
13	malfunction		aircraft malfunction	항공기 오작동

➕ **본문 문장 속에서 단어의 의미를 우리말로 해석해 보세요.**

Commercial airplanes generally travel airways / similar to roads, / although they are not physical structures.

→ 일반적으로   항공기는   로 운항한다 / 도로와 유사한 / 그 항공로들이
      은 아니지만.

STEP **2** · 수능 기출 제대로 풀기

D 다음 글의 밑줄 친 부분 중, 어법상 틀린 것은?

Commercial airplanes generally travel airways similar to roads, although they are not physical structures. Airways have fixed widths and defined altitudes, ① which separate traffic moving in opposite directions. Vertical separation of aircraft allows some flights ② to pass over airports while other processes occur below. Air travel usually covers long distances, with short periods of intense pilot activity at takeoff and landing and long periods of lower pilot activity while in the air, the portion of the flight ③ known as the "long haul." During the long-haul portion of a flight, pilots spend more time assessing aircraft status than ④ searching out nearby planes. This is because collisions between aircraft usually occur in the surrounding area of airports, while crashes due to aircraft malfunction ⑤ tends to occur during long-haul flight.

*altitude: 고도
** long haul: 장거리 비행

정답과 해설 p.25

01 Commercial airplanes generally travel airways / similar to roads, / although they are
not physical structures.
　　　　　　　　　　　　　　　　　　　　　형용사구　　　　　　~에도 불구하고(양보절)

02 Airways have fixed widths and defined altitudes, / which separate traffic / moving in
opposite directions.
　　　　　　　　　　　　　　　　　　관계대명사 계속적 용법　　　　　　　　　　현재분사

03 Vertical separation of aircraft allows / some flights to pass over airports / while other
processes occur below.
　　　　　　allow+목적어+목적격 보어(to부정사)

04 Air travel usually covers long distances, / with short periods of intense pilot activity
at takeoff and landing / and long periods of lower pilot activity while in the air, / the
portion of the flight known as the "long haul."
　　~라고 알려진　　　　　　　　　　　　　　　　　　　　they are 생략
　　　　　　　　　　　　　　　　과거분사 수식

05 During the long-haul portion of a flight, / pilots spend more time / assessing aircraft
status / than searching out nearby planes.
　　　　　　　　　　　　　　　　비교급
　　　　　　　　　　　spend+시간+-ing: ~하는 데 시간을 보내다

06 This is because collisions between aircraft usually occur / in the surrounding area of
airports, / while crashes due to aircraft malfunction tend to occur / during long-haul
flight.
　　　　　　　주어(복수)　　　　　　　　　　　　　　　　수 일치

01 일반적으로 민간 항공기commercial airplane는 항공로airway로 운항한다 / 도로와 유사한 / 물리적 구조물structure은
아니지만.

02 항공로에는 고정된 폭fixed width과 규정된 고도defined altitude가 있으며, / 그것들이 통행을 분리한다 / 반대 방향으로
움직이는.

03 항공기 간의 상하 간격vertical separation은 허용한다 / 일부 비행기가 공항 위를 통과할 수 있도록 / 아래에서 다른
과정이 이루어지는 동안.

04 항공 여행은 보통 장거리에 걸치는데, / 이륙과 착륙takeoff and landing 시 고강도intense로 조종사 활동을 하는 짧은
시간과 / 공중에 있는 동안 저강도로 조종사 활동을 하는 긴 시간이 있다 / '장거리 비행'이라고 알려진 비행 부분인.

05 비행에서 장거리 비행 부분 동안 / 조종사들은 더 많은 시간을 보낸다 / 항공기 상태를 평가하는 데assess / 근처의
비행기를 탐색하는 것보다.

06 이는 항공기 간의 충돌collision이 대개 발생하기 때문이다 / 공항 주변 지역에서, / 반면 항공기 오작동aircraft
malfunction으로 인한 추락crash은 발생하는 경향이 있다 / 장거리 비행 중에.

① Airways have fixed widths and defined altitudes, which
separates / separate traffic moving in opposite
directions.

선행사가 복수명사구인 fixed widths and defined altitudes이므로 관계
대명사 뒤에 복수동사 separate를 쓴다.

② Air travel usually covers long distances, with short
periods of intense pilot activity at takeoff and landing
and long periods of lower pilot activity during / while
in the air.

문맥상 they(=pilots) are가 생략된 부사절 축약 구문이므로 접속사 while
을 쓴다. 전치사 during 뒤에는 시간 명사구가 나온다.

정답 ① separate ② while

E

STEP 1 • 수능에 *진짜* 나오는 *단어*

✔ 문제에 나오는 단어들을 확인하세요.

01	be good at	~을 잘하다	He (✔ is) (good) (at) singing.	그는 노래를 잘한다.
02	suspect	v. 의심하다	many scientists ( )	많은 과학자들이 의심하다
03	compound	n. 화학적 화합물	( )s in leaves	잎에 있는 화합물들
04	state	n. 상태	a confused ( )	혼란스러운 상태
05	nutrient	n. 영양분	low in ( )	영양분이 적은
06	as ~ as possible	가능한 한 ~하게	( ) little ( ) ( )	가능한 한 적게
07	motion	n. 움직임	in slow ( )	느린 동작으로
08	rest	v. 쉬다	( ) sixteen hours a day	하루에 16시간을 쉬다
09	unconscious	a. 의식이 없는	be ( ) while sleeping	수면 중에 의식이 없다
10	shrink	v. 줄어들다	( ) in the wash	빨래로 줄어들다
11	skull	n. 두개골	fill half of its ( )	두개골의 반을 채우다

⊕ 본문 문장 속에서 단어들을 확인해 보세요.

Therefore / they tend to move as little as possible / — and when they do move, / they often look / as though they're in slow motion.

그래서 / 그것들은 가능한 한 적게 움직이는 경향이 있다 / 그리고 그것들이 실제로 움직일 때에는, / 흔히 그것들은 보인다 / 마치 느린 동작으로 움직이는 것처럼.

문제를 풀기 전에 단어들을 **30초** 동안 다시 확인하세요.

01	be good at	✎ ~을 잘하다	He is good at singing.	그는 노래를 잘한다.
02	suspect		many scientists suspect	많은 과학자들이 의심하다
03	compound		compounds in leaves	잎에 있는 화합물들
04	state		a confused state	혼란스러운 상태
05	nutrient		low in nutrient	영양분이 적은
06	as ~ as possible		as little as possible	가능한 한 적게
07	motion		in slow motion	느린 동작으로
08	rest		rest sixteen hours a day	하루에 16시간을 쉬다
09	unconscious		be unconscious while sleeping	수면 중에 의식이 없다
10	shrink		shrink in the wash	빨래로 줄어들다
11	skull		fill half of its skull	두개골의 반을 채우다

➕ **본문 문장 속에서 단어의 의미를 우리말로 해석해 보세요.**

Therefore / they tend to move as little as possible / — and when they do move, / they often look / as though they're in slow motion.

→ 그래서 / 그것들은   움직이는 경향이 있다 / 그리고 그것들이 실제로 움직일 때에는, / 흔히 그것들은 보인다 / 마치 느린   으로 움직이는 것처럼.

STEP 2 · 수능 기출 제대로 풀기

E

다음 글의 밑줄 친 부분 중, 어법상 틀린 것은?

If there's one thing koalas are good at, it's sleeping. For a long time many scientists suspected that koalas were so lethargic ① <u>because</u> the compounds in eucalyptus leaves kept the cute little animals in a drugged-out state. But more recent research has shown that the leaves are simply so low in nutrients ② <u>that</u> koalas have almost no energy. Therefore they tend to move as little as possible — and when they ③ <u>do</u> move, they often look as though they're in slow motion. They rest sixteen to eighteen hours a day and spend most of that unconscious. In fact, koalas spend little time thinking; their brains actually appear to ④ <u>have shrunk</u> over the last few centuries. The koala is the only known animal ⑤ <u>its</u> brain only fills half of its skull.

*lethargic: 무기력한
**drugged-out: 몽롱한, 취한

정답과 해설 p.25

01 If there's one thing koalas are good at, / it's sleeping.
　　　　　　　　　　　　　　└┈┈┈┈┘ 목적격 관계대명사 that 생략

02 For a long time / many scientists suspected / that koalas were so lethargic / because the
　　　　　　　　　　　　　　　　　　　　　　명사절 접속사 that(목적어)　　　　　　　접속사
compounds in eucalyptus leaves / kept the cute little animals in a drugged-out state.
　주어　　　└┈┈┈┈┘　　　　　　동사

03 But / more recent research has shown / that the leaves are simply so low in nutrients /
　　　　　　　　　　　　　　　　　　명사절 접속사 that(목적어)　　　　　so ~ that…: 너무 ~해서 …하다
that koalas have almost no energy.

04 Therefore / they tend to move as little as possible / — and when they do move, / they
　　　　　　　　　　　　　　　　　　　　　　　　　　　　　　　　　　동사 강조
often look / as though they're in slow motion.
　　　　　　마치 ~처럼

05 They rest sixteen to eighteen hours a day / and spend most of that unconscious.

06 In fact, / koalas spend little time thinking; / their brains actually appear to
　　　shrink-shrank-shrunk　　　　　　　　　　　　　　　　　~처럼 보인다
have shrunk / over the last few centuries.
have p.p.: appear보다 과거의 시점을 나타냄

07 The koala is the only known animal / whose brain only fills half of its skull.
　　　　　　　　　　　　　　　└┈┈┈┈┘ 소유격 관계대명사절

01 코알라가 잘하는be good at 것이 한 가지 있다면, / 그것은 자는 것이다.

02 오랫동안 / 많은 과학자들은 의심했다suspect / 코알라들이 너무 무기력한 상태에 있다고 / 유칼립투스 잎 속의 화합물 compounds in eucalyptus leaves이 / 그 작고 귀여운 동물들을 몽롱한 상태로in a drugged-out state 만들기 때문에.

03 그러나 / 더 최근의 연구는 보여 주었다 / 그 잎들이 단순히 영양분nutrient이 너무나도 적어서 / 코알라가 거의 에너지가 없는 것임을.

04 그래서 / 코알라들은 가능한 한 적게as little as possible 움직이는 경향이 있다 / 그리고 그것들이 실제로 움직일 때에는, / 흔히 그것들은 보인다 / 마치 느린 동작으로in slow motion 움직이는 것처럼.

05 그것들은 하루에 16시간에서 18시간 동안 휴식을 취하는데rest, / 의식이 없는unconscious 상태로 그 시간의 대부분을 보낸다.

06 사실 / 코알라는 생각하는 데에 시간을 거의 사용하지 않는데 / 그것들의 뇌는 실제로 줄어든shrink 것처럼 보인다 / 지난 몇 세기 동안.

07 코알라는 알려진 유일한 동물이다 / 뇌가 겨우 두개골의 절반을 채우는fill half of its skull.

구문 Check up	① If there's one thing koalas are good / good at , it's sleeping.	② In fact, koalas spend little time thinking; their brains actually appear to shrink / to have shrunk over the last few centuries.
	one thing 다음에 목적격 관계대명사 that이 생략되어 있으므로 관계대 명사절은 동사 또는 전치사의 목적어가 빠진 불완전한 구조여야 한다. 따라서 전치사로 끝나는 good at이 적절하다.	over the last few centuries로 보아 '과거에 줄어든' 것처럼 보인다는 의미로, 주절보다 먼저 일어난 사건을 묘사하는 to have p.p. 형태(to have shrunk)를 써야 한다.

STEP 1 • 수능에 진짜 나오는 단어

✔ 문제에 나오는 단어들을 확인하세요.

시간이 없다면 색으로 표시된 단어만이라도 꼭 외우고 넘어가세요!

01	liquid	n. 액체	(✔ liquid) or solid	액체 또는 고체
02	flow	v. 흐르다, 액체처럼 움직이다	House cats ( ).	집고양이가 흐물거리며 움직인다.
03	furry	a. 털로 덮인, 털이 많은	( ) pets	털로 덮인 애완동물
04	adapt	v. 맞추다, 조절하다	( ) to the shape	모양에 맞게 조절하다
05	container	n. 그릇, 용기	the shape of the ( )	용기의 모양
06	fluid	n. 액체, 유동체	( )s such as water	물과 같은 액체
07	apply	v. 적용하다	( ) rheology	유동학을 적용하다
08	branch	n. 가지, 분야	the ( ) of physics	물리학의 한 분야
09	deformation	n. 변형, 변화	the ( ) of matter	물질의 변화
10	calculate	v. 계산하다	( ) the time	시간을 계산하다
11	take up	차지하다, 넘겨받다	( ) ( ) the space	공간을 차지하다
12	circumstance	n. 상황, 환경	depending on the ( )s	환경에 따라
13	minimize	v. 최소화하다	( ) its contact	접촉을 최소화하다

➕ 본문 문장 속에서 단어들을 확인해 보세요.

So he applied rheology, / the branch of physics / that deals with the deformation of matter, / to calculate the time / it takes for cats to take up the space of a vase or bathroom sink.

그래서 그는 유동학을 적용했다 / 물리학의 한 분야인 / 물질의 변화를 다루는 / 시간을 계산하기 위해 / 고양이가 꽃병 또는 욕조의 공간을 차지하는 데 걸리는.

01	liquid	🖉 액체	liquid or solid	액체 또는 고체
02	flow		House cats flow.	집고양이가 흐물거리며 움직인다.
03	furry		furry pets	털로 덮인 애완동물
04	adapt		adapt to the shape	모양에 맞게 조절하다
05	container		the shape of the container	용기의 모양
06	fluid		fluids such as water	물과 같은 액체
07	apply		apply rheology	유동학을 적용하다
08	branch		the branch of physics	물리학의 한 분야
09	deformation		the deformation of matter	물질의 변화
10	calculate		calculate the time	시간을 계산하다
11	take up		take up the space	공간을 차지하다
12	circumstance		depending on the circumstances	환경에 따라
13	minimize		minimize its contact	접촉을 최소화하다

➕ **본문 문장 속에서 단어의 의미를 우리말로 해석해 보세요.**

So he applied rheology, / the branch of physics / that deals with the deformation of matter, / to calculate the time / it takes for cats to take up the space of a vase or bathroom sink.

→ 그래서 그는 유동학을 ⬚⬚⬚⬚⬚ / 물리학의 한 ⬚⬚⬚⬚⬚ 인 / 물질의 ⬚⬚⬚⬚⬚ 를 다루는 / 시간을 ⬚⬚⬚⬚⬚ 위해 / 고양이가 꽃병 또는 욕조의 ⬚⬚⬚⬚⬚ 데 걸리는.

STEP 2 • 수능 기출 제대로 풀기

F

다음 글의 밑줄 친 부분 중, 어법상 틀린 것은?

Are cats liquid or solid? That's the kind of question that could win a scientist an Ig Nobel Prize, a parody of the Nobel Prize that honors research that "makes people laugh, then think." But it wasn't with this in mind ① that Marc-Antoine Fardin, a physicist at Paris Diderot University, set out to find out whether house cats flow. Fardin noticed that these furry pets can adapt to the shape of the container they sit in ② similarly to what fluids such as water do. So he applied rheology, the branch of physics that deals with the deformation of matter, to calculate the time ③ it takes for cats to take up the space of a vase or bathroom sink. The conclusion? Cats can be either liquid or solid, depending on the circumstances. A cat in a small box will behave like a fluid, ④ filled up all the space. But a cat in a bathtub full of water will try to minimize its contact with it and ⑤ behave very much like a solid.

정답과 해설 p.26

01 Are cats liquid or solid? // That's the kind of question / that could win a scientist an Ig
주격 관계대명사
Nobel Prize, / a parody of the Nobel Prize / that honors research / that "makes people
동격   주격 관계대명사절   사역동사(make)+목적어
laugh, then think."   +목적격 보어(동사원형)

02 But / it wasn't with this in mind / that Marc-Antoine Fardin, a physicist at Paris Diderot
it ~ that 강조구문(with this in mind 강조)
University, / set out to find out / whether house cats flow.
부사적 용법(목적)   명사절 접속사: ~인지 아닌지

03 Fardin noticed / that these furry pets can adapt to the shape of the container / they sit
명사절 접속사(noticed의 목적어)   목적격 관계대명사 생략
in / similarly to what fluids such as water do.
관계대명사 what절

04 So he applied rheology, / the branch of physics / that deals with the deformation
주격 관계대명사
of matter, / to calculate the time / it takes for cats to take up the space of a vase or
부사적 용법(목적)   it takes+시간+for 목적격+to부정사: ~이 …하는 데 ~만큼 걸리다
bathroom sink.

05 The conclusion? // Cats can be either liquid or solid, / depending on the circumstances.
either A or B: A 또는 B 둘 중 하나
// A cat in a small box will behave / like a fluid, / filling up all the space.
분사구문(=as it fills ~)

06 But a cat in a bathtub full of water / will try to minimize its contact with it / and behave
which is 생략   병렬 연결
very much like a solid.

---

01 고양이는 액체liquid일까 고체일까? // 이는 종류의 질문이다 / 이그 노벨상을 과학자가 타게 할 수 있는 (질문) / 노벨상의 패러디인 (이그 노벨상) / 연구에 경의를 표하는 / "사람들을 웃게 한 후 생각을 하게 만드는".

02 하지만 / 이런 생각을 하면서가 아니었다 / Paris Diderot 대학의 물리학자인 Marc-Antoine Fardin이 / 알아내는 것을 시작한 것은 / 집고양이가 액체처럼 흐물거리며 움직이는지flow 아닌지를.

03 Fardin은 알아냈다 / 털로 덮인furry 이 애완동물이 용기container의 모양에 맞게 조절할adapt 수 있다는 것을 / 그들이 들어가 앉아 있는 / 물과 같은 액체fluid가 하는 것과 유사하게.

04 그래서 그는 유동학을 적용했다apply / 물리학의 한 분야branch인 / 물질의 변화deformation를 다루는 / 시간을 계산하기calculate 위해 / 고양이가 꽃병 또는 욕조의 공간을 차지하는take up 데 걸리는.

05 결론은? // 고양이는 액체도 될 수 있고 고체도 될 수 있다 / 환경circumstance에 따라. // 작은 상자 안의 고양이는 행동할 것이다 / 액체처럼 / 그 모든 공간을 채우며.

06 하지만 물로 가득 찬 욕조의 고양이는 / 그것과의 접촉을 최소화하려고minimize 노력하면서 / 고체와 매우 유사하게 움직일 것이다.

구문 Check up

① That's the kind of question that could win a scientist an Ig Nobel Prize, a parody of the Nobel Prize that honors research that "makes people laugh, then think / thinks ."

앞서 나온 동사 makes가 아닌, makes의 목적격보어 laugh와 병렬연결이 되어야 하므로 think가 적절하다.

② Fardin noticed that these furry pets can adapt to the shape of the container they sit in similarly to that / what fluids such as water do.

앞에 선행사가 없고 뒤에 불완전한 문장이 오므로 선행사를 포함한 관계대명사 what이 적절하다.

정답 ① think ② what

STEP 1 • 수능에 진짜 나오는 단어

✔️ 문제에 나오는 단어들을 확인하세요.

시간이 없다면 색으로 표시된 단어만이라도 꼭 외우고 넘어가세요!

01	describe	v. 설명하다, 묘사하다	(✔️ describe) an event	사건을 묘사하다
02	familial	a. 가족의, 혈통적인	( ) relationships	가족 관계
03	consider	v. 고려하다, 여기다	( ) it strange	그것을 이상하게 여기다
04	absurd	a. 터무니없는, 말도 안 되는	( ) questions	터무니 없는 질문
05	relative	n. 친척	female ( )s	여자 친척
06	distinguish	v. 구별하다	( ) colors	색을 구별하다
07	confusing	a. 혼란스러운	The words are ( ).	그 단어들은 혼란스럽다.
08	make sense of	~을 이해하다	( ) ( ) ( ) a situation	상황을 이해하다
09	kin	n. 친족	one's blood ( )	혈족

➕ 본문 문장 속에서 단어들을 확인해 보세요.

Many African language speakers would consider it absurd / to use a single word like "cousin" / to describe both male and female relatives.

많은 아프리카 언어 사용자들은 불합리하다고 여길 것이다 / "cousin"과 같은 한 단어를 사용하는 것을 / 남성과 여성 친척 양쪽 모두를 묘사하는 데.

문제를 풀기 전에 단어들을 30초 동안 다시 확인하세요.

01	describe	✎ 설명하다, 묘사하다	describe an event	사건을 묘사하다
02	familial		familial relationships	가족 관계
03	consider		consider it strange	그것을 이상하게 여기다
04	absurd		absurd questions	터무니 없는 질문
05	relative		female relatives	여자 친척
06	distinguish		distinguish colors	색을 구별하다
07	confusing		The words are confusing.	그 단어들은 혼란스럽다.
08	make sense of		make sense of a situation	상황을 이해하다
09	kin		one's blood kin	혈족

⊕ 본문 문장 속에서 단어의 의미를 우리말로 해석해 보세요.

Many African language speakers would consider it absurd / to use a single word like "cousin" / to describe both male and female relatives.

→ 많은 아프리카 언어 사용자들은 　　　　　　　고 　　　　　　　 / "cousin"과 같은 한 단어를 사용하는 것을 / 남성과 여성 　　　　　　　 양쪽 모두를 　　　　　　　데.

제한시간 70초

난이도 ★★★☆☆

STEP 2 • 수능 기출 제대로 풀기

G (A), (B), (C)의 각 네모 안에서 어법에 맞는 표현으로 가장 적절한 것은?

English speakers have one of the simplest systems for describing familial relationships. Many African language speakers would consider it absurd to use a single word like "cousin" to describe both male and female relatives, or not to distinguish whether the person (A) described / describing is related by blood to the speaker's father or to his mother. To be unable to distinguish a brother-in-law as the brother of one's wife or the husband of one's sister would seem confusing within the structure of personal relationships existing in many cultures. Similarly, how is it possible to make sense of a situation (B) which / in which a single word "uncle" applies to the brother of one's father and to the brother of one's mother? The Hawaiian language uses the same term to refer to one's father and to the father's brother. People of Northern Burma, who think in the Jinghpaw language, (C) has / have eighteen basic terms for describing their kin. Not one of them can be directly translated into English.

	(A)		(B)		(C)
①	described	……	which	……	have
②	described	……	in which	……	has
③	described	……	in which	……	have
④	describing	……	which	……	has
⑤	describing	……	in which	……	has

정답과 해설 p.26

01 English speakers have one of the simplest systems / for describing familial relationships.
one of+the 최상급+복수 명사: 가장 ~한 것들 중 하나

02 Many African language speakers would consider it absurd / [to use a single word like
가목적어   진목적어1(to부정사)   ~인지 아닌지
"cousin" / to describe both male and female relatives], / or [not to distinguish / whether
부사적 용법(~하기 위해서)   진목적어2(to부정사)
the person described is related by blood to the speaker's father or to his mother].
과거분사

03 To be unable to distinguish a brother-in-law / as the brother of one's wife or the
주어(to부정사)
husband of one's sister / would seem confusing / within the structure of personal
relationships / existing in many cultures.
분사(명사 수식)

04 Similarly, / how is it possible / to make sense of a situation / in which a single word
가주어   진주어(to부정사)   전치사+관계대명사절
"uncle" applies / to the brother of one's father and to the brother of one's mother?
자동사(주어만 있으면 완전)

05 The Hawaiian language uses the same term / to refer to one's father and to the father's
부사적 용법(~하기 위해서)
brother.

06 People of Northern Burma, / (who think in the Jinghpaw language), / have eighteen
주어(복수)   삽입절(계속적 용법)   수 일치
basic terms for describing their kin. // Not one of them can be directly translated into
English.

---

01 영어 사용자들은 가장 단순한 체계들 중 하나를 가진다 / 가족 관계를 묘사하기describe familial relationships 위한.

02 많은 아프리카 언어 사용자들은 불합리하다absurd고 여길 것이다consider / "cousin"과 같은 한 단어를 사용하는 것을 / 남성과 여성 친척relative 양쪽 모두를 묘사하는 데, / 또는 구별하지 않는 것을 / 묘사되는 사람이 말하는 사람의 아버지와 혈연 관계인지 아니면 어머니와 혈연 관계인지.

03 brother-in-law를 구별할distinguish 수 없다는 것은 / 아내의 남자형제인지 여자형제의 남편인지 / 혼란스럽게confusing 보일 것이다 / 인간관계의 구조 내에서 / 많은 문화에 존재하는.

04 마찬가지로, / 어떻게 가능하겠는가 / 상황을 이해하는make sense of 것이 / "uncle"이라는 한 단어가 적용되는 (상황) / 아버지의 형제와 어머니의 형제에게?

05 하와이 언어는 동일한 용어를 사용하여 / 아버지와 아버지의 남자형제를 지칭한다.

06 Northern Burma의 사람들은 / Jinghpaw 언어로 사고하는 (사람들) / 그들의 친족kin을 묘사하기 위한 18개의 기본 용어를 가진다. // 이 용어 중 어떤 것도 영어로 바로 번역될 수 없다.

---

① Many African language speakers would consider absurd / it absurd to use a single word like "cousin" to describe both male and female relatives.

<consider+목적어+목적격 보어> 구조로, 목적어(to부정사)가 길어져 뒤로 가는 대신에 가목적어 it을 쓰므로 it absurd가 적절하다.

② People of Northern Burma, who think / thinks in the Jinghpaw language, have eighteen basic terms for describing their kin.

관계대명사절의 주어가 앞의 선행사 People이므로 복수 취급하여 think를 쓴다.

DAY 08

A

빈칸 추론 Ⅰ ✚

STEP 1 • 수능에 *진짜* 나오는 *단어*

✔ 문제에 나오는 단어들을 확인하세요.

시간이 없다면 색으로 표시된 단어만이라도 꼭 외우고 넘어가세요!

01	describe	v. 묘사하다	(✔ describe) the environment as extreme	환경을 극심하다고 묘사하다
02	harsh	a. 혹독한	a very ( ) environment	대단히 혹독한 환경
03	obvious	a. 명백한	an ( ) fact	명백한 사실
04	desert	n. 사막	an oasis in the ( )	사막의 오아시스
05	physiological	a. 생리적인	( ) needs	생리적 욕구
06	characteristic	n. 특성	individual ( )s	개인적인 특성
07	tolerance	n. 내성, 관용	( ) to cold	추위에 대한 내성
08	cactus (*pl.* cacti)	n. 선인장	a ( ) with flowers on top	위에 꽃이 핀 선인장
09	lazy	a. 태만한, 게으른, 성의 없는	a ( ) assumption	성의 없는 가정
10	ecologist	n. 생태학자	a noted ( )	저명한 생태학자
11	with care	조심스럽게, 신중하게	use the word ( ) ( )	그 단어를 조심스럽게 사용하다

✚ 본문 문장 속에서 단어들을 확인해 보세요.

But this only means / that these conditions are extreme *for us*, / given our particular physiological characteristics and tolerances.

하지만 이것은 의미할 뿐이다 / 이런 환경이 '우리에게' 극심하다는 / 우리의 특정한 생리적 특징과 내성을 고려할 때.

01	describe	✎ 묘사하다	describe the environment as extreme	환경을 극심하다고 묘사하다
02	harsh		a very harsh environment	대단히 혹독한 환경
03	obvious		an obvious fact	명백한 사실
04	desert		an oasis in the desert	사막의 오아시스
05	physiological		physiological needs	생리적 욕구
06	characteristic		individual characteristics	개인적인 특성
07	tolerance		tolerance to cold	추위에 대한 내성
08	cactus		a cactus with flowers on top	위에 꽃이 핀 선인장
09	lazy		a lazy assumption	성의 없는 가정
10	ecologist		a noted ecologist	저명한 생태학자
11	with care		use the word with care	그 단어를 조심스럽게 사용하다

⊕ **본문 문장 속에서 단어의 의미를 우리말로 해석해 보세요.**

But this only means / that these conditions are extreme *for us*, / given our particular physiological characteristics and tolerances.

→ 하지만 이것은 의미할 뿐이다 / 이런 환경이 '우리에게' 극심하다는 / ⬛⬛⬛⬛⬛⬛⬛⬛⬛⬛⬛⬛⬛⬛⬛⬛⬛ 을 고려할 때.

DAY **08** • A

STEP **2** • 수능 기출 제대로 풀기

A

다음 빈칸에 들어갈 말로 가장 적절한 것은?

It seems natural to describe certain environmental conditions as 'extreme', 'harsh', 'benign' or 'stressful'. It may seem obvious when conditions are 'extreme': the midday heat of a desert, the cold of an Antarctic winter, the salinity of the Great Salt Lake. But this only means that these conditions are extreme *for us*, given our particular physiological characteristics and tolerances. To a cactus there is nothing extreme about the desert conditions in which cacti have evolved; nor are the icy lands of Antarctica an extreme environment for penguins. It is lazy and dangerous for the ecologist to assume that _____. Rather, the ecologist should try to gain a worm's-eye or plant's-eye view of the environment: to see the world as others see it. Emotive words like harsh and benign, even relativities such as hot and cold, should be used by ecologists only with care.

*benign: 온화한 **salinity: 염도

① complex organisms are superior to simple ones

② technologies help us survive extreme environments

③ ecological diversity is supported by extreme environments

④ all other organisms sense the environment in the way we do

⑤ species adapt to environmental changes in predictable ways

정답과 해설 **p.28**

01 It seems natural / to describe certain environmental conditions / as 'extreme', 'harsh',
가주어   진주어

'benign' or 'stressful'. // It may seem obvious / when conditions are 'extreme': / the
대명사(=앞 문장)

midday heat of a desert, / the cold of an Antarctic winter, / the salinity of the Great Salt
extreme conditions에 대한 예시

Lake.

02 But this only means / that these conditions are extreme *for us*, / given our particular ·
접속사(~것)   명사구   독립분사구문(~을 고려할 때)

physiological characteristics and tolerances.

03   -thing으로 끝나는 대명사는 형용사가 뒤에서 수식

To a cactus / there is nothing extreme about the desert conditions / in which cacti have
                                               전치사+관계대명사절

evolved; / nor are the icy lands of Antarctica / an extreme environment for penguins.
부정 동의(nor+대동사+주어)   주격보어

04 It is lazy and dangerous / for the ecologist / to assume that all other organisms sense
가주어   의미상 주어   진주어

the environment / in the way we do. // Rather, / the ecologist should try to gain a
                    대동사(=sense)

worm's-eye or plant's-eye view of the environment: / to see the world as others see it.
                                               부사적 용법(~하기 위해)

05 Emotive words like harsh and benign, / even relativities such as hot and cold, / should
주어   전치사(~처럼)   삽입구(주어 보충)   조동사 수동태

be used by ecologists only with care.
                      with+추상명사: 부사(=carefully)

01 자연스러워 보인다 / 특정한 환경 조건을 묘사하는describe 것은 / '극심하다', '혹독하다harsh', '온화하다' 혹은 '스트레스가 된다'고. // 이것은 명백해obvious 보일지도 모른다 / 조건이 '극심한' 경우에 / 사막desert 한낮의 열기, / 남극 겨울의 추위, / 그레이트솔트호의 염도와 같이.

02 하지만 이것은 의미할 뿐이다 / 이런 환경이 '우리에게' 극심하다는 것을 / 우리의 특정한 생리적 특징physiological characteristic과 내성tolerance을 고려할 때.

03 선인장cactus에게 / 사막의 환경 조건은 전혀 극심하지 않다 / 선인장들이 진화해 온 / 마찬가지로 얼음에 뒤덮인 남극 땅은 ~이 아니다 / 펭귄에게 극심한 환경이.

04 성의 없고lazy 위험하다 / 생태학자ecologist가 / 모든 다른 유기체가 환경을 느낀다고 추정하는 것은 / 우리가 느끼는 방식대로. // 오히려 / 생태학자는 환경에 대한 벌레의 관점이나 식물의 관점을 얻기 위해 노력해야 한다 / 다른 유기체가 세계를 보는 방식으로 세계를 바라보고자.

05 혹독한, 온화한 등 감정이 실린 단어들은 / 심지어 덥고 추운 것과 같은 상대적인 단어들 / 생태학자들에 의해 오로지 신중하게with care 사용되어야 한다.

구문 Check up

① These conditions are extreme *for us*, giving / given our particular physiological characteristics and tolerances.

'~을 고려할 때'라는 의미의 독립분사구문 given이 적절하다.

② It is lazy and dangerous for the ecologist to assume that all other organisms sense the environment in the way we do / are .

앞에 나온 일반동사 sense를 대신하는 대동사 자리이므로 do가 적절하다.

정답 ① given ② do

B

STEP 1 • 수능에 *진짜* 나오는 *단어*

✔️ 문제에 나오는 단어들을 확인하세요.

시간이 없다면 색으로 표시된 단어만이라도 꼭 외우고 넘어가세요!

01	blow	n. 타격, 한 방	receiving help could be a (✔️ blow)	도움을 받는 것이 타격이 될 수 있다
02	self-esteem	n. 자존감	a blow to ( )	자존감에 대한 타격
03	examine	v. 검토하다, 조사하다	( ) the possibility	가능성을 검토하다
04	threat	n. 위협	the ( ) to self-esteem	자존감에 대한 위협
05	perceive	v. 인지하다, 지각하다	( ) help as supportive and loving	도움을 협력적이고 애정 있는 것으로 여기다
06	threatening	a. 위협적인	see help as ( )	도움을 위협적인 것으로 보다
07	interpret	v. 해석하다, 이해하다	( ) the sentence	문장을 해석하다
08	imply	v. 암시하다, 넌지시 드러내다, 의미하다	( ) criticism	비난을 암시하다
09	incompetence	n. 무능	imply ( )	무능함을 암시하다
10	undermine	v. (~의 토대를) 손상시키다, 훼손하다	( ) the potential positive effects	잠재적인 긍정적 영향을 손상시키다
11	self-concept	n. 자아 개념, 자아상	one's ( ) rests on one's ability	자아 개념이 실력에 달려 있다
12	ego	n. 자아	a blow to one's ( )	자아에 대한 타격

➕ 본문 문장 속에서 단어들을 확인해 보세요.

According to the threat to self-esteem model, / help can be perceived as supportive and loving, / or it can be seen as threatening / if that help is interpreted / as implying incompetence.

자존감에 대한 위협 이론에 따르면, / 도움은 협력적이고 애정 있는 것으로 인식될 수도 있고, / 혹은 그것은 위협적으로 보여질 수 있다 / 만약 그 도움이 해석된다면 / 무능함을 암시하는 것으로.

문제를 풀기 전에 단어들을 **30초** 동안 다시 확인하세요.

01	blow	🖋 타격, 한방	receiving help could be a blow	도움을 받는 것이 타격이 될 수 있다
02	self-esteem		a blow to self-esteem	자존감에 대한 타격
03	examine		examine the possibility	가능성을 검토하다
04	threat		the threat to self-esteem	자존감에 대한 위협
05	perceive		perceive help as supportive and loving	도움을 협력적이고 애정 있는 것으로 여기다
06	threatening		see help as threatening	도움을 위협적인 것으로 보다
07	interpret		interpret the sentence	문장을 해석하다
08	imply		imply criticism	비난을 암시하다
09	incompetence		imply incompetence	무능함을 암시하다
10	undermine		undermine the potential positive effects	잠재적인 긍정적 영향을 손상시키다
11	self-concept		one's self-concept rests on one's ability	자아 개념이 실력에 달려 있다
12	ego		a blow to one's ego	자아에 대한 타격

➕ **본문 문장 속에서 단어의 의미를 우리말로 해석해 보세요.**

According to the threat to self-esteem model, / help can be perceived as supportive and loving, / or it can be seen as threatening / if that help is interpreted / as implying incompetence.

➡ ＿＿＿＿＿에 대한 ＿＿＿＿＿ 이론에 따르면, / 도움은 협력적이고 애정 있는 것으로 ＿＿＿＿＿ 수도 있고, / 혹은 그것은 ＿＿＿＿＿으로 보여질 수 있다 / 만약 그 도움이 ＿＿＿＿＿ 된다면 / ＿＿＿＿＿을 ＿＿＿＿＿하는 것으로.

STEP **2** • 수능 기출 제대로 풀기

B   다음 빈칸에 들어갈 말로 가장 적절한 것은?

There are several reasons why support may not be effective. One possible reason is that receiving help could be a blow to self-esteem. A recent study by Christopher Burke and Jessica Goren at Lehigh University examined this possibility. According to the threat to self-esteem model, help can be perceived as supportive and loving, or it can be seen as threatening if that help is interpreted as implying incompetence. According to Burke and Goren, support is especially likely to be seen as threatening if it is in an area that is self-relevant or self-defining — that is, in an area where your own success and achievement are especially important. Receiving help with a self-relevant task can _____, and this can undermine the potential positive effects of the help. For example, if your self-concept rests, in part, on your great cooking ability, it may be a blow to your ego when a friend helps you prepare a meal for guests because it suggests that you're not the master chef you thought you were.

① make you feel bad about yourself

② improve your ability to deal with challenges

③ be seen as a way of asking for another favor

④ trick you into thinking that you were successful

⑤ discourage the person trying to model your behavior

정답과 해설 p.28

01 There are several reasons / why support may not be effective. // One possible reason is
명사절 접속사(보어절 연결)　　　　관계부사절
/ that receiving help could be a blow to self-esteem.
　　　동명사 주어

02 A recent study by Christopher Burke and Jessica Goren at Lehigh University / examined
this possibility. // According to the threat to self-esteem model, / help can be perceived
　　　　　　　　　　　　　　　　　　　　　　　　A be perceived as B: A가 B로 인식되다
as supportive and loving, / or it can be seen as threatening / if that help is interpreted
　　　　　　　　　A be seen as B: A가 B로 보여지다　　　　　　A be interpreted as B: A가 B로 해석되다
as implying incompetence.

03 According to Burke and Goren, / support is especially likely to be seen as threatening /
if it is in an area / that is self-relevant or self-defining / — that is, in an area / where your
　　　　　　　주격 관계대명사절　　　　　　즉　　　　　　관계부사절
own success and achievement are especially important.

04 Receiving help with a self-relevant task / can make you feel bad about yourself, / and
동명사 주어　　　　　　　　　　　　5형식 동사　　목적격 보어(동사원형)
this can undermine the potential positive effects of the help.
　　　　　　　　　　　　　　　　　　　　목적어

05 For example, / if your self-concept rests, in part, on your great cooking ability, / it may
　　　　　　　　　　　　　　　삽입구
be a blow to your ego / when a friend helps you prepare a meal for guests / because it
　　　　　　　　　　　　　　　　5형식 동사+목적어+목적격 보어(동사원형)
suggests / that you're not the master chef / you thought you were.
　　　명사절 접속사　　　　　　관계대명사절(생략된 관계대명사 that이 were의 보어)

---

01 몇몇 이유들이 있다 / 왜 도움이 효과적이지 않을 수 있는지에 대한. // 한 가지 가능한 이유는 / 도움을 받는 것이 자존감에 타격a blow to self-esteem이 될 수 있다는 것이다.

02 Lehigh 대학의 Christopher Burke와 Jessica Goren에 의한 한 최근 연구는 / 이 가능성을 검토했다examine. // 자존감에 대한 위협threat 이론에 따르면, / 도움은 협력적이고 애정 있는 것으로 인식될perceived 수도 있고, / 혹은 그것은 위협적threatening으로 보여질 수 있다 / 만약 그 도움이 무능함을 암시하는imply incompetence 것으로 해석된다면interpreted.

03 Burke와 Goren에 따르면, / 도움은 특히 위협적인 것으로 보여질 가능성이 있다 / 도움이 영역 안에 있을 경우 / 자기 연관적이거나 자기 정의적인 / 즉, 영역에 있을 경우 / 당신 자신의 성공과 성취가 특히 중요한 (영역).

04 자기 연관적인 일로 도움을 받는 것은 / 당신이 당신 자신에 대해 기분 나쁘게 느끼도록 만들 수 있고, / 이것은 도움의 잠재적인 긍정적 영향을 손상시킬undermine 수 있다.

05 예를 들어, / 만약 당신의 자아 개념self-concept이 어느 정도는 당신의 훌륭한 요리 실력에 달려 있다면, / 당신의 자아ego에 타격이 될 수 있다 / 친구가 당신이 손님들을 위해 식사를 준비하는 것을 도울 때 / 왜냐하면 이는 암시하기 때문이다 / 당신이 유능한 요리사가 아니라는 점을 / 당신 자신이 그렇다고 생각했던 (요리사).

구문 Check up

① One possible reason is that receive / receiving help could be a blow to self-esteem.

명사절(that절)의 주어로 기능해야 하므로 동명사 receiving을 쓴다.

② Receiving help with a self-relevant task can make you feel / to feel bad about yourself.

5형식 사역 동사 make의 목적격 보어 자리에는 동사원형을 써야 하므로 feel이 적절하다.

정답 ① receiving ② feel

C
STEP 1 • 수능에 *진짜* 나오는 *단어*

✔ 문제에 나오는 단어들을 확인하세요.

시간이 없다면 색으로 표시된 단어만이라도 꼭 외우고 넘어가세요!

01	self-handicap	v. 자기불구화하다(실패의 구실을 만들고자 최선을 다하지 않음)	overcome (✔ self-handicap)ping	자기불구화를 극복하다
02	engage in	~에 관여하다	( ) ( ) behaviour	행동에 관여하다
03	chance	n. 가능성	( )s of succeeding	성공의 가능성
04	intentionally	ad. 의도적으로	( ) harm the chances	가능성을 의도적으로 해치다
05	decent	a. 적당한	a ( ) time	적당한 시간
06	conclude	v. 결론을 내리다	( ) about oneself	자기자신에 대해 결론 내리다
07	blow	n. 타격, 세게 때림	a pretty hard ( )	꽤 강한 타격
08	self-esteem	n. 자존감	your ( )	당신의 자존감
09	be bound to	~할 수밖에 없다	( ) ( ) ( ) get a C	C를 받을 수밖에 없다
10	paradox	n. 역설	seem like a ( )	역설처럼 보이다
11	deliberately	ad. 의도적으로, 신중하게	( ) harm the chances	가능성을 의도적으로 해치다

⊕ 본문 문장 속에서 단어들을 확인해 보세요.

Self-handicapping **seems like a** paradox, / **because people are** deliberately **harming** / **their** chances **of success.**

자기불구화 현상은 역설처럼 보인다 / 사람들이 의도적으로 해치고 있기 때문에 / 성공의 가능성을.

문제를 풀기 전에 단어들을 **30초** 동안 다시 확인하세요.

01	self-handicap	🖊 자기불구화하다	overcome self-handicapping	자기불구화를 극복하다
02	engage in		engage in behaviour	행동에 관여하다
03	chance		chances of succeeding	성공의 가능성
04	intentionally		intentionally harm the chances	가능성을 의도적으로 해치다
05	decent		a decent time	적당한 시간
06	conclude		conclude about oneself	자신에 대해 결론 내리다
07	blow		a pretty hard blow	꽤 강한 타격
08	self-esteem		your self-esteem	당신의 자존감
09	be bound to		be bound to get a C	C를 받을 수밖에 없다
10	paradox		seem like a paradox	역설처럼 보이다
11	deliberately		deliberately harm the chances	가능성을 의도적으로 해치다

➕ 본문 문장 속에서 단어의 의미를 우리말로 해석해 보세요.

Self-handicapping seems like a paradox, / because people are deliberately harming / their chances of success.

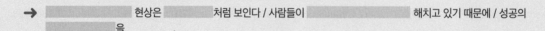

➡ ▇▇▇▇▇ 현상은 ▇▇▇▇ 처럼 보인다 / 사람들이 ▇▇▇▇▇▇▇ 해치고 있기 때문에 / 성공의 ▇▇▇▇▇ 을.

218

STEP 2 · 수능 기출 제대로 풀기

C 다음 빈칸에 들어갈 말로 가장 적절한 것은?

When self-handicapping, you're engaging in behaviour that you know will harm your chances of succeeding: you know that you won't do as well on the test if you go out the night before, but you do it anyway. Why would anyone intentionally harm their chances of success? Well, here's a possible answer. Say that you do study hard. You go to bed at a decent time and get eight hours of sleep. Then you take the maths test, but don't do well: you only get a C. What can you conclude about yourself? Probably that you're just not good at maths, which is a pretty hard blow to your self-esteem. But if you self-handicap, you'll never be in this position because _____. You were bound to get a C, you can tell yourself, because you went out till 1 a.m. That C doesn't mean that you're bad at maths; it just means that you like to party. Self-handicapping seems like a paradox, because people are deliberately harming their chances of success.

① getting some rest from studying is necessary

② failure serves as the foundation for success

③ you're creating a reason for your failure

④ studying is not about winning or losing

⑤ you have already achieved a lot

정답과 해설 p.29

01 When self-handicapping, / you're engaging in behaviour / **주격 관계대명사절** [that you know will harm
접속사가 있는 분사구문 your chances of succeeding]: // you know / that you won't do as well on the test / **삽입구문** if you
go out the night before, / but you do it anyway.
명사절 접속사
= go out the night before

02 Why would anyone intentionally harm their chances of success? // Well, here's a
possible answer.

03 **명사절 접속사** Say / that you do study hard. // You go to bed at a decent time / and get eight hours of
sleep. // Then you take the maths test, / but don't do well: / you only get a C.
동사 강조 **콜론: 구체적 설명**

04 What can you conclude about yourself? // Probably that you're just not good at maths,
명사절 접속사 (앞 문장 conclude의 목적어)
/ which is a pretty hard blow / to your self-esteem.
계속적 용법의 관계대명사(= and it)

05 But / if you self-handicap, / you'll never be in this position / because you're creating a
reason for your failure.

06 You were bound to get a C, / you can tell yourself, / because you went out till 1 a.m. //
That C doesn't mean that you're bad at maths; // it just means that you like to party.
명사절 접속사 **세미콜론: 문장과 문장 연결** **명사절 접속사**

07 Self-handicapping seems like a paradox, / because people are deliberately harming
their chances of success.
부사(동사 수식)

01 자기불구화할self-handicap 때, / 당신은 행동에 관여하고 있다engage in / 성공의 가능성chances of succeeding을
해칠 것으로 당신이 아는 (행동). // 당신은 알고 있지만 / 그만큼 시험을 잘 치지 못할 것이라는 것을 / 전날 밤에 밖에
나가면, / 어쨌든 당신은 그것을 한다.

02 어떤 사람이 왜 의도적으로intentionally 성공의 가능성을 해치겠는가? // 자, 여기에 가능한 답이 있다.

03 말해 보자 / 당신이 공부를 열심히 한다고. // 당신은 적당한decent 시간에 잠자리에 들고 / 8시간 동안 잠을 잔다. //
그러고 나서 당신은 수학 시험에 응시하지만, / 잘 치지 못한다. / 당신은 겨우 C를 받는다.

04 당신은 자신에 대해 어떤 결론을 내릴conclude 수 있는가? // 아마도 당신은 단지 수학을 잘하지 못해서라고 (결론을 내릴
수 있다), / 그리고 그것은 꽤 강한 타격a pretty hard blow이다 / 당신의 자존감self-esteem에.

05 하지만 / 만약 당신이 자기불구화한다면, / 당신은 결코 이런 상황에 처하지 않을 것이다 / 당신이 실패에 대한 이유를
만들기 때문에.

06 당신이 C를 받을 수밖에 없었다고be bound to, / 당신은 스스로에게 말할 수 있다 / 당신이 새벽 1시까지 밖에 나가 있었기
때문에. // 그 C는 당신이 수학을 못한다는 것을 의미하지는 않는다. // 그것은 단지 당신이 파티하는 것을 좋아한다는 것을
의미한다.

07 자기불구화 현상은 역설paradox처럼 보인다 / 사람들이 의도적으로deliberately 성공의 가능성을 해치고 있기 때문에.

구문 Check up

① When self-handicapping, you're engaging in behaviour
what / that you know will harm your chances of
succeeding.

behaviour를 선행사로 하는 주격 관계대명사절이므로, that이 적절하다.

② Self-handicapping seems like a paradox, because
people are deliberate / deliberately harming their
chances of success.

are ~ harming이라는 현재진행시제 동사를 꾸미도록 부사 deliberately
를 쓴다.

D

STEP 1 • 수능에 진짜 나오는 단어

✔ 문제에 나오는 단어들을 확인하세요.

시간이 없다면 색으로 표시된 단어만이라도 꼭 외우고 넘어가세요!

01	genetics	n. 유전학	the growing field of (✔ genetics)	성장하는 유전학 분야
02	suspect	v. 의심하다, 짐작하다	( ) that it is false	그것이 가짜라고 의심하다
03	gene	n. 유전자	the same ( )s	동일한 유전자
04	obey	v. 복종하다	( ) the law	법을 지키다
05	identical	a. 일란성의, 동일한	( ) twins	일란성 쌍둥이
06	instruct	v. 명령하다, 지시하다	a specific gene ( )s one twin	특정 유전자가 한 쌍둥이에게 명령하다
07	initiate	v. 일으키다, 시작하다	( ) the disease	병을 일으키다
08	turn off	~을 끄다	( ) ( ) the cancer gene	암 유전자를 꺼버리다
09	toxin	n. 독소	chemical ( )s	화학적 독소
10	contribute to	~의 원인이 되다, ~에 기여하다	( ) ( ) cancer	암의 원인이 되다
11	relatively	ad. 비교적, 상대적으로	( ) new	상대적으로 새로운
12	preference	n. 선호(도)	( ) for food	음식 선호도
13	fatal	a. 치명적인	( ) diseases	치명적인 병
14	genetic blueprint	유전자 청사진, 게놈 지도	influence the ( ) ( )	게놈 지도에 영향을 주다

⊕ 본문 문장 속에서 단어들을 확인해 보세요.

A specific gene instructed one twin / to develop cancer, / but in the other / the same gene did not initiate the disease.

특정 유전자가 쌍둥이 중 한 명에게 명령했다 / 암에 걸리도록 / 하지만 나머지 한 명에서는 / 똑같은 유전자가 그 질병을 일으키지 않았다.

01	genetics	🖉 유전학	the growing field of genetics	성장하는 유전학 분야
02	suspect		suspect that it is false	그것이 가짜라고 의심하다
03	gene		the same genes	동일한 유전자
04	obey		obey the law	법을 지키다
05	identical		identical twins	일란성 쌍둥이
06	instruct		a specific gene instructs one twin	특정 유전자가 한 쌍둥이에게 명령하다
07	initiate		initiate the disease	병을 일으키다
08	turn off		turn off the cancer gene	암 유전자를 꺼버리다
09	toxin		chemical toxins	화학적 독소
10	contribute to		contribute to cancer	암의 원인이 되다
11	relatively		relatively new	상대적으로 새로운
12	preference		preference for food	음식 선호도
13	fatal		fatal diseases	치명적인 병
14	genetic blueprint		influence the genetic blueprint	게놈 지도에 영향을 주다

➕ 본문 문장 속에서 단어의 의미를 우리말로 해석해 보세요.

A specific gene instructed one twin / to develop cancer, / but in the other / the same gene did not initiate the disease.

→ 특정   가 쌍둥이 중 한 명에게   / 암에 걸리도록 / 하지만 나머지 한 명에서는 / 똑같은 유전자가 그 질병을   않았다.

STEP **2** • 수능 기출 제대로 풀기

D 다음 빈칸에 들어갈 말로 가장 적절한 것은?

The growing field of genetics is showing us what many scientists have suspected for years — _____ . This information helps us better understand that genes are under our control and not something we must obey. Consider identical twins; both individuals are given the same genes. In mid-life, one twin develops cancer, and the other lives a long healthy life without cancer. A specific gene instructed one twin to develop cancer, but in the other the same gene did not initiate the disease. One possibility is that the healthy twin had a diet that turned off the cancer gene — the same gene that instructed the other person to get sick. For many years, scientists have recognized other environmental factors, such as chemical toxins (tobacco for example), can contribute to cancer through their actions on genes. The notion that food has a specific influence on gene expression is relatively new.

① identical twins have the same genetic makeup

② our preference for food is influenced by genes

③ balanced diet is essential for our mental health

④ genetic engineering can cure some fatal diseases

⑤ foods can immediately influence the genetic blueprint

정답과 해설 p.29

01 The growing field of genetics is showing us / what many scientists have suspected for
show+간접목적어+직접목적어(관계대명사 what절)
years / — foods can immediately influence the genetic blueprint.

02 This information helps us better understand / that genes are under our control / and
help+목적어+목적격 보어(동사원형)   명사절 접속사
not something we must obey.
목적격 관계대명사절

03 Consider identical twins; / both individuals are given the same genes. // In mid-life, /
be given+목적어: ~을 받다
one twin develops cancer, / and the other lives a long healthy life / without cancer.
부정대명사(나머지 하나)

04 A specific gene instructed one twin / to develop cancer, / but in the other / the same
instruct+목적어+목적격 보어(to부정사)
gene did not initiate the disease.

05 One possibility is / that the healthy twin had a diet / that turned off the cancer gene /
명사절 접속사(보어)   주격 관계대명사절
— the same gene that instructed the other person to get sick.
주격 관계대명사절
명사절 접속사 that 생략

06 For many years, / scientists have recognized / other environmental factors, such as
~와 같은
chemical toxins (tobacco for example), / can contribute to cancer / through their
actions on genes.

07 The notion [that food has a specific influence on gene expression] / is relatively new.
주어   동격절(The notion 부가 설명)   동사

01 성장하고 있는 유전학 분야the growing field of genetics는 우리에게 보여 주고 있다 / 많은 과학자가 여러 해 동안
짐작해왔던suspect 것을 / 즉, 식품이 유전자 청사진the genetic blueprint에 직접 영향을 줄 수 있다는 것을.

02 이 정보는 우리가 더 잘 이해하도록 도와준다 / 유전자gene가 우리의 통제 하에 있는 것이지 / 우리가 복종해야obey 하는
것이 아니라는 것을.

03 일란성 쌍둥이identical twins를 생각해 보자. / 두 사람은 모두 똑같은 유전자를 부여 받는다. // 중년에, / 쌍둥이 중 한
명은 암에 걸리고, / 다른 한 명은 건강하게 오래 산다 / 암 없이.

04 특정 유전자가 쌍둥이 중 한 명에게 명령했다instruct / 암에 걸리도록 / 하지만 나머지 한 명에서는 / 똑같은 유전자가 그
질병을 일으키지initiate the disease 않았다.

05 한 가지 가능성은 / 쌍둥이 중 건강한 사람이 식사를 했다는 것이다 / 암 유전자를 꺼버리는turn off the cancer gene / 즉
나머지 한 명이 병에 걸리도록 명령했던 그 똑같은 유전자를.

06 여러 해 동안 / 과학자들은 인정해 왔다 / 화학적 독소chemical toxins(예를 들어 담배)와 같은 다른 환경적 요인들이 /
암의 원인이 될 수 있다는contribute to cancer 것을 / 유전자에 작용하여.

07 음식이 유전자 발현에 특정한 영향을 미친다는 생각은 / 비교적 새로운relatively new 것이다.

구문 Check up

① The growing field of genetics is showing us that /
  what many scientists have suspected for years.

동사 show의 직접목적어 자리에 명사가 와야 하고, 뒤에 불완전한 문장
이 오므로 선행사를 포함하는 관계대명사 what을 써야 한다.

② In mid-life, one twin develops cancer, and others / the
  other lives a long healthy life without cancer.

문맥상 쌍둥이 중 나머지 한 명이므로 the other가 적절하다.

정답 ① what ② the other

STEP 1 • 수능에 *진짜* 나오는 *단어*

✔ **문제에 나오는 단어들을 확인하세요.**

시간이 없다면 색으로 표시된 단어만이라도 꼭 외우고 넘어가세요!

01	pharmaceutical	a. 제약의	the (✔ pharmaceutical) giant		거대 제약회사
02	executive	n. 간부	highly motivated ( )s		매우 동기부여된 간부들
03	take a role	역할을 하다	( ) ( ) more active ( )		더 적극적인 역할을 하다
04	innovation	n. 혁신	lead ( )		혁신을 이끌다
05	radical	a. 급진적인	do something ( )		급진적인 것을 하다
06	generate	v. 만들다, 생성하다	( ) ideas		생각을 만들다
07	competitor	n. 경쟁자	a top ( )		주요 경쟁자
08	soar	v. 치솟다	Energy ( )s.		에너지가 치솟다.
09	crush	v. 짓밟다, 깨부수다	( ) a top competitor		주요 경쟁자를 짓밟다
10	reverse	v. 반대로 하다	( ) their roles		그들의 역할을 반대로 하다
11	threat	n. 위협	defend against ( )s		위협에 방어하다
12	urgency	n. 다급함	the ( ) of innovation		혁신의 다급함
13	apparent	a. 명확한	The urgency of innovation was ( ).		혁신의 다급함이 명확해졌다.
14	irrational	a. 비이성적인	( ) practice		비이성적인 실행
15	in terms of	~의 관점에서	( ) ( ) ( ) losses		손실의 관점에서

➕ **본문 문장 속에서 단어들을 확인해 보세요.**

At the pharmaceutical giant Merck, / CEO Kenneth Frazier decided to motivate his executives / to take a more active role / in leading innovation and change.

거대 제약회사인 Merck에서 / CEO인 Kenneth Frazier는 그의 간부들에게 동기를 부여하기로 결심하였다 / 더 적극적인 역할을 하도록 / 혁신과 변화를 이끄는 데.

No.	단어		예문	뜻
01	pharmaceutical	제약의	the pharmaceutical giant	거대 제약회사
02	executive		highly motivated executives	매우 동기부여된 간부들
03	take a role		take a more active role	더 적극적인 역할을 하다
04	innovation		lead innovation	혁신을 이끌다
05	radical		do something radical	급진적인 것을 하다
06	generate		generate ideas	생각을 만들다
07	competitor		a top competitor	주요 경쟁자
08	soar		Energy soars.	에너지가 치솟다.
09	crush		crush a top competitor	주요 경쟁자를 짓밟다
10	reverse		reverse their roles	그들의 역할을 반대로 하다
11	threat		defend against threats	위협에 방어하다
12	urgency		the urgency of innovation	혁신의 다급함
13	apparent		The urgency of innovation was apparent.	혁신의 다급함이 명확해졌다.
14	irrational		irrational practice	비이성적인 실행
15	in terms of		in terms of losses	손실의 관점에서

⊕ **본문 문장 속에서 단어의 의미를 우리말로 해석해 보세요.**

At the pharmaceutical giant Merck, / CEO Kenneth Frazier decided to motivate his executives / to take a more active role / in leading innovation and change.

→ 거대 _____ 회사인 Merck에서 / CEO인 Kenneth Frazier는 그의 _____ 에게 동기를 부여하기로 결심하였다 / _____ / _____ 과 변화를 이끄는 데.

STEP 2 • 수능 기출 제대로 풀기

E

다음 빈칸에 들어갈 말로 가장 적절한 것은?

At the pharmaceutical giant Merck, CEO Kenneth Frazier decided to motivate his executives to take a more active role in leading innovation and change. He asked them to do something radical: generate ideas that would put Merck out of business. For the next two hours, the executives worked in groups, pretending to be one of Merck's top competitors. Energy soared as they developed ideas for drugs that would crush theirs and key markets they had missed. Then, their challenge was to reverse their roles and figure out how to defend against these threats. This "kill the company" exercise is powerful because _____. When deliberating about innovation opportunities, the leaders weren't inclined to take risks. When they considered how their competitors could put them out of business, they realized that it was a risk not to innovate. The urgency of innovation was apparent.

*crush: 짓밟다
**deliberate: 심사숙고하다

① the unknown is more helpful than the negative

② it highlights the progress they've already made

③ it is not irrational but is consumer-based practice

④ it reframes a gain-framed activity in terms of losses

⑤ they discuss how well it fits their profit-sharing plans

정답과 해설 p.29

01 At the pharmaceutical giant Merck, / CEO Kenneth Frazier decided to <u>motivate</u>
<u>his executives</u> / to take a more active role / in leading innovation and change.
motivate+목적어+목적격 보어(to부정사)

02 He asked them to do something radical: / generate ideas that would put Merck out of
ask+목적어+목적격 보어(to부정사)   주격 관계대명사절
business. // For the next two hours, / the executives worked in groups, / <u>pretending to</u>
<u>be one of Merck's top competitors.</u>   분사구문: ~하면서

03 Energy soared / as they developed ideas / for drugs that would crush theirs / and key
                                                              주격 관계대명사절
markets they had missed.
         목적격 관계대명사절

04 Then, / their challenge was to reverse their roles / and figure out how to defend against
                          to부정사 병렬연결(주격보어)
these threats. // This "kill the company" exercise is powerful / because it reframes a
gain-framed activity / in terms of losses.

05 When deliberating about innovation opportunities, / the leaders weren't inclined to
접속사가 있는 분사구문
take risks.

06 When they considered / how their competitors could put them out of business, / they
                                      의문사절
realized / that it was a risk not to innovate. // The urgency of innovation was apparent.
         가주어   진주어(to부정사)

01 거대 제약회사the pharmaceutical giant인 Merck에서 / CEO인 Kenneth Frazier는 간부들에게 동기를 부여하기로 motivate executives 결심하였다 / 보다 적극적인 역할을 취하도록take a more active role / 혁신innovation과 변화를 이끄는 데.

02 그는 그들이 급진적인 것을 하도록do something radical 요청하였다 / Merck를 사업에서 몰아낼 수도 있는 아이디어들을 만들어내라generate ideas. // 다음 두 시간 동안 / 회사 간부들은 그룹으로 작업을 하였다 / Merck의 주요 경쟁사competitor 가운데 하나인 체하면서.

03 에너지가 치솟았다soar / 그들이 아이디어를 만들어내는 동안 / 그들의 약을 짓밟을crush 만한 약에 대한 / 그리고 그들이 놓쳤던 주요 시장(에 대한).

04 그리고 나서, / 그들의 과제는 그들의 역할을 반대로 하는 것이었다reverse their roles / 그리고 이러한 위험을 어떻게 방어할defend against threats 수 있는지를 알아내는 것. // 이러한 "회사 무너뜨리기" 활동은 강력하다 / 수익에 맞춰 구조화된 활동을 재구조화하기 때문에 / 손실의 관점으로.

05 혁신 기회에 대해 심사숙고할 때, / 리더들은 위험을 무릅쓰지 않는 경향이 있었다.

06 그들이 고려했을 때 / 경쟁자들이 그들을 어떻게 사업에서 몰아낼 수 있을지를, / 그들은 깨달았다 / 혁신하지 않는 것이 위험한 것이라는 것을. // 혁신의 다급함urgency이 명확해졌다apparent.

① The executives worked in groups, pretend / pretending to be one of Merck's top competitors.

앞 문장과 연결하는 접속사와 주어가 없기 때문에 분사구문이 와야 한다. 따라서 pretending이 정답이다.

② When deliberating about innovation opportunities, the leaders weren't inclined taking / to take risks.

be inclined to는 '~하는 경향이 있다'라는 뜻으로 to take가 적절하다.

F

STEP 1 • 수능에 *진짜* 나오는 *단어*

✔ 문제에 나오는 단어들을 확인하세요.

시간이 없다면 색으로 표시된 단어만이라도 꼭 외우고 넘어가세요!

01	advise	v. 충고하다, 조언하다	(✔ advise) your kids	아이들에게 조언하다
02	expand	v. 확장하다	( ) your network of friends	친구의 범위를 확장하다
03	potential	a. 잠재적인	( ) business partners	잠재적인 사업 파트너
04	process	n. 과정, 절차	throughout this ( )	이 과정 내내
05	benefit	n. 이익	social ( )	사회적 이익
06	retired	a. 은퇴한	a ( ) FBI profiler	은퇴한 FBI 프로파일러
07	emphasize	v. 강조하다	( ) the need	필요성을 강조하다
08	assume	v. 가정하다, 추정하다	safe to ( )	가정하기에 안전한
09	polite	a. 공손한	be ( )	공손하다
10	criminal	n. 범죄자	deal with a ( )	범죄자를 다루다
11	manipulation	n. 조작, 속임수	result ( )	결과 조작
12	deceit	n. 사기, 기만	the art of ( )	사기의 기술
13	superficial	a. 표면적인, 피상적인	a person's ( ) qualities	사람의 피상적인 특성

✚ 본문 문장 속에서 단어들을 확인해 보세요.

After all, / you expand your network of friends / and create potential business partners / by meeting strangers.

결국, / 당신은 친구의 범위를 확장하고 / 잠재적인 사업 파트너를 만든다 / 낯선 사람들을 만남으로써.

문제를 풀기 전에 단어들을 **30초** 동안 다시 확인하세요.

01	advise	충고하다, 조언하다	advise your kids	아이들에게 조언하다
02	expand		expand your network of friends	친구의 범위를 확장하다
03	potential		potential business partners	잠재적인 사업 파트너
04	process		throughout this process	이 과정 내내
05	benefit		social benefit	사회적 이익
06	retired		a retired FBI profiler	은퇴한 FBI 프로파일러
07	emphasize		emphasize the need	필요성을 강조하다
08	assume		safe to assume	가정하기에 안전한
09	polite		be polite	공손하다
10	criminal		deal with a criminal	범죄자를 다루다
11	manipulation		result manipulation	결과 조작
12	deceit		the art of deceit	사기의 기술
13	superficial		a person's superficial qualities	사람의 피상적인 특성

➕ 본문 문장 속에서 단어의 의미를 우리말로 해석해 보세요.

After all, / you expand your network of friends / and create potential business partners / by meeting strangers.

→ 결국, / 당신은 친구의 범위를 ⬚⬚⬚⬚⬚⬚⬚⬚⬚ / ⬚⬚⬚⬚⬚⬚⬚⬚⬚ 사업 파트너를 만든다 / 낯선 사람들을 만남으로써.

STEP **2** · 수능 기출 제대로 풀기

F 다음 빈칸에 들어갈 말로 가장 적절한 것은?

Do you advise your kids to keep away from strangers? That's a tall order for adults. After all, you expand your network of friends and create potential business partners by meeting strangers. Throughout this process, however, analyzing people to understand their personalities is not all about potential economic or social benefit. There is your safety to think about, as well as the safety of your loved ones. For that reason, Mary Ellen O'Toole, who is a retired FBI profiler, emphasizes the need to _____ in order to understand them. It is not safe, for instance, to assume that a stranger is a good neighbor, just because they're polite. Seeing them follow a routine of going out every morning well-dressed doesn't mean that's the whole story. In fact, O'Toole says that when you are dealing with a criminal, even your feelings may fail you. That's because criminals have perfected the art of manipulation and deceit.

*tall order: 무리한 요구

① narrow down your network in social media

② go beyond a person's superficial qualities

③ focus on intelligence rather than wealth

④ trust your first impressions of others

⑤ take advantage of criminals

정답과 해설 p.30

01 Do you advise your kids / to keep away from strangers? // That's a tall order for adults.
advise+목적어+목적격 보어(to부정사)
// After all, / you expand your network of friends / and create potential business
partners / by meeting strangers.
by+-ing: ~함으로써

02 Throughout this process, / however, / [analyzing people to understand their
동명사 주어(단수 취급)   to부정사의 부사적 용법(목적)
personalities] / is not all about potential economic or social benefit. // There is your
동사 부분 부정
safety to think about, / as well as the safety of your loved ones.
to부정사의 형용사적 용법

03 For that reason, / Mary Ellen O'Toole, who is a retired FBI profiler, / emphasizes the
need / to go beyond a person's superficial qualities / in order to understand them. // It
형용사적 용법   ~하기 위해서(목적)   가주어
is not safe, / for instance, / [to assume that a stranger is a good neighbor, / just because
진주어   명사절 접속사(assume의 목적어)
they're polite].

04 [Seeing them follow a routine of going out every morning well-dressed] / doesn't mean
동명사 주어(단수 취급)
지각동사(see)+목적어+목적격 보어(동사원형)   동사(수 일치)
that's the whole story.

05 In fact, / O'Toole says / that when you are dealing with a criminal, / even your feelings
명사절 접속사
may fail you. // That's because criminals have perfected the art of manipulation and
이것은 ~ 때문이다(뒤에 원인)
deceit.

01 당신은 당신의 아이들에게 조언하는가advise / 낯선 사람을 멀리 하라고? // 그것은 어른들에게는 무리한 요구이다.
// 결국, / 당신은 당신의 친구의 범위를 확장하고expand / 잠재적인potential 사업 파트너를 만든다 / 낯선 사람들을
만남으로써.

02 이 과정process에서, / 그러나 / 그들의 성격을 이해하기 위해 사람들을 분석하는 것은 / 잠재적인 경제적 또는 사회적
이익benefit에 대한 것만은 아니다. // 당신의 안전도 생각해봐야 한다 / 당신이 사랑하는 사람들의 안전뿐 아니라.

03 그런 이유로, / 은퇴한retired FBI 프로파일러인 Mary Ellen O'Toole은 / 필요성을 강조한다emphasize / 사람의
피상적인superficial 특성을 넘어설 / 그들을 이해하기 위해. // 안전하지 않다 / 예를 들어, / 낯선 이가 좋은 이웃이라고
가정하는assume 것은 / 단지 그들이 공손하다polite는 이유로.

04 매일 아침 잘 차려 입고 외출하는 그들을 보는 것이 / 그것이 전부임을 의미하지는 않는다.

05 사실, / O'Toole은 말한다 / 당신이 범죄자criminal를 다룰 때, / 심지어 당신의 느낌도 당신을 틀리게 할 수 있다고. //
그것은 왜냐하면 범죄자들이 조작manipulation과 사기deceit의 기술에 통달했기 때문이다.

① It / That is not safe, for instance, to assume that a stranger is a good neighbor, just because they're polite.

to부정사구(to assume)가 진주어로 쓰인 <가주어-진주어> 구문이므로 가주어 It을 쓴다.

② Seeing them follow / to follow a routine of going out every morning well-dressed doesn't mean that's the whole story.

지각동사(see)의 목적격 보어는 목적어와 목적격 보어가 능동 관계일 때 동사원형 또는 현재분사 형태만 가능하므로 follow가 정답이다.

정답 ① It ② follow

✔ 문제에 나오는 단어들을 확인하세요.

시간이 없다면 색으로 표시된 단어만이라도 꼭 외우고 넘어가세요!

01	region	n. 지역	a desert (✔ region)	사막 지역
02	grow	v. 재배하다	( ) green vegetables	녹색 채소를 재배하다
03	packed with	~로 가득한	be ( ) ( ) books	책으로 가득하다
04	vital	a. 필수적인	a ( ) role	필수적인 역할
05	nutrient	n. 영양분	vital ( )s	필수 영양분
06	raise	v. 기르다, 재배하다	( ) children	아이를 양육하다
07	crop	n. 곡물	raise ( )s	곡물을 재배하다
08	exposure	n. 노출, (영향을) 받음	no ( ) to nutrition advice	영양과 관련된 조언을 접하지 못함
09	sufficient	a. 충분한	( ) protein	충분한 단백질
10	deficiency	n. 결핍	iron ( )	철분 결핍
11	diversify	v. 다양화하다	( ) diets	식단을 다양화하다
12	assistance	n. 지원, 원조	nutritional ( )	영양적인 지원

⊕ 본문 문장 속에서 단어들을 확인해 보세요.

In many regions of Central America, / native people can but do not grow green vegetables / packed with vital nutrients such as vitamin A.

중미의 많은 지역에서 / 토착민들은 할 수는 있지만 녹색 채소를 재배하지 않는다 / 비타민 A와 같은 필수 영양분이 가득한.

01	region	🖉 지역	a desert region	사막 지역
02	grow		grow green vegetables	녹색 채소를 재배하다
03	packed with		be packed with books	책으로 가득하다
04	vital		a vital role	필수적인 역할
05	nutrient		vital nutrients	필수 영양분
06	raise		raise children	아이를 양육하다
07	crop		raise crops	곡물을 재배하다
08	exposure		no exposure to nutrition advice	영양과 관련된 조언을 접하지 못함
09	sufficient		sufficient protein	충분한 단백질
10	deficiency		iron deficiency	철분 결핍
11	diversify		diversify diets	식단을 다양화하다
12	assistance		nutritional assistance	영양적인 지원

➕ **본문 문장 속에서 단어의 의미를 우리말로 해석해 보세요.**

In many regions of Central America, / native people can but do not grow green vegetables / packed with vital nutrients such as vitamin A.

→ 중미의 많은 _____ 에서 / 토착민들은 할 수 있지만 녹색 채소를 _____ 않는다 / 비타민 A와 같은 _____.

G 다음 빈칸에 들어갈 말로 가장 적절한 것은?

In many regions of Central America, native people can but do not grow green vegetables packed with vital nutrients such as vitamin A. Generally speaking, the people do not have a tradition of raising these crops. They often have limited education in general and almost no exposure to health and nutrition advice, and they grow what feeds the most people. They often have plenty of tortillas and beans, so they have sufficient protein, and they eat until full. Yet the lack of micronutrients leads to their children developing blindness, iron deficiency, and other growth disorders. In these situations, families have to be educated about nutrition, encouraged to diversify their diets, plant more green vegetables, and sometimes receive nutritional assistance to _____
_____.

*micronutrient: 미량 영양소

① eliminate obesity

② improve digestion

③ correct imbalances

④ consume more protein

⑤ preserve their tradition

정답과 해설 p.30

01   In many regions of Central America, / native people can but do not grow green
vegetables / packed with vital nutrients such as vitamin A.
         과거분사(명사 수식)

02   Generally speaking, / the people do not have a tradition of raising these crops.
   일반적으로 말해서

03   They often have limited education in general / and almost no exposure to health and
                목적어1   목적어2
nutrition advice, / and they grow what feeds the most people.
                          관계대명사 what절(grow의 목적어)

04   They often have plenty of tortillas and beans, / so they have sufficient protein, / and
                       they are 생략
they eat until full.

05   Yet / the lack of micronutrients / leads to their children / developing blindness, iron
                                 동명사의 의미상 주어   동명사(leads to의 목적어)
deficiency, and other growth disorders.

06   In these situations, / families have to be educated about nutrition, / encouraged to
                                조동사 수동태(~되어야 한다)   being 생략 분사구문
diversify their diets, / plant more green vegetables, / and sometimes receive nutritional
                               and로 연결되는 병렬구조(to부정사)
assistance] / to correct imbalances.
            to부정사의 부사적 용법(목적)

01   중미의 많은 지역region에서 / 토착민들은 녹색 채소를 재배할grow 수는 있지만, 재배하지 않는다 / 비타민 A와 같은 필수 영양분이 가득한packed with vital nutrients.

02   일반적으로 말해서, / 이 사람들은 이러한 곡물을 재배하는raise crops 전통을 가지고 있지 않다.

03   그들은 흔히 일반적으로 제한된 교육을 받고, / 건강이나 영양과 관련된 조언을 거의 접하지 못하며no exposure, / 최대한 많은 사람들을 먹일 수 있는 것을 재배한다.

04   그들은 흔히 많은 tortilla와 콩을 먹어서 / 충분한 단백질sufficient protein을 섭취하며 / 배부를 때까지 먹는다.

05   하지만 / 미량 영양소의 부족은 / 그들의 자녀에게 초래한다 / 실명, 철분 결핍iron deficiency, 그리고 다른 발육 장애의 발병을.

06   이러한 상황에서 / 가정은 영양에 대한 교육을 받아야 한다 / 식단을 다양화하고diversify, / 보다 많은 녹색 채소를 심고, / 때로는 영양적 지원nutritional assistance을 받도록 권장받으며 / 불균형을 바로잡기 위해.

구문 Check up

① They often have plenty of tortillas and beans, so they have sufficient protein, and they eat until   full / is full .

접속사 until 다음에 they are가 생략되고 보어가 바로 이어지는 구조이다. 따라서 full이 적절하다.

② Families have to be educated about nutrition, encouraged to diversify their diets, plant more green vegetables, and sometimes   receive / received   nutritional assistance.

(being) encouraged의 보어인 to부정사를 병렬 연결하고 있으므로 to가 생략된 receive를 쓴다.

정답 ① full ② receive

문제에 나오는 단어들을 확인하세요.

시간이 없다면 색으로 표시된 단어만이라도 꼭 외우고 넘어가세요!

01	rebel	*n.* 반항아, 반대자 *v.* 반항[저항]하다	the (✓ rebel) of the family	집안의 반항아
02	turn A off from B	A가 B에 흥미를 잃게 하다	( ) some people ( ) ( ) an idea	일부 사람들이 어떤 생각에 흥미를 잃게 하다
03	**alternative**	*n.* 대안	look for ( )s	대안을 찾다
04	reject	*v.* 거부하다	strongly ( ) popular opinion	대중적인 의견에 강하게 반대하다
05	in favor of	~을 위해, ~을 지지하여	( ) ( ) ( ) maintaining your uniqueness	여러분의 고유성을 지키기 위해
06	**independence**	*n.* 독립(성)	achieve ( )	독립을 이루다
07	majority	*n.* 대다수	present the ( ) option	대다수의 선택을 제시하다
08	trick	*v.* 속이다	be ( )ed into believing a lie	속아서 거짓말을 믿다
09	suit	*v.* ~에 맞다	( ) the purpose	목적에 맞다
10	**mainstream**	*n.* 주류, 대세	outside the ( )	주류가 아닌
11	loyalty	*n.* 충성도	a strong brand ( )	강력한 브랜드 충성도
12	reversal	*n.* 반전	a ( ) of the situation	상황의 반전
13	conformity	*n.* 순응	( ) to the rules	규칙에 대한 순응

➕ 본문 문장 속에서 단어들을 확인해 보세요.

Saying, "Everyone is doing it" / may turn some people off from an idea.

"모두가 그렇게 하고 있다."라고 말하는 것은 / 일부 사람들이 어떤 생각에 흥미를 잃게 할지도 모른다.

01	rebel	✎ 반항아, 반대자 반항[저항]하다	the rebel of the family	집안의 반항아
02	turn A off from B		turn some people off from an idea	일부 사람들이 어떤 생각에 흥미를 잃게 하다
03	alternative		look for alternatives	대안을 찾다
04	reject		strongly reject popular opinion	대중적인 의견에 강하게 반대하다
05	in favor of		in favor of maintaining your uniqueness	여러분의 고유성을 지키기 위해
06	independence		achieve independence	독립을 이루다
07	majority		present the majority option	대다수의 선택을 제시하다
08	trick		be tricked into believing a lie	속아서 거짓말을 믿다
09	suit		suit the purpose	목적에 맞다
10	mainstream		outside the mainstream	주류가 아닌
11	loyalty		a strong brand loyalty	강력한 브랜드 충성도
12	reversal		a reversal of the situation	상황의 반전
13	conformity		conformity to the rules	규칙에 대한 순응

⊕ 본문 문장 속에서 단어의 의미를 우리말로 해석해 보세요.

Saying, "Everyone is doing it" / may turn some people off from an idea.

➡ "모두가 그렇게 하고 있다."라고 말하는 것은 / ▇▇▇▇▇▇▇▇▇▇ 지도 모른다.

STEP **2** • 수능 기출 제대로 풀기

A 다음 빈칸에 들어갈 말로 가장 적절한 것은?

Rebels may think they're rebels, but clever marketers influence them just like the rest of us. Saying, "Everyone is doing it" may turn some people off from an idea. These people will look for alternatives, which (if cleverly planned) can be exactly what a marketer or persuader wants you to believe. If I want you to consider an idea, and know you strongly reject popular opinion in favor of maintaining your independence and uniqueness, I would present the majority option first, which you would reject in favor of my actual preference. We are often tricked when we try to maintain a position of defiance. People use this _____ to make us "independently" choose an option which suits their purposes. Some brands have taken full effect of our defiance towards the mainstream and positioned themselves as rebels; which has created even stronger brand loyalty.

*defiance: 반항

① reversal

② imitation

③ repetition

④ conformity

⑤ collaboration

정답과 해설 p.32

01 **접속사 that 생략**
Rebels may think they're rebels, / but clever marketers influence them just like the rest
마치 ~처럼
of us.

02 Saying, "Everyone is doing it" / may turn some people off from an idea. // These people
주어(동명사구)   타동사+목적어+부사
will look for alternatives, / which (if cleverly planned) can be / exactly [what a marketer
선행사   삽입절(=if they are ~ planned)   명사절(can be의 보어)
or persuader wants you to believe].

03 If I want you to consider an idea, / and know you strongly reject popular opinion / in
            └------- 병렬 연결 -------┘
favor of maintaining your independence and uniqueness, / I would present the majority
                                                                            선행사
option first, / which you would reject in favor of my actual preference.
            계속적 용법(선행사 보충)

04 We are often tricked / when we try to maintain a position of defiance. // People use this
            사역동사+목적어+원형부정사
reversal / to make us "independently" choose an option / which suits their purposes.
        부사적 용법(목적)   주격 관계대명사절

05 Some brands have taken full effect of our defiance towards the mainstream / and
            └----- 병렬 연결 -----┘
positioned themselves as rebels; / which has created even stronger brand loyalty.
                                계속적 용법(세미콜론 앞 내용을 보충 설명)

01 반항자rebel들은 본인이 반항자라고 생각할지도 모르지만, / 영리한 마케터들은 나머지 우리에게 하는 것처럼 그들에게도
영향을 준다.

02 "모두가 그렇게 하고 있다."라고 말하는 것은 / 일부 사람들이 어떤 생각에 흥미를 잃게 할turn some people off from
an idea지도 모른다. // 이 사람들은 대안alternative을 찾을 것이고, / 그것은 (만약 영리하게 계획된다면) ~일 수 있다 /
정확히 마케터나 설득하는 사람이 여러분더러 믿기를 원하는 것.

03 만약 내가 여러분이 어떤 아이디어를 고려하길 바라는데, / 여러분이 대중적인 의견을 강하게 거부한다reject는 것을
안다면, / 자신의 독립성independence과 고유성을 지키기 위해in favor of / 나는 대다수majority가 선택하는 것을 먼저
제시할 것이고, / 여러분은 내 실제 선호에 맞게 그것을 거부할 것이다.

04 우리는 종종 속는다trick / 우리가 반항의 입장을 지키려 할 때. // 사람들은 이러한 반전reversal을 사용한다 / 우리가
선택지를 '독자적으로' 택하도록 만들기 위해 / 그들의 목적에 맞는suit.

05 일부 브랜드들은 주류mainstream에 대한 우리의 반항을 완전히 활용해 / 스스로를 반항자로 자리매김해 왔고, / 이는
훨씬 더 강력한 브랜드 충성도loyalty를 만들었다.

구문 Check up

① Say / Saying "Everyone is doing it" may turn some people off from an idea.

may turn 앞에 주어가 필요하므로 동명사 Saying을 쓴다.

② I would present the majority option first, what / which you would reject in favor of my actual preference.

선행사 the majority option을 보충 설명하는 관계대명사로 which가 적절하다. what은 선행사가 없을 때 쓴다.

정답 ① Saying ② which

240

B

STEP 1 • 수능에 *진짜* 나오는 *단어*

✔ 문제에 나오는 단어들을 확인하세요.

시간이 없다면 색으로 표시된 단어만이라도 꼭 외우고 넘어가세요!

01	define	v. 정의하다	(✔ define) the word	단어를 정의하다
02	position	n. 직책, 지위	hold a senior ( )	고위직에 있다
03	subordinate	n. 부하	the position as a ( )	부하로서의 지위
04	empower	v. ~에게 힘(권한, 능력)을 주다	( ) leaders	리더들에게 힘을 주다
05	analyst	n. 분석가	a leadership ( )	리더십 분석가
06	refer to A as B	A를 B라고 지칭하다, 부르다	( ) ( ) them ( ) "citizens"	그들을 '시민'이라고 부르다
07	constituent	n. 구성원(유권자), 구성 요소	have the full support of ( )s	유권자들의 전폭적 지지를 받다
08	wind up ~ing	결국 ~하게 되다	( ) ( ) be( ) a leader	결국 리더가 되다
09	objective	n. 목적, 목표	when ( )s change	목표가 바뀔 때
10	attend	v. 참석하다	( ) a concert	콘서트에 참석하다
11	formally	ad. 공식적으로	He is ( ) my boss.	그는 공식적으로 나의 상사이다.
12	regardless of	~와 관련 없이	( ) ( ) the fact	그 사실과는 관련 없이
13	rigid	a. 융통성 없는, 엄격한	a ( ) rule	엄중한 규칙
14	fluid	a. 유동적인, 가변적인	a ( ) relationship	유동적인 관계
15	apparent	a. 명백한	It is ( ).	이는 명백하다.

➕ 본문 문장 속에서 단어들을 확인해 보세요.

Followers can be defined / by their position as subordinates / or by their behavior of going along with leaders' wishes.

추종자는 정의될 수 있다 / 부하라는 직책에 의해 / 혹은 리더의 바람에 따르는 행동에 의해.

01	define	정의하다	define the word	단어를 정의하다
02	position		hold a senior position	고위직에 있다
03	subordinate		the position as a subordinate	부하로서의 지위
04	empower		empower leaders	리더들에게 힘을 주다
05	analyst		a leadership analyst	리더쉽 분석가
06	refer to A as B		refer to them as "citizens"	그들을 '시민'이라고 부르다
07	constituent		have the full support of constituents	유권자들의 전폭적 지지를 받다
08	wind up ~ing		wind up being a leader	결국 리더가 되다
09	objective		when objectives change	목표가 바뀔 때
10	attend		attend a concert	콘서트에 참석하다
11	formally		He is formally my boss.	그는 공식적으로 나의 상사이다.
12	regardless of		regardless of the fact	그 사실과는 관련 없이
13	rigid		a rigid rule	엄중한 규칙
14	fluid		a fluid relationship	유동적인 관계
15	apparent		It is apparent.	이는 명백하다.

➕ 본문 문장 속에서 단어의 의미를 우리말로 해석해 보세요.

Followers can be defined / by their position as subordinates / or by their behavior of going along with leaders' wishes.

➔ 추종자는 　　　　　　　 수 있다 / 　　　　　　　 라는 　　　　　　　 에 의해 / 혹은 리더의 바람에 따르는 행동에 의해.

STEP **2** • 수능 기출 제대로 풀기

B 다음 빈칸에 들어갈 말로 가장 적절한 것은?

Followers can be defined by their position as subordinates or by their behavior of going along with leaders' wishes. But followers also have power to lead. Followers empower leaders as well as vice versa. This has led some leadership analysts like Ronald Heifetz to avoid using the word *followers* and refer to the others in a power relationship as "citizens" or "constituents." Heifetz is correct that too simple a view of followers can produce misunderstanding. In modern life, most people wind up being both leaders and followers, and the categories can become quite _____ . Our behavior as followers changes as our objectives change. If I trust your judgment in music more than my own, I may follow your lead on which concert we attend (even though you may be formally my subordinate in position). But if I am an expert on fishing, you may follow my lead on where we fish, regardless of our formal positions or the fact that I followed your lead on concerts yesterday.

*vice versa: 반대로, 거꾸로

① rigid

② unfair

③ fluid

④ stable

⑤ apparent

정답과 해설 **p.32**

STEP 3 • 수능 지문 제대로 복습하기

01 Followers can be defined / by their position as subordinates / or by their behavior of
병렬연결
going along with leaders' wishes. // But followers also have power to lead. // Followers
to부정사의 형용사적 용법
empower leaders / as well as vice versa.

02 This has led some leadership analysts like Ronald Heifetz / to avoid using the word
5형식 동사   목적어   목적격 보어(to부정사)
followers / and refer to the others in a power relationship / as "citizens" or "constituents."
병렬연결

03 Heifetz is correct / that too simple a view of followers / can produce misunderstanding.
too+형용사+관사+명사: 너무 (형용사)한 (명사)

04 In modern life, / most people wind up being both leaders and followers, / and the
wind up+동명사: 결국 ~하다
categories can become quite fluid.

05 Our behavior as followers changes / as our objectives change. // If I trust your judgment
전치사(~로서)   접속사(~함에 따라)
in music more than my own, / I may follow your lead / on which concert we attend / (even
의문사절(전치사 on의 목적어)
though you may be formally my subordinate in position).

06 But if I am an expert on fishing, / you may follow my lead on where we fish, / regardless
의문사절(전치사 on의 목적어)
of our formal positions / or the fact that I followed your lead on concerts yesterday.
병렬연결   동격의 that(=the fact)

---

01 추종자는 정의define될 수 있다 / 부하subordinate라는 직책position에 의해 / 혹은 리더의 바람에 따르는 행동에 의해.
// 그러나 추종자도 이끌 힘이 있다. // 추종자는 리더에게 힘을 주기도empower 하고 / 그 반대도 마찬가지이다.

02 이는 Ronald Heifetz와 같은 일부 리더십 분석가analyst들로 하여금 / '추종자'라는 단어를 사용하는 것을 피하게 한다 /
그리고 권력 관계에 있는 다른 사람들을 지칭하게refer to ~ as ...한다 / "시민" 또는 "구성원constituent"으로.

03 Heifetz는 옳다 / 추종자에 대한 너무 단순한 관점이 / 오해를 불러일으킬 수 있다는 점에 있어서.

04 현대의 삶에서, / 대부분의 사람들은 결국 리더와 추종자 둘 다가 되고wind up being, / 그 범주는 꽤 유동적fluid일 수 있다.

05 추종자로서의 우리의 행동이 바뀐다 / 우리의 목표objective가 변함에 따라. // 만약 내가 음악에 대한 나의 판단보다
당신의 판단을 더 신뢰한다면, / 나는 당신의 주도를 따를 수 있다 / 우리가 어떤 콘서트에 참석할지attend에 대해서는 /
(당신이 비록 공식적으로formally 지위상 나의 부하일지라도).

06 하지만 내가 낚시 전문가라면, / 낚시할 장소에 대해서는 당신이 나를 따를 수 있다, / 공식적인 지위에 관계없이 / 혹은
내가 어제 콘서트에 대해 당신을 따랐다는 사실과는 관계없이regardless of.

구문 Check up

① Heifetz is correct that a too simple view / too simple a view of followers can produce misunderstanding.

② Our behavior as followers change / changes as our objectives change.

'너무 (형용사)한 (명사)'를 나타낼 때에는 <too+형용사+관사+명사>의 어순을 따르므로 too simple a view가 정답이다.

주어가 behavior이므로 단수로 수일치하여 changes를 쓴다.

정답 ① too simple a view ② changes

STEP 1 • 수능에 *진짜* 나오는 *단어*

☑ 문제에 나오는 단어들을 확인하세요.

시간이 없다면 색으로 표시된 단어만이라도 꼭 외우고 넘어가세요!

01	general	a. 일반적인	a (✓ general) attitude		일반적인 태도
02	mechanism	n. 기제, 메커니즘, 방법	a ( ) for the mind		정신을 위한 메커니즘
03	waistline	n. 허리 둘레	affect our ( )s		우리 허리 둘레에 영향을 미치다
04	function	n. 함수	as a ( )		함수로서
05	consume	v. 소비하다	( ) food		음식을 소비하다
06	comparison	n. 비교	by a ( )		비교를 통해
07	alternative	n. 대안, 선택	( )s of the food		이 음식의 대안
08	ounce	n. <무게> 온스(28.35그램)	10 ( )s		10온스
09	satisfied	a. 만족하는	be perfectly ( )		완벽히 만족하다
10	equally	ad. 똑같이	feel ( ) happy		똑같이 행복감을 느끼다
11	nourishment	n. 영양분	daily ( )		일일 영양분

⊕ 본문 문장 속에서 단어들을 확인해 보세요.

We decide / how much to eat / not simply as a function / of how much food we actually consume, / but by a comparison to its alternatives.

우리는 결정한다 / 얼마나 많이 먹을지를, / 단순히 함수로서가 아니라 / 우리가 실제로 얼마나 많은 음식을 소비할지의 (함수) / 그것의 대안과의 비교를 통해서.

문제를 풀기 전에 단어들을 30초 동안 다시 확인하세요.

01	general	🖉 일반적인	a general attitude	일반적인 태도
02	mechanism		a mechanism for the mind	정신을 위한 메커니즘
03	waistline		affect our waistlines	우리 허리 둘레에 영향을 미치다
04	function		as a function	함수로서
05	consume		consume food	음식을 소비하다
06	comparison		by a comparison	비교를 통해
07	alternative		alternatives of the food	이 음식의 대안
08	ounce		10 ounces	10온스
09	satisfied		be perfectly satisfied	완벽히 만족하다
10	equally		feel equally happy	똑같이 행복감을 느끼다
11	nourishment		daily nourishment	일일 영양분

➕ **본문 문장 속에서 단어의 의미를 우리말로 해석해 보세요.**

We decide / how much to eat / not simply as a function / of how much food we actually consume, / but by a comparison to its alternatives.

→ 우리는 결정한다 / 얼마나 많이 먹을지를, / 단순히   로서가 아니라 / 우리가 실제로 얼마나 많은 음식을
지의 (함수) / 그것의   과의   를 통해서.

제한시간 80초
난이도 ★★★★★

STEP **2** • 수능 기출 제대로 풀기

C 다음 빈칸에 들어갈 말로 가장 적절한 것은?

_____ works as a general mechanism for the mind, in many ways and across many different areas of life. For example, Brian Wansink, author of *Mindless Eating*, showed that it can also affect our waistlines. We decide how much to eat not simply as a function of how much food we actually consume, but by a comparison to its alternatives. Say we have to choose between three burgers on a menu, at 8, 10, and 12 ounces. We are likely to pick the 10-ounce burger and be perfectly satisfied at the end of the meal. But if our options are instead 10, 12, and 14 ounces, we are likely again to choose the middle one, and again feel equally happy and satisfied with the 12-ounce burger at the end of the meal, even though we ate more, which we did not need in order to get our daily nourishment or in order to feel full.

① Originality

② Relativity

③ Visualization

④ Imitation

⑤ Forgetfulness

정답과 해설 p.32

01 Relativity works / as a general mechanism for the mind, / in many ways / and across
　　　　　　　　　　전치사(~로서)
many different areas of life.

02 For example, / Brian Wansink, author of *Mindless Eating*, / showed / that it can also
　　　　　　　　　└─── 동격 ───┘　　　　　　　　　　　　　　　　명사절 접속사
affect our waistlines.

　　　　　　　　　　　　　　　not A but B: A가 아니라 B
03 We decide / how much to eat / not simply as a function / of how much food we actually
　　　　　　　의문사절(동사 decide의 목적어)　　　　　　　　　　　　의문사절(전치사 of의 목적어)
consume, / but by a comparison to its alternatives.

04 Say / we have to choose / between three burgers on a menu, / at 8, 10, and 12 ounces.
　　명사절 접속사 that 생략
　　　　　　　　　　　　　　　　┌──────── 병렬 연결 ────────┐
05 We are likely to pick the 10-ounce burger / and be perfectly satisfied at the end of the
　　　be likely+to부정사: ~일 것이다
meal.

06 But / if our options are instead 10, 12, and 14 ounces, / we are likely again to choose
　　　　　　　　　　　　　　부사
the middle one, / and again feel equally happy and satisfied / with the 12-ounce burger
　　　　　　　　　　　　　감각동사(feel)+주격보어(형용사)
/ at the end of the meal, / even though we ate more, / [which we did not need / in order
　　　　　　　　　　　　　　　　　선행사(문장)　　　　　　계속적 용법의 관계대명사
to get our daily nourishment / or in order to feel full].
　　　　　　　　병렬 연결

01 상대성은 작용한다 / 정신을 위한 일반적인 메커니즘a general mechanism으로 / 여러 면에서 / 그리고 삶의 많은 다른 영역에 걸쳐.

02 예를 들어, / 〈Mindless Eating〉의 저자 Brian Wansink는 / 보여주었다 / 그것이 우리의 허리 둘레waistline에도 영향을 미칠 수 있다는 것을.

03 우리는 결정한다 / 얼마나 많이 먹을지를, / 단순히 함수function로서가 아니라 / 우리가 실제로 얼마나 많은 음식을 소비할지consume의 (함수) / 그것의 대안alternative과의 비교를 통해서by a comparison.

04 생각해보자 / 우리가 선택해야 한다고 / 메뉴에 있는 버거 세 개 중에서 / 8온스ounce, 10온스, 12온스의.

05 우리는 10온스 버거를 고를 것이다 / 그리고 식사가 끝날 때쯤이면 완벽하게 만족할satisfied 수 있을 것이다.

06 하지만 / 만약 대신에 우리의 선택권이 10온스, 12온스, 14온스라면, / 우리는 다시 중간의 것을 선택할 것이고, / 똑같이equally 행복감과 만족감을 다시 느낄 수 있을 것이다 / 12온스의 햄버거에 / 식사가 끝날 때 / 비록 우리가 더 많이 먹었더라도, / 그리고 (더 많이 먹는 건) 필요하지 않았다 / 일일 영양분nourishment을 섭취하기 위해 / 또는 포만감을 느끼기 위해.

<table>
<tr><td>구문 Check up</td><td>① For example, Brian Wansink, author of *Mindless Eating*, showing / showed that it can also affect our waistlines.</td><td>② We are likely to pick the 10-ounce burger and be perfectly satisfying / satisfied at the end of the meal.</td></tr>
<tr><td></td><td>문장의 동사 자리이므로, 문맥에 맞추어 과거시제인 showed를 쓴다.</td><td>분사의 의미상 주어 we가 '만족을 느낀다'는 의미가 되도록 과거분사 satisfied를 쓴다.</td></tr>
</table>

빈칸 추론 Ⅱ ✛

STEP 1 • 수능에 *진짜* 나오는 *단어*

✔ 문제에 나오는 단어들을 확인하세요.

시간이 없다면 색으로 표시된 단어만이라도 꼭 외우고 넘어가세요!

01	contemporary	a. 현대의	the (✔ contemporary) Buddhist	현대 불교인
02	**remarkable**	a. 주목할 만한, 놀라운	a ( ) book	놀라운 책
03	precious	a. 소중한	make life ( )	삶을 소중하게 만들다
04	struggle	n. 고행, 고투, 분투	a ( ) to escape	벗어나려는 고투
05	unstable	a. 불안정한	( ) beauty	불안정한 아름다움
06	inevitable	a. 피할 수 없는	an ( ) part of life	삶의 피할 수 없는 부분
07	wound	n. 상처	a severe ( )	심한 상처
08	companion	n. 동반자	intimate ( )s	친한 동반자
09	cast	n. 색조, 빛깔	a red ( )	붉은 빛
10	twilight	n. 황혼	the cast of ( )	황혼의 색조
11	mountainside	n. 산 중턱, 산허리	across a ( )	산 중턱을 가로질러
12	last	v. 지속하다	( ) only a moment	오직 한 순간만 지속하다
13	fragility	n. 연약함	the ( ) of Mother Nature	대자연의 연약함
14	diversity	n. 다양성	a ( ) of opinions	의견의 다양성

✛ 본문 문장 속에서 단어들을 확인해 보세요.

When he was dying, / the contemporary Buddhist teacher Dainin Katagiri wrote a remarkable book / called *Returning to Silence*.

죽음을 앞두고 / 현대의 불교 스승인 Dainin Katagiri는 주목할 만한 책을 집필했다 / <침묵으로의 회귀>라는.

01	contemporary	현대의	the contemporary Buddhist	현대 불교인
02	remarkable		a remarkable book	놀라운 책
03	precious		make life precious	삶을 소중하게 만들다
04	struggle		a struggle to escape	벗어나려는 고투
05	unstable		unstable beauty	불안정한 아름다움
06	inevitable		an inevitable part of life	삶의 피할 수 없는 부분
07	wound		a severe wound	심한 상처
08	companion		intimate companions	친한 동반자
09	cast		a red cast	붉은 빛
10	twilight		the cast of twilight	황혼의 색조
11	mountainside		across a mountainside	산 중턱을 가로질러
12	last		last only a moment	오직 한 순간만 지속하다
13	fragility		the fragility of Mother Nature	대자연의 연약함
14	diversity		a diversity of opinions	의견의 다양성

➕ 본문 문장 속에서 단어의 의미를 우리말로 해석해 보세요.

When he was dying, / the contemporary Buddhist teacher Dainin Katagiri wrote a remarkable book / called *Returning to Silence*.

→ 죽음을 앞두고 / _____ 불교 스승인 Dainin Katagiri는 _____ 책을 집필했다 / <침묵으로의 회귀>라는.

STEP **2** • 수능 기출 제대로 풀기

D

다음 빈칸에 들어갈 말로 가장 적절한 것은?

When he was dying, the contemporary Buddhist teacher Dainin Katagiri wrote a remarkable book called *Returning to Silence*. Life, he wrote, "is a dangerous situation." It is the weakness of life that makes it precious; his words are filled with the very fact of his own life passing away. "The china bowl is beautiful because sooner or later it will break.... The life of the bowl is always existing in a dangerous situation." Such is our struggle: this unstable beauty. This inevitable wound. We forget — how easily we forget — that love and loss are intimate companions, that we love the real flower so much more than the plastic one and love the cast of twilight across a mountainside lasting only a moment. It is this very _____ that opens our hearts.

① fragility

② stability

③ harmony

④ satisfaction

⑤ diversity

정답과 해설 p.33

01 When he was dying, / the contemporary Buddhist teacher Dainin Katagiri wrote a
remarkable book / called *Returning to Silence*.
　　　　　　　　　　과거분사

02 Life, / (he wrote), / "is a dangerous situation." // It is the weakness of life / that makes it
　주어　　삽입구　　　동사　　　　　　　　　　　　　　It ~ that 강조구문
precious; / his words are filled / with the very fact of his own life passing away.
　　　　　　　　　　　　　　　　전치사　　의미상 주어　　동명사

03 "The china bowl is beautiful / because sooner or later it will break.... // The life of the
bowl is always existing / in a dangerous situation."

04 Such is our struggle: / this unstable beauty. // This inevitable wound.
명사: 그런 것

05 We forget / — (how easily we forget) — / [that love and loss are intimate companions],
　　　　　　　　삽입절　　　　　　　　[ ]: forget의 목적절
/ [that we love the real flower so much more than the plastic one / and love the cast of
twilight across a mountainside / lasting only a moment].
　　　　　　전치사구　　　　　　　　현재분사

06 It is this very fragility / that opens our hearts.
　　　It ~ that 강조구문

01 죽음을 앞두고, / 현대의 불교contemporary Buddhist 스승인 Dainin Katagiri는 주목할 만한 책a remarkable book을
집필했다 / <침묵으로의 회귀>라는.

02 삶이란 / 그는 썼다 / "위험한 상황이다."라고. // 바로 삶의 취약함이다 / 삶을 소중하게 만드는make life precious 것은. /
그의 글은 채워져 있다 / 자신의 삶이 끝나가고 있다는 바로 그 사실로.

03 "자기 그릇은 아름답다 / 언젠가 깨질 것이기 때문에…. // 그 그릇의 생명은 늘 놓여 있다 / 위험한 상황에."

04 그런 것이 우리의 고행struggle이다. / 이 불안정한 아름다움the unstable beauty. // 이 피할 수 없는 상처the inevitable
wound.

05 우리는 잊어버린다 / — 얼마나 쉽게 우리가 잊는가 — / 사랑과 상실이 친밀한 동반자intimate companion라는 것을, /
우리가 진짜 꽃을 플라스틱 꽃보다 훨씬 더 사랑하고 / 산 중턱을 가로지르는across a mountainside 황혼의 색조the cast
of twilight를 사랑한다는 것을 / 한 순간만 지속하는last only a moment.

06 바로 이 연약함fragility이다 / 우리의 마음을 여는 것은.

구문 Check up	① The life of the bowl is always existed / existing in a dangerous situation.	② It is this very fragility that open / opens our hearts.
	동사 exist는 자동사이기 때문에 수동태로 쓰지 않는다. 따라서 existing 이 적절하다.	It-that 강조구문으로, 동사는 강조하고 있는 명사구 this very fragility에 수 일치시켜 opens를 쓴다.

정답 ① existing ② opens

252

E

STEP 1 • 수능에 *진짜* 나오는 *단어*

✔ **문제에 나오는 단어들을 확인하세요.**

시간이 없다면 색으로 표시된 단어만이라도 꼭 외우고 넘어가세요!

01	capacity	n. 능력	develop the (✔ capacity)	능력을 발달시키다
02	solitude	n. 혼자 있음, (즐거운) 고독	the capacity for ( )	혼자 있을 수 있는 능력
03	presence	n. 존재	in the ( ) of others	다른 사람들이 있을 때
04	attentive	a. 관심을 가져주는	an ( ) other	관심을 가져주는 타인
05	silence	n. 고요	consider the ( )s	고요함을 생각하다
06	increasingly	ad. 점점	feel ( ) aware	점점 알아가다
07	available	a. (함께할) 시간이 있는	be ( ) to her	그녀에게 시간을 내어 줄 수 있다
08	comfortable	a. 편안한	be ( ) with it	그것을 편안해 하다
09	imagination	n. 상상	her ( )	그녀의 상상
10	hardship	n. 고난, 곤경	endure many ( )s	많은 고난을 견디다
11	attachment	n. 애착	an early ( ) to parents	부모에 대한 초기 애착

➕ **본문 문장 속에서 단어들을 확인해 보세요.**

Gradually, / the bath, taken alone, / is a time / when the child is comfortable with her imagination.

점차적으로, / 혼자서 하는 목욕은 / 시간이 된다 / 그 아이가 상상을 하며 편안해 하는.

01	capacity	🖉 능력	develop the capacity	능력을 발달시키다
02	solitude		the capacity for solitude	혼자 있을 수 있는 능력
03	presence		in the presence of others	다른 사람들이 있을 때
04	attentive		an attentive other	관심을 가져주는 타인
05	silence		consider the silences	고요함을 생각하다
06	increasingly		feel increasingly aware	점점 알아가다
07	available		be available to her	그녀에게 시간을 내어줄 수 있다
08	comfortable		be comfortable with it	그것을 편안해 하다
09	imagination		her imagination	그녀의 상상
10	hardship		endure many hardships	많은 고난을 견디다
11	attachment		an early attachment to parents	부모에 대한 초기 애착

➕ 본문 문장 속에서 단어의 의미를 우리말로 해석해 보세요.

Gradually, / the bath, taken alone, / is a time / when the child is comfortable with her imagination.

➜ 점차적으로, / 혼자서 하는 목욕은 / 시간이 된다 / 그 아이가 ＿＿＿＿＿＿＿을 하며 ＿＿＿＿＿＿＿＿＿.

STEP **2** • 수능 기출 제대로 풀기

E 다음 빈칸에 들어갈 말로 가장 적절한 것은?

Children develop the capacity for solitude in the presence of an attentive other. Consider the silences that fall when you take a young boy on a quiet walk in nature. The child comes to feel increasingly aware of what it is to be alone in nature, supported by being "with" someone who is introducing him to this experience. Gradually, the child takes walks alone. Or imagine a mother giving her two-year-old daughter a bath, allowing the girl's reverie with her bath toys as she makes up stories and learns to be alone with her thoughts, all the while knowing her mother is present and available to her. Gradually, the bath, taken alone, is a time when the child is comfortable with her imagination. _____ enables solitude.

*reverie: 공상

① Hardship

② Attachment

③ Creativity

④ Compliment

⑤ Responsibility

정답과 해설 p.33

01 Children develop the capacity for solitude / in the presence of an attentive other.

02 Consider the silences that fall / when you take a young boy on a quiet walk in nature.
명령문(~하라)   주격 관계대명사절

의문사(무엇인지, 어떤 것인지)
03 The child comes to feel increasingly aware / of what it is to be alone in nature, /
      ~하게 되다   가주어   진주어(to부정사)
supported by being "with" someone / who is introducing him to this experience.
분사구문   주격 관계대명사

04 Gradually, / the child takes walks alone.

동명사 giving의 의미상의 주어
05 Or / imagine a mother giving her two-year-old daughter a bath, / allowing the girl's
명령문   동명사: 수여동사(give)+간접목적어+직접목적어   분사구문
reverie with her bath toys / [as she makes up stories / and learns to be alone with her
                              부사절 접속사(시간)
thoughts, / all the while knowing / her mother is present and available to her].
        접속사가 남아있는 분사구문   명사절 접속사 that 생략

06 Gradually, / the bath, taken alone, / is a time / when the child is comfortable with her
                          과거분사   관계부사
imagination.

07 Attachment enables solitude.

01 아이들은 혼자 있을 수 있는 능력the capacity for solitude을 발달시킨다 / 관심을 가져주는 타인이 있을 때in the presence of an attentive other.

02 다가오는 고요함silence을 생각해 보라 / 여러분이 어린 소년을 자연에서 조용히 산책시킬 때.

03 그 아이는 점점increasingly 알아가게 된다 / 자연 속에서 혼자 있는 것이 어떤 것인지에 대해 / 누군가와 '함께' 있다는 것에 의해 도움을 받아 / 그에게 이러한 경험을 처음으로 하게 한 (누군가).

04 점차적으로, / 그 아이는 혼자 산책한다.

05 또는 / 두 살짜리 딸아이를 목욕시키는 엄마를 생각해 보라 / 딸이 목욕 장난감을 가지고 공상에 잠길 수 있게 하는 (엄마를) / 딸이 이야기를 만들고 / 생각을 하며 혼자 있는 법을 배우는 동안 / (딸이) 알고 있는 내내 / 엄마가 함께 있고 엄마가 자신에게 시간을 내어줄 수 있다는available to her 것을.

06 점차적으로, / 혼자서 하는 목욕은 / 시간이 된다 / 그 아이가 상상imagination을 하며 편안해 하는comfortable.

07 애착attachment은 혼자 있는 것을 가능하게 한다.

구문 Check up

① Consider the silences that fall when you take a young boy on a quiet / quietly walk in nature.

명사 walk를 수식하므로 형용사 quiet를 쓴다.

② Gradually, the bath, taking / taken alone, is a time when the child is comfortable with her imagination.

명사 the bath를 수식하는 분사로, '목욕'은 사람에 의해 행해지는 것이므로 수동의 의미를 담아 과거분사 taken으로 쓴다.

DAY 09

F

STEP 1 • 수능에 *진짜* 나오는 *단어*

✔ 문제에 나오는 단어들을 확인하세요.

시간이 없다면 색으로 표시된 단어만이라도 꼭 외우고 넘어가세요!

01	widely	ad. 아주, 크게, 널리	vary (✔ widely)	아주 다양하다
02	preservability	n. 보존 가능성, 저장 가능성	the ( ) of the data in the cloud	클라우드에 있는 데이터의 보존 가능성
03	intact	a. (훼손되지 않고) 온전한	remain ( )	온전하게 남아 있다
04	suspend	v. 멈추다, 중단하다	Nothing can ( ) time.	어떤 것도 시간을 멈출 수는 없다.
05	slip	v. 빠져나가다, 미끄러지다	( ) between our fingers	우리 손가락 사이를 빠져나가다
06	challenge	v. 이의를 제기하다, 반박하다	( ) the conclusion	결론에 이의를 제기하다
07	mysteriously	ad. 희한하게, 불가사의하게	( ) disappear	희한하게도 사라지다
08	slight	a. 약간의, 조금의	a ( ) change	약간의 변화
09	accidental	a. 우연한, 돌발적인	an ( ) meeting	우연한 만남
10	otherwise	ad. 그렇지 않(았)으면	He worked hard; ( ) he would have failed.	그는 열심히 노력했다. 그렇지 않았다면 그는 실패했을 것이다.
11	everlasting	a. 영원한	an ( ) love	영원한 사랑
12	scarcity	n. 부족, 결핍, 희소성	the ( ) of water	물 부족
13	permanency	n. 영속성	stability and ( )	안정성과 영속성

➕ 본문 문장 속에서 단어들을 확인해 보세요.

Even though the design, activities, and membership of social media / might change over time, / the content of what people posted / usually remains intact.

비록 소셜 미디어의 디자인, 활동, 멤버십이 / 시간이 흐르며 바뀔지도 모르겠지만, / 사람들이 게시했던 내용은 / 보통 온전하게 남아 있다.

문제를 풀기 전에 단어들을 **30초** 동안 다시 확인하세요.

01	widely	✎ 아주, 크게, 널리	vary widely	아주 다양하다
02	preservability		the preservability of the data in the cloud	클라우드에 있는 데이터의 보존 가능성
03	intact		remain intact	온전하게 남아 있다
04	suspend		Nothing can suspend time.	어떤 것도 시간을 멈출 수는 없다.
05	slip		slip between our fingers	우리 손가락 사이를 빠져나가다
06	challenge		challenge the conclusion	결론에 이의를 제기하다
07	mysteriously		mysteriously disappear	희한하게도 사라지다
08	slight		a slight change	약간의 변화
09	accidental		an accidental meeting	우연한 만남
10	otherwise		He worked hard; otherwise he would have failed.	그는 열심히 노력했다. 그렇지 않았다면 그는 실패했을 것이다.
11	everlasting		an everlasting love	영원한 사랑
12	scarcity		the scarcity of water	물 부족
13	permanency		stability and permanency	안정성과 영속성

⊕ 본문 문장 속에서 단어의 의미를 우리말로 해석해 보세요.

Even though the design, activities, and membership of social media / might change over time, / the content of what people posted / usually remains intact.

→ 비록 소셜 미디어의 디자인, 활동, 멤버십이 / 시간이 흐르며 바뀔지도 모르겠지만, / 사람들이 게시했던 내용은 / 보통   .

STEP 2 • 수능 기출 제대로 풀기

F 다음 빈칸에 들어갈 말로 가장 적절한 것은?

Online environments vary widely in how easily you can save whatever happens there, what I call its *recordability* and *preservability*. Even though the design, activities, and membership of social media might change over time, the content of what people posted usually remains intact. Email, video, audio, and text messages can be saved. When perfect preservation is possible, time has been suspended. Whenever you want, you can go back to reexamine those events from the past. In other situations, _____ slips between our fingers, even challenging our reality testing about whether something existed at all, as when an email that we seem to remember receiving mysteriously disappears from our inbox. The slightest accidental tap of the finger can send an otherwise everlasting document into nothingness.

① scarcity

② creativity

③ acceleration

④ permanency

⑤ mysteriousness

정답과 해설 p.34

01 Online environments vary widely / in how easily you can save whatever happens there,
자동사
/ what I call its *recordability* and *preservability*.
동격

02 **Even though** the design, activities, and membership of social media / might change
접속사(비록 ~일지라도)
over time, / the content of what people posted / usually **remains intact.** // Email, video,
2형식 동사+형용사
audio, and text messages / **can be saved.**
조동사 수동태

03 When perfect preservation is possible, / time **has been suspended.** // **Whenever** you
현재완료 수동태   복합관계부사(~할 때마다)
want, / you can go back / **to reexamine** those events from the past.
부사적 용법(목적)

04 In other situations, / permanency slips between our fingers, / even challenging our
분사구문
reality testing about **whether** something existed at all, / **as** when an email [that we
명사절 접속사(about의 목적절)   ~와 마찬가지로
seem to **remember receiving**] / mysteriously **disappears** from our inbox.
remember+동명사: (이미) ~한 것을 기억하다   자동사(주어만 있으면 완전)

05 The slightest accidental tap of the finger / can send an otherwise everlasting document
into nothingness.

---

01 온라인 환경은 아주widely 다양하다 / 거기서 무슨 일이 일어나든 간에 여러분이 얼마나 쉽게 저장할 수 있는지 하는
면에서 / 즉 내가 그것의 '기록 가능성'과 '저장 가능성preservability'이라고 부르는 것.

02 비록 소셜 미디어의 디자인, 활동, 멤버십이 / 시간이 흐르며 바뀔지도 모르겠지만, / 사람들이 게시했던 내용은 / 보통
온전하게intact 남아 있다. // 이메일, 동영상, 음성, 텍스트 메시지는 / 저장될 수 있다.

03 완벽한 보존이 가능할 때, / 시간은 멈춰suspend 있다. // 여러분이 원할 때마다 / 여러분은 되돌아갈 수 있다 / 그러한
과거의 사건들을 다시 돌아보기 위해.

04 다른 상황에서는, / 영속성permanency은 우리 손가락 사이로 빠져나가slip 버리고 / 어떤 것이 어떻게든 존재했었는지에
대한 현실 검증에 이의를 제기하기challenge까지 한다 / 마치 우리가 받았다고 기억하는 듯한 이메일이 ~할 때와
마찬가지로 / 우리의 수신함에서 희한하게도mysteriously 사라질.

05 손가락으로 우연히 살짝 톡 건드린 것the slightest accidental tap이 / 만일 그렇게 하지 않았으면otherwise
영원히everlasting 존재했을 문서를 무(無)의 상태로 보낼 수 있다.

---

① The content of what people posted usually remain / remains intact.

핵심 주어인 The content가 단수명사이므로 동사 역시 단수형인 remains
가 적절하다.

② Permanency slips between our fingers, even challenging our reality testing about that / whether something existed at all.

'~인지 아닌지'라는 의미로 about의 목적절을 이끌 수 있도록 접속사
whether를 써야 한다.

정답 ① remains ② whether

STEP 1 · 수능에 진짜 나오는 단어

✔ 문제에 나오는 단어들을 확인하세요.

시간이 없다면 색으로 표시된 단어만이라도 꼭 외우고 넘어가세요!

01	slow-changing	a. 천천히 변화하는	a (✓ slow-changing) machine	천천히 변화하는 기계
02	overnight	ad. 하룻밤 사이에	completely change ( )	하룻밤 사이에 완전히 변하다
03	unstable	a. 불안정한	feel ( )	불안정하다고 느끼다
04	norm	n. 전형적 행동 양식, 규범	My ( ) is to wake up at 7 in the morning.	내 전형적 행동 양식은 아침 7시에 깨는 것이다.
05	habitual	a. 습관적인	a ( ) routine	습관적인 일상
06	repetition	n. 반복	the ( ) of a certain behavior	특정한 행동의 반복
07	accept	v. 받아들이다, 수용하다	( ) the truth	진실을 받아들이다
08	thankful	a. 고마워하는	I'm ( ) for your presence.	나는 네 존재에 고마워.

➕ 본문 문장 속에서 단어들을 확인해 보세요.

If your brain could completely change overnight, / you would be unstable.

만약 여러분의 뇌가 하룻밤 사이에 완전히 바뀔 수 있다면 / 여러분은 불안정해질 것이다.

01	slow-changing	✎ 천천히 변화하는	a slow-changing machine	천천히 변화하는 기계
02	overnight		completely change overnight	하룻밤 사이에 완전히 변하다
03	unstable		feel unstable	불안정하다고 느끼다
04	norm		My norm is to wake up at 7 in the morning.	내 전형적 행동 양식은 아침 7시에 깨는 것이다.
05	habitual		a habitual routine	습관적인 일상
06	repetition		the repetition of a certain behavior	특정한 행동의 반복
07	accept		accept the truth	진실을 받아들이다
08	thankful		I'm thankful for your presence.	나는 네 존재에 고마워.

➕ 본문 문장 속에서 단어의 의미를 우리말로 해석해 보세요.

If your brain could completely change overnight, / you would be unstable.

→ 만약 여러분의 뇌가 _____ 수 있다면 / 여러분은 _____ 것이다.

제한시간 70초

난이도 ★★★☆☆

STEP **2** • 수능 기출 제대로 풀기

G 다음 빈칸에 들어갈 말로 가장 적절한 것은?

What is the true nature of the brain? The brain is a slow-changing machine, and that's a good thing. If your brain could completely change overnight, you would be unstable. Let's just say that your norm is to wake up, read the paper with coffee and a bagel, walk your dog, and watch the news. This is your habitual routine. Then one night, you get a phone call at 3 a.m. and have to run outside in your underwear to check on your neighbors. What if your brain latched on to this new routine and you continued to run outside at 3 a.m. every night in your underwear? Nobody would want that, so it's a good thing our brains require more repetition than that! Let's accept and be thankful for the _____ our slow-changing brains provide us.

*latch on to: ~을 자기 것으로 하다

① stability

② maturity

③ curiosity

④ variability

⑤ productivity

정답과 해설 **p.34**

01 What is the true nature of the brain?

02 The brain is a slow-changing machine, / and that's a good thing.
지시대명사(and 앞 내용)

03 If your brain could completely change overnight, / you would be unstable.
가정법 과거: 현재 사실 반대(if+주어+과거시제 동사 ~, 주어+조동사 과거형+동사원형 …)

04 Let's just say / that your norm is to wake up, / read the paper with coffee and a bagel, /
주격보어(to부정사구 병렬: A, B, C, and D)
walk your dog, / and watch the news. // This is your habitual routine.

05 Then one night, / you get a phone call at 3 a.m. / and have to run outside in your
underwear / to check on your neighbors.
부사적 용법(~하기 위해)

06 What if your brain latched on to this new routine / and you continued to run outside at
what if+주어+과거시제 동사 ~?: 가정법 과거(현재 ~하지 않지만 ~하다면 어떨까?)
3 a.m. every night in your underwear?

07 Nobody would want that, / so it's a good thing our brains require more repetition than
가주어   명사절 접속사 that 생략   진주어
that!

08 Let's accept and be thankful for the stability / our slow-changing brains provide us.
목적격 관계대명사절

---

01 뇌의 진정한 본질은 무엇인가?

02 뇌는 천천히 변화하는slow-changing 기계이며, / 이는 좋은 것이다.

03 만약 여러분의 뇌가 하룻밤 사이에overnight 완전히 바뀔 수 있다면 / 여러분은 불안정해질unstable 것이다.

04 ~라고 해 보자 / 여러분의 전형적 행동 양식norm이 잠에서 깨어 / 커피와 베이글을 가지고 신문을 읽고 / 개를 산책시키고 / 뉴스를 보는 것이라고. // 이것은 여러분의 습관적인habitual 일상이다.

05 그런데 어느 밤, / 여러분은 새벽 3시에 전화를 받고 / 속옷 차림으로 뛰쳐나가야 한다 / 이웃을 살펴보러.

06 만약 여러분의 뇌가 이 새로운 일상을 자기 것으로 만들어, / 여러분이 매일 밤 새벽 3시에 계속 속옷만 입고 밖으로 뛰쳐나가야 한다면 어떻겠는가?

07 누구도 그러길 원치 않을 것이며, / 그렇기에 좋은 것이다 / 우리 뇌가 이보다 더 많은 반복repetition을 요한다는 것은!

08 안정감을 받아들이고accept 고마워하자be thankful / 천천히 변화하는 우리 뇌가 우리에게 주는.

구문 Check up

① Let's just say that your norm is to wake up, read the paper with coffee and a bagel, walk your dog, and **watch / watches** the news.

is의 보어인 to부정사가 A, B, C, and D 형태로 병렬 연결되므로 watch가 적절하다.

② Nobody would want that, so it's a good thing our brains require more repetition **as / than** that!

앞에 비교급(more)이 나오므로 than이 적절하다.

☑ 종합 성적표

구분	공부한 날 ❶	결과 분석			틀린 이유 ❸
		출처	풀이 시간 ❷	채점 결과 (O, ✕)	
Day 7	월 일	학력평가 기출 2023년	분 초		
		학력평가 기출 2022년	분 초		
		학력평가 기출 2021년	분 초		
		학력평가 기출 2020년	분 초		
		학력평가 기출 2019년	분 초		
		학력평가 기출 2018년	분 초		
		학력평가 기출 2017년	분 초		
Day 8	월 일	학력평가 기출 2023년	분 초		
		학력평가 기출 2022년	분 초		
		학력평가 기출 2021년	분 초		
		학력평가 기출 2020년	분 초		
		학력평가 기출 2019년	분 초		
		학력평가 기출 2018년	분 초		
		학력평가 기출 2017년	분 초		
Day 9	월 일	학력평가 기출 2023년	분 초		
		학력평가 기출 2022년	분 초		
		학력평가 기출 2021년	분 초		
		학력평가 기출 2020년	분 초		
		학력평가 기출 2019년	분 초		
		학력평가 기출 2018년	분 초		
		학력평가 기출 2017년	분 초		

3일간
공부한 내용을
다시 보니,
……

❶ **매일 지문을 하루 계획에 맞춰 풀었다. vs. 내가 한 약속을 못 지켰다.**

<매3영 고2 기출>은 단순 문제풀이를 위한 책이 아니라, 매일 규칙적으로 영어를 공부하는 습관을 잡는 책입니다. 따라서 푸는 문제 개수는 상황에 따라 다르더라도 '매일' 학습하는 것이 중요합니다.

❷ **주어진 시간을 자꾸 넘긴다?**

풀이 시간이 계속해서 권장 시간을 넘긴다면 실전 훈련이 부족하다는 신호입니다. 아직 조급함을 가질 필요는 없지만, 매일의 문제 풀이에 더 긴장감 있게 임해보세요.

❸ **틀린 이유 맞춤 솔루션:** 오답 이유에 따라 다음 해결책을 참고하세요.

(1) 단어를 많이 몰라서

▶ <STEP 1 단어>에 제시된 필수 어휘를 매일 챙겨보고, SELF-TEST까지 꼼꼼히 진행합니다.

(2) 문장 해석이 잘 안 돼서

▶ <STEP 3 지문 복습>의 구문 첨삭과 끊어읽기 해설을 정독하며 문장구조를 보는 눈을 길러보세요.

(3) 해석은 되지만 내용이 이해가 안 되거나, 선택지로 연결을 못 해서

▶ <정답과 해설>의 해설과 오답풀이를 참고해 틀린 이유를 깊이 고민하고 정리해 보세요.

!

결론적으로, 내가 **취약한 부분**은 [   ] 이다. **취약점을 보완하기 위해서** 나는 [   ] 을/를 해야겠다.

3일 뒤 다시 봐야 할 문항과, 꼭 다시 외워야 할 사항·구문 등이 있는 페이지는 지금 바로 접어 두세요.

<매3영>이 제시하는 3단계로

유형 3일 훈련

DAY

10~12

DAY 10

STEP 1 • 수능에 진짜 나오는 단어

문제에 나오는 단어들을 확인하세요.

#	단어	뜻	예시	해석
01	democracy	n. 민주주의	early (✓ democracy) in Europe	유럽의 초기 민주주의
02	thrive	v. 번성하다	( ) in this area	이 지역에서 번성하다
03	prosper	v. 번영하다	( ) in business	사업이 번영하다
04	precisely	ad. 바로, 정확히	( ) the same	정확히 똑같은
05	ruler	n. 통치자	European ( )s	유럽의 통치자들
06	remarkably	ad. 현저하게	( ) weak	현저히 약한
07	assess	v. 평가하다	( ) production efficiency	생산 효율을 평가하다
08	substantial	a. 상당한	( ) taxes	상당한 세금
09	illustrate	v. 설명하다, (분명히) 보여주다	( ) the point	요점을 보여주다
10	revenue	n. (정부나 기관의) 수입, 세입	how little ( ) they collected	그들이 얼마나 적은 세입을 거뒀는지
11	huge	a. 막대한, 거대한	a ( ) amount of revenue	막대한 액수의 세입
12	awfully	ad. 엄청나게, 정말, 몹시	an ( ) long time	엄청나게 오랜 시간
13	medieval	a. 중세의	in ( ) times	중세 시대
14	extract	v. 뜯어내다, 뽑아내다	( ) much more	훨씬 더 많이 뜯어내다

⊕ **본문 문장 속에서 단어들을 확인해 보세요.**

The irony of early democracy in Europe is / that it thrived and prospered / precisely because European rulers for a very long time were remarkably weak.

유럽 초기 민주주의의 아이러니는 / 그것이 번성하고 번영했다는 것이다 / 바로 유럽의 통치자들이 매우 오랫동안 현저하게 약했기 때문에.

267

01	democracy	🖊 민주주의	early democracy in Europe	유럽의 초기 민주주의
02	thrive		thrive in this area	이 지역에서 번성하다
03	prosper		prosper in business	사업이 번영하다
04	precisely		precisely the same	정확히 똑같은
05	ruler		European rulers	유럽의 통치자들
06	remarkably		remarkably weak	현저히 약한
07	assess		assess production efficiency	생산 효율을 평가하다
08	substantial		substantial taxes	상당한 세금
09	illustrate		illustrate the point	요점을 보여주다
10	revenue		how little revenue they collected	그들이 얼마나 적은 세입을 거뒀는지
11	huge		a huge amount of revenue	막대한 액수의 세입
12	awfully		an awfully long time	엄청나게 오랜 시간
13	medieval		in medieval times	중세 시대
14	extract		extract much more	훨씬 더 많이 뜯어내다

➕ **본문 문장 속에서 단어의 의미를 우리말로 해석해 보세요.**

The irony of early democracy in Europe is / that it thrived and prospered / precisely because European rulers for a very long time were remarkably weak.

➔ 　　　　　　　의 아이러니는 / 그것이　　　　　　　는 것이다 /　　　　　　　이 매우 오랫동안
　　　　　　　때문에.

STEP **2** • 수능 기출 제대로 풀기

A 다음 글에서 전체 흐름과 관계 <u>없는</u> 문장은?

The irony of early democracy in Europe is that it thrived and prospered precisely because European rulers for a very long time were remarkably weak. ① For more than a millennium after the fall of Rome, European rulers lacked the ability to assess what their people were producing and to levy substantial taxes based on this. ② The most striking way to illustrate European weakness is to show how little revenue they collected. ③ For this reason, tax collectors in Europe were able to collect a huge amount of revenue and therefore had a great influence on how society should function. ④ Europeans would eventually develop strong systems of revenue collection, but it took them an awfully long time to do so. ⑤ In medieval times, and for part of the early modern era, Chinese emperors and Muslim caliphs were able to extract much more of economic production than any European ruler with the exception of small city-states.

*levy: 부과하다
**caliph: 칼리프(과거 이슬람 국가의 통치자)

정답과 해설 **p.35**

01　The irony of early democracy in Europe is / [that it thrived and prospered / precisely
　　　　　　　　　　　　　　　　　　　주격 보어(명사절)　　　　　　　　　　　　　　바로 ~ 때문이다
because European rulers for a very long time were remarkably weak]. // For more than a
　　　　　　　　　　　　　　　　　　　　　　　　　　　　　　　　　　전치사(~ 동안)
millennium after the fall of Rome, / European rulers lacked the ability / to assess what
their people were producing / and to levy substantial taxes based on this.
　　　　　　　　　　　병렬구조(형용사적 용법)

02　The most striking way to illustrate European weakness / is to show how little revenue
　　주어　　　　　　　　　　　　형용사적 용법　　　　　　　동사　주격 보어(명사구)
they collected.

03　For this reason, / tax collectors in Europe / were able to collect a huge amount of
　　　　　　　　　　　주어(복수)　　　　　　　　동사1
revenue / and therefore had a great influence / on how society should function.
　　　　　　　　　　　동사2　　　　　　　　　　　전치사의 목적어

04　Europeans would eventually develop strong systems of revenue collection, / but it took
them an awfully long time to do so. // In medieval times, / and for part of the early
it takes A+시간+to-V: A가 ~하는 데 …의 시간이 걸리다
modern era, / Chinese emperors and Muslim caliphs / were able to extract much more
　　　　　　　　　　　　　　　　　　　　　　　　　　　　　　　　　　비교급 수식(훨씬)
of economic production / than any European ruler / with the exception of small city-
states.

01　유럽 초기 민주주의democracy의 아이러니는 / 그것이 번성하고 번영했다thrive and prosper는 것이다 / 바로precisely
유럽의 통치자들이 매우 오랫동안 현저하게remarkably 약했기 때문에. // 로마의 멸망 후 천 년 넘게, / 유럽의
통치자ruler들은 능력이 부족했다 / 백성들이 생산하고 있던 것을 평가하고assess, / 이를 바탕으로 상당한substantial
세금을 부과할.

02　유럽의 약함을 설명하는illustrate 가장 눈에 띄는 방법은 / 그들이 거둔 세입revenue이 얼마나 적은지를 보여주는 것이다.

03　(이러한 이유로, / 유럽의 세금 징수원은 / 막대한huge 액수의 세입을 거둘 수 있었고, / 그리하여 큰 영향을 미쳤다 /
사회가 어떻게 기능해야 할지에.)

04　유럽인들은 결국 강력한 세입 징수 시스템을 개발했지만, / 그렇게 하는 데는 엄청나게awfully 오랜 시간이 걸렸다. //
중세medieval 시대와 / 초기 근대의 일부 동안, / 중국의 황제들과 이슬람 문명의 칼리프들은 / 훨씬 더 많은 경제적
생산물을 뜯어낼extract 수 있었다 / 그 어떤 유럽 통치자보다도 / 작은 도시 국가들을 제외하고.

구문 Check up	① European rulers lacked the ability to assess what their people were producing and levied / to levy substantial taxes based on this.	② The most striking way to illustrate European weakness is shown / to show how little revenue they collected.
	to assess와 병렬 연결되도록 to levy를 쓴다. 동사 lacked와 병렬하여 levied를 쓰면 '생산물을 평가할 능력이 부족'한데 '상당한 세금을 부과했다'는 의미여서 어색하다.	문맥상 주어인 'The ~ way'가 '보여주는' 것이므로 to show를 써야 한다.

정답 ① to levy ② to show

✔ 문제에 나오는 단어들을 확인하세요.

01	inflationary	a. 인플레이션의	(✓ inflationary) risk	인플레이션에 관한 위험성
02	refer to	~을 나타내다, ~와 관련 있다	The word ( )s ( ) a kind of bird.	이 단어는 새의 한 종류를 의미한다.
03	uncertainty	n. 불확실성	refer to ( )	불확실성과 관련 있다
04	regarding	prep. ~에 대한(대하여)	uncertainty ( ) the future real value	미래 실질 가치에 대한 불확실성
05	investment	n. 투자	the future real value of one's ( )s	개인 투자의 미래 실질 가치
06	account	n. 계좌	in a bank ( )	은행 계좌에
07	fee	n. 수수료	have no ( )s	수수료가 없다
08	interest	n. 이자	pay ( )	이자를 갚다
09	earn	v. 벌다	( ) interest	이자를 벌다
10	in advance	미리	know ( ) ( )	미리 알다
11	firm	n. 회사	a law ( )	법률 사무소(로펌)
12	revenue	n. 수익, 수입	your firm's total ( )	당신 회사의 총수입
13	differentiate	v. 구별하다	( ) between two diseases	두 질병을 구별하다

➕ 본문 문장 속에서 단어들을 확인해 보세요.

Inflationary **risk** refers to uncertainty / regarding **the future real value of one's** investments.

인플레이션에 관한 **위험성**은 불확실성과 관련되어 있다 / **개인 투자**의 미래 실질 가치에 대한.

01	inflationary	🖉 인플레이션의	inflationary risk	인플레이션에 관한 위험성
02	refer to		The word refers to a kind of bird.	이 단어는 새의 한 종류를 의미한다.
03	uncertainty		refer to uncertainty	불확실성과 관련 있다
04	regarding		uncertainty regarding the future real value	미래 실질 가치에 대한 불확실성
05	investment		the future real value of one's investments	개인 투자의 미래 실질 가치
06	account		in a bank account	은행 계좌에
07	fee		have no fees	수수료가 없다
08	interest		pay interest	이자를 갚다
09	earn		earn interest	이자를 벌다
10	in advance		know in advance	미리 알다
11	firm		a law firm	법률 사무소(로펌)
12	revenue		your firm's total revenue	당신 회사의 총수입
13	differentiate		differentiate between two diseases	두 질병을 구별하다

➕ 본문 문장 속에서 단어의 의미를 우리말로 해석해 보세요.

Inflationary **risk** refers to uncertainty / regarding **the future real value of one's** investments.

→   위험성은   / 개인   의 미래 실질
가치   .

STEP **2** • 수능 기출 제대로 풀기

B

다음 글에서 전체 흐름과 관계 <u>없는</u> 문장은?

Inflationary risk refers to uncertainty regarding the future real value of one's investments. Say, for instance, that you hold $100 in a bank account that has no fees and accrues no interest. If left untouched there will always be $100 in that bank account. ① If you keep that money in the bank for a year, during which inflation is 100 percent, you've still got $100. ② Only now, if you take it out and put it in your wallet, you'll only be able to purchase half the goods you could have bought a year ago. ③ In other words, if inflation increases faster than the amount of interest you are earning, this will decrease the purchasing power of your investments over time. ④ It would be very useful to know in advance what would happen to your firm's total revenue if you increased your product's price. ⑤ That's why we differentiate between nominal value and real value.

*accrue: 생기다
**nominal: 명목의, 액면(상)의

정답과 해설 p.35

01 Inflatory risk refers to uncertainty / regarding the future real value of one's
전치사(~에 관한)
investments.

02 Say, for instance, / that you hold $100 in a bank account / that has no fees and accrues
명사절 접속사   주격 관계대명사절
no interest. // If left untouched / there will always be $100 in that bank account.
    it is 생략

03 If you keep that money in the bank for a year, / during which inflation is 100 percent, /
                    전치사+관계대명사절
you've still got $100.

04 Only now, / if you take it out and put it in your wallet, / you'll only be able to purchase
            시간과 조건의 부사절에서는 현재가 미래를 대신함
           could have p.p.: ~할 수도 있었다
half the goods / you could have bought a year ago.
           목적격 관계대명사절

05 In other words, / if inflation increases faster / than the amount of interest you are
           비교급+than: ~보다 더 ···한   목적격 관계대명사절
earning, / this will decrease the purchasing power of your investments / over time.

06 It would be very useful / [to know in advance / what would happen to your firm's total
가주어   진주어(to부정사)   의문사절(to know의 목적어)
revenue / if you increased your product's price].

07 That's why we differentiate between nominal value and real value.
이것이 ~한 이유다(뒤에 결과)

01 인플레이션에 관한inflatory 위험성은 불확실성과 관련되어 있다refer to uncertainty / 개인 투자investment의 미래 실질 가치에 대한regarding.

02 예를 들어보자, / 당신이 은행 계좌account에 100달러를 가지고 있다고 / 수수료fee가 없고 이자interest가 생기지 않는. // 그대로 내버려 두면, / 그 은행 계좌에는 항상 100달러가 있을 것이다.

03 만약 당신이 1년 동안 은행에 그 돈을 보관하고, / 그 기간에 인플레이션이 100퍼센트라면, / 당신은 여전히 100달러만 가지고 있는 것이다.

04 이제, / 만약 당신이 그 돈을 인출해서 당신의 지갑에 넣어둔다면, / 당신은 물건들의 절반만 구매할 수 있게 될 것이다 / 1년 전에 당신이 살 수도 있었던.

05 다시 말하자면, / 만약 인플레이션이 더 빨리 증가한다면 / 당신이 받고 있는earn 이자의 양보다, / 이것은 당신 투자의 구매력을 감소시킬 것이다 / 시간이 지남에 따라.

06 (매우 유용할 것이다 / 미리in advance 아는 것은 / 당신 회사firm의 총수입total revenue에 어떤 일이 일어날지를 / 만약 당신이 당신의 상품의 가격을 올린다면.)

07 그것이 우리가 명목 가치와 실질 가치를 구별하는differentiate 이유이다.

구문 Check up

① If you keep that money in the bank for a year, which / during which inflation is 100 percent, you've still got $100.

뒤따르는 절이 완전하므로 관계부사 when의 기능을 수행하는 <전치사+관계대명사> during which를 쓴다.

② It would be very useful to know in advance what / that would happen to your firm's total revenue if you increased your product's price.

to know의 목적어 자리에 명사절이 와야 하고, 뒤따르는 절에 주어가 없어 불완전하므로 의문사 what이 와야 한다.

STEP 1 • 수능에 *진짜* 나오는 *단어*

✔ 문제에 나오는 단어들을 확인하세요.

시간이 없다면 색으로 표시된 단어만이라도 꼭 외우고 넘어가세요!

01	ethically	ad. 윤리적으로	(✔ ethically) correct		윤리적으로 옳은
02	market	v. 판촉하다, 마케팅하다	( ) products		제품을 판촉하다
03	dilemma	n. 딜레마, 난제	a ( ) for psychologists		심리학자들의 딜레마
04	manipulate	v. 조종하다, 조작하다	( ) children into purchasing		아이들을 조종해서 구매하게 하다
05	admit to	~을 인정하다	( ) ( ) taking advantage		이용한 것을 인정하다
06	competitive	a. 경쟁력 있는	remain ( )		경쟁력을 유지하다
07	unfavorable	a. 부정적인, 호의적이지 않은	in an ( ) way		부정적인 방식으로
08	vulnerability	n. 취약성	their emotional ( )		그들의 정서적 취약성
09	inadequateness	n. 부적절함	feelings of ( )		부적절하다고 느끼는 감정
10	instant	a. 즉각적인, 순간적인	( ) emotions		즉각적인 감정
11	material	a. 물질적인	( ) possessions		물질적 소유물
12	possession	n. 소유(물)	Material ( )s are important.		물질적 소유물이 중요하다.

✚ 본문 문장 속에서 단어들을 확인해 보세요.

The constant feelings of inadequateness / created by advertising / have been suggested / to contribute to children becoming fixated / with instant gratification / and beliefs that material possessions are important.

끊임없이 부적절하다고 느끼는 감정은 / 광고에 의해 만들어진 (감정) / 언급되어 왔다 / 아이들이 집착하게 되는 데 기여한다고 / 즉각적인 만족감에 / 그리고 물질적 소유물이 중요하다는 믿음에.

문제를 풀기 전에 단어들을 **30초** 동안 다시 확인하세요.

01	ethically	🖊 윤리적으로	ethically correct	윤리적으로 옳은
02	market		market products	제품을 판촉하다
03	dilemma		a dilemma for psychologists	심리학자들의 딜레마
04	manipulate		manipulate children into purchasing	아이들을 조종해서 구매하게 하다
05	admit to		admit to taking advantage	이용한 것을 인정하다
06	competitive		remain competitive	경쟁력을 유지하다
07	unfavorable		in an unfavorable way	부정적인 방식으로
08	vulnerability		their emotional vulnerability	그들의 정서적 취약성
09	inadequateness		feelings of inadequateness	부적절하다고 느끼는 감정
10	instant		instant emotions	즉각적인 감정
11	material		material possessions	물질적 소유물
12	possession		Material possessions are important.	물질적 소유물이 중요하다.

➕ 본문 문장 속에서 단어의 의미를 우리말로 해석해 보세요.

The constant feelings of inadequateness / created by advertising / have been suggested / to contribute to children becoming fixated / with instant gratification / and beliefs that material possessions are important.

→ 끊임없이 _____ 하다고 느끼는 감정은 / 광고에 의해 만들어진 (감정) / 언급되어 왔다 / 아이들이 집착하게 되는 데 기여한 다고 / _____ 만족감에 / 그리고 _____ 이 중요하다는 믿음에.

제한시간 70초
난이도 ★★★☆☆

STEP **2** • 수능 기출 제대로 풀기

C

다음 글에서 전체 흐름과 관계 <u>없는</u> 문장은?

Academics, politicians, marketers and others have in the past debated whether or not it is ethically correct to market products and services directly to young consumers. ① This is also a dilemma for psychologists who have questioned whether they ought to help advertisers manipulate children into purchasing more products they have seen advertised. ② Advertisers have admitted to taking advantage of the fact that it is easy to make children feel that they are losers if they do not own the 'right' products. ③ When products become more popular, more competitors enter the marketplace and marketers lower their marketing costs to remain competitive. ④ Clever advertising informs children that they will be viewed by their peers in an unfavorable way if they do not have the products that are advertised, thereby playing on their emotional vulnerabilities. ⑤ The constant feelings of inadequateness created by advertising have been suggested to contribute to children becoming fixated with instant gratification and beliefs that material possessions are important.

*fixated: 집착하는
**gratification: 만족(감)

정답과 해설 p.36

01 Academics, politicians, marketers and others have in the past debated / whether or not
it is ethically correct / to market products and services / directly to young consumers.
가주어 삽입구 / 명사절 접속사(~인지 아닌지) / 진주어(to부정사)

02 This is also a dilemma for psychologists / [who have questioned / whether they ought
주격 관계대명사절 / 명사절 접속사(~인지 아닌지)
to help advertisers / manipulate children into purchasing more products / they have
원형부정사(to help의 목적격보어) / 목적격 관계대명사절
seen advertised].

03 Advertisers have admitted to taking advantage of the fact / that it is easy to make
가주어 진주어
admit to+동명사: ~한 것을 인정하다 동격의 that(=the fact)
children feel / that they are losers / if they do not own the 'right' products.
명사절 접속사(feel의 목적어)

04 When products become more popular, / more competitors enter the marketplace / and
marketers lower their marketing costs / to remain competitive.
remain+주격 보어(형용사)

05 Clever advertising informs children / [that they will be viewed by their peers / in an
4형식 동사 간접목적어 직접목적어(that절)
unfavorable way / if they do not have the products / that are advertised], / thereby
주격 관계대명사절
playing on their emotional vulnerabilities.
분사구문

06 The constant feelings of inadequateness / created by advertising / have been suggested
주어(복수) 과거분사 수 일치
/ to contribute to [children becoming fixated / with instant gratification / and beliefs
동명사의 의미상 주어(children)+동명사(becoming~)
that material possessions are important].
동격의 that(=beliefs)

01 지금까지 대학 교수, 정치인, 마케팅 담당자, 그리고 그 외의 사람들은 논쟁해왔다 / 윤리적으로ethically 옳은지 그렇지
않은지를 / 제품과 서비스를 판촉하는market 것이 / 어린 소비자들에게 직접.

02 이것은 또한 심리학자들에게도 딜레마dilemma이다 / 의문을 가진 / 그들이 광고주들을 도와야 할지 / 아이들이 제품을 더
많이 사도록 조종하는manipulate 것을 / 그들(아이들)이 광고되는 것을 본 (제품).

03 광고주들은 사실을 이용한 것을 인정했다admit to / 아이들이 느끼도록 만드는 것이 쉽다는 (사실) / 자신이 패배자라고 /
그 '적절한' 제품을 소유하고 있지 않으면.

04 (제품이 더 인기 있어질 때 / 더 많은 경쟁자들이 시장에 진출하고 / 마케팅 담당자들은 그들의 마케팅 비용을 줄인다 /
경쟁력을 유지하기remain competitive 위해.)

05 영리한 광고는 아이들에게 알려 준다 / 아이들이 자신의 또래 친구들에게 보일 것이라고 / 부정적으로in an
unfavorable way / 만약 그들이 제품을 가지고 있지 않으면 / 광고되는 (제품) / 그로 인해 (광고는) 아이들의 정서적인
취약성vulnerability을 이용한다.

06 끊임없이 부적절하다고 느끼는 감정feelings of inadequateness은 / 광고에 의해 만들어진 (감정) / 언급되어 왔다 /
아이들이 집착하게 되는 데 기여한다고 / 즉각적인instant 만족감에 / 그리고 물질적 소유물material possession이
중요하다는 믿음에.

① Advertisers have admitted to taking advantage of the
fact which / that it is easy to make children feel that
they are losers.

명사 the fact를 추가로 설명하는 완전한 절이 뒤따르므로 동격의 접속사
that을 쓴다.

② More competitors enter the marketplace and
marketers lower their marketing costs to remain
competitive / competitively .

2형식 동사 remain 뒤 주격보어 자리에는 형용사를 쓴다. 따라서
competitive가 적절하다.

구문 Check up

정답 ① that ② competitive

D

STEP **1** • 수능에 *진짜* 나오는 *단어*

 문제에 나오는 단어들을 확인하세요.

시간이 없다면 색으로 표시된 단어만이라도 꼭 외우고 넘어가세요!

01	interconnect	v. 서로 연결하다	Oceans are (✓ interconnect)ed.	대양은 서로 연결되어 있다.
02	geographical	a. 지리적인	( ) boundaries	지리적 경계
03	basin	n. 분지, 유역	the ocean ( )	대양의 분지
04	rotate	v. 회전하다, 돌다	The water slowly ( )s.	물은 천천히 돈다.
05	organism	n. 유기체	marine ( )s	해양 유기체
06	dispersal	n. 분산, 이산	the ( ) of their young	새끼의 분산
07	larva (*pl.* larvae)	n. 유충, 애벌레	their young or ( )e	그들의 새끼나 유충
08	region	n. 지역, 지대	near-shore ( )s	근해 지역
09	inhabit	v. 서식하다, 거주하다	( )ed by a variety of organisms	다양한 유기체에 의해 서식되는(다양한 유기체가 서식하는)
10	differ	v. 다르다	( )ing ecological tolerances	다른 생태학적 내성
11	ecological	a. 생태학적인, 생태계의	( ) system	생태계
12	tolerance	n. 내성	ecological ( )s	생태학적 내성
13	barrier	n. 장벽, 방해물	( )s to the movement	이동에 대한 방해물

⊕ 본문 문장 속에서 단어들을 확인해 보세요.

The major oceans are all interconnected, / so that their geographical boundaries are less clear / than those of the continents.

주요 대양은 모두 서로 연결되어 있어, / 그것들의 지리적 경계가 덜 명확하다 / 대륙의 경계보다.

문제를 풀기 전에 단어들을 **30초** 동안 다시 확인하세요.

01	interconnect	🖉 서로 연결하다	Oceans are interconnected.	대양은 서로 연결되어 있다.
02	geographical		geographical boundaries	지리적 경계
03	basin		the ocean basin	대양의 분지
04	rotate		The water slowly rotates.	물은 천천히 돈다.
05	organism		marine organisms	해양 유기체
06	dispersal		the dispersal of their young	새끼의 분산
07	larva		their young or larvae	그들의 새끼나 유충
08	region		near-shore regions	근해 지역
09	inhabit		inhabited by a variety of organisms	다양한 유기체에 의해 서식되는 (다양한 유기체가 서식하는)
10	differ		differing ecological tolerances	다른 생태학적 내성
11	ecological		ecological system	생태계
12	tolerance		ecological tolerances	생태학적 내성
13	barrier		barriers to the movement	이동에 대한 방해물

➕ **본문 문장 속에서 단어의 의미를 우리말로 해석해 보세요.**

The major oceans are all interconnected, / so that their geographical boundaries are less clear / than those of the continents.

➔ 주요 대양은 모두   있어, / 그것들의   경계가 덜 명확하다 / 대륙의 경계보다.

제한시간 80초
난이도 ★★★★☆

STEP **2** • 수능 기출 제대로 풀기

D 다음 글에서 전체 흐름과 관계 <u>없는</u> 문장은?

The major oceans are all interconnected, so that their geographical boundaries are less clear than those of the continents. As a result, their biotas show fewer clear differences than those on land. ① The oceans themselves are continually moving because the water within each ocean basin slowly rotates. ② These moving waters carry marine organisms from place to place, and also help the dispersal of their young or larvae. ③ In other words, coastal ocean currents not only move animals much less often than expected, but they also trap animals within near-shore regions. ④ Furthermore, the gradients between the environments of different areas of ocean water mass are very gradual and often extend over wide areas that are inhabited by a great variety of organisms of differing ecological tolerances. ⑤ There are no firm boundaries within the open oceans although there may be barriers to the movement of organisms.

*biota: 생물 군집
**gradient: 변화도

정답과 해설 p.36

01 The major oceans are all interconnected, / so that their geographical boundaries are
less clear / than those of the continents.
less ~ than(비교급)   (=boundaries)
그래서(결과)

02 As a result, / their biotas show fewer clear differences / than those on land.
fewer ~ than(비교급)   (=biotas)

03 The oceans themselves are continually moving / because the water within each ocean
basin slowly rotates.
접속사(이유) 주어
동사(단수)

04 These moving waters carry marine organisms / from place to place, / and also help the
dispersal of their young or larvae.

05 In other words, / coastal ocean currents not only move animals / much less often than
즉   not only A but also B: A뿐만 아니라 B도   비교급 강조
expected, / but they also trap animals within near-shore regions.

06 Furthermore, / [the gradients between the environments of different areas of ocean
주어(복수)
water mass] / are very gradual / and often extend over wide areas / that are inhabited by
동사 병렬연결   주격 관계대명사절
a great variety of organisms of differing ecological tolerances.

07 There are no firm boundaries / within the open oceans / although there may be barriers
~일지라도(양보)
to the movement of organisms.

01 주요 대양은 모두 서로 연결되어be interconnected 있어, / 그것들의 지리적 경계geographical boundary가 덜 명확하다
/ 대륙의 경계보다.

02 결과적으로 / 그들의 생물 군집은 명확한 차이를 덜 보여준다 / 육지에서의 생물 군집보다.

03 대양 자체가 끊임없이 움직인다 / 각 해저 분지ocean basin 안에서 물이 천천히 회전하기slowly rotate 때문에.

04 이 이동하는 물은 해양 생물marine organisms을 운반하며 / 여기저기로, / 또한 그들의 새끼나 유충larvae의
분산dispersal을 돕는다.

05 (즉 / 연안 해류는 동물들을 이동시킬 뿐 아니라 / 예상보다 훨씬 덜, / 근해 지역 내near-shore region로 동물을 가두기도
한다.)

06 더욱이 / 다양한 지역의 대양 해수 덩어리 환경 사이의 변화도는 / 매우 점진적이며, / 종종 넓은 지역으로 확장된다 /
생태학적 내성ecological tolerance이 다른differing 매우 다양한 유기체에 의해 거주되는be inhabited.

07 확실한 경계는 없다 / 넓은 대양에 / 유기체의 이동에 방해물barrier이 있을 수 있지만.

① Coastal ocean currents not only move animals very
/ much less often than expected, but they also trap
animals within nearshore regions.

② The gradients between the environments of different
areas of ocean water mass is / are very gradual and
often extend over wide areas.

비교급은 much, far, even, a lot 등으로 강조할 수 있으므로 much가 정답
이다. very는 원급 또는 최상급을 강조한다.

주어가 The gradients이므로 동사와 수 일치하면 are를 써야 한다.

정답 ① much ② are

E

STEP 1 · 수능에 *진짜* 나오는 *단어*

✔ 문제에 나오는 단어들을 확인하세요.

시간이 없다면 색으로 표시된 단어만이라도 꼭 외우고 넘어가세요!

01	erroneously	ad. 잘못되게, 틀리게	assume (✔ erroneously)	잘못 추정하다
02	**evidence**	n. 증거	( ) to suggest	시사하는 증거
03	comparative	a. 비교하는	the study of ( ) cultures	비교 문화 연구
04	content	n. 내용	cultural ( )	문화적인 내용
05	**attitude**	n. 태도	a friendly ( )	친근한 태도
06	behavioral	a. 행동의, 행동에 대한	( ) patterns	행동 양식
07	accomplish	v. 완수하다, 성취하다	( ) the task	과업을 완수하다
08	**efficiency**	n. 효율성	similar ( )	유사한 효율성
09	enhance	v. 강화하다, 향상시키다	( ) particularly	특별히 강화하다
10	adaptation	n. 적응(성)	enhance the ( ) to life	삶에 대한 적응성을 강화하다
11	adapt	v. 적응하다	( ) to the environment	환경에 적응하다
12	**lack**	v. 부족하다	( ) survival skills	생존 기술이 부족하다
13	track	v. 좇다, 추적하다	( ) a wounded animal	상처 난 동물을 추적하다

⊕ 본문 문장 속에서 단어들을 확인해 보세요.

The traditional Hadza hunter has not learned algebra / because such knowledge would not particularly enhance his adaptation / to life in the East African grasslands.

전통적인 Hadza 사냥꾼은 대수학을 학습하지 않았다 / 그런 지식이 적응성을 특별히 강화해주지 않기 때문에 / 동아프리카 목초지에서의 삶에 대한.

01	erroneously	✎ 잘못되게, 틀리게	assume erroneously	잘못 추정하다
02	evidence		evidence to suggest	시사하는 증거
03	comparative		the study of comparative cultures	비교 문화 연구
04	content		cultural content	문화적인 내용
05	attitude		a friendly attitude	친근한 태도
06	behavioral		behavioral patterns	행동 양식
07	accomplish		accomplish the task	과업을 완수하다
08	efficiency		similar efficiency	유사한 효율성
09	enhance		enhance particularly	특별히 강화하다
10	adaptation		enhance the adaptation to life	삶에 대한 적응성을 강화하다
11	adapt		adapt to the environment	환경에 적응하다
12	lack		lack survival skills	생존 기술이 부족하다
13	track		track a wounded animal	상처 난 동물을 추적하다

➕ **본문 문장 속에서 단어의 의미를 우리말로 해석해 보세요.**

The traditional Hadza hunter has not learned algebra / because such knowledge would not particularly enhance his adaptation / to life in the East African grasslands.

➡ 전통적인 Hadza 사냥꾼은 대수학을 학습하지 않았다 / 그런 지식이   을 특별히   않기 때문에 / 동아프리카 목초지에서의 삶에 대한.

STEP **2** • 수능 기출 제대로 풀기

E

다음 글에서 전체 흐름과 관계 없는 문장은?

People often assume erroneously that if a Hadza adult of Tanzania does not know how to solve an algebraic equation, then he must be less intelligent than we are. ① Yet there is no evidence to suggest that people from some cultures are fast learners and people from others are slow learners. ② The study of comparative cultures has taught us that people in different cultures learn different cultural content (attitudes, values, ideas, and behavioral patterns) and that they accomplish this with similar efficiency. ③ The traditional Hadza hunter has not learned algebra because such knowledge would not particularly enhance his adaptation to life in the East African grasslands. ④ Consequently, he failed to adapt to the environment of the grasslands because he lacked survival skills. ⑤ However, he would know how to track a wounded bush buck that he has not seen for three days and where to find groundwater.

*algebraic equation: 대수 방정식
**bush buck: 부시 벅(아프리카 영양)

정답과 해설 p.36

STEP 3 · 수능 지문 제대로 복습하기

01 People often assume erroneously / [that if a Hadza adult of Tanzania does not know /
how to solve an algebraic equation, / then he must be less intelligent than we are].
that절 안에 if 조건절이 있는 구조
목적어(that절) / 목적어(의문사+to부정사) / 강한 추측: ~임에 틀림없다 / 대동사(=are intelligent)

02 Yet there is no evidence [to suggest / that people from some cultures are fast learners /
and people from others are slow learners].
형용사적 용법 / 부정대명사(=other cultures)

03 The study of comparative cultures / has taught us / [that people in different cultures
learn different cultural content (attitudes, values, ideas, and behavioral patterns)] /
and [that they accomplish this / with similar efficiency].
수여동사+간접목적어+직접목적어(that절) / 병렬연결(that절)

04 The traditional Hadza hunter has not learned algebra / because such knowledge would
not particularly enhance his adaptation / to life in the East African grasslands.
현재완료

05 Consequently, / he failed to adapt / to the environment of the grasslands / because he
lacked survival skills.
fail+to부정사: ~하지 못하다

06 However, / he would know how to track a wounded bush buck / that he has not seen for
three days / and where to find groundwater.
동사 / 목적어1(의문사+to부정사) / 목적격 관계대명사절 / 목적어2(의문사+to부정사)

01 사람들은 종종 잘못 추정한다assume erroneously / 만약 Tanzania의 Hadza의 한 성인이 모른다면 / 대수 방정식을 푸는 방법을 / 그가 우리보다 덜 똑똑함에 틀림없다고.

02 그러나 보여주는 증거evidence to suggest는 없다 / 어떤 문화의 사람은 빠른 학습자이고 / 다른 문화의 사람은 느린 학습자라는 것을.

03 비교 문화comparative culture 연구는 / 우리에게 가르쳐왔다 / 다른 문화의 사람들이 다른 문화적인 내용cultural content(태도attitude, 가치관, 생각, 그리고 행동 양식behavioral pattern)을 배운다고 / 그리고 그들이 이것을 성취한다accomplish고 / 유사한 효율성similar efficiency을 갖고.

04 전통적인 Hadza 사냥꾼은 대수학을 학습하지 않았다 / 그런 지식이 적응성adaptation을 특별히 강화해주지enhance 않기 때문에 / 동아프리카 목초지에서의 삶에 대한.

05 (결과적으로, / 그는 적응하는adapt 데 실패했다 / 목초지의 환경에 / 생존 기술이 부족했기lack survival skills 때문에.)

06 그러나, / 그는 상처 입은 부시 벅을 어떻게 추적하는지track를 알 것이다 / 3일 동안 보지 못한 / 그리고 어디에서 지하수를 찾을 수 있는지를 (알 것이다).

구문 Check up

① The study of comparative cultures have / has taught us that people in different cultures learn different cultural content.

주어가 The study이기 때문에 이것에 수 일치하여 has를 쓴다.

② Consequently, he failed to adapt / adaptation to the environment of the grasslands because he lacked survival skills.

동사 failed 다음에 to부정사가 오는 구문이므로 동사 adapt를 쓴다.

정답 ① has ② adapt

STEP 1 • 수능에 진짜 나오는 단어

✔ 문제에 나오는 단어들을 확인하세요.

시간이 없다면 색으로 표시된 단어만이라도 꼭 외우고 넘어가세요!

01	defence	n. 방어	natural (✔ defence)	자연적 방어
02	immune	a. 면역의	the ( ) system	면역 체계
03	complicated	a. 복잡한	a ( ) system	복잡한 체계
04	mobilize	v. 가동하다, 동원하다	The body is ( )d.	신체는 가동된다.
05	produce	v. 생산하다	( ) special cells	특별한 세포를 만들어내다
06	army	n. 군대	a kind of ( )	일종의 군대
07	recover	v. 회복하다	The person ( )s.	그 사람은 회복한다.
08	equipment	n. 장비, 장치	the molecular ( )	분자로 된 장비
09	particular	a. 특정한	that ( ) battle	그 특정한 전투
10	infection	n. 감염	any following ( )	모든 후속 감염
11	weakened	a. 약해진	the ( ) immune system	약해진 면역 체계
12	resistance	n. 저항, 저항력	weaken ( )	저항력을 약화시키다
13	measles	n. 홍역	a disease like the ( )	홍역과 같은 질병

⊕ 본문 문장 속에서 단어들을 확인해 보세요.

After that, / the immune system remembers the molecular equipment / that it developed for that particular battle, / and any following infection by the same kind of parasite / is beaten off so quickly / that we don't notice it.

그 후, / 면역 체계가 분자로 된 장비를 기억해서 / 그 특정한 전투를 위해 발달시켰던, / 똑같은 균에 대한 모든 후속 감염은 / 너무 빨리 퇴치되어 / 우리는 그것을 알아차리지도 못한다.

문제를 풀기 전에 단어들을 30초 동안 다시 확인하세요.

01	defence	🖉 방어	natural defence	자연적 방어
02	immune		the immune system	면역 체계
03	complicated		a complicated system	복잡한 체계
04	mobilize		The body is mobilized.	신체는 가동된다.
05	produce		produce special cells	특별한 세포를 만들어내다
06	army		a kind of army	일종의 군대
07	recover		The person recovers.	그 사람은 회복한다.
08	equipment		the molecular equipment	분자로 된 장비
09	particular		that particular battle	그 특정한 전투
10	infection		any following infection	모든 후속 감염
11	weakened		the weakened immune system	약해진 면역 체계
12	resistance		weaken resistance	저항력을 약화시키다
13	measles		a disease like the measles	홍역과 같은 질병

➕ 본문 문장 속에서 단어의 의미를 우리말로 해석해 보세요.

After that, / the immune system remembers the molecular equipment / that it developed for that particular battle, / and any following infection by the same kind of parasite / is beaten off so quickly / that we don't notice it.

→ 그 후, / ▨▨▨▨▨ 가 분자로 된 ▨▨▨▨▨ 를 기억해서 / 그 ▨▨▨▨▨ 전투를 위해 발달시켰던, / 똑같은 균에 대한 ▨▨▨▨▨ 은 / 너무 빨리 퇴치되어 / 우리는 그것을 알아차리지도 못한다.

STEP **2** • 수능 기출 제대로 풀기

F

다음 글에서 전체 흐름과 관계 <u>없는</u> 문장은?

The body has an effective system of natural defence against parasites, called the immune system. The immune system is so complicated that it would take a whole book to explain it. ① Briefly, when it senses a dangerous parasite, the body is mobilized to produce special cells, which are carried by the blood into battle like a kind of army. ② Usually the immune system wins, and the person recovers. ③ After that, the immune system remembers the molecular equipment that it developed for that particular battle, and any following infection by the same kind of parasite is beaten off so quickly that we don't notice it. ④ As a result, the weakened immune system leads to infection, and the infection causes damage to the immune system, which further weakens resistance. ⑤ That is why, once you have had a disease like the measles or chicken pox, you're unlikely to get it again.

*parasite: 기생충, 균
**molecular: 분자의

정답과 해설 p.37

STEP 3 · 수능 지문 제대로 복습하기

01 The body has an effective system of natural defence / against parasites, / called the immune system.
보어(선행사와 동격)　　　　　　　　　　　　　　　　　　　　　과거분사

02 The immune system is so complicated / that it would take a whole book / to explain it.
　　　　　　　　　so 형용사/부사 that …: 너무 ~해서 …하다

03 Briefly, / when it senses a dangerous parasite, / the body is mobilized / to produce
special cells, / which are carried by the blood into battle / like a kind of army.
선행사(복수)　　　주격 관계대명사(계속적 용법)　　　　　　　　　수동태(be+p.p.)

04 Usually the immune system wins, / and the person recovers. // After that, / the immune
system remembers the molecular equipment / that it developed for that particular
　　　　　　　　　　　　　　　　　　　　　　목적격 관계대명사
battle, / and any following infection by the same kind of parasite / is beaten off
　　　　　　　　　　　　　　　　　　　　　　　　　　　　　　수동태(be+p.p.)
so quickly / that we don't notice it.
so 형용사/부사 that …: 너무 ~해서 …하다

05 As a result, / the weakened immune system leads to infection, / and the infection
　　　　　　　　과거분사
causes damage to the immune system, / which further weakens resistance.
　　　　　　　　　　　　　　　　　주격 관계대명사(계속적 용법)

06 That is why, / once you have had a disease like the measles or chicken pox, / you're
　　　　　　접속사(일단 ~하면)
the reason 생략　　현재완료
unlikely to get it again.

---

01 신체는 효율적인 자연적 방어natural defence 체계를 갖고 있다 / 병균에 대항하는 / 면역 체계the immune system라 불리는.

02 면역 체계는 너무나 복잡해서complicated / 책 한 권이 있어야 할 것이다 / 그것을 설명하려면.

03 간단히 말해 / 면역 체계가 위험한 균을 감지할 때, / 신체는 가동되며be mobilized / 특별한 세포를 만들어내기produce 위해, / 그 세포는 혈액에 의해 전쟁터로 운반된다 / 마치 군대army처럼.

04 보통은 면역 체계가 승리하고, / 그 사람은 회복한다recover. // 그 후, / 면역 체계가 분자로 된 장비equipment를 기억해서 / 그 특정한particular 전투를 위해 발달시켰던, / 똑같은 균에 대한 모든 후속 감염infection은 / 너무 빨리 퇴치되어 / 우리는 그것을 알아차리지도 못한다.

05 (그 결과 / 약해진weakened 면역 체계는 감염을 일으키고, / 그 감염은 면역 체계에 손상을 일으켜, / 더 나아가 저항력resistance을 약화시킨다.)

06 그것이 이유이다 / 당신이 홍역the measles이나 천연두와 같은 질병을 한 번 앓고 나면, / 그것에 다시 걸릴 가능성은 거의 없어지는.

구문 Check up

① The body has an effective system of natural defence against parasites, calling / called the immune system.

② Briefly, when it senses a dangerous parasite, the body is mobilized to produce special cells, that / which are carried by the blood into battle like a kind of army.

수식을 받는 명사(an effective system)와 분사의 관계가 수동이므로 과거분사 called가 적절하다.

관계대명사 that은 계속적 용법으로 쓸 수 없으므로 which가 적절하다.

정답 ① called ② which

STEP 1 • 수능에 *진짜* 나오는 *단어*

✔️ **문제에 나오는 단어들을 확인하세요.**

시간이 없다면 색으로 표시된 단어만이라도 꼭 외우고 넘어가세요!

01	humidity	n. 습도	data on (✔️ humidity)		습도에 관한 자료
02	pressure	n. 압력	air ( )		기압
03	force	n. 힘, 세기	wind ( )		바람의 세기
04	radiation	n. 복사열	the Earth ( )		지구 복사열
05	near	v. 접근하다, 다가가다	The tornado ( )ed the area.		토네이도가 그 지역에 접근했다.
06	delivery	n. 배달	( ) systems		배달 시스템
07	transportation	n. 교통수단, 운송(업)	public ( )		공공 교통수단
08	carrier	n. 운반 장치, 운반차	transportation ( )s		수송 수단들
09	pollute	v. 오염시키다	( ) the air		공기를 오염시키다
10	atmosphere	n. 대기	pollute the ( )		대기를 오염시키다
11	relevant	a. 유의미한, 관련 있는	( ) data		유의미한 자료
12	accurate	a. 정확한	( ) predictions		정확한 예측
13	prediction	n. 예측	( )s about the future		미래에 대한 예측

➕ **본문 문장 속에서 단어들을 확인해 보세요.**

With drone delivery systems, / fewer transportation carriers will be traveling on roads / and polluting the atmosphere.

드론 배달 시스템으로, / 더 적은 수송 수단들이 도로 위를 주행하며 / 대기를 오염시킬 것이다.

01	humidity	습도	data on humidity	습도에 관한 자료
02	pressure		air pressure	기압
03	force		wind force	바람의 세기
04	radiation		the Earth radiation	지구 복사열
05	near		The tornado neared the area.	토네이도가 그 지역에 접근했다.
06	delivery		delivery systems	배달 시스템
07	transportation		public transportation	공공 교통수단
08	carrier		transportation carriers	수송 수단들
09	pollute		pollute the air	공기를 오염시키다
10	atmosphere		pollute the atmosphere	대기를 오염시키다
11	relevant		relevant data	유의미한 자료
12	accurate		accurate predictions	정확한 예측
13	prediction		predictions about the future	미래에 대한 예측

➕ 본문 문장 속에서 단어의 의미를 우리말로 해석해 보세요.

With drone delivery systems, / fewer transportation carriers will be traveling on roads / and polluting the atmosphere.

➔ 드론 _____ 시스템으로, / 더 적은 _____ 이 도로 위를 주행하며 / _____ 것이다.

STEP **2** • 수능 기출 제대로 풀기

G

다음 글에서 전체 흐름과 관계 <u>없는</u> 문장은?

The use of drones in science has been increasing. Drones may be useful to collect all kinds of research data. ① For instance, in meteorology drones can collect data on humidity, pressure, temperature, wind force, radiation, etc. ② In case of nearing tornados or hurricanes, people can seek safety with the help of the data gathered by drones. ③ With drone delivery systems, fewer transportation carriers will be traveling on roads and polluting the atmosphere. ④ Drones can gather relevant data in places that were previously difficult or costly to reach — data that may provide new scientific knowledge about the atmosphere and the climate. ⑤ Such knowledge may improve existing climate models and provide more accurate predictions.

*meteorology: 기상학

정답과 해설 p.37

01 The use of drones in science / has been increasing. // Drones may be useful / to collect
have been+-ing(현재완료 진행): 과거부터 쭉 지금까지 해오다
all kinds of research data.

02 For instance, / in meteorology / drones can collect data / on humidity, pressure,
temperature, wind force, radiation, etc.

03 In case of nearing tornados or hurricanes, / people can seek safety / with the help
현재분사
of the data / gathered by drones.
과거분사(명사 수식)

04 With drone delivery systems, / fewer transportation carriers will be traveling on roads /
and polluting the atmosphere.
will be에 등위접속사 and로 병렬연결

05 Drones can gather relevant data in places / that were previously difficult or costly to
주격 관계대명사절
reach / — data that may provide new scientific knowledge about the atmosphere and
주격 관계대명사절
the climate.

06 Such knowledge may improve existing climate models / and provide more accurate
predictions.

01 과학 분야에서 드론의 사용이 / 증가해 오고 있다. // 드론은 도움이 될 수 있다 / 모든 종류의 연구 자료를 수집하는 데.

02 예를 들면, / 기상학 분야에서 / 드론은 자료를 수집할 수 있다 / 습도humidity, 기압pressure, 온도, 바람의 세기wind force, 복사열radiation 등에 관한.

03 토네이도나 허리케인이 접근하는near 경우에 / 사람들은 안전을 추구할 수 있다 / 정보의 도움으로 / 드론에 의해 수집된.

04 (드론 배달 시스템delivery system으로, / 더 적은 수송 수단transportation carrier들이 도로 위를 주행하며 / 대기를 오염시킬pollute the atmosphere 것이다.)

05 드론은 장소에서 유의미한 자료relevant data를 모을 수 있다 / 이전에는 도달하기 어렵거나 비용이 많이 들었던 (장소) / 즉, 대기와 기후에 관한 새로운 과학적 지식을 제공할 자료(를 모을 수 있다).

06 그러한 지식은 기존의 기후 모형을 개선하고 / 더 정확한 예측accurate prediction을 제공할 것이다.

① In case of nearing tornados or hurricanes, people can seek safety with the help of the data gather / gathered by drones.

문장의 동사는 seek이고 접속사가 없기 때문에 다른 동사가 연결될 수 없다. 따라서 gather는 data를 수식하는 분사형 gathered로 쓴다.

② Drones can gather relevant data in places that was / were previously difficult or costly to reach.

주격 관계대명사 that 뒤의 동사는 선행사 places에 수 일치시켜 were로 쓴다.

정답 ① gathered ② were

294

주어진 문장 넣기 ➕

STEP 1 • 수능에 *진짜* 나오는 *단어*

✔ 문제에 나오는 단어들을 확인하세요.

시간이 없다면 색으로 표시된 단어만이라도 꼭 외우고 넘어가세요!

01	fundamental	a. 근본적인	the (✔ fundamental) nature	근본적인 본질
02	experimental	a. 실험의	the ( ) method	실험 방법
03	manipulation	n. 조작	( ) and control	조작과 통제
04	variable	n. 변인, 변수 a. 가변적인	a ( ) of interest	관심 변인
05	identify	v. 식별하다, 확인하다	( ) the causes of events	사건의 원인을 식별하다
06	underlying	a. 근본적인, 기저에 있는	the ( ) reason	근본적인 이유
07	overstate	v. 강조하다	cannot be ( )d	아무리 강조해도 지나치지 않다
08	correlate	v. 상관관계를 보여주다, 서로 관련시키다	( )d variables	상관관계가 있는 변인들
09	supplement	n. 보충(제)	take vitamin ( )s	비타민 보충제를 섭취하다
10	health effect	건강상 영향	the ( ) ( )s of vitamins	비타민의 건강상 영향
11	constant	a. 일정한, 변함없는	hold everything else ( )	다른 모든 것을 일정하게 유지하다

➕ 본문 문장 속에서 단어들을 확인해 보세요.

The fundamental nature of the experimental method / is manipulation and control.

실험 방법의 근본적인 본질은 / 조작과 통제이다.

01	fundamental	🖊 근본적인	the fundamental nature	근본적인 본질
02	experimental		the experimental method	실험 방법
03	manipulation		manipulation and control	조작과 통제
04	variable		a variable of interest	관심 변인
05	identify		identify the causes of events	사건의 원인을 식별하다
06	underlying		the underlying reason	근본적인 이유
07	overstate		cannot be overstated	아무리 강조해도 지나치지 않다
08	correlate		correlated variables	상관관계가 있는 변인들
09	supplement		take vitamin supplements	비타민 보충제를 섭취하다
10	health effect		the health effects of vitamins	비타민의 건강상 영향
11	constant		hold everything else constant	다른 모든 것을 일정하게 유지하다

➕ 본문 문장 속에서 단어의 의미를 우리말로 해석해 보세요.

The fundamental nature of the experimental method / is manipulation and control.

→ _____의 _____ 본질은 / _____과 _____이다.

STEP **2** • 수능 기출 제대로 풀기

A
글의 흐름으로 보아, 주어진 문장이 들어가기에 가장 적절한 곳은?

Rather, we have to create a situation that doesn't actually occur in the real world.

The fundamental nature of the experimental method is manipulation and control. Scientists manipulate a variable of interest, and see if there's a difference. At the same time, they attempt to control for the potential effects of all other variables. The importance of controlled experiments in identifying the underlying causes of events cannot be overstated. (①) In the real-uncontrolled-world, variables are often correlated. (②) For example, people who take vitamin supplements may have different eating and exercise habits than people who don't take vitamins. (③) As a result, if we want to study the health effects of vitamins, we can't merely observe the real world, since any of these factors (the vitamins, diet, or exercise) may affect health. (④) That's just what scientific experiments do. (⑤) They try to separate the naturally occurring relationship in the world by manipulating one specific variable at a time, while holding everything else constant.

정답과 해설 **p.39**

01 The fundamental nature of the experimental method / is manipulation and control. //
주어   동사(단수)
Scientists manipulate a variable of interest, / and see if there's a difference. // At the
                                  ~인지 아닌지(= whether)
same time, / they attempt to control for the potential effects of all other variables. //
The importance of controlled experiments / in identifying the underlying causes of
                                    ~할 때, ~하는 데 (있어)
events / cannot be overstated.
        아무리 강조해도 지나치지 않다

02 In the real-uncontrolled-world, / variables are often correlated. // For example, / people
who take vitamin supplements / may have different eating and exercise habits / than
주격 관계대명사절   ~와는 다른
people who don't take vitamins.
            주격 관계대명사절

03 As a result, / if we want to study the health effects of vitamins, / we can't merely
observe the real world, / since any of these factors (the vitamins, diet, or exercise) /
              ~ 때문에   동사(단수: 선행사에 수 일치)
may affect health. // Rather, / we have to create a situation / that doesn't actually occur
                                            주격 관계대명사절
in the real world.

04 That's just what scientific experiments do. // They try to separate the naturally
지시대명사(= create a situation that doesn't actually occur ~)   ~하려고 (노력)하다
occurring relationship in the world / by manipulating one specific variable at a time, /
현재분사구
while holding everything else constant.
접속사를 남긴 분사구문(=while they hold ~)

01 실험experimental 방법의 근본적인fundamental 본질은 / 조작manipulation과 통제이다. // 과학자들은 관심
변인variable을 조작하고, / 차이가 있는지 확인한다. // 동시에, / 그들은 다른 모든 변인의 잠재적 영향을 통제하려고
시도한다. // 통제된 실험의 중요성은 / 사건의 근본적인underlying 원인을 식별하는identify 데 있어 / 아무리 강조해도
지나치지 않다cannot be overstated.

02 현실의 통제되지 않은 세계에서, / 변인들은 종종 상관관계가 있다correlate. // 예를 들어, / 비타민 보충제supplement를
섭취하는 사람들은 / 다른 식습관과 운동 습관을 지닐 수 있다 / 비타민을 섭취하지 않는 사람들과는.

03 그 결과, / 만약 우리가 비타민의 건강상 영향health effect을 연구하고 싶다면, / 우리는 단지 현실 세계만 관찰할 수
없는데, / 왜냐하면 이러한 요소(비타민, 식단, 운동) 중 어느 것이든 / 건강에 영향을 미칠 수 있기 때문이다. // 오히려, /
우리는 상황을 만들어야 한다 / 현실 세계에서 실제로 일어나지 않는.

04 그것이 바로 과학 실험이 하는 일이다. // 그것들은 세상에서 자연적으로 발생하는 관계를 분리하려고 애쓴다 / 한 번에
하나의 특정 변인을 조작하여 / 그 밖의 다른 모든 것을 일정하게constant 유지하면서.

구문 Check up

① The fundamental nature of the experimental method
   are / is manipulation and control.

핵심 주어가 단수명사인 'The ~ nature'이므로 단수동사 is가 적합하다.

② Rather, we have to create a situation that / where
   doesn't actually occur in the real world.

뒤에 주어 없는 불완전한 절이 나오는 것으로 보아 관계대명사 that이 적
합하다.

정답 ① is ② that

298

B

STEP 1 • 수능에 *진짜* 나오는 *단어*

✔ 문제에 나오는 단어들을 확인하세요.

시간이 없다면 색으로 표시된 단어만이라도 꼭 외우고 넘어가세요!

01	capacity	n. 능력	the (✔ capacity) to produce chemicals	화학 물질을 생산하는 능력
02	inherit	v. 물려받다	the capacity is ( )ed	능력이 유전되다
03	adaptation	n. 적응	( ) involves changes.	적응은 변화를 수반한다.
04	acclimation	n. (환경 변화에 대한) 순응, 적응	( ) training	(환경) 적응 훈련
05	organism	n. 유기체, 생물	an individual ( )'s change	개별 유기체의 변화
06	alter	v. 바꾸다, 변경하다	an ( )ed environment	바뀐 환경
07	concentration	n. 농도	increase the ( )	농도를 높이다
08	temporary	a. 일시적인	a ( ) change	일시적인 변화
09	intensely	ad. 강렬히	( ) sunny environments	햇빛이 강렬한 환경
10	thrive	v. 번영하다	be likely to ( )	번영할 가능성이 높다
11	subsequent	a. 이후의, 차후의	( ) generations	이후 세대
12	distinctive	a. 특징적인, 독특한	the ( ) long neck of a giraffe	기린의 특징적인 긴 목
13	happen to	우연히 ~하게 되다	( ) ( ) have long necks	우연히 긴 목을 갖게 되다
14	advantage	n. 유리함, 이점	have an ( )	이점을 갖다

⊕ 본문 문장 속에서 단어들을 확인해 보세요.

Adaptation involves changes in a population, / with characteristics / that are passed from one generation to the next.

적응은 개체군의 변화를 수반한다 / 특성들과 함께 / 한 세대로부터 다음으로 전해지는.

01	capacity	✎ 능력	the capacity to produce chemicals	화학 물질을 생산하는 능력
02	inherit		the capacity is inherited	능력이 유전되다
03	adaptation		Adaptation involves changes.	적응은 변화를 수반한다.
04	acclimation		acclimation training	(환경) 적응 훈련
05	organism		an individual organism's change	개별 유기체의 변화
06	alter		an altered environment	바뀐 환경
07	concentration		increase the concentration	농도를 높이다
08	temporary		a temporary change	일시적인 변화
09	intensely		intensely sunny environments	햇빛이 강력한 환경
10	thrive		be likely to thrive	번영할 가능성이 높다
11	subsequent		subsequent generations	이후 세대
12	distinctive		the distinctive long neck of a giraffe	기린의 특징적인 긴 목
13	happen to		happen to have long necks	우연히 긴 목을 갖게 되다
14	advantage		have an advantage	이점을 갖다

➕ 본문 문장 속에서 단어의 의미를 우리말로 해석해 보세요.

Adaptation involves changes in a population, / with characteristics / that are passed from one generation to the next.

→ ▓▓▓▓▓▓▓▓ 개체군의 ▓▓▓▓▓▓▓▓▓ / 특성들과 함께 / 한 세대로부터 다음으로 전해지는.

STEP **2** • 수능 기출 제대로 풀기

B 글의 흐름으로 보아, 주어진 문장이 들어가기에 가장 적절한 곳은?

> However, the capacity to produce skin pigments is inherited.

Adaptation involves changes in a population, with characteristics that are passed from one generation to the next. This is different from acclimation — an individual organism's changes in response to an altered environment. (①) For example, if you spend the summer outside, you may acclimate to the sunlight: your skin will increase its concentration of dark pigments that protect you from the sun. (②) This is a temporary change, and you won't pass the temporary change on to future generations. (③) For populations living in intensely sunny environments, individuals with a good ability to produce skin pigments are more likely to thrive, or to survive, than people with a poor ability to produce pigments, and that trait becomes increasingly common in subsequent generations. (④) If you look around, you can find countless examples of adaptation. (⑤) The distinctive long neck of a giraffe, for example, developed as individuals that happened to have longer necks had an advantage in feeding on the leaves of tall trees.

*pigment: 색소

정답과 해설 **p.39**

01 Adaptation involves changes in a population, / with characteristics / that are passed
from one generation to the next.
　　　　　　　　　　　　　　　　　　　　　　　　주격 관계대명사절

02 This is different from acclimation / — an individual organism's changes / in response
　　　　　　　　　　　　　　　동격
to an altered environment.

03 For example, / if you spend the summer outside, / you may acclimate to the sunlight: /
your skin will increase its concentration of dark pigments / that protect you from the
　　　　　　　　　　　　　　　　　　　　　　　　　　　　주격 관계대명사절
sun.

04 This is a temporary change, / and you won't pass the temporary change on / to future
generations. // However, / the capacity to produce skin pigments / is inherited.
　　　　　　　　　　　　　　　　　　to부정사의 형용사적 용법

05 For populations living in intensely sunny environments, / individuals with a good
　　　　　　　　　　현재분사구(명사 수식)　　　　　　　　　주어
ability to produce skin pigments / are more likely to thrive, or to survive, / than people
　　　to부정사의 형용사적 용법　　　동사(수 일치)
with a poor ability to produce pigments, / and that trait becomes increasingly common
　　　　　　　to부정사의 형용사적 용법
/ in subsequent generations.

06 If you look around, / you can find countless examples of adaptation. // The distinctive
long neck of a giraffe, / for example, / developed / as individuals that happened to have
　　　　　　　　　　　　　　　　　　동사　　　접속사(이유)　주어　　　주격 관계대명사절
longer necks / had an advantage in feeding on the leaves of tall trees.
　　　　　　동사

01 적응adaptation은 개체군의 변화를 수반한다 / 특성들과 함께 / 한 세대로부터 다음 세대로 전해지는.

02 이것은 순응acclimation과는 다르다 / — 개별 유기체organism의 변화 / 바뀐altered 환경에 반응한.

03 예를 들어, / 당신이 여름을 야외에서 보낸다면, / 당신은 햇빛에 순응하게 될 것이다. / 당신의 피부는 어두운 색소의
농도concentration를 높일 것이다 / 당신을 태양으로부터 보호하는.

04 이것은 일시적인temporary 변화이고, / 당신은 그 일시적인 변화를 물려주지 않을 것이다 / 미래 세대에. // 하지만, / 피부
색소를 생산하는 능력capacity은 / 유전된다be inherited.

05 햇빛이 강렬한intensely sunny 환경에 사는 사람들의 경우, / 피부 색소를 생산하는 능력이 좋은 사람들이 / 더
번영하거나thrive 생존할 가능성이 높다 / 색소를 생산하는 능력이 좋지 않은 사람들보다 / 그리고 그 특징은 더욱
흔해진다 / 이후subsequent 세대에서.

06 주변을 둘러보면, / 당신은 적응의 수많은 사례를 찾을 수 있다. // 기린의 특징적인distinctive 긴 목은 / 발달했다 / 예를
들어 / 우연히happen to 더 긴 목을 갖게 된 개체들이 / 높은 나무의 잎을 먹는 데 유리했기have an advantage 때문에.

① Your skin will increase its concentration of dark
pigments that / what protect you from the sun.

② The distinctive long neck of a giraffe, for example,
developed / developing as individuals that happened
to have longer necks had an advantage in feeding on
the leaves of tall trees.

선행사가 있고 뒤따르는 절이 불완전하므로 관계대명사 that을 써야 한
다.

주절의 동사가 없으므로 과거형 동사 developed를 써야 한다. as 이하는
부사절이다.

정답 ① that ② developed

✔ 문제에 나오는 단어들을 확인하세요.

시간이 없다면 색으로 표시된 단어만이라도 꼭 외우고 넘어가세요!

01	transfer	n. 이전, 이동	(✔ transfer) of a risk	위험의 이전
02	inherit	v. 이어받다, 상속받다	(　　　　) another risk	다른 위험을 이어받다
03	uncertainty	n. 불확실성	arise from (　　　　　)	불확실성으로부터 발생하다
04	party	n. 당사자	contract with a (　　　)	당사자와 계약하다
05	experienced	a. 숙련된, 능숙한	a party who is (　　　　　)	숙련된 당사자
06	associated	a. 관련된	the (　　　　　) risk	관련된 위험
07	capital	n. 자본	the (　　　　) cost	자본 비용
08	equipment	n. 장비	the tooling and (　　　　　)	도구 및 장비
09	manufacturer	n. 제조업자	a leading (　　　　　)	선도적인 제조업자
10	component	n. 부품	major (　　　　　)s	주요 부품들
11	supplier	n. 공급업자	(　　　　　)s familiar with the component	그 부품에 정통한 공급업자들
12	relieve	v. 덜어주다	(　　　　) him of the risk	그에게 위험을 덜어주다
13	management	n. 관리	careful (　　　　　)	신중한 관리

⊕ 본문 문장 속에서 단어들을 확인해 보세요.

One way to avoid such risk / is to contract with a party / who is experienced and knows how to do it.

그러한 위험을 피할 수 있는 한 가지 방식은 / 당사자와 계약하는 것이다 / 숙련되었으며 그것을 하는 방법을 알고 있는.

303

01	transfer	✏ 이전, 이동	transfer of a risk	위험의 이전
02	inherit		inherit another risk	다른 위험을 이어받다
03	uncertainty		arise from uncertainty	불확실성으로부터 발생하다
04	party		contract with a party	당사자와 계약하다
05	experienced		a party who is experienced	숙련된 당사자
06	associated		the associated risk	관련된 위험
07	capital		the capital cost	자본 비용
08	equipment		the tooling and equipment	도구 및 장비
09	manufacturer		a leading manufacturer	선도적인 제조업자
10	component		major components	주요 부품들
11	supplier		suppliers familiar with the components	부품에 정통한 공급업자들
12	relieve		relieve him of the risk	그에게 위험을 덜어주다
13	management		careful management	신중한 관리

➕ **본문 문장 속에서 단어의 의미를 우리말로 해석해 보세요.**

One way to avoid such risk / is to contract with a party / who is experienced and knows how to do it.

→ 그러한 위험을 피할 수 있는 한 가지 방식은 /   와 계약하는 것이다 /   그것을 하는 방법을 알고 있는.

STEP **2** • 수능 기출 제대로 풀기

C 글의 흐름으로 보아, 주어진 문장이 들어가기에 가장 적절한 곳은?

However, transfer of one kind of risk often means inheriting another kind.

Risk often arises from uncertainty about how to approach a problem or situation. (①) One way to avoid such risk is to contract with a party who is experienced and knows how to do it. (②) For example, to minimize the financial risk associated with the capital cost of tooling and equipment for production of a large, complex system, a manufacturer might subcontract the production of the system's major components to suppliers familiar with those components. (③) This relieves the manufacturer of the financial risk associated with the tooling and equipment to produce these components. (④) For example, subcontracting work for the components puts the manufacturer in the position of relying on outsiders, which increases the risks associated with quality control, scheduling, and the performance of the end-item system. (⑤) But these risks often can be reduced through careful management of the suppliers.

*subcontract: 하청을 주다(일감을 다른 사람에게 맡기다)

정답과 해설 **p.40**

01 Risk often arises from uncertainty / about how to approach a problem or situation.

02 One way to avoid such risk / is [to contract with a party / who is experienced and knows
                             to부정사 명사적 용법(주격 보어)
                         to부정사 형용사적 용법   *주격 관계대명사절*
how to do it].

03 For example, / [to minimize the financial risk / associated with the capital cost of
                 to부정사 부사적 용법(목적)   *과거분사구*
tooling and equipment / for production of a large, complex system], / a manufacturer
might subcontract the production of the system's major components / to suppliers
familiar with those components.
형용사구 수식

04 This relieves the manufacturer of the financial risk / [associated with the tooling
                                    과거분사구
and equipment / to produce these components].
                 to부정사 형용사적 용법

05 However, / transfer of one kind of risk / often means / inheriting another kind.
                                 mean+동명사: ~하는 것을 의미하다

06 For example, / subcontracting work for the components / puts the manufacturer in the
               동명사 주어(단수 취급)   *동사*
position of relying on outsiders, / which increases the risks / associated with quality
                      계속적 용법(=and it)   *과거분사구*
control, scheduling, and the performance of the end-item system.

07 But / these risks often can be reduced / through careful management of the suppliers.

01 위험은 종종 불확실성uncertainty으로부터 발생한다 / 문제나 상황에 접근하는 방법에 대한.

02 그러한 위험을 피할 수 있는 한 가지 방식은 / 당사자party와 계약하는 것이다 / 숙련되었으며experienced 그것을 하는
방법을 알고 있는.

03 예를 들어, / 재정적 위험을 최소화하기 위해 / 도구 및 장비equipment의 자본 비용the capital cost과
관련된associated / 크고 복잡한 시스템의 생산을 위한 (도구 및 장비), / 제조업자manufacturer는 시스템의 주요
부품component 생산을 하청 줄지도 모른다 / 그러한 부품들에 정통한 공급업자supplier들에게.

04 이것은 제조업자에게 재정적 위험을 덜어준다relieve / 도구 및 장비와 관련된 / 이러한 부품을 생산하기 위한.

05 그러나, / 한 종류의 위험의 이전transfer은 / 종종 의미한다 / 다른 종류(의 위험)를 이어받는inherit 것을.

06 예를 들어, / 부품에 대한 작업을 하청 주는 것은 / 제조업자를 외부 업자들에게 의존하는 처지에 놓는다 / 그리고 이는
위험들을 증가시킨다 / 품질 관리, 일정 관리, 완제품 시스템의 성능과 관련된.

07 그러나 / 이러한 위험들은 종종 감소될 수 있다 / 공급업자들의 신중한 관리management를 통해.

구문 Check up	① One way to avoid such risk is to contract with a party who is experienced and know / knows how to do it.	② However, transfer of one kind of risk often means inherited / inheriting another kind.
	주격 관계대명사절의 동사구가 병렬 연결되어 있다. 선행사 a party에 수 일치하여 knows를 쓴다.	<mean+동명사(~하는 것을 의미하다)> 구문이므로 inheriting이 적절하다.

D

STEP 1 • 수능에 *진짜* 나오는 *단어*

✔️ 문제에 나오는 단어들을 확인하세요.

시간이 없다면 색으로 표시된 단어만이라도 꼭 외우고 넘어가세요!

01	cease	v. 멈추다	(✔️ cease) to function	기능을 멈추다
02	function	n. 기능 v. 기능하다	significant ( )s	주요한 기능들
03	transplant	n. 이식 v. 이식하다, 옮겨 심다	the first heart ( )	첫 번째 심장 이식
04	surgeon	n. 외과 의사	a heart ( )	심장 외과 의사
05	era	n. 시대	a new ( ) of medicine	의학의 새로운 시대
06	realization	n. 인식, 깨달음	an important ( )	중요한 깨달음
07	organ	n. 장기	a human ( )	인간의 장기
08	transplantation	n. 이식 (수술)	organs for ( )	이식 수술용 장기
09	brain death	뇌사	have ( ) ( )	뇌사에 빠지다
10	recommendation	n. 권고, 추천	make a ( )	권고하다
11	absence	n. 부재, 없음	the ( ) of all activity	모든 활동의 부재
12	nervous system	신경계	the central ( ) ( )	중추 신경계
13	adopt	v. 받아들이다, 채택하다	( ) the recommendation	권고를 받아들이다
14	modification	n. 수정, 변경	a ( ) in plans	계획의 변경

➕ 본문 문장 속에서 단어들을 확인해 보세요.

The recommendation has since been adopted, / with some modifications, / almost everywhere.

그 권고는 그 후 받아들여졌다 / 일부 수정을 거쳐 / 거의 모든 곳에서.

01	cease	멈추다	cease to function	기능을 멈추다
02	function		significant functions	주요한 기능들
03	transplant		the first heart transplant	첫 번째 심장 이식
04	surgeon		a heart surgeon	심장 외과 의사
05	era		a new era of medicine	의학의 새로운 시대
06	realization		an important realization	중요한 깨달음
07	organ		a human organ	인간의 장기
08	transplantation		organs for transplantation	이식 수술용 장기
09	brain death		have brain death	뇌사에 빠지다
10	recommendation		make a recommendation	권고하다
11	absence		the absence of all activity	모든 활동의 부재
12	nervous system		the central nervous system	중추 신경계
13	adopt		adopt the recommendation	권고를 받아들이다
14	modification		a modification in plans	계획의 변경

➕ 본문 문장 속에서 단어의 의미를 우리말로 해석해 보세요.

The recommendation has since been adopted, / with some modifications, / almost everywhere.

→ 그 _____ 는 그후 _____ 졌다 / 일부 _____ 을 거쳐 / 거의 모든 곳에서.

STEP **2** • 수능 기출 제대로 풀기

 D 글의 흐름으로 보아, 주어진 문장이 들어가기에 가장 적절한 곳은?

In some cases, their brains had ceased to function altogether.

Of all the medical achievements of the 1960s, the most widely known was the first heart transplant, performed by the South African surgeon Christiaan Barnard in 1967. (①) The patient's death 18 days later did not weaken the spirits of those who welcomed a new era of medicine. (②) The ability to perform heart transplants was linked to the development of respirators, which had been introduced to hospitals in the 1950s. (③) Respirators could save many lives, but not all those whose hearts kept beating ever recovered any other significant functions. (④) The realization that such patients could be a source of organs for transplantation led to the setting up of the Harvard Brain Death Committee, and to its recommendation that the absence of all "discernible central nervous system activity" should be "a new criterion for death". (⑤) The recommendation has since been adopted, with some modifications, almost everywhere.

*respirator: 인공호흡기
**discernible: 식별 가능한
***criterion: 기준

정답과 해설 **p.40**

01 Of all the medical achievements of the 1960s, / the most widely known / was the first
of all: 모든 ~중에서
heart transplant, / performed by the South African surgeon Christiaan Barnard in 1967.
과거분사

02 The patient's death 18 days later / did not weaken the spirits of those / who welcomed
주격 관계대명사절
a new era of medicine.

03 The ability to perform heart transplants / was linked to the development of respirators,
to부정사의 형용사적 용법   선행사
/ which had been introduced to hospitals in the 1950s.
=and they

부분부정: 다는 아니다
04 Respirators could save many lives, / but not all those whose hearts kept beating / ever
소유격 관계대명사절
recovered any other significant functions. // In some cases, / their brains had ceased to
cease+to부정사: ~하기를 멈추다
function altogether.

05 The realization that such patients could be a source of organs for transplantation / led
that 동격절(The realization 부가 설명)
to the setting up of the Harvard Brain Death Committee, / and to its recommendation /
that the absence of all "discernible central nervous system activity" should be "a new
that 동격절(its recommendation 부가 설명)
criterion for death".

부사: 그 후
06 The recommendation has since been adopted, / with some modifications, / almost
현재완료(계속)
everywhere.

01 1960년대의 모든 의학적 성취 중에서 / 가장 널리 알려진 것은 / 최초의 심장 이식the first heart transplant이었다
/1967년 남아프리카 공화국의 외과 의사surgeon Christiaan Barnard에 의해서 행해진.

02 18일 후에 그 환자가 사망한 것은 / 사람들의 사기를 떨어뜨리지 않았다 / 의학의 새로운 시대a new era of medicine를
환영하는.

03 심장 이식을 할 수 있는 능력은 / 인공호흡기의 개발과 관련이 있었다 / 그리고 그것들은 1950년대에 병원에 도입되었다.

04 인공호흡기는 많은 생명을 구할 수 있었지만, / 심장이 계속해서 뛰는 사람들이 모두 다 / 어떤 다른 중요한 기능을 회복한
것은 아니었다. // 어떤 경우에는 / 그들의 뇌가 완전히 기능을 멈추었다cease to function.

05 그러한 환자들이 이식 수술transplantation용 장기organ 공급자가 될 수 있다는 인식realization은 / 하버드 뇌사
위원회Brain Death Committee의 설립으로 이어졌다 / 그리고 그 위원회의 권고로도 / 모든 '식별 가능한 중추
신경계central nervous system 활동'의 부재absence는 '사망의 새로운 기준'이 되어야 한다는.

06 그 권고recommendation는 그 후 받아들여졌다adopt / 일부 수정modification을 거쳐 / 거의 모든 곳에서.

구문 Check up

① Not all those who / whose hearts kept beating ever
recovered any other significant functions.

선행사인 'those의 심장'이라는 의미를 나타내야 하므로 소유격 관계대명
사 whose를 쓴다.

② The recommendation has since adopted / been
adopted , with some modifications, almost everywhere.

권고가 '받아들여지다'라는 수동의 의미로 쓰였으므로 been adopted가
적절하다.

정답 ① whose ② been adopted

E

STEP 1 • 수능에 진짜 나오는 단어

✔ 문제에 나오는 단어들을 확인하세요.

시간이 없다면 색으로 표시된 단어만이라도 꼭 외우고 넘어가세요!

01	container	n. 용기, 그릇	a closed (✔ container)	폐쇄된 용기
02	be credited with	~에 대해 공로를 인정받다	( ) ( ) ( ) inventing the first computer	최초의 컴퓨터를 발명한 것으로 공로를 인정받다
03	vacuum	n. 진공	a ( ) cleaner	진공청소기
04	claim	v. 주장하다 n. 주장; 청구	( ) to be the first	최초라고 주장하다
05	coin	v. 신조어를 만들다	( ) a term	용어를 만들다
06	nature	n. 속성	devices of this ( )	이런 속성의 기기들
07	inappropriate	a. 부적절한	an ( ) name	부적절한 이름
08	rapid	a. 빠른	( ) air movement	빠른 공기의 움직임
09	suction	n. 흡입	create ( )	흡입을 만들다 (=흡입하다)
10	handy	a. 편리한, 간편한	a ( ) device	편리한 기기
11	be stuck with	~을 어쩔 수 없이 하다	( ) ( ) ( ) the name	그 이름을 어쩔 수 없이 쓰다
12	reference	n. 언급, 참조	find a ( )	언급을 찾다
13	prior to	~ 이전에	( ) ( ) the meeting	모임 전에
14	file	v. 제출하다	( ) a manual	매뉴얼을 제출하다
15	intended	a. 의도된	( ) invention	의도된 발명품

➕ 본문 문장 속에서 단어들을 확인해 보세요.

In fact, / he only claimed to be the first / to coin the term "vacuum cleaner" for devices of this nature, / which may explain / why he is so credited.

사실 / 그는 단지 최초의 사람이라고 주장했고 / 이런 속성을 가진 장치들에 대해 '진공청소기'라는 용어를 만든, / 이 점이 설명해 줄 수도 있다 / 그가 그렇게 공로를 인정받는 이유를.

01	container	용기, 그릇	a closed container	폐쇄된 용기
02	be credited with		be credited with inventing the first computer	최초의 컴퓨터를 발명한 것으로 공로를 인정받다
03	vacuum		a vacuum cleaner	진공청소기
04	claim		claim to be the first	최초라고 주장하다
05	coin		coin a term	용어를 만들다
06	nature		devices of this nature	이런 속성의 기기들
07	inappropriate		an inappropriate name	부적절한 이름
08	rapid		rapid air movement	빠른 공기의 움직임
09	suction		create suction	흡입을 만들다(=흡입하다)
10	handy		a handy device	편리한 기기
11	be stuck with		be stuck with the name	그 이름을 어쩔 수 없이 쓰다
12	reference		find a reference	언급을 찾다
13	prior to		prior to the meeting	모임 전에
14	file		file a manual	매뉴얼을 제출하다
15	intended		intended invention	의도된 발명품

➕ **본문 문장 속에서 단어의 의미를 우리말로 해석해 보세요.**

In fact, / he only claimed to be the first / to coin the term "vacuum cleaner" for devices of this nature, / which may explain / why he is so credited.

→ 사실 / 그는 단지 최초의 사람이라고 _____ / 이런 _____ 을 가진 장치들에 대해 '_____'라는 용어를 _____, / 이 점이 설명해 줄 수도 있다 / 그가 그렇게 _____ 이유를.

STEP **2** · 수능 기출 제대로 풀기

E 글의 흐름으로 보아, 주어진 문장이 들어가기에 가장 적절한 것은?

Rather, it is the air moving through a small hole into a closed container, as a result of air being blown out of the container by a fan on the inside.

Hubert Cecil Booth is often credited with inventing the first powered mobile vacuum cleaner. (①) In fact, he only claimed to be the first to coin the term "vacuum cleaner" for devices of this nature, which may explain why he is so credited. (②) As we all know, the term "vacuum" is an inappropriate name, because there exists no vacuum in a vacuum cleaner. (③) But I suppose a "rapid air movement in a closed container to create suction" cleaner would not sound as scientific or be as handy a name. (④) Anyway, we are stuck with it historically, and it is hard to find any references to "vacuum" prior to Booth. (⑤) Interestingly, Booth himself did not use the term "vacuum" when he filed a provisional specification describing in general terms his intended invention.

*provisional specification: 임시 제품 설명서

정답과 해설 p.40

01 Hubert Cecil Booth is often credited / with inventing the first powered mobile
동명사
vacuum cleaner.

02 In fact, / he only claimed to be the first / [to coin the term "vacuum cleaner" for
to부정사의 형용사적 용법
devices of this nature], / which may explain / why he is so credited.
관계대명사 계속적 용법   may explain의 목적어(의문사+주어+동사)

03 As we all know, / the term "vacuum" is an inappropriate name, / because there exists
no vacuum in a vacuum cleaner. // Rather, / it is the air / [moving through a small hole
분사(명사 수식)
into a closed container, / as a result of air being blown out of the container / by a fan
의미상 주어   동명사(being p.p.: ~되는 것)
on the inside].

04 But I suppose / a "rapid air movement in a closed container to create suction" cleaner /
접속사 that 생략
주어
would not sound as scientific / or be as handy a name.
동사구   as+형+a(n)+명(그토록 ~한 …)

05 Anyway, / we are stuck with it historically, / and it is hard to find any references to
가주어   진주어
"vacuum" / prior to Booth.

06 Interestingly, / Booth himself did not use the term "vacuum" / when he filed a
주어 강조
provisional specification / describing in general terms his intended invention.
현재분사(명사 수식)

01 Herbert Cecil Booth는 공로를 자주 인정받는다be credited with / 최초의 이동식 전동 진공청소기vacuum cleaner를
발명한 것으로.

02 사실 / 그는 단지 최초의 사람이라고 주장했었다claim to be the first / 이런 속성을 가진 장치들devices of this nature에
대해 '진공청소기'라는 용어를 만든coin the term, / 그리고 그것은 설명해 줄 수도 있다 / 그가 그렇게 공로를 인정받는
이유를.

03 우리 모두가 알고 있듯이, / '진공'이라는 용어는 부적절한inappropriate 이름인데, / 왜냐하면 진공청소기에는 진공이
없기 때문이다. // 오히려, / 그것은 공기이다 / 작은 구멍을 통해 폐쇄된 용기container 안으로 유입되는 / 공기가
용기에서 밖으로 배출된 결과로 / 내부에 있는 송풍기를 통해서.

04 그러나 나는 생각한다 / '흡입을 만들기create suction 위한 폐쇄된 용기 안에서의 빠른 공기의 흐름rapid air movement'
청소기는 / 과학적으로 들리지 않는다고 / 또는 편리한handy 이름도 (아니라고).

05 어쨌든 / 우리는 역사적으로 그것을 어쩔 수 없이 쓰고be stuck with 있으며, / '진공'에 대한 어떠한 언급도 찾기find any
references가 어렵다 / Booth 이전에prior to.

06 흥미롭게도 / Booth 자신은 '진공'이라는 용어를 사용하지 않았다 / 임시 제품 설명서를 제출할file 때 / 자신이 의도한
발명품intended invention을 일반적인 용어로 설명하는.

| 구문 Check up | ① Hubert Cecil Booth is often credited with invent / inventing the first powered mobile vacuum cleaner.

전치사의 목적어로는 명사나 동명사 등이 오며 동사는 올 수 없다. 따라서 inventing이 적절하다. | ② But I suppose a "rapid air movement in a closed container to create suction" cleaner would be such / as handy a name.

<as+형+a(n)+명> 어순에 따라 as를 써야 한다. such는 <such+a(n)+형+명> 어순으로 쓴다. |

STEP 1 • 수능에 *진짜* 나오는 *단어*

✔ 문제에 나오는 단어들을 확인하세요.

시간이 없다면 색으로 표시된 단어만이라도 꼭 외우고 넘어가세요!

01	track	v. 추적하다	(✔ track) online	온라인으로 추적하다
02	violate	v. 침해하다, 위반하다	( ) privacy	사생활을 침해하다
03	accumulate	v. 축적하다	( ) personal information	개인정보를 축적하다
04	greet	v. 맞이하다, 인사하다	( ) users like old friends	오랜 친구처럼 사용자들을 맞이한다
05	customer	n. 고객	( ) service	고객 서비스
06	estate	n. 재산, 소유권	real ( )	부동산
07	property	n. 재산, 부동산	intellectual ( )	지적 재산
08	trick	n. 재주, 기술	amazing ( )s	놀라운 기술
09	benefit	v. ~에게 도움이(득이) 되다 n. 이익	( ) individuals	개인들에게 도움이 되다
10	save A B	A에게 B를 덜어주다	( ) us the pain of last-minute stress	우리에게 막판 스트레스의 고통을 덜어주다
11	chore	n. 잡일, 허드렛일	the ( ) of having to enter names	이름을 입력해야만 하는 귀찮은 일
12	purchase	n. 구입 v. 구입하다	make a ( )	구입하다

⊕ 본문 문장 속에서 단어들을 확인해 보세요.

For example, / cookies save users the chore / of having to enter names and addresses into e-commerce websites / every time they make a purchase.

예컨대, / cookie는 사용자에게 귀찮은 일을 덜어 준다 / 전자상거래 사이트에 이름과 주소를 입력해야만 하는 / 매번 구입할 때마다.

No.	단어	뜻	표현	표현 뜻
01	track	✎ 추적하다	track online	온라인으로 추적하다
02	violate		violate privacy	사생활을 침해하다
03	accumulate		accumulate personal information	개인정보를 축적하다
04	greet		greet users like old friends	오랜 친구처럼 사용자들을 맞이한다
05	customer		customer service	고객 서비스
06	estate		real estate	부동산
07	property		intellectual property	지적 재산
08	trick		amazing tricks	놀라운 기술
09	benefit		benefit individuals	개인들에게 도움이 되다
10	save A B		save us the pain of last-minute stress	우리에게 막판 스트레스의 고통을 덜어주다
11	chore		the chore of having to enter names	이름을 입력해야만 하는 귀찮은 일
12	purchase		make a purchase	구입하다

➕ 본문 문장 속에서 단어의 의미를 우리말로 해석해 보세요.

For example, / cookies save users the chore / of having to enter names and addresses into e-commerce websites / every time they make a purchase.

→ 예컨대, / cookie는 ▓▓▓▓▓▓▓▓▓▓▓▓▓▓▓▓▓▓▓▓▓▓▓▓▓▓ / 전자상거래 사이트에 이름과 주소를 입력해야만 하는 / 매번 ▓▓▓▓▓▓▓▓ 때마다.

STEP **2** • 수능 기출 제대로 풀기

F

글의 흐름으로 보아, 주어진 문장이 들어가기에 가장 적절한 곳은?

> However, concerns have been raised that cookies, which can track what people do online, may be violating privacy by helping companies or government agencies accumulate personal information.

Favorite websites sometimes greet users like old friends. Online bookstores welcome their customers by name and suggest new books they might like to read. (①) Real estate sites tell their visitors about new properties that have come on the market. (②) These tricks are made possible by cookies, small files that an Internet server stores inside individuals' web browsers so it can remember them. (③) Therefore, cookies can greatly benefit individuals. (④) For example, cookies save users the chore of having to enter names and addresses into e-commerce websites every time they make a purchase. (⑤) Security is another concern: Cookies make shared computers far less secure and offer hackers many ways to break into systems.

정답과 해설 **p.41**

01 Favorite websites sometimes greet users / like old friends. // Online bookstores welcome their customers by name / and suggest new books they might like to read. // Real estate sites tell their visitors / about new properties that have come on the market.

that 생략
목적격 관계대명사절
주격 관계대명사절

02 These tricks are made possible by cookies, / small files that an Internet server stores inside individuals' web browsers / so it can remember them. // Therefore, cookies can greatly benefit individuals.

동격
be made+형용사: ~하게 되다(5형식 수동태)
목적격 관계대명사절
~하도록(목적)

03 For example, / cookies save users the chore / of having to enter names and addresses into e-commerce websites / every time they make a purchase.

save+간접목적어+직접목적어: ~에게서 …을 덜어주다
=whenever

04 However, / concerns have been raised / [that cookies, which can track what people do online, / may be violating privacy / by helping companies or government agencies accumulate personal information].

동격의 that절(=concerns)
의문사절(can track의 목적어)
help+목적어(A)+목적격 보어(동사원형): A가 ~하는 것을 돕다

05 Security is another concern: / Cookies make shared computers far less secure / and offer hackers many ways / to break into systems.

콜론(:): 추가 설명
비교급 강조
to부정사의 형용사적 용법

---

01 즐겨 찾는 웹사이트들은 때때로 사용자들을 맞이한다greet / 오랜 친구처럼. // 온라인 서점은 이름으로 고객customer들을 환영하며, / 그들이 읽고 싶어할 수도 있는 새로운 도서를 제안해 준다. // 부동산real estate 사이트는 방문자들에게 알려 준다 / 시장에 나온 새로운 부동산property에 대해.

02 이러한 기술trick은 cookie에 의해 가능한 것이다 / 인터넷 서버가 개인의 웹 브라우저 안에 저장하는 작은 파일인 / 사용자들을 기억해 낼 수 있도록. // 그러므로 cookie는 개인에게 매우 도움이 될benefit 수 있다.

03 예컨대, / cookie는 사용자로부터 귀찮은 일을 덜어 준다save users the chore / 전자상거래 사이트에 이름과 주소를 입력해야만 하는 / 매번 구입할make a purchase 때마다.

04 하지만, / 우려가 제기돼 왔다 / 사람들이 온라인에서 무엇을 하는지에 대해 추적할track 수 있는 cookie가 / 사생활을 침해할 violate privacy 수 있다는 / 기업체나 정부기관으로 하여금 개인정보를 축적하도록accumulate personal information 도움으로써.

05 보안은 또 다른 우려인데, / cookie는 공유 컴퓨터를 훨씬 덜 안전하게 하고 / 해커들에게 많은 방법을 제공한다 / 시스템에 침입하게 할.

구문 Check up

① Real estate sites tell their visitors about new properties what / that have come on the market.

② Security is another concern: Cookies make shared computers far less secure and offer hackers many ways break / to break into systems.

선행사가 있으므로 관계대명사 that이 적합하다. what은 선행사 뒤에 오지 않는다.

이 문장의 동사는 make와 offer이므로 ways 다음에 오는 break는 명사를 수식하는 형용사적 용법의 to부정사인 to break로 쓴다.

정답 ① that ② to break

주어진 문장 넣기 ✚

STEP 1 • 수능에 *진짜* 나오는 *단어*

✔ 문제에 나오는 단어들을 확인하세요.

시간이 없다면 색으로 표시된 단어만이라도 꼭 외우고 넘어가세요!

01	application	n. 적용	many practical (✔ application)s	많은 실제적인 적용들
02	fruition	n. 결실	come to ( )	결실을 맺다
03	mow	v. 베다, 깎다	( ) grass	잔디를 깎다
04	straw	n. 짚, 지푸라기	mow and tie ( )	짚을 베고 묶다
05	pour	v. 붓다, 쏟다	( ) oil into a frying pan	프라이팬에 오일을 붓다
06	grain	n. 낟알	pour ( ) into sacks	낟알을 자루 안으로 쏟아붓다
07	market	v. 유통하다	a machine was ( )ed	기계가 유통되었다
08	patent	n. 특허권	a ( ) for a typewriter	타자기에 대한 특허권
09	issue	v. 발급하다	The patent was ( )d.	특허가 발급되었다.
10	commercially	ad. 상업적으로	( ) available	상업적으로 이용 가능한
11	eager	a. 열망하는	( ) to learn	배우려고 열망하는
12	ancestor	n. 조상	His ( )s are French.	그의 조상은 프랑스인이다.
13	hasten	v. 앞당기다	( ) the process	과정을 앞당기다
14	innovative	a. 혁신적인	an ( ) cycle	혁신적인 순환
15	radically	ad. 급격하게	a ( ) new approach	급격하게 새로운 접근법

➕ 본문 문장 속에서 단어들을 확인해 보세요.

A machine was invented / that mowed, threshed, and tied straw into bundles / and poured grain into sacks.

기계가 발명되었다 / (곡식을) 베고, 타작하고 짚을 다발로 묶고, / 낟알을 자루 안으로 쏟아 부어 주는 (기계).

01	application	✎ 적용	many practical applications	많은 실제적인 적용들
02	fruition		come to fruition	결실을 맺다
03	mow		mow grass	잔디를 깎다
04	straw		mow and tie straw	짚을 베고 묶다
05	pour		pour oil into a frying pan	프라이팬에 오일을 붓다
06	grain		pour grain into sacks	낟알을 자루 안으로 쏟아붓다
07	market		a machine was marketed	기계가 유통되었다
08	patent		a patent for a typewriter	타자기에 대한 특허권
09	issue		The patent was issued.	특허가 발급되었다.
10	commercially		commercially available	상업적으로 이용 가능한
11	eager		eager to learn	배우려고 열망하는
12	ancestor		His ancestors are French.	그의 조상은 프랑스인이다.
13	hasten		hasten the process	과정을 앞당기다
14	innovative		an innovative cycle	혁신적인 순환
15	radically		a radically new approach	급격하게 새로운 접근법

➕ 본문 문장 속에서 단어의 의미를 우리말로 해석해 보세요.

A machine was invented / that mowed, threshed, and tied straw into bundles / and poured grain into sacks.

→ 기계가 발명되었다 / (곡식을)   , 타작하고   을 다발로 묶고, /   을 자루 안으로   (기계).

STEP **2** • 수능 기출 제대로 풀기

G 글의 흐름으로 보아, 주어진 문장이 들어가기에 가장 적절한 곳은?

> Today, such delays between ideas and application are almost unthinkable.

Scientific discoveries are being brought to fruition at a faster rate than ever before. (①) For example, in 1836, a machine was invented that mowed, threshed, and tied straw into bundles and poured grain into sacks. (②) The machine was based on technology that even then was twenty years old, but it was not until 1930 that such a machine actually was marketed. (③) The first English patent for a typewriter was issued in 1714, but another 150 years passed before typewriters were commercially available. (④) It is not that we are more eager or more ambitious than our ancestors but that we have, over time, invented all sorts of social devices to hasten the process. (⑤) Thus, we find that the time between the first and second stages of the innovative cycle — between idea and application — has been cut radically.

*thresh : 타작하다

정답과 해설 p.41

01 Scientific discoveries are being brought to fruition / at a faster rate than ever before.
현재 진행형 수동태

02 For example, / in 1836, / a machine was invented / that mowed, threshed, and tied
straw into bundles / and poured grain into sacks.
주격 관계대명사절

부사 삽입구
03 The machine was based on technology / that even then was twenty years old, / but
it was not until 1930 that such a machine actually was marketed.
주격 관계대명사절
it was not until 시간 that ~: '시간'이 되어서야 비로소 ~했다

04 The first English patent for a typewriter / was issued in 1714, / but another 150 years
수동태
passed / before typewriters were commercially available.

05 Today, / such delays between ideas and application / are almost unthinkable. // It
주어   수 일치(복수)
is not that we are more eager or more ambitious / than our ancestors / but that we
━━━━━━━━━ not A, but B: A가 아니라 B ━━━━━━━━━
have, over time, invented all sorts of social devices / to hasten the process.
━━━ 현재완료 ━━━   to부정사의 형용사적 용법

06 Thus, / we find / that the time between the first and second stages of the innovative
that절의 주어
cycle / — between idea and application — / has been cut radically.
that절의 동사

01 과학적 발견들은 결실fruition을 맺고 있다 / 과거 어느 때보다 더 빠른 속도로.

02 예를 들어, / 1836년에 / 기계가 발명되었다 / (곡식을) 베고mow, 타작하고, 짚straw을 다발로 묶고, / 낟알grain을 자루
안으로 쏟아 부어 주는pour (기계).

03 그 기계는 기술에 기초하였다 / 심지어 그 당시에 20년이 된 (기술) / 그러나, 1930년이 되어서야 비로소 그러한 기계가
실제로 유통되었다be marketed.

04 타자기에 대한 최초의 영국 특허권patent은 / 1714년에 발급되었다be issued / 그러나 150년이 더 지났다 / 타자기가
상업적으로commercially 판매되기 전에.

05 오늘날, / 아이디어와 적용application 사이의 그러한 지연은 / 거의 생각할 수 없다. // 그것은 우리가 더 간절하거나more
eager 열망이 더 강해서가 아니라 / 우리 조상ancestor들보다 / 시간이 지나면서 우리가 모든 종류의 사회적 장치들을
발명해 왔기 때문이다 / 그 과정을 앞당기는hasten (사회적 장치들).

06 그러므로, / 우리는 알게 된다 / 혁신적인innovative 순환의 첫 번째와 두 번째 단계 사이의 시간 / 즉, 아이디어와 적용
사이의 시간이 / 급격히radically 줄었다는 것을.

① The machine was based on technology that / what
even then was twenty years old.

선행사인 technology가 있으므로 주격 관계대명사 that을 써야 한다.
what은 선행사가 필요하지 않다.

② But it was not until 1930 that such a machine actually
was marketed / was marketing .

주어와 서술어의 관계가 능동인지 수동인지 판단하는 문제이다. that절
의 주어 a machine은 '유통하는(능동)' 것이 아니라 '유통되는(수동)' 것이
므로 was marketed로 쓴다.

정답 ① that ② was marketed

A

STEP **1** • 수능에 *진짜* 나오는 *단어*

✔ 문제에 나오는 단어들을 확인하세요.

시간이 없다면 색으로 표시된 단어만이라도 꼭 외우고 넘어가세요!

01	assumption	n. 가정, 추정	a common (✔ assumption)	흔한 가정
02	reason	n. 이유, 이성 v. 추론하다	both ( ) and emotion	이성과 감정 둘 다
03	get by	~로 (그럭저럭) 살아가다	( ) ( ) on a small salary	적은 급여로 살아가다
04	eventually	ad. 결국	Any reason ( ) leads to a feeling.	어떤 이유든 결국 감정으로 이어진다.
05	wholegrain	a. 통곡물로 만든	a ( ) cereal	통곡물로 만든 시리얼
06	deep-seated	a. 뿌리 깊은	a set of ( ) values	뿌리 깊은 일련의 가치관
07	list	v. 나열하다, 열거하다	( ) all the reasons	모든 이유를 열거하다
08	be based on	~에 근거하다, 바탕을 두다	( ) ( ) ( ) facts	사실에 근거하다
09	loved one	사랑하는 사람 (연인, 가족, 친구 등)	spend more time with our ( ) ( )s	우리가 사랑하는 사람들과 더 많은 시간을 보내다
10	ultimately	ad. 결국, 궁극적으로	He ( ) accepted the deal.	그는 결국 거래를 받아들였다.

✚ 본문 문장 속에서 단어들을 확인해 보세요.

A common but incorrect assumption / is that we are creatures of reason / when, in fact, we are creatures of both reason and emotion.

일반적이지만 잘못된 가정은 / 우리가 이성의 피조물이라는 것이다 / 사실 우리는 이성과 감정 둘 다의 피조물인 상황에서.

01	assumption	가정, 추정	a common assumption	흔한 가정
02	reason		both reason and emotion	이성과 감정 둘 다
03	get by		get by on a small salary	적은 급여로 살아가다
04	eventually		Any reason eventually leads to a feeling.	어떤 이유든 결국 감정으로 이어진다.
05	wholegrain		a wholegrain cereal	통곡물로 만든 시리얼
06	deep-seated		a set of deep-seated values	뿌리 깊은 일련의 가치관
07	list		list all the reasons	모든 이유를 열거하다
08	be based on		be based on facts	사실에 근거하다
09	loved one		spend more time with our loved ones	우리가 사랑하는 사람들과 더 많은 시간을 보내다
10	ultimately		He ultimately accepted the deal.	그는 결국 거래를 받아들였다.

➕ 본문 문장 속에서 단어의 의미를 우리말로 해석해 보세요.

A common but incorrect assumption / is that we are creatures of reason / when, in fact, we are creatures of both reason and emotion.

→ 잘못된 은 / 우리가 이성의 피조물이라는 것이다 / 사실 우리는 의 피조물인 상황에서.

STEP **2** • 수능 기출 제대로 풀기

A 주어진 글 다음에 이어질 글의 순서로 가장 적절한 것은?

A common but incorrect assumption is that we are creatures of reason when, in fact, we are creatures of both reason and emotion. We cannot get by on reason alone since any reason always eventually leads to a feeling. Should I get a wholegrain cereal or a chocolate cereal?

(A) These deep-seated values, feelings, and emotions we have are rarely a result of reasoning, but can certainly be influenced by reasoning. We have values, feelings, and emotions before we begin to reason and long before we begin to reason effectively.

(B) I can list all the reasons I want, but the reasons have to be based on something. For example, if my goal is to eat healthy, I can choose the wholegrain cereal, but what is my reason for wanting to be healthy?

(C) I can list more and more reasons such as wanting to live longer, spending more quality time with loved ones, etc., but what are the reasons for those reasons? You should be able to see by now that reasons are ultimately based on non-reason such as values, feelings, or emotions.

① (A) — (C) — (B)   ② (B) — (A) — (C)

③ (B) — (C) — (A)   ④ (C) — (A) — (B)

⑤ (C) — (B) — (A)

정답과 해설 p.43

01 A common but incorrect assumption / is that we are creatures of reason / when, in
접속사(시간)
fact, we are creatures of both reason and emotion. // We cannot get by on reason alone
주격보어 삽입구
/ since any reason always eventually leads to a feeling. // Should I get a wholegrain
both A and B: A와 B 둘 다
접속사(이유)
cereal or a chocolate cereal?

02 I can list all the reasons I want, / but the reasons have to be based on something. // For
목적격 관계대명사 생략
example, / if my goal is to eat healthy, / I can choose the wholegrain cereal, / but what
is my reason for wanting to be healthy?
주격보어(~하는 것)

03 I can list more and more reasons / such as wanting to live longer, / spending more
~와 같은 동명사구
quality time with loved ones, etc., / but what are the reasons for those reasons? // You
should be able to see by now / that reasons are ultimately based on non-reason / such
동사구(~할 수 있어야 한다) 목적절(완전한 명사절)
as values, feelings, or emotions.

04 These deep-seated values, feelings, and emotions we have / are rarely a result of
목적격 관계대명사 생략
주어(복수명사구) 동사1
reasoning, / but can certainly be influenced by reasoning. // We have values, feelings,
and emotions / before we begin to reason / and long before we begin to reason
동사2(조동사 수동태)
시간 접속사1 시간 접속사2(~하기 오래 전에)
effectively.

01 일반적이지만 잘못된 가정assumption은 / 우리가 이성reason의 피조물이라는 것이다 / 사실 우리는 이성과 감정 둘 다의 피조물인 상황에서. // 우리는 이성만으로 살아갈get by 수 없다 / 어떤 이성이든 항상 결국eventually 감정으로 이어지므로. // 나는 통곡물wholegrain 시리얼을 선택해야 할까, 혹은 초콜릿 시리얼을 선택해야 할까?

02 나는 내가 원하는 모든 이유를 열거할list 수 있지만, / 그 이유는 뭔가에 근거를 둬야be based on 한다. // 예를 들어 / 내 목표가 건강하게 먹는 것이라면 / 나는 통곡물 시리얼을 선택해도 되지만, / 건강해지고 싶다는 것을 뒷받침하는 나의 이유는 무엇일까?

03 나는 더 많고 많은 이유를 열거할 수 있다 / 더 오래 살고 싶다는 것과 같은 / 사랑하는 사람loved one들과 양질의 시간을 더 보내고 싶다는 것 등등 / 하지만 그러한 이유를 뒷받침하는 이유는 무엇인가? // 이제 여러분은 알 수 있을 것이다 / 이유란 것이 궁극적으로ultimately 비이성에 근거한다는 것을 / 가치, 느낌, 또는 감정과 같은.

04 우리가 가진 이러한 뿌리 깊은deep-seated 가치, 느낌, 감정은 / 추론의 산물인 경우가 거의 없지만, / 물론 추론의 영향을 받을 수 있다. // 우리는 가치, 느낌, 감정을 가진다 / 우리가 추론을 시작하기 전에 / 그리고 우리가 효과적으로 추론을 시작하기 훨씬 전에.

구문 Check up	① These deep-seated values, feelings, and emotions we have to be / are rarely a result of reasoning.	② You should be able to see by now what / that reasons are ultimately based on non-reason such as values, feelings, or emotions.
	we have 앞이 주어인 복수명사구이므로 동사가 필요하다. 따라서 are가 적절하다.	동사구 should be able to see에 연결되는 목적어로 수동태(be based on) 가 포함된 완전한 문장이 나온다. 따라서 접속사 that이 적절하다.

정답 ① are ② that

B

STEP 1 • 수능에 *진짜* 나오는 *단어*

✔ 문제에 나오는 단어들을 확인하세요.

시간이 없다면 색으로 표시된 단어만이라도 꼭 외우고 넘어가세요!

01	receptor	n. 수용체	touch (✔ receptor)s	촉감 수용체
02	evenly	ad. 골고루	be spread ( )	골고루 퍼져 있다
03	apart	ad. 떨어져서	far ( )	멀리 떨어져서
04	individually	ad. 각각, 개별적으로	feel the fingers ( )	손가락들을 각각 느끼다
05	so that	~하기 위해	( ) ( ) you don't see it	당신이 그것을 보지 않게 하기 위해
06	probably	ad. 아마	you will ( ) think	당신은 아마 생각할 것이다
07	tell	v. 구별하다	be able to ( ) easily	쉽게 구별할 수 있다
08	poke	v. 찌르다	( ) you in the back	당신의 등을 찌르다
09	separate	a. 서로 떨어져 있는	five thousand ( ) touch receptors	5천 개의 서로 떨어져 있는 촉감 수용체
10	far	ad. 훨씬 (비교급 강조)	( ) fewer touch receptors	훨씬 적은 촉감 수용체

➕ 본문 문장 속에서 단어들을 확인해 보세요.

But / if the fingers are spread far apart, / you can feel them individually.

하지만 / 만약 손가락끼리 멀리 떨어져 있다면, / 당신은 그것들을 각각 느낄 수 있다.

문제를 풀기 전에 단어들을 **30초** 동안 다시 확인하세요.

01	receptor	🖉 수용체	touch receptors	촉감 수용체
02	evenly		be spread evenly	골고루 퍼져 있다
03	apart		far apart	멀리 떨어져서
04	individually		feel the fingers individually	손가락들을 각각 느끼다
05	so that		so that you don't see it	당신이 그것을 보지 않게 하기 위해
06	probably		you will probably think	당신은 아마 생각할 것이다
07	tell		be able to tell easily	쉽게 구별할 수 있다
08	poke		poke you in the back	당신의 등을 찌르다
09	separate		five thousand separate touch receptors	5천 개의 서로 떨어져 있는 촉감 수용체
10	far		far fewer touch receptors	훨씬 적은 촉감 수용체

➕ **본문 문장 속에서 단어의 의미를 우리말로 해석해 보세요.**

But / if the fingers are spread far apart, / you can feel them individually.

→ 하지만 / 만약 손가락끼리 멀리 _____ 있다면, / 당신은 그것들을 _____ 느낄 수 있다.

328

STEP **2** • 수능 기출 제대로 풀기

B 주어진 글 다음에 이어질 글의 순서로 가장 적절한 것은?

Touch receptors are spread over all parts of the body, but they are not spread evenly. Most of the touch receptors are found in your fingertips, tongue, and lips.

(A) But if the fingers are spread far apart, you can feel them individually. Yet if the person does the same thing on the back of your hand (with your eyes closed, so that you don't see how many fingers are being used), you probably will be able to tell easily, even when the fingers are close together.

(B) You can test this for yourself. Have someone poke you in the back with one, two, or three fingers and try to guess how many fingers the person used. If the fingers are close together, you will probably think it was only one.

(C) On the tip of each of your fingers, for example, there are about five thousand separate touch receptors. In other parts of the body there are far fewer. In the skin of your back, the touch receptors may be as much as 2 inches apart.

① (A) — (C) — (B)　　② (B) — (A) — (C)

③ (B) — (C) — (A)　　④ (C) — (A) — (B)

⑤ (C) — (B) — (A)

정답과 해설 p.43

01 Touch receptors are spread over all parts of the body, / but they are not spread evenly.
// Most of the touch receptors are found / in your fingertips, tongue, and lips.
부분+of+전체   수 일치(복수)

02 On the tip of each of your fingers, / for example, / there are about five thousand
부사(대략, 약)
separate touch receptors. // In other parts of the body / there are far fewer. // In the
skin of your back, / the touch receptors may be as much as 2 inches apart.
as 형용사/부사 as ~: ~만큼 …한(하게)

03 You can test this for yourself. // [Have someone poke you in the back / with one, two, or
5형식 동사 목적어   목적격 보어(동사원형)
three fingers] / and [try to guess / how many fingers the person used].
┌─ 병렬연결(명령문) ─┐
의문사절(to guess의 목적어)

04 If the fingers are close together, / you will probably think / it was only one.
명사절 접속사 that 생략
시간과 조건의 부사절에서는 현재가 미래를 대신함

05 But / if the fingers are spread far apart, / you can feel them individually.
부사(동사 수식)

06 Yet / if the person does the same thing on the back of your hand / (with your eyes
closed, / so that you don't see / how many fingers are being used), / you probably will
with+명사+과거분사: (명사)가 ~된 채로
~하기 위해(목적)   의문사절(see의 목적어)
be able to tell easily, / even when the fingers are close together.

---

01 촉감 수용체receptor는 신체 곳곳에 퍼져 있지만, / 골고루evenly 퍼져 있지는 않다. // 대부분의 촉감 수용체는 발견된다
/ 손가락 끝, 혀, 그리고 입술에서.

02 각각의 손가락 끝에는, / 예를 들어, / 약 5천 개의 서로 떨어져 있는separate 촉감 수용체가 있다. // 몸의 다른 부분에서는
/ 훨씬far 더 적다. // 당신의 등 피부에는, / 촉감 수용체가 2인치만큼 떨어져apart 있을 수도 있다.

03 당신은 스스로 이것을 테스트해 볼 수 있다. // 누군가에게 당신의 등을 찌르게poke 하라 / 한 손가락, 두 손가락, 또는 세
손가락으로 / 그리고 추측해 보라 / 그 사람이 얼마나 많은 손가락을 사용했는지.

04 만약 손가락이 서로 가까이 붙어 있다면, / 당신은 아마probably 생각할 것이다 / 그것이 한 개라고.

05 하지만 / 만약 손가락끼리 멀리 떨어져 있다면, / 당신은 그것들을 각각individually 느낄 수 있다.

06 하지만 / 만약 그 사람이 당신의 손등에 같은 행동을 한다면 / (당신의 눈을 감은 채로, / 당신이 모르게 하기 위해so that /
몇 개의 손가락이 사용되고 있는지), / 당신은 아마 쉽게 구별할tell 수 있을 것이다 / 손가락이 서로 가까이 있을 때조차도.

구문 Check up

① Have someone poke you in the back with one, two, or three fingers and try / trying to guess how many fingers the person used.

② But if the fingers are spread far apart, you can feel them individual / individually .

명령문 두 개가 and로 병렬연결되는 구조이므로 try를 쓴다.

'손가락들을 개별적으로 느낄 수 있다'는 내용이므로 3형식 동사 feel을 수식하는 부사 individually가 적절하다.

정답 ① try ② individually

✔ 문제에 나오는 단어들을 확인하세요.

시간이 없다면 색으로 표시된 단어만이라도 꼭 외우고 넘어가세요!

01	survey	n. 설문 조사 v. 조사하다	in one (✔ survey)	한 조사에서
02	assistance	n. 지원	(　　　　　) to the poor	빈곤층 지원
03	framing	n. 틀, 구성	the (　　　　) of a question	질문의 구성
04	heavily	ad. 크게, 아주	(　　　　) influence the answer	답변에 크게 영향을 미치다
05	obtain	v. 얻다	(　　　　) a true measure	진정한 척도를 얻다
06	measure	n. 척도 v. 측정하다	a (　　　　) of what people think	사람들이 생각하는 것에 대한 척도
07	welfare	n. 복지	(　　　　) programmes	복지 프로그램들
08	in favour	찬성하는	Only 21 percent were (　　) (　　　　).	단지 21퍼센트만이 찬성했다.
09	refer to	~를 나타내다, 지칭하다	(　　) (　　) those programmes	그 프로그램들을 나타내다
10	portray	v. 묘사하다	Newspapers (　　　　) it.	신문들이 그것을 묘사한다.

➕ 본문 문장 속에서 단어들을 확인해 보세요.

In one survey, / 61 percent of Americans said / that they supported / the government spending more on 'assistance to the poor'.

한 조사에서, / 61%의 미국인들이 말했다 / 그들은 지지한다고 / 정부가 '빈곤층 지원'에 더 많은 돈을 쓰는 것을.

문제를 풀기 전에 단어들을 **30초** 동안 다시 확인하세요.

01	survey	🖊 설문 조사, 조사하다	in one survey	한 조사에서
02	assistance		assistance to the poor	빈곤층 지원
03	framing		the framing of a question	질문의 구성
04	heavily		heavily influence the answer	답변에 크게 영향을 미치다
05	obtain		obtain a true measure	진정한 척도를 얻다
06	measure		a measure of what people think	사람들이 생각하는 것에 대한 척도
07	welfare		welfare programmes	복지 프로그램들
08	in favour		Only 21 percent were in favour.	단지 21퍼센트만이 찬성했다.
09	refer to		refer to those programmes	그 프로그램들을 나타내다
10	portray		Newspapers portray it.	신문들이 그것을 묘사한다.

➕ 본문 문장 속에서 단어의 의미를 우리말로 해석해 보세요.

In one survey, / 61 percent of Americans said / that they supported / the government spending more on 'assistance to the poor'.

➡ 한 _____에서, / 61%의 미국인들이 말했다 / 그들은 지지한다고 / 정부가 '빈곤층 _____'에 더 많은 돈을 쓰는 것을.

STEP **2** • 수능 기출 제대로 **풀기**

 주어진 글 다음에 이어질 글의 순서로 가장 적절한 것은?

In one survey, 61 percent of Americans said that they supported the government spending more on 'assistance to the poor'.

(A) Therefore, the framing of a question can heavily influence the answer in many ways, which matters if your aim is to obtain a 'true measure' of what people think. And next time you hear a politician say 'surveys prove that the majority of the people agree with me', be very wary.

(B) But when the same population was asked whether they supported spending more government money on 'welfare', only 21 percent were in favour. In other words, if you ask people about individual welfare programmes — such as giving financial help to people who have long-term illnesses and paying for school meals for families with low income — people are broadly in favour of them.

(C) But if you ask about 'welfare' — which refers to those exact same programmes that you've just listed — they're against it. The word 'welfare' has negative connotations, perhaps because of the way many politicians and newspapers portray it.

*wary: 조심성 있는
**connotation: 함축

① (A) — (C) — (B)   ② (B) — (A) — (C)

③ (B) — (C) — (A)   ④ (C) — (A) — (B)

⑤ (C) — (B) — (A)

정답과 해설 **p.44**

01 In one survey, / 61 percent of Americans said / that they supported / the government
명사절 접속사　　　　동명사의 의미상 주어
spending more on 'assistance to the poor'.
동명사(supported의 목적어)

02 But / when the same population was asked / whether they supported spending more
~인지 아닌지　　　　　동명사(supported의 목적어)
government money on 'welfare', / only 21 percent were in favour.
of the population 생략　수 일치(복수)

03 In other words, / if you ask people about individual welfare programmes / — such as
다시 말해
[giving financial help to people who have long-term illnesses] and [paying for school
주격 관계대명사절　　　　　　병렬 연결(such as에 연결)
meals for families with low income] — / people are broadly in favour of them.

04 But / if you ask about 'welfare' / — which refers to those exact same programmes / that
you've just listed — / they're against it.
목적격 관계대명사절

05 The word 'welfare' has negative connotations, / perhaps because of the way many
politicians and newspapers portray it.　　　　　　　　　　　관계부사 생략

06 Therefore, / the framing of a question can heavily influence the answer / in many ways,
/ which matters / if your aim is to obtain a 'true measure' of what people think.
= and it　　　　　　　　　　　　　　　　　　　　　관계대명사절(전치사의 목적어)

07 And / next time you hear a politician say / 'surveys prove that the majority of the
부사절 접속사(시간)　지각동사(hear)+목적어+목적격보어(동사원형)　명사절 접속사　부분+of+전체
people agree with me', / be very wary.
수 일치(복수)　　　명령문

01 한 조사survey에서, / 61%의 미국인들이 말했다 / 그들은 지지한다고 / 정부가 '빈곤층 지원assistance to the poor'에
더 많은 돈을 쓰는 것을.

02 그러나 / 같은 모집단이 질문을 받았을 때 / 그들이 '복지welfare'에 더 많은 정부 예산을 쓰는 것을 지지하는지, / 단지
21%만이 찬성했다be in favour.

03 다시 말해, / 만약 당신이 개별 복지 프로그램들에 대해 사람들에게 물어보면 / 장기 질환을 가진 사람들에게 재정적 도움을
주는 것 / 그리고 저소득 가정의 급식 비용을 대주는 것과 같은 (프로그램들) / 사람들은 대체로 그것들에 찬성한다.

04 그러나 / 만약 당신이 '복지'에 관해 질문한다면 / 정확히 동일한 프로그램을 나타내는refer to (복지) / 당신이 방금 열거한
(프로그램) / 그들은 그것에 반대한다.

05 '복지'라는 단어는 부정적인 함축된 의미를 가지고 있다 / 아마도 방식 때문인지 / 많은 정치인들과 신문들이 그것을
묘사하는portray (방식).

06 따라서, / 질문의 구성framing은 답변에 크게 영향을 미칠heavily influence 수 있다 / 여러 가지 방식으로, / 이는
중요하다 / 당신의 목표가 사람들이 생각하는 것에 대한 '진정한 척도'를 얻는obtain a 'true measure' 것이라면.

07 그리고 / 다음 번에 당신이 한 정치인이 말하는 것을 듣게 될 때, / '설문 조사는 대다수의 국민들이 나에게 동의한다는 것을
입증한다'고 / 매우 조심하라.

구문 Check up	① The word 'welfare' has negative connotations, perhaps because / because of the way many politicians and newspapers portray it.	② It matters if your aim is to obtain a 'true measure' of which / what people think.
	뒤에 명사구(the way ~)가 오므로 because of를 쓴다.	전치사 of의 목적어 역할을 하면서 불완전한 문장을 연결할 수 있도록 선행사(명사)를 포함하는 관계대명사 what을 쓴다.

D

STEP 1 • 수능에 *진짜* 나오는 *단어*

✔ 문제에 나오는 단어들을 확인하세요.

시간이 없다면 색으로 표시된 단어만이라도 꼭 외우고 넘어가세요!

01	**regardless of**	~에 상관없이	(✔ regardless) (of) distance	거리와 상관없이
02	agriculture	n. 농경, 농업	( ) and society	농업과 사회
03	undeniable	a. 부인할 수 없는	( ) evidence	부인할 수 없는 증거
04	**support**	v. 부양하다, 지지하다	( ) a family	가족을 부양하다
05	**require**	v. 필요로 하다, 요구하다	( ) a license	면허를 필요로 하다
06	sustain	v. 지탱하다, 부양하다	( ) many people	많은 사람들을 지탱하다
07	qualitative	a. 질적인	( ) changes	질적인 변화
08	estimate	n. 추정치 v. 추정[추산]하다	a rough ( )	대략적인 추정
09	vary	v. 다양하다	Estimates ( ).	추정치는 다양하다.
10	point to	~을 보여주다, ~을 가리키다	( ) ( ) an increase	증가를 보여주다
11	establish	v. 확립하다	( ) agriculture	농업을 확립하다
12	store	v. 저장하다	( ) food	음식을 저장하다
13	**create**	v. 만들다	( ) a society with haves and have-nots	가진 자와 못 가진 자로 이루어진 사회를 만들다

⊕ 본문 문장 속에서 단어들을 확인해 보세요.

Regardless of **whether the people existing after** agriculture **were happier, healthier, or neither, / it is** undeniable **that there were more of them.**

농경 **이후에 존재했던 사람들이 더 행복했든, 더 건강했든, 아니면 둘 다 아니었든 간에** 상관없이 **/ 더 많은 수의 사람들이 있었다는 것은** 부인할 수 없다.

01	regardless of	✎ ~에 상관없이	regardless of distance	거리와 상관없이
02	agriculture		agriculture and society	농업과 사회
03	undeniable		undeniable evidence	부인할 수 없는 증거
04	support		support a family	가족을 부양하다
05	require		require a license	면허를 필요로 하다
06	sustain		sustain many people	많은 사람들을 지탱하다
07	qualitative		qualitative changes	질적인 변화
08	estimate		a rough estimate	대략적인 추정
09	vary		Estimates vary.	추정치는 다양하다.
10	point to		point to an increase	증가를 보여주다
11	establish		establish agriculture	농업을 확립하다
12	store		store food	음식을 저장하다
13	create		create a society with haves and have-nots	가진 자와 못 가진 자로 이루어진 사회를 만들다

➕ **본문 문장 속에서 단어의 의미를 우리말로 해석해 보세요.**

Regardless of whether the people existing after agriculture were happier, healthier, or neither, / it is undeniable that there were more of them.

→   ＿＿＿＿＿＿ 이후에 존재했던 사람들이 더 행복했든, 더 건강했든, 아니면 둘 다 아니었든 간에 ＿＿＿＿＿＿＿＿ / 더 많은 수의 사람들이 있었다는 것은 ＿＿＿＿＿＿＿.

제한시간 80초
난이도 ★★★★★

STEP **2** • 수능 기출 제대로 풀기

D 주어진 글 다음에 이어질 글의 순서로 가장 적절한 것은?

Regardless of whether the people existing after agriculture were happier, healthier, or neither, it is undeniable that there were more of them. Agriculture both supports and requires more people to grow the crops that sustain them.

(A) And a larger population doesn't just mean increasing the size of everything, like buying a bigger box of cereal for a larger family. It brings qualitative changes in the way people live.

(B) Estimates vary, of course, but evidence points to an increase in the human population from 1-5 million people worldwide to a few hundred million once agriculture had become established.

(C) For example, more people means more kinds of diseases, particularly when those people are sedentary. Those groups of people can also store food for long periods, which creates a society with haves and have-nots.

*sedentary: 한 곳에 정착해 있는

① (A) — (C) — (B)　　　② (B) — (A) — (C)

③ (B) — (C) — (A)　　　④ (C) — (A) — (B)

⑤ (C) — (B) — (A)

정답과 해설 p.44

01 Regardless of [whether the people existing after agriculture were happier, healthier, or
현재분사
whether절(전치사 of의 목적어)
neither], / it is undeniable / that there were more of them.
가주어   진주어(that절)

02 Agriculture both supports and requires more people / [to grow the crops / that sustain
both A and B: A와 B 둘 다(A, B 자리에 동사 병렬)   to부정사의 부사적 용법   주격 관계대명사절
them].
동명사

03 Estimates vary, of course, / but evidence points to an increase in the human population
/ from 1-5 million people worldwide to a few hundred million / once agriculture had
접속사(일단 ~ 한 후)
become established.
과거완료

04 And a larger population doesn't just mean increasing the size of everything, / like
mean+동명사: ~하는 것을 뜻하다   전치사
buying a bigger box of cereal for a larger family.
동명사

05 It brings qualitative changes / in the way people live. // For example, / more people
means more kinds of diseases, / particularly when those people are sedentary.
관계부사절

06 Those groups of people can also store food for long periods, / which creates a society
선행사   =and it
with haves and have-nots.

01 농경agriculture 이후에 존재했던 사람들이 더 행복했든, 더 건강했든, 아니면 둘 다 아니었든 간에 상관없이regardless of,
/ 부인할 수 없다undeniable / 더 많은 수의 사람들이 있었다는 것은.

02 농경은 더 많은 사람을 부양하고support 필요로 한다require / 농작물을 기르기 위해 / 그들을 지탱해sustain 주는.

03 물론, 추정치estimate는 다양하지만vary, / 증거는 인구가 증가했다는 것을 보여준다point to / 전 세계적으로 1~5백만
명에서 수억 명으로 / 일단 농경이 확립된become established 후.

04 그리고 더 많은 인구는 단지 모든 것의 규모를 확장하는 것을 의미하지는 않는다 / 더 큰 가족을 위해 더 큰 상자의
시리얼을 사는 것 같이.

05 그것은 질적인 변화qualitative changes를 가져온다 / 사람들의 생활 방식에. // 예를 들어 / 더 많은 사람은 더 많은
종류의 질병을 의미하는데, / 특히 그 사람들이 한 곳에 정착해 있을 때 그렇다.

06 그러한 사람들의 집단은 또한 음식을 장기간 보관할store food 수 있고, / 이것은 가진 자와 가지지 못한 자로 이루어진
사회를 만들어 낸다create a society with haves and have-nots.

① Regardless of if / whether the people existing after agriculture were happier, healthier, or neither, it is undeniable that there were more of them.

if, whether는 모두 '~인지 아닌지'라는 의미로 쓰이지만, 전치사의 목적어일 때는 whether만 쓴다.

② Those groups of people can also store food for long periods, that / which creates a society with haves and have-nots.

문장을 연결하고 주어나 목적어 등을 대신하는 관계대명사는 that, which 모두 가능하지만 콤마(,)를 써서 연결할 때는 which를 쓴다.

정답 ① whether ② which

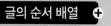

글의 순서 배열

STEP 1 • 수능에 진짜 나오는 단어

✔ 문제에 나오는 단어들을 확인하세요.

시간이 없다면 색으로 표시된 단어만이라도 꼭 외우고 넘어가세요!

No.	단어	뜻	표현	의미
01	assessment	n. 평가	direct (✔ assessment)	직접적인 평가
02	measure	n. 측정 v. 측정하다	a ( ) of understanding	이해 측정
03	accurate	a. 정확한	( ) measures	정확한 측정
04	inquiry	n. 탐구, 조사	in an ( )	조사에서
05	process	n. 과정	the ( )es of inquiry	탐구 과정
06	be capable of	~할 수 있다	( ) ( ) ( ) applying	적용할 수 있다
07	apply	v. 적용하다	( ) skillfully	능숙하게 적용하다
08	disciplinary	a. 학과의	a ( ) strategy	학과의 전략
09	misinterpret	v. 잘못 이해하다	( ) the content	내용을 잘못 이해하다
10	assess	v. 평가하다	( ) a skill	기술을 평가하다
11	investigation	n. 관찰	assess a skill with ( )s	관찰로 기술을 평가하다
12	interconnect	v. 서로 연결하다	The skill and the content are ( )ed.	기술과 내용은 서로 연결되어 있다.
13	analysis	n. 분석	do the pattern ( )	패턴 분석을 하다
14	properly	ad. 올바르게	do the analysis ( )	분석을 올바르게 하다

● 본문 문장 속에서 단어들을 확인해 보세요.

Sometimes / students will understand the processes of inquiry well, / and be capable of skillfully applying / social studies disciplinary strategies.

때때로 / 학생들은 탐구 과정을 잘 이해할 것이다 / 그리고 능숙하게 적용할 수 있을 것이다 / 사회 학과의 전략을.

단어 다시보기 문제를 풀기 전에 단어들을 **30초** 동안 다시 확인하세요.

01	assessment	✎ 평가	direct assessment	직접적인 평가
02	measure		a measure of understanding	이해 측정
03	accurate		accurate measures	정확한 측정
04	inquiry		in an inquiry	조사에서
05	process		the processes of inquiry	탐구 과정
06	be capable of		be capable of applying	적용할 수 있다
07	apply		apply skillfully	능숙하게 적용하다
08	disciplinary		a disciplinary strategy	학과의 전략
09	misinterpret		misinterpret the content	내용을 잘못 이해하다
10	assess		assess a skill	기술을 평가하다
11	investigation		assess a skill with investigations	관찰로 기술을 평가하다
12	interconnect		The skill and the content are interconnected.	기술과 내용은 서로 연결되어 있다.
13	analysis		do the pattern analysis	패턴 분석을 하다
14	properly		do the analysis properly	분석을 올바르게 하다

➕ **본문 문장 속에서 단어의 의미를 우리말로 해석해 보세요.**

Sometimes / students will understand the processes of inquiry well, / and be capable of skillfully applying / social studies disciplinary strategies.

→ 때때로 / 학생들은   을 잘 이해할 것이다 / 그리고 능숙하게   것이다 / 사회   전략을.

STEP **2** • 수능 기출 제대로 풀기

E 주어진 글 다음에 이어질 글의 순서로 가장 적절한 것은?

Testing strategies relating to direct assessment of content knowledge still have their value in an inquiry-driven classroom.

(A) For these reasons, we need a measure of a student's content understanding. To do this right, we need to make sure our assessment is getting us accurate measures of whether our students understand the content they use in an inquiry.

(B) However, it also could be that they did not understand the content that they were trying to build patterns with. Sometimes students will understand the processes of inquiry well, and be capable of skillfully applying social studies disciplinary strategies, yet fail to do so because they misinterpret the content.

(C) Let's pretend for a moment that we wanted to ignore content and only assess a student's skill with investigations. The problem is that the skills and the content are interconnected. When a student fails at pattern analysis, it could be because they do not understand how to do the pattern analysis properly.

*inquiry-driven classroom: 탐구 주도형 교실

① (A) — (C) — (B)   ② (B) — (A) — (C)

③ (B) — (C) — (A)   ④ (C) — (A) — (B)

⑤ (C) — (B) — (A)

정답과 해설 p.45

01 Testing strategies relating to direct assessment of content knowledge / still have their
주어(복수)   현재분사(명사 수식)   동사
value / in an inquiry-driven classroom.

02 Let's pretend (for a moment) / that we wanted to ignore content and only assess
청유문(~하자)   삽입구   명사절 접속사(목적어)
a student's skill with investigations. // The problem is / that the skills and the content
명사절 접속사(보어)
are interconnected.

03 When a student fails at pattern analysis, / it could be / because they do not understand
/ how to do the pattern analysis properly.
의문사+to부정사(목적어)

04 However, / it also could be / [that they did not understand the content / that they were
주격보어(명사절)   목적격 관계대명사절
trying to build patterns with].

05 ────────── 병렬 연결 ──────────
Sometimes / students will understand the processes of inquiry well, / and be capable
of skillfully applying social studies disciplinary strategies, / yet fail to do so / because
등위접속사(하지만)
they misinterpret the content.

06 For these reasons, / we need a measure of a student's content understanding. // To do
this right, / we need to make sure / our assessment is getting us accurate measures / of
부사적 용법(목적)   명사절 접속사 that 생략
whether our students understand the content / they use in an inquiry.
명사절 접속사: ~인지 아닌지   목적격 관계대명사절

01 내용 지식에 대한 직접 평가direct assessment와 관련된 테스트 전략은 / 여전히 그 가치를 지닌다 / 탐구 주도형 교실에서.

02 잠시 가정해 보자 / 우리가 내용을 무시하고 관찰을 통해 학생의 기술만을 평가하기assess a skill with investigations를
원한다고. // 문제는 / 기술과 내용이 서로 연결되어 있다는be interconnected 것이다.

03 학생이 패턴 분석에 실패하면 / 그것은 ~일 수 있다 / 학생이 이해하지 못하기 때문일 / 패턴 분석을 올바르게 수행하는do the
pattern analysis properly 방법을.

04 그러나 / 또한 ~일 수도 있다 / 그들이 내용을 이해하지 못한 것 / 그들이 패턴을 만들려고 하는 (내용).

05 때때로 / 학생들은 탐구inquiry 과정process을 잘 이해하고 / 사회 학과의 전략disciplinary strategies을 능숙하게
적용할 능력이 있다be capable of skillfully applying / 하지만 그렇게 하지 못할 것이다 / 그들이 내용을 잘못
해석하기misinterpret the content 때문에.

06 이러한 이유로 / 우리는 학생의 내용 이해에 대한 측정measure이 필요하다. // 이것을 올바르게 하기 위해서 / 우리는
확실하게 할 필요가 있다 / 평가가 우리로 하여금 정확한 측정accurate measures을 하게 하는지를 / 학생들이 내용을
이해했는지 여부에 대한 (측정) / 탐구에서 사용하는 (내용).

구문 Check up

① Testing strategies relating to direct assessment of
content knowledge still have / has their value in an
inquiry-driven classroom.

이 문장의 주어는 strategies로 복수이므로 have를 쓴다. 동사 바로 앞에
있는 명사 knowledge를 주어로 착각하지 말아야 한다.

② Sometimes students will understand the processes
of inquiry well, and be / are capable of skillfully
applying social studies disciplinary strategies.

앞에 조동사 will이 있고 접속사 and로 연결되는 것이므로 understand와
마찬가지로 원형인 be가 적절하다.

글의 순서 배열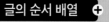

STEP 1 • 수능에 *진짜* 나오는 *단어*

✔ 문제에 나오는 단어들을 확인하세요.

시간이 없다면 색으로 표시된 단어만이라도 꼭 외우고 넘어가세요!

01	redundant	a. 넘치는, 중복된	seem (✔ redundant)	중복된 것처럼 보이다
02	versatile	a. 다재다능한, 활용도가 높은	the most ( ) pants	가장 활용도가 높은 바지
03	wardrobe	n. 옷장	in your ( )	당신의 옷장 속에 있는
04	neutral	a. 중립적인, 무난한	a particularly ( ) color	특별히 무난한 색
05	amount	n. 양	tiny ( )s	소량
06	thread	n. 실	a needle and ( )	바늘과 실
07	commonly	ad. 흔하게	most ( ) used	가장 흔하게 사용되는
08	chemical	a. 화학적인	the ( ) properties	화학적 특성
09	dye	n. 염료, 물감	blue ( )	청색 염료
10	temperature	n. 온도	in hot ( )s	높은 온도에서
11	eventually	ad. 결국, 마침내	( ) achieve	마침내 얻다
12	achieve	v. 얻다, 성취하다	( ) the feeling	느낌을 얻다
13	laborer	n. 노동자	choice for ( )s	노동자들의 선택

➕ 본문 문장 속에서 단어들을 확인해 보세요.

While jeans are probably the most versatile pants in your wardrobe, / blue actually isn't a particularly neutral color.

청바지는 당신의 옷장에서 아마도 가장 활용도가 높은 바지이지만 / 사실은 파란색이 특별히 무난한 색은 아니다.

01	redundant	넘치는, 중복된	seem redundant	중복된 것처럼 보이다
02	versatile		the most versatile pants	가장 활용도가 높은 바지
03	wardrobe		in your wardrobe	당신의 옷장 속에 있는
04	neutral		a particularly neutral color	특별히 무난한 색
05	amount		tiny amounts	소량
06	thread		a needle and thread	바늘과 실
07	commonly		most commonly used	가장 흔하게 사용되는
08	chemical		the chemical properties	화학적 특성
09	dye		blue dye	청색 염료
10	temperature		in hot temperatures	높은 온도에서
11	eventually		eventually achieve	마침내 얻다
12	achieve		achieve the feeling	느낌을 얻다
13	laborer		choice for laborers	노동자들의 선택

➕ **본문 문장 속에서 단어의 의미를 우리말로 해석해 보세요.**

While jeans are probably the most versatile pants in your wardrobe, / blue actually isn't a particularly neutral color.

➜   청바지는 당신의   에서 아마도   이지만 / 사실은 파란색이   은 아니다.

STEP **2** · 수능 기출 제대로 풀기

F

주어진 글 다음에 이어질 글의 순서로 가장 적절한 것은?

Calling your pants "blue jeans" almost seems redundant because practically all denim is blue. While jeans are probably the most versatile pants in your wardrobe, blue actually isn't a particularly neutral color.

(A) The natural indigo dye used in the first jeans, on the other hand, would stick only to the outside of the threads. When the indigo-dyed denim is washed, tiny amounts of that dye get washed away, and the thread comes with them.

(B) Ever wonder why it's the most commonly used hue? Blue was the chosen color for denim because of the chemical properties of blue dye. Most dyes will permeate fabric in hot temperatures, making the color stick.

(C) The more denim was washed, the softer it would get, eventually achieving that worn-in, made-just-for-me feeling you probably get with your favorite jeans. That softness made jeans the trousers of choice for laborers.

*hue: 색상
**permeate: 스며[배어]들다

① (A) — (C) — (B)　　　　② (B) — (A) — (C)

③ (B) — (C) — (A)　　　　④ (C) — (A) — (B)

⑤ (C) — (B) — (A)

정답과 해설 p.45

01 Calling your pants "blue jeans" / almost seems redundant / because practically all
동명사(단수 취급)   동사
denim is blue. // While jeans are probably the most versatile pants in your wardrobe, /
~인 반면에   the+최상급(가장 ~한)
blue actually isn't a particularly neutral color.

02 Ever wonder / why it's the most commonly used hue? // Blue was the chosen
의문사절(목적어)   과거분사
color for denim / because of the chemical properties of blue dye.
because of+명사(구)

03 Most dyes will permeate fabric / in hot temperatures, / making the color stick.
                                                                분사구문(=and they will make~)
                                                                사역동사(make)+목적어+목적격 보어(동사원형)

04 The natural indigo dye / used in the first jeans, / on the other hand, / would stick only
                              과거분사구   반면에
to the outside of the threads.

05 When the indigo-dyed denim is washed, / tiny amounts of that dye get washed away, /
                   과거분사   수동태(be+p.p.)   주어(복수)   수 일치
and the thread comes with them.

06 The more denim was washed, / the softer it would get, / eventually achieving that
the 비교급, ~ the 비교급 …: ~할수록 더 …하다   분사구문(=and it achieved ~)
worn-in, made-just-for-me feeling / you probably get with your favorite jeans. // That
                                목적격 관계대명사 생략
softness made jeans / the trousers of choice for laborers.
5형식 동사(make)+목적어+목적격 보어(명사)

01 바지를 "파란 청바지"라 부르는 것은 / 거의 표현이 중복된redundant 것처럼 보인다 / 거의 모든 데님이 파란색이기
때문에. // 청바지는 당신의 옷장wardrobe에서 아마도 가장 활용도가 높은versatile 바지이지만 / 사실은 파란색이
특별히 무난한neutral 색은 아니다.

02 궁금해 해 본 적이 있는가 / 왜 파란색이 (청바지에) 가장 흔하게commonly 사용되는 색상인지? // 파란색은 데님의
색깔로 선택되었다 / 청색 염료dye의 화학적chemical 특성 때문에.

03 대부분의 염료는 천에 스며들게 된다 / 높은 온도temperature에서 / 색이 들러붙게 하며.

04 천연 남색 염료는 / 최초의 청바지에 사용되었던 / 반면에 / 옷감의 바깥 쪽에만 들러붙었다.

05 남색으로 염색된 데님을 빨 때, / 그 염료 중 소량tiny amounts은 씻겨 나가게 되고 / 실thread이 그 염료와 함께 나오게
된다.

06 데님을 더 많이 빨수록, / 더 부드러워지게 되고, / 마침내eventually 닳아 해진, 나만을 위해 만들어졌다는 바로 그
느낌을 얻게 된다achieve / 당신이 아마 가장 좋아하는 청바지로부터 얻는 (느낌). // 이 부드러움은 청바지를 만들었다 /
노동자laborer들이 선택한 바지로.

구문 Check up

① Blue was the chosen color for denim because / because of the chemical properties of blue dye.

② Most dyes will permeate fabric in hot temperatures, making the color stick / to stick .

뒤에 명사구가 이어지고 있으므로 전치사와 함께 쓰인 because of가 적절하다. because 뒤에는 절이 온다.

사역동사(make)의 목적격 보어로 동사원형인 stick이 적절하다.

STEP 1 · 수능에 진짜 나오는 단어

✔ 문제에 나오는 단어들을 확인하세요.

시간이 없다면 색으로 표시된 단어만이라도 꼭 외우고 넘어가세요!

01	evolution	n. 진화	the theory of (✔ evolution)	진화 이론
02	elbow	n. 팔꿈치	( )s for fouling	반칙을 할 수 있는 팔꿈치
03	enable	v. ~을 가능하게 하다	( ) me to buy	내가 사는 것을 가능하게 하다
04	ritualized	a. 의례화된	a ( ) action	의례화된 행동
05	aggression	n. 공격	ritualized ( )	의례화된 공격
06	instinct	n. 본능	a natural ( )	자연적 본능
07	rough-and-tumble play	거친 (신체) 놀이	the rules for ( ) ( )	거친 신체 놀이의 규칙들
08	gene	n. 유전자	a human ( )	인간의 유전자
09	identical	a. 동일한	an ( ) set of ideas	동일한 생각 체계
10	entirely	ad. 전적으로, 완전히	These ideas are ( ) imaginary.	이러한 생각들은 전적으로 가상이다.
11	work in concert with	~와 협력하다	( ) ( ) ( ) ( ) teammates	팀원들과 협력하다
12	opposing	a. 서로 겨루는(대립하는)	the ( ) team	상대팀

➕ 본문 문장 속에서 단어들을 확인해 보세요.

Other animals that engage strangers in ritualized aggression / do so largely by instinct.

의례화된 공격에 낯선 동물을 끌어들이는 다른 동물들은 / 주로 본능에 의해 그렇게 한다.

문제를 풀기 전에 단어들을 30초 동안 다시 확인하세요.

01	evolution	✏ 진화	the theory of evolution	진화 이론
02	elbow		elbows for fouling	반칙을 할 수 있는 팔꿈치
03	enable		enable me to buy	내가 사는 것을 가능하게 하다
04	ritualized		a ritualized action	의례화된 행동
05	aggression		ritualized aggression	의례화된 공격
06	instinct		a natural instinct	자연적 본능
07	rough-and-tumble play		the rules for rough-and-tumble play	거친 신체 놀이의 규칙들
08	gene		a human gene	인간의 유전자
09	identical		an identical set of ideas	동일한 생각 체계
10	entirely		These ideas are entirely imaginary.	이러한 생각들은 전적으로 가상이다.
11	work in concert with		work in concert with teammates	팀원들과 협력하다
12	opposing		the opposing team	상대팀

➕ **본문 문장 속에서 단어의 의미를 우리말로 해석해 보세요.**

Other animals that engage strangers in ritualized aggression / do so largely by instinct.

→ ▨▨▨▨▨ 에 낯선 동물을 끌어들이는 다른 동물들은 / 주로 ▨▨▨▨▨ 에 의해 그렇게 한다.

제한시간 80초
난이도 ★★★★☆

STEP **2** • 수능 기출 제대로 풀기

G 주어진 글 다음에 이어질 글의 순서로 가장 적절한 것은?

Evolution did not give humans the ability to play soccer. True, it produced legs for kicking and elbows for fouling, but all that this enables us to do is perhaps practice penalty kicks alone.

(A) Other animals that engage strangers in ritualized aggression do so largely by instinct — puppies throughout the world have the rules for rough-and-tumble play built into their genes.

(B) But human teenagers have no such genes for soccer. They can nevertheless play the game with complete strangers because they have all learned an identical set of ideas about soccer. These ideas are entirely imaginary, but if everyone shares them, we can all play the game.

(C) To get into a game with the strangers we find in the schoolyard on any given afternoon, we not only have to work in concert with ten teammates we may never have met before, we also need to know that the eleven players on the opposing team are playing by the same rules.

① (A) — (C) — (B)   ② (B) — (A) — (C)

③ (B) — (C) — (A)   ④ (C) — (A) — (B)

⑤ (C) — (B) — (A)

정답과 해설 p.46

01 Evolution did not give humans / the ability to play soccer. // True, it produced legs for
   to부정사의 형용사적 용법
kicking and elbows for fouling, / but all that this enables us to do / is perhaps practice
                                    주어(오직 ~한 것이라고는)   주격 보어(=to practice)
penalty kicks alone.

02 [To get into a game with the strangers / we find in the schoolyard on any given
   to부정사의 부사적 용법(~하려면)   목적격 관계대명사절
afternoon], / we not only have to work in concert with ten teammates / we may never
                 not only A (but) also B: A뿐만 아니라 B도   목적격 관계대명사절
have met before, / we also need to know / that the eleven players on the opposing team
                                            명사절 접속사
are playing by the same rules.

03 Other animals [that engage strangers in ritualized aggression] / do so largely by instinct
                   주격 관계대명사절   =engage strangers
/ — puppies throughout the world / have the rules for rough-and-tumble play / built
   대시: 예를 들어 설명   과거분사
into their genes.

04 But human teenagers have no such genes for soccer. // They can nevertheless play the
                              형용사(명사 수식)
game with complete strangers / because they have all learned an identical set of ideas
                                접속사(이유)
about soccer.

05 These ideas are entirely imaginary, / but if everyone shares them, / we can all play the game.
                                          접속사(조건)

01 진화evolution는 인간에게 주지 않았다 / 축구를 할 수 있는 능력을. // 실제로, 그것은 찰 수 있는 다리와 반칙을 할 수 있는 팔꿈치elbow를 생기게 했다 / 그러나 이것이 우리에게 할 수 있게enable 하는 것이라고는 / 아마도 혼자서 페널티 킥을 연습하는 것뿐이다.

02 낯선 사람들과 경기를 시작하기 위해서는 / 우리가 어느 날 오후에 학교 운동장에서 만난 (낯선 사람들), / 우리는 열 명의 팀 구성원들과 조화를 이루어야work in concert with 할 뿐만 아니라 / 전에 만난 적이 없는 (열 명의 팀 구성원), / 또한 우리는 알 필요가 있다 / 상대편opposing team 열한 명의 선수들이 / 같은 규칙으로 경기를 하고 있다는 것을.

03 의례화된 공격ritualized aggression에 낯선 동물을 끌어들이는 다른 동물들은 / 주로 본능instinct에 의해 그렇게 한다. / 전세계의 강아지들은 / 거친 놀이rough-and-tumble play에 대한 규칙들을 가지고 있다 / 그들의 유전자에genes 내재된.

04 그러나 십대 인간들은 축구에 대한 그러한 유전자를 가지고 있지 않다. // 그럼에도 불구하고 그들은 완전히 낯선 사람들과 경기를 할 수 있다 / 모두 축구에 대한 동일한identical 생각 체계를 배워 왔기 때문이다.

05 이러한 생각들은 전적으로entirely 가상이다 / 그러나 모두가 그러한 생각들을 공유한다면 / 우리는 모두 경기를 할 수 있다.

구문 Check up

① All that this enables us to do is perhaps practices /
practice penalty kicks alone.

본동사 is 뒤로 주격보어가 필요한데, 주어가 'all ~ do'의 형태로 '오직 ~한 것이라고는'의 의미를 나타낼 때는 to부정사 주격보어의 to가 생략될 수 있다. 따라서 practice가 적절하다.

② Other animals that engage / engages strangers in
ritualized aggression do so largely by instinct.

주격 관계대명사 that 뒤의 동사는 선행사(Other animals)에 수 일치하므로 engage가 답으로 와야 한다.

정답 ① practice ② engage

☑ 종합 성적표

구분	공부한 날 ❶	결과 분석			틀린 이유 ❸
		출처	풀이 시간 ❷	채점 결과 (O, X)	
Day **10**	월 일	학력평가 기출 2023년	분 초		
		학력평가 기출 2022년	분 초		
		학력평가 기출 2021년	분 초		
		학력평가 기출 2020년	분 초		
		학력평가 기출 2019년	분 초		
		학력평가 기출 2018년	분 초		
		학력평가 기출 2017년	분 초		
Day **11**	월 일	학력평가 기출 2023년	분 초		
		학력평가 기출 2022년	분 초		
		학력평가 기출 2021년	분 초		
		학력평가 기출 2020년	분 초		
		학력평가 기출 2019년	분 초		
		학력평가 기출 2017년	분 초		
		학력평가 기출 2016년	분 초		
Day **12**	월 일	학력평가 기출 2023년	분 초		
		학력평가 기출 2022년	분 초		
		학력평가 기출 2021년	분 초		
		학력평가 기출 2020년	분 초		
		학력평가 기출 2019년	분 초		
		학력평가 기출 2018년	분 초		
		학력평가 기출 2016년	분 초		

3일간
공부한 내용을
다시 보니,
……

❶ **매일 지문을 하루 계획에 맞춰 풀었다. vs. 내가 한 약속을 못 지켰다.**

<매3영 고2 기출>은 단순 문제풀이를 위한 책이 아니라, 매일 규칙적으로 영어를 공부하는 습관을 잡는 책입니다. 따라서 푸는 문제 개수는 상황에 따라 다르더라도 '매일' 학습하는 것이 중요합니다.

❷ **주어진 시간을 자꾸 넘긴다?**

풀이 시간이 계속해서 권장 시간을 넘긴다면 실전 훈련이 부족하다는 신호입니다. 아직 조급함을 가질 필요는 없지만, 매일의 문제 풀이에 더 긴장감 있게 임해보세요.

❸ **틀린 이유 맞춤 솔루션:** 오답 이유에 따라 다음 해결책을 참고하세요.

(1) 단어를 많이 몰라서

▶ <STEP 1 단어>에 제시된 필수 어휘를 매일 챙겨보고, SELF-TEST까지 꼼꼼히 진행합니다.

(2) 문장 해석이 잘 안 돼서

▶ <STEP 3 지문 복습>의 구문 첨삭과 끊어읽기 해설을 정독하며 문장구조를 보는 눈을 길러보세요.

(3) 해석은 되지만 내용이 이해가 안 되거나, 선택지로 연결을 못 해서

▶ <정답과 해설>의 해설과 오답풀이를 참고해 틀린 이유를 깊이 고민하고 정리해 보세요.

! 결론적으로, 내가 **취약한 부분**은 [   ] 이다. **취약점을 보완하기 위해서** 나는

[   ] 을/를 해야겠다.

3일 뒤 다시 봐야 할 문항과, 꼭 다시 외워야 할 사항·구문 등이 있는 페이지는 지금 바로 접어 두세요.

<매3영>이 제시하는 3단계로

유형 2일 훈련

DAY

13~14

DAY 13

A

STEP **1** • 수능에 *진짜* 나오는 *단어*

요약문 완성 ⊕

✔ 문제에 나오는 단어들을 확인하세요.

시간이 없다면 색으로 표시된 단어만이라도 꼭 외우고 넘어가세요!

01	conduct	v. 수행하다	(✔ conduct) a psychological study	심리학 연구를 수행하다
02	motivation	n. 동기	the ( )s for helping	도와주려는 동기
03	assistance	n. 도움	other forms of ( )	다른 형태의 도움
04	discomfort	n. 불편, 곤란	reduce another's ( )	다른 사람의 불편을 줄이다
05	stem from	~에서 비롯되다	( ) ( ) differences	차이에서 비롯되다
06	initial	a. 초기의	their ( ) impressions	그들의 첫인상
07	discharge	v. 해소하다, 방출하다	( ) that emotional distress	그 감정적 고통을 해소하다
08	empathize with	~에 공감하다	( ) ( ) their pain	그들의 고통에 공감하다
09	victim	n. 희생자	the ( )s of the attack	그 공격의 희생자들
10	struggle	v. 고생하다, 분투하다	( ) to escape	탈출하려고 고생하다
11	decline	n. 감소	a ( ) in motivation	동기의 감소
12	discourage	v. 낙담시키다	be ( )d by failures	실패에 의해 낙담하다
13	maximization	n. 극대화	profit ( )	이윤 극대화

⊕ 본문 문장 속에서 단어들을 확인해 보세요.

In 2006, / researchers conducted a study on the motivations for helping / after the September 11th terrorist attacks against the United States.

2006년에 / 연구자들은 도와주려는 동기에 관한 연구를 수행했다 / 미국에 대한 9.11 테러 공격 이후.

문제를 풀기 전에 단어들을 **30초** 동안 다시 확인하세요.

01	conduct	✎ 수행하다	conduct a psychological study	심리학 연구를 수행하다
02	motivation		the motivations for helping	도와주려는 동기
03	assistance		other forms of assistance	다른 형태의 도움
04	discomfort		reduce another's discomfort	다른 사람의 불편을 줄이다
05	stem from		stem from differences	차이에서 비롯되다
06	initial		their initial impressions	그들의 첫인상
07	discharge		discharge that emotional distress	그 감정적 고통을 해소하다
08	empathize with		empathize with their pain	그들의 고통에 공감하다
09	victim		the victims of the attack	그 공격의 희생자들
10	struggle		struggle to escape	탈출하려고 고생하다
11	decline		a decline in motivation	동기의 감소
12	discourage		be discouraged by failures	실패에 의해 낙담하다
13	maximization		profit maximization	이윤 극대화

➕ **본문 문장 속에서 단어의 의미를 우리말로 해석해 보세요.**

In 2006, / researchers conducted a study on the motivations for helping / after the September 11th terrorist attacks against the United States.

→ 2006년에 / 연구자들은   / 미국에 대한 9.11 테러 공격 이후.

STEP **2** • 수능 기출 제대로 풀기

 다음 글의 내용을 한 문장으로 요약하고자 한다. 빈칸 (A), (B)에 들어갈 말로 가장 적절한 것은?

In 2006, researchers conducted a study on the motivations for helping after the September 11th terrorist attacks against the United States. In the study, they found that individuals who gave money, blood, goods, or other forms of assistance because of other-focused motives (giving to reduce another's discomfort) were almost four times more likely to still be giving support one year later than those whose original motivation was to reduce personal distress. This effect likely stems from differences in emotional arousal. The events of September 11th emotionally affected people throughout the United States. Those who gave to reduce their own distress reduced their emotional arousal with their initial gift, discharging that emotional distress. However, those who gave to reduce others' distress did not stop empathizing with victims who continued to struggle long after the attacks.

*distress: (정신적) 고통   **arousal: 자극

> A study found that the act of giving was less likely to be ____(A)____ when driven by self-centered motives rather than by other-focused motives, possibly because of the ____(B)____ in emotional arousal.

	(A)		(B)
①	sustained	……	decline
②	sustained	……	maximization
③	indirect	……	variation
④	discouraged	……	reduction
⑤	discouraged	……	increase

정답과 해설 **p.47**

01 In 2006, / researchers conducted a study on the motivations for helping / after the September 11th terrorist attacks against the United States.

02 In the study, / they found / [that individuals who gave money, blood, goods, or other
목적어(명사절)
주어   주격 관계대명사절
forms of assistance / because of other-focused motives (giving to reduce another's
명사구 동격
discomfort) / were almost four times more likely / to still be giving support one year
수 일치(복수)
later / than those whose original motivation was to reduce personal distress].
소유격 관계대명사절

03 This effect likely stems from differences in emotional arousal. // The events of
September 11th / emotionally affected people throughout the United States. //
주어
Those who gave to reduce their own distress / reduced their emotional arousal with
주격 관계대명사절   동사
their initial gift, / discharging that emotional distress. // However, / those who gave
분사구문(능동)   주격 관계대명사절
to reduce others' distress / did not stop empathizing with victims / who continued to
~하기를 멈추다   주격 관계대명사절
struggle long after the attacks.

04 → A study found / that the act of giving was less likely to be sustained / when driven by
it was
~할 가능성이 더 적다
self-centered motives / rather than by other-focused motives, / possibly because of the
decline in emotional arousal.

01 2006년에 / 연구자들은 도와주려는 동기motivation에 관한 연구를 수행했다conduct / 미국에 대한 9.11 테러 공격 이후.

02 그 연구에서, / 그들은 발견했다 / 돈, 혈액, 물품, 또는 다른 형태의 도움assistance을 주었던 사람들이 / 타인에게 초점을 맞춘 동기(다른 사람의 불편discomfort을 줄여주려고 베푸는 것) 때문에 / 가능성이 거의 네 배 더 높다는 것을 / 1년 뒤에도 여전히 지원을 제공할 / 원래 동기가 자기 고통을 줄이는 것이었던 사람들에 비해.

03 이 결과는 감정적 자극의 차이에서 비롯된stem from 것 같다. // 9.11의 사건들은 / 미국 전역의 사람들에게 감정적으로 영향을 미쳤다. // 자기 자신의 고통을 줄이고자 베푼 사람들은 / 초기의initial 베품을 통해 감정적 자극을 줄였다 / 그 감정적 고통을 해소하면서discharge. // 하지만, / 다른 사람들의 고통을 줄이기 위해 베푼 사람들은 / 피해자들에게 공감하기empathize with victims를 멈추지 않았다 / 공격 이후 오랫동안 계속해서 고생하는struggle.

04 → 한 연구에서 밝히기로, / 베푸는 행위가 지속될 가능성이 더 낮았는데 / 자기중심적 동기에 의해 유도될 때 / 타인에 초점을 맞춘 동기보다는 / 이것은 아마도 감정적 자극의 감소decline 때문이었다.

---

① Individuals were almost four times more likely to still be giving support one year later than those who / whose original motivation was to reduce personal distress.

뒷문장에서 빠진 부분은 소유격(their)이므로 소유격 관계대명사 whose 가 정답이다.

② Those who gave to reduce others' distress did not stop to empathize / empathizing with victims who continued to struggle long after the attacks.

문맥상 '공감하기를 멈추지' 않았다는 의미로 empathizing을 써야 한다.

B

STEP 1 • 수능에 진짜 나오는 단어

✔ 문제에 나오는 단어들을 확인하세요.

시간이 없다면 색으로 표시된 단어만이라도 꼭 외우고 넘어가세요!

01	irony	n. 아이러니	the great (✔ irony) of performance psychology	퍼포먼스 심리학의 큰 아이러니
02	as far as	~하는 한	( ) ( ) ( ) he is able	그가 능력이 있는 한
03	indulge	v. (특정한 욕구를) 충족시키다	( ) the passion for art	예술에 대한 열정을 충족시키다(마음껏 다하다)
04	skepticism	n. 회의(론)	indulge one's inner ( )	내면의 회의에 빠지다
05	logic	n. 논리	the ( ) of sports	스포츠의 논리
06	athlete	n. 운동선수	between a scientist and an ( )	과학자와 운동선수 사이의
07	stock in trade	일상적인 것[요소], 상투적인 것	Doubt is a scientist's ( ) ( ) ( ).	의심은 과학자의 일상적인 업무이다.
08	evidence	n. 증거	focus on the ( )	증거에 집중하다
09	refute	v. 반박하다	( ) a theory	이론을 반박하다
10	accordingly	ad. 이에 따라	improve the theory ( )	그에 따라 이론을 개선하다
11	immune to	~에 영향을 받지 않는	( ) ( ) doubt	의심에 영향을 받지 않는
12	uncertainty	n. 불확실성	doubt and ( )	의심과 불확실성
13	rational	a. 이성적인	from a ( ) perspective	이성적인 시각에서 보면
14	convince	v. 확신시키다	( ) himself he will win	자신이 이길 것이라고 확신하다
15	proportion A to B	A를 B에 할당하다, B에 맞춰 A를 조절하다	( ) one's belief ( ) the evidence	신념을 증거에 할당하다

⊕ 본문 문장 속에서 단어들을 확인해 보세요.

Progress is made / by focusing on the evidence / that refutes a theory / and by improving the theory accordingly.

진보는 이루어진다 / 증거에 집중함으로써 / 이론을 반박하는 / 그리고 그에 따라 이론을 개선함으로써.

01	irony	아이러니	the great irony of performance psychology	퍼포먼스 심리학의 큰 아이러니
02	as far as		as far as he is able	그가 능력이 있는 한
03	indulge		indulge the passion for art	예술에 대한 열정을 충족시키다 (마음껏 다하다)
04	skepticism		indulge one's inner skepticism	내면의 회의에 빠지다
05	logic		the logic of sports	스포츠의 논리
06	athlete		between a scientist and an athlete	과학자와 운동선수 사이의
07	stock in trade		Doubt is a scientist's stock in trade.	의심은 과학자의 일상적인 업무이다.
08	evidence		focus on the evidence	증거에 집중하다
09	refute		refute a theory	이론을 반박하다
10	accordingly		improve the theory accordingly	그에 따라 이론을 개선하다
11	immune to		immune to doubt	의심에 영향을 받지 않는
12	uncertainty		doubt and uncertainty	의심과 불확실성
13	rational		from a rational perspective	이성적인 시각에서 보면
14	convince		convince himself he will win	자신이 이길 것이라고 확신하다
15	proportion A to B		proportion one's belief to the evidence	신념을 증거에 할당하다

⊕ 본문 문장 속에서 단어의 의미를 우리말로 해석해 보세요.

Progress is made / by focusing on the evidence / that refutes a theory / and by improving the theory accordingly.

➔ 진보는 이루어진다 / _____ 에 집중함으로써 / 이론을 _____ / 그리고 _____ 이론을 개선함으로써.

STEP **2** • 수능 기출 제대로 풀기

B 다음 글의 내용을 한 문장으로 요약하고자 한다. 빈칸 (A), (B)에 들어갈 말로 가장 적절한 것은?

The great irony of performance psychology is that it teaches each sportsman to believe, as far as he is able, that he will win. No man doubts. No man indulges his inner skepticism. That is the logic of sports psychology. But only one man *can* win. That is the logic of sport. Note the difference between a scientist and an athlete. Doubt is a scientist's stock in trade. Progress is made by focusing on the evidence that refutes a theory and by improving the theory accordingly. Skepticism is the rocket fuel of scientific advance. But doubt, to an athlete, is poison. Progress is made by ignoring the evidence; it is about creating a mindset that is immune to doubt and uncertainty. Just to reiterate: From a rational perspective, this is nothing less than crazy. Why should an athlete convince himself he will win when he knows that there is every possibility he will lose? Because, to win, one must proportion one's belief, not to the evidence, but to whatever the mind can usefully get away with.

*reiterate: 되풀이하다

Unlike scientists whose ____(A)____ attitude is needed to make scientific progress, sports psychology says that to succeed, athletes must ____(B)____ feelings of uncertainty about whether they can win.

	(A)		(B)		(A)		(B)
①	confident	⋯⋯	keep	②	skeptical	⋯⋯	eliminate
③	arrogant	⋯⋯	express	④	critical	⋯⋯	keep
⑤	stubborn	⋯⋯	eliminate				

정답과 해설 p.47

STEP 3 • 수능 지문 제대로 복습하기

01 The great irony of performance psychology is / that it teaches each sportsman [to believe, (as far as he is able), / that he will win].

02 No man doubts. // No man indulges his inner skepticism. // That is the logic of sports psychology. // But only one man *can* win. // That is the logic of sport.

03 Note the difference between a scientist and an athlete. // Doubt is a scientist's stock in trade. // Progress is made / [by focusing on the evidence / that refutes a theory] / and [by improving the theory accordingly]. // Skepticism is the rocket fuel of scientific advance.

04 But doubt, (to an athlete), is poison. // Progress is made by ignoring the evidence; / it is about creating a mindset / that is immune to doubt and uncertainty.

05 Just to reiterate: / From a rational perspective, / this is nothing less than crazy. // Why should an athlete convince himself he will win / when he knows / [that there is every possibility he will lose]? // Because, / to win, / one must proportion one's belief, / not to the evidence, / but to whatever the mind can usefully get away with.

06 → Unlike scientists / [whose skeptical attitude is needed to make scientific progress], / sports psychology says / that to succeed, / athletes must eliminate feelings of uncertainty / about whether they can win.

01 퍼포먼스 심리학의 큰 아이러니irony는 / 개개의 운동선수들이 믿도록 가르친다는 것이다, / 그가 능력이 있는 한as far as, / 이길 것이라고.

02 어느 누구도 의심하지 않는다. // 어느 누구도 내면의 회의에 빠지지 않는다indulge one's skepticism. // 그것이 스포츠 심리학의 논리logic이다. // 하지만 오직 한 사람만이 이길 수 '있다'. // 그것이 스포츠의 논리이다.

03 과학자와 운동선수athlete의 차이점을 주목하라. // 의심은 과학자의 일상적인 업무stock in trade이다. // 진보는 이루어진다 / 증거evidence에 집중함으로써 / 이론을 반박하는refute / 그리고 그에 따라accordingly 이론을 개선함으로써. // 회의론은 과학적 진보의 추진 연료이다.

04 하지만 운동선수에게 의심은 독이다. // 진보는 증거를 무시함으로써 만들어진다 / 그것은 사고방식을 만드는 것이다 / 의심과 불확실성uncertainty에 영향을 받지 않는immune to.

05 다시 한번 되풀이하자면 / 이성적인rational 시각에서 보면, / 이건 미친 짓이나 다름없다. // 왜 운동선수는 자신이 이길 것이라고 확신해야convince oneself 하는가 / 그가 알면서도 / 자신이 질 거라는 모든 가능성이 있다는 것을? // 왜냐하면, / 이기기 위해서, / 선수는 자신의 신념을 할당해야proportion 하기 때문이다 / 증거가 아니라, / 무엇이든 마음이 유용하게 해낼 수 있는 것에.

06 → 과학자들과는 달리 / 과학적 진보를 이루기 위해 회의적인 태도가 요구되는, / 스포츠 심리학은 말한다 / 성공하기 위해서는 / 운동선수들이 불확실한 감정을 없애야 한다고 / 그들이 이길 수 있는지에 대한.

① The great irony of performance psychology is that it teaches each sportsman believe / to believe , as far as he is able, that he will win.

5형식 동사 teach의 목적격 보어 자리에는 to부정사를 써야 하므로 to believe가 정답이다.

② Why should an athlete convince himself he will win when he knows what / that there is every possibility he will lose?

know의 목적어로 자리에 명사가 와야 하고, 뒤따르는 절이 완전하므로 명사절 접속사 that이 적절하다.

정답 ① to believe ② that

✔ 문제에 나오는 단어들을 확인하세요.

시간이 없다면 색으로 표시된 단어만이라도 꼭 외우고 넘어가세요!

01	primary	a. 최초의, 주된	a (✔ primary) care	1차 진료
02	physician	n. (내과) 의사	a ( ) in Boston	Boston의 한 의사
03	willpower	n. 의지력	change their ( )	그들의 의지력을 바꾸다
04	motivation	n. 동기	boost their ( )	그들의 동기를 북돋다
05	slight	a. 약간의, 조금의	a ( ) decline	약간의 감소
06	architecture	n. 구조, 건축	the choice ( )	선택 구조
07	arrange	v. 놓다, 배열하다	how drinks are ( )d	음료가 놓여 있는 방식
08	cash register	금전 등록기(계산대)	next to the ( ) ( )	금전 등록기 옆에
09	available	a. 이용 가능한	Water is ( ).	물은 이용 가능하다.
10	meanwhile	ad. 그 동안에, 한편	( ), sales of bottled water increased.	한편, 물병 판매는 증가했다.
11	perform	v. 수행하다	the study ( )ed by him	그에 의해 수행된 연구
12	consumption	n. 소비	lower the ( )	소비를 낮추다
13	placement	n. 배치	the ( ) of drinks	음료의 배치

⊕ 본문 문장 속에서 단어들을 확인해 보세요.

She believed / she could improve the eating habits of thousands of hospital staff and visitors / without changing their willpower or motivation in the slightest way.

그녀는 믿었다 / 그녀가 수천 명의 병원 직원들과 방문객들의 식습관을 개선할 수 있다고 / 의지력이나 동기를 최소한의 방식으로도 바꾸지 않고.

문제를 풀기 전에 단어들을 30초 동안 다시 확인하세요.

01	primary	✎ 최초의, 주된	a primary care	1차 진료
02	physician		a physician in Boston	Boston의 한 의사
03	willpower		change their willpower	그들의 의지력을 바꾸다
04	motivation		boost their motivation	그들의 동기를 북돋다
05	slight		a slight decline	약간의 감소
06	architecture		the choice architecture	선택 구조
07	arrange		how drinks are arranged	음료가 놓여 있는 방식
08	cash register		next to the cash register	금전 등록기 옆에
09	available		Water is available.	물은 이용 가능하다.
10	meanwhile		Meanwhile, sales of bottled water increased.	한편, 물병 판매는 증가했다.
11	perform		the study performed by him	그에 의해 수행된 연구
12	consumption		lower the consumption	소비를 낮추다
13	placement		the placement of drinks	음료의 배치

➕ 본문 문장 속에서 단어의 의미를 우리말로 해석해 보세요.

She believed / she could improve the eating habits of thousands of hospital staff and visitors / without changing their willpower or motivation in the slightest way.

→ 그녀는 믿었다 / 그녀가 수천 명의 병원 직원들과 방문객들의 식습관을 개선할 수 있다고 / ＿＿＿＿＿＿＿＿이나 ＿＿＿＿＿＿＿＿를 ＿＿＿＿＿＿＿＿방식으로도 바꾸지 않고.

2021 6월 학평 40번 문제

제한시간 80초
난이도 ★★★★☆

STEP **2** • 수능 기출 제대로 풀기

C 다음 글의 내용을 한 문장으로 요약하고자 한다. 빈칸 (A), (B)에 들어갈 말로 가장 적절한 것은?

Anne Thorndike, a primary care physician in Boston, had a crazy idea. She believed she could improve the eating habits of thousands of hospital staff and visitors without changing their willpower or motivation in the slightest way. In fact, she didn't plan on talking to them at all. Thorndike designed a study to alter the "choice architecture" of the hospital cafeteria. She started by changing how drinks were arranged in the room. Originally, the refrigerators located next to the cash registers in the cafeteria were filled with only soda. She added water as an option to each one. Additionally, she placed baskets of bottled water next to the food stations throughout the room. Soda was still in the primary refrigerators, but water was now available at all drink locations. Over the next three months, the number of soda sales at the hospital dropped by 11.4 percent. Meanwhile, sales of bottled water increased by 25.8 percent.

↓

The study performed by Thorndike showed that the _____(A)_____ of drinks at the hospital cafeteria influenced the choices people made, which _____(B)_____ the consumption of soda.

(A)	(B)	(A)	(B)
① placement	⋯⋯ lowered	② placement	⋯⋯ boosted
③ price	⋯⋯ lowered	④ price	⋯⋯ boosted
⑤ flavor	⋯⋯ maintained		

정답과 해설 p.48

01 Anne Thorndike, a primary care physician in Boston, / had a crazy idea. // She believed / she could improve the eating habits of thousands of hospital staff and visitors / without changing their willpower or motivation in the slightest way.

동격
명사절 접속사 that 생략
without+동명사: ~하지 않고

02 In fact, / she didn't plan on talking to them at all. // Thorndike designed a study / to alter the "choice architecture" of the hospital cafeteria. // She started / by changing how drinks were arranged in the room.

by+동명사: ~함으로써
관계부사절(how와 선행사 the way는 함께 쓰지 않음)

03 Originally, / the refrigerators located next to the cash registers in the cafeteria / were filled with only soda. // She added water / as an option / to each one. // Additionally, / she placed baskets of bottled water / next to the food stations throughout the room.

주어   과거분사   동사(복수)
add A to B: A를 B에 추가하다

04 Soda was still in the primary refrigerators, / but water was now available / at all drink locations. // Over the next three months, / the number of soda sales at the hospital dropped / by 11.4 percent. // Meanwhile, / sales of bottled water increased / by 25.8 percent.

동사   by+숫자: ~만큼
주어(the number of+복수명사)
한편

05 → The study performed by Thorndike / showed / [that the placement of drinks at the hospital cafeteria / influenced the choices people made, / which lowered the consumption of soda].

과거분사   명사절 접속사
목적격 관계대명사 생략   = and it

01 Boston의 1차 진료 의사a primary care physician인 Anne Thorndike는 / 아주 좋은 생각을 했다. // 그녀는 믿었다 / 그녀가 수천 명의 병원 직원들과 방문객들의 식습관을 개선할 수 있다고 / 의지력이나 동기willpower or motivation를 아주 조금도in the slightest way 바꾸지 않고.

02 사실, / 그녀는 그들과 대화할 계획을 전혀 세우지 않았다. // Thorndike는 연구를 설계했다 / 병원 구내식당의 "선택 구조architecture"를 바꾸기 위해서. // 그녀는 시작했다 / 공간 안에 음료가 놓여 있는be arranged 방식을 바꾸는 것으로.

03 원래, / 구내식당 내의 금전 등록기cash register 옆에 있는 냉장고들은 / 탄산음료로만 채워져 있었다. // 그녀는 물을 추가했다 / 선택 사항으로 / 각각의 냉장고에. // 게다가, / 그녀는 물병이 담긴 바구니들을 놓았다 / 공간 전체에 있는 배식대 옆에.

04 탄산음료는 여전히 본래의 냉장고에 있었지만, / 물은 이제 이용 가능했다available / 음료를 둔 모든 곳에서. // 다음 3개월 동안, / 병원의 탄산음료 판매 숫자는 떨어졌다 / 11.4퍼센트만큼. // 한편Meanwhile, / 물병의 판매는 증가했다 / 25.8퍼센트만큼.

05 → Thorndike에 의해 수행된performed by Thorndike 연구는 / 보여주었다 / 병원 구내식당의 음료 배치placement가 / 사람들이 하는 선택에 영향을 주어, / 탄산음료의 소비consumption를 낮춘다는 것을.

구문 Check up

① She started by change / changing how drinks were arranged in the room.

<by+동명사(~함으로써)> 구문이므로 동명사 changing을 쓴다.

② Originally, the refrigerators located next to the cash registers in the cafeteria was / were filled with only soda.

수식을 받는 주어 the refrigerators가 복수이므로, 동사도 복수형인 were로 쓴다.

정답 ① changing ② were

D

STEP 1 • 수능에 진짜 나오는 단어

✔ 문제에 나오는 단어들을 확인하세요.

시간이 없다면 색으로 표시된 단어만이라도 꼭 외우고 넘어가세요!

01	excessive	a. 지나친, 과도한	(✔ excessive) tension	지나친 긴장
02	dependence	n. 의존	our ( ) on technology	기술에 대한 우리의 의존
03	generate	v. 초래하다, 야기하다	( ) growth	성장을 야기하다
04	diversification	n. 다양화, 다양성	a lower productive ( )	더 낮은 생산적 다양화
05	abundance	n. 풍요	material ( )	물질적 풍요
06	in itself	그 자체로	resource abundance ( ) ( )	자원의 풍요 그 자체로
07	abundant	a. 풍부한	( ) natural resources	풍부한 천연자원
08	outgrow	v. (성장하여) ~에서 벗어나다	( ) dependence	의존에서 벗어나다
09	diversify	v. 다양화하다	( ) economic activity	경제 활동을 다양화하다
10	trap	v. 가두다 n. 덫	be ( )ped	갇히다
11	capital	n. 자본(금), 자원	natural ( )	자연 자본
12	exclude	v. 배제하다	( ) other types of capital	다른 형태의 자본을 배제하다
13	interfere with	~을 저해하다	( ) ( ) economic growth	경제 성장을 저해하다

✚ 본문 문장 속에서 단어들을 확인해 보세요.

But some developing countries are trapped / in their dependence on their large natural resources.

하지만 일부 개발 도상국들은 갇혀 있다 / 자국의 많은 천연자원에 대한 의존에.

01	excessive	🖉 지나친, 과도한	excessive tension	지나친 긴장
02	dependence		our dependence on technology	기술에 대한 우리의 의존
03	generate		generate growth	성장을 야기하다
04	diversification		a lower productive diversification	더 낮은 생산적 다양화
05	abundance		material abundance	물질적 풍요
06	in itself		resource abundance in itself	자원의 풍요 그 자체로
07	abundant		abundant natural resources	풍부한 천연자원
08	outgrow		outgrow dependence	의존에서 벗어나다
09	diversify		diversify economic activity	경제 활동을 다양화하다
10	trap		be trapped	갇히다
11	capital		natural capital	자연 자본
12	exclude		exclude other types of capital	다른 형태의 자본을 배제하다
13	interfere with		interfere with economic growth	경제 성장을 저해하다

➕ **본문 문장 속에서 단어의 의미를 우리말로 해석해 보세요.**

But some developing countries are trapped / in their dependence on their large natural resources.

➜   하지만 일부 개발 도상국들은   / 자국의 많은 천연자원에 대한   에.

STEP **2** • 수능 기출 제대로 풀기

D 다음 글의 내용을 한 문장으로 요약하고자 한다. 빈칸 (A)와 (B)에 들어갈 말로 가장 적절한 것은?

Some natural resource-rich developing countries tend to create an excessive dependence on their natural resources, which generates a lower productive diversification and a lower rate of growth. Resource abundance in itself need not do any harm: many countries have abundant natural resources and have managed to outgrow their dependence on them by diversifying their economic activity. That is the case of Canada, Australia, or the US, to name the most important ones. But some developing countries are trapped in their dependence on their large natural resources. They suffer from a series of problems since a heavy dependence on natural capital tends to exclude other types of capital and thereby interfere with economic growth.

> Relying on rich natural resources without _____(A)_____ economic activities can be a _____(B)_____ to economic growth.

	(A)		(B)
①	varying	......	barrier
②	varying	......	shortcut
③	limiting	......	challenge
④	limiting	......	barrier
⑤	connecting	......	shortcut

정답과 해설 **p.48**

01 Some natural resource-rich developing countries / tend to create an excessive
~하는 경향이 있다
dependence on their natural resources, / which generates a lower productive
=and it generates ~
diversification / and a lower rate of growth.

02 Resource abundance in itself / need not do any harm: / many countries have abundant
그 자체로   동사1
natural resources / and have managed to outgrow their dependence on them / by
동사2(manage to+동사원형: 가까스로 ~하다)
diversifying their economic activity.

03 That is the case of Canada, Australia, or the US, / to name the most important ones. //
But some developing countries are trapped / in their dependence on their large natural
수동태: 갇히다
resources.

04 They suffer from a series of problems / since a heavy dependence on natural capital
(=some developing countries)   =because   tends to 생략
tends to exclude other types of capital / and thereby interfere with economic growth.
그로 인해, 그리하여

05 → Relying on rich natural resources without varying economic activities / can be a
동명사(주어)
barrier to economic growth.

01 천연자원이 풍부한 일부 개발 도상국들은 / 자국의 천연자원에 대한 지나친 의존an excessive dependence을 초래하는
경향이 있으며, / 이로 인해 더 낮은 생산적 다양화a lower productive diversification를 초래한다generate / 그리고 더
낮은 성장률을.

02 자원의 풍요resource abundance가 그 자체로in itself / 해가 되어야 하는 것은 아니다. / 많은 나라들이 풍부한
천연자원abundant natural resource을 가지고 있으며 / 그것(풍부한 천연자원)에 대한 의존에서 가까스로
벗어났다outgrow / 자국의 경제 활동을 다양화함diversify으로써.

03 캐나다, 호주, 또는 미국의 경우가 그러하다 / 가장 중요한 나라들을 꼽자면. // 하지만 일부 개발 도상국들은 갇혀 있다be
trapped / 자국의 많은 천연자원에 대한 의존에.

04 그들은 일련의 문제를 겪고 있다 / 자연 자본natural capital에 대한 과도한 의존은 다른 형태의 자본을 배제하고exclude
/ 그로 인해 경제 성장을 저해하는interfere with economic growth 경향이 있기 때문에.

05 → 경제 활동을 다양화하지 않은 채 풍부한 천연자원에 의존하는 것은 / 경제 성장에 장애가 될 수 있다.

구문 Check up

① But some developing countries trap / are trapped in their dependence on their large natural resources.

개발도상국이 '갇히다'라는 수동의 의미가 적절하기 때문에 are trapped 로 쓴다.

② Rely / Relying on rich natural resources without varying economic activities can be a barrier to economic growth.

동사가 can be이고 주어가 없기 때문에 주어가 될 수 있는 동명사 Relying 으로 써야 한다.

DAY 13

E

STEP 1 • 수능에 진짜 나오는 단어

요약문 완성 ✛

✔️ 문제에 나오는 단어들을 확인하세요.

시간이 없다면 색으로 표시된 단어만이라도 꼭 외우고 넘어가세요!

01	adorable	a. 귀여운	an (✔ adorable) creature	귀여운 생명체
02	urge	n. 충동	an overwhelming ( )	압도적인 충동
03	squeeze	v. 쥐어짜다, 꽉 쥐다	( ) that cuteness	그런 귀여움을 꽉 쥐다
04	pinch	v. 꼬집다	( ) the cheek	볼을 꼬집다
05	cuddle	v. 껴안다	( ) a teddy bear	곰 인형을 껴안다
06	aggression	n. 공격성	cute ( )	귀여운 공격성
07	compulsion	n. 충동	( ) to cuddle that cuteness	그런 귀여움을 껴안고 싶은 충동
08	neurological	a. 신경학적인	a complex ( ) response	복잡한 신경학적 반응
09	overloaded	a. 과부하된	emotionally ( )	감정적으로 과부하된
10	temper	v. 조절하다, 완화하다	a ( )ing mechanism	조절 기제
11	perceive	v. 인지하다	( ) a change	변화를 인지하다
12	regulate	v. 조절하다	( ) temperature	온도를 조절하다

✛ 본문 문장 속에서 단어들을 확인해 보세요.

When we see an adorable creature, / we must fight an overwhelming urge / to squeeze that cuteness.

우리가 귀여운 생명체를 볼 때, / 우리는 압도적인 충동과 싸워야 한다 / 그 귀여운 것을 꽉 쥐고자 하는.

01	adorable	🖊 귀여운	an adorable creature	귀여운 생명체
02	urge		an overwhelming urge	압도적인 충동
03	squeeze		squeeze that cuteness	그런 귀여움을 꽉 쥐다
04	pinch		pinch the cheek	볼을 꼬집다
05	cuddle		cuddle a teddy bear	곰 인형을 껴안다
06	aggression		cute aggression	귀여운 공격성
07	compulsion		compulsion to cuddle that cuteness	그런 귀여움을 껴안고 싶은 충동
08	neurological		a complex neurological response	복잡한 신경학적 반응
09	overloaded		emotionally overloaded	감정적으로 과부하된
10	temper		a tempering mechanism	조절 기제
11	perceive		perceive a change	변화를 인지하다
12	regulate		regulate temperature	온도를 조절하다

➕ 본문 문장 속에서 단어의 의미를 우리말로 해석해 보세요.

When we see an adorable creature, / we must fight an overwhelming urge / to squeeze that cuteness.

➡ 우리가 ＿＿＿＿＿＿＿ 생명체를 볼 때, / 우리는 압도적인 ＿＿＿＿＿＿＿ 과 싸워야 한다 / 그 귀여운 것을 ＿＿＿＿＿＿＿ 하는.

제한시간 80초
난이도 ★★★★☆

STEP 2 • 수능 기출 제대로 풀기

E 다음 글의 내용을 한 문장으로 요약하고자 한다. 빈칸 (A)와 (B)에 들어갈 말로 가장 적절한 것은?

When we see an adorable creature, we must fight an overwhelming urge to squeeze that cuteness. And pinch it, and cuddle it, and maybe even bite it. This is a perfectly normal psychological tick — an oxymoron called "cute aggression" — and even though it sounds cruel, it's not about causing harm at all. In fact, strangely enough, this compulsion may actually make us more caring. The first study to look at cute aggression in the human brain has now revealed that this is a complex neurological response, involving several parts of the brain. The researchers propose that cute aggression may stop us from becoming so emotionally overloaded that we are unable to look after things that are super cute. "Cute aggression may serve as a tempering mechanism that allows us to function and actually take care of something we might first perceive as overwhelmingly cute," explains the lead author, Stavropoulos.

*oxymoron: 모순 어법

According to research, cute aggression may act as a neurological response to _____(A)_____ excessive emotions and make us _____(B)_____ for cute creatures.

	(A)		(B)		(A)		(B)
①	evaluate	⋯⋯	care	②	regulate	⋯⋯	care
③	accept	⋯⋯	search	④	induce	⋯⋯	search
⑤	display	⋯⋯	speak				

정답과 해설 p.49

01 When we see an adorable creature, / we must fight an overwhelming urge / to squeeze that cuteness. // And pinch it, and cuddle it, and maybe even bite it.
to부정사의 형용사적 용법

02 This is a perfectly normal psychological tick / — an oxymoron called "cute aggression"
과거분사구
— / and even though it sounds cruel, / it's not about causing harm at all.
비록 ~이지만

03 In fact, strangely enough, / this compulsion may actually make us more caring. // The
make+목적어+목적격 보어(형용사)
first study to look at cute aggression in the human brain / has now revealed that this
to부정사의 형용사적 용법   명사절 접속사
is a complex neurological response, / involving several parts of the brain.

04 명사절 접속사
The researchers propose / that cute aggression may stop us / from becoming so
emotionally overloaded / that we are unable to look after things that are super cute.
so ~ that …: 너무 ~해서 …하다   주격 관계대명사절

05 "Cute aggression may serve as a tempering mechanism / [that allows us to function
to 생략   that 생략   주격 관계대명사   목적격보어1
and actually take care of something we might first perceive as overwhelmingly cute],"
목적격보어2   목적격 관계대명사절
/ explains the lead author, Stavropoulos.

06 → According to research, / cute aggression may act as a neurological response / to
regulate excessive emotions / and make us care for cute creatures.
to부정사의 형용사적 용법

01 우리가 귀여운 생명체adorable creature를 볼 때, / 우리는 압도적인 충동overwhelming urge과 싸워야 한다 / 그 귀여운 것을 꽉 쥐고자 하는squeeze that cuteness. // 그리고 꼬집고pinch, 꼭 껴안고cuddle, 심지어 깨물고 싶은.

02 이것은 완전히 정상적인 심리학적 행동이다 / 즉 '귀여운 공격성cute aggression'이라 불리는 모순 어법이며, / 비록 이것이 잔인하게 들리기는 하지만, / 이것은 해를 끼치는 것에 관한 것은 결코 아니다.

03 사실, 충분히 이상하게도, / 이러한 충동compulsion은 실제로는 우리로 하여금 (남을) 더 잘 보살피게 한다. // 인간 뇌의 귀여운 공격성을 살펴본 최초의 연구가 / 이제 드러냈다 / 이것이 복잡한 신경학적인 반응neurological response이라는 것을 / 뇌의 여러 부분과 관련된.

04 연구자들은 제시한다 / 귀여운 공격성이 우리를 막을지도 모른다고 / 너무 감정적으로 과부하되어서emotionally overloaded / 정말 귀여운 것을 돌볼 수 없게 되는 것으로부터.

05 "귀여운 공격성은 조절 기제a tempering mechanism로 기능할지도 모른다 / 우리가 제대로 기능하고 실제로 무언가를 돌볼 수 있도록 하는 (기제) / 처음에 압도적으로 귀엽다고 인지하는perceive (무언가)"라고 / 주 저자인 Stavropoulos는 설명한다.

06 → 연구에 따르면, / 귀여운 공격성은 신경학적인 반응으로서 역할을 할지 모른다 / 과도한 감정emotion을 조절하고regulate / 우리로 하여금 귀여운 생명체를 돌보게 하는.

구문 Check up

① In fact, strangely enough, this compulsion may actually make us more caring / more caringly .

목적격보어 자리에 올 품사를 고르는 문제이므로 형용사의 비교급인 more caring이 적절하다.

② Cute aggression may stop us from becoming so emotionally overloaded that / which we are unable to look after things.

'너무 ~해서 …하다'라는 뜻의 <so ~ that> 구문이므로, 접속사 that을 써야 한다.

정답 ① more caring ② that

F

STEP 1 • 수능에 *진짜* 나오는 *단어*

✔ 문제에 나오는 단어들을 확인하세요.

01	primary	a. (교육) 초등의, 기초의	a (✔ primary) school teacher	초등학교 선생님
02	fractional	a. (수학) 분수의	understand ( ) parts	분수 부분을 이해하다
03	commonplace	a. 아주 흔한	( ) in primary classrooms	초등학교 교실에서 아주 흔한
04	reference	n. 언급 대상, 참고, 기준	a commonplace ( )	흔한 언급 대상
05	discourse	n. 담화	a classroom ( ) about mathematics	수학에 대한 교실 담화
06	puzzled	a. 의아해하는, 어리둥절한	look ( )	의아해 보이다
07	serve	v. (음식을) 차려내다, ~의 역할을 하다	( ) as a warning	경고의 역할을 하다
08	referent	n. 언급, 지시 대상	a common ( )	흔한 지시 대상
09	interference	n. 간섭	a source of ( )	간섭의 원천
10	preoccupied	a. (어떤 생각에) 사로잡힌, 몰두한	( ) with something else	뭔가 다른 것에 사로잡힌
11	texture	n. 질감	chunky ( )	덩어리진 질감
12	attempt	v. 시도하다, 노력하다	( ) to teach a lesson	어떤 교훈을 가르치려 하다

➕ 본문 문장 속에서 단어들을 확인해 보세요.

Even the slight difference of being unfamiliar with pumpkin pie / can serve as a source of interference for the student.

호박파이에 친숙하지 않다는 그 작은 차이조차 / 학생에게는 간섭의 원천 역할을 할 수 있다.

01	primary	✎ (교육) 초등의, 기초의	a primary school teacher	초등학교 선생님
02	fractional		understand fractional parts	분수 부분을 이해하다
03	commonplace		commonplace in primary classrooms	초등학교 교실에서 아주 흔한
04	reference		a commonplace reference	흔한 언급 대상
05	discourse		a classroom discourse about mathematics	수학에 대한 교실 담화
06	puzzled		look puzzled	의아해 보이다
07	serve		serve as a warning	경고의 역할을 하다
08	referent		a common referent	흔한 지시 대상
09	interference		a source of interference	간섭의 원천
10	preoccupied		preoccupied with something else	뭔가 다른 것에 사로잡힌
11	texture		chunky texture	덩어리진 질감
12	attempt		attempt to teach a lesson	어떤 교훈을 가르치려 하다

➕ 본문 문장 속에서 단어의 의미를 우리말로 해석해 보세요.

Even the slight difference of being unfamiliar with pumpkin pie / can serve as a source of interference for the student.

➡ 호박파이에 친숙하지 않다는 그 작은 차이조차 / 학생에게는 _____의 원천 _____ 수 있다.

제한시간 80초
난이도 ★★★★☆

STEP **2** · 수능 기출 제대로 풀기

F 다음 글의 내용을 한 문장으로 요약하고자 한다. 빈칸 (A), (B)에 들어갈 말로 가장 적절한 것은?

A primary school teacher is helping students to understand fractional parts by using what she thinks is a commonplace reference. "Today, we're going to talk about cutting up a Thanksgiving holiday favorite — pumpkin pie." She continues with an explanation of parts. Well into her discourse, a young African American boy, looking puzzled, asks, "What is pumpkin pie?" Most African Americans are likely to serve sweet potato pie for holiday dinners. In fact, one of the ways that African American parents explain pumpkin pie to their children is to say that it is something like sweet potato pie. For them, sweet potato pie is the common referent. Even the slight difference of being unfamiliar with pumpkin pie can serve as a source of interference for the student. Rather than be engaged actively in the lesson, he may have been preoccupied with trying to imagine pumpkin pie: What does it taste like? How does it smell? Is its texture chunky like apple or cherry pie? In the mind of a child, all of these questions can become more of the focus than the subject of fractions that the teacher is attempting to teach.

*fraction: 분수

Even small differences in _____(A)_____ knowledge have the potential to affect students' _____(B)_____.

	(A)		(B)		(A)		(B)
①	cultural	·····	learning	②	cultural	·····	responsibility
③	mathematical	·····	imagination	④	mathematical	·····	intelligence
⑤	nutritional	·····	development				

정답과 해설 p.49

01 A primary school teacher is helping students to understand fractional parts / by using
help+목적어+to부정사: ~이 …하도록 돕다
what she thinks is a commonplace reference. // "Today, we're going to talk about
삽입절(그녀가 생각하기로)
cutting up a Thanksgiving holiday favorite — / pumpkin pie." // She continues with
an explanation of parts. // Well into her discourse, / a young African American boy, /
looking puzzled, / asks, / "What is pumpkin pie?"
분사구문(문장 중간에 삽입)

02 Most African Americans are likely to serve sweet potato pie for holiday dinners. // In
be likely to+동사원형: ~하는 경향이 있다, ~할 가능성이 있다
fact, / one of the ways / that African American parents explain pumpkin pie to their
one of the+복수명사: ~ 중 하나   ways 수식(that: 관계부사 역할)
children / is to say / that it is something like sweet potato pie. // For them, / sweet
동사(단수) 주격보어
potato pie is the common referent.

03 Even the slight difference of being unfamiliar with pumpkin pie / can serve as a source
of interference for the student. // Rather than be engaged actively in the lesson, / he
~라기보다, ~ 대신
may have been preoccupied with trying to imagine pumpkin pie: / What does it taste
과거에 대한 추측(~했을지도 모른다)
like? / How does it smell? / Is its texture chunky like apple or cherry pie? // In the mind
of a child, / all of these questions can become more of the focus / than the subject of
fractions / that the teacher is attempting to teach.
                목적격 관계대명사절

04 Even small differences in cultural knowledge / have the potential to affect students'
                                                                     형용사적 용법
learning.

01 한 초등학교primary school 선생님이 학생들이 분수fractional 부분을 이해하도록 돕고 있는 중이다 / 그녀가 아주 흔한 언급
대상a commonplace reference이라고 생각한 것을 사용해. // "오늘, 우리는 추수감사절에 인기 있는 걸 자르는 것에 대해
이야기할 거예요 / 즉, 호박파이." // 그녀는 (분수) 부분에 대한 설명을 이어간다. // 그녀의 담화discourse에 열심히 몰두하던
/ 한 어린 아프리카계 미국인 소년이 / 의아한puzzled 표정으로 / 질문한다. / "호박파이가 뭐예요?"

02 대부분의 아프리카계 미국인들은 고구마파이를 명절 만찬으로 차리는serve 경향이 있다. // 사실 / 방식 중 하나는 /
아프리카계 미국인 부모가 자식들에게 호박파이에 관해 설명하는 / 말하는 것이다 / 그게 고구마파이 같은 거라고. //
그들에게는 / 고구마파이가 흔히 언급되는 것referent이다.

03 호박파이에 친숙하지 않다는 그 작은 차이조차 / 학생에게는 간섭interference의 원천 역할을 할serve as 수 있다. // 수업에
적극적으로 참여하기보다는, / 그는 호박파이를 상상하려고 노력하는 데 사로잡혀preoccupied 있었을지도 모른다. / 그건
무슨 맛일까? / 무슨 냄새가 날까? / 그것의 질감texture은 사과나 체리 파이처럼 덩어리졌을까? // 아이의 마음속에서 / 이런
모든 질문들은 / 더 초점이 될 수 있다 / 분수라는 주제보다 / 선생님이 가르치려 시도하는attempt.

04 → 문화적 지식의 작은 차이조차도 / 학생들의 학습에 영향을 미칠 잠재력이 있다.

구문 Check up

① Well into her discourse, a young African American boy, looking puzzling / puzzled , asks, "What is pumpkin pie?"

a young African American boy가 '의아함을 느끼는' 것이므로 과거분사 puzzled를 쓴다.

② In fact, one of the ways that African American parents explain pumpkin pie to their children are / is to say that it is something like sweet potato pie.

<one of the+복수명사> 주어는 단수 취급하므로 is를 쓴다.

정답 ① puzzled ② is

DAY 13

STEP 1 • 수능에 *진짜* 나오는 *단어*

요약문 완성 ➕

✔ 문제에 나오는 단어들을 확인하세요.

시간이 없다면 색으로 표시된 단어만이라도 꼭 외우고 넘어가세요!

01	unequal	a. 불평등한	an (✔ unequal) balance of power	힘의 불평등한 균형
02	distribution	n. 분배	the ( ) of wealth	부의 분배
03	degree	n. 정도	the ( ) to which power imbalance is accepted	힘의 불균형이 받아들여지는 정도
04	inequality	n. 불평등	( ) should be minimal.	불평등은 최소여야 한다.
05	norm	n. 규범	Social ( )s are rules of behavior.	사회적 규범은 행동의 규칙이다.
06	allocate	v. 할당하다	( ) a place in society	사회에서의 위치를 할당하다
07	hierarchy	n. 계층, 위계	obey the social ( )	사회 계층에 복종하다
08	division	n. 구분	a hierarchical ( )	계층적 구분
09	convenience	n. 편의	for the sake of ( )	편의를 위해
10	fluidity	n. 유동성	( ) within the society	사회 내 유동성

➕ 본문 문장 속에서 단어들을 확인해 보세요.

Power distance is the term / used to refer to / how widely an unequal distribution of power is accepted / by the members of a culture.

'권력 거리'는 용어이다 / 가리키고자 사용되는 / 권력의 불평등한 분배가 얼마나 널리 수용되는지 / 한 문화의 구성원들에 의해.

문제를 풀기 전에 단어들을 30초 동안 다시 확인하세요.

01	unequal	🖉 불평등한	an unequal balance of power	힘의 불평등한 균형
02	distribution		the distribution of wealth	부의 분배
03	degree		the degree to which power imbalance is accepted	힘의 불균형이 받아들여지는 정도
04	inequality		Inequality should be minimal.	불평등은 최소여야 한다.
05	norm		Social norms are rules of behavior.	사회적 규범은 행동의 규칙이다.
06	allocate		allocate a place in society	사회에서의 위치를 할당하다
07	hierarchy		obey the social hierarchy	사회 계층에 복종하다
08	division		a hierarchical division	계층적 구분
09	convenience		for the sake of convenience	편의를 위해
10	fluidity		fluidity within the society	사회 내 유동성

➕ 본문 문장 속에서 단어의 의미를 우리말로 해석해 보세요.

Power distance is the term / used to refer to / how widely an unequal distribution of power is accepted / by the members of a culture.

➔ '권력 거리'는 용어이다 / 가리키고자 사용되는 / ▇▇▇▇▇▇▇▇▇▇▇가 얼마나 널리 수용되는지 / 한 문화의 구성원들에 의해.

378

STEP **2** • 수능 기출 제대로 풀기

G
다음 글의 내용을 한 문장으로 요약하고자 한다. 빈칸 (A), (B)에 들어갈 말로 가장 적절한 것은?

Power distance is the term used to refer to how widely an unequal distribution of power is accepted by the members of a culture. It relates to the degree to which the less powerful members of a society accept their inequality in power and consider it the norm. In cultures with high acceptance of power distance (e.g., India, Brazil, Greece, Mexico, and the Philippines), people are not viewed as equals, and everyone has a clearly defined or allocated place in the social hierarchy. In cultures with low acceptance of power distance (e.g., Finland, Norway, New Zealand, and Israel), people believe inequality should be minimal, and a hierarchical division is viewed as one of convenience only. In these cultures, there is more fluidity within the social hierarchy, and it is relatively easy for individuals to move up the social hierarchy based on their individual efforts and achievements.

Unlike cultures with high acceptance of power distance, where members are more _____(A)_____ to accept inequality, cultures with low acceptance of power distance allow more _____(B)_____ within the social hierarchy.

	(A)		(B)			(A)		(B)
①	willing	……	mobility		②	willing	……	assistance
③	reluctant	……	resistance		④	reluctant	……	flexibility
⑤	afraid	……	openness					

정답과 해설 p.49

STEP 3 • 수능 지문 제대로 복습하기

01 *Power distance* is the term / used to refer to / how widely an unequal distribution of power is accepted / by the members of a culture. // It relates to the degree / to which the less powerful members of a society / accept their inequality in power / and consider it the norm.

02 In cultures with high acceptance of power distance / (e.g., India, Brazil, Greece, Mexico, and the Philippines), / people are not viewed as equals, / and everyone has a clearly defined or allocated place in the social hierarchy.

03 In cultures with low acceptance of power distance / (e.g., Finland, Norway, New Zealand, and Israel), / people believe inequality should be minimal, / and a hierarchical division is viewed as one of convenience only. // In these cultures, / there is more fluidity within the social hierarchy, / and it is relatively easy / for individuals to move up the social hierarchy / based on their individual efforts and achievements.

04 → Unlike cultures with high acceptance of power distance, / where members are more willing to accept inequality, / cultures with low acceptance of power distance / allow more mobility within the social hierarchy.

01 '권력 거리'는 용어이다 / 가리키고자 사용되는 / 권력의 불평등한unequal 분배distribution가 얼마나 널리 수용되는지 / 한 문화의 구성원들에 의해. // 그것은 정도degree와 관련돼 있다 / 권력이 덜한 사회 구성원들이 / 권력에서의 불평등inequality을 수용하고 / 그것을 규범norm으로 여기는.

02 권력 거리를 높게 수용하는 문화들에서 / (가령 인도, 브라질, 그리스, 멕시코, 그리고 필리핀) / 사람들은 평등하다고 여겨지지 않으며, / 모든 사람은 사회 계층hierarchy 내에서 명확히 정해지거나 할당된allocate 입지를 가진다.

03 권력 거리가 낮게 수용되는 문화들에서는 / (가령 핀란드, 노르웨이, 뉴질랜드, 그리고 이스라엘) / 사람들은 불평등이 최소여야만 한다고 믿으며, / 계층적 구분은 오직 편의convenience상 구분division으로 여겨진다. // 이러한 문화에서는 / 사회 계층 내에 유동성fluidity이 더 크며, / 상대적으로 쉽다 / 개인이 사회 계층을 상승시키기가 / 자신의 개인적 노력과 성취를 토대로.

04 → 권력 거리가 높이 수용되는 문화와 달리, / 구성원들이 불평등을 더 기꺼이 수용하는 / 권력 거리에 대한 수용 정도가 낮은 문화는 / 사회 계층 내 더 많은 이동을 허락한다.

구문 Check up

① It relates to the degree which / to which the less powerful members of a society accept their inequality in power and consider it the norm.

뒤에 <accept+목적어>와 <consider+목적어+목적격보어>가 모두 완전하게 연결되므로 <전치사+관계대명사> 형태의 to which를 쓴다.

② It is relatively easy for individuals to move up the social hierarchy based on its / their individual efforts and achievements.

individuals의 소유격을 나타내는 대명사로 their가 적절하다.

정답 ① to which ② their

A

STEP **1** • 수능에 진짜 나오는 단어

✔️ 문제에 나오는 단어들을 확인하세요.

시간이 없다면 색으로 표시된 단어만이라도 꼭 외우고 넘어가세요!

01	out of ordinary	평범하지 않은	events or experiences that are (✔️ out) (of) (ordinary)	평범하지 않은 사건이나 경험
02	**access**	v. 접근하다	( ) the memories	기억에 접근하다
03	particular	a. 특정한, 특별한 n. 세부 사항	that ( ) breakfast	그 특정한 아침 식사
04	generic	a. 일반적인	a sort of ( ) impression of a breakfast	아침 식사에 대한 일종의 일반적인 인상
05	**impression**	n. 인상	make a good ( )	좋은 인상을 만들다
06	merge	v. 병합하다, 합치다	( ) similar events	유사한 사건들을 병합하다
07	**efficient**	a. 효율적인	an ( ) thing to do	하기에 효율적인 일
08	extract	v. 추출하다	( ) abstract rules	추상적인 규칙을 추출하다
09	routine	a. 일상적인, 틀에 박힌	( ) duties	일상적인 일
10	**content**	n. 내용	the overall ( ) of the behavior	그 행동의 전반적 내용
11	distinctive	a. 특이한, 독특한	unless they were especially ( )	그것이 아주 특이하지 않다면
12	spill	v. 쏟다	( ) tomato sauce on the dress shirt	와이셔츠에 토마토소스를 쏟다

➕ 본문 문장 속에서 단어들을 확인해 보세요.

Your memory merges similar events / not only because it's more efficient to do so, / but also because this is fundamental to how we learn things / — our brains extract abstract rules / that tie experiences together.

여러분의 기억력은 유사한 사건들을 병합하는데 / 그렇게 하는 것이 더 효율적일 뿐만 아니라, / 이것은 우리가 어떤 것들을 배우는 방법의 기본이기 때문이다. / 우리의 뇌는 추상적인 규칙들을 추출한다 / 경험을 함께 묶는.

문제를 풀기 전에 단어들을 **30초** 동안 다시 확인하세요.

01	out of ordinary	✎ 평범하지 않은	events or experiences that are out of ordinary	평범하지 않은 사건이나 경험
02	access		access the memories	기억에 접근하다
03	particular		that particular breakfast	그 특정한 아침 식사
04	generic		a sort of generic impression of a breakfast	아침 식사에 대한 일종의 일반적인 인상
05	impression		make a good impression	좋은 인상을 만들다
06	merge		merge similar events	유사한 사건들을 병합하다
07	efficient		an efficient thing to do	하기에 효율적인 일
08	extract		extract abstract rules	추상적인 규칙을 추출하다
09	routine		routine duties	일상적인 일
10	content		the overall content of the behavior	그 행동의 전반적 내용
11	distinctive		unless they were especially distinctive	그것이 아주 특이하지 않다면
12	spill		spill tomato sauce on the dress shirt	와이셔츠에 토마토소스를 쏟다

➕ 본문 문장 속에서 단어의 의미를 우리말로 해석해 보세요.

Your memory merges similar events / not only because it's more efficient to do so, / but also because this is fundamental to how we learn things / — our brains extract abstract rules / that tie experiences together.

→ 여러분의 기억력은 _____ / 그렇게 하는 것이 _____ 뿐만 아니라, / 이것은 우리가 어떤 것들을 배우는 방법의 기본이기 때문이다. / 우리의 뇌는 _____ / 경험을 함께 묶는.

STEP **2** • 수능 기출 제대로 풀기

 다음 글을 읽고, 물음에 답하시오.

Events or experiences that are out of ordinary tend to be remembered better because there is nothing competing with them when your brain tries to access them from its storehouse of remembered events. In other words, the reason it can be (a) difficult to remember what you ate for breakfast two Thursdays ago is that there was probably nothing special about that Thursday or that particular breakfast — consequently, all your breakfast memories combine together into a sort of generic impression of a breakfast. Your memory (b) merges similar events not only because it's more efficient to do so, but also because this is fundamental to how we learn things — our brains extract abstract rules that tie experiences together.

This is especially true for things that are (c) routine. If your breakfast is always the same — cereal with milk, a glass of orange juice, and a cup of coffee for instance — there is no easy way for your brain to extract the details from one particular breakfast. Ironically, then, for behaviors that are routinized, you can remember the generic content of the behavior (such as the things you ate, since you always eat the same thing), but (d) particulars to that one instance can be very difficult to call up (such as the sound of a garbage truck going by or a bird that passed by your window) *unless* they were especially distinctive. On the other hand, if you did something unique that broke your routine — perhaps you had leftover pizza for breakfast and spilled tomato sauce on your dress shirt — you are (e) less likely to remember it.

[A-1] 윗글의 제목으로 가장 적절한 것은?

① Repetition Makes Your Memory Sharp!
② How Does Your Memory Get Distorted?
③ What to Consider in Routinizing Your Work
④ Merging Experiences: Key to Remembering Details
⑤ The More Unique Events, the More Vivid Recollection

[A-2] 밑줄 친 (a)~(e) 중에서 문맥상 낱말의 쓰임이 적절하지 <u>않은</u> 것은?

① (a)
② (b)
③ (c)
④ (d)
⑤ (e)

정답과 해설 **p.51**

383

01 Events or experiences that are out of ordinary / tend to be remembered better / because there is nothing competing with them / when your brain tries to access them from its storehouse of remembered events.

02 In other words, / the reason it can be difficult / to remember what you ate for breakfast two Thursdays ago / is that there was probably nothing special / about that Thursday or that particular breakfast / — consequently, / all your breakfast memories combine together / into a sort of generic impression of a breakfast.

03 Your memory merges similar events / not only because it's more efficient to do so, / but also because this is fundamental to how we learn things / — our brains extract abstract rules / that tie experiences together. // This is especially true for things that are routine.

04 If your breakfast is always the same / — (cereal with milk, a glass of orange juice, and a cup of coffee for instance) / — there is no easy way / for your brain to extract the details from one particular breakfast. // Ironically, then, / for behaviors that are routinized, / you can remember the generic content of the behavior / (such as the things you ate, / since you always eat the same thing), / but particulars to that one instance can be very difficult to call up / (such as the sound of a garbage truck going by / or a bird that passed by your window) / *unless* they were especially distinctive.

05 On the other hand, / if you did something unique / that broke your routine / — (perhaps you had leftover pizza for breakfast / and spilled tomato sauce on your dress shirt) — / you are less likely to remember it.

---

01 평범하지 않은out of ordinary 사건이나 경험은 / 더 잘 기억되는 경향이 있는데 / 그 이유는 그것과 경쟁하는 것이 없기 때문이다 / 당신의 뇌가 기억된 사건들의 창고에서 그것에 접근하려고access 할 때.

02 다시 말해, / 기억하기 어려울 수 있는 이유는 / 2주 전 목요일에 아침 식사로 무엇을 먹었는지 / 아마도 특별한 것이 없었기 때문이다 / 그 목요일이나 그 특정particular 아침 식사에 대해 / 그 결과, / 당신의 모든 아침 식사 기억은 합쳐진다 / 아침 식사에 대한 일종의 일반적인 인상a sort of generic impression으로.

03 여러분의 기억력은 유사한 사건들을 병합하는데merge, / 그렇게 하는 것이 더 효율적일efficient 뿐만 아니라, / 이것은 우리가 어떤 것들을 배우는 방법의 기본이기 때문이다 / 우리의 뇌는 추상적인 규칙들을 추출한다extract / 경험을 함께 묶는. // 이것은 일상적인routine 것들에 특히 해당된다.

04 만약 당신의 아침 식사가 항상 같다면 / 가령 우유와 시리얼, 오렌지 주스 한 잔, 커피 한 잔 / 쉬운 방법이 없다 / 당신의 뇌가 특정한 한 아침 식사에서 그 세부 사항을 추출할. // 그럼 아이러니하게도 / 일상화된 행동의 경우, / 당신은 그 행동의 일반적인 내용content은 기억할 수 있지만 / (당신이 먹었던 것처럼, / 당신은 항상 같은 것을 먹기 때문에) / 그 한 가지 예의 세부 사항들은 기억하기 매우 어려울 수 있다 / (쓰레기 트럭이 지나가는 소리나 / 창문을 지나치는 새소리 등) / 그것이 매우 특이하지distinctive '않다면'.

05 반면에, / 만약 당신이 특이한 일을 했다면 / 당신의 일상을 깨뜨리는 / 어쩌면 당신은 아침 식사로 남은 피자를 먹고 / 와이셔츠에 토마토소스를 쏟았을spill 수도 있다 / 당신은 그것을 덜(→ 더) 기억하기 쉽다.

B

STEP 1 • 수능에 *진짜* 나오는 *단어*

✔ **문제에 나오는 단어들을 확인하세요.**

시간이 없다면 색으로 표시된 단어만이라도 꼭 외우고 넘어가세요!

01	board	v. ~에 탑승하다	(✔ board) a flight	비행기에 탑승하다
02	aisle seat	(비행기의) 통로 쪽 좌석	sit in the ( ) ( )	통로 쪽 좌석에 앉다
03	overhead bin	(비행기의) 머리 위 짐칸	a bag in the ( ) ( )	짐칸에 있는 가방
04	take off	이륙하다	a flight ( )s ( )	비행기가 이륙하다
05	tightly	ad. 꽉, 단단히	grab the seat ( )	좌석을 꽉 잡다
06	meanwhile	ad. 그러는 동안	( ) = at the same time	그러는 동안
07	neatly	ad. 가지런히	put away crayons ( )	크레용을 가지런히 치워 놓다
08	bumpy	a. 울퉁불퉁한	a ( ) road	울퉁불퉁한 길
09	land	v. 착륙하다	( ) soon	곧 착륙하다
10	descent	n. 하강	begin the ( )	하강을 시작하다
11	fasten one's seat belt	안전벨트를 매다	everyone ( )s ( ) ( ) ( )s	모두가 안전벨트를 매다
12	encounter	v. 만나다, 마주치다	( ) a difficulty	어려움에 부딪히다
13	rough	a. 거친	the ( ) weather	악천후(거친 날씨)

➕ **본문 문장 속에서 단어들을 확인해 보세요.**

The pilot told everyone / to fasten their seat belts / and remain calm, / as they had encountered rough weather.

조종사는 모든 사람들에게 말했다 / 안전벨트를 매라고 / 그리고 침착하라고 / 거친 날씨를 만났기 때문에.

01	board	~에 탑승하다	board a flight	비행기에 탑승하다
02	aisle seat		sit in the aisle seat	통로 쪽 좌석에 앉다
03	overhead bin		a bag in the overhead bin	짐칸에 있는 가방
04	take off		a flight takes off	비행기가 이륙하다
05	tightly		grab the seat tightly	좌석을 꽉 잡다
06	meanwhile		meanwhile = at the same time	그러는 동안
07	neatly		put away crayons neatly	크레용을 가지런히 치워 놓다
08	bumpy		a bumpy road	울퉁불퉁한 길
09	land		land soon	곧 착륙하다
10	descent		begin the descent	하강을 시작하다
11	fasten one's seat belt		everyone fastens their seat belts	모두가 안전벨트를 매다
12	encounter		encounter a difficulty	어려움에 부딪히다
13	rough		the rough weather	악천후

⊕ 본문 문장 속에서 단어의 의미를 우리말로 해석해 보세요.

The pilot told everyone / to fasten their seat belts / and remain calm, / as they had encountered rough weather.

➜ 조종사는 모든 사람들에게 말했다 /   / 그리고 침착하라고 /   날씨를   때문에.

386

STEP **2** • 수능 기출 제대로 풀기

B   다음 글을 읽고, 물음에 답하시오.

(A) A businessman boarded a flight. Arriving at his seat, he greeted his travel companions: a middle-aged woman sitting at the window, and a little boy sitting in the aisle seat. After putting his bag in the overhead bin, he took his place between them. After the flight took off, he began a conversation with the little boy. He appeared to be about the same age as his son and was busy with a coloring book.

(B) As the plane rose and fell several times, people got nervous and sat up in their seats. The man was also nervous and grabbing his seat as tightly as he could. Meanwhile, the little boy was sitting quietly beside him. His coloring book and crayons were put away neatly in the seat pocket in front of him, and his hands were calmly resting on his legs. Incredibly, he didn't seem worried at all.

(C) Then, suddenly, the turbulence ended. The pilot apologized for the bumpy ride and announced that they would be landing soon. As the plane began its descent, the man said to the little boy, "You are just a little boy, but I have never met a braver person in all my life! Tell me, how is it that you remained so calm while all of us adults were so afraid?" Looking him in the eyes, he said, "My father is the pilot, and he's taking me home."

*turbulence: 난기류

(D) He asked the boy a few usual questions, such as his age, his hobbies, as well as his favorite animal. He found it strange that such a young boy would be traveling alone, so he decided to keep an eye on him to make sure he was okay. About an hour into the flight, the plane suddenly began experiencing turbulence. The pilot told everyone to fasten their seat belts and remain calm, as they had encountered rough weather.

[B-1] 주어진 글 (A)에 이어질 내용을 순서에 맞게 배열한 것으로 가장 적절한 것은?

① (B) – (D) – (C)
② (C) – (B) – (D)
③ (C) – (D) – (B)
④ (D) – (B) – (C)
⑤ (D) – (C) – (B)

[B-2] 윗글에 관한 내용으로 적절하지 <u>않은</u> 것은?

① 사업가는 중년 여성과 소년 사이에 앉았다.
② 비행기가 오르락내리락하자 사람들은 긴장했다.
③ 소년은 색칠 공부 책과 크레용을 가방에 넣었다.
④ 소년은 자신의 아버지가 조종사라고 말했다.
⑤ 조종사는 사람들에게 안전벨트를 매고 침착하라고 말했다.

정답과 해설 p.51

01 A businessman boarded a flight. // Arriving at his seat, / he greeted his travel companions:
분사구문
/ a middle-aged woman sitting at the window, / and a little boy sitting in the aisle seat. //
현재분사 현재분사
After putting his bag in the overhead bin, / he took his place between them.
접속사가 남아있는 분사구문

02 After the flight took off, / he began a conversation with the little boy. // He appeared to
~한 것으로 보이다
be about the same age as his son / and was busy with a coloring book. // He asked the
간접목적어
boy a few usual questions, / such as his age, his hobbies, as well as his favorite animal.
직접목적어
// He found it strange / that such a young boy would be traveling alone, / so he decided
가목적어 진목적어
to keep an eye on him / to make sure he was okay.
부사적 용법(목적)

03 About an hour into the flight, / the plane suddenly began experiencing turbulence.
약, 대략
// The pilot told everyone / to fasten their seat belts / and remain calm, / as they had
5형식 동사 목적어 목적격 보어(to부정사) 접속사(~ 때문에)
encountered rough weather.

04 As the plane rose and fell several times, / people got nervous and sat up in their
seats. // The man was also nervous / and grabbing his seat as tightly as he could. //
as+형용사/부사+as+주어+can: 최대한, 가능한 한 ~한(하게)
Meanwhile, the little boy was sitting quietly beside him. // His coloring book and
crayons were put away neatly in the seat pocket in front of him, / and his hands were
calmly resting on his legs. // Incredibly, he didn't seem worried at all.
문장 수식 부사

05 Then, suddenly, the turbulence ended. // The pilot apologized for the bumpy ride / and
announced that they would be landing soon. // As the plane began its descent, / the
명사절 접속사
man said to the little boy, / "You are just a little boy, / but I have never met a braver
person in all my life! // Tell me, / how is it that you remained so calm / while all of us
가주어 진주어
adults were so afraid?" // Looking him in the eyes, / he said, / "My father is the pilot,
분사구문
and he's taking me home."

01 한 사업가가 비행기에 탑승했다board. // 그의 자리에 도착한 후, / 그는 여행 동반자들과 인사를 나누었다 / 창가에 앉아 있는 중년 여성과 / 통로 쪽 좌석aisle seat에 앉아 있는 어린 소년. // 가방을 머리 위 짐칸overhead bin에 넣은 후, / 그는 그들 사이에 앉았다.

02 비행기가 이륙한take off 후, / 그는 어린 소년과 대화를 시작했다. // 그는 그의 아들과 나이가 비슷해 보였고 / 색칠 공부 책을 칠하느라 바빴다. // 그는 소년에게 몇 가지 일상적인 질문을 했다 / 그의 나이, 취미, 좋아하는 동물과 같은. // 그는 이상하다고 생각했다 / 그런 어린 소년이 혼자 여행하는 것이, / 그래서 그를 지켜보기로 했다 / 그가 괜찮은지 확인하기 위해.

03 비행 시작 1시간여 만에 / 비행기가 갑자기 난기류를 타기 시작했다. // 조종사는 모든 사람들에게 말했다 / 안전벨트를 매라고fasten one's seat belts / 그리고 침착하라고 / 거친rough 날씨를 만났기encounter 때문에.

04 비행기가 여러 차례 오르락내리락하자 / 사람들은 긴장해 자리에 똑바로 앉았다. // 그 남자도 긴장해서 / 그의 좌석을 최대한 꽉tightly 잡고 있었다. // 그러는 동안에도Meanwhile, 어린 소년은 조용히 그의 옆에 앉아 있었다. // 그의 색칠 공부 책과 크레용은 앞 좌석 주머니에 가지런히neatly 치워져 있었고, / 그의 손은 차분히 다리에 놓여 있었다. // 놀랍게도, 그는 전혀 걱정하지 않는 것처럼 보였다.

05 그러다가, 갑자기, 난기류가 끝이 났다. // 조종사는 험난한bumpy 비행에 대해 사과하고 / 그들이 곧 착륙할land 것이라고 알렸다. // 비행기가 하강descent하기 시작했을 때, / 그 남자는 어린 소년에게 말했다, / "너는 어린 소년일 뿐이지만, / 나는 평생 동안 더 용감한 사람을 만난 적이 없어! / 말해 주렴, / 어떻게 그렇게 침착하게 있었는지 / 어른들 모두가 두려워하는데?" // 그의 눈을 바라보며, / 그는 말했다. / "저희 아버지께서 조종사이신데, / 아버지께서 저를 집으로 데려가고 있는 중이에요."

STEP 1 • 수능에 진짜 나오는 단어

✔ 문제에 나오는 단어들을 확인하세요.

시간이 없다면 색으로 표시된 단어만이라도 꼭 외우고 넘어가세요!

01	associate	v. 연관시키다	(✔ associate) our sense of worthiness with our performance	우리의 자부심을 성적과 연관시키다
02	rooted in	~에 뿌리를 둔	( ) ( ) truth	사실에 뿌리를 둔
03	descriptive	a. 설명하는, 묘사적인	( ) of your value	당신의 가치를 설명하는
04	virtue	n. 미덕	reflection of the ( )	미덕의 반영
05	unreasonable	a. 부당한, 지나친	( ) pressure	부당한 압력
06	certification	n. 자격(증)	the ( ) test	자격 시험
07	attend to	~에 주의를 기울이다	( ) ( ) the task	과제에 주의를 기울이다
08	term	n. 말, 용어	in positive ( )s	긍정적인 말로
09	rationalize	v. 합리화하다	( ) past test performance	과거 시험 성적들을 합리화하다
10	variable	n. 변수	secondary ( )s	부차적인 변수들
11	relieve	v. 완화하다	( ) the stress	스트레스를 완화하다
12	affirm	v. 확인하다	( ) your value	당신의 가치를 확인하다
13	dedication	n. 헌신	( ) to the challenge	과제에 대한 헌신
14	head on	정면으로	meet the challenge ( ) ( )	과제에 정면으로 맞서다

➕ 본문 문장 속에서 단어들을 확인해 보세요.

Believing that test performance is a reflection of your virtue / places unreasonable pressure / on your performance.

시험 성적이 여러분의 미덕을 반영하는 것이라고 믿는 것은 / 부당한 압력을 가한다 / 여러분의 수행에.

문제를 풀기 전에 단어들을 **30초** 동안 다시 확인하세요.

01	associate	✏ 연관시키다	associate our sense of worthiness with our performance	우리의 자부심을 성적과 연관시키다
02	rooted in		rooted in truth	사실에 뿌리를 둔
03	descriptive		descriptive of your value	당신의 가치를 설명하는
04	virtue		reflection of the virtue	미덕의 반영
05	unreasonable		unreasonable pressure	부당한 압력
06	certification		the certification test	자격 시험
07	attend to		attend to the task	과제에 주의를 기울이다
08	term		in positive terms	긍정적인 말로
09	rationalize		rationalize past test performance	과거 시험 성적들을 합리화하다
10	variable		secondary variables	부차적인 변수들
11	relieve		relieve the stress	스트레스를 완화하다
12	affirm		affirm your value	당신의 가치를 확인하다
13	dedication		dedication to the challenge	과제에 대한 헌신
14	head on		meet the challenge head on	과제에 정면으로 맞서다

➕ **본문 문장 속에서 단어의 의미를 우리말로 해석해 보세요.**

Believing that test performance is a reflection of your virtue / places unreasonable pressure / on your performance.

➡ 시험 성적이 여러분의 ⬛⬛⬛⬛ 을 반영하는 것이라고 믿는 것은 / ⬛⬛⬛⬛ 압력을 가한다 / 여러분의 수행에.

STEP **2** · 수능 기출 제대로 풀기

C 다음 글을 읽고, 물음에 답하시오.

Test scores are not a measure of self-worth; however, we often associate our sense of worthiness with our performance on an exam. Thoughts such as "If I don't pass this test, I'm a failure" are mental traps not rooted in truth. Failing a test is failing a test, nothing more. It is in no way (a) <u>descriptive</u> of your value as a person. Believing that test performance is a reflection of your virtue places (b) <u>unreasonable</u> pressure on your performance. Not passing the certification test only means that your certification status has been delayed. (c) <u>Maintaining</u> a positive attitude is therefore important. If you have studied hard, reaffirm this mentally and believe that you will do well. If, on the other hand, you did not study as hard as you should have or wanted to, (d) <u>accept</u> that as beyond your control for now and attend to the task of doing the best you can. If things do not go well this time, you know what needs to be done in preparation for the next exam. Talk to yourself in positive terms. Avoid rationalizing past or future test performance by placing the blame on secondary variables. Thoughts such as, "I didn't have enough time," or "I should have …," (e) <u>relieve</u> the stress of test-taking. Take control by affirming your value, self-worth, and dedication to meeting the test challenge head on. Repeat to yourself "I can and I will pass this exam."

[C-1] 윗글의 제목으로 가장 적절한 것은?

① Attitude Toward a Test: It's Just a Test
② Some Stress Is Good for Performance
③ Studying Together Works for a Test
④ Repetition: The Road to Perfection
⑤ Sound Body: The Key to Success

[C-2] 밑줄 친 (a)~(e) 중에서 문맥상 낱말의 쓰임이 적절하지 <u>않은</u> 것은?

① (a)
② (b)
③ (c)
④ (d)
⑤ (e)

정답과 해설 **p.52**

01 Test scores are not a measure of self-worth; // however, / we often associate our sense of worthiness / with our performance on an exam. // Thoughts such as "If I don't pass this test, I'm a failure" / are mental traps / not rooted in truth. // Failing a test is failing a test, / nothing more. // It is in no way descriptive of your value as a person.

02 Believing that test performance is a reflection of your virtue / places unreasonable pressure on your performance. // Not passing the certification test / only means / that your certification status has been delayed.

03 Maintaining a positive attitude / is therefore important. // If you have studied hard, / reaffirm this mentally / and believe that you will do well. // If, on the other hand, you did not study / as hard as you should have or wanted to, / accept that / as beyond your control for now / and attend to the task of doing the best you can.

04 If things do not go well this time, / you know / what needs to be done / in preparation for the next exam. // Talk to yourself in positive terms. // Avoid rationalizing past or future test performance / by placing the blame on secondary variables. // Thoughts such as, "I didn't have enough time," or "I should have …," / relieve the stress of test-taking. // Take control / by affirming your value, self-worth, and dedication / to meeting the test challenge head on. // Repeat to yourself / "I can and I will pass this exam."

---

01 시험 점수는 자부심의 척도가 아니다. // 하지만 / 우리는 흔히 우리의 자부심을 연관시킨다associate / 우리의 시험 성적과. // "이 시험에 합격하지 못하면 나는 실패자야."와 같은 생각은 / 정신적 함정이다 / 사실에 뿌리를 두고 있지 않은not rooted in truth. // 시험에 실패하는 것은 시험에 실패하는 것이지, / 그 이상이 아니다. // 그것은 결코 사람으로서의 여러분의 가치를 설명하지descriptive of 않는다.

02 시험 성적이 여러분의 미덕virtue을 반영하는 것이라고 믿는 것은 / 여러분의 수행에 부당한unreasonable 압력을 가한다. // 자격certification 시험을 통과하지 못한 것은 / 단지 의미할 따름이다 / 여러분의 자격 지위가 지연되었다는 것을.

03 긍정적인 태도를 유지하는 것이 / 그러므로 중요하다. // 만약 여러분이 열심히 공부했다면, / 마음속으로 이것을 재확인하라 / 그리고 좋은 성적이 나올 것이라고 믿으라. // 다른 한편, 만약 여러분이 공부하지 않았다면, / 여러분이 했어야 하거나 원하는 만큼 열심히 / 그것을 받아들여라 / 여러분이 지금으로서는 어찌할 수 없는 것으로 / 그리고 여러분이 할 수 있는 최선의 것을 하는 과제에 주의를 기울이라attend to.

04 만약 이번에 잘 되지 않는다면, / 알게 된다 / 무엇이 되어 있어야 하는지 / 다음 시험 준비에서는. // 긍정적인 말term로 자신에게 이야기하라. // 과거 또는 미래의 시험 성적을 합리화하는rationalize 것을 피하라 / 부차적인 변수variable에 책임을 지움으로써. // "나는 시간이 충분하지 않았어."라거나 "내가 그랬어야 했는데…"와 같은 생각은 / 시험을 보는 것의 스트레스를 완화시킨다relieve(→ 악화시킨다). // 통제권을 잡으라 / 자신의 가치, 자부심, 그리고 헌신dedication을 확인함affirm으로써 / 시험 과제에 정면으로head on 맞서는 것에 대한 (헌신). // 자신에게 되풀이해 말하라 / "난 이 시험에 합격할 수 있고 합격할 거야."라고.

DAY 14

장문의 이해 ➕

D STEP 1 • 수능에 *진짜* 나오는 *단어*

✔ 문제에 나오는 단어들을 확인하세요.

시간이 없다면 색으로 표시된 단어만이라도 꼭 외우고 넘어가세요!

01	aviation	n. 항공 산업	commercial (✔ aviation)	민간 항공 산업
02	**submit**	v. 제출하다	( ) reports	보고서를 제출하다
03	**numerous**	a. 많은	( ) improvements	많은 개선점
04	self-induced	a. 스스로 만들어낸	severe ( ) social pressures	스스로 만들어낸 심한 사회적 압박감
05	**semi-anonymous**	a. 반익명의	( ) reports	반익명의 보고서
06	detach	v. 분리하다, 떼어내다	( ) the contact information	연락처를 떼어내다
07	penalty	n. 벌금	a civil ( )	벌금형
08	**invoke**	v. 실시하다	( ) a civil penalty	벌금형을 실시하다
09	suspension	n. 중지, 보류	certificate ( )	면허 정지
10	exempt A from B	A를 B로부터 면제해주다	( ) him ( ) punishment	그를 처벌에서 면제해주다

➕ 본문 문장 속에서 단어들을 확인해 보세요.

U.S. commercial aviation has long had an extremely effective system / for encouraging pilots to submit reports of errors.

미국 민항 산업에는 매우 효과적인 시스템이 오랫동안 있었다 / 조종사들이 오류 보고서를 제출하도록 장려하는.

01	aviation	항공 산업	commercial aviation	민간 항공 산업
02	submit		submit reports	보고서를 제출하다
03	numerous		numerous improvements	많은 개선점
04	self-induced		severe self-induced social pressures	스스로 만들어낸 심한 사회적 압박감
05	semi-anonymous		semi-anonymous reports	반익명의 보고서
06	detach		detach the contact information	연락처를 떼어내다
07	penalty		a civil penalty	벌금형
08	invoke		invoke a civil penalty	벌금형을 실시하다
09	suspension		certificate suspension	면허 정지
10	exempt A from B		exempt him from punishment	그를 처벌에서 면제해주다

➕ **본문 문장 속에서 단어의 의미를 우리말로 해석해 보세요.**

U.S. commercial aviation has long had an extremely effective system / for encouraging pilots to submit reports of errors.

➜ 미국   에는 매우 효과적인 시스템이 오랫동안 있었다 / 조종사들이 오류 보고서를   장려하는.

STEP **2** • 수능 기출 제대로 풀기

 다음 글을 읽고, 물음에 답하시오.

U.S. commercial aviation has long had an extremely effective system for encouraging pilots to submit reports of errors. The program has resulted in numerous improvements to aviation safety. It wasn't easy to establish: pilots had severe self-induced social pressures against (a) admitting to errors. Moreover, to whom would they report them? Certainly not to their employers. Not even to the Federal Aviation Authority (FAA), for then they would probably be punished. The solution was to let the National Aeronautics and Space Administration (NASA) set up a (b) voluntary accident reporting system whereby pilots could submit semi-anonymous reports of errors they had made or observed in others. Once NASA personnel had acquired the necessary information, they would (c) detach the contact information from the report and mail it back to the pilot. This meant that NASA no longer knew who had reported the error, which made it impossible for the airline companies or the FAA (which enforced penalties against errors) to find out who had (d) rejected the report. If the FAA had independently noticed the error and tried to invoke a civil penalty or certificate suspension, the receipt of self-report automatically exempted the pilot from punishment. When a sufficient number of similar errors had been collected, NASA would analyze them and issue reports and recommendations to the airlines and to the FAA. These reports also helped the pilots realize that their error reports were (e) valuable tools for increasing safety.

[D-1] 윗글의 제목으로 가장 적절한 것은?

① Aviation Safety Built on Anonymous Reports
② More Flexible Manuals Mean Ignored Safety
③ Great Inventions from Unexpected Mistakes
④ Controversies over New Safety Regulations
⑤ Who Is Innovating Technology in the Air?

[D-2] 밑줄 친 (a)~(e) 중에서 문맥상 낱말의 쓰임이 적절하지 않은 것은?

① (a)
② (b)
③ (c)
④ (d)
⑤ (e)

정답과 해설 p.52

01
U.S. commercial aviation has long had an extremely effective system / for encouraging
현재완료(계속)
pilots to submit reports of errors. // The program has resulted in numerous
encourage+목적어+목적격 보어(to부정사)
improvements / to aviation safety. // It wasn't easy to establish: / pilots had severe
전치사(~에 대해)   to부정사의 부사적 용법(형용사 수식)
self-induced social pressures / against admitting to errors.

02
Moreover, to whom would they report them? // Certainly not to their employers. //
전치사+의문대명사
Not even to the Federal Aviation Authority (FAA), / for then they would probably be
등위접속사(=because)
punished.

03
The solution was to let the National Aeronautics and Space Administration (NASA) /
to부정사의 명사적 용법(보어)
[set up a voluntary accident reporting system / whereby pilots could submit
let의 목적격 보어(원형부정사구)   (=where, 관계부사)
semi-anonymous reports of errors / they had made or observed in others].
목적격 관계대명사절

04
Once NASA personnel had acquired the necessary information, / they would detach
일단 ~하면
the contact information from the report / and mail it back to the pilot. // This meant
that NASA no longer knew / who had reported the error, / which made it impossible /
명사절 접속사   의문사절(knew의 목적어)   관계대명사 계속적 용법 가목적어
for the airline companies or the FAA (which enforced penalties against errors) / to find
to부정사의 의미상의 주어   진목적어(to부정사)
out who had rejected the report. // If the FAA had independently noticed the error /
and tried to invoke a civil penalty or certificate suspension, / the receipt of self-report
automatically exempted the pilot from punishment.
exempt A from B: A가 B를 면하게 하다

05
When a sufficient number of similar errors had been collected, / NASA would analyze
them / and issue reports and recommendations to the airlines and to the FAA. // These
reports also helped the pilots realize / that their error reports were valuable tools / for
help+목적어+목적격 보어(동사원형)   명사절 접속사
increasing safety.

01 미국 민항 산업commercial aviation에는 매우 효과적인 시스템이 오랫동안 있었다 / 조종사들이 오류 보고서를 제출하도록submit report 장려하는. // 이 프로그램은 많은 개선점numerous improvement들을 만들어 왔다 / 항공 안전에 있어. // 그것은 정착시키기 쉽지 않았다 / 조종사들은 스스로 만들어 낸 심한 사회적 압박감severe self-induced social pressure을 느꼈다 / 오류를 인정하는 것에 대해.

02 더구나, 누구에게 그 오류들을 보고한단 말인가? // 분명 그들의 고용주에게는 아닐 것이다. // 미국 연방항공청(FAA)에게는 더욱 아닐 것이다 / 처벌을 받을 수도 있기에.

03 해결책은 항공우주국(NASA)에게 시키는 것이었다 / 자발적인 사고 보고 체계를 만들도록 / 조종사들이 반익명의 오류 보고서semi-anonymous report를 제출할 수 있게 하는 / 그들이 저지른 오류나 다른 조종사에게서 목격한.

04 일단 NASA 인사부가 필요한 정보를 얻어내면, / 그들은 보고서에 있던 연락처를 떼어냈다detach the contact information / 그리고 조종사들에게 돌려 보냈다. // 이것은 NASA가 더 이상 알지 못한다는 것을 의미했다 / 오류를 누가 보고했는지를, / 그리고 이는 불가능하게 만들었다 / (오류에 대해 제재를 가할 수 있는) 항공사나 FAA가 / 누가 보고서를 거절했는지(→제출했는지) 아는 것을. // 만일 FAA가 독립적으로 오류를 발견하고 / 벌금형 또는 면허정지를 실시하려고invoke a civil penalty or certificate suspension하면, / 자기 보고서의 접수가 자동으로 해당 조종사가 처벌받는 것을 면하게exempt해주었다.

05 유사한 오류가 충분히 수집되면, / NASA는 그것들을 분석했다 / 그리고 보고서와 권고안을 항공사들과 FAA에 발송하곤 했다. // 이러한 보고서는 또한 조종사들로 하여금 깨닫게 하는 데 도움을 주었다 / 그들의 오류 보고서가 유용한 도구였다는 것을 / 안전을 높이는 데.

STEP 1 • 수능에 진짜 나오는 단어

✔ 문제에 나오는 단어들을 확인하세요.

시간이 없다면 색으로 표시된 단어만이라도 꼭 외우고 넘어가세요!

01	passer-by	n. 지나가는 사람, 행인	ask a (✔ passer-by) for directions	지나가는 사람에게 방향을 묻다
02	**spare change**	잔돈	give away ( ) ( )	잔돈을 주다
03	spot	n. 장소	a dry ( )	건조한 곳
04	engagement	n. 약혼	an ( ) ring	약혼 반지
05	appraise	v. 감정하다, 평가하다	( ) it for $100	그것을 100달러로 감정하다
06	**return**	v. 반납하다, 돌려주다	( ) the book	그 책을 반납하다
07	reunite	v. 재회하다, 재회하게 하다	They're happily ( )d.	그들은 행복하게 재회한다.
08	deed	n. 행동	a good ( )	선한 행동
09	fateful	a. 운명적인	the ( ) day	운명적인 날
10	donation	n. 기부	give a ( )	기부금을 보내다
11	solid	a. 견고한	a ( ) plan	견고한 계획

➕ 본문 문장 속에서 단어들을 확인해 보세요.

He lived on a street corner in Kansas City, / holding out a cup / and asking passers-by for spare change.

그는 Kansas City의 길모퉁이에서 살았다 / 컵을 내밀어 / 지나가는 사람들에게 잔돈을 구걸하며.

01	passer-by	지나가는 사람, 행인	ask a passer-by for directions	지나가는 사람에게 방향을 묻다
02	spare change		give away spare change	잔돈을 주다
03	spot		a dry spot	건조한 곳
04	engagement		an engagement ring	약혼 반지
05	appraise		appraise it for $100	그것을 100달러로 감정하다
06	return		return the book	그 책을 반납하다
07	reunite		They're happily reunited.	그들은 행복하게 재회한다.
08	deed		a good deed	선한 행동
09	fateful		the fateful day	운명적인 날
10	donation		give a donation	기부금을 보내다
11	solid		a solid plan	견고한 계획

➕ **본문 문장 속에서 단어의 의미를 우리말로 해석해 보세요.**

He lived on a street corner in Kansas City, / holding out a cup / and asking passers-by for spare change.

➡ 그는 Kansas City의 길모퉁이에서 살았다 / 컵을 내밀어 /   에게   을 구걸하며.

제한시간 110초
난이도 E-1 ★★★☆☆
      E-2 ★★★☆☆

STEP **2** • 수능 기출 제대로 풀기

E 다음 글을 읽고, 물음에 답하시오.

(A) Six months ago, 55-year-old Billy Ray Harris was homeless. He lived on a street corner in Kansas City, holding out a cup and asking passers-by for spare change. But then, one day, his life changed. In February, Sarah Darling passed Harris at his usual spot and dropped some change into his cup. But she also accidentally dropped in her engagement ring. Though Harris considered selling the ring — he got it appraised for $4,000 — a few days later, he returned the ring to Darling. "I am not trying to say that I am a saint, but I am no devil either," he said at the time.

(B) They were happily reunited, and Harris is now working on his relationship with them. And the Kansas City community hasn't forgotten about Harris and his good deed. "I still see some of the same people," he says, "but only now, instead of coming up and giving me change, they're coming up shaking my hand and saying, 'Hey, good job'." Since the fateful day that Darling's ring landed in his cup, Harris's life has turned completely around. "I want to thank all the people that helped me out," he says.

(C) As a way to say thank you, Darling gave Harris all the cash she had with her. Then her husband, Bill Krejci, launched a Give Forward page to collect money for Harris. As of mid-morning Tuesday, close to $152,000 had been donated. Over the weekend, he spoke with Harris about what he's planning to do with the donations, and knew that he had a very solid plan of making it happen.

(D) The fund raised far more than any of them expected — in just three months, people donated more than $190,000. Harris talked to a lawyer, who helped him put the money in a trust. Since then, he's been able to buy a car and even put money down on a house, which he's fixing up himself. And that's not all: After he appeared on TV, his family members who had been searching for him for 16 years were able to find him.

*trust: 신탁 (재산)

[E-1] 주어진 글 (A)에 이어질 내용을 순서에 맞게 배열한 것으로 가장 적절한 것은?

① (B) — (D) — (C)
② (C) — (B) — (D)
③ (C) — (D) — (B)
④ (D) — (B) — (C)
⑤ (D) — (C) — (B)

[E-2] 윗글에 관한 내용으로 적절하지 <u>않은</u> 것은?

① Darling은 Harris의 컵에 반지를 떨어뜨렸다.
② Kansas City 지역 사회는 Harris의 선행을 잊지 않았다.
③ Darling은 감사 표시로 Harris에게 지녔던 현금 전부를 주었다.
④ Harris를 위한 모금액은 예상에 미치지 못했다.
⑤ Harris의 TV 출연 후 가족들이 그를 찾을 수 있었다.

정답과 해설 p.53

01   Six months ago, / 55-year-old Billy Ray Harris / was homeless. // He lived on a street corner in Kansas City, / holding out a cup / and asking passers-by for spare change.

동시동작의 분사구문   병렬 구조

02   But then, one day, / his life changed. // In February, / Sarah Darling passed Harris at his usual spot / and dropped some change into his cup. // But she also accidentally dropped in her engagement ring.

03   Though Harris considered selling the ring / — he got it appraised for $4,000 — / a few days later, he returned the ring to Darling. // "I am not trying to say / that I am a saint, / but I am no devil either," / he said at the time. // As a way to say thank you, / Darling gave Harris / all the cash she had with her. // Then / her husband, Bill Krejci, / launched a Give Forward page / to collect money for Harris.

get+목적어+목적격 보어(과거분사)

목적격 관계대명사 생략

to부정사의 부사적 용법(목적)

04   As of mid-morning Tuesday, / close to $152,000 had been donated. // Over the weekend, / he spoke with Harris / about what he's planning to do with the donations, / and knew that he had a very solid plan of making it happen.

~의 시점에서

의문사절(전치사 about의 목적어)

05   The fund raised far more than any of them expected / — in just three months, / people donated more than $190,000. // Harris talked to a lawyer, / who helped him put the money in a trust. // Since then, / he's been able to buy a car / and even put money down on a house, / which he's fixing up himself. // And that's not all: / After he appeared on TV, / his family members who had been searching for him for 16 years / were able to find him.

전치사: ~이후로   현재완료

주격 관계대명사절

06   They were happily reunited, / and Harris is now working on his relationship with them. // And the Kansas City community hasn't forgotten / about Harris and his good deed. // "I still see some of the same people," / he says, / "but only now, / instead of coming up and giving me change, / they're coming up shaking my hand / and saying, 'Hey, good job'." // Since the fateful day / that Darling's ring landed in his cup, / Harris's life has turned completely around. // "I want to thank all the people / that helped me out," / he says.

전치사: ~이후로   관계부사절

주격 관계대명사절

01 6개월 전에 / 55세의 Billy Ray Harris는 / 노숙자였다. // 그는 Kansas City의 길모퉁이에서 살았다 / 컵을 내밀어 / 지나가는 사람들passers-by에게 잔돈spare change을 구걸하며.

02 그러나 그러던 어느 날 / 그의 인생이 바뀌었다. // 2월에 / Sarah Darling이 항상 그 자리spot에 있던 Harris를 지나갔고 / 그의 컵에 약간의 잔돈을 떨어뜨렸다. // 그러나 그녀는 또한 우연히도 그녀의 약혼반지engagement ring까지 떨어뜨렸다.

03 비록 Harris가 그 반지를 파는 것에 대해 생각했지만 / 그는 그것을 4,000달러로 감정받았다appraise / 며칠 후, 그는 그 반지를 Darling에게 돌려주었다return. // "나는 말하려는 것은 아닙니다 / 내가 성자라고 / 하지만 나는 악마도 아닙니다."라고 / 그때 그는 말했다. // 감사를 표할 한 가지 방법으로 / Darling은 Harris에게 주었다 / 그녀가 지니고 있던 현금 전부를. // 그러고 나서 / 그녀의 남편 Bill Krejci가 / Give Forward 페이지를 시작하였다 / Harris를 위한 돈을 모금하기 위해.

04 화요일 오전 중간쯤에 / 거의 152,000달러가 기부되었다. // 주말 동안, / 그는 Harris와 이야기를 나누었다 / 그 기부금donation을 가지고 무엇을 하고자 계획하는지에 대해 / 그리고 그가 그것을 실현시킬 매우 확고한 계획solid plan을 가지고 있다는 것을 알게 되었다.

05 그들 중 누가 예상했던 것보다 훨씬 더 많은 기금이 모아졌다 / 단 3개월 만에 / 사람들이 190,000달러 이상을 기부하였다. // Harris는 변호사와 이야기하였는데 / 그 변호사는 그가 돈을 신탁에 넣도록 도와주었다. // 그 때 이후로, / 그는 차를 살 수 있게 되었고, / 집에 돈(보증금)을 걸었으며, / 그 집을 그가 직접 고치고 있다. // 그리고 그것이 전부가 아니다 / 그가 TV에 출연하고 난 후 / 16년 동안 그를 찾고 있었던 가족들이 / 그를 찾을 수 있었다.

06 그들은 행복하게 재결합하였고be reunited / Harris는 이제 그들과의 관계를 위해 애쓰고 있다. // 그리고 Kansas City 지역 사회는 잊지 않았다 / Harris와 그의 선행good deed에 대해. // "나는 여전히 똑같은 사람 중 몇몇을 봅니다."라고, / 그는 말한다 / "하지만 단지 지금은 / 그들이 다가와서 나에게 잔돈을 주는 대신에, / 다가와 악수를 하고 / '이봐, 참 훌륭한 일을 했어'라고 말합니다."라고. // 그 운명의 날the fateful day 이후로 / Darling의 반지가 그의 컵에 떨어졌던 / Harris의 인생은 완전히 달라졌다. // "나는 모든 사람들에게 감사하고 싶습니다 / 나를 도와주었던,"라고 / 그는 말한다.

F

STEP 1 • 수능에 *진짜* 나오는 *단어*

✔ 문제에 나오는 단어들을 확인하세요.

시간이 없다면 색으로 표시된 단어만이라도 꼭 외우고 넘어가세요!

01	experiment	n. 실험	an influential (✓ experiment)	영향력 있는 실험
02	resident	n. 거주자	Illinois ( )s	Illinois 거주자들
03	welfare	n. 복지	about ( )	복지에 대한
04	confident	a. 자신감 있는, 확신하는	the most ( )	가장 확신하는
05	disturbingly	ad. 충격적이게도	more ( )	더 충격적이게도
06	response	n. 응답, 대답	this sort of ( )	이러한 종류의 응답
07	factual	a. 사실적인	their ( ) beliefs	그들의 사실적 믿음
08	wired	a. (뇌가 신경망으로) 구성된	how our brains are ( )	우리의 뇌가 어떻게 구성되는지
09	substantial	a. 상당한	a ( ) body of research	상당한 양의 연구
10	interpret	v. 해석하다	( ) information	정보를 해석하다
11	reinforce	v. 강화하다	( ) their preexisting views	그들의 기존의 견해들을 강화하다
12	dismiss	v. 묵살하다, 멀리 보내다	( ) information	정보를 멀리하다
13	entertain	v. (생각 등을) 품다	( ) facts	사실을 받아들이다
14	consistency	n. 일관성, 지속성	seek ( )	일관성을 추구하다

➕ 본문 문장 속에서 단어들을 확인해 보세요.

There is a substantial body of psychological research / showing that people tend to interpret information / with an eye toward reinforcing their preexisting views.

상당한 양의 심리학적인 연구조사가 있다 / 사람들이 정보를 해석하는 경향이 있다는 것을 보여주는 / 그들의 기존의 견해들을 강화하는 쪽으로의 시각을 가지고.

01	experiment	🖉 실험	an influential experiment	영향력 있는 실험
02	resident		Illinois residents	Illinois 거주자들
03	welfare		about welfare	복지에 대한
04	confident		the most confident	가장 확신하는
05	disturbingly		more disturbingly	더 충격적이게도
06	response		this sort of response	이러한 종류의 응답
07	factual		their factual beliefs	그들의 사실적 믿음
08	wired		how our brains are wired	우리의 뇌가 어떻게 구성되는지
09	substantial		a substantial body of research	상당한 양의 연구
10	interpret		interpret information	정보를 해석하다
11	reinforce		reinforce their preexisting views	그들의 기존의 견해들을 강화하다
12	dismiss		dismiss information	정보를 멀리하다
13	entertain		entertain facts	사실을 받아들이다
14	consistency		seek consistency	일관성을 추구하다

➕ **본문 문장 속에서 단어의 의미를 우리말로 해석해 보세요.**

There is a substantial body of psychological research / showing that people tend to interpret information / with an eye toward reinforcing their preexisting views.

→ _____ 양의 심리학적인 연구조사가 있다 / 사람들이 _____ 경향이 있다는 것을 보여주는 / 그들의 기존의 견해들을 _____ 쪽으로의 시각을 가지고.

STEP **2** • 수능 기출 제대로 풀기

F 다음 글을 읽고, 물음에 답하시오.

In 2000, James Kuklinski of the University of Illinois led an influential experiment in which more than 1,000 Illinois residents were asked questions about welfare. More than half indicated that they were confident that their answers were correct — but in fact, only three percent of the people got more than half of the questions right. Perhaps more disturbingly, the ones who were the most confident they were right were generally the ones who knew the least about the topic. Kuklinski calls this sort of response the "I know I'm right" syndrome. "It implies not only that most people will resist correcting their factual beliefs," he wrote, "but also that the very people who most need to correct them will be least likely to do so." How can we have things so wrong and be so sure that we're right? Part of the answer lies in the way our brains are wired. Generally, people tend to seek _____. There is a substantial body of psychological research showing that people tend to interpret information with an eye toward reinforcing their preexisting views. If we believe something about the world, we are more likely to passively accept as truth any information that confirms our beliefs, and actively dismiss information that doesn't. This is known as "motivated reasoning." Whether or not the consistent information is accurate, we might accept it as fact, as confirmation of our beliefs. This makes us more confident in said beliefs, and even less likely to entertain facts that contradict them.

[F-1] 위 글의 제목으로 가장 적절한 것은?

① Belief Wins Over Fact
② Still Judge by Appearance?
③ All You Need Is Motivation
④ Facilitate Rational Reasoning
⑤ Correct Errors at the Right Time

[F-2] 위 글의 빈칸에 들어갈 말로 가장 적절한 것은?

① diversity
② accuracy
③ popularity
④ consistency
⑤ collaboration

정답과 해설 **p.54**

01 In 2000, / James Kuklinski of the University of Illinois led an influential experiment / in which more than 1,000 Illinois residents / were asked questions about welfare. // More than half indicated / that they were confident / that their answers were correct / — but in fact, / only three percent of the people / got more than half of the questions right.

02 Perhaps more disturbingly, / the ones who were the most confident they were right / were generally the ones / who knew the least about the topic. // Kuklinski calls this sort of response / the "I know I'm right" syndrome.

03 "It implies / not only that most people will resist correcting their factual beliefs," / he wrote, / "but also that the very people / who most need to correct them / will be least likely to do so."

04 How can we have things so wrong / and be so sure / that we're right? // Part of the answer lies / in the way our brains are wired.

05 Generally, / people tend to seek consistency. // There is a substantial body of psychological research / showing that people tend to interpret information / with an eye toward reinforcing their preexisting views. // If we believe something about the world, / we are more likely to passively accept as truth / any information [that confirms our beliefs], / and actively dismiss information that doesn't. // This is known as "motivated reasoning."

06 Whether or not the consistent information is accurate, / we might accept it as fact, / as confirmation of our beliefs. // This makes us more confident / in said beliefs, / and even less likely to entertain facts / that contradict them.

01 2000년에 / Illinois 대학의 James Kuklinski가 영향력 있는 실험experiment을 이끌었다 / 1,000명이 넘는 Illinois의 거주자resident들이 / 복지welfare에 대한 질문을 받은. // 절반이 넘는 응답자들이 말했다 / 확신한다confident고 / 그들의 답이 맞다고 / 하지만 사실은 / 오직 그 사람들의 3퍼센트만이 / 질문의 답을 절반 넘게 맞혔다.

02 아마도 더 충격적인 것은more disturbingly, / 그들이 맞았다고 가장 확신했던 사람들이 / 사람들이었다 / 그 주제에 대해 대체로 가장 적게 알았던. // Kuklinski는 이러한 종류의 응답response을 불렀다 / "내가 맞았다는 것을 나는 안다"는 신드롬이라고.

03 "이것은 의미한다 / 대부분의 사람들이 그들의 사실적factual 믿음을 고치는 것에 저항할 뿐만 아니라" / 그가 말했다 / "또한 바로 그 사람들이 / 그것들을(자기가 믿고 있는 사실들을) 가장 고쳐야 할 필요가 있는 / 그렇게 할(고칠) 가능성이 가장 적다는 것을."

04 어떻게 우리는 그렇게 틀리고도, / 그렇게 확신할 수 있을까 / 우리가 맞다고? // 정답의 일부는 있다 / 우리의 뇌가 구성된wired 방식에.

05 일반적으로, / 사람들은 일관성consistency을 추구하는 경향이 있다. // 상당한substantial 양의 심리학적인 연구조사가 있다 / 사람들이 정보를 해석하는interpret 경향이 있다는 것을 보여주는 / 그들의 기존의 견해들을 강화하는reinforce 쪽으로의 시각을 가지고. // 만약에 우리가 세상에 대해 무언가를 믿는다면, / 우리는 수동적으로 사실이라고 받아들이는 경향이 더 있다 / 우리의 믿음을 확인해주는 어떠한 정보라도, / 그리고 그렇지 않은 정보는 적극적으로 멀리하는dismiss (경향이 더 있다). // 이것은 "의도적 합리화"라고 알려져 있다.

06 일관성이 있는 정보가 정확하든 아니든 간에, / 우리는 그것을 사실로 받아들일 것이다 / 우리의 믿음에 대한 확인으로서. // 이것은 우리가 더 확신을 갖게 만들고 / (말로) 서술한 믿음에, / 그리고 심지어 사실을 받아들일entertain 가능성을 더 낮게 만든다 / 그것들에 모순되는 (사실).

✔ 문제에 나오는 단어들을 확인하세요.

시간이 없다면 색으로 표시된 단어만이라도 꼭 외우고 넘어가세요!

01	deaf	a. 청각장애의	(✓ deaf) students	청각장애의 학생들
02	district	n. 지역	school ( )	학군
03	enroll	v. 입학시키다, 입학하다	( ) at the university	대학에 입학하다
04	caution	v. 주의를 주다	( ) him	그에게 주의를 주다
05	assessment	n. 평가	( ) results	평가 결과
06	prompt	v. 자극하다, 촉발하다	( ) her to listen	그녀가 남의 말을 듣도록 유도하다
07	appreciation	n. 이해	( ) for writing	글쓰기에 대한 이해
08	keep in touch	연락하다	( ) ( ) ( ) with her	그녀와 연락을 하다
09	reunite	v. 다시 만나다	( ) soon	곧 다시 만나다

⊕ 본문 문장 속에서 단어들을 확인해 보세요.

They said / they would be moving to the district / and planned to enroll their deaf daughter / as a first grader.

그들은 말했다 / 이 지역으로 이사 와서 / 청각장애인 딸을 입학시킬 것이라고 / 1학년으로.

01	deaf	✎ 청각장애의	deaf students	청각장애의 학생들
02	district		school district	학군
03	enroll		enroll at the university	대학에 입학하다
04	caution		caution him	그에게 주의를 주다
05	assessment		assessment results	평가 결과
06	prompt		prompt her to listen	그녀가 남의 말을 듣도록 유도하다
07	appreciation		appreciation for writing	글쓰기에 대한 이해
08	keep in touch		keep in touch with her	그녀와 연락을 하다
09	reunite		reunite soon	곧 다시 만나다

➕ **본문 문장 속에서 단어의 의미를 우리말로 해석해 보세요.**

They said / they would be moving to the district / and planned to enroll their deaf daughter / as a first grader.

➡ 그들은 말했다 / 이   으로 이사 와서 /   딸을   것이라고 / 1학년으로.

STEP **2** · 수능 기출 제대로 풀기

G 다음 글을 읽고, 물음에 답하시오.

(A) In the late 1990s, a family visited the public elementary school where I taught deaf students. They said they would be moving to the district and planned to enroll their deaf daughter as a first grader. They were upset that their child's kindergarten teacher cautioned them not to have high hopes for her academically. Based upon assessment results, the teacher painted a hopeless picture for their little girl's future. Standing behind them was Kathy, a beautiful five-year-old with long shiny brown hair and dark flashing eyes. The whole time her parents were there, she didn't make a sound or use sign language, even when her parents prompted her.

(B) That day Kathy discovered the power of the pen. From then on, she had a new appreciation for writing. She is a young woman now and has become an excellent writer, public speaker, and student leader. During her senior year in high school, Kathy became the Douglas County Rodeo Queen, and the following year, she enrolled at the University of Northern Colorado to become a teacher. Kathy keeps in touch, and I especially treasure her emails with term papers attached. This young lady wields a very powerful pen!

*wield: 잘 다루다, 휘두르다

(C) After a few weeks with Kathy, I discovered I was dealing with a very bright, very strong-willed child. Although I was able to engage her in a variety of learning activities, writing was a constant struggle. I tried everything to interest her in writing class, but she would refuse to write anything.

(D) One day, Kathy got off her bus and stood in front of the school crying. The staff member there did not know enough sign language to ask her why she was crying. Finally, the staff member took Kathy into the office where she handed Kathy a pen and notepad. Kathy wrote: "PAC BAK." Immediately she realized the girl left her backpack on the bus. She called the bus back to school, and soon Kathy was reunited with her backpack.

[G-1] 주어진 글 (A)에 이어질 내용을 순서에 맞게 배열한 것으로 가장 적절한 것은?

① (B) — (D) — (C)
② (C) — (B) — (D)
③ (C) — (D) — (B)
④ (D) — (B) — (C)
⑤ (D) — (C) — (B)

[G-2] 위 글의 Kathy에 관한 내용으로 적절하지 <u>않은</u> 것은?

① 청각 장애를 가지고 있었다.
② 'I'와 처음 만났을 때 다섯 살이었다.
③ 교사가 되려고 대학에 진학했다.
④ 초등학교 작문 수업 시간에 글쓰기를 거부하곤 했다.
⑤ 버스에 두고 내린 가방을 되찾지 못했다.

정답과 해설 **p.55**

01 In the late 1990s, / a family visited the public elementary school / 관계부사 where I taught deaf students. // They said / they would be moving to the district / and planned to enroll their deaf daughter / as a first grader. 동사1 동사2

02 They were upset / that their child's kindergarten teacher cautioned them / not to have high hopes for her academically. // Based upon assessment results, / the teacher painted a hopeless picture for their little girl's future. caution+목적어+목적격 보어(to부정사)

03 도치(분사구+동사+주어) 동격 Standing behind them was Kathy, / a beautiful five-year-old with long shiny brown hair and dark flashing eyes. // The whole time her parents were there, / she didn't make a sound / or use sign language, / even when her parents prompted her.

04 After a few weeks with Kathy, / I discovered / I was dealing with a very bright, very strong-willed child. // Although I was able to engage her in a variety of learning activities, / writing was a constant struggle.

05 to부정사의 부사적 용법 refuse+목적어(to부정사) I tried everything / to interest her in writing class, / but she would refuse to write anything. // One day, / Kathy got off her bus / and stood in front of the school crying. // The staff member there did not know enough sign language / to ask her why she was crying. enough+명사+to부정사: ~할 만큼 충분한

06 관계부사 hand+간접목적어+직접목적어 Finally, / the staff member took Kathy into the office / where she handed Kathy a pen and notepad. // Kathy wrote: PAC BAK." // Immediately she realized / the girl left her backpack on the bus. // She called the bus back to school, / and soon Kathy was reunited with her backpack.

07 That day / Kathy discovered the power of the pen. // From then on, / she had a new appreciation for writing. // She is a young woman now / and has become an excellent writer, public speaker, and student leader.

08 During her senior year in high school, / Kathy became the Douglas County Rodeo Queen, / and the following year, / she enrolled at the University of Northern Colorado / to become a teacher. // Kathy keeps in touch, / and I especially treasure her emails / with term papers attached. // This young lady wields a very powerful pen! with+명사+과거분사: (명사)가 ~된 채로

---

01 1990년대 후반에, / 공립 초등학교로 한 가족이 방문하였다 / 내가 청각장애인deaf students 을 가르치는. // 그들은 말했다 / 이 지역district 으로 이사 와서 / 청각장애인 딸을 입학시키기enroll로 계획했다고 /1학년으로.

02 부모들은 언짢아했다 / 딸의 유치원 선생님이 그들에게 주의를 주어서caution / 딸에 대하여 학업적으로 큰 희망을 갖지 말라고. // 평가 결과assessment result에 근거하여 / 그 선생님은 그들의 어린 딸의 미래에 대하여 희망 없는 그림(전망)을 그렸다.

03 부모 뒤에는 Kathy가 서 있었다 / 빛나는 긴 갈색 머리와 반짝이는 짙은색 눈을 한 예쁜 다섯 살 난 아이. // 부모가 있는 내내, / 그녀는 소리를 내거나 / 수화를 사용하거나 하지 않았다 / 심지어 부모가 시켜도prompt.

04 Kathy와 함께한 몇 주가 지난 후, / 나는 발견하였다 / 내가 매우 영리하고 의지력이 강한 아이를 맡고 있다는 것을. // 나는 그녀를 다양한 학습 활동에 참여하게 할 수 있었지만, / 글쓰기는 계속 힘든 일이었다.

05 나는 모든 것을 시도했다 / 그녀가 작문 시간에 흥미를 갖도록 / 그러나 그녀는 어떤 것도 쓰는 것을 거부하곤 했다. // 어느 날, / Kathy는 버스에서 내린 후 / 학교 앞에서 울며 서 있었다. // 거기에 있던 학교 직원은 충분한 수화를 알지 못했다 / 그녀가 왜 울고 있는지 물어볼 만큼.

06 마침내, / 그 직원은 Kathy를 사무실로 데려와서 / 그곳에서 펜과 메모장을 건네주었다. // Kathy는 "PAC BAK"이라고 썼다. // 그녀는 즉시 알아차렸다 / 아이가 버스에 책가방을 놓고 왔다는 것을. // 그녀는 버스를 다시 학교로 불렀고, / 곧 Kathy는 자신의 책가방과 다시 만날 수reunite 있었다.

07 그 날 / Kathy는 펜의 힘을 발견하였다. // 그때부터, / 그녀는 글쓰기에 대해 새롭게 인식a new appreciation for writing하게 되었다. // 그녀는 지금은 젊은 여성이고, / 뛰어난 작가, 연설가, 학생 리더이다.

08 그녀의 고등학교 졸업반 때, / Kathy는 Douglas County Rodeo Queen이 되었고, / 다음 해에 / University of Northern Colorado에 입학하였다 / 교사가 되려고. // Kathy는 계속 연락을 해 오고keep in touch 있으며, / 나는 특히 그녀의 이메일을 소중하게 여긴다 / 학기말 과제가 첨부된. // 이 젊은 여성은 매우 뛰어난 필력을 발휘한다!

☑ **종합 성적표**

구분	공부한 날 ❶	결과 분석			틀린 이유 ❸
		출처	풀이 시간 ❷	채점 결과 (O, X)	
Day 13	월 일	학력평가 기출 2023년	분 초		
		학력평가 기출 2022년	분 초		
		학력평가 기출 2021년	분 초		
		학력평가 기출 2020년	분 초		
		학력평가 기출 2019년	분 초		
		학력평가 기출 2018년	분 초		
		학력평가 기출 2017년	분 초		
Day 14	월 일	학력평가 기출 2023년	분 초		
		학력평가 기출 2022년	분 초		
		학력평가 기출 2021년	분 초		
		학력평가 기출 2020년	분 초		
		학력평가 기출 2019년	분 초		
		학력평가 기출 2018년	분 초		
		학력평가 기출 2017년	분 초		

2일간
공부한 내용을
다시 보니,
......

❶ **매일 지문을 하루 계획에 맞춰 풀었다. vs. 내가 한 약속을 못 지켰다.**

<매3영 고2 기출>은 단순 문제풀이를 위한 책이 아니라, 매일 규칙적으로 영어를 공부하는 습관을 잡는 책입니다. 따라서 푸는 문제 개수는 상황에 따라 다르더라도 '매일' 학습하는 것이 중요합니다.

❷ **주어진 시간을 자꾸 넘긴다?**

풀이 시간이 계속해서 권장 시간을 넘긴다면 실전 훈련이 부족하다는 신호입니다. 아직 조급함을 가질 필요는 없지만, 매일의 문제 풀이에 더 긴장감 있게 임해보세요.

❸ **틀린 이유 맞춤 솔루션**: 오답 이유에 따라 다음 해결책을 참고하세요.

(1) 단어를 많이 몰라서

▶ <STEP 1 단어>에 제시된 필수 어휘를 매일 챙겨보고, SELF-TEST까지 꼼꼼히 진행합니다.

(2) 문장 해석이 잘 안 돼서

▶ <STEP 3 지문 복습>의 구문 첨삭과 끊어읽기 해설을 정독하며 문장구조를 보는 눈을 길러보세요.

(3) 해석은 되지만 내용이 이해가 안 되거나, 선택지로 연결을 못 해서

▶ <정답과 해설>의 해설과 오답풀이를 참고해 틀린 이유를 깊이 고민하고 정리해 보세요.

!

결론적으로, 내가 **취약한 부분**은 [ ] 이다. **취약점을 보완하기 위해서** 나는
[ ] 을/를 해야겠다.

3일 뒤 다시 봐야 할 문항과, 꼭 다시 외워야 할 사항·구문 등이 있는 페이지는 지금 바로 접어 두세요.

Memo

Memo

매일 3단계로 푸는 영어독해

고2

전국연합 학력평가 기출

정답 및 해설

고2

매일
3단계로 푸는
영어독해

전국연합
학력평가 기출

정답 및 해설

A 정답 ④ 33% 2023 6월 학평

해석 교육은 지식의 나무 줄기에 초점을 맞추면서, 나뭇가지, 잔가지, 잎이 모두 공통의 핵심에서 나오는 방식을 밝혀야 한다. 사고를 위한 도구는 이 핵심에서 비롯되어, 다양한 분야의 실무자들이 혁신 과정에 대한 경험을 공유하고 창의적 활동 사이의 연결 고리를 발견할 수 있는 공통 언어를 제공한다. 교육과정 전반에 걸쳐 동일한 용어가 사용될 때, 학생들은 서로 다른 과목들과 수업들을 연결하기 시작한다. 글쓰기 수업에서 추상을 연습하고, 회화나 그림 그리기 수업에서 추상을 연습하고, 그리고 모든 경우에 이를 추상으로 일컫는다면, 그들(학생들)은 학문의 경계를 넘어 사고하는 법을 이해하기 시작한다. 그들은 자기 생각을 하나의 개념과 표현 방식에서 다른 방식으로 바꾸는 법을 알게 된다. 용어들과 도구들이 보편적 상상력의 일부로 제시될 때 학문들을 연결하는 것은 자연스럽게 이루어진다.

해설 여러 분야에 걸쳐 통일된 용어를 사용할 때 학생들은 분야 간 연결 학습을 더 잘할 수 있다는 내용이므로, 글의 주제로 가장 적절한 것은 ④ '커리큘럼 통합을 위해 공통된 언어를 사용할 필요성'이다. 글 중간의 'When the same terms are employed ~'와 마지막 문장이 핵심을 잘 제시한다.

오답 풀이

선택률	보기 해석
① 12%	분야 간 유의미한 연결고리를 찾을 때의 어려움
② 11%	다양한 분야에 공통된 용어를 적용하는 것의 단점
③ 30%	커리큘럼의 다양화가 학생들의 창의력에 미치는 영향
⑤ 15%	추상적인 생각을 구체적 표현으로 바꾸는 것의 유용함

구문 풀이 1행

Education must focus on the trunk of the tree of knowledge, revealing **the ways in which** the branches, twigs, and leaves all emerge from a common core.

→ <전치사+관계대명사>가 the ways를 꾸민다.

구문 플러스 선행사 the way

방법의 선행사 the way는 관계부사 how 대신 <전치사+관계대명사> 형태의 in which와 함께 쓰인다. that과도 종종 쓰인다.

The way in which he spoke hurt them.
The way that she sings is truly fascinating.

B 정답 ⑤ 84% 2022 3월 학평

해석 친구나 가족의 조언은 모든 것 중에서 가장 선의로 하는 말이지만, 새로운 습관에 자신을 맞추는 최선의 방법은 아니다. 핫 요가가 여러분 친구의 삶을 바꿔 놓았을지 모르지만, 그것이 핫 요가가 여러분에게

맞는 운동(습관)임을 의미할까? 우리 모두에게는 새벽 4시 30분에 일어나는 새로운 습관이 자신의 삶을 바꿨고 우리도 그렇게 해야 한다고 '확언하는' 친구들이 있다. 나는 엄청 일찍 일어나는 것이 사람들의 삶을 때로는 좋은 방식으로 때로는 그렇지 않게 바꾼다는 것을 의심하지 않는다. 그러나 주의하라. 이 습관이 특히 잠을 더 적게 자는 것을 의미한다면 그것이 실제로 여러분의 삶을 더 낫게 만들지 알 수 없다. 그러니 친구에게 효과가 있었던 것을 시도해 볼 수 있지만, 친구의 해결책이 여러분을 똑같은 방식으로 바꾸지 않는다고 해도 자책하지 말라. 이 모든 접근법은 추측과 우연을 포함한다. 그리고 그것이 여러분의 삶의 변화를 위해 노력하는 좋은 방법은 아니다.

해설 새로운 습관에 대한 친구의 조언이 나에게도 통할지는 알 수 없다는 내용이므로, 정답은 ⑤ '타인에게 유익했던 습관이 자신에게는 효과가 없을 수 있다.'이다.

오답 풀이

선택률	오답 풀이
① 1%	잘못 들인 습관에 대해 언급하지 않았다.
② 2%	습관을 들일 수 있는지 없는지가 핵심이 아니다.
③ 4%	친구나 가족의 조언이라도 나에게 맞지 않을 수 있다는 내용이다.
④ 7%	좋은 습관의 유용성은 글의 핵심이 아니다.

구문 풀이 7행

You don't know **if** this habit will actually make your life better, especially **if** it means you get less sleep.

→ 첫 번째 if는 know의 목적어절(명사절)을 이끄는 접속사로, '~인지 아닌지'를 의미한다. 두 번째 if는 부사절을 이끄는 접속사로, '~라면'을 의미한다.

구문 플러스 접속사 if

· 명사절 접속사: ~인지 아닌지
· 부사절 접속사: (조건) 만약 ~라면 / (양보) ~하더라도

I don't know **if** I can do that.
　　　　　~인지 아닌지
I can do that **if** you show me how.
　　　　　만약 ~라면
The party was fun, **if** a bit overcrowded.
　　　　　~했긴 해도

C 정답 ③ 75% 2021 3월 학평

해석 생태계에 해를 끼치는 것에 대한 두려움은 우리가 초래하는 (환경) 파괴를 최소화하는 것을 목표로 해야 한다는 건전한 환경 보호주의자 원칙을 바탕으로 하지만, 이 원칙이 '자연의 균형'이라는 오래된 생각과 혼동될지도 모른다는 위험이 있다. 이것은 그 자체를 유지하려고 노

력하고 우리가 바꾸어서는 안 되는 완벽한 자연의 질서를 전제로 한다. 그것은 목가적인 것은 물론 낭만적인 개념이지만 정적인 상태를 전제로 하기 때문에 매우 잘못된 인식을 준다. 생태계는 역동적이고, 일부는 겉보기에는 변하지 않는 채로 인간의 수명과 비교해 보면 오랜 기간 동안 지속될지 모르지만, 그것은 결국 변할 것임에 틀림없고 정말 변한다. 생물 종(種)들은 생겼다 사라지고 기후는 변하며 동식물 군집은 달라진 환경에 적응하고 미세하게 자세히 검토하면 그런 적응과 결과적인 변화는 항상 일어나고 있는 것으로 보일 수 있다. '자연의 균형'은 잘못된 통념이다. 지구는 역동적이고, 지구의 서식자들이 함께 사는 모습[생활 방식]도 그러하다.

해설 '자연의 균형,' 즉 자연이 정적인 상태라는 생각은 잘못되었음을 지적하며 ③ '자연은 정적이지 않고 역동적으로 계속 변한다'고 말하는 내용이다.

오답 풀이

선택률	오답 풀이
① 4%	기후 변화 적응에 대한 언급은 없다.
② 10%	'자연의 균형'은 잘못된 통념이다.
④ 3%	적자생존의 원칙에 대하 언급은 없다.
⑤ 7%	생태계의 균형은 이루어지지 않는다.

구문 풀이 13행

Our planet is dynamic, and **so are the arrangements by which** its inhabitants live together.
→ '~도 역시/또한 (그러하다)'라는 의미의 so 뒤에 '(be)동사-주어'의 어순으로 쓰여 있으며, '전치사+관계대명사(by which)'가 주어 the arrangements를 수식하고 있다.

구문 플러스 동의 구문

긍정 동의: <so + 조동사, be, do/does/did + S> → ~도 그렇다
부정 동의: <nor/neither + 조동사, be, do/does/did + S> → ~도 …않다

He's busy this week, and **so am I**. → '나도 바쁘다'
I can't swim, **nor can Jake**. → 'Jake도 수영 못한다'

D 정답 ⑤ 74% 2020 9월 학평

해석 웃음의 능력은 인간의 독특한 특징이라고 오랫동안 여겨져 왔다. (기원후 2세기) Samosata의 재치 있는 Lucian은 인간을 당나귀와 구별하는 방법으로 한쪽은 웃고 다른 한쪽은 그렇지 않다는 것을 지적했다. 모든 사회에서 유머는 규범을 강화하고 행동을 규제하면서, 개인적인 의사소통에서뿐만 아니라 사회적 그룹들을 형성하는 힘으로서도 중요하다. "각각 특정한 시간, 각각의 시대, 사실상 각각의 순간은 웃음에 대한 그 자체의 조건과 주제를 가지고 있다… 그 당시에 널리 퍼져있는 수된 사고, 관심사, 흥미, 활동, 관계, 그리고 방식 때문에." 고대 그리스와 같은 다른 문화를 연구하는 누군가의 궁극적인 목표는 유물, 역사적 사건들, 혹은 사회적 집단화의 총 합계 이상이었던 사람들 그 자체를 이해하는 것이다. 이 목표에 직접적으로 접근하는 한 가지 방법은 그 문화의 유머를 연구하는 것이다. Goethe가 적절하게 언급한 대로, "사람들이 무

엇을 웃는다고 생각하는지만큼 그들의 특성을 명확히 보여주는 것도 없다."

해설 첫 문장이 이 글의 주제문으로 유머가 인간의 특징이며 유머를 통해 사회 규범과 행동을 알 수 있다고 정의 내리고 있으므로 ⑤ '문화를 이해하는 도구로서의 유머'가 적절하다.

오답 풀이

선택률	보기 해석
① 4%	전형적인 문화적 동화 과정
② 10%	우정을 쌓는 데 웃음의 기능
③ 4%	문화 간의 경쟁력을 위한 교육적인 필요성
④ 6%	사회적 문제를 비판하는 데 있어서 유머의 역할

구문 풀이 4행

In all societies humor is important not only **in individual communication** but also **as a molding force** of social groups, reinforcing their norms and regulating behavior.
→ 전치사구가 접속사 not only ~ but also에 의해 병렬구조로 연결되어 있다.

구문 플러스 병렬 구조

형태가 같은 것끼리 접속사로 연결하여 쉽게 글의 구조를 파악하게 해준다.
They saw him **jump**, **snatch up slippers** and **run into the fence**.
목적격 보어(동사원형)가 and로 연결

E 정답 ⑤ 50% 2019 6월 학평

해석 이 세상에서 똑똑하거나 능력이 있는 것만으로는 충분하지 않다. 사람들은 때때로 그들이 재능을 볼 때 그것을 알아차리지 못한다. 그들의 시야는 우리가 주는 첫인상에 의해 가려지고, 이것은 우리가 원하는 일 또는 우리가 원하는 관계를 잃게 할 수 있다. 우리가 우리 스스로를 보여주는 방식은 만약 우리가 그러한 보여주기를 적극적으로 계발한다면 우리가 제시할 기술들에 대해 더 설득력 있게 말해줄 수 있다. 어느 누구도 다른 사람들에게 그들(자신)이 누구인지를 보여줄 기회를 제공받기 전에 목록에서 지워지는 것을 좋아하지 않는다. 당신이 다른 사람을 만나는 그 순간부터 당신의 이야기를 말할 수 있는 것은 당신이 고려되어야 할 누군가이고 그 자리에 적합한 사람이라는 메시지를 전달하기 위해서 적극적으로 계발되어야만 하는 기술이다. 그러한 이유로, 우리 모두는 올바른 방식으로 적절한 것들을 말하는 방법과 다른 사람에게 호소하는 방식으로 우리 스스로를 보여주는 방법, 즉 훌륭한 첫인상을 재단하는 것을 배우는 게 중요하다.

해설 첫인상에 많은 부분들이 가려지고 자신의 재능도 가려질 수 있기 때문에 ⑤ '자신을 잘 보여줄 수 있는 법을 계발할 필요'가 있다는 내용이다.

선택률	보기 해석
① 6%	대중 앞에서 자신을 보여주는 데 있어서의 어려움
② 7%	첫인상으로 남을 평가하는 것의 위험
③ 17%	좋은 인상을 만들지 못하게 하는 요인들
④ 18%	자신을 드러내는 기술을 향상시키는 데 도움이 되는 전략들

구문 풀이 7행

Being able to tell your story from the moment you meet other people **is** a skill that must be actively cultivated, ~

→ 동명사 주어는 단수 취급하기 때문에 동사도 주어에 맞게 is로 쓴다.

구문 플러스' 동명사 주어

동명사가 주어 역할일 때는 동사를 단수 취급한다.

In this ever-changing world, **being smart or competent isn't** enough.

F 정답 ③ 71% *2018 9월 학평*

해석 비록 우리가 아이들의 발달에 미치는 디지털 기술의 모든 신경학적인 영향을 알지 못하지만, 우리는 모든 스크린 타임이 동등하게 만들어지지 않는다는 사실을 분명히 알고 있다. 예를 들어, 전자책을 읽는 것, 할머니와 화상 통화를 하는 것, 혹은 당신이 방금 찍은 아이의 사진을 아이에게 보여주는 것은 많은 부모와 교육자를 걱정시키는 수동적으로 TV를 시청하는 스크린 타임과 같지 않다. 그래서 아이들이 '얼마나 많이' 스크린과 상호작용하는가에 집중하기보다는, 그 대신에 부모와 교육자는 아이들이 '무엇'과 상호작용하고 있는가와 '누가' 그들과 그들의 경험에 대해 이야기하고 있는가로 초점을 돌리고 있다. 비록 부모가 아이에게 스크린을 건네주고 떠나고 싶은 유혹을 느낄 수 있으나, 아이들에게 미디어에 대한 경험을 안내해 주는 것은 그들이 비판적 사고력과 미디어 정보 독해력과 같은 중요한 21세기 핵심 역량을 발달시키는 데 도움을 준다.

해설 아이들이 얼마나 많이 스크린에 노출되는가보다 그들이 스크린을 통해 무엇과 상호작용하는가에 집중해야 한다는 글이다. 따라서 주제는 ③ '아이들이 스크린을 통해 어떤 경험을 하는가의 중요성'이다.

오답 풀이

선택률	보기 해석
① 6%	아이들의 스크린 매체 중독의 예측 변수
② 7%	아이들이 스크린 매체를 선호하는 이유
④ 10%	스크린 타임의 양이 아이들의 사회적 기술에 미치는 영향
⑤ 4%	아이들의 신체 활동에 대한 부모의 통제 필요성

구문 풀이 9행

Though parents may be tempted to hand a child a screen and walk away, guiding children's media experiences **helps them build** important 21st Century skills, such as critical thinking and media literacy.

→ help는 목적어 다음에 목적격 보어로 동사원형 또는 to부정사가 온다.

구문 플러스' 준사역동사 help

준사역동사 help의 목적격 보어는 동사원형 또는 to부정사의 형태를 취한다.

Jeremy helped his brother **to get** ready for the interview.
We all helped Irene **clean** the kitchen after dinner.

G 정답 ④ 70% *2017 9월 학평*

해석 개인적인 고난을 경험한 많은 부모들은 그들의 자녀가 더 나은 삶을 살기를 바란다. 자녀가 불쾌한 경험을 겪지 않도록 해주고자 하는 것은 고귀한 목적이고, 그것은 당연히 자녀에 대한 사랑과 염려로부터 나오는 것이다. 그러나 이러한 부모들이 깨닫지 못하는 것은 그들이 단기적으로는 자녀의 삶을 좀 더 즐겁게 만들어 주고 있을지 모르지만, 장기적으로는 자녀가 자신감, 정신력, 그리고 중요한 대인 기술을 습득하지 못하게 막고 있을지도 모른다는 것이다. 19세기의 영국 작가인 Samuel Smiles는 "희망, 욕망, 그리고 분투의 여지를 남기지 않은 채 자신의 노력 없이 이루어진 모든 소망에 대한 완전한 만족보다 인간에게 가해지는 더 심한 저주가 과연 있을까 하는 의문이 든다."라고 썼다. 건전한 발달을 위해 아이는 실패를 다루고 어려운 시기를 거쳐 발버둥 치며 고통스러운 감정을 경험할 필요가 있다.

해설 이 글의 주제문은 마지막 문장이다. 즉 건전한 성장은 실패와 그 감정에 대한 경험을 통해 이루어질 수 있다는 것이 핵심 내용이므로, 정답은 ④ '부모가 자식이 어려움을 경험하게 놔둘 필요성'이다.

오답 풀이

선택률	보기 해석
① 5%	전통적인 아이 양육 관행의 이점
② 6%	아이들의 육체적 발달에 주요한 요소들
③ 15%	아이에 대한 부모의 정서적 지지의 중요성
⑤ 2%	부모와 아이 사이의 관점의 차이

구문 풀이 2행

To want to spare children from having to go through unpleasant experiences is a noble aim, and it naturally stems from love and concern for the child.

→ to부정사 주어는 단수 취급한다(is).

구문 플러스' to부정사 주어

to부정사구가 주어 역할일 때는 동사를 단수 취급한다.

To swim in the sea is fun.
(= **Swimming in the sea** is fun.)

 요지 / 주제 추론

글의 요지 또는 주제 추론은 글의 전체적인 내용을 파악하고 말하고자 하는 바를 압축한 답을 찾는 유형이다.

① 첫 문장에서 주제 또는 핵심 소재가 제시되는지 살펴본다.
② 요지 문제의 경우, 특정 한 문장을 그대로 번역하여 답으로 만드는 경우가 흔했지만, 최근에는 중후반부 두세 문장 내용을 조합해 요약하는 형태로도 출제되곤 한다.
③ 주제 문제의 경우, 지문에서 언급되지 않은 것을 다루거나, 지문에서 언급된 것을 다루더라도 너무 포괄적이거나 너무 구체적인 선택지는 정답에서 제외한다.

A 정답 ④ 65%　　　*2023 3월 학평*

해석　승리는 다른 사람이 보고 있다는, 남을 의식하는 인식을 촉발한다. 아무도 여러분을 모르고 주의를 기울이고 있지 않다면 눈에 띄지 않게 움직이기가 훨씬 더 쉽다. 여러분은 일을 망치고 난폭해지고 비열해져도 되는데, 아무도 여러분이 거기 있음을 알지조차 못하기 때문이다. 하지만 여러분이 이기기 시작하거나, 다른 사람이 알아차리기 시작하는 순간부터, 여러분은 관찰되고 있다는 것을 갑자기 인식한다. 여러분은 평가받고 있다. 여러분은 다른 사람이 여러분의 실수와 약점을 발견할 것이라고 걱정하고, 여러분이 좋은 본보기이자 훌륭한 시민이고 다른 사람이 존경할 수 있는 지도자가 될 수 있도록 여러분 본래의 성격을 숨기기 시작한다. 그것에 문제는 없다. 하지만 자기 자신을 기쁘게 하는 대신 타인을 기쁘게 하는 결정을 내리면서, 진정한 자신이 되는 것을 희생하며 그렇게 한다면, 여러분은 그 지위에 그리 오래 머물지 못할 것이다. 여러분이 자신의 모습에 관해 사과하기 시작하는 순간, 여러분은 성장을 멈추고, 승리를 멈추게 된다. 영원히.

해설　성공 이후 남의 눈을 의식하여 진정한 자기 모습대로 살지 못하면 그 성공을 오래 누릴 수 없다는 내용이다. 첫 문장과 마지막 세 문장에 주제가 잘 제시된다. 따라서 제목으로는 ④ '덫에 걸린 승리자들: 너무 남을 의식하여 자기 자신이 되지 못한다'이다.

오답 풀이

선택률	보기 해석
① 14%	인생이라는 경주에서 이기려면 남을 그만 판단하라
② 3%	왜 실망은 비판보다 더 마음 아픈가
③ 13%	승리 vs. 패배: 위험할 정도로 잘못된 사고방식
⑤ 2%	정직이 적을 친구로 돌릴 최선의 방책인가?

구문 풀이　2행

It's **a lot easier** to move under the radar when no one knows you and no one is paying attention.

→ a lot은 비교급을 수식할 때 '훨씬'이라는 뜻이다.

구문 플러스⁺　비교급 강조 부사

비교급을 수식하는 부사로는 a lot, even, still, much, far 등이 있다. very는 비교급을 수식하지 못한다.

much better 훨씬 더 좋은
work **even** harder 훨씬 더 노력하다
cf. a **very** young man → 원급 수식(매우)
　　the **very** most important thing → 최상급 수식(바로 그)

B 정답 ③ 95%　　　*2022 3월 학평*

해석　우리는 더 글로벌한 사회로 나아가고 있지만, 다양한 민족 집단들은 전통적으로 상당히 다르게 일을 하고 있어, 개방적인 아이를 만들 때는 새로운 관점이 가치가 있다. 광범위한 다문화 경험은 아이들을 더 창의적으로 만들고 (얼마나 많은 생각을 떠올릴 수 있는지와 연상 능력으로 측정됨) 아이들이 자신의 생각을 확장하기 위해 다른 문화로부터 관습에 얽매이지 않는 생각을 포착할 수 있게 한다. 부모로서 가능한 한 자주 자녀가 다른 문화를 접하게 해야 한다. 할 수 있다면 자녀와 다른 나라로 여행하고, 가능하면 거기서 살라. 둘 다 가능하지 않다면, 지역 축제 탐방하기와 다른 문화에 대한 도서관 책 빌리기, 집에서 다른 문화의 음식 요리하기와 같이 국내에서 할 수 있는 일이 많다.

해설　아이들에게 광범위한 다문화 경험을 시키라는 내용이므로 정답은 ③ '자녀가 다른 문화를 가능한 한 자주 접할 수 있게 해야 한다.'이다.

오답 풀이

선택률	오답 풀이
① 1%	전통문화가 아닌, 다문화가 핵심이다.
② 0%	문제에 대한 탐구는 언급하지 않았다.
④ 1%	자녀의 실수에 대해 언급하지 않았다.
⑤ 1%	경험한 것을 돌이켜 보는 것에 대해 언급하지 않았다.

구문 풀이　8행

If you can, travel with your child to other countries; live there **if (it is) possible**.

→ if가 이끄는 조건 부사절에서 문맥상 유추 가능한 <주어+동사>가 생략되었다. 생략된 주어 it은 'to live there'의 의미이다.

구문 플러스⁺　부사절 축약 구문

시간, 조건, 양보의 부사절에서 유추 가능한 <대명사 주어+be동사>가 생략되는 경우를 말한다.

While (you are) on the plane, you are not allowed to use your smartphone. → being 생략+접속사 남긴 분사구문으로도 분석 가능
If (it is) possible, I'll lend you a hand.
→ it: 'to lend you a hand'를 받는 대명사

C 정답 ① 75%　　　*2021 9월 학평*

해석　화려한 고층 건물, 금융 본부, 관광 센터, 기념품 행상인들이 Battery Park City로 나아가기 전에, 세계 무역 센터 뒤편의 지역은 거대하고 험오스러운 쓰레기 매립지였다. 1982년, 예술가 Agnes Denes는 비록 일시적이긴 하지만 그 매립지를 다시 원래의 뿌리로 되돌리기로 결정했다. Denes는 Public Art Fund로부터 Manhattan에서 지금까지 본 가장 의미심장하며 환상적인 공공 사업 작품 중 하나를 만들어 달라는 의뢰를 받았다. 그녀의 콘셉트는 전통적인 조형물이 아니라 대중이 미술을 보는 방식을 바꾼 살아있는 설치 조형물이었다. 예술의 이름으로, Denes는 반짝이는 쌍둥이 빌딩의 그림자에 아름다운 황금 밀밭을 만들었다.

(그녀의 작품인) <Wheatfield—A Confrontation>을 위해, Denes와 자원 봉사자들은 4에이커의 땅에서 쓰레기를 치운 다음 그 지역 위에 황색 빛깔의 너울거리는 곡물을 심었다. 수개월의 농사와 관개 후에 밀밭은 무성해져 있었고 준비가 되었다. 그 예술가와 그녀의 자원 봉사자들은 수천 파운드의 밀을 수확하여 뉴욕의 푸드 뱅크에 기부하였고, 뉴욕 사람들의 마음과 몸에 모두 영양분을 공급해 주었다.

해설 세계 무역 센터 뒤편의 지역이 원래 쓰레기 매립지였다가 공공 사업 예술 작품인 밀밭으로 바뀌었다는 것이 이 글의 주된 내용이므로 ① '살아있는 공공 예술이 쓰레기 매립지에서 자라나다'가 제목으로 적절하다.

오답 풀이

선택률	보기 해석
② 7%	왜 예술이 도시 지역에서 서서히 사라지는가?
③ 5%	뉴욕: 세계의 마천루 수도
④ 4%	예술이 나이 든 사람들과 젊은 사람들의 차이를 좁히다
⑤ 7%	어떻게 도시 확장이 식량 생산에 영향을 줄 수 있는가

구문 풀이 1행

Before the fancy high-rises, financial headquarters, tourist centers, and souvenir peddlers made their way to Battery Park City, **the area behind the World Trade Center was a giant, gross landfill**.

→ 'the area ~'는 Battery Park City라는 고유명사를 설명하기 위한 동격 구문이다.

구문 플러스 동격 구문

고유명사 등 설명이 필요한 단어 뒤에 콤마, 콜론, 줄표(—)를 쓰고 부연 설명을 추가하는 것이다.

Julie, my sister, is the only doctor in town.
→ Julie를 모르는 사람들에게 '내 동생'임을 설명

D 정답 ③ 76% *2020 6월 학평*

해석 많은 발명품들은 수천 년 전에 발명이 되어서 그것들의 정확한 기원을 아는 것은 어려울 수 있다. 때때로 과학자들은 초기 발명품의 모형을 발견하고 이 모형으로부터 그것이 얼마나 오래되었고 어디에서 왔는지를 정확하게 우리에게 말해 줄 수 있다. 그러나 미래에 다른 과학자들이 세계의 다른 곳에서 똑같은 발명품의 훨씬 더 오래된 모형을 발견할 가능성이 항상 존재한다. 사실 우리는 고대 발명품들의 역사를 계속해서 발견하고 있다. 이것의 한 예는 도자기라는 발명품이다. 수 년 동안 고고학자들은 그들이 기원전 9,000년으로 거슬러 올라가는 항아리를 발견한 근동지역(현대의 이란 근처)에서 도자기가 처음 발명되었다고 믿었다. 그러나, 1960년대에 기원전 10,000년의 더 오래된 항아리가 일본의 혼슈섬에서 발견되었다. 미래에 고고학자들이 다른 어딘가에서 훨씬 더 오래된 항아리를 발견할 가능성은 언제나 존재한다.

해설 발명품의 기원이 더 오래된 것을 발견할 가능성이 높다는 것이

이 글의 주된 내용이므로 ③ '발명품의 기원: 끝없는 여행'이 적절하다.

오답 풀이

선택률	보기 해석
① 4%	어떻게 진짜와 가짜를 구별할 수 있는가?
② 8%	고대 도자기의 물질을 탐구하기
④ 7%	과거로부터 배우고, 더 나아지기 위해 변하다
⑤ 3%	인류 문명의 추진력으로서의 과학

구문 풀이 4행

However, there is always the possibility **that** in the future other scientists will discover an even older model of the same invention in a different part of the world.

→ that절이 앞의 명사의 내용을 추가 설명하는 것으로, 문장성분이 빠진 부분이 없을 때 이를 동격절이라고 한다.

구문 플러스 동격절

that절이 앞의 명사를 추가 설명하며, 문장성분이 완전할 때 이를 동격절이라고 한다.

There exists a possibility **that** he went there.
　　　　　　　　　that절: a possibility의 내용

E 정답 ⑤ 89% *2019 9월 학평*

해석 요즘 들어 전동 스쿠터가 빠르게 캠퍼스의 주요 요소가 되고 있다. 그들의 빠른(가파른) 인기 상승은 스쿠터가 가져다주는 편리함 덕분이지만, 문제가 없는 것은 아니다. 스쿠터 회사는 안전 규정을 제공하고 있지만 이 규정들이 탑승자들에게 항상 지켜지는 것은 아니다. 학생들은 탑승하는 동안 무모할 수 있고, 일부는 한 대의 스쿠터에 두 명이 한꺼번에 탑승하기도 한다. 대학들은 이미 전동 교통수단을 제한하기 위해 보행자 전용 구역과 같은 특정한 규정들을 두고 있다. 그러나 그들은 특히 전동 스쿠터를 대상으로 하여 더 많은 것을 해야 한다. 전동 스쿠터를 이용하는 학생들과 그들 주변의 사람들의 안전을 지키기 위하여 관계자들은 학생들이 규정을 위반했을 때 신호로 정지시키고 경고를 주는 교통정리원을 두는 등 더 엄격한 규정을 강화할 것을 검토해야 한다.

해설 편리해서 전동 스쿠터가 많이 보급되었지만, 사건사고가 많아지면서 대학 내 스쿠터 이용에 대한 규정 강화를 검토해야 한다고 주장하고 있으므로 정답은 ⑤이다.

오답 풀이

선택률	오답 풀이
① 3%	미성년자의 전동 스쿠터 사용 금지에 대한 언급은 없다.
② 2%	전동 스쿠터 충전 시설에 대한 언급은 없다.
③ 2%	대중교통 할인 제도에 대해 말한 바가 없다.
④ 1%	셔틀버스에 대한 언급도 없다.

Students can be reckless while they ride, **some even having two people** on one scooter at a time.

→ 분사구문은 접속사와 주어를 생략하고 동사를 분사의 형태로 쓰지만, 주절의 주어와 다르면 주어를 생략할 수 없다.

구문 플러스' 독립분사구문(의미상 주어가 따로 있는 분사구문)

주절의 주어와 다르면 분사구문의 의미상 주어를 생략할 수 없다.

The computer being out of order. I didn't finish my work.
의미상 주어　　분사구문

유형 플러스' 필자의 주장

목적, 심경에 이어 가장 쉬운 대의파악 유형으로, 요지와 마찬가지로 한글 선택지로 구성된다.

① 흔히 명령문, should, must, need to를 포함한 주제문을 거의 그대로 번역한 선택지가 정답이다. 최근에는 한 문장에 주장을 제시하지 않고 두세 문장에 나눠 제시한 후 이를 적절히 요약하는 형태로도 나온다.
② 글의 중후반부를 집중적으로 읽으면 금방 풀린다.

F 정답 ② 63%　　　　　2018 6월 학평

해석　당신은 왜 도서관에 가는가? 그렇다, 책 때문이다. 그리고 당신은 그 책들이 이야기를 들려주기 때문에 책을 좋아한다. 당신은 이야기에 몰입하거나 다른 사람의 삶 속으로 들어가 보기를 바란다. 한 형태의 도서관에서는, 비록 그곳에는 책이 한 권도 없지만 당신은 그렇게 할 수 있다. Human Library에서는, 특별한 인생 이야기를 가진 사람들이 자원해서 "책"이 된다. 정해진 시간 동안, 당신은 그들에게 질문할 수 있고 그들의 이야기를 들을 수 있는데, 이것은 당신이 책에서 발견할 수 있는 그 어떤 것만큼이나 매력적이고 감동적이다. 그 이야기들 중 많은 것들은 일종의 고정관념과 관련이 있다. 당신은 피난민, 외상 후 스트레스 장애로 고통받는 군인 또는 노숙자와 이야기할 수 있다. Human Library는 사람들이 기존의 관념에 도전하도록 격려하는데, 즉, 그렇지 않았더라면 섣부른 판단을 내렸을 누군가에 대해 진정으로 알고, 그 사람으로부터 배울 수 있도록 해준다.

해설　책 대신 다른 사람들의 인생 이야기를 들을 수 있는 도서관을 소개하는 글이므로 제목으로는 ② '사람이 책인 장소'가 가장 적절하다.

오답 풀이

선택률	보기 해석
① 6%	언어를 배우는 데 유용한 책
③ 10%	도서관: 당신의 학문적 연구의 출발점
④ 13%	Human Library에서 사람을 선택하는 방법
⑤ 5%	책 애호가의 감동적인 이야기!

The Human Library encourages people to challenge their own existing notions — to truly get to know, and learn from, someone

(whom) they might otherwise make quick judgements about.

→ 전치사 about의 목적어 역할을 하는 관계대명사 who(m)가 생략되었다.

구문 플러스' 관계대명사의 생략 (1)

목적격 관계대명사 또는 <주격 관계대명사+be동사>는 생략할 수 있다.

• Tell me everything **(that)** you know.
• The girl **(who is)** wearing a red skirt is my sister.

G 정답 ③ 52%　　　　　2017 9월 학평

해석　1947년 사해 사본이 발견되었을 때 고고학자들은 새롭게 발견되는 각각의 문서마다 포상금을 걸었다. 다량의 추가 두루마리가 발견되는 대신에 포상금을 늘리기 위한 목적으로 그것들은 그저 갈가리 찢겼다. 이와 유사하게 19세기 중국에서는 공룡의 뼈를 발견하는 것에 대해 포상금이 주어졌다. 농부들은 그들의 토지에서 몇 개를 찾아내어 그것들을 조각으로 부수고 많은 돈을 벌었다. 현대의 장려금 또한, 더 나을 것이 없다. 회사의 이사회는 달성된 목표에 대해 보너스를 주겠다고 약속한다. 그리고 무슨 일이 일어나는가? 관리자들은 사업을 키우는 것보다 목표치를 낮추는 것에 더 많은 에너지를 투자한다. 사람들은 그들에게 가장 이익이 되는 것을 행하는 방식으로 장려금에 반응한다. 주목할 만한 것은 첫째로 장려금이 시행될 때 사람들의 행동이 얼마나 빠르게, 그리고 급격하게 변화하는가이며, 두 번째로는 사람들이 장려금의 이면에 있는 높은 차원의 의도가 아니라 장려금 그 자체에 반응한다는 사실이다.

해설　포상금의 원래 목적과 달리 많은 부작용을 예시로 보여주고 주제문이 마지막에 나오는 미괄식 구성이다. 따라서 정답은 ③ '포상이 원래의 목적과 다르게 작동한다'이다.

오답 풀이

선택률	보기 해석
① 9%	황금빛 과거의 영광을 되살리다
② 6%	이기주의가 팀워크를 약화시키는 방법
④ 24%	비물질적인 상여금: 더 우수한 동기부여
⑤ 7%	문화적인 유물은 관광을 부흥시키는 것이 된다!

Instead of lots of extra scrolls being found, they were simply torn apart **to increase the reward**.

→ to increase ~는 목적을 나타내는 to부정사로 부사적 용법에 해당한다.

구문 플러스' to부정사의 부사적 용법

to부정사(to+동사원형)는 부사적 용법으로 쓰일 때 목적, 이유, 조건, 결과 등의 의미를 나타낸다.

• I went to the shop **to buy** a cup. (목적: '~하기 위하여')
• I'm glad **to meet** you again. (원인: '~해서')
• He grew up **to be** a doctor. (결과: '~해서 …하다')
• English is not easy **to learn**. (형용사 수식: '~하기에')

 제목 추론

필자의 주장이나 주제 찾기와 비슷한 유형인 제목 추론 유형은 글의 전체적인 내용을 파악하는 것이 필요하다. 다음과 같은 전략으로 해결한다.

① 중심 내용을 상징적이고 함축적으로 나타내는 표현을 찾는다.
② 글의 내용을 포괄하는 제목을 선택한다. 특정 내용만을 지엽적으로 나타내는 제목은 피한다.
③ 반복되는 주요 어휘의 유의어로 표현된 제목이 없는지 눈여겨본다. 주요 어휘가 그대로 포함된 함정 선택지가 아닌지 꼭 더블체크해야 한다.

A 정답 ② 82%　　　　　　　　　　2023 3월 학평

해석　개업식날, Isabel은 초조한 기대감을 품고 카페에 매우 일찍 도착한다. 그녀는 카페를 둘러보지만, 뭔가 빠졌다는 느낌을 떨쳐낼 수 없다. 컵과 숟가락, 접시를 차려 놓으며 Isabel의 의심은 커진다. 그녀는 카페를 완벽하게 만들기 위해 자신이 무엇을 더 할 수 있을지를 상상하려 애쓰면서 주변을 둘러보지만, 아무것도 머릿속에 떠오르지 않는다. 그때, 갑작스러운 영감의 폭발과 함께, Isabel은 붓을 쥐고 꽃과 나무를 더해서 텅 빈 벽을 풍경화로 변화시킨다. 그림을 그리면서, 그녀의 불안도 서서히 사라지기 시작한다. 아름답게 완성된 자신의 작품을 보며, 그녀는 카페가 성공할 거라고 확신한다. '자, 성공이 확실히 보장되지는 않았지만, 나는 분명 이룰 거야.'라고 스스로 생각한다.

해설　카페 개업을 앞둔 Isabel이 뭔가 부족한 느낌에 초조해하다가 갑작스레 영감을 받아 벽화를 그린 뒤 자신감을 찾았다는 내용이다. 따라서 ② '의심하는 → 자신 있는'이 심경 변화로 가장 적절하다.

오답 풀이

선택률	보기 해석
① 1%	평온한 → 놀란
③ 12%	부러운 → 기쁜
④ 1%	고마운 → 겁에 질린
⑤ 2%	무관심한 → 불안한

구문 풀이　2행

She looks around the cafe, but she can't shake off **the feeling that** something is missing.
→ 동격의 that절이 앞의 the feeling의 내용을 자세히 설명하고 있다.

구문 플러스⁺　동격절을 유도하는 추상명사

동격의 that절은 흔히 fact, idea, news, rumor, view, evidence, feeling 등의 추상명사와 어울려 쓰인다.

the evidence that he stole the necklace
the rumor that the boss will leave the company

B 정답 ③ 89%　　　　　　　　　　2022 9월 학평

해석　위 그래프는 2020년 OECD에서의 원유 수요의 부문별 분포를 보여 준다. 48.6%를 차지하는 도로 교통 부문은 OECD 회원국들에서 가장 큰 원유 수요 부문이었다. 석유화학 부문의 원유 수요 비율은 도로 교통 부문의 원유 수요 비율의 삼 분의 일이었다. 기타 산업 부문과 석유화학 부문 사이의 원유 수요 차이는 항공 부문과 전기 발전 부문 사이의 원유 수요 차이보다 작았다(→컸다). 주거, 상업, 그리고 농업 부문의 원유 수요는 OECD의 총 원유 수요의 9.8%를 차지했는데, 이는 전체 부문 중 네 번째로 컸다. 해상 벙커 부문의 원유 수요 비율은 철도와 국내 수로 부문의 원유 수요 비율의 두 배였다.

해설　기타 산업과 석유화학 부문의 비율 차이(16.2%-12.6%=3.6%p)는 항공, 전기 발전 부문의 비율 차이(4.4%-3%=1.4%p)보다 크다. 즉, ③이 도표의 내용과 일치하지 않는다.

오답 풀이

선택률	오답 풀이
① 1%	도로교통 부문 비율은 48.6%로, 가장 큰 비율을 차지한다.
② 2%	석유화학 부문 비율(16.2%)이 도로 교통 부문 비율(48.6%)의 삼 분의 일이다.
④ 3%	주거, 상업, 농업 부문 비율은 9.8%로, 네 번째이다.
⑤ 3%	해상 벙커 부문 비율(3.6%)은 철도와 국내 수로 부문 비율(1.8%)의 두 배이다.

구문 풀이　5행

The difference in oil demand between the Other industry sector and the Petrochemicals sector **was** smaller than the difference in oil demand between the Aviation sector and the Electricity generation sector.
→ 주어가 긴 문장이다. 동사의 수 일치는 the difference에 해야 한다.

구문 플러스⁺　긴 주어와 수 일치

주어에 관계대명사절 등의 수식이 길게 붙거나, 주어와 동사 사이에 부사구가 길어질 경우, 동사의 수 일치에 특히 유의해야 한다.

The climatic change severely occurring on our planet, which directly influences the trees and other plants, **is** getting worse.

C 정답 ④ 90%　　　　　　　　　　2021 6월 학평

해석　위의 표는 2014년과 2018년, 전세계의 천연가스 생산 상위 7개 국가들을 보여준다. 미국, 러시아, 이란은 2014년과 2018년 모두 상위 3개 천연가스 생산 국가였다. 2014년과 2018년 각각, 러시아와 이란 간의 천연가스 생산량 차이는 4,000억 세제곱미터보다 더 컸다. 비록 캐나다의 천연가스 생산량은 증가했지만 캐나다는 2014년보다 2018년에 낮은 순위를 기록했다. 2014년과 2018년 사이, 중국의 천연가스 생산 증가량은 카타르의 그것의 3배 이상(→미만)이었다. 호주는 2014년 상위 7개 천연가스 생산 국가에 포함되지 않았는데 2018년에 7위에 올랐다.

해설　2014년과 2018년 사이 중국의 천연가스 생산 증가량은 440억 세제곱 미터이고, 카타르의 생산 증가량은 210억 세제곱미터이다. 즉 중국의 생산 증가량이 카타르의 세 배에는 미치지 못하므로 ④가 정답이다.

선택률	오답 풀이
① 1%	미국, 러시아, 이란은 항상 상위 3개 국가였다.
② 3%	러시아와 이란 간의 천연가스 생산량 차이는 4,000억 세제곱미터보다 더 컸다.
③ 3%	캐나다의 경우, 생산량은 증가했지만 순위는 낮아졌다.
⑤ 1%	2014년 리스트에 없던 호주가 2018년에 7위에 올랐다.

구문 풀이 7행

Between 2014 and 2018, the increase in natural gas production in China was **more than three times that** in Qatar.

→ '~의 몇 배'는 <숫자+times+(대)명사구>로 표현한다. times와 (대)명사구 사이에 전치사 of를 쓰지 않음에 주의한다.

구문 플러스+ 배수 표현

'~의 몇 배'를 표현하는 방식에는 <숫자+times+(대)명사구>, <숫자+times+as+형용사/부사+as>, 또는 <숫자+times+비교급+than> 등이 있다. 단, 2배를 표현할 때에는 two times라고 쓰지 않고 twice라고 쓴다.

- This price is **three times the price of the last year**.
- James is **twice as tall as** Lucy.
- I spent **three times more days** on the project **than last year**.

D 정답 ① 91% *2020 11월 학평*

해석 11살 소년 Ryan은 최대한 빨리 집으로 달려갔다. 마침내, 여름 방학이 시작되었다! 그가 집으로 들어갔을 때 그의 엄마는 냉장고 앞에 서서 그를 기다리고 있었다. 그녀는 그에게 가방을 싸라고 말했다. Ryan의 심장이 풍선처럼 날아올랐다. '왜 가방을 싸지? 우리 디즈니랜드라도 가나?' 그는 마지막으로 부모님이 자신을 데리고 휴가를 갔던 때가 (언제인지) 기억나지 않았다. 그의 두 눈이 반짝거렸다. "너는 Tim 삼촌과 Gina 숙모와 함께 여름을 보내게 될 거야." Ryan은 (불만으로) 신음을 냈다. "여름 내내요?" "그래. 여름 내내." 그가 느꼈던 기대감이 순식간에 사라졌다. 끔찍한 3주 내내, 그는 삼촌과 숙모의 농장에서 지내게 될 것이었다. 그는 한숨을 쉬었다.

해설 여름 방학을 맞아 디즈니랜드라도 갈지 기대했던 Ryan이 방학 동안 삼촌네 농장에 있을 거라는 말에 실망했다는 내용이다. 따라서 ① '신난 → 실망한'이 심경 변화로 가장 적절하다.

선택률	보기 해석
② 1%	분노한 → 후회하는
③ 1%	짜증 난 → 만족한
④ 2%	초조한 → 느긋한
⑤ 1%	만족한 → 질투하는

구문 풀이 1행

Ryan, an **eleven-year-old** boy, ran home **as fast as** he **could**.

→ <수사+명사>가 결합되어 복합형용사를 이루면, 수사가 복수(eleven)더라도 명사는 단수형(year)으로 쓴다.

→ <as+원급+as ~ can[could]> 구문은 '최대한 ~한/하게'의 의미이다.

구문 플러스+ 원급비교 관용표현

as+원급+as ~ can[could] = as+원급+as possible

= 최대한 ~한/하게

Answer me **as soon as possible.**
Find out **as much** information **as you can.**

E 정답 ④ 79% *2019 3월 학평*

해석 위 두 원그래프는 2014년의 지역별 자연재해 횟수와 피해액을 보여 준다. 다섯 지역 중 아시아의 자연재해 횟수가 가장 많았으며, 유럽의 비율의 2배가 넘는 36%를 차지했다. 아메리카가 23%를 차지하면서 자연재해 횟수가 두 번째로 많았다. 오세아니아의 자연재해 횟수가 가장 적었으며 아프리카의 자연재해 횟수의 3분의 1도 안 되었다. 아시아의 피해액이 가장 많았으며 아메리카와 유럽을 합친 액수보다 더 많았다(→ 더 적었다). 아프리카가 비록 자연재해 횟수에서는 3위를 차지했지만 피해액은 가장 적었다.

해설 2014년 아메리카와 유럽의 피해액은 각각 5,326억 달러와 2,386억 달러로, 이 둘을 합한 액수는 7,712억 달러인데, 아시아의 피해액은 이보다 적은 7,211억 달러이다. 그러므로 ④에서 more를 less로 고쳐야 한다.

선택률	오답 풀이
① 5%	아시아가 가장 자연재해 횟수가 많다.
② 2%	두 번째로 자연재해의 횟수가 많은 곳은 아메리카이다.
③ 6%	오세아니아는 재해 횟수가 가장 적다.
⑤ 6%	아프리카는 횟수에 비해 피해액이 적다.

구문 풀이 7행

The amount of damage in Asia was the largest and more than the **combined** amount of Americas and Europe.

→ combined는 명사 amount를 수식하는 과거분사이다.

구문 플러스+ 과거분사

<동사+-ed> 형태인 과거분사는 동사의 성질을 가지면서 형용사 역할을 한다. 명사의 앞이나 뒤에서 수식하거나 보어로 쓰이며, 과거분사는 완료나 수동의 의미를 나타낸다.

- This is the **saved** money. (money 앞에서 수식)
- She is a girl **loved** by him. (a girl 뒤에서 수식)
- I had my leg **broken** in the accident. (목적격 보어 역할)

해석 우리 1960년 졸업생들은 중요한 50주년 동창회를 맞아 다시 모일 것이었지만, 나는 오고 가는 여비를 감당할 수 없어서 안타깝게도 동창회에 가지 못할 거라고 나의 네 아이 중 한 명에게 슬프게 얘기했었다. 그러던 어느 날 저녁에 막내딸인 Kelly가 내게 봉투 하나를 건네며 "이거 이따 읽어보세요."라고 말했다. 그 봉투 속 편지는 모든 연령대에서 오래된 우정이 얼마나 중요한지, 그리고 "내 50주년 동창회가 내 인생 단 한 번뿐인 행사이므로" 내가 꼭 "참석해야 한다"고 온통 잔소리하고 있었다. 안에는 Syracuse 왕복 항공권과 약 200달러의 현금이 들어 있었다. 그 편지에는 사 남매 모두가 만나서 나를 동창회에 보내기 위해 자신들의 돈을 모으는 데 동의했다고 쓰여 있었다. "그리고 돈을 갚을 생각조차 하지 마세요!" 나는 (놀라서) 어안이 벙벙해진 채 할 말을 잃고 거기 앉아 있었다. 그리고 나는 눈물을 흘렸다.

해설 여비가 없어 동창회에 가지 못할 줄 알고 아쉬워했던 필자가 자녀들의 도움을 받아 동창회에 갈 수 있게 되자 감격했다는 내용이다. 따라서 ③ '슬픈 → 감동한'이 답으로 적절하다.

오답 풀이

선택률	보기 해석
① 3%	질투하는 → 만족한
② 13%	(당황·공포로) 어쩔 줄 모르는 → 안도한
④ 5%	신난 → 실망한
⑤ 2%	겁에 질린 → 무관심한

구문 풀이 1행

~ **regretfully,** I was going to miss the reunion because I just couldn't afford the trip.

→ regretfully는 문장 전체(I was going to miss ~)를 꾸미는 부사이다.

 플러스 부사의 수식

부사는 동사, 형용사, 다른 부사, 문장 전체를 수식한다. 또한, 준동사(to부정사, 동명사, 분사)도 원칙적으로 부사의 수식을 받는다.

old **enough** to drive (형용사 수식)

Fortunately, we made it on time. (문장 수식)

I advise you to drive **carefully**. (to부정사 수식)

 플러스 심경 파악

문학적 이야기 글을 읽고, 필자 또는 주요 인물의 심경 (변화)을 추론하는 유형이다. 대체로 매우 쉬운 편이다.

① 동사, 형용사, 부사 등 심경이나 분위기를 나타내는 단서 위주로 글을 빠르게 훑듯이 읽는다.

② 심경 변화 유형의 경우, 지문에는 반드시 흐름을 반전시키는 역접어 (however, nevertheless, suddenly 등)가 있다. 이 역접어를 중심으로 글을 전반부와 후반부로 나누고, 키워드를 따로 파악한다.

해석 위 그래프는 2010년에 전통적인 형식만, 다운로드 음악만, 또는 둘 다 소비한 다른 연령 집단의 음악 청취자들의 비율을 보여준다. 15~24세 집단을 제외한 각 연령 집단에서 다운로드 음악만을 들었던 사람들이 최저 비율을 차지했다. 연령 집단의 나이가 많을수록, 두 형식을 모두 들은 사람들의 비율은 점차 낮아졌다. 25~34세 집단에는 전통적인 형식만을 들은 사람들과 다운로드 음악만을 들은 사람들 간의 퍼센트포인트 격차가 다른 연령 집단보다 더 좁았다. 45~54세 집단에서 전통적인 형식만을 들은 사람들이 60퍼센트 이상(→미만)을 차지하며, 나머지 유형의 음악을 들은 사람들보다 수가 더 많았다. 55~64세 연령 집단의 70% 이상은 전통적인 형식만을 들었다.

해설 45~54세 집단에서 전통적인 형식만을 들은 사람들이 54퍼센트이므로 ④가 도표의 내용과 일치하지 않는다.

오답 풀이

선택률	오답 풀이
① 13%	다운로드 음악은 15~24세를 제외하고 최저 비율이다.
② 7%	나이와 반비례로 두 가지 형식으로 음악을 듣는 비율이 낮아졌다.
③ 8%	25~34세에서 두 가지 음악 형식의 비율차가 가장 적다.
⑤ 2%	55~64세는 70퍼센트 이상이 전통적인 형식만 들었다.

구문 풀이 5행

The older the age group was, **the lower** the percentage of those who listened to both was.

→ <the 비교급 ~, the 비교급 …>는 '~할수록 더 …한'의 의미이다.

플러스 도표의 이해

막대 그래프나 선, 원 그래프 등의 정보를 파악하는 유형으로 대부분 도표와 지문 내용이 다른 문장을 찾는 것이다. 아래의 전략으로 해결한다.

① 도표의 제목이나 지문의 첫 문장으로 어떤 것에 대한 내용인지 파악한다. 도표의 비교 항목들도 확인한다.

② 글의 문장을 도표와 하나씩 비교하며 일치 여부를 확인한다. 도표 유형에는 비교급, 최상급, 배수 표현들이 자주 나오므로 미리 알아 둔다.

③ 숫자는 자세하게 계산하지 말고, 상대적으로 더 큰지 적은지 등 대략적으로만 파악한다.

A 정답 ③ 51%
2023 3월 학평

해석 '완벽함이 좋음의 적이 되게 두지 말라'는 표현은 누구나 들어 본 적이 있다. 여러분이 장애물을 극복해서, 여러분의 아이디어가 오랫동안 꿈꿔 왔던 해결책을 기반으로 한 방책이 될 수 있도록 하고 싶다면, 전부 아니면 전무라고 여기는 사고방식을 가져서는 안 된다. 여러분은 기꺼이 여러분의 아이디어를 바꾸고, 다른 사람들이 그 결과에 영향을 미치도록 해야 한다. 결과가 여러분이 원했던 것과 조금 다르거나, 심지어 원했던 것보다 조금 '못해도' 괜찮다고 여겨야 한다. 여러분이 수질 오염 방지법을 추진하고 있다고 가정해 보자. 설령 (결과로) 나타난 것이 여러분이 원했던 만큼 자금을 충분하게 지원받지 못했거나, 여러분이 처음에 이 법안을 고안한 방식과 일치하지 않더라도, 여러분은 힘든 지역의 아이들이 깨끗한 물을 확실히 이용할 수 있게 하는 데 여전히 성공하는 것이다. 중요한 것은 바로 여러분의 아이디어와 노력 덕분에 '그들'이 더 안전하리라는 것이다. 완벽한가? 아니다. 더 해야 할 일이 있는가? 당연하다. 하지만 거의 모든 경우에, 바늘이 앞으로 가게 돕는 것이 전혀 돕지 않는 것보다 훨씬 더 낫다.

해설 완벽하지 않거나 처음 생각한 것과 다르더라도 일단 아이디어를 실행하는 것이 중요하다는 내용이다. 따라서 ③ '상황이 허락하는 한 최대한 차이를 만들어가는 것'이 밑줄 부분의 의미로 적절하다.

오답 풀이

선택률	보기 해석
① 7%	완벽을 찬양하는 데 시간과 돈을 쓰는 것
② 11%	좋은 대의명분을 위해 비용 절감 전략을 제안하는 것
④ 19%	원래 목표를 수정하기 전에 자원을 체크하는 것
⑤ 12%	가난한 어린이들의 교육을 도울 기부금을 모으는 것

구문 풀이 2행

If you want to get over an obstacle **so that** your idea can become the solution-based policy you've long dreamed of, you can't have an all-or-nothing mentality.

→ so that은 여기서 목적(~하도록)의 의미를 나타내는 부사절을 이끈다.

 플러스⁺ 부사절 접속사 so that

① ~하기 위해서, ~하도록 / ② (…해서) ~하다
→ 둘 중 문맥에 맞는 것으로 해석한다.

I bought a new dress **so that** I could wear it to the party.

B 정답 ① 50%
2022 6월 학평

해석 고객들을 즐겁게 하는 데 관심이 있는 기업들에게, 뛰어난 가치와 서비스는 기업 문화 전반의 일부가 된다. 예를 들어, 해마다, 고객 만족이라는 측면에서 Pazano는 서비스업 중 최상위 또는 상위권을 차지

한다. 고객을 만족시키기 위한 그 기업의 열정은 그것의 신조에 요약되어 있고, 이는 그 기업의 고급 호텔이 진정으로 기억될만한 경험을 제공할 것을 약속한다. 고객 중심 기업은 경쟁사 대비 높은 고객 만족을 제공하고자 하지만, 고객 만족을 '최대화'하려고 하지는 않는다. 기업은 가격을 낮추거나 서비스를 증진시킴으로써 고객 만족을 항상 높일 수 있다. 하지만 이것은 더 낮은 이윤으로 이어질지도 모른다. 따라서, 마케팅의 목적은 수익을 내면서 고객 가치를 창출하는 것이다. 이것은 매우 미묘한 균형을 필요로 한다. 즉 마케팅 담당자는 더 많은 고객 가치와 만족을 계속해서 창출해야 하지만, '집을 거저나 다름없이 팔아서는' 안 된다는 것이다.

해설 기업들이 고객 만족을 높일 때, 수익이 나는 선까지만 고객 만족을 높일 수 있다는 내용이다. 따라서 '집을 거저나 다름없이 팔아서는' 안 된다는 것은 ① '기업의 수익성을 위태롭게 (할 정도로 무리)해서는' 안 된다는 의미이다.

오답 풀이

선택률	보기 해석
② 5%	경쟁자의 장점을 간과해서는
③ 10%	기업의 평판을 손상시켜서는
④ 20%	더 많은 고객 불만을 창출해서는
⑤ 15%	고객 지향적인 마케팅을 버려서는

구문 풀이 4행

The company's passion for satisfying customers is summed up in its credo, **which** promises **that** its luxury hotels will deliver a truly memorable experience.

→ 콤마 뒤의 which는 콤마 앞의 its credo에 대해 이어 설명하기 위한 계속적 용법의 관계대명사이고, that은 동사 promise의 목적어절을 이끄는 명사절 접속사이다.

구문 **플러스⁺** 관계대명사 that과 명사절 접속사 that의 구분

관계대명사 that과 명사절 접속사 that의 구분은 뒤따르는 절이 완전한지 여부로 나뉜다.

• I want that shirt **that** is blue.
→ 관계대명사 that (뒤따르는 절이 불완전)
• I didn't know **that** he likes you.
→ 명사절 접속사 that (뒤따르는 절이 완전)

C 정답 ④ 56%
2021 9월 학평

해석 창의적인 팀은 역설적인 특징을 보인다. 그것은 우리가 상호 배타적이거나 모순된다고 가정할 법한 생각과 행동의 경향을 보여준다. 예를 들어, 최고의 작업을 수행하기 위해서는 팀이 해결하려는 문제와 관련된 주제에 대한 깊은 지식과 수반되는 과정의 숙달이 필요하다. 그러나

동시에, 팀에게는 널리 퍼져 있는 지혜나 일을 하는 입증된 방법에 구애받지 않는 신선한 관점이 필요하다. 종종 '초심자의 마음'이라고 불리는 이것은 신참의 관점이다. 즉, 이런 사람들은 호기심 많고, 심지어 장난기 넘치고, 질문이 아무리 순진해 보이더라도 무엇이든 기꺼이 물어보는데, 이것은 자신이 무엇을 모르는지 모르기 때문이다. 따라서 <u>모순되는 특징들을 한데 모으는 것</u>이 새로운 아이디어의 과정을 가속화할 수 있다.

답에 근접하다'라는 숙어인데, 밑줄 친 부분에서는 이것을 colder로 바꾸어 반의어로 썼다.

선택률	보기 해석
② 10%	대중의 비평 때문에 명성을 잃었다
③ 25%	새로운 예술 트렌드를 따르려 하지 않았다
④ 11%	덜 열정적으로 남의 예술 작품을 감상했다
⑤ 22%	자기 자신의 스타일을 만들어 나가기보다 대가의 스타일을 모방했다

구문 풀이 7행

Had Beethoven been able to distinguish an extraordinary from an ordinary work, he would have accepted his composition immediately as a hit.

→ 원래 'If Beethoven had been ~'이었던 가정법 과거완료 종속절에서 if를 생략하고 <Had+주어+p.p. ~> 어순을 썼다.

구문 플러스 가정법 도치

가정법 종속절에서 if가 생략될 때의 3가지 형태
① if S were ~ → Were S ~
② if S had p.p. ~ → Had S p.p. ~
③ if S should+동사원형~ → Should S+동사원형 ~

Were you in my shoes, what would you do?
Should you have any questions, please email me.

F 정답 ① 32%   *2019 11월 학평*

해석 크라우드 펀딩은 프로젝트 자금을 확보하는 새롭고 더 협력적인 방법이다. 그것은 세계 어디서든 가치 있는 대의명분을 위한 기부를 요청하는 것, 그리고 기부자들과 프로젝트 펀딩을 만들고 이후 프로젝트 파트너가 되는 것과 같이 다양한 방법으로 이용될 수 있다. 본질적으로, 크라우드 펀딩은 소셜 네트워킹과 벤처 자본주의의 융합이다. 소셜 네트워킹이 사람들이 서로 의사소통하고 상호작용하는 방식에 관한 전통적인 규칙을 다시 쓴 것과 마찬가지로, 온갖 다양한 형태의 크라우드 펀딩은 미래에 기업과 다른 프로젝트가 자금을 얻는 방식에 관한 규칙을 다시 쓸 잠재력을 가진다. 크라우드 펀딩은 기업 자금 조달의 민주화로 여겨질 수 있다. 자본 조달과 할당을 비교적 소규모의 고정된 소수에 한정하는 대신에, 크라우드 펀딩은 인터넷에 연결된 모든 사람이 인터넷에 접속하는 모든 사람의 집단 지혜와 쌈짓돈에 접근할 수 있게 해준다.

해설 사람들이 소셜 네트워크를 통해 직접 프로젝트를 기획하고 펀딩하는 크라우드 펀딩에 관해 설명하는 글이다. '기업 자금 조달의 민주화'라는 표현은 기존과는 달리 인터넷만 있으면 '대중이 프로젝트 자금 조달에 직접 참여할 수 있다는 의미로 볼 수 있다. 따라서 ① '더 많은 사람들이 사업 자금 조달에 관여할 수 있다.'가 적절하다.

선택률	보기 해석
② 9%	더 많은 사람들이 신제품 개발에 참여할 것이다.
③ 21%	크라우드펀딩은 전통적 방식의 재원 조달을 강화할 수 있다.
④ 31%	크라우드펀딩은 소셜 네트워크가 자금 조달을 용이하게 만들지 못하게 한다.
⑤ 7%	인터넷은 한 회사의 직원들이 서로 소통하도록 돕는다.

구문 풀이 2행

It **can be used** in different ways such as **requesting** donations for a worthy cause anywhere in the world **and generating** funding for a project with the contributors **then becoming** partners in the project.

→ <can be+p.p.>는 조동사 수동태이다.

→ 동명사구 <requesting ~ and generating ~>이 병렬 연결되었다. then becoming은 generating과 한 덩어리로, '창출하고 ~가 되는' 행위가 하나로 취급된다.

구문 플러스 조동사 수동태

조동사 뒤에는 동사원형이 나오므로, 수동태는 <조동사+be p.p.> 형태가 된다.

Answers **can be written or presented** orally.

G 정답 ⑤ 67%   *2019 3월 학평*

해석 신체는 문제를 축적하는 경향이 있으며, 그것은 흔히 하나의 작고 사소해 보이는 불균형에서 시작한다. 이 문제는 또 다른 미묘한 불균형을 유발하고, 그것이 또 다른 불균형을, 그다음 몇 개의 더 많은 불균형을 유발한다. 결국 여러분은 어떤 증상을 갖게 된다. 그것은 마치 일련의 도미노를 한 줄로 세워 놓는 것과 같다. 여러분은 첫 번째 도미노를 쓰러뜨리기만 하면 되는데, 그러면 많은 다른 것들도 또한 쓰러질 것이다. 마지막 도미노를 쓰러뜨린 것은 무엇인가? 분명히, 그것은 그것의 바로 앞 혹은 앞의 앞에 있던 것이 아니라, 첫 번째 도미노이다. 신체도 같은 방식으로 작동한다. 최초의 문제는 흔히 눈에 띄지 않는다. 뒤쪽의 '도미노' 중 몇 개가 쓰러지고 나서야 비로소 좀 더 분명한 단서와 증상이 나타난다. 결국 여러분은 두통, 피로, 또는 우울증, 심지어 질병까지도 얻게 된다. 여러분이 마지막 도미노, 즉 최종 결과인 증상만을 치료하려 한다면, 그 문제의 원인은 해결되지 않는다. 최초의 도미노가 원인, 즉 가장 중요한 문제이다.

해설 신체도 '도미노와 똑같이' 작동한다는 말은 처음 것부터 쓰러지기 시작해 마지막 것까지 쓰러지듯이 '맨 처음의 원인이 있고 그것이 다른 불균형을 계속 낳다가 증상으로 나온다'는 의미와 같다. 따라서 ⑤ '최종 증상은 최초의 사소한 문제에서 생겨난다'가 밑줄 친 부분의 의미로 가장 적절하다.

선택률	보기 해석
① 7%	질병을 치료하는 데 정해진 순서는 없다.

② 8%	사소한 건강 문제는 저절로 해결된다.
③ 7%	여러분은 나이를 먹어가면서 점점 더 무기력해진다.
④ 9%	최종 결과인 증상을 치료하기에 너무 늦은 때란 없다.

구문 풀이 4행

All you need to do is **knock down** the first one and many others will fall too.

→ 주어가 <all+주어 ~ do> 형태로 the only thing의 의미를 나타내면 be동사의 보어 자리에 to를 생략한 원형부정사가 나올 수 있다.

유형 플러스 함축적 의미 추론

글의 전체적인 맥락 속에서 밑줄 친 어구가 의미하는 바를 추론하는 유형이다. 글의 핵심에 관련된 비유적인 표현에 밑줄이 있고, 그 의미를 재진술하는 선택지를 골라야 하는 경우가 대부분이다.

① 글의 핵심 소재와 주제를 잘 파악해야 한다.
② 지문의 밑줄 친 어구를 선택지의 표현으로 바꾸어 써도 기존의 맥락과 의미가 유지되어야 한다.

A 정답 ④ 78%   *2023 6월 학평*

해석 1627년 잉글랜드 Essex주 Black Notley에서 태어난 John Ray는 마을 대장장이의 아들이었다. 16세에 그는 Cambridge 대학교에 들어가서 폭넓게 공부하고 그리스어부터 수학까지 강의를 하다가 1660년에 성직자의 길로 들어섰다. 1650년 병에서 회복하고자 그는 자연을 산책하기 시작했고, 식물학에 대한 관심을 키웠다. 부유한 학생이자 후원자였던 Francis Willughby와 함께 Ray는 1660년대에 영국과 유럽을 여행하며 식물과 동물을 연구하고 수집했다. 그는 1673년 Margaret Oakley와 결혼했고, Willughby 집안을 떠난 뒤에는 77세까지 Black Notley에서 조용히 살았다. 그는 동식물 목록을 만들기 위해 표본을 연구하면서 말년을 보냈다. 그는 식물과 그 형태, 기능뿐만 아니라 신학과 자기 여행에 관한 20편 이상의 저서를 썼다.

해설 'Accompanied by his wealthy student and supporter Francis Willughby, ~'에 따르면, John Ray의 유럽 여행에는 Francis Willughby가 동행했다. 따라서 내용과 일치하지 않는 것은 ④이다.

오답 풀이

선택률	오답 풀이
① 4%	~ was the son of the village blacksmith.
② 6%	At 16, he went to Cambridge University, ~ before joining the priesthood in 1660.
③ 6%	To recover from an illness in 1650, he had taken to nature walks ~
⑤ 4%	He spent his later years studying samples in order to assemble plant and animal catalogues.

구문 풀이 11행

He wrote more than twenty works on theology and his travels, **as well as** on plants and their form and function.

→ <A as well as B(B뿐 아니라 A도)> 구문으로, A와 B가 <on+명사> 형태로 병렬 연결되었다.

구문 플러스⁺ A as well as B

• <A as well as B>의 A, B는 문법적 성격이 같다.
• <A as well as B>가 주어 자리에 오면, 동사는 A에 수 일치한다.

I enjoy exploring the city by bike **as well as** on foot. → 전치사구 병렬
Tim, **as well as** other boys, enjoys playing soccer.
A(단수)   B(복수)   동사(단수)

B 정답 ⑤ 92%   *2022 9월 학평*

해석 Carl-Gustaf Rossby는 Bergen 대학에서 노르웨이 기상학자인 Vilhelm Bjerknes와 함께 일했던 저명한 스칸디나비아 연구자들 중 한 명이었다. Stockholm에서 성장하면서, Rossby는 전통적인 교육을 받았

다. 그는 1918년에 University of Stockholm에서 수리 물리학 학위를 받았지만, Bjerknes의 강의를 듣고 나서, 짐작하건대 Stockholm에 지루함을 느껴, Bergen에 새로 설립된 지구 물리학 연구소로 옮겼다. 1925년에 Rossby는 스웨덴-미국 재단으로부터 장학금을 받아 미국으로 갔고, 그곳에서 미국 기상국에 합류했다. 일기 예보에 대한 그의 실질적인 경험을 일부 바탕으로 하여, Rossby는 고온 기단과 저온 기단 사이의 경계에서 발생하는 사이클론 순환을 설명하는 "polar front theory"의 지지자가 되었다. 1947년에 Rossby는 University of Stockholm에 그를 위해 마련된 기상 연구소장 자리를 받아들였고, 10년 후 생을 마감할 때까지 그곳에서 재직했다.

해설 마지막 문장에 따르면, Rossby는 University of Stockholm에 마련된 직책을 수락했으므로 ⑤가 일치하지 않는다.

오답 풀이

선택률	오답 풀이
① 1%	While growing up in Stockholm, Rossby received a traditional education.
② 1%	He earned a degree in mathematical physics at the University of Stockholm
③ 3%	In 1925, Rossby received a scholarship
④ 1%	Rossby had become a supporter of the "polar front theory,"

구문 풀이 4행

He earned a degree in mathematical physics at the University of Stockholm in 1918, but **after hearing a lecture by Bjerknes**, and **apparently bored with Stockholm**, he moved to the newly established Geophysical Institute in Bergen.

→ 분사구문 after ~ Bjerknes와 apparently ~ Stockholm이 and로 병렬 연결되고 있다. 분사구문의 주어는 주절의 주어와 같은 he이고, he와의 능·수동 관계에 따라 hearing은 능동태, bored는 수동태로 쓰였다.

구문 플러스⁺ 분사구문의 능·수동

<접속사+주어+동사>의 부사절을 분사구문으로 나타낼 때, 주어와 동사의 능·수동 관계에 따라 분사를 현재분사 혹은 과거분사의 형태로 쓴다.

• Because **she had** no food to eat, she went to the supermarket.
  → **Having** no food to eat, she went to the supermarket.
  현재분사(능동)
• As **he was encouraged** to do what he wants, he applied for the job.
  → **Encouraged** to do what he wants, he applied for the job.
  과거분사(수동)

C 정답 ③ 93%   *2021 3월 학평*

해석 Ingrid Bergman은 1915년 8월 29일에 스웨덴의 스톡홀름에서

태어났다. 그녀의 어머니는 독일인이었고 아버지는 스웨덴인이었다. 그녀의 어머니는 그녀가 세 살 때 돌아가셨고, 아버지는 그녀가 열두 살 때 돌아가셨다. 결국 그녀는 Uncle Otto와 Aunt Hulda에 의해 키워졌다. 그녀는 어릴 때부터 연기에 관심이 있었다. 그녀가 열일곱 살 때 스톡홀름에 있는 Royal Dramatic Theater School에 다녔다. 그녀는 연극으로 데뷔했지만 영화계에서 일하는 데 더 관심이 있었다. 1940년대 초에 그녀는 할리우드에서 스타의 지위를 얻었고 영화의 여주인공으로 많은 역할을 맡았다. Bergman은 굉장한 연기 재능과 천사 같은 자연미와 영화에서 최상의 것을 얻으려고 기꺼이 열심히 일하려는 태도를 가진 것으로 여겨졌다. 그녀는 다섯 개의 언어에 유창했고 다양한 영화, 연극, 그리고 TV 작품에 출연했다.

해설 Bergman은 연극을 통해 데뷔했으나 영화에 더 관심이 있었으므로 ③이 불일치하는 내용이다.

오답 풀이

선택률	오답 풀이
① 1%	Her mother was German and her father Swedish.
② 1%	When she was 17, she attended the Royal Dramatic Theater School
④ 1%	In the early 1940s, she gained star status in Hollywood
⑤ 1%	She was fluent in five languages

구문 풀이 2행

Her mother was German **and** her father **(was)** Swedish.
→ 등위접속사 and 뒤에서 중복되는 동사 was를 생략했다.

구문 **플러스⁺** 등위접속사 생략 구문

등위접속사 and, or, but, so 뒤에서 앞말과의 중복을 피하기 위해 뒷말 일부를 생략하기도 한다.

The spices were borrowed from India, **and** tomatoes **(were borrowed)** from South America.

D 정답 ③ 85% *2020 3월 학평*

해석 네덜란드의 수학자이자 천문학자인 Christiaan Huygens는 1629년 헤이그에서 태어났다. 그는 대학에서 법과 수학을 공부했고, 그런 후에 처음에는 수학에서, 그다음 광학에서 망원경을 연구하고 본인만의 렌즈를 갈면서 상당 기간을 자기 연구에 헌신했다. Huygens는 영국을 몇 차례 방문했고, 1689년에 아이작 뉴턴을 만났다. 빛에 관한 연구 외에도 Huygens는 힘과 운동을 연구했으나, 뉴턴의 만유인력 법칙을 받아들이지 않았다. Huygens의 광범위한 업적에는 시계추에 대한 그의 연구의 결과물인, 당대의 가장 정확한 시계 중 몇몇이 포함되었다. 자신의 망원경을 사용하여 수행된 그의 천문학 연구에는 토성의 위성 중 가장 큰 타이탄의 발견과 토성의 고리에 대한 최초의 정확한 기술이 포함되었다.

해설 Huygens는 뉴턴의 만유인력 법칙을 받아들이지 않았다고 하므로 ③이 일치하지 않는다.

오답 풀이

선택률	오답 풀이
① 4%	studied law and mathematics at his university
② 3%	met Isaac Newton in 1689
④ 3%	Huygens' wide-ranging achievements included some of the most accurate clocks of his time
⑤ 2%	His astronomical work, carried out using his own telescopes

구문 풀이 9행

His astronomical work, **carried out using his own telescopes**, included the discovery of Titan, the largest of Saturn's moons, and the first correct description of Saturn's rings.

→ carried out은 분사로, 앞에 which was가 생략된 것으로 볼 수 있다.

구문 **플러스⁺** 〈주격 관계대명사+be동사〉 생략

관계대명사절이 주로 수동태나 진행형일 때 〈주격 관계대명사+be동사〉는 생략되곤 한다. 원칙적으로 주격 관계대명사를 단독 생략하지는 않는다.

He worked at the store **(which is) located** next to the City Hall.
which만 생략은 X

E 정답 ④ 85% *2019 3월 학평*

해석 Alexander Young Jackson(모든 사람들이 그를 A. Y.라고 불렀다)은 1882년에 Montreal의 한 가난한 가정에서 태어났다. 그가 어렸을 때 그의 아버지는 그들을 저버렸고, A. Y.는 12살 때 그의 형제와 자매를 부양하는 것을 돕기 위해 일을 해야만 했다. 인쇄소에서 일을 하면서 그는 미술에 관심을 가지게 되었고, 신선하고 새로운 방식으로 풍경화를 그리기 시작했다. 기차로 Ontario 북부를 횡단하는 여행을 하면서, A. Y.와 몇 명의 다른 화가들은 그들이 보는 모든 것을 그렸다. 자칭 'Group of Seven'은 여행의 결과물들을 한데 모아 1920년에 Toronto에서 미술 전시회를 열었다. 그 전시회에서 그들의 그림은 '미쳐버린 예술'이라고 호되게 비판을 받았다. 그러나 그는 계속 그림을 그리고, 여행을 하고, 전시회를 열었고, 1974년 82세의 나이로 사망할 무렵에 A. Y. Jackson은 천재 화가이자 현대 풍경화의 개척자로 인정받았다.

해설 Toronto에서 한 A. Y. Jackson의 전시는 최악의 혹평을 받았으므로 ④가 불일치하는 내용이다.

오답 풀이

선택률	오답 풀이
① 2%	was born to a poor family in Montreal in 1882
② 2%	Working in a print shop, he became interested in art
③ 2%	Traveling by train across northern Ontario
⑤ 6%	was acknowledged as a painting genius and a pioneer of modern landscape art

구문 풀이 9행

That was the show **where their paintings were severely**

criticized as "art gone mad."

→ 관계부사는 접속사와 부사 역할을 하는 것으로, where는 장소나 공간을 대신한다.

 플러스 관계부사 where

관계부사 where는 문장을 연결하며 장소나 공간을 대신하고, <전치사+관계대명사>와 바꿔쓸 수 있다.

This is the hotel **where** we stayed.
= This is the hotel **at which** we stayed.

F 정답 ④ 87% *2018 9월 학평*

해석 Shah Rukh Khan은 인도의 영화배우이자 제작자이다. Khan은 대학에서 경제학을 공부했지만 Delhi의 Theatre Action Group에서 많은 시간을 보냈고, 그곳에서 연기를 공부했다. Bollywood에서 전업으로 일을 하기 위해 Delhi에서 Mumbai로 이주했고, 이는 그에게 큰 명성을 가져다주었다. "King of Bollywood" 또는 "King Khan"으로 매체에서 불리면서 그는 80편이 넘는 Bollywood 영화에 출연했다. 2007년에 프랑스 정부는 영화에 대한 공로로 Khan에게 the Order of Arts and Letters를 수여하였다. 그는 정기적으로 인도 문화에서 가장 영향력 있는 인물들 목록에 등재되며, 2008년에는 세계에서 가장 영향력 있는 인물 50인 중 한 명으로 선정되었다. Khan의 박애주의적인 노력은 의료 서비스와 재난 구호를 제공해왔으며, 그는 2011년에 아동 교육에 대한 후원으로 UNESCO에서 Pyramide con Marni 상을 받았다.

해설 Khan이 세계에서 가장 영향력 있는 인물 50인 중 한 명으로 선정된 것은 2008년이다. 따라서 글의 내용과 일치하지 않는 것은 ④ '2007년에 세계에서 가장 영향력 있는 50인 중 한 명으로 선정되었다.'이다.

오답 풀이

선택률	오답 풀이
① 3%	Shah Rukh Khan is an Indian film actor and producer.
② 3%	Khan studied economics in college
③ 2%	he has appeared in more than 80 Bollywood films
⑤ 5%	he was honored with UNESCO's Pyramide con Marni award in 2011 for his support of children's education

구문 풀이 8행

He is regularly featured on lists of the most influential people in Indian culture, and in 2008, he was chosen as **one of the 50 most powerful people** in the world.

→ <one of+the 최상급+복수명사>는 '가장 ~한 것들 중 하나'라는 표현이다.

 플러스 one of+the 최상급+복수명사

one of는 '~ 중에 하나'의 의미로 뒤에 복수명사가 온다. 그러나 <one of+the 최상급+복수명사>가 주어로 쓰이면 동사는 단수로 수 일치시킨다.

• This is **one of** the most expensive **books** in our store.
• **One of** the smartest **people** in the world **is** Albert Einstein.

G 정답 ⑤ 78% *2016 6월 학평*

해석 tarsier는 쥐보다 그다지 크지 않은 작은 영장류이다. 전체 몸통보다 훨씬 더 긴 가는 꼬리 때문에 쥐와의 유사성이 더욱 부각된다. 모든 tarsier는 완전히 야행성이고 이러한 생활 방식을 위하여 많은 뛰어난 신체적 적응 장치들을 가지고 있다. 그들은 뛰어난 청력을 가지고 있다. tarsier는 또한 몸 크기에 비해 굉장히 큰 눈을 가지고 있는데 눈이 얼굴 크기의 약 1/4을 차지한다. tarsier의 서식지는 보통 열대 우림 지역이며, 그들은 빽빽한 대나무 숲에서 발견된다. 낮 동안에는 나무 둥치의 구멍이나 어둡고 두꺼운 엉킨 초목에 누워 있기도 한다. 밤에는 벌레, 거미, 그리고 작은 도마뱀을 사냥한다. tarsier는 머리를 최소 180도로 돌릴 수 있는데, 이는 먹이를 찾기 위한 넓은 시야를 확보해 준다.

해설 주어진 지문에 따르면, tarsier는 벌레, 거미 그리고 작은 도마뱀을 사냥한다고 하므로, 채식 위주의 먹잇감을 찾는다는 ⑤가 내용과 일치하지 않는다.

오답 풀이

선택률	오답 풀이
① 8%	their thin tail, which is much longer than their overall body length
② 5%	have an excellent sense of hearing
③ 5%	their eyes make up nearly one-fourth the size of their faces
④ 4%	The habitat of the tarsier is generally tropical rain forest

구문 풀이 3행

All tarsiers are completely nocturnal and have **a number of remarkable physical adaptations** for this lifestyle.

→ <a number of+복수명사(많은 ~)>이다.

 플러스 a number of vs. the number of

• a number of+복수명사: 많은 ~ → 복수 취급
• the number of+복수명사: ~의 수 → 단수 취급

A number of students these days **report** loneliness.
The number of students suffering from loneliness **is** increasing.

유형 **플러스** 내용 (불)일치

글의 세부적인 정보가 선택지와 일치 또는 불일치하는지를 판단하는 유형이다. 다음과 같은 전략으로 해결한다.

① 글의 도입부에서 중심 소재가 무엇인지 빠르게 파악한다.
② 선택지를 먼저 훑어보고 지문에서 어떤 정보를 확인해야 하는지 확인한다.
③ 지문과 선택지의 순서는 동일하기 때문에, 선택지와 지문의 내용을 순서대로 꼼꼼하게 대조한다.

A 정답 ③ 41% *2023 3월 학평*

해석 Robert Blattberg와 Steven Hoch는 변화하는 환경에서 일관성이 항상 장점인지가 분명하지 않다는 것과, 인간이 판단하는 것의 이점 중 하나는 변화를 감지하는 능력이라는 것에 주목했다. 따라서 변화하는 환경에서는 인간의 판단과 통계 모형을 결합하는 것이 유리할 수 있다. Blattberg와 Hoch는 슈퍼마켓 관리자들에게 특정한 제품에 대한 수요를 예측하게 한 다음, 이 판단을 지난 데이터에 근거한 통계 모형의 예측과 평균을 내어 종합적인 예측을 생성해 봄으로써 이러한 가능성을 조사했다. (그들의) 논리는 통계 모형들은 변동 없는 조건을 부정하기(→ 가정하기) 때문에, 경쟁자들이 취한 행동이나 신제품의 도입과 같은 새로운 사건이 수요에 미치는 영향을 설명할 수 없다는 것이었다. 그러나 인간은 이러한 새로운 요인들을 자신들의 판단에 통합할 수 있다. 종합된 것, 즉 인간의 판단과 통계 모형의 평균이 통계 모델이나 관리자들이 단독으로 처리하는 것보다 더 정확하다는 것이 증명되었다.

해설 통계 모형은 새로운 사건이 수요에 미치는 영향을 설명하지 못한다는 내용으로 보아, 인간과 달리 '변화를 감지하기' 어렵다는 것을 알 수 있다. 이는 통계 모형이 기본적으로 변동 없는 상황을 '부인하는' 것이 아니라 '전제하기' 때문이므로, ③ deny를 assume으로 고쳐야 문맥상 옳다.

오답 풀이

선택률	보기 해석
① 7%	advantageous(유리한)
② 9%	past(지난)
④ 36%	incorporate(통합하다)
⑤ 7%	accurate(정확한)

구문 풀이 13행

The composite — or average of human judgments and statistical models — **proved to be more accurate** than either the statistical models or the managers working alone.
→ <prove to be+형용사> 형태의 2형식 구문이다.

구문 플러스 prove 2형식

2형식 동사 prove(~라고 판명되다)는 <(to be)+형용사>를 보어로 취한다.
The rumor proved **(to be) true**.

B 정답 ⑤ 30% *2022 3월 학평*

해석 정상 과학은 정확히 무엇을 포함하는가? Thomas Kuhn에 따르면, 그것은 주로 '문제 해결'이라는 문제이다. 패러다임이 아무리 성공적이더라도, 그것은 항상 특정한 문제들, 즉 그것이 쉽게 수용할 수 없는 현상이나 이론의 예측과 실험적 사실 사이의 불일치에 부딪힐 것이다. 정상 과학자들의 일은, 패러다임에 가능한 한 변화를 거의 주지 않으면서 이러한 사소한 문제들을 제거하려고 노력하는 것이다. 그래서 정상 과학은 보수적인 활동으로, 그것을 실행하는 사람은 극히 중대한 발견을 하고자 노력하고 있지 않고, 오히려 단지 현존하는 패러다임을 발전시키고 확장하려는 것이다. Kuhn의 말로 하자면, 정상 과학은 '사실이나 이론의 참신함을 목표로 하지 않으며, 성공적일 때에는 찾아내는 것이 없다.' 무엇보다도 Kuhn은 정상 과학자들이 패러다임을 '시험'하려 노력하지 않는다는 것을 강조했다. 오히려 그들은 패러다임을 의심하지 않고 받아들이고, 그것이 설정한 한계 안에서 자신의 연구를 수행한다. 만약 정상 과학자가 패러다임에 부합하는(→ 상충하는) 실험 결과를 얻는다면, 그들은 보통 자신의 실험 기술에 결함이 있는 것으로 여기고, 패러다임이 틀린 것은 아니라고 여길 것이다.

해설 과학자가 본인의 실험 기술을 탓하는 것은 실험 결과가 기존 패러다임과 일치하지 '않아야' 일어날 수 있는 상황이다. 따라서 ⑤ '부합하는'은 적절하지 않다. (과학자의 생각: 기존 패러다임에 맞는 실험 결과가 나와야 하는데 그렇지 않은 것을 보니, 내가 기술적으로 무언가 잘못했구나! 패러다임은 잘못되었을 리가 없으니까.)

오답 풀이

선택률	보기 해석
① 5%	encounter(부딪히다)
② 16%	eliminate(제거하다)
③ 15%	conservative(보수적인)
④ 32%	unquestioningly(의심하지 않고)

구문 풀이 10행

In Kuhn's words, 'normal science does not aim at novelties of fact or theory, and **(when successful)** finds none'.
→ 'when (it is) successful'이라는 부사절이 and 뒤 동사인 finds 앞에 삽입되어 있다.

구문 플러스 삽입구문

독립적인 부사 같은 역할을 하며, 문장 앞이나 중간에 콤마로 삽입될 때가 있다. (콤마가 생략되기도 함)

They are, **as far as I know**, unreliable people.
(그들은 내가 아는 한 못 미더운 사람들이다.)

C 정답 ④ 49% *2021 6월 학평*

해석 사진이 생생한 색으로 되어 있지 않았던 시기로 돌아가 보자. 그 기간 동안, 사람들은 오늘날 우리처럼 사진을 "흑백 사진"이라고 부르기보다는 "사진"이라고 불렀다. 색의 가능성은 존재하지 않았고, 따라서 "흑백"이라는 형용사를 삽입하는 것은 불필요했다. 하지만, 우리가 컬러 사진의 존재 전에 "흑백"이라는 어구를 포함시켰다고 가정해 보자. 그 현실을 강조함으로써, 우리는 현재의 한계를 의식하게 되고, 따라서 새로운 가능성과 잠재적 기회에 마음을 연다. 제1차 세계대전은 우리가 제2차 세계대전에 깊이 휘말린 후에야 비로소 그 이름이 붙여졌다. 1940년대의 끔찍한 시기 이전에, 제1차 세계대전은 단순히 "대전쟁" 또는, 더 나쁘게는, "모든 전쟁을 끝내는 전쟁"이라고 불렸다. 만약 우리가 1918년으로 돌아가 그것을 "제1차 세계대전"이라고 불렀더라면 어땠을까? 그러한 명칭은 두 번째 세계적 충돌의 가능성을 정부와 개인에게 <u>예측할 수 없는</u>(→ 더 큰) 현실로 만들었을지도 모른다. 우리가 그것들을 명시적으로 인지했을 때, 우리는 문제들을 의식하게 된다.

해설 1918년에 이미 "제1차 세계대전"이라는 명칭을 사용했다면 제2차 세계대전 발발의 가능성을 의식하게 되었을 것이라는 내용이므로 ④ '예측할 수 없는'은 적절하지 않다.

오답 풀이

선택률	보기 해석
① 10%	unnecessary(불필요한)
② 12%	highlight(강조하다)
③ 18%	after(이후에)
⑤ 9%	identify(인지하다)

구문 풀이 12행

What if we **had called** it "World War I" back in 1918?
→ What if는 '~라면 어떨까?'라는 뜻으로, 여기서는 과거완료 시제와 결합해 과거 상황의 반대를 가정하고 있다.

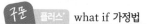

what if 가정법

① what if+주어+과거시제 ~?
  : (현재 ~하지 않지만) ~한다면 어떨까?
② what if+주어+had p.p. ~?
  : (과거에 ~하지 않았지만) ~했다면 어땠을까?

What if we **lost** the game?
우리가 혹시 경기에 지면 어떡하지?
What if you **had accepted** the offer?
네가 그 제안을 만일 받아들였다면 어땠을까?
cf. What if the rumor **is** true? → 직설법
  (사실인지 아닌지 모르는 상황)

D 정답 ③ 50% *2020 6월 학평*

해석 갑작스러운 성공이나 상금은 아주 위험할 수 있다. 신경학적으로 흥분과 에너지의 강력한 분출을 유발하는 화학물질들이 뇌에서 분비되고, 이 경험을 반복하고자 하는 욕구로 이어진다. 그것이 어떤 종류의 중독 또는 광적 행동의 출발점일 수 있다. 또한, 이익이 빨리 얻어질 때, 우리는 진정한 성공이 정말 지속되기 위해서는 노력을 통해야 한다는 기본적인 지혜를 보지 못하는 경향이 있다. 우리는 그처럼 <u>어렵게 얻은</u>(→갑작스러운) 이익에 있어 운이 하는 역할을 고려하지 않는다. 우리는 그만큼의 돈이나 관심을 얻어 느끼는 그 황홀감을 되찾기 위해 계속해서 시도한다. 우리는 우월감의 감정을 느낀다. 우리는 특히 우리에게 경고를 하려고 하는 사람에게 저항하고, 그들은 이해하지 못한다고 스스로에게 이

야기한다. 이것은 지속될 수 없기 때문에 우리는 더욱 큰 고통이 되는 필연적인 추락을 경험하고, 그것은 사이클의 침체기로 이어진다. 도박꾼들이 가장 이러기 쉽지만, 이것은 거품 경제일 때의 사업가들과 대중으로부터 갑작스러운 관심을 얻은 사람들에게도 똑같이 적용된다.

해설 노력을 통해 힘들게 얻은 진정한 성공이 아니라 운이 좋아 쉽게 얻은 이익임에도 불구하고 운의 역할(기여도)을 고려하지 않음을 문제 삼는 것이므로 ③ '어렵게 얻은'은 적절하지 않다.

오답 풀이

선택률	보기 해석
① 6%	repeat(반복하다)
② 14%	lose(잃다)
④ 18%	resistant(저항하는)
⑤ 9%	fall(추락)

구문 풀이 11행

Because this cannot be sustained, we experience an inevitable fall ~
→ 이유를 나타내는 because는 뒤에 주어, 동사가 오는 접속사이다. 같은 의미의 전치사인 because of와 구별해 둔다.

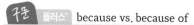

because vs. because of

because와 because of는 둘 다 이유를 나타내지만 because of 뒤에는 명사(구)가, because 뒤에는 절이 온다.

He couldn't finish his work **because of** his laziness.
→ He couldn't finish his work **because** he was lazy.

E 정답 ④ 39% *2019 9월 학평*

해석 언론의 자유와 종교적 관용의 옹호자였던 Voltaire는 논란이 많았던 인물이었다. 예를 들어 그는 "나는 여러분이 하는 말을 싫어하지만 그것을 말할 여러분의 권리를 사력을 다해 옹호할 것이다."라고 말했다고 여겨지는데, 그것은 여러분이 경멸하는 의견조차도 들어볼 만하다는 생각에 대한 강력한 변론이었다. 하지만 18세기 유럽에서는 가톨릭교회가 무엇이 출판될 수 있는지를 엄격히 통제하였다. Voltaire의 많은 희곡과 책이 검열을 받았고 공개적으로 불태워졌으며, 세력이 있는 귀족을 모욕했기 때문에 파리의 Bastille 감옥에 수감되기까지 하였다. 하지만 이 중 어떤 것도 그가 그의 주변 사람들의 편견과 가식에 도전하는 것을 멈추게 하지 못했다. 그의 철학 단편 소설인 <Candide>에서, 그는 당대의 다른 사상가들이 표명했던 인류와 우주에 대한 종교적인 낙관론을 완전히 <u>지지했고</u>(→훼손했고), 이를 매우 재미있는 방식으로 하여 그 책은 즉시 베스트셀러가 되었다. 현명하게도, Voltaire는 속표지에서 자신의 이름을 지웠는데, 만약 그렇지 않았다면 그 책의 출판은 종교적 신념을 조롱한 이유로 다시 그를 감옥에 갇히게 했을지도 모른다.

해설 Voltaire는 당시 종교적인 낙관론과 반대에 있었기 때문에 문맥상 ④ '지지한다'는 적절하지 않다.

오답 풀이

선택률	보기 해석
① 9%	defense(변론)
② 7%	control(통제하다)
③ 16%	insult(모욕하다)
⑤ 27%	off(없어져)

구문 풀이 15행

Wisely, Voltaire left his name off the title page, **otherwise** its publication **would have landed** him in prison again ~

→ if절 대신 otherwise가 가정을 나타내고 그 뒤에 주절이 나온 가정법 과거완료이다.

구문 플러스' 가정법 과거완료

일반적으로 가정법 과거완료는 <if+주어+had+p.p., ~ would/could+ have p.p.>로 나타내는데, if절 대신 다른 표현이 올 수도 있다.

She studied hard; **otherwise**, she **would have failed**.
= if she hadn't studied hard

F 정답 ① 37% *2018 9월 학평*

해석 사회 심리학의 한 현상인 Pratfall Effect는 한 개인의 인지된 매력도가 그 사람이 실수를 한 후에 그 사람의 인지된 능력에 따라 증가 또는 감소한다고 말한다. 유명 인사들은 일반적으로 능력 있는 사람으로 여겨지고 특정한 측면에서 종종 흠이 없고 완벽하다고도 보이기 때문에, 실수를 저지르는 것은 그 사람의 인간미를 다른 사람들에게 사랑스럽게 만들 것이다. 기본적으로 실수를 전혀 저지르지 않는 사람들은 이따금 실수를 저지르는 사람들에 비해 덜 매력적이거나 덜 호감을 주는 것으로 인지된다. 완벽성, 혹은 그 자질을 개인들에게 귀속하는 것은 일반 대중들이 (자신과) 관련지을 수 없는 인지된 거리감을 만들며 실수를 전혀 저지르지 않는 사람들을 덜 매력적이고 덜 호감이 가는 것으로 인지되게 만든다. 하지만 이것은 또한 정반대의 효과도 가지는데, 인지된 평균 혹은 그 이하의 능력을 가진 사람이 실수를 저지른다면, 그 사람은 다른 사람들에게 덜 매력적이고 호감일 것이다.

해설 개인의 인지된(perceived) 능력에 따라 실수를 한 뒤 그 개인에 대한 평가가 달라진다는 내용의 글이다. 실수를 전혀 하지 않는 완벽한 사람은 대중들과 거리감을 만들어(creates)내며, 반대로 유능하지 않은 이가 실수를 하면 그들을 덜(less) 매력적으로 만든다는 내용이다. 따라서 정답으로는 ①이 가장 적절하다.

오답 풀이

선택률	보기 해석
② 11%	perceived(인지된), narrows(좁히다), more(더)
③ 41%	perceived(인지된), creates(만들다), more(더)
④ 5%	hidden(숨겨진), creates(만들다), less(덜)
⑤ 3%	hidden(숨겨진), narrows(좁히다), less(덜)

구문 풀이 12행

However, this can also have the opposite effect — **if** a perceived average or less than average competent person **makes** a mistake, he or she will be less attractive and likable to others.

→ 접속사 if가 이끄는 부사절이라서 미래를 현재시제(makes)로 나타냈다.

구문 플러스' 미래시제를 대신해 쓰이는 현재시제

시간과 조건의 부사절에서는 현재시제가 미래를 대신한다.

If it **rains** tomorrow. we won't be able to go on a picnic.
접속사(조건)

G 정답 ② 57% *2017 9월 학평*

해석 Dworkin은 어떤 한 종류의 기회의 평등에 관한 고전적 주장을 제시한다. Dworkin의 관점에서 정의는 한 사람의 운명이 운이 아닌 그 사람의 통제 내에 있는 것들에 의해 결정되는 것을 요구한다. 행복에 있어서의 차이가 개인의 통제 밖에 있는 환경에 의해 결정된다면, 그 차이는 불공평하다. 이 주장에 따르면, 개인의 선택이나 취향의 차이에 의해 만들어진 행복의 불평등은 허용 가능하다. 그러나 우리는 개인의 책임이 아니면서 개인이 자신이 중요하게 여기는 것을 성취하지 못하게 막는 요소에 의해 만들어지는 행복의 불평등을 제거하기 위해 노력해야 한다. 우리는 기회의 평등 또는 기본적인 자원에의 접근의 평등을 보장함으로써 그렇게 한다.

해설 글에 따르면, 행복이 운이라는 외부적인 환경에 좌우된다면 그것은 불공평하지만(unjust) 개인의 선택일 때에는 불평등이 허용 가능하다(acceptable). 따라서 기회의 평등을 보장함으로써(ensuring) 외부적 요인에 의한 행복의 불평등을 개선해야 한다. 따라서 정답으로는 ②가 가장 적절하다.

오답 풀이

선택률	보기 해석
① 9%	fair(공평한), acceptable(허용 가능한), neglecting(무시함)
③ 15%	unjust(불공평한), intolerable(참을 수 없는), ensuring(보장함)
④ 4%	fair(공평한), intolerable(참을 수 없는), neglecting(무시함)
⑤ 13%	unjust(불공평한), acceptable(허용 가능한), neglecting(무시함)

구문 풀이 2행

From Dworkin's view, justice **requires that** a person's fate **be determined** by things that are within that person's control, not by luck.

→ 주장, 요구, 명령, 제안의 동사 뒤에 나오는 목적절이 '~해야 한다'라는 당위의 의미를 나타내면, that절 동사 자리에 <(should)+동사원형>이 쓰인다. 여기서도 require(요구하다) 뒤의 that절이 '~해야 한다'는 의미이므로 (should) be determined 형태가 왔다.

구문 플러스⁺ that 목적절의 should 생략

주장 - insist
요구 - request, ask, demand
명령 - command, order   + that S **(should) V**
제안 - suggest, propose   ~해야 하다
충고 - recommend, advise

She **requested** that the meeting **be rescheduled**.
The doctor **advised** that he **not smoke**.

 유형 플러스⁺ 어휘의 이해

어휘의 이해 문제는 짝지어진 두 개의 반의어나 철자가 유사한 어휘 세 쌍 중 적절한 것을 고르는 유형과 밑줄 친 다섯 개의 어휘 중 문맥에 맞지 않는 것을 고르는 유형으로 출제된다. 최근에는 후자가 압도적으로 많이 출제된다.

① 짝지어진 어휘가 반의어인지, 철자가 비슷한 것인지 먼저 살펴본다. 반의어 공부를 평소에 해 놓으면 도움이 된다.
② 밑줄 친 어휘 중 고르는 문제는 주어진 어휘와 반대되는 의미의 단어를 넣어보고 흐름이 매끄러운지 확인한다.

A 정답 ④ 39% — 2023 6월 학평

해석 연구 심리학자들은 종종 '자기 보고 데이터'로 작업을 하는데, 이는 자신의 행동에 대한 참가자들의 구두 설명으로 구성되어 있다. 변인을 측정하기 위해 설문지, 면접 또는 성격 목록이 사용될 때마다 여기 해당한다. 자기 보고 방법은 꽤 유용할 수 있다. 이것은 사람들이 자신을 풀타임으로 관찰할 수 있는 독특한 기회를 갖는다는 사실을 이용한다. 그러나, 자기 보고는 몇 가지 종류의 왜곡으로 오염될 수 있다. 이러한 왜곡 중 가장 문제가 되는 하나는 사회적 바람직성 편향인데, 이것은 자신에 관한 질문에 사회적으로 용인되는 답을 제공하는 경향이다. 이러한 편향에 영향을 받은 피실험자들은 특히 민감한 문제에 관해 질문받을 때 호의적인 인상을 만들기 위해 추가로 노력한다. 예를 들어 설문 조사 응답자들 중 많은 수가 사실은 하지 않았다고 밝혀도 될 때 선거에서 투표했다고 하거나 자선 단체에 기부했다고 보고할 것이다.

해설 ④의 주어 subjects는 문맥상 민감한 문제에 관해 '질문을 받는' 대상이다. 따라서 능동태 동사 ask 대신 수동태 동사 are asked를 써야 한다.

오답 풀이

선택률	오답 풀이
① 14%	복합관계부사(~할 때마다)이다.
② 12%	주어 people을 받는 재귀대명사이다.
③ 15%	과거분사 approved를 꾸미는 부사이다.
⑤ 20%	voted와 병렬 연결되는 과거시제 동사이다.

구문 풀이 11행

~ many survey respondents will report that they **voted in an election or gave to a charity** when in fact it is possible to determine that they **did not**.

→ 'voted ~ or gave ~'의 의미를 받아오면서 부정의 의미를 함께 나타내기 위해 대동사 did not을 사용했다. 즉 did not을 풀어 쓰면 'did not vote ~ or give ~'와 같다.

구문 플러스 대동사

앞에 나온 동사를 그대로 반복하지 않으면서 대신하는 표현이다. 조동사, be동사, do가 활용된다.

He thought she was at home while she **wasn't**.
(= wasn't at home)
He said he would help me, but he **didn't**.
(= didn't help me)

B 정답 ⑤ 43% — 2022 6월 학평

해석 World Bank와 같은 기관들은 "선진" 국가와 "개발도상" 국가를 구별하기 위해 부를 사용하지만, 그들은 또한 발전이 경제 성장 그 이상이라는 것에 동의한다. "발전"은 또한, 경제 성장에 의해 야기되거나 경제 성장을 수반하는 사회적이고 환경적인 변화도 포함할 수 있으며, 그 변화의 일부는 긍정적이고 따라서 (일부는) 부정적일지도 모른다. 경제 성장이 인간과 지구에 어떤 영향을 미치고 있는지에 대한 문제가 다루어질 필요가 있다는 인식이 커졌고 — 그리고 계속해서 커지고 있다. 국가들은 경제 활동이나 프로젝트의 해로운 영향을 피해가 나타난 이후보다 그것이 계획되는 때인 초기에 줄이려고 노력하는 것이 비용이 덜 들고 훨씬 적은 고통을 야기한다는 것을 서서히 깨닫고 있다. 이것을 하는 것은 쉽지 않고 항상 불완전하다. 그러나 그러한 노력의 필요성에 대한 인식은 새로운 제품과 서비스를 만드는 데만 집중했던 이전의 널리 퍼진 태도가 나타냈던 것보다 더 큰 이해와 도덕적 관심을 나타낸다.

해설 ⑤의 대동사가 대신하는 동사구가 앞에 나온 일반동사구 'indicates a greater understanding and moral concern'이므로, 대동사로 be동사가 아닌 do동사를 써야 한다. 전체적인 시제에 맞추어 did를 쓴다.

오답 풀이

선택률	오답 풀이
① 6%	부사적 용법(~하기 위해서)의 to부정사이다.
② 18%	<부분을 나타내는 명사(some) + of + 관계대명사>가 쓰인 것으로, 선행사는 the social ~ changes이다.
③ 17%	동사 needs는 that절의 동사로, that절의 주어가 the question이므로 단수로 수일치한다.
④ 16%	비교급 less를 수식하는 부사로 much의 쓰임은 적절하다.

구문 풀이 8행

Countries are slowly learning that **it** is cheaper and causes much less suffering **to try to reduce the harmful effects of an economic activity or project at the beginning, when it is planned**, than after the damage appears.

→ that절에 <가주어-진주어> 구문과 비교급 구문이 쓰였다. 가주어는 it이고, 진주어는 to부정사구(to try ~ planned)이며, 내용적으로는 시점에 따른 비교가 이루어지고 있다.

구문 플러스 가주어 it과 진주어 to부정사구

to부정사는 문장의 주어가 될 수 있는데(명사적 용법), to부정사구가 너무 길어지면 진주어인 to부정사구 대신 가주어 it을 문장 앞에 사용한다.

· **To play tennis** is pleasant.
→ **It** is pleasant **to play tennis**.

C 정답 ⑤ 27% — 2021 3월 학평

해석 오늘날 조직, 지도자, 그리고 가족의 요구에 관해 곰곰이 생각할 때 우리는 독특한 특성 중 하나가 포용성이라는 것을 깨닫는다. 왜 그런가? 포용성은 모든 사람이 자신의 관계에서 궁극적으로 원하는 것인 협력을 뒷받침하기 때문이다. 그러나 대다수의 지도자, 조직, 그리고 가족은 여전히 오래된 패러다임의 언어를 사용하고 있고, 거기서는 한 사람이, 보통 가장 연장자, 가장 교육을 많이 받은 사람, 그리고/또는 가장 부유한 사람인데, 모든 결정을 내리고 토론이나 다른 사람을 포함시키는 것이 거의 없이 그들의 결정이 지배하고 결과적으로 배타성을 초래한다. 오늘날 이 사람은 어떤 조직의 이사, 최고 경영자, 또는 다른 상급 지도자일 수 있다. 다른 사람들이 자신의 생각을 제시할 필요가 없는데 왜냐하면 그것은 부적절한 것으로 여겨지기 때문이다. 그러나 연구에 따르면 문제 해결에 있어서 배타성은, 심지어 천재와 함께하는 것이더라도, 포용성만큼 효과적이지 않은데, 포용성이 있는 경우에는 모든 사람의 생각을 듣게 되고 해결책은 협력을 통해 발전된다.

해설 ⑤ 뒤에 필수 문장성분을 모두 갖춘 완전한 절이 오기 때문에 관계대명사 which를 관계부사 where로 바꿔 써야 한다.

오답 풀이

선택률	오답 풀이
① 8%	<one of + 복수명사>는 단수 취급한다.
② 21%	관계대명사 what절이 support의 목적어 역할을 한다.
③ 18%	분사구문으로, result in은 항상 능동으로 쓰이므로 현재분사로 쓴다.
④ 23%	수동태로 쓰인 be considered의 목적격 보어로 형용사가 적절하다.

구문 풀이 4행

Yet **the majority of leaders, organizations, and families are** still using the language of the old paradigm ~

→ 주어가 <부분을 나타내는 표현 of 전체 명사>일 때에는 뒤의 전체 명사에 수일치한다.

구문 플러스' 부분+of+전체 주어의 수일치

<부분+of+전체>가 주어로 나오면 전체 명사에 수일치한다. 부분을 나타내는 표현으로는 all, most, half, some, none, percent(s) 등이 있다.

Most of the students are awake.
　　전체(복수)　복수
All of the information is correct.
　　전체(불가산)　단수

D 정답 ⑤ 65%　　　　　　　　　*2020 3월 학평*

해석 일반적으로 민간 항공기는 물리적 구조물은 아니지만 도로와 유사한 항공로로 운항한다. 항공로에는 고정된 폭과 규정된 고도가 있으며, 그것들이 반대 방향으로 움직이는 통행을 분리한다. 항공기 간에 상하 간격을 둠으로써 아래에서 다른 과정이 이루어지는 동안 일부 비행기가 공항 위를 통과할 수 있게 된다. 항공 여행은 보통 장거리에 걸치는데, 이륙과 착륙 시 고강도로 조종사 활동을 하는 짧은 시간과, '장거리 비행'이라고 알려진 비행 부분인, 공중에 있는 동안 저강도로 조종사 활동을 하는 긴 시간이 있다. 비행에서 장거리 비행 부분 동안 조종사들은 근처의 비행기를 탐색하는 것보다 항공기 상태를 평가하는 데 더 많은 시간을

보낸다. 이는 항공기 간의 충돌은 대개 공항 주변 지역에서 발생하는 반면, 항공기 오작동으로 인한 추락은 장거리 비행 중에 발생하는 경향이 있기 때문이다.

해설 ⑤ while이 이끄는 부사절에서 복수 명사 crashes가 주어이기 때문에 동사 tends는 tend로 바꿔 써야 한다.

오답 풀이

선택률	오답 풀이
① 6%	fixed ~ altitudes를 설명하는 계속적 용법의 관계대명사이다.
② 5%	allow는 목적격 보어로 to부정사를 취한다.
③ 12%	the portion ~ flight를 수식하는 분사로 과거분사 형태가 적절하다.
④ 9%	spend+시간+-ing(~하는 데 시간을 보내다)이 쓰였다.

구문 풀이 4행

Vertical separation of aircraft **allows** some flights **to pass over** airports while other processes occur below.

→ <allow+목적어+목적격 보어>의 5형식 문장으로 목적격 보어로 to부정사가 왔다.

 플러스' 목적격 보어 - to부정사

동사 want, allow, enable, encourage 등은 목적어 다음에 목적격 보어로 to부정사가 온다.

I just want him **to try** it again.

E 정답 ⑤ 26%　　　　　　　　　*2019 3월 학평*

해석 코알라가 잘하는 것이 한 가지 있다면, 그것은 자는 것이다. 오랫동안 많은 과학자들은 유칼립투스 잎 속의 화합물이 그 작고 귀여운 동물들을 몽롱한 상태로 만들어서 코알라들이 그렇게도 무기력한 상태에 있는 것이라고 의심했다. 그러나 더 최근의 연구는 그 잎들이 단순히 영양분이 너무나도 적기 때문에 코알라가 거의 에너지가 없는 것임을 보여 주었다. 그래서 코알라들은 가능한 한 적게 움직이는 경향이 있다. 그리고 그것들이 실제로 움직일 때에는, 흔히 그것들은 마치 슬로 모션으로 움직이는 것처럼 보인다. 그것들은 하루에 16시간에서 18시간 동안 휴식을 취하는데, 의식이 없는 상태로 그 시간의 대부분을 보낸다. 사실 코알라는 생각을 하는 데에 시간을 거의 사용하지 않는데, 그것들의 뇌는 실제로 지난 몇 세기 동안 크기가 줄어든 것처럼 보인다. 코알라는 뇌가 겨우 두개골의 절반을 채운다고 알려진 유일한 동물이다.

해설 두 개의 절을 연결하고 선행사 the only known animal의 소유격의 역할을 해야 하므로 ⑤ its를 관계대명사 whose로 바꿔야 한다.

오답 풀이

선택률	오답 풀이
① 6%	이유를 나타내는 접속사 because가 쓰였다.
② 11%	so ~ that … 구문(너무 ~해서 …하다)으로, so low 다음에 결과의 that절이 이어진다.

③ 22%	강조 동사 do가 move를 강조하고 있다.
④ 33%	to have shrunk는 본동사 appear보다 이전 시제를 나타낸다.

구문 풀이 6행

~ when they do move, they often look **as though** they're in slow motion.

→ as though는 as if와 의미가 같으며 '마치 ~처럼'으로 해석한다.

구문 플러스⁺ as though = as if

as though 다음에 과거형이 나오고, 주절이 현재이면 현재 사실의 반대를 가정하는 것일 수 있다.

He acts **as though he got the answer**.

(=actually, he doesn't have the answer)

F 정답 ④ 49%   *2018 9월 학평*

해석 고양이는 액체일까 고체일까? 이는 "사람들을 웃게 한 후 생각을 하게 만드는" 연구에 경의를 표하는, 노벨상의 패러디인 이그 노벨상을 과학자가 타게 할 수 있는 종류의 질문이다. 하지만 Paris Diderot 대학의 물리학자인 Marc-Antoine Fardin은 이런 생각을 하면서 집고양이가 액체처럼 흐물거리며 움직이는지 아닌지를 알아내는 것을 시작한 것은 아니었다. Fardin은 털로 덮인 이 애완동물이 물과 같은 액체가 하는 것과 유사하게 그들이 들어가 앉아 있는 용기의 모양에 맞게 조절할 수 있다는 것을 알아냈다. 그래서 그는 고양이가 꽃병 또는 욕조의 공간을 채우는 데 걸리는 시간을 계산하기 위해 물질의 변화를 다루는 물리학의 한 분야인 유동학을 적용했다. 결론은? 고양이는 환경에 따라 액체도 될 수 있고 고체도 될 수 있다. 작은 상자 안의 고양이는 그 모든 공간을 채우며 액체처럼 행동할 것이다. 하지만 물로 가득 찬 욕조의 고양이는 그것과의 접촉을 최소화하려고 노력하면서 고체와 매우 유사하게 움직일 것이다.

해설 주절의 주어(A cat)와 분사의 관계가 능동이므로 ④ filled를 현재분사 filling으로 고쳐야 한다.

오답 풀이

선택률	오답 풀이
① 7%	it ~ that 강조구문에 쓰인 that은 적절하다.
② 21%	동사구(adapt to the shape)를 수식해야 하므로 부사 형태는 적절하다.
③ 14%	시간이 걸린다는 의미로 <it takes+시간>을 쓴다. 이때 it은 원칙적으로 that 등 다른 대명사로 바꿀 수 없다.
⑤ 7%	조동사 will에 이어지므로 동사원형이 나온다.

구문 풀이 7행

So he applied rheology, the branch of physics that deals with the deformation of matter, to calculate the time it takes **for cats** to take up the space of a vase or bathroom sink.

→ to부정사인 to take up 앞에 의미상의 주어 for cats가 온 것이다.

구문 플러스⁺ to부정사의 의미상의 주어

절의 주어와 to부정사의 행위 주체가 다를 때 to부정사 앞에 <for+목적격>의 형태로 의미상의 주어를 쓴다. 단, to부정사가 사람의 성격을 나타내는 형용사의 뒤에 쓰일 경우 의미상의 주어는 <of+목적격> 형태가 된다.

• It was the easiest way **for him** to find out the answer.
• It was foolish **of you** to say such a thing.

G 정답 ③ 63%   *2017 9월 학평*

해석 영어 사용자들은 가족 관계를 묘사하기 위한 가장 단순한 체계들 중 하나를 가진다. 많은 아프리카 언어 사용자들은 남성과 여성 친척 양쪽 모두를 묘사하는 데 "cousin"과 같은 한 단어를 사용하는 것, 또는 묘사되는 사람이 말하는 사람의 아버지와 혈연 관계인지 아니면 어머니와 혈연 관계인지 구별하지 않는 것을 불합리하다고 여길 것이다. brother-in-law를 아내의 남자형제인지 여자형제의 남편인지 구별할 수 없다는 것은 많은 문화에 존재하는 인간관계의 구조 내에서 혼란스럽게 보일 것이다. 마찬가지로, "uncle"이라는 한 단어가 아버지의 형제와 어머니의 형제에게 적용되는 상황을 이해하는 것이 어떻게 가능하겠는가? 하와이 언어는 동일한 용어를 사용하여 아버지와 아버지의 남자형제를 지칭한다. Jinghpaw 언어로 사고하는 Northern Burma의 사람들은 그들의 친족을 묘사하기 위한 18개의 기본 용어를 가진다. 이 용어 중 어떤 것도 영어로 바로 번역될 수 없다.

해설 (A)에서 the person은 행위의 대상이므로 과거분사 described를 써야 한다. (B) 이하는 a situation을 수식하는 관계사절로서 완전한 문장이므로 in which를 써야 한다. (C)에서는 주어인 People of Northern Burma와의 수 일치를 위해 have를 써야 한다. 따라서 정답은 ③이다.

오답 풀이

선택률	오답 풀이
① 12%	(B) 관계사절에 주어, 목적어 등이 빠진 부분이 없고 의미상 전치사가 필요하므로 <전치사+관계대명사>로 쓴다. 이 in which는 where로 바꿔도 된다.
② 14%	(C) 주어인 People of Northern Burma와 수 일치해야 한다.
④ 4%	(A) describe의 the person은 '묘사하는' 행위의 대상이므로 과거분사로 써야 한다.
⑤ 4%	—

구문 풀이 2행

Many African language speakers would **consider it absurd to use** a single word like "cousin" to describe both male and female relatives ~

→ <consider+목적어+목적격 보어>의 5형식 문장으로 목적어인 to부정사가 길어서 가목적어 it을 대신 앞에 썼다.

구문 플러스⁺ 가목적어 it (1)

5형식 문장에서 목적어가 길어지거나 직접적으로 목적어 자리에 사용할 수 없는 형태의 목적어를 쓸 때 가목적어 it을 활용한다.

• 가목적어 it이 포함된 문장의 형태
  주어 + 5형식 동사 + it(가목적어) + 목적격 보어 + 진목적어

• 가목적어를 쓸 수 있는 5형식 동사의 예
  believe, make, consider, find, think 등

• 진목적어의 형태
  ① to부정사 ② that 명사절 ③ what 명사절 등
  → 가목적어 it은 that이나 this로 바꿔 쓸 수 없다.

유형 플러스⁺ 어법의 이해

어법의 이해는 다섯 개의 밑줄 친 표현 중 틀린 것을 고르거나 네모 안에 주어진 두 표현 중 적절한 것을 고르는 유형으로 출제된다. 다음과 같은 해법으로 접근한다.

① 자주 출제되는 문법 사항들이 있다. 주어, 동사의 수 일치, 병렬구조, 태, 분사(구문), to부정사, 동명사, 목적어의 형태, 관계사 등은 평소에 정리해 두도록 한다.
② 문장의 기본 요소인 주어와 동사를 기준으로 파악한다. 길어진 주어를 찾거나 동사의 형태를 찾는 등의 전략이 도움이 된다.

A 정답 ④ 40%   *2023 3월 학평*

해석 특정한 환경 조건이 '극심하다', '혹독하다', '온화하다' 혹은 '스트레스가 된다'고 묘사하는 것은 자연스러워 보인다. 이것은 사막 한낮의 열기, 남극 겨울의 추위, 그레이트솔트호의 염도와 같이 (환경) 조건이 '극심한' 경우에 명백해 보일지도 모른다. 하지만 이것은 우리의 특정한 생리적 특징과 내성을 고려할 때 이런 환경이 '우리에게' 극심하다는 의미일 뿐이다. 선인장에게 선인장들이 진화해 온 사막의 환경 조건은 전혀 극심하지 않으며, 마찬가지로 펭귄에게 얼음에 뒤덮인 남극 땅은 극심한 환경이 아니다. 생태학자가 <u>모든 다른 유기체가 우리가 느끼는 방식대로 환경을 느낀다</u>고 추정하는 것은 성의 없고 위험하다. 오히려 생태학자는 다른 유기체가 세계를 보는 방식으로 세계를 바라보고자 환경에 대한 벌레의 관점이나 식물의 관점을 얻기 위해 노력해야 한다. 혹독한, 온화한 등 감정이 실린 단어들, 심지어 덥고 추운 것과 같은 상대적인 단어들은 생태학자들에 의해 오로지 신중하게 사용되어야 한다.

해설 특정 환경을 '극심하다', '혹독하다' 등 감정적인 언어를 사용해 표현할 때에는 각별한 주의가 필요하다는 내용이다. 특히 빈칸 뒤에서, 생태학자라면 다른 유기체가 세상을 바라보는 시각을 고려하고자 노력해야 한다고 언급한다. 이로 미루어볼 때, '다른 유기체도 다 우리처럼 세상을 인식할 것이라고' 섣불리 가정하지 말라는 충고가 빈칸에 어울린다. 따라서 정답은 ④ '모든 다른 유기체가 우리가 느끼는 방식대로 환경을 느낀다'이다.

오답 풀이

선택률	보기 해석
① 10%	복잡한 유기체가 단순한 유기체보다 우월하다
② 13%	기술은 우리가 극심한 환경에서 살아남도록 도와준다
③ 24%	생태적 다양성은 극심한 환경들에 의해 뒷받침된다
⑤ 12%	(생물) 종들은 예측 가능한 방식으로 환경 변화에 적응한다

구문 풀이 6행

~ **nor are the icy lands of Antarctica** an extreme environment for penguins.
→ <부정어+be+주어> 어순의 도치 구문이다.

 플러스 부정어구의 도치

부정어구(not, never, nor, no sooner, hardly, scarcely, only+부사구 등)가 문장 맨 앞에 나오면 주어와 동사는 의문문 어순으로 도치된다.

Never can I forget my first meeting with Cindy.
　　　조동사+주어+동사원형
Hardly did we speak to each other after the fight.
　　　do/does/did+주어+동사원형

B 정답 ① 40%   *2022 9월 학평*

해석 왜 도움이 효과적이지 않을 수 있는지에 대한 몇몇 이유들이 있다. 한 가지 가능한 이유는 도움을 받는 것이 자존감에 타격이 될 수 있다는 것이다. Lehigh 대학의 Christopher Burke와 Jessica Goren에 의한 한 최근 연구는 이 가능성을 검토했다. 자존감에 대한 위협 이론에 따르면, 도움은 협력적이고 애정 있는 것으로 인식될 수도 있고, 혹은 만약 그 도움이 무능함을 암시하는 것으로 해석된다면 위협적으로 보여질 수 있다. Burke와 Goren에 따르면 도움이 자기 연관적이거나 자기 정의적인 영역—즉, 당신 자신의 성공과 성취가 특히 중요한 영역—안에 있는 경우, 그것은 특히 위협적인 것으로 보여질 가능성이 있다. 자기 연관적인 일로 도움을 받는 것은 <u>당신이 당신 자신에 대해 기분 나쁘게 느끼도록 만들</u> 수 있고, 이것은 도움의 잠재적인 긍정적 영향을 손상시킬 수 있다. 예를 들어, 만약 당신의 자아 개념이 어느 정도는 당신의 훌륭한 요리 실력에 달려 있다면, 친구가 당신이 손님들을 위해 식사를 준비하는 것을 도울 때 이는 당신의 자아에 타격이 될 수 있는데, 왜냐하면 이는 당신이 자신이 그렇다고 생각했던 유능한 요리사가 아니라는 점을 암시하기 때문이다.

해설 자아 개념이 달려 있는 영역에서 도움을 주는 것은, 오히려 자아에 타격을 준다는 내용이다. 따라서, 자기 연관적인 일로 도움을 받는 것은 ① '당신이 당신 자신에 대해 기분 나쁘게 느끼도록 만들' 수 있다.

오답 풀이

선택률	보기 해석
② 22%	도전들을 처리할 수 있는 능력을 향상시킬
③ 9%	다른 호의를 요청하는 방법으로 보일
④ 20%	당신이 성공적이었다고 생각하도록 속일
⑤ 9%	당신의 행동을 따르려고 노력하는 사람을 단념시킬

구문 풀이 12행

~ it may be a blow to your ego when a friend helps you prepare a meal for guests because it suggests that you're not the master chef **you thought you were**.
→ the master chef를 꾸미는 (that) you thought you were에서 관계대명사 that이 생략되었다.

 플러스 관계대명사의 생략 (2)

선행사가 관계절의 보어일 때 관계대명사로는 that이 쓰이며, 이 that은 생략 가능하다.

I'm not the man **(that)** I used to be.
　　　　　　　used to be의 보어

C 정답 ③ 55%

해석 자기불구화를 할 때, 당신은 당신이 알기에 성공의 가능성을 해칠 행동에 관여하고 있다: 당신은 전날 밤에 밖에 나가면 그만큼 시험을 잘 치지 못할 것이라는 것을 알고 있지만, 어쨌든 당신은 그것을 한다. 어떤 사람이 왜 의도적으로 성공의 가능성을 해치겠는가? 자, 여기에 가능한 답이 있다. 공부를 열심히 한다고 말해 보자. 당신은 적당한 시간에 잠자리에 들고 8시간 동안 잠을 잔다. 그리고 나서 당신은 수학 시험에 응시하지만, 잘 치지 못한다: 당신은 겨우 C를 받는다. 당신은 자신에 대해 어떤 결론을 내릴 수 있는가? 아마도 당신은 단지 수학을 잘하지 못해서라고(결론을 내릴 수 있다), 그리고 그것은 당신의 자존감에 꽤 큰 타격이다. 하지만 만약 당신이 자기불구화를 한다면, 당신이 실패에 대한 이유를 만들기 때문에 당신은 결코 이런 상황에 처하지 않을 것이다. 당신이 새벽 1시까지 밖에 나가 있었기 때문에 C를 받을 수밖에 없었다고, 당신은 스스로에게 말할 수 있다. 그 C는 당신이 수학을 못한다는 것을 의미하지는 않는다; 그것은 단지 당신이 파티하는 것을 좋아한다는 것을 의미한다. 사람들이 의도적으로 성공의 가능성을 해치고 있기 때문에, 자기불구화 현상은 역설처럼 보인다.

해설 공부를 열심히 했는데도 C를 받아 자존감에 타격을 받는 일을 방지하기 위하여 일부러 열심히 공부를 하지 않는 자기불구화를 한다는 내용의 글이다. 즉, 자기불구화를 하는 것은 ③ '당신이 실패에 대한 이유를 만들기' 위함이다.

오답 풀이

선택률	보기 해석
① 12%	공부로부터 휴식을 취하는 것은 필수적이기
② 17%	실패가 성공의 기반으로 기능하기
④ 9%	공부는 이기고 지는 것이 아니기
⑤ 5%	당신은 이미 많은 것을 성취하였기

구문 풀이 1행

When self-handicapping, you're engaging in behaviour that **you know** will harm your chances of succeeding:
→ 관계사절에 <주어+동사>의 삽입 구문이 끼어든 형태이다. 이 때 삽입 구문의 동사는 인식이나 확신의 의미를 가진 동사가 쓰인다.

구문 플러스° 관계대명사 삽입절

주격 관계대명사 뒤에 '주어+동사(think, believe, claim 등)'가 삽입되는 경우가 있는데, 이 경우 관계대명사절은 '(명사)가 (동사)하기에 ~한'으로 해석된다.

I'm not sure about the clues **which they claim are compelling clues**.
그들이 주장하기에 강력한 단서들인
It was something **that other people think he stole**.
다른 사람들이 생각하기에 그가 훔쳤던

D 정답 ⑤ 46% 2020 3월 학평

해석 성장하고 있는 유전학 분야는 많은 과학자가 여러 해 동안 짐작해왔던 것, 즉 식품이 유전자 청사진에 직접 영향을 줄 수 있다는 것을 우

리에게 보여 주고 있다. 이 정보는 유전자가 우리의 통제 하에 있는 것이지 우리가 복종해야 하는 것이 아니라는 것을 더 잘 이해하도록 도와준다. 일란성 쌍둥이를 생각해 보자. 두 사람은 모두 똑같은 유전자를 부여받는다. 중년에, 쌍둥이 중 한 명은 암에 걸리고, 다른 한 명은 암 없이 건강하게 오래 산다. 특정 유전자가 쌍둥이 중 한 명에게 암에 걸리도록 명령했지만, 나머지 한 명에서는 똑같은 유전자가 그 질병을 일으키지 않았다. 한 가지 가능성은 쌍둥이 중 건강한 사람이 암 유전자, 즉 나머지 한 명이 병에 걸리도록 명령했던 그 똑같은 유전자를 꺼버리는 식사를 했다는 것이다. 여러 해 동안 과학자들은 화학적 독소(예를 들어 담배)와 같은 다른 환경적 요인들이 유전자에 작용하여 암의 원인이 될 수 있다는 것을 인정해 왔다. 음식이 유전자 발현에 특정한 영향을 미친다는 생각은 비교적 새로운 것이다.

해설 마지막 문장에 결론이 나오는 글로 음식이 유전자 발현에 영향을 준다고 했기 때문에 ⑤ '식품이 유전자 청사진에 직접 영향을 줄 수 있다'가 빈칸에 적절하다.

오답 풀이

선택률	보기 해석
① 16%	일란성 쌍둥이는 똑같은 유전적 구성을 지닌다
② 15%	음식에 대한 우리의 선호도는 유전자의 영향을 받는다
③ 6%	균형 잡힌 식단이 우리의 정신 건강에 필수적이다
④ 15%	유전 공학은 몇몇 치명적인 질병을 치료할 수 있다

구문 풀이 10행

For many years, scientists have recognized other environmental factors, such as chemical toxins (tobacco for example), ~
→ 기간을 나타낼 때 전치사 for를 쓰는데 과거부터 현재까지의 시간을 나타내기 때문에 현재완료와 자주 쓰인다.

구문 플러스° during vs. for

during과 for는 둘 다 '동안'의 의미이지만 during은 기간을 나타내는 명사, for는 구체적인 시간과 함께 쓰인다.
- He went to my grandfather **during** summer vacation.
- She has been studying **for** three hours.

E 정답 ④ 38% 2019 6월 학평

해석 거대 제약회사인 Merck에서 CEO인 Kenneth Frazier는 혁신과 변화를 이끄는 데 그의 간부들이 보다 적극적인 역할을 취하도록 동기를 부여하기로 결심하였다. 그는 그들이 급진적인 무엇인가를 하도록 요청하였다. Merck를 사업에서 몰아낼 수도 있는 아이디어들을 만들어내라는 것이었다. 다음 두 시간 동안 회사 간부들은 Merck의 주요 경쟁사 가운데 하나인 체하면서, 그룹으로 작업을 하였다. 그들이 자사의 약을 짓밟을 만한 약과 그들이 놓쳤던 주요 시장에 대한 아이디어를 만들어내는 동안 에너지가 치솟았다. 그러고 나서, 그들의 과제는 그들의 역할을 반대로 하여 이러한 위협을 어떻게 방어할 수 있는지를 알아내는 것이었다. 이러한 "회사 무너뜨리기" 활동은 수익에 맞춰 구조화된 활동을 손실의 관점으로 재구조화하기 때문에 강력하다. 혁신 기회에 대해 심사숙고

할 때, 리더들은 위험을 무릅쓰지 않는 경향이 있었다. 그들이 경쟁자들이 그들을 어떻게 사업에서 몰아낼 수 있을지를 고려했을 때, 그들은 혁신하지 않는 것이 위험한 것이라는 것을 깨달았다. 혁신의 다급함이 명확해졌다.

해설 주요 경쟁사를 설정하고 '자사 제품을 무너뜨릴' 아이디어를 만드는 과정에서 혁신에 대한 필요성을 절감했다는 내용이다. 따라서 빈칸에는 ④ '수익에 맞춰 구조화된 활동을 손실의 관점으로 재구조화하기'가 가장 적절하다.

오답 풀이

선택률	보기 해석
① 16%	알려지지 않은 것이 부정적인 것보다 더 도움이 되기
② 16%	그것은 그들이 이미 만든 진전을 강조하기
③ 16%	비합리적인 것이 아니라 소비자 위주의 실행이기
⑤ 11%	그들은 얼마나 그것이 그들의 이익 분배 계획에 잘 부합하는지 논의하기

구문 풀이 10행

When deliberating about innovation opportunities, the leaders weren't inclined to take risks.
→ 접속사가 있는 분사구문은 대부분 의미를 명확하게 하기 위해 접속사를 그대로 둔다.

구문 **플러스'** 접속사가 있는 분사구문

일반적으로 분사구문은 접속사와 주어를 생략하고 동사를 분사로 바꾸어 쓰지만, 의미를 분명하게 하기 위해 일부러 접속사를 남겨두기도 한다.
We often make mistakes **when speaking** in English.

F 정답 ② 41% *2018 6월 학평*

해석 당신은 당신의 아이들에게 낯선 사람을 멀리 하라고 조언하는가? 그것은 어른들에게는 무리한 요구이다. 결국, 당신은 낯선 사람들을 만남으로써 당신의 친구의 범위를 확장하고 잠재적인 사업 파트너를 만든다. 그러나 이 과정에서, 사람들의 성격을 이해하기 위해 그들을 분석하는 것은 잠재적인 경제적 또는 사회적 이익에 대한 것만은 아니다. 당신이 사랑하는 사람들의 안전뿐 아니라, 당신의 안전도 생각해봐야 한다. 그런 이유로, 은퇴한 FBI 프로파일러인 Mary Ellen O'Toole은 그들을 이해하기 위해 사람의 피상적인 특성을 넘어설 필요성을 강조한다. 예를 들어, 단지 낯선 이들이 공손하다는 이유로 그들이 좋은 이웃이라고 가정하는 것은 안전하지 않다. 매일 아침 잘 차려 입고 외출하는 그들을 보는 것이 전부는 아니다. 사실, O'Toole은 당신이 범죄자를 다룰 때, 심지어 당신의 느낌도 당신을 틀리게 할 수 있다고 말한다. 그것은 범죄자들이 조작과 사기의 기술에 통달했기 때문이다.

해설 안전을 위해 낯선 사람을 정확히 분석하고 이해하기 위해서는 겉으로 드러나는 것을 넘어서야 한다는 이야기이므로, 빈칸에 들어갈 말은 ② '사람의 피상적인 특성을 넘어설'이다.

오답 풀이

선택률	보기 해석
① 17%	소셜미디어에서 사람을 만나는 범위를 줄일
③ 11%	부보다 재능에 집중할
④ 17%	다른 사람에 대한 당신의 첫인상을 믿을
⑤ 11%	범죄자들을 이용할

구문 풀이 3행

Throughout this process, however, analyzing people to understand their personalities is **not all** about potential economic or social benefit.
→ not all은 '전부 ~인 것은 아니다'라는 부분 부정이다.

구문 **플러스'** 부분 부정

not all, not always, not every와 같은 표현은 '모두(항상) 그런 것은 아니다'의 의미로 일부를 부정한다.
Not every student in my class **wears** glasses.
→ **Some students** in my class **don't** wear glasses.

G 정답 ③ 59% *2017 9월 학평*

해석 중미의 많은 지역에서 토착민들은 비타민 A와 같은 필수 영양분이 가득한 녹색 채소를 재배할 수는 있지만, 재배하지 않는다. 일반적으로 말해서, 이 사람들은 이러한 곡물을 재배하는 전통을 가지고 있지 않다. 그들은 흔히 일반적으로 제한된 교육을 받고, 건강이나 영양과 관련된 조언을 거의 접하지 못하며, 최대한 많은 사람들을 먹일 수 있는 식량을 재배한다. 그들은 흔히 많은 tortilla와 콩을 먹어서 충분한 단백질을 섭취하며 배부를 때까지 먹는다. 하지만 미량 영양소의 부족은 그들의 자녀에게 실명, 철분 결핍, 그리고 다른 발육 장애의 발병을 초래한다. 이러한 상황에서 가정은 불균형을 바로잡기 위해 식단을 다양화하고 보다 많은 녹색 채소를 심고, 때로는 영양적 지원을 받도록 권장 받으며, 영양에 대한 교육을 받아야 한다.

해설 토착민이 교육의 미비와 전통적인 상황으로 인해 영양 불균형이라는 설명 뒤로 그런 ③ '불균형을 바로잡기' 위한 영양 교육의 필요성을 말하고 있다.

오답 풀이

선택률	보기 해석
① 7%	비만을 제거하기
② 12%	소화를 향상시키기
④ 13%	더 많은 단백질을 섭취하기
⑤ 6%	그들의 전통을 보존하기

구문 풀이 7행

Yet the lack of micronutrients leads to **their children developing** blindness, iron deficiency, and other growth disorders.
→ 동사 leads to의 목적어로 동명사가 쓰이고 있으며, 동명사의 의미상

주어가 동명사 바로 앞에 목적격으로 표시되었다.

 플러스⁺ 동명사의 의미상 주어

동명사의 의미상 주어는 목적격이나 소유격으로 쓴다. 의미상 주어가 문맥
상 명확하거나 불특정 일반인일 때는 생략한다.

I hate **Peter** telling a lie.
My father is sure of **my brother's** passing the exam.

A 정답 ① 39%   *2023 9월 학평*

해석 반항자들은 본인이 반항자라고 생각할지도 모르지만, 영리한 마케터들은 (반항자가 아닌) 나머지 우리에게 하는 것처럼 그들에게도 영향을 준다. "모두가 그렇게 하고 있다."라고 말하는 것은 일부 사람들이 어떤 생각에 대해 흥미를 잃게 할지도 모른다. 이 사람들은 대안을 찾을 것이고, 그것은 (만약 영리하게 계획된다면) 정확히 마케터나 설득하는 사람이 여러분더러 믿기를 원하는 것일 수 있다. 만약 내가 여러분이 어떤 아이디어를 고려하길 바라는데, 여러분이 자신의 독립성과 고유성을 지키기 위해 대중적인 의견을 강하게 거부한다는 것을 안다면, 나는 대다수가 선택하는 것을 먼저 제시할 것이고, 여러분은 내 실제 선호에 맞게 그것을 거부할 것이다. 우리는 반항의 입장을 지키려 할 때 종종 속는다. 사람들은 우리가 그들의 목적에 맞는 선택지를 '독자적으로' 택하도록 만들기 위해 이러한 **반전**을 사용한다. 일부 브랜드들은 주류에 대한 우리의 반항을 완전히 활용해 스스로를 반항자로 자리매김해 왔고, 이는 훨씬 더 강력한 브랜드 충성도를 만들었다.

해설 주류를 거부하는 반항자들의 속성을 이용한 마케팅 전략을 설명하는 글이다. 마케터의 실제 의도가 대중적 의견과 반대되는 것을 납득시키려는 것일 때, 대중적 의견을 반항자들에게 먼저 제시하면, 반항자들은 그에 반대하면서 '자발적으로' 마케터의 의도 쪽으로 향한다는 것이다. 이것은 ① '반전'이라는 말로 가장 정확히 요약된다.

오답 풀이

선택률	보기 해석
② 20%	imitation(모방)
③ 20%	repetition(반복)
④ 13%	conformity(순응)
⑤ 9%	collaboration(협력)

구문 풀이 9행

People use this reversal to make us **"independently" choose** an option which suits their purposes.

→ 원형부정사 choose를 꾸미기 위해 부사 independently를 썼다. make의 목적격보어로 착각하지 않도록 한다.

구문 플러스 형용사 vs. 부사

실전 빈출 포인트

1) 보어 자리에는 형용사가 온다.
2) 명사 아닌 것을 꾸미려면 부사를 쓴다.
3) 준동사를 수식하려면 부사를 쓴다.

Pets make us **happy**(happily). → 목적격보어
A good joke makes us **instantly**(instant) happy.
       └ 형용사 수식

She decided to **quickly**(quick) finish her work.
      to부정사 수식(가운데 삽입)

B 정답 ③ 39%   *2022 6월 학평*

해석 추종자는 부하라는 직책이나 리더의 바람에 따르는 행동에 의해 정의될 수 있다. 그러나 추종자도 이끌 힘이 있다. 추종자는 리더에게 힘을 주기도 하고 그 반대도 마찬가지이다. 이로 인해 Ronald Heifetz와 같은 일부 리더십 분석가들은 '추종자'라는 단어를 사용하는 것을 피하고 권력 관계에 있는 다른 사람들을 "시민" 또는 "구성원"으로 지칭하게 되었다. 추종자에 대한 너무 단순한 관점이 오해를 불러일으킬 수 있다는 Heifetz의 말은 옳다. 현대의 삶에서, 대부분의 사람들은 결국 리더와 추종자 둘 다가 되고, 그 범주는 꽤 **유동적**일 수 있다. 우리의 목표가 변함에 따라 추종자로서의 우리의 행동도 바뀐다. 만약 내가 음악에 대한 나의 판단보다 당신의 판단을 더 신뢰한다면, 우리가 어떤 콘서트에 참석할지에 대해서는 당신의 주도를 따를 수 있다(당신이 비록 공식적으로 지위상 나의 부하일지라도). 하지만 내가 낚시 전문가라면, 공식적인 지위나 내가 어제 콘서트에 대해 당신을 따랐다는 사실과는 관계없이, 낚시할 장소에 대해서는 당신이 나를 따를 수 있다.

해설 상황에 따라 추종자도 리더의 역할을 할 수 있고, 리더도 추종자의 역할을 할 수 있다는 내용이므로, 추종자와 리더의 범주는 ③ '유동적'이라고 함이 자연스럽다.

오답 풀이

선택률	보기 해석
① 14%	rigid(엄격한)
② 15%	unfair(불공정한)
④ 20%	stable(안정적인)
⑤ 13%	apparent(명백한)

구문 풀이 6행

Heifetz is correct that **too simple a view of followers** can produce misunderstanding.

→ <too+형/부+관사+명사> 어순이다.

구문 플러스 주의할 관사의 어순

too+형/부+a(n)+명
so+형/부+a(n)+명   vs.   such+a(n)+형+명
as+형/부+a(n)+명

too simple a puzzle 너무 쉬운 문제
so smart a boy 몹시 똑똑한 소년
as great a poet as ever lived 여태 없었던 위대한 시인
cf. **such** a nice gentleman 그토록 친절한 신사

C 정답 ② 46%   *2021 9월 학평*

해석 상대성은 여러 면에서 그리고 삶의 많은 다른 영역에 걸쳐 정신을 위한 일반적인 메커니즘으로 작용한다. 예를 들어, <Mindless

Eating>의 저자 Brian Wansink는 그것이 우리의 허리 둘레에 도 영향을 미칠 수 있다는 것을 보여주었다. 우리는 어느 정도로 먹을지를, 단순히 우리가 실제로 얼마나 많은 음식을 소비할지의 함수로서가 아니라 그것의 선택(대안)과의 비교를 통해서 결정한다. 우리가 메뉴에 있는 8온스, 10온스, 12온스의 버거 세 개 중 하나를 선택해야 한다고 하자. 우리는 10온스 버거를 고르고 식사가 끝날 때쯤이면 완벽하게 만족할 수 있을 것이다. 하지만 만약 대신에 우리의 선택권이 10온스, 12온스, 14온스라면, 우리는 다시 중간의 것을 선택할 것이고, 비록 우리가 더 많이 먹었더라도, 식사가 끝날 때 일일 양분을 섭취하거나 포만감을 느끼기 위해 필요하지 않았던 12온스의 햄버거에 똑같이 행복감과 만족감을 다시 느낄 수 있을 것이다.

해설 우리가 무엇을 먹을지 결정하는 것이 선택(대안)과의 비교를 통해서 이루어진다고 하였으므로 ② '상대성'이 작용한다고 하는 것이 자연스럽다.

오답 풀이

선택률	보기 해석
① 13%	Originality(독창성)
③ 20%	Visualization(시각화)
④ 13%	Imitation(모방)
⑤ 6%	Forgetfulness(건망증)

구문 풀이 4행

We decide how much to eat **not** simply as a function of how much food we actually consume, **but** by a comparison to its alternatives.
→ 'not A but B' 구조로 전치사구가 병렬연결되고 있으며, 첫 번째 전치사구는 simply라는 부사의 수식을 받고 있다.

 상관접속사

상관접속사는 등위접속사(and, but, or 등)와 의미를 좀 더 보강해주는 단어들이 짝을 이룬 접속사로, 대개 같은 품사나 형태의 어구를 연결한다.

- not A but B: A가 아니라 B
  She is crying **not** because you touched her **but** because her dad is not here.
- either A or B: A와 B 둘 중 하나
  I will **either** play tennis **or** go hiking.

D 정답 ① 57%   *2020 3월 학평*

해석 현대의 불교 스승인 Dainin Katagiri는 죽음을 앞두고 <침묵으로의 회귀>라는 주목할 만한 책을 집필했다. 그는 삶이란 "위험한 상황이다."라고 썼다. 삶을 소중하게 만드는 것은 바로 삶의 취약함이며, 그의 글은 자신의 삶이 끝나가고 있다는 바로 그 사실로 채워져 있다. "자기 그릇은 언젠가 깨질 것이기 때문에 아름답다… 그 그릇의 생명은 늘 위험한 상황에 놓여 있다." 그런 것이 우리의 고행이다. 이 불안정한 아름다움. 이 피할 수 없는 상처. 우리는 사랑과 상실이 친밀한 동반자라는 것을, 우리가 진짜 꽃을 플라스틱 꽃보다 훨씬 더 사랑하고 산 중턱을 가로지르는 한 순간만 지속하는 황혼의 색조를 사랑한다는 것을 잊어버린다 (우리가 이것을 얼마나 쉽게 잊는가). 우리의 마음을 여는 것은 바로 이 연약함이다.

해설 삶이 아름답고 소중한 이유는 그릇처럼 깨지기 쉽기 때문이라고 하고 있기 때문에 빈칸에는 ① '연약함'이 자연스럽다.

오답 풀이

선택률	보기 해석
② 17%	stability(안정감)
③ 8%	harmony(조화)
④ 10%	satisfaction(만족감)
⑤ 6%	diversity(다양성)

구문 풀이 3행

It is the weakness of life **that** makes it precious; his words are filled with the very fact of his own life passing away.
→ <it ~ that> 강조구문으로, '…한 것은 바로 ~이다'라는 의미이다.

 플러스 〈it ~ that〉 강조구문

강조하고 싶은 명사구 또는 부사구를 it ~ that 사이에 넣어 강조하는 것이다.

We first met last year.
→ **It was** last year **that** we first met.
Cindy ate my hotdog.
→ **It was** Cindy **who** ate my hotdog.
   (강조어구가 사람이면 who를 쓰기도 함)

E 정답 ② 26%   *2019 9월 학평*

해석 아이들은 관심을 가져주는 타인이 있을 때 혼자 있을 수 있는 능력을 발달시킨다. 여러분이 어린 아이를 자연에서 조용히 산책시킬 때 다가오는 고요를 생각해 보라. 그 아이는, 그에게 이러한 경험을 처음으로 하게 한 누군가와 '함께' 있다는 것에 의해 도움을 받아, 자연 속에서 혼자 있는 것이 어떤 것인지에 대해 점점 알아 가는 것을 느끼게 된다. 점차적으로, 그 아이는 혼자 산책한다. 또는 두 살짜리 딸아이를 목욕시키는 엄마가, 딸이 엄마와 함께 있고 엄마가 자신에게 시간을 내어줄 수 있다는 것을 알고 있는 내내, 이야기를 만들고 생각을 하며 혼자 있는 법을 배우면서 목욕 장난감을 가지고 공상에 잠길 수 있게 하는 것을 생각해 보라. 점차적으로, 혼자서 하는 목욕은 그 아이가 상상을 하며 편안해 하는 시간이 된다. 애착은 혼자 있는 것을 가능하게 한다.

해설 주제문인 첫 문장에서, 관심을 가져주는(즉, 애착을 느끼는) 타인이 있을 때 아이들이 혼자 있을 수 있는 능력을 발달시킬 수 있다고 하였으므로 빈칸에는 ② '애착'이 자연스럽다.

오답 풀이

선택률	보기 해석
① 9%	Hardship(고난)
③ 46%	Creativity(창조성)
④ 8%	Compliment(칭찬)
⑤ 7%	Responsibility(책임감)

Gradually, the bath, taken alone, is a time **when** the child is comfortable with her imagination.

→ 시간 선행사 a time을 꾸미는 관계부사 when이다.

 플러스⁺ **관계부사 when**

관계부사 when은 문장을 연결하며 시간을 대신하고, <전치사+관계대명사>와 바꿔쓸 수 있다.

July is the month **when** many families go on vacation.
= July is the month **on which** many families go on vacation.

F 정답 ④ 33% *2018 9월 학평*

해석 온라인 환경은 거기서 무슨 일이 일어나든 간에 얼마나 쉽게 저장할 수 있는지에 따라 아주 다양하고, 나는 이를 가리켜 그것(온라인 환경)의 '기록 가능성'과 '저장 가능성'이라고 부른다. 비록 소셜 미디어의 디자인, 활동, 멤버십이 시간이 흐르며 바뀔지도 모르겠지만, 사람들이 게시했던 내용은 보통 (훼손되지 않고) 온전하게 남아 있다. 이메일, 동영상, 음성, 텍스트 메시지는 저장될 수 있다. 완벽한 보존이 가능할 때, 시간은 멈춰 있다. 여러분은 원할 때마다 되돌아가서 그러한 과거의 사건들을 다시 돌아볼 수 있다. 다른 상황에서는, 우리가 받았다고 기억하는 듯한 이메일이 우리의 수신함에서 희한하게도 사라질 때와 마찬가지로, 영속성은 우리 손가락 사이로 빠져나가 버리고, 어떤 것이 어떻게든 존재했었는지에 대한 현실 검증에 이의를 제기하기까지 한다. 손가락으로 우연히 살짝 톡 건드린 것이, 만일 그렇게 하지 않았으면 영원히 존재했을 문서를 무(無)의 상태로 보낼 수 있다.

해설 빈칸 문장을 보충하는 마지막 문장에서, 우연히 건드리지 않더라면 '영원히 존재했을' 문서를 날리는 경우를 언급하고 있다. 이를 근거로 볼 때, 데이터의 ④ '영속성'이 우리 손을 벗어나는 경우가 있다는 내용이 적절하다.

오답 풀이

선택률	보기 해석
① 13%	scarcity(희소성)
② 13%	creativity(창의력)
③ 12%	acceleration(가속)
⑤ 18%	mysteriousness(불가사의함)

구문 풀이 6행

When perfect preservation is possible, time **has been suspended**.

→ <have been+과거분사>는 현재완료 수동태이다.

 플러스⁺ **현재완료 수동태**

현재완료와 수동태의 결합으로, <have/has+been+과거분사>의 형태이다.

The desk **has not been used** for 10 years.
'사용되는' 대상(수동태)   기간 표현(현재완료)

G 정답 ① 76% *2017 11월 학평*

해석 뇌의 진정한 본질은 무엇인가? 뇌는 천천히 변화하는 기계이며, 이는 좋은 것이다. 만약 여러분의 뇌가 하룻밤 사이에 완전히 바뀔 수 있다면 여러분은 불안정해질 것이다. 여러분의 전형적 행동 양식이 잠에서 깨서, 커피와 베이글을 가지고 신문을 읽고, 개를 산책시키고, 뉴스를 보는 것이라고 해 보자. 이것은 여러분의 습관적인 일상이다. 그런데 어느 밤, 여러분은 새벽 3시에 전화를 받고 속옷 차림으로 이웃을 살펴보러 뛰쳐나가야 한다. 만약 여러분의 뇌가 이 새로운 일상을 자기 것으로 만들어, 여러분이 매일 밤 새벽 3시에 계속 속옷만 입고 밖으로 뛰쳐나가야 한다면 어떻겠는가? 누구도 그러길 원치 않을 것이며, 그렇기에 우리 뇌가 이보다 더 많은 반복을 요한다는 것은 좋은 것이다! 천천히 변화하는 우리 뇌가 우리에게 주는 안정감을 받아들이고 고마워하자.

해설 뇌는 여러 차례의 반복을 통해 천천히 변한다(slow-changing)는 내용으로 보아, ① '안정감'을 빈칸에 넣는 것이 적절하다.

오답 풀이

선택률	보기 해석
② 6%	maturity(성숙함)
③ 3%	curiosity(호기심)
④ 6%	variability(가변성)
⑤ 6%	productivity(생산성)

구문 풀이 9행

Nobody would want that, so **it**'s a good thing **(that)** our brains require more repetition than that!

→ <가주어 it-진주어 that절> 구문이다.

 플러스⁺ **가주어 it과 진주어 that절**

to부정사구 주어와 마찬가지로, that절 주어 또한 가주어로 흔히 대체된다. 이는 긴 주어를 피하기 위함이다.

It is certain **that she will graduate**. → It: '그것' X

유형 플러스⁺ **빈칸 추론**

지문 내용을 근거로 빈칸에 들어갈 어구를 찾는 유형이다. 순서, 삽입과 함께 고난도 유형으로 꼽힌다.

① 빈칸에 들어갈 말과 동일한 맥락의 내용이 예시, 재진술 등의 형태로 제시될 수 있다. 이 경우 해당 내용과 같은 의미가 되도록 빈칸을 채운다.
② 빈칸에 들어갈 말과 반대되는 맥락의 내용이 대조, 대비, 비교 등의 형태로 함께 제시될 수 있다. 이 경우 해당 내용과 반대의 의미가 되도록 빈칸을 채운다.

A 정답 ③ 33%   *2023 9월 학평*

해석 유럽 초기 민주주의의 아이러니는 바로 유럽의 통치자들이 매우 오랫동안 현저하게 약했기 때문에 그것이 번성하고 번영했다는 것이다. 로마의 멸망 후 천 년 넘게, 유럽의 통치자들은 백성들이 생산하고 있던 것을 평가해 이를 바탕으로 상당한 세금을 부과할 능력이 부족했다. 유럽의 약함을 설명하는 가장 눈에 띄는 방법은 그들이 거둔 세입이 얼마나 적은지를 보여주는 것이다. (이러한 이유로, 유럽의 세금 징수원은 막대한 액수의 세입을 거둘 수 있었고, 그리하여 사회가 어떻게 기능해야 할지에 큰 영향을 미쳤다.) 유럽인들은 결국 강력한 세입 징수 시스템을 개발했지만, 그렇게 하는 데는 엄청나게 오랜 시간이 걸렸다. 중세 시대와 초기 근대의 일부 동안, 중국의 황제들과 이슬람 문명의 칼리프들은 작은 도시 국가들을 제외한 그 어떤 유럽 통치자들보다도 훨씬 더 많은 경제적 생산물을 뜯어낼 수 있었다.

해설 유럽 통치자들의 힘이 약했다는 것을 유럽의 적은 세입으로 알 수 있다는 내용인데, ③은 세입이 '막대했다'고 하므로 내용상 모순된다. 따라서 흐름상 어색한 것은 ③이다.

오답 풀이

선택률	오답 풀이
① 4%	유럽 통치자들이 '약했다'는 것을 보여주는 예로 '세금 징수 능력 부족'을 언급한다.
② 18%	①과 같은 맥락으로, 유럽 통치자들이 세금을 얼마 거두지 못했다는 사실을 언급한다.
④ 27%	강력한 세금 징수 시스템을 만들기까지 너무 오랜 시간이 걸렸다는 말은 세금 징수의 발판을 마련할 힘이 그만큼 부족했다는 뜻이다. 즉 ②-④가 자연스럽게 연결된다.
⑤ 18%	다른 문화권 통치자들은 훨씬 많이 거뒀다는 비교를 통해 주제를 뒷받침한다.

구문 풀이 9행

Europeans would eventually develop strong systems of revenue collection, but **it took them an awfully long time to do so**.
→ <it takes A+시간+to-V(A가 ~하는 데 …의 시간이 걸리다)> 구문이다.

 플러스 <it takes+시간> 구문

it takes A+시간+to-V
= it takes+시간+for A+to-V

It took **me a year to learn** French.
= It took **a year for me to learn** French.

B 정답 ④ 55%   *2022 6월 학평*

해석 인플레이션에 관한 위험성은 개인 투자의 미래 실질 가치에 대한 불확실성과 관련되어 있다. 예를 들어, 당신이 수수료가 없고 이자가 생기지 않는 은행 계좌에 100달러를 가지고 있다고 하자. 그대로 내버려 두면, 그 은행 계좌에는 항상 100달러가 있을 것이다. 만약 당신이 1년 동안 은행에 그 돈을 보관하고 그 기간에 인플레이션이 100퍼센트라면, 당신은 여전히 100달러만 가지고 있는 것이다. 이제, 만약 당신이 그 돈을 인출해서 당신의 지갑에 넣어둔다면, 당신은 1년 전에 당신이 살 수도 있었던 물건들의 절반만 구매할 수 있게 될 것이다. 다시 말하자면, 만약 인플레이션이 당신이 받고 있는 이자의 양보다 더 빨리 증가한다면, 이것은 시간이 지남에 따라 당신 투자의 구매력을 감소시킬 것이다. (만약 당신이 당신의 상품의 가격을 올린다면 당신 회사의 총수입에 어떤 일이 일어날지를 미리 아는 것은 매우 유용할 것이다.) 그것이 우리가 명목 가치와 실질 가치를 구별하는 이유이다.

해설 인플레이션으로 인한 화폐의 실질 가치 변화에 대해 설명하는 글이다. 화폐의 명목 가치가 같아도 인플레이션에 따라 그 실질 가치가 달라질 수 있다는 것이 이 글의 핵심으로, ④ '상품 가격에 따라 회사의 총수입이 어떻게 변할지 미리 아는 것은 유용하다'는 문장은 이 글과 무관하다.

오답 풀이

선택률	오답 풀이
① 5%	화폐의 명목 가치에는 변화가 없음을 예시를 들어 설명하고 있다.
② 17%	화폐의 실질 가치가 변화하였음을 예시를 들어 설명하고 있다.
③ 16%	인플레이션에 따라 화폐의 실제 구매력(실질 가치)이 달라짐을 설명하고 있다.
⑤ 7%	명목 가치와 실질 가치를 구별해야 함을 이야기하고 있다.

구문 풀이 4행

If you keep that money in the bank for a year, **during which inflation is 100 percent,** you've still got $100.
→ <전치사+관계대명사> during which가 이끄는 계속적 용법의 관계대명사절이 쓰이고 있다. 선행사는 a year이다.

플러스 전치사+관계대명사

관계대명사절에서 선행사(관계대명사)의 원래 위치가 전치사의 목적어 자리일 경우, 해당 전치사를 관계대명사 앞에 쓸 수 있다. <전치사+관계대명사> 뒤에는 완전한 문장이 나온다.

The house has a beautiful garden **on which** we often have picnics.   <주어+동사+목적어>가 있는 완전한 문장

The report provides information **on which** decisions will be based.   be based on의 on이 관계대명사 앞으로 이동

C 정답 ③ 66% 2021 3월 학평

해석 지금까지 대학 교수, 정치인, 마케팅 담당자, 그리고 그 외의 사람들은 제품과 서비스를 어린 소비자들에게 직접 판촉하는 것이 윤리적으로 옳은지 그렇지 않은지를 논쟁해 왔다. 이것은 또한 아이들이 광고되는 것을 본 제품을 더 많이 사도록 광고주들이 아이들을 조종하는 것을 도와야 할지 의문을 가진 심리학자들에게도 딜레마이다. 광고주들은 아이들이 그 '적절한' 제품을 소유하고 있지 않으면 자신이 패배자라고 느끼게 만드는 것이 쉽다는 사실을 이용한 것을 인정했다. (제품이 더 인기 있어질 때 더 많은 경쟁자들이 시장에 진출하고 마케팅 담당자들은 경쟁력을 유지하기 위해 그들의 마케팅 비용을 줄인다.) 영리한 광고는 아이들에게 만약 그들이 광고되는 제품을 가지고 있지 않으면 자신의 또래 친구들에게 부정적으로 보일 것이라고 알려 주고, 그로 인해 아이들의 정서적인 취약성을 이용한다. 광고가 만들어 내는, 끊임없이 부적절하다고 느끼는 감정은 아이들이 즉각적인 만족감과 물질적 소유물이 중요하다는 믿음에 집착하게 되는 데 기여한다고 언급되어 왔다.

해설 아이들에게 직접적으로 광고를 하는 것에 대한 부정적 시각이 이 글의 주제이므로 ③ '경쟁력 유지를 위해 마케팅 비용을 줄인다'는 부자연스럽다.

오답 풀이

선택률	오답 풀이
① 3%	아이들에 대한 판촉을 도와야 하는지가 딜레마라고 말하고 있다.
② 6%	광고를 통해 아이들의 패배감을 이용하기 쉽다고 말하고 있다.
④ 17%	광고가 아이들의 정서적 취약성을 이용한다고 말하고 있다.
⑤ 5%	광고가 아이들에게 미치는 부정적 영향을 설명하고 있다.

구문 풀이 1행

Academics, politicians, marketers and others have in the past debated **whether or not** it is ethically correct to market products and services / directly to young consumers.

→ 'whether (or not)'은 '~인지 아닌지'의 의미를 가지며, 명사절을 이끈다. 접속사 if도 같은 의미의 명사절 접속사로 쓸 수 있지만, if절은 'or not'과 함께 쓸 수 없음에 주의한다.

구문 플러스 접속사 whether

whether은 명사절을 이끄는 접속사로도 쓰이고, 부사절을 이끄는 접속사로도 쓰인다. 명사절을 이끌 때에는 '~인지 아닌지'의 의미로 쓰이고, 부사절을 이끌 때에는 '~이든지 간에'의 의미로 쓰인다.

I wonder **whether you would accept it or not**. (명사절)
Whether you win or lose, we shall respect the process. (부사절)
보통 주절과 콤마로 분리

D 정답 ③ 57% 2020 9월 학평

해석 주요 대양은 모두 서로 연결되어 있어, 그것들의 지리적 경계가 대륙의 경계보다 덜 명확하다. 결과적으로 그들의 생물 군집은 육지에서의 생물 군집보다 명확한 차이를 덜 보여준다. 각 해저분지 안에서 물이

천천히 회전하기 때문에 대양 자체가 끊임없이 움직인다. 이 이동하는 물은 해양 생물을 여기저기로 운반하며, 또한 그들의 새끼나 유충의 분산을 돕는다. (즉 연안 해류는 예상보다 훨씬 덜 동물들을 이동시킬 뿐 아니라 근해 지역 내로 동물을 가두기도 한다.) 더욱이 다양한 지역의 대양 해수 덩어리 환경 사이의 변화도는 매우 점진적이며, 종종 생태학적 내성이 다른 매우 다양한 유기체가 서식하는 넓은 지역으로 확장된다. 유기체의 이동에 방해물이 있을 수 있지만, 넓은 대양에 확실한 경계는 없다.

해설 대양은 대륙과 달리 물이 이동하기 때문에 경계가 덜 명확하다고 말하고 있다. 따라서 ③ '해류가 동물들을 덜 이동시킨다'는 문장은 이 글과 무관하다.

오답 풀이

선택률	오답 풀이
① 3%	대양의 지리적 경계가 대륙보다 덜 명확함을 말하고 있다.
② 7%	대양의 움직임이 해양 생물을 이동시킨다고 말하고 있다.
④ 24%	대양의 이동이 미치는 생태학적 영향을 말하고 있다. 첨가의 Furthermore가 있어 앞에 나오지 않은 내용을 추가하는 것이 어색하지 않다.
⑤ 6%	분명한 경계가 없다는 주제가 반복된다.

구문 풀이 7행

~ coastal ocean currents **not only** move animals much less often than expected, **but** they **also** trap animals within near-shore regions.

→ <not only A but also B>는 'A뿐만 아니라 B도'의 의미로 A, B에는 같은 형태 구문이 온다.

구문 플러스 not only A but also B

<not only A but also B>는 'A뿐만 아니라 B도'의 의미로 <B as well as A>와 같다.

He **not only** did his homework **but also** cooked dinner.
→ He cooked dinner **as well as** did his homework.

E 정답 ④ 54% 2019 6월 학평

해석 사람들은 종종 만약 Tanzania의 Hadza의 한 어른이 대수 방정식을 푸는 방법을 모른다면, 그가 우리보다 덜 똑똑함에 틀림없다고 잘못 추정한다. 그러나 어떤 문화의 사람은 빠른 학습자이고 다른 문화의 사람은 느린 학습자라는 것을 보여주는 증거는 없다. 비교 문화 연구는 우리에게 다른 문화의 사람들이 다른 문화적인 내용(태도, 가치관, 생각, 그리고 행동 양식)을 배운다는 것과 그들이 이것을 유사한 정도의 효율성으로 성취한다는 것을 가르쳐왔다. 전통적인 Hadza 사냥꾼은 대수학 지식이 동아프리카 목초지에서의 삶에 대한 적응성을 특별히 강화해주지 않기 때문에 그것을 학습하지 않았다. (결과적으로, 그는 생존 기술이 부족했기 때문에 목초지의 환경에 적응하는 데 실패했다.) 그러나, 그는 3일 동안 보지 못한 상처 입은 부시 벅을 어떻게 추적하는지와 어디에서 지하수를 찾을 수 있는지를 알 것이다.

해설 문화에 따라 자신들이 배우는 내용이 다르므로 다른 태도, 가치관 등을 갖게 된다는 내용이 이 글의 주제이므로 ④ '생존 기술 부족으로 목초지 환경 적응에 실패했다'는 부자연스럽다.

오답 풀이

선택률	오답 풀이
① 8%	문화에 따라 사람들의 학습 속도(능력)을 판단할 수 없다며 문화의 상대성을 말하고 있다.
② 12%	문화에 따라 서로 다른 문화 내용이 습득되지만 효율성은 비슷하다는 내용이 언급된다. 이는 문화적 상대성을 뒷받침하는 설명이다.
③ 16%	문화의 상대성의 예로 전통적인 Hadza 사냥꾼이 나온다.
⑤ 8%	전통적인 Hadza 사냥꾼이 알고 있을 내용은 비록 대수 방정식과는 무관하지만 자기 환경에 적합한 내용일 것이라는 부연 설명이다.

구문 풀이 1행

People often assume erroneously that if a Hadza adult of Tanzania does not know how to solve an algebraic equation, then he **must** be less intelligent than we are.

→ 조동사 must는 '~해야 한다'는 의무로 많이 쓰이지만, 이 문장처럼 확신을 나타낼 때도 쓴다.

구문 플러스 must의 의미

must는 '~임에 틀림없다'는 확신을 나타낼 때 쓸 수 있다. 이때 반의어는 cannot(~일 리가 없다)이다.

It **must** be true. (그것은 사실임에 틀림없다.)
↔ It **cannot be** true. (그건 사실일 리 없다.)

F 정답 ④ 50%   *2018 6월 학평*

해석 신체는 면역 체계라 불리는, 병균에 대항하는 효율적인 자연적 방어 체계를 갖고 있다. 면역 체계는 너무나 복잡해서 그것을 설명하려면 책 한 권이 있어야 할 것이다. 간단히 말해, 면역 체계가 위험한 균을 감지할 때, 신체는 특별한 세포를 만들어내기 위해 가동되며, 그 세포는 마치 군대처럼 혈액에 의해 전쟁터로 운반된다. 보통은 면역 체계가 승리하고, 그 사람은 회복한다. 그 후, 면역 체계는 그 특정한 전투를 위해 발달시켰던 분자로 된 장비를 기억해서, 똑같은 균에 대한 모든 후속 감염은 너무 빨리 퇴치되어 우리는 그것을 알아차리지도 못한다. (그 결과, 약해진 면역 체계는 감염을 일으키고, 그 감염은 면역 체계에 손상을 일으켜, 더 나아가 저항력을 약화시킨다.) 그것이 당신이 홍역이나 천연두와 같은 질병을 한 번 앓고 나면, 그것에 다시 걸릴 가능성은 거의 없어지는 이유이다.

해설 면역 체계가 작동하는 방식과 그것의 효율성에 대한 글이므로, ④ '그 결과, 약해진 면역 체계는 감염을 일으키고, 그 감염은 면역체계에 손상을 일으켜, 더 나아가 저항력을 약화시킨다.'는 글의 흐름상 어울리지 않는다.

오답 풀이

선택률	오답 풀이
① 10%	면역 체계가 작동하는 방식을 설명하고 있다.
② 19%	면역 체계가 효율적으로 작동해 사람이 회복한다는 내용이다.
③ 10%	한 번 감염을 퇴치하고 나면 후속 감염은 더 잘 퇴치할 수 있다는 설명이다.
⑤ 9%	구체적인 예시를 들어 면역 체계의 효율성을 뒷받침하고 있다.

구문 풀이 2행

The immune system is **so** complicated **that** it would take a whole book to explain it.

→ <so ~ that …>은 '너무 ~해서 …하다'는 의미의 구문이다.

구문 플러스 so 형용사/부사 that

<so 형용사/부사 that>은 '너무 ~해서 …하다'의 의미로 that 뒤에는 완전한 절이 오며, 의미에 따라 <enough to부정사> 또는 <too ~ to부정사>로 바꿀 수 있다.

The painting was **so** realistic **that** it looked like a photograph.
= The painting was realistic **enough to look** like a photograph.
This job offer is **so** good **that** it **can't** be true.
= This job offer is **too** good **to** be true.

G 정답 ③ 66%   *2017 9월 학평*

해석 과학 분야에서 드론의 사용이 증가해 오고 있다. 드론은 모든 종류의 연구 자료를 수집하는 데 도움이 될 수 있다. 예를 들면, 기상학 분야에서 드론은 습도, 기압, 온도, 바람의 세기, 복사열 등에 관한 자료를 수집할 수 있다. 토네이도나 허리케인이 접근하는 경우에 사람들은 드론에 의해 수집된 정보의 도움으로 안전을 추구할 수 있다. (드론 배달 시스템으로, 도로 위를 주행하며 대기를 오염시키는 수송 수단이 적어질 것이다.) 드론은 이전에는 도달하기 어렵거나 비용이 많이 들었던 장소에서 유의미한 자료, 즉, 대기와 기후에 관한 새로운 과학적 지식을 제공할 자료를 모을 수 있다. 그러한 지식은 기존의 기후 모형을 개선하고 더 정확한 예측을 제공할 것이다.

해설 드론이 대기와 기후의 자료 수집에 주요한 역할을 한다는 내용이다. 하지만 ③은 드론 배달 시스템으로 인해 대기 오염이 줄어들 것이라는 의미이므로 흐름상 무관하다.

오답 풀이

선택률	오답 풀이
① 6%	기상학에서 드론의 역할을 말하고 있다.
② 7%	기후 변화의 자료를 수집하는 드론을 말하고 있다.
④ 6%	대기와 기후에 대한 새로운 과학 자료를 드론으로 쉽게 얻을 수 있는 이점을 말하고 있다.
⑤ 12%	드론으로 수집한 자료를 통해 얻을 수 있는 점을 말하고 있다.

In case of nearing tornados or hurricanes, people can seek safety
with the help of the data **gathered by drones**.

→ 과거분사가 길어져서 명사 뒤에서 수식하는 형태이다.

유형 플러스 무관한 문장 찾기

무관한 문장 유형은 지문 안에서 문맥을 방해하거나 주제와 동떨어진 문장
을 찾는 문제이다. 다음과 같은 해법으로 해결하도록 한다.

① 번호가 없는 글 초반부의 문장에서 주어진 지문의 전반적인 흐름을 파악
   하여 주제와 중심 소재를 알아둔다.
② 핵심어가 있더라도, 글의 다른 부분에서 언급되지 않는 다른 소재가 함께
   언급된다면 정답일 확률이 높다.
③ 역접어 없이 글의 전체적 내용과 반대되는 문장이 나오지 않는지 살펴본
   다.
④ 지시어나 대명사가 문맥 속에서 자연스러운지 확인한다.

A 정답 ④ 45% *2023 6월 학평*

【해석】 실험 방법의 근본적인 본질은 조작과 통제이다. 과학자들은 관심 변인을 조작하고, 차이가 있는지 확인한다. 동시에, 다른 모든 변인의 잠재적 영향을 통제하려고 시도한다. 사건의 근본적인 원인을 식별하는 데 있어 통제된 실험의 중요성은 아무리 강조해도 지나치지 않다. 현실의 통제되지 않은 세계에서, 변인들은 종종 상관관계가 있다. 예를 들어, 비타민 보충제를 섭취하는 사람들은 비타민을 섭취하지 않는 사람들과는 다른 식습관과 운동 습관을 지닐 수 있다. 그 결과, 만약 우리가 비타민의 건강상 영향을 연구하고 싶다면, 우리는 단지 현실 세계만 관찰할 수 없는데, 왜냐하면 이러한 요소(비타민, 식단, 운동) 중 어느 것이든 건강에 영향을 미칠 수 있기 때문이다. 오히려, 우리는 현실 세계에서 실제로 일어나지 않는 상황을 만들어야 한다. 그것이 바로 과학 실험이 하는 일이다. 그것들은 그 밖의 다른 모든 것을 일정하게 유지하면서, 한 번에 하나의 특정 변인을 조작하여 세상에서 자연적으로 발생하는 관계를 분리하려고 애쓴다.

【해설】 ④ 앞에서 비타민 보충제 효과 연구를 예로 들어, 우리가 현실 세계만 관찰해서는 제대로 된 변수 측정을 하기 어렵다고 설명한다. 그런데 ④ 뒤에서는 바로 '그것'이 과학 실험에서 일어난다고 하므로, 흐름이 어색하게 끊긴다. 이때 주어진 문장을 ④에 넣어보면, ④ 앞에 이어서 '오히려' 현실 세계를 보면 결과가 잘 안 나오기 때문에 '통제된' 환경을 설정해야 한다는 내용이 자연스럽게 연결된다. 따라서 답으로 적절한 것은 ④이다.

【오답 풀이】

선택률	오답 풀이
① 9%	앞에서 통제된 실험 환경이 중요함을 언급하고, 뒤에서 '현실 세계'는 통제되지 않은 환경임을 덧붙이고 있다.
② 18%	비타민 보충제를 섭취하는 사람들을 연구하는 예시를 언급한다.
③ 19%	앞에서 비타민 보충제를 섭취하는 사람들은 섭취하지 않는 사람들과 생활 습관이 다를 거라고 언급하고, 뒤이어 '그렇기 때문에' 현실 세계에서 이들을 그대로 연구하면 보충제가 아닌 다른 요인들이 결과에 간섭할 수도 있다는 내용이 자연스럽게 연결된다.
⑤ 9%	앞의 scientific experiments가 뒤에서 They로 연결된다.

【구문 풀이】 4행

Scientists manipulate a variable of interest, and see **if** there's a difference.

→ whether로 바꿀 수 있는 명사절 접속사 if이다.

 【플러스】 if/whether와 어울려 쓰이는 동사

if/whether 명사절과 자주 함께 쓰이는 동사
: check(확인하다), see(알아보다), doubt(의심하다), question(의문을 갖다), be not sure[uncertain](불확실하다) 등

We **doubt if** it will snow as forecast.
I'll **see if** she is available.

B 정답 ③ 49% *2022 9월 학평*

【해석】 적응은 한 세대로부터 다음 세대로 전해지는 특성과 함께 개체군의 변화를 수반한다. 이것은 순응 — 바뀐 환경에 반응한 개별 유기체의 변화 — 과는 다르다. 예를 들어, 당신이 여름을 야외에서 보낸다면, 당신은 햇빛에 순응하게 될 것이다. 당신의 피부는 당신을 태양으로부터 보호하는 어두운 색소의 농도를 높일 것이다. 이것은 일시적인 변화이고, 당신은 그 일시적인 변화를 미래 세대에 물려주지 않을 것이다. 하지만, 피부 색소를 생산하는 능력은 유전된다. 햇빛이 강렬한 환경에 사는 사람들의 경우, 피부 색소를 생산하는 능력이 좋은 사람들이 색소 생산 능력이 좋지 않은 사람들보다 더 번영하거나 생존할 가능성이 높고, 그 특징은 이후 세대에서 더욱 흔해진다. 주변을 둘러보면, 당신은 적응의 수많은 사례를 찾을 수 있다. 예를 들어, 기린의 특징적인 긴 목은 우연히 더 긴 목을 갖게 된 개체들이 높은 나무의 잎을 먹는 데 유리했기 때문에 발달했다.

【해설】 ③ 이전까지는 순응(유전되지 않는, 개별 유기체의 일시적인 변화)에 대해 이야기하다가, ③ 이후에는 갑자기 적응(유전되는 특징)에 대한 이야기가 등장한다. 즉, ③에서 흐름이 어색하게 끊기므로, However로 시작하는 주어진 문장을 넣어 전환을 자연스럽게 만들어 주어야 한다.

【오답 풀이】

선택률	오답 풀이
① 7%	'순응(개별 유기체의 변화)'에 대한 구체적 예시가 이어진다.
② 17%	앞서 설명한 '순응'이 유전되지는 않음을 설명한다.
④ 21%	앞서 설명한 '색소 생산 능력의 유전'을 '적응'으로 명명하며 적응의 다른 예시들을 소개하려 한다.
⑤ 6%	적응의 구체적 예시로 기린의 예시가 이어진다.

【구문 풀이】 8행

For populations living in intensely sunny environments, individuals with a good ability **to produce skin pigments** are more likely to thrive, or to survive, than people with a poor ability **to produce pigments**, and that trait becomes increasingly common in subsequent generations.

→ 형용사적 용법의 to부정사구가 앞의 ability를 수식하고 있다.

 【플러스】 to부정사

to부정사는 명사, 형용사, 부사 역할을 한다

• It is easy **to judge people based on their actions**. (주어—명사 역할)
• I need many people **to care animals**. (명사 수식—형용사 역할)
• She goes to school **to learn many things**. (목적—부사 역할)

해석 위험은 종종 문제나 상황에 접근하는 방법에 대한 불확실성으로부터 발생한다. 그러한 위험을 피할 수 있는 한 가지 방식은 숙련되고 일 처리 방법을 알고 있는 당사자와 계약하는 것이다. 예를 들어, 크고 복잡한 시스템의 생산을 위한 도구 및 장비의 자본 비용과 관련된 재정적 위험을 최소화하기 위해, 제조업자는 시스템의 주요 부품 생산을 그러한 부품들에 정통한 공급 업자들에게 하청을 줄지도 모른다. 이것은 제조업자에게 이러한 부품을 생산하기 위한 도구 및 장비와 관련된 재정적 위험을 덜어 준다. 그러나, 한 종류의 위험의 이전은 종종 다른 종류의 위험을 이어받는 것을 의미한다. 예를 들어, 부품에 대한 작업을 하청주는 것은 제조 업자를 외부 업자들에 의존하게 만들고, 이는 품질 관리, 일정 관리, 완제품 시스템의 성능과 관련된 위험들을 증가시킨다. 그러나 이러한 위험들은 공급업자들의 신중한 관리를 통해 종종 감소될 수 있다.

해설 ④ 이전까지는 부품 생산을 하청 주는 것의 장점에 대해 이야기하다가, ④ 이후에는 갑자기 하청의 부작용에 대한 이야기가 등장한다. 즉, ④에서 흐름이 어색하게 끊기므로, However로 시작하는 주어진 문장을 넣어 전환을 자연스럽게 만들어주어야 한다.

오답 풀이

선택률	오답 풀이
① 3%	불확실성에서 오는 위험과 이를 피하는 방법에 대한 이야기가 이어지고 있다.
② 10%	숙련된 당사자와 계약하는 내용이 구체적인 예시로 이어지고 있다.
③ 21%	주요 부품 생산의 하청 이야기와 그 장점에 대한 이야기가 이어지고 있다.
⑤ 5%	하청으로 인해 새로 발생하는 위험과 이를 관리하는 방법에 대한 이야기가 이어지고 있다.

구문 풀이 3행

For example, to minimize the financial risk **(which is)** associated with the capital cost of tooling and equipment for production of a large, complex system, a manufacturer might subcontract the production of the system's major components to suppliers **(who are)** familiar with those components.

→ <주격관계대명사+be동사>가 생략되어 과거분사와 형용사가 바로 앞의 선행사를 수식하는 형태가 되었다.

구문 플러스 선행사를 후치 수식하는 형용사구

<주격관계대명사+be동사>가 생략되면 be동사 뒤의 분사구 또는 형용사구가 선행사를 후치 수식하는 형태가 된다.

He is looking at the guy **(who is)** wearing a red shirt.
　　　　　　　　　　　　　　현재분사구

해석 1960년대의 모든 의학적 성취 중에서 가장 널리 알려진 것은 1967년 남아프리카 공화국의 외과 의사 Christiaan Barnard에 의해서 행해진 최초의 심장 이식이었다. 18일 후에 그 환자가 사망한 것은 의학

의 새로운 시대를 환영하는 사람들의 사기를 떨어뜨리지 않았다. 심장이식을 할 수 있는 능력은 1950년대에 병원에 도입된 인공호흡기의 개발과 관련이 있었다. 인공호흡기는 많은 생명을 구할 수 있었지만, 심장이 계속해서 뛰는 사람들이 모두 다 어떤 다른 중요한 기능을 회복한 것은 아니었다. 어떤 경우에는 그들의 뇌가 완전히 기능을 멈추었다. 그러한 환자들이 이식 수술용 장기 공급자가 될 수 있다는 인식으로 인해 하버드 뇌사 위원회가 설립되었고, 모든 '식별 가능한 중추 신경계 활동'의 부재는 '사망의 새로운 기준'이 되어야 한다는 그 위원회의 권고로 이어졌다. 그 권고는 그 후 일부 수정을 거쳐 거의 모든 곳에서 받아들여졌다.

해설 ④ 앞은 인공호흡기가 많은 생명을 살리기는 했지만 모두 다 회복한 것은 아니었다는 내용인데, ④ 뒤에서는 '그런' 환자들이 장기 기증의 원천이 될 수 있었다는 내용이다. '그런 환자들'이 ④ 앞에서 충분히 부연되지 않아서 흐름이 끊기는 상황이다. 이때 주어진 문장을 보면, ④ 앞의 '회복하지 못한 환자들'을 their로 가리키며, 이들의 신체 기능이 완전히 멈춰버리기도 했다는 부연 설명을 이어 가고 있다. 이렇듯 '신체 기능을 잃은 이들'을 ④ 뒤에서는 장기 기증에 참여시키기로 했다고 언급하는 것이다. 따라서 ④가 답으로 적절하다.

오답 풀이

선택률	오답 풀이
① 5%	심장 이식의 시작과 함께 새로운 의학 시대가 태동하려 했다는 내용이 앞뒤로 자연스럽게 전개된다.
② 8%	심장 이식이 인공호흡기 발달로도 이어졌다는 내용이 자연스럽게 연결된다.
③ 8%	앞서 언급된 인공호흡기 발달로 많은 생명이 살아났지만, 모두가 그러지는 못했다는 내용 흐름이 자연스럽다.
⑤ 8%	앞서 언급된 권고안(recommendation)이 그대로 다시 언급되며 글의 결론을 이끈다.

구문 풀이 8행

Respirators could save many lives, but not all those **whose** hearts kept beating ever recovered any other significant functions.

→ 관계대명사 whose는 선행사의 소유격을 나타낸다.

구문 플러스 소유격 관계대명사

소유격 관계대명사 whose 뒤에는 관사 없는 명사로 시작하는 완전한 절이 나온다.

Have you heard stories about people **whose** hair turned white overnight?

해석 Herbert Cecil Booth는 최초의 이동식 전동 진공청소기를 발명한 것으로 공로를 자주 인정받는다. 사실 그는 단지 이런 속성을 가진 장치들에 대해 '진공청소기'라는 용어를 만든 최초의 사람이라고 주장했었고, 이 점이 그가 그렇게 공로를 인정받는 이유를 설명해 줄 수도 있다. 우리 모두 알고 있듯이, '진공'이라는 용어는 부적절한 이름인데, 왜냐하면 진공청소기에는 진공이 없기 때문이다. 오히려 (더 정확히 말하면), 그것은 내부에 있는 공기가 송풍기에 의해서 용기 밖으로 배출되었다가 (다시) 작은 구멍을 통해 밀폐된 용기 안으로 유입되는 것이다. 그러나 나

는 '흡입을 만들기 위한, 폐쇄된 용기 안에서의 빠른 공기의 흐름' 청소기라는 말이 과학적으로 들리지 않고, 편리한 이름도 아니라고 생각한다. 어쨌든 우리는 역사적으로 그것을 어쩔 수 없이 사용하고 있으며, Booth 이전에 '진공'에 대한 어떠한 언급도 찾기가 어렵다. 흥미롭게도 Booth 자신은 자신이 의도한 발명품을 일반적인 용어로 설명하는 임시 제품 설명서를 제출할 때 '진공'이라는 용어를 사용하지 않았다.

해설 ③ 앞에서 '진공'이라는 명칭이 부적절함을 지적한 후, ③ 이후 a "rapid air ~" cleaner라는 명칭도 부적절하다고 지적하는데, 두 문장이 역접의 접속사 But으로 연결되어 있어 흐름이 어색하다. 따라서 주어진 문장을 ③에 넣어 내용을 연결하는 것이 자연스럽다.

오답 풀이

선택률	오답 풀이
① 5%	진공청소기 발명과 그 명명에 관한 이야기가 이어진다.
② 9%	'진공'이라는 용어의 부적절함에 대해 지적한다.
④ 25%	'진공'청소기라고 부를 수 밖에 없던 이유들을 나열한다.
⑤ 9%	Booth도 제품 설명서에 '진공'이라는 표현을 쓰지 않았다고 부연설명하고 있다.

구문 풀이 5행

he only claimed to be the first to coin the term "vacuum cleaner" for devices of this nature, which may explain **why he is so credited**.
→ <why+주어+동사~>의 의문사절이 동사 explain의 목적어 역할을 하고 있다.

구문 플러스 간접의문문

의문문이 문장의 주어, 보어, 목적어 역할을 할 때 <의문사+주어+동사~>의 어순으로 쓰는 것에 주의한다.

Have you decided **what you're going to do**?
┈> what are you going to do(X)

F 정답 ⑤ 48%　　　　　*2017 9월 학평*

해석 즐겨 찾는 웹사이트들은 때때로 사용자들을 오랜 친구처럼 맞이한다. 온라인 서점은 이름으로 고객들을 환영하며, 그들이 읽고 싶어 할 수도 있는 새로운 도서를 제안해 준다. 부동산 사이트는 시장에 나온 새로운 부동산에 대해 방문자들에게 알려 준다. 이러한 기술은 인터넷 서버가 사용자들을 기억해 낼 수 있도록 개인의 웹 브라우저 안에 저장하는 작은 파일인 cookie에 의해 가능한 것이다. 그러므로 cookie는 개인에게 매우 도움이 될 수 있다. 예컨대, cookie는 사용자가 매번 구입할 때마다 전자상거래 사이트에 이름과 주소를 입력해야만 하는 귀찮은 일을 덜어 준다. 하지만 사람들이 온라인에서 무엇을 하는지에 대해 추적할 수 있는 cookie가 기업체나 정부기관으로 하여금 개인정보를 축적하도록 도움으로써 사생활을 침해할 수 있다는 우려가 제기돼 왔다. 보안은 또다른 우려인데, cookie는 공유 컴퓨터를 훨씬 덜 안전하게 하고 해커들이 시스템에 침입하게 할 많은 방법을 제공한다.

해설 ⑤ 앞은 쿠키의 장점을 말하는데, ⑤ 이후에서는 쿠키에 대한 우려를 말하고 있어 흐름이 어색하게 끊긴다. 따라서, However로 시작하

는 주어진 문장을 ⑤에 넣어 내용을 전환하는 것이 자연스럽다.

오답 풀이

선택률	오답 풀이
① 8%	웹사이트들이 사용자들을 오랜 친구처럼 맞이하는 예시들이 이어진다.
② 7%	앞의 예시들이 쿠키에 의해 가능하다고 말한 뒤, 쿠키에 대해 설명한다.
③ 13%	쿠키가 개인에게 도움이 될 수 있다고 말한다.
④ 22%	쿠키가 어떻게 도움이 되는지 구체적인 예를 든다.

구문 풀이 10행

For example, cookies save users the chore of having to enter names and addresses into e-commerce websites **every time** they make a purchase.
→ 주절 뒤에 <every time S V> 시간 부사절이 나왔다.

구문 플러스 주의할 시간 부사절 접속사

every time(=whenever) S V: ~할 때마다
next time S V: 다음에 ~할 때
the moment(=as soon as) S V: ~하자마자, ~한 순간

Every time he talks about Cindy, he smiles.
You may return the book **next time** we meet.
The moment she came in, I fell in love with her.

G 정답 ④ 65%　　　　　*2016 9월 학평*

해석 과학적 발견들은 과거 어느 때보다 더 빠른 속도로 결실을 맺고 있다. 예를 들어, 1836년에 곡식을 베고 타작하고 짚을 다발로 묶고, 낟알을 자루 안으로 쏟아 부어 주는 기계가 발명되었다. 그 기계는 심지어 그 당시에 20년이 된 기술에 기초하였다. 그러나, 1930년이 되어서야 비로소 그러한 기계가 실제로 유통되었다. 타자기에 대한 최초의 영국 특허권은 1974년에 발급되었다. 그러나 타자기가 상업적으로 판매되기까지는 150년이란 시간이 걸렸다. 오늘날 아이디어와 적용 사이의 그러한 지연은 거의 생각할 수 없다. 그것은 우리가 우리 조상들보다 더 간절하거나 열망이 더 강해서가 아니라, 시간이 지나면서 우리가 그 과정을 앞당기는 모든 종류의 사회적 장치들을 발명해 왔기 때문이다. 그러므로, 혁신적인 순환의 첫 번째와 두 번째 단계 사이의 시간, 즉 아이디어와 적용 사이의 시간이 급격히 줄었다는 것을 우리는 알게 된다.

해설 ④ 앞에서는 과학적 발견이 느리게 적용되었던 과거를 설명하다가, ④ 이후에서는 그 적용이 앞당겨진 현재에 대해 설명한다. 따라서 ④에 주어진 문장을 넣어 과거에서 현재 상황으로 내용을 자연스럽게 전환해 주어야 한다.

오답 풀이

선택률	오답 풀이
① 6%	과거에는 과학적 발견이 느리게 적용되었음을 예시로 설명한다.
② 6%	첫 번째 예시(곡식 처리 기계)에 대한 내용이 이어지고 있다.

③ 8%	첫 번째 예시에서 두 번째 예시(타자기)로 이어지고 있다.
⑤ 15%	사회적 장치가 발명되어, 이에 따라(Thus) 아이디어와 적용 사이의 시간이 줄었다고 말하며 마무리한다.

구문 풀이 11행

~ we have, over time, invented all sorts of social devices **to hasten** the process.

→ to부정사구가 앞에 있는 명사 social devices를 수식한다.

 유형 플러스 주어진 문장 넣기

다섯 군데의 빈칸 중에 주어진 문장이 들어갈 위치를 찾는 문제로 문장과 문장 사이의 연결이 자연스럽도록 해야 한다.

① 먼저 핵심 소재를 파악한다. 주어진 문장을 먼저 읽어 내용을 파악한다.

② 정관사, 대명사, 지시어 등을 살펴보아 문장 간의 관계를 유추한다.

③ 흐름이 갑자기 어색해지는 부분이 있다면 주어진 문장을 대입해본다.

A 정답 ③ 69%　　　　　2023 3월 학평

해석 일반적이지만 잘못된 가정은 우리가 이성의 피조물이라는 것이지만, 사실 우리는 이성과 감정 둘 다의 피조물이다. 어떤 이성이든 항상 결국 감정으로 이어지므로, 우리는 이성만으로 살아갈 수 없다. (예컨대) 나는 통곡물 시리얼을 선택해야 할까, 혹은 초콜릿 시리얼을 선택해야 할까?

(B) 나는 내가 원하는 모든 이유를 열거할 수 있지만, 그 이유는 뭔가에 근거를 둬야 한다. 예를 들어 건강하게 먹는 것이 내 목표라면 나는 통곡물 시리얼을 선택해도 되지만, 건강해지고 싶다는 것을 뒷받침하는 나의 이유는 무엇일까?

(C) 더 오래 살고 싶다, 사랑하는 사람들과 양질의 시간을 더 보내고 싶다 등등 많고 많은 이유를 더 열거할 수 있지만, 그러한 이유를 뒷받침하는 이유는 무엇인가? 이제 여러분은 이유란 것이 궁극적으로 가치, 느낌, 또는 감정과 같은 비이성에 근거함을 알 수 있을 것이다.

(A) 우리가 가진 이러한 뿌리 깊은 가치, 느낌, 감정은 추론의 산물인 경우가 거의 없지만, 물론 추론의 영향을 받을 수 있다. 우리는 추론을 시작하기 전, (정확히는) 효과적으로 추론을 시작하기 훨씬 전에 가치, 느낌, 감정을 가진다.

해설 주어진 글은 우리가 이성과 감정에 둘 다 영향을 받는다고 언급하며, 시리얼을 선택하는 경우를 가정한다. (B)는 둘 중 한 시리얼을 '원하는 이유'가 많더라도 그 이유가 다시 뭔가에 근거를 두고 있어야 할 것이라고 설명하며, '건강해지고 싶다'는 이유를 한 예로 든다. (C)는 건강해지고 싶다는 이유 이면에도 또 이유가 있을 것인데, 그 이유를 찾다 보면 결국 '감정'이 뒤에 있음을 알게 될 것이라고 한다. 마지막으로 (A)는 결국 우리가 이유를 따지기 (오래) 전부터 감정에 영향을 받는다는 결론으로 향한다. 따라서 ③ '(B)-(C)-(A)'가 글의 순서로 가장 자연스럽다.

오답 풀이

선택률	오답 풀이
① 3%	(A)의 These deep-seated values, feelings, and emotions로 이어질 만한 내용이 주어진 글에 언급되지 않았다.
② 12%	(B)의 마지막이 '대체 건강해지고 싶은 것 이면의 이유는 뭘까'라는 질문으로 끝났는데, (A)는 '이유'에 관한 언급 없이 'These ~ emotions'를 언급한다.
④ 8%	주어진 글이 '두 시리얼 중 어느 것을 선택할까'라는 질문으로 끝났는데, (C)의 첫 문장은 시리얼 선택에 관해 더 설명하지 않은 채 '더 오래 살고 싶어서 ~'와 같은 엉뚱한 이유를 언급한다.
⑤ 6%	④와 동일

구문 풀이 3행

We cannot get by on reason alone **since** any reason always eventually leads to a feeling.

→ since는 여기서 '~ 때문에'라는 의미이다.

구문 플러스 부사절 접속사 since

① 시간(~ 이후로) → 주절에 현재완료 시제가 옴
② 이유(~ 때문에)

We've been friends **since** we were young. → 시간
Since it's raining, we should stay inside. → 이유

B 정답 ⑤ 40%　　　　　2022 6월 학평

해석 촉감 수용체는 신체 곳곳에 퍼져 있지만 골고루 퍼져 있지는 않다. 대부분의 촉감 수용체는 손가락 끝, 혀, 그리고 입술에서 발견된다.

(C) 예를 들어, 각각의 손가락 끝에는 약 5천 개의 서로 떨어져 있는 촉감 수용체가 있다. 몸의 다른 부분에서는 훨씬 더 적다. 당신의 등 피부에는 촉감 수용체가 2인치만큼 떨어져 있을 수도 있다.

(B) 당신은 스스로 이것을 테스트해 볼 수 있다. 누군가에게 당신의 등을 한 손가락, 두 손가락, 또는 세 손가락으로 찌르게 하고 그 사람이 얼마나 많은 손가락을 사용했는지 추측해 보라. 만약 손가락이 서로 가까이 붙어 있다면, 당신은 아마 그것이 한 개라고 생각할 것이다.

(A) 하지만 만약 손가락끼리 멀리 떨어져 있다면, 당신은 그것들을 각각 느낄 수 있다. 하지만 만약 그 사람이 당신의 손등에 같은 행동을 한다면 (몇 개의 손가락이 사용되고 있는지 모르게 하기 위해 당신의 눈을 감은 채로), 당신은 아마 손가락이 서로 가까이 있을 때조차도 쉽게 구별할 수 있을 것이다.

해설 주어진 글에 따르면 촉감 수용체는 신체 곳곳에 불균형하게 퍼져 있는데, (C)에서는 예를 들어 등 피부에는 촉감 수용체가 서로 멀리 떨어져 있다고 한다. 이어서 (B)에서는 실제로 찔러보기 테스트를 해 보면 이를 알 수 있다고 하는데, (A)에서는 '등과 달리' 손등은 촉감 수용체가 촘촘히 많다는 대비를 제시한다. 따라서 정답은 ⑤ '(C)-(B)-(A)'이다.

오답 풀이

선택률	오답 풀이
① 4%	(B)의 '등 찔러보기' 이야기가 (A)의 '손등 찔러보기' 이야기보다 먼저 나와야 역접의 접속사 But의 쓰임이 자연스럽다.
② 16%	(C)의 '등 피부에서의 촉감 수용체의 분포' 이야기가 (B)의 '등 찔러보기' 이야기보다 먼저 나와야 흐름이 자연스럽다.
③ 17%	②와 동일
④ 23%	①과 동일

구문 풀이 5행

Yet if the person does the same thing on the back of your hand (**with your eyes closed**, so that you don't see how many fingers are being used), you probably will be able to tell easily, even when the fingers are close together.

→ 'with+명사+분사'는 '~가 …한/된 채로'라는 의미로, 분사는 명사와의 능·수동 관계에 따라 현재분사 혹은 과거분사가 쓰인다.

구문 플러스 with+명사+분사

'with+명사+현재분사'는 '~가 ...한 채로'라는 의미로, 명사와 분사와의 관계가 능동이다. 한편 'with+명사+과거분사'는 '~가 ...된 채로'라는 의미로, 명사와 분사와의 관계가 수동이다.

· She spoke **with tears falling down her cheeks**.
  → tears가 '굴러떨어지는' 주체(능동)
· Jack stood **with his arms folded**.
  → his arms가 '접히는' 대상(수동)

C 정답 ③ 60%   *2021 6월 학평*

해석 한 조사에서, 61%의 미국인들이 정부가 '빈곤층 지원'에 더 많은 돈을 쓰는 것을 지지한다고 말했다.
(B) 그러나 같은 모집단이 '복지'에 더 많은 정부 예산을 쓰는 것을 지지하느냐는 질문을 받았을 때, 단지 21%만이 찬성했다. 다시 말해, 만약 당신이 장기 질환을 가진 사람들에게 재정적 도움을 주는 것이나 저소득 가정의 급식비를 대주는 것과 같은 개별 복지 프로그램들에 대해 사람들에게 물어보면, 사람들은 대체로 그것들에 찬성한다.
(C) 그러나 만약 당신이 '복지'에 관해 질문한다면 — 방금 열거한 것과 정확히 동일한 프로그램을 나타내는 — 그들은 그것에 반대한다. '복지'라는 단어는 아마도 많은 정치인들과 신문들이 그것을 묘사하는 방식 때문인지, 부정적인 함축된 의미를 가지고 있다.
(A) 따라서, 질문의 프레이밍은 여러 가지 방식으로 답변에 큰 영향을 미칠 수 있으며, 이는 당신의 목표가 사람들이 생각하는 것에 대한 '진정한 척도'를 얻는 것이라면 중요하다. 그리고 다음 번에 한 정치인이 '설문 조사에서 입증하기로, 대다수의 국민들이 나에게 동의합니다'라고 말하는 것을 듣게 된다면, 매우 조심하라.

해설 '빈곤층에 대한 지원'이라고 표현했을 때에는 많은 미국인들이 이를 지지하였으나, (B) '복지'라고 표현을 바꾸자 지지율이 대폭 감소하였다는 내용이다. 다시 말해, 미국인들은 개별 복지 프로그램들에 대해서는 대체로 찬성하지만, (C) '복지'라는 표현에 대해서는 부정적으로 반응한다. (A) 이에 대한 결론은, 질문의 프레이밍이 답변에 큰 영향을 미친다는 것이다. 따라서 정답은 ③ '(B)-(C)-(A)'이다.

오답 풀이

선택률	오답 풀이
① 4%	주어진 글에서 '질문'이 언급되지 않는데 '질문의 프레이밍'을 말하는 (A)가 먼저 연결될 수는 없다.
② 15%	(C)는 (B)와 똑같은 배경 상황에서 단어만 바꿔 말하는 경우를 예로 드는 것이므로 결론인 (A)보다 먼저 나와야 한다.
④ 8%	주어진 글에 '열거된 프로그램'이 없는데 '이 프로그램'에 반대할 것이라는 내용의 (C)를 연결할 수는 없다.
⑤ 11%	(B)의 individual welfare programmes가 먼저 나오고 이를 지칭하는 (C)의 those exact same programmes가 후에 나와야 한다.

구문 풀이 5행

~ next time you **hear** a politician **say** 'surveys prove that the majority of the people agree with me', **be very wary**.
→ 시간 부사절이 앞에 붙은 명령문(be ~ wary)이다. 시간 부사절은

<hear+목적어+원형부정사>의 5형식 구조이다.

구문 플러스 지각/사역동사의 5형식 구조

지각동사: see, watch, observe, hear, feel 등
사역동사: make, have, let
→ 목적어가 목적격보어를 행하는 주체일 때(능동), 원형부정사를 목적격보어로 취할 수 있음

I **saw** him **carry[carrying]** the box.
  목적어   목적격보어(him이 '상자를 나르는' 주체)
She **made** him **do** the dishes.
  목적어   목적격보어(him이 '설거지하는' 주체)

D 정답 ② 44%   *2020 3월 학평*

해석 농경 이후에 존재했던 사람들이 더 행복했든, 더 건강했든, 아니면 둘 다 아니었든 간에 상관없이, 더 많은 수의 사람들이 있었다는 것은 부인할 수 없다. 농경은 더 많은 사람을 부양하는 동시에, 그들을 지탱해주는 농작물을 기를 더 많은 사람을 필요로 한다.
(B) 물론, 추정치는 다양하지만, 증거는 농경이 확립된 후 전 세계적으로 인구가 1~5백만 명에서 수억 명으로 증가했다는 것을 보여준다.
(A) 그리고 더 큰 가족을 위해 더 큰 상자의 시리얼을 사는 것 같이, 더 많은 인구는 단지 모든 것의 규모를 확장하는 것을 의미하지는 않는다. 그것은 사람들의 생활 방식에 질적인 변화를 가져온다.
(C) 예를 들어 더 많은 사람은 더 많은 종류의 질병을 의미하는데, 특히 그 사람들이 한 곳에 정착해 있을 때 그렇다. 그러한 사람들의 집단은 또한 음식을 장기간 보관할 수 있고, 이것은 가진 자와 가지지 못한 자로 이루어진 사회를 만들어 낸다.

해설 농경 이후의 사회는 많은 인구를 필요로 한다는 주어진 글 뒤에, (B)에서 그 인구 수의 추정치를 설명하고, (A)에서 이러한 인구 증가가 규모의 확장만을 의미하는 것이 아니라 질적인 변화를 가져온다고 말한다. 그 후 (C)에서 질적인 변화의 예를 드는 것이 자연스럽다. 따라서 정답은 ② '(B)-(A)-(C)'이다.

오답 풀이

선택률	오답 풀이
① 8%	주어진 글과 (B)는 농경으로 인한 인구 증가라는 한 가지 소재로 묶이는데, (A)는 '질적 변화'라는 다른 소재로 넘어간다. 따라서 (A)보다 (B)가 먼저 나와야 한다.
③ 14%	(A)에서 '질적 변화'라는 일반적 표현이 먼저 나와야 (C)에서 '질병 확산'이라는 구체적 예를 드는 것이 자연스럽다.
④ 14%	인구 증가를 언급하는 주어진 글 뒤에 갑자기 '질병 확산'을 언급하는 (C)를 연결할 수는 없다.
⑤ 16%	④와 동일

구문 풀이 12행

Those groups of people can also store food for long periods, **which** creates a society with haves and have-nots.
→ 동사구인 'store food for long periods'를 선행사로 받는 계속적 용법의 which이다.

E 정답 ⑤ 50%　　　　　　　　　　　　　　　2019 9월 학평

해석 내용 지식에 대한 직접 평가와 관련된 테스트 전략은 여전히 탐구 주도형 교실에서 그 가치를 지닌다.
(C) 우리가 내용을 무시하고 관찰을 통해 학생의 기술만을 평가하기를 원한다고 잠시 가정해 보자. 문제는 기술과 내용이 서로 연결되어 있다는 것이다. 학생이 패턴 분석에 실패하면 그것은 학생이 패턴 분석을 올바르게 수행하는 방법을 이해하지 못하기 때문일 수 있다.
(B) 그러나 또한 패턴을 만들려고 하는 내용을 이해하지 못한 것일 수도 있다. 때때로 학생들은 탐구 과정을 잘 이해하고 사회 학과의 전략을 능숙하게 적용할 능력이 있지만 내용을 잘못 해석하기 때문에 그렇게 하지 못할 것이다.
(A) 이러한 이유로 우리는 학생의 내용 이해에 대한 측정이 필요하다. 이것을 올바르게 하기 위해서 우리의 평가가 학생들이 탐구에서 사용하는 내용을 이해했는지 여부에 대한 정확한 측정을 하게 하는지 확실하게 할 필요가 있다.

해설 내용 지식에 대한 직접 평가가 탐구 주도형 교실에서도 여전히 가치를 지닌다고 말하면서 (C)에서 사례를 가정하여 설명한다. 한 학생이 패턴 분석을 제대로 수행하지 못하는 것이 내용을 이해하지 못해서일 수 있다는 설명이 (B)에서 이어지고, 그러므로 내용 지식에 대한 측정이 필요하다는 (A)로 마무리되는 것이 흐름상 적절하다. 따라서 정답은 ⑤ '(C)-(B)-(A)'이다.

오답 풀이

선택률	오답 풀이
① 4%	(A)는 이 글의 결론에 해당하므로 맨 앞에 올 수 없다.
② 12%	(B)는 앞부분에 대한 반대 설명이므로 (C)의 뒤에 와야 한다.
③ 15%	②와 동일
④ 17%	(A)는 이 글의 결론에 해당하므로 (B) 앞에 올 수 없다.

구문 풀이 1행

Testing strategies **relating to direct assessment of content knowledge** still have their value ~
→ 여기서 relating은 앞의 명사 strategies를 수식하는 현재분사이다.

F 정답 ② 69%　　　　　　　　　　　　　　　2018 9월 학평

해석 거의 모든 데님이 파란색이기 때문에 바지를 "파란 청바지"라 부르는 것은 거의 표현이 중복된 것처럼 보인다. 청바지는 당신의 옷장에서 아마도 당신의 가장 활용도가 높은 바지이겠지만, 사실은 파란색이 특별히 무난한 색은 아니다.
(B) 왜 파란색이 (청바지에) 가장 흔하게 사용되는 색상인지 궁금해 해 본 적이 있는가? 파란색은 청색 염료의 화학적 특성 때문에 데님의 색깔로 선택되었다. 대부분의 염료는 높은 온도에서 색이 천에 들러붙게 하며 스며들게 된다.
(A) 반면에 최초의 청바지에 사용되었던 천연 남색 염료는 옷감의 바깥쪽에만 들러붙었다. 남색으로 염색된 데님을 빨 때, 그 염료 중 소량은 씻겨 나가게 되고 실이 그 염료와 함께 나오게 된다.
(C) 데님을 더 많이 빨수록, 더 부드러워지게 되고, 마침내 당신이 아마 가장 좋아하는 청바지로부터 얻는, 닳아 해지고 나만을 위해 만들어졌다는 바로 그 느낌을 얻게 된다. 이 부드러움은 청바지를 노동자들이 선택한 바지로 만들었다.

해설 청바지의 파란색이 무난한 색상은 아니라는 주어진 문장 뒤에, 그럼에도 불구하고 파란색이 청바지에 사용된 이유를 묻는 (B)가 이어지고, 대부분의 염료와는 다른 파란 염료의 특성을 설명하는 (A)가 이어져야 한다. 마지막으로 청바지를 빨수록 부드러워지고, 그 때문에 노동자들이 청바지를 가장 많이 선택하게 되었다는 내용의 (C)가 이어져야 자연스럽다. 따라서 정답은 ② '(B)-(A)-(C)'이다.

오답 풀이

선택률	오답 풀이
① 8%	(A)는 (B)에서 언급된 '파란색의 화학적 특성'을 설명하므로 (B) 뒤에 와야 한다.
③ 12%	(C)는 노동자들이 청바지를 선택했다는 결론을 제시하므로 가장 마지막에 와야 한다.
④ 5%	①과 동일
⑤ 4%	(A) 후반부와 (C) 초반부가 둘 다 '데님 세탁'을 언급한다. 즉 (A)에서 마무리되지 못한 내용이 (C)로 이어지는 것이므로 (A)-(C)의 순서가 바르다.

구문 풀이 13행

The more denim was washed, **the softer** it would get, eventually achieving that worn-in, made-just-for-me feeling you probably get with your favorite jeans.
→ <the 비교급 ~, the 비교급 …>은 '~할수록 더 …하다'라는 비교급 표현이다.

구문 플러스* the 비교급, the 비교급

<the 비교급 주어+동사, the 비교급 주어+동사>는 '~할수록 더 …하다'의 의미로 'The sooner, the better.(빠르면 빠를수록 좋다.)'처럼 속담으로 자주 쓰인다.

The earlier we start to research, **the more** information we can get.

G 정답 ④ 56% 2016 9월 학평

해석 진화는 인간에게 축구를 할 수 있는 능력을 주지 않았다. 실제로, 그것은 찰 수 있는 다리와 반칙을 할 수 있는 팔꿈치를 생기게 했으나, 이것이 우리에게 가능케 하는 일이라고는 아마도 혼자서 페널티 킥을 연습하는 것뿐이다.

(C) 우리가 어느 날 오후에 학교 운동장에서 만난 낯선 사람들과 경기를 시작하기 위해서는 전에 만난 적이 없는 열 명의 팀 구성원들과 조화를 이루어야 할 뿐만 아니라 또한 상대편 열 명의 선수들이 같은 규칙으로 경기를 하고 있다는 것을 알 필요가 있다.

(A) 의례화된 공격에 낯선 동물을 끌어들이는 다른 동물들은 주로 본능에 의해 그렇게 한다. 전세계의 강아지들은 그들의 유전자에 내재된 거친 놀이에 대한 규칙들을 가지고 있다.

(B) 그러나 십 대 인간들은 축구에 대한 그러한 유전자를 가지고 있지 않다. 그럼에도 불구하고 그들은 모두 축구에 대한 동일한 생각 체계를 배워 왔기 때문에 그들은 완전히 낯선 사람들과 경기를 할 수 있다. 이러한 생각들은 전적으로 가상이지만, 모두가 그러한 생각체계를 공유한다면 우리는 그 누구와도 경기를 할 수 있다.

해설 인간에게 혼자 축구할 능력이 주어지지 않았다는 주어진 글 뒤로, 축구를 하려면 규칙을 알아야 한다는 내용의 (C)가 먼저 연결된다. 이어서 (A)는 다른 동물들의 경우 본능과 유전자에 의해 놀이를 함께한다고 설명하고, (B)는 다시 인간에 관한 이야기로 돌아와 글을 마무리한다. 따라서 글의 순서로 가장 적절한 것은 ④ '(C)-(A)-(B)'이다.

오답 풀이

선택률	오답 풀이
① 6%	주어진 글과 (A)까지는 자연스러워 보일 수 있지만, (A) 뒤에 (C)를 연결하려면 소재가 동물에서 인간으로 다시 바뀐다는 것을 예고하는 역접어가 나와야 한다. 하지만 (C)에는 역접어가 없다.
② 11%	주어진 글도 (B)도 인간이 본능적으로 축구를 할 수 없다는 내용인데, 두 단락을 But으로 연결하면 어색하다.
③ 16%	②와 동일
⑤ 11%	(C)와 (B)가 모두 인간에 관한 내용인데 두 단락을 But으로 연결하면 어색하다.

구문 풀이 1행

True, it produced legs for kicking and elbows for fouling, but **all that this enables us to do** is perhaps **practice** penalty kicks alone.

→ 주어가 <all+주어 ~ do>의 형태로 the only thing(오직 ~한 것이라고는)의 의미를 나타낼 때, be동사의 보어인 to부정사에서 to가 생략될 수 있다.

구문 플러스* 주격보어 자리의 원형부정사

주격보어인 to부정사에서 to가 생략되려면 다음 조건을 따른다.
• 주어가 what 또는 all로 시작할 것
• 주어의 마지막이 do동사일 것
• 문장의 본동사가 be동사일 것

What she needs to **do** is **improve** her communication skills.
All you have to **do** is **listen** carefully.
All she **did** was **apologize** for her mistake.

유형 플러스* 글의 순서 배열

주어진 글 뒤에 (A), (B), (C)의 글을 순서대로 배치하는 유형이다.

단서가 될 수 있는 표현들

인칭대명사	성(性)과 수가 일치하는 명사를 포함하는 문장 뒤에 이어져야 한다.
지시대명사	명사가 언급된 문장 뒤에 이어져야 하며 수 일치에 주의해야 한다.
one, the other, another	one이 먼저 나오고, 뒤에 추가의 another나 두 당사자 중 '상대방'을 가리키는 the other를 연결해준다.
(the) others	some과 연결된 경우 some이 포함된 단락 뒤에 위치해야 한다.
reason(s)	앞에 나온 원인에 관한 결론을 이끄는 문장으로 원인이 포함된 단락 뒤에 위치해야 한다.

A 정답 ① 40%   *2023 9월 학평*

해석 2006년에 연구자들은 미국에 대한 9.11 테러 공격 이후 도와주려는 동기에 관한 연구를 수행했다. 그 연구에서, 그들은 타인에게 초점을 맞춘 동기(다른 사람의 불편을 줄여주려고 베푸는 것) 때문에 돈, 혈액, 물품, 또는 다른 형태의 도움을 주었던 사람들이 원래 동기가 자기 고통을 줄이는 것이었던 사람들에 비해 1년 뒤에도 여전히 지원을 제공할 가능성이 거의 네 배 더 높다는 것을 발견했다. 이 결과는 감정적 자극의 차이에서 비롯된 것 같다. 9.11의 사건들은 미국 전역의 사람들에게 감정적으로 영향을 미쳤다. 자기 자신의 고통을 줄이고자 베푼 사람들은 초기의 베풂을 통해 그 감정적 고통을 해소하면서 감정적 자극을 줄였다. 하지만, 다른 사람들의 고통을 줄이기 위해 베푼 사람들은 공격 이후 오랫동안 계속해서 고생하는 피해자들에게 계속 공감했다.
→ 한 연구에서 밝히기로, 베푸는 행위가 타인에 초점을 맞춘 동기보다는 자기중심적 동기에 의해 유도될 때 (A) 지속될 가능성이 더 낮은데, 이것은 아마도 감정적 자극의 (B) 감소 때문이었다.

해설 마지막 세 문장에 따르면, 9.11 테러 이후 자기 자신의 감정적 고통을 줄이기 위해 피해자들을 도왔던 사람들은 타인에 초점을 맞춘 동기를 지녔던 사람들에 비해 도움을 지속하지(sustained) 못했다. 이는 도움을 주는 행위를 통해 그들의 감정적 고통과 자극이 줄어들었기(decline) 때문이다. 따라서 요약문에는 ① '지속될 - 감소'가 들어가야 적절하다.

오답 풀이

선택률	보기 해석
② 18%	sustained(지속될), maximization(극대화)
③ 7%	indirect(간접적일), variation(변화)
④ 22%	discouraged(단념될), reduction(감소)
⑤ 14%	discouraged(단념될), increase(증가)

구문 풀이 11행

However, those who gave to reduce others' distress did not **stop empathizing** with victims who continued to struggle long after the attacks.
→ <stop V-ing(~하기를 멈추다)>와 <stop to-V(~하기 위해 멈추다)>를 구별해서 기억해 둔다.

구문 플러스 to부정사와 동명사를 모두 목적어로 취하는 동사

의미 차이가 있는지 없는지 나누어 기억한다.

- 의미 차이가 없는 동사: love, like, start, begin, continue, cease
- 의미 차이가 있는 동사

remember / forget	+ to-V: (앞으로) ~할 일을 기억하다/잊다
	+ V-ing: (이미) ~한 일을 기억하다/잊다
regret	+ to-V: ~하게 되어 유감이다
	+ V-ing: ~한 것을 후회하다
mean	+ to-V: ~할 작정이다
	+ V-ing: ~을 뜻하다

cf. 동명사를 목적어로 취하지만, 의미상 주의할 동사

try	+ V-ing: 한번 ~해보다
	+ to-V: ~하려고 노력하다 → 부사적 용법
stop	+ V-ing: ~하기를 관두다
	+ to-V: ~하려고 멈추다 → 부사적 용법

B 정답 ② 47%   *2022 6월 학평*

해석 퍼포먼스 심리학의 큰 아이러니는 개개의 운동선수들이 능력이 있는 한 이길 것이라고 믿도록 가르친다는 것이다. 어느 누구도 의심하지 않는다. 어느 누구도 내면의 회의에 빠지지 않는다. 그것이 스포츠 심리학의 논리이다. 하지만 오직 한 사람만이 이길 수 '있다'. 그것이 스포츠의 논리이다. 과학자와 운동선수의 차이점을 주목하라. 의심은 과학자의 일상적인 업무이다. 진보는 이론을 반박하는 증거에 집중하고 그에 따라 이론을 개선함으로써 이루어진다. 회의론은 과학적 진보의 추진 연료이다. 하지만 운동선수에게 의심은 독이다. 진보는 증거를 무시함으로써 만들어진다. 그것은 의심과 불확실성에 영향을 받지 않는 사고방식을 만드는 것이다. 다시 한번 되풀이하자면, 이성적인 시각에서 보면 이건 미친 짓이나 다름없다. 왜 운동선수는 자신이 질 거라는 모든 가능성이 있다는 것을 알면서도 이길 것이라고 확신해야 하는가? 왜냐하면, 이기기 위해서, 선수는 증거가 아니라 무엇이든 마음이 유용하게 해낼 수 있는 것에 자신의 신념을 할당해야 하기 때문이다.
→ 과학적 진보를 이루기 위해 (A) 회의적인 태도가 요구되는 과학자들과는 달리, 스포츠 심리학은 운동선수들이 성공하기 위해서는 그들이 이길 수 있는지에 대한 불확실한 감정을 (B) 없애야 한다고 말한다.

해설 과학자들은 의심이 일상적인 업무일만큼 회의적인(skeptical) 태도가 필요하지만, 반대로 운동 선수들에게는 그러한 회의적 태도가 독이 되므로 그것을 없애야(eliminate) 한다는 내용이다. 따라서 정답은 ② 이다.

오답 풀이

선택률	보기 해석
① 20%	confident(자신감 있는), keep(유지하다)
③ 8%	arrogant(거만한), express(표현하다)
④ 14%	critical(비판적인), keep(유지하다)
⑤ 10%	stubborn(고집 센), eliminate(없애다)

구문 풀이 12행

Because, to win, one must proportion one's belief, not to the evidence, but to **whatever the mind can usefully get away with.**
→ 여기서 복합관계대명사 whatever는 명사절을 이끌고, anything that으로 바꾸어 쓸 수 있다.

whatever는 명사절(~하는 것은 무엇이든)을 이끌 수도 있고, 부사절(~하는 것이 무엇이든지)을 이끌 수도 있다.

- Do **whatever** you can.
  → whatever이 명사절(do의 목적어)을 이끈다. anything that으로 바꾸어 쓸 수 있다.
- I'll follow my heart **whatever** they say.
  → whatever이 부사절을 이끈다. no matter what으로 바꾸어 쓸 수 있다.

C 정답 ① 57% *2021 6월 학평*

해석 Boston의 1차 진료 의사(지역 병원 의사)인 Anne Thorndike는 아주 좋은 생각을 했다. 그녀는 의지력이나 동기를 아주 조금도 바꾸지 않고 수천 명의 병원 직원들과 방문객들의 식습관을 개선할 수 있다고 믿었다. 사실, 그녀는 그들과 대화할 계획을 아예 세우지 않았다. Thorndike는 병원 구내식당의 "선택 구조"를 바꾸기 위해서 연구를 설계했다. 그녀는 공간 안에 음료가 놓여 있는 방식을 바꾸는 것으로 시작했다. 원래, 구내식당 내의 금전등록기 옆에 있는 냉장고들은 탄산음료로만 채워져 있었다. 그녀는 각각의 냉장고에 선택 사항으로 물을 추가했다. 게다가, 그녀는 공간 전체에 있는 음식을 두는 장소 옆에 물병이 담긴 바구니들을 놓았다. 탄산음료는 여전히 본래의 냉장고에 있었지만, 물은 이제 음료를 둔 모든 곳에서 이용 가능하게 되었다. 다음 3개월 동안, 병원의 탄산음료 판매 숫자는 11.4퍼센트만큼 떨어졌다. 한편, 물병의 판매는 25.8퍼센트만큼 증가했다.
→ Thorndike에 의해 수행된 연구는 병원 구내식당의 음료 (A) 배치가 사람들이 하는 선택에 영향을 주어, 탄산음료의 소비를 (B) 낮춘다는 것을 보여주었다.

해설 Thorndike가 탄산음료의 소비를 낮추기(lowered) 위하여 병원 구내식당 음료 배치(placement)를 바꾸었다는 내용이다. 따라서 정답은 ①이다.

오답 풀이

선택률	보기 해석
② 17%	placement(배치), boosted(북돋웠다)
③ 12%	price(가격), lowered(낮췄다)
④ 10%	price(가격), boosted(북돋웠다)
⑤ 3%	flavor(맛), maintained(유지했다)

구문 풀이 2행

She believed she could improve the eating habits of thousands of hospital staff and visitors **without changing** their willpower or motivation in the slightest way.
→ <without -ing>은 '~하지 않은 채'라는 뜻이다.

- in -ing: ~하는 데 있어, ~할 때
- on -ing: ~하자마자
- by -ing: ~함으로써
- without -ing: ~하지 않은 채

He takes pride **in helping** others succeed.
On entering the room, he noticed a strange smell.
He improved his English **by watching** movies.
She managed to solve the puzzle **without asking** for help.

D 정답 ① 56% *2020 3월 학평*

해석 천연자원이 풍부한 일부 개발 도상국들은 자국의 천연자원에 대한 지나친 의존을 초래하는 경향이 있으며, 이로 인해 더 낮은 생산적 다양화와 더 낮은 성장률을 초래한다. 자원의 풍요가 그 자체로 해가 되어야 하는 것은 아니다. 많은 나라들이 풍부한 천연자원을 가지고 있으며 자국의 경제 활동을 다양화함으로써 그것(풍부한 천연자원)에 대한 의존에서 가까스로 벗어났다. 가장 중요한 나라들을 꼽자면 캐나다, 호주, 또는 미국의 경우가 그러하다. 하지만 일부 개발 도상국들은 자국의 많은 천연자원에 대한 의존에 갇혀 있다. 자연 자본에 대한 과도한 의존은 다른 형태의 자본을 배제하고 그로 인해 경제 성장을 저해하는 경향이 있기 때문에 그들은 일련의 문제를 겪고 있다.
→ 경제 활동을 (A) 다양화하지 않은 채 풍부한 천연자원에 의존하는 것은 경제 성장에 (B) 장애가 될 수 있다.

해설 천연자원에 대한 의존으로 인해 생산력이 저하되고 성장률이 낮아지는 등 장애(barrier)가 되기 때문에 경제 활동을 다양화하여(varying) 천연자원에 대한 의존을 벗어나야 한다고 말하고 있다. 따라서 정답은 ①이다.

오답 풀이

선택률	보기 해석
② 11%	varying(다양화하지), shortcut(지름길)
③ 8%	limiting(제한하지), challenge(난제)
④ 19%	limiting(제한하지), barrier(장애)
⑤ 3%	connecting(연결하지), shortcut(지름길)

구문 풀이 3행

Resource abundance **in itself** need not do any harm: many countries have abundant natural resources and have managed to outgrow their dependence on them by diversifying their economic activity.
→ in itself는 '그 자체'라는 뜻의 관용표현이다.

- in inself: 그 자체
- by oneself: 혼자(=alone)
- for oneself: 혼자 힘으로, 스스로

The artwork was a masterpiece **in itself**.
He lived **by himself** throughout his life.
She decided to travel the world **for herself**.

E 정답 ② 52%   *2019 9월 학평*

해석 우리가 귀여운 생명체를 볼 때, 우리는 그 귀여운 것을 꼭 쥐고자 하는 압도적인 충동과 싸워야 한다. 그리고 꼬집고, 꼭 껴안고, 심지어 깨물고 싶을 수도 있다. 이것은 완전히 정상적인 심리학적 행동, 즉 '귀여운 공격성'이라 불리는 모순 어법이며, 비록 이것이 잔인하게 들리기는 하지만, 이것은 해를 끼치는 것에 관한 것은 결코 아니다. 사실, 충분히 이상하게도, 이러한 충동은 실제로는 우리로 하여금 (남을) 더 잘 보살피게 한다. 인간 뇌에서 귀여운 공격성을 살펴본 최초의 연구가 이것이 뇌의 여러 부분과 관련된 복잡한 신경학적 반응이라는 것을 이제 드러냈다. 연구자들은 귀여운 공격성이 우리가 너무 감정적으로 과부하되어서 정말 귀여운 것들을 돌볼 수 없게 되는 것을 막을지도 모른다고 제시한다. "귀여운 공격성은 우리가 제대로 기능하도록 해 주고, 우리가 처음에 압도적으로 귀엽다고 인지하는 것을 실제로 돌볼 수 있도록 해 주는 조절 기제로 기능할지도 모른다."라고 주 저자인 Stavropoulos는 설명한다.
→ 연구에 따르면, 귀여운 공격성은 과도한 감정을 (A) 조절하고 귀여운 생명체를 (B) 돌보게 하는 신경학적인 반응으로서 역할을 할지 모른다.

해설 글에 따르면, 귀여운 것에 대한 과도한 충동은 감정을 조절하고 (regulate) 귀여운 것을 돌보게(care) 하는 감정을 불러 일으킨다. 따라서 정답은 ②이다.

오답 풀이

선택률	보기 해석
① 26%	evaluate(평가하다), care(돌보다)
③ 11%	accept(인정하다), search(찾다)
④ 5%	induce(유도하다), search(찾다)
⑤ 3%	display(보여주다), speak(말하다)

구문 풀이 5행

~ this compulsion may actually **make us more caring**.
→ 5형식 동사 make 다음에 목적어(us)가 오고 목적격 보어로 형용사가 왔다.

구문 플러스 5형식 문장

<동사+목적어+목적격 보어>의 순으로 쓰며 목적격 보어로 형용사, 명사, 동사원형, to부정사 등이 온다.

- She **kept me warm**. (형용사)
- They **called her Mary**. (명사)
- It **makes her look** like a rabbit. (동사원형)
- I **want him to finish** the work. (to부정사)

F 정답 ① 58%   *2018 9월 학평*

해석 한 초등학교 선생님이 아주 흔히 언급된다고 생각한 것을 사용해 학생들이 분수 부분을 이해하도록 돕고 있는 중이다. "오늘, 우리는 추수감사절에 인기 있는 호박파이를 자르는 것에 대해 이야기할 거예요." 그녀는 (분수) 부분에 대한 설명을 이어간다. 그녀의 이야기에 열심히 몰두하던 한 어린 아프리카계 미국인 소년이 의아한 표정으로 질문한다. "호박파이가 뭐예요?" 대부분의 아프리카계 미국인들은 고구마파이를 명절 만찬으로 차리는 경향이 있다. 사실 아프리카계 미국인 부모가 자식들에게 호박파이에 관해 설명하는 방식 중 하나는 그게 고구마파이 같은 거라고 말하는 것이다. 그들에게는 고구마파이가 흔히 언급되는 것이다. 호박파이에 친숙하지 않다는 그 작은 차이조차, 학생에게는 간섭의 원인이 될 수 있다. 수업에 적극적으로 참여하기보다는, 그는 호박파이를 상상하려고 노력하는 데 사로잡혀 있었을지도 모른다. 그건 무슨 맛일까? 무슨 냄새가 날까? 그것의 질감은 사과나 체리 파이처럼 덩어리졌을까? 아이의 마음속에서 이런 모든 질문들은 선생님이 가르치려 시도하는 분수라는 주제보다 더 초점이 될 수 있다.
→ (A) 문화적 지식의 작은 차이조차도 학생들의 (B) 학습에 영향을 미칠 잠재력이 있다.

해설 교사가 흔하다고 생각한 문화적(cultural) 대상을 예로 들어 수업할 때, 문화권이 다른 학생이 있다면 그 예를 이해하기 어려울 것이므로 학습(learning)에 간섭이 일어날 수 있다는 내용이다. 따라서 요약문에 들어갈 말로 적절한 것은 ①이다.

오답 풀이

선택률	보기 해석
② 8%	cultural(문화적), responsibility(책임)
③ 13%	mathematical(수학적), imagination(상상력)
④ 7%	mathematical(수학적), intelligence(지능)
⑤ 3%	nutritional(영양적), development(발달)

구문 풀이 5행

Well into her discourse, a young African American boy, looking **puzzled,** asks, "What is pumpkin pie?"
→ 감정 표현과 관련된 동사는 기본적으로 타동사이므로, '감정을 느낀다'는 의미를 나타내려면 과거분사로 흔히 쓴다.

구문 플러스 감정 타동사의 분사형

- 감정을 '유발하는' 주체 → 현재분사로 설명
- 감정을 '느끼는' 대상 → 과거분사로 설명

a **satisfying** game → game이 만족을 유발
satisfied customers → customers가 만족을 느낌

G 정답 ① 29%   *2017 11월 학평*

해석 '권력 거리'는 한 문화의 구성원들이 권력의 불평등한 분배를 얼마나 널리 수용하는지 가리키고자 사용되는 용어이다. 그것은 권력이 덜한 사회 구성원들이 권력 불평등을 수용하고 그것을 규범으로 여기는 정

도와 관련돼 있다. 권력 거리를 높게 수용하는 문화들(가령 인도, 브라질, 그리스, 멕시코, 그리고 필리핀)에서, 사람들은 평등하다고 여겨지지 않으며, 모든 사람은 사회 계층 내에서 명확히 정해지거나 할당된 입지를 가진다. 권력 거리가 낮게 수용되는 문화들(가령 핀란드, 노르웨이, 뉴질랜드, 그리고 이스라엘)에서는, 사람들은 불평등이 최소여야만 한다고 믿으며, 계층적 구분은 오직 편의상 구분으로 여겨진다. 이러한 문화에서는 사회 계층 내에 유동성이 더 크며, 개인이 개인적 노력과 성취를 토대로 사회 계층을 상승시키기가 상대적으로 쉽다.

→ 권력 거리가 높이 수용되는 문화에서 구성원들이 불평등을 더 (A) 기꺼이 수용하는 것과는 달리, 권력 거리에 대한 수용 정도가 낮은 문화에서는 사회 계층 내 더 많은 (B) 이동을 허락한다.

해설 '권력 거리'는 구성원이 사회적 불평등을 수용하는 정도를 가리키는 개념으로, 권력 거리에 대한 수용을 더 잘 받아들이는(willing) 문화에서는 사람들이 평등하게 취급받지 않지만, 권력 거리를 적게 수용하는 문화에서는 계층간 이동(mobility)이 더 자유롭다고 한다. 따라서 요약문에 들어갈 말로 적절한 것은 ①이다.

오답 풀이

선택률	보기 해석
② 18%	willing(기꺼이 ~하는), assistance(도움)
③ 12%	reluctant(마지못해 하는), resistance(저항)
④ 22%	reluctant(마지못해 하는), flexibility(유연성)
⑤ 3%	afraid(두려워하는), openness(개방성)

구문 풀이 2행

It relates to the degree **to which** the less powerful members of a society accept their inequality in power and consider it the norm.
→ <전치사+관계대명사> 뒤로 accept 3형식과 consider 5형식이 완전하게 연결되었다. 이 'to which ~'는 the degree를 수식한다.

유형 플러스 요약문 완성

요약문 완성 유형은 지문의 내용을 요약한 문장의 빈칸에 들어갈 알맞은 표현을 고르는 문제이다. 다음과 같은 해법으로 접근한다.

① 요약문을 먼저 읽어 요지나 주제를 파악한다. 요약문의 내용을 염두에 두고 지문을 읽으면서 핵심어에 주목한다.
② 핵심어와 반복되는 어휘를 표시해 두었다가 선택지의 표현과 비교해 본다. 보통 지문에 사용되지 않은 표현이 답일 경우가 많으므로 유의한다.

A 정답 1. ⑤ 51%　2. ⑤ 58%　　　　*2023 6월 학평*

해석 평범하지 않은 사건이나 경험이 더 잘 기억되는 경향이 있는데, 그 이유는 당신의 뇌가 기억된 사건들의 창고에서 그것에 접근하려 할 때 그것과 경쟁하는 것이 없기 때문이다. 다시 말해, 2주 전 목요일에 아침 식사로 무엇을 먹었는지 기억하기 어려울 수 있는 이유는 아마도 그 목요일이나 그 특정 아침 식사에 대해 특별한 것이 없었기 때문이다. 그 결과, 당신의 모든 아침 식사 기억은 아침 식사에 대한 일종의 일반적인 인상으로 합쳐진다. 여러분의 기억력은 유사한 사건들을 병합하는데, 그렇게 하는 것이 더 효율적일 뿐만 아니라, 이것은 우리가 어떤 것들을 배우는 방법의 기본이기 때문이다. 우리의 뇌는 경험을 함께 묶는 추상적인 규칙들을 추출한다.
이것은 일상적인 것들에 특히 해당된다. 만약 당신의 아침 식사가 항상 같다면(가령 우유와 시리얼, 오렌지 주스 한 잔, 커피 한 잔), 당신의 뇌가 특정한 한 아침 식사에서 그 세부 사항을 추출하는 것은 쉽지 않다. 그럼 아이러니하게도, 일상화된 행동의 경우, 당신은 그 행동의 일반적인 내용(당신이 먹었던 것처럼, 당신은 항상 같은 것을 먹기 때문에)은 기억할 수 있지만, 그 한 가지 예의 세부 사항들(쓰레기 트럭이 지나가는 소리나 창문을 지나치는 새소리 등)은 그것이 매우 특이하지 '않다면' 기억하기 매우 어려울 수 있다. 반면에, 만약 당신이 당신의 일상을 깨뜨리는 특이한 일을 했다면 — 어쩌면 당신은 아침 식사로 남은 피자를 먹고 드레스 셔츠에 토마토소스를 쏟았을 수도 있다 — 당신은 그것을 덜(→ 더) 기억하기 쉽다.

A1
해설 특별한 사건일수록 기억이 잘 난다는 내용의 첫 문장이 주제문이다. 따라서 제목으로 가장 적절한 것은 ⑤ '사건이 더 특이할수록 기억은 더 생생하다'이다.

오답 풀이

선택률	보기 해석
① 9%	반복이 기억력을 예리하게 만든다!
② 10%	당신의 기억은 어떻게 왜곡되는가?
③ 8%	작업을 일상화할 때의 고려사항
④ 21%	경험들을 병합하기: 세부 사항을 기억하는 데 핵심

A2
해설 마지막 문장의 On the other hand 뒤로는 아침에 평소와 다른 메뉴를 먹고 토마토소스까지 옷에 쏟은 '특별한' 상황을 언급하고 있다. 이 경우 첫 문장에서 언급했듯 기억이 '더 잘' 날 것이므로, (e)에는 less 대신 more를 써야 문맥상 적합하다. 따라서 어색한 낱말은 ⑤이다.

오답 풀이

선택률	보기 해석
① 11%	difficult(어려운)
② 4%	merges(병합하다)
③ 12%	routine(일상적인)

| ④ 16% | particulars(세부 사항) |

구문 풀이 **14행**

~ **particulars to that one instance can be very difficult to call up** (such as the sound of a garbage truck going by or a bird that passed by your window) ~.
→ 본래 가주어-진주어가 포함된 <it is very difficult to call up particulars to that one instance ~>에서, 진주어인 to부정사의 목적어를 문장 전체의 주어로 올려 <particulars ~ can be very difficult to call up>으로 바꾸었다.

구문 **플러스** 목적어 상승 구문

<가주어-진주어> 구문에서 to부정사의 목적어를 문장 전체의 주어로 올려 문장을 다시 구성한 형태를 말한다. 문장에 difficult, easy, hard, impossible 등의 형용사가 있을 때 이런 재구성이 가능하다.

Music is **easy** for us **to appreciate**.
(= It is **easy** for us **to appreciate** music.)

B 정답 1. ④ 83%　2. ③ 85%　　　　*2022 6월 학평*

해석 (A) 한 사업가가 비행기에 탑승했다. 그의 자리에 도착한 후, 그는 여행 동반자들과 인사를 나누었다. (그 동반자들이란) 창가에 앉아 있는 중년 여성과 통로 쪽 좌석에 앉아 있는 어린 소년이었다. 가방을 머리 위 짐칸에 넣은 후, 그는 그들 사이에 앉았다. 비행기가 이륙한 후, 그는 어린 소년과 대화를 시작했다. 그는 그의 아들과 나이가 비슷해 보였고 색칠 공부 책을 칠하느라 바빴다.
(D) 그는 소년에게 그의 나이, 취미, 좋아하는 동물과 같은 몇 가지 일상적인 질문을 했다. 그는 그런 어린 소년이 혼자 여행하는 것이 이상하다고 생각해서 그가 괜찮은지 확인하기 위해 그를 지켜보기로 했다. 비행 시작 1시간여 만에 비행기가 갑자기 난기류를 타기 시작했다. 조종사는 악천후를 만났기 때문에, 안전벨트를 매고 침착하라고 모든 사람들에게 말했다.
(B) 비행기가 여러 차례 오르락내리락하자 사람들은 긴장해 자리에 똑바로 앉았다. 그 남자도 긴장해서 그의 좌석을 최대한 꽉 잡고 있었다. 그러는 동안에도, 어린 소년은 조용히 그의 옆에 앉아 있었다. 그의 색칠 공부 책과 크레용은 앞 좌석 주머니에 가지런히 치워져 있었고, 그의 손은 차분히 다리에 놓여 있었다. 놀랍게도, 그는 전혀 걱정하지 않는 것처럼 보였다.
(C) 그러다가 갑자기 난기류가 끝이 났다. 조종사는 험난한 비행에 대해 사과하고 그들이 곧 착륙할 것이라고 알렸다. 비행기가 하강하기 시작했을 때, 그 남자는 어린 소년에게 말했다, "너는 어린 소년일 뿐이지만, 나는 평생 동안 더 용감한 사람을 만난 적이 없어! 어른들 모두가 두려워하는데 어떻게 그렇게 침착하게 있었는지 말해 주겠니?" 그의 눈을 바라보며, 그는 말했다. "저희 아버지께서 조종사이신데, 아버지께서 저를 집으로 데려가고 있는 중이에요."

B1

해설 (D)에서 비행기가 난기류를 겪기 시작하고, (B)에서 이에 대한 사람들의 반응이 이어진 뒤, (C)에서 왜 소년이 난기류에 당황하지 않았는지 그 이유를 설명하는 흐름이 자연스럽다. 따라서 정답은 ④ '(D)-(B)-(C)'이다.

오답 풀이

선택률	오답 풀이
① 3%	난기류가 시작되는 (D)가 (B)보다 먼저 나와야 한다.
② 3%	난기류가 종료되는 (C)가 맨 마지막에 나와야 한다.
③ 4%	②와 동일
⑤ 5%	②와 동일

B2

해설 (B)에서 소년은 색칠 공부 책과 크레용을 가방이 아닌 좌석 주머니에 넣었다고 하므로, 일치하지 않는 것은 ③이다.

오답 풀이

선택률	오답 풀이
① 4%	(A) he took his place between them
② 2%	(B) As the plane rose and fell several times, people got nervous
④ 3%	(C) he said, "My father is the pilot, and he's taking me home."
⑤ 5%	(D) The pilot told everyone to fasten their seat belts and remain calm

구문 풀이 18행

He found **it** strange **that such a young boy would be traveling alone**, so he decided to keep an eye on him to make sure he was okay.
→ '가목적어-진목적어' 구문이 쓰였다. 가목적어는 it이고, 진목적어는 that절이다.

C 정답 1. ① 79% 2. ⑤ 41% *2021 3월 학평*

해석 시험 점수는 자부심의 척도가 아니지만, 우리는 흔히 우리의 자부심과 우리의 시험 성적을 연관시킨다. "이 시험에 합격하지 못하면 나는 실패자야."와 같은 생각은 사실에 뿌리를 두고 있지 않은 정신적 함정이다. 시험에 실패하는 것은 시험에 실패하는 것이지, 그 이상이 아니다. 그것은 결코 사람으로서의 여러분의 가치를 설명하지 않는다. 시험 성적이 여러분의 미덕을 반영하는 것이라고 믿는 것은 여러분의 수행에 부당한 압력을 가한다. 자격 시험을 통과하지 못한 것은 단지 여러분의 자격 지위가 지연되었다는 것을 의미할 따름이다. 그러므로 긍정적인 태도를 유지하는 것이 중요하다. 만약 여러분이 열심히 공부했다면, 마음속으로 이것을 재확인하고 좋은 성적이 나올 것이라고 믿으라. 다른 한편, 만약 여러분이 했어야 하거나 원하는 만큼 열심히 공부하지 않았다면, 지금으로서는 여러분이 어찌할 수 없는 것으로 그것을 받아들이고 여러분이 할 수 있는 최선의 것을 하는 과제에 주의를 기울이라. 만약 이번에 잘 되지 않는다면, 다음 시험 준비에서는 무엇을 해야 될지 알게 된다. 긍정적인 말로 자신에게 이야기하라. 부차적인 변수에 책임을 지워 과거 또는 미래의 시험 성적을 합리화하는 것을 피하라. "나는 시간이 충분하지 않았어."라거나 "내가 그랬어야 했는데…"와 같은 생각은 시험을 보는 것의 스트레스를 완화시킨다(→ 악화시킨다). 자신의 가치, 자부심, 그리고 시험 과제에 정면으로 맞서는 것에 대한 헌신을 확인함으로써 통제권을 잡으라. "난 할 수 있고 이 시험에 합격할 거야."라고 자신에게 되풀이해 말하라.

C1

해설 시험 성적은 시험 성적일 뿐, 인간으로서의 가치나 미덕을 결정 짓는 것은 아니라는 내용이므로 제목으로는 ① '시험에 대한 태도: 시험일 뿐이다'가 가장 적절하다.

오답 풀이

선택률	보기 해석
② 6%	약간의 스트레스는 성적에 좋다
③ 5%	같이 공부하는 것은 시험에 도움이 된다
④ 5%	반복: 완벽으로의 길
⑤ 4%	건강한 몸: 성공의 열쇠

C2

해설 부차적인 변수에 책임을 지우지 말라고 하였으므로, "나는 시간이 충분하지 않았어." 또는 "내가 그랬어야 했는데…"와 같은 합리화 과정이 스트레스를 ⑤ '완화시킨다'는 설명은 부적절하다. 문맥상 relieve 대신 compound(악화시킨다)가 적절하다.

오답 풀이

선택률	보기 해석
① 7%	descriptive(설명하는)
② 25%	unreasonable(부당한)
③ 10%	Maintaining(유지하기)
④ 15%	accept(받아들이다)

구문 풀이 6행

Not passing the certification test only **means** that your certification status has been delayed.
→ 동명사의 부정은 동명사 바로 앞에 부정어(not)를 쓰고, 동명사 주어는 단수 취급한다.

구문 플러스 준동사(동명사, to부정사, 분사)의 부정

준동사를 부정할 때는 준동사 바로 앞에 부정어(not, never 등)를 쓴다.

I'm sorry for **not coming earlier**.
I decided **never to meet him**.
Not knowing the answer, he felt nervous.

D 정답 1. ① 68% 2. ④ 51% *2020 9월 학평*

해석 미국 민항 산업에는 조종사들이 오류 보고서를 제출하도록 장려하는 매우 효과적인 시스템이 오랫동안 있었다. 이 프로그램은 항공 안

전에 있어 많은 개선점들을 만들어 왔다. 정착이 쉽지는 않았다. 조종사들은 오류를 인정하는 것에 대해 스스로 만들어낸 심한 사회적 압박감을 느꼈다. 더구나, 누구에게 그 오류들을 보고한단 말인가? 분명 그들의 고용주에게는 아닐 것이다. 처벌을 받을 수도 있기에, 미국 연방항공청(FAA)에게는 더욱 아닐 것이다. 해결책은 항공우주국(NASA)에게 조종사들이 그들이 저지른 오류나 다른 조종사에게서 목격한 오류에 대해 반익명의 오류 보고서를 제출할 수 있게 하는 자발적인 사고 보고 체계를 만들도록 시키는 것이었다. 일단 NASA 인사부가 필요한 정보를 얻어내면, 보고서에 있던 연락처를 떼어내어 조종사들에게 돌려 보냈다. 이것은 NASA가 오류를 누가 보고했는지를 더 이상 알지 못한다는 것을 의미했고, 이는 (오류에 대해 제재를 가할 수 있는) 항공사나 FAA가 누가 보고서를 거절했는지(→제출했는지) 아는 것을 불가능하게 만들었다. 만일 FAA가 독립적으로 오류를 발견하고 벌금형 또는 면허정지를 실시하려고 하면, 자기 보고서의 접수가 자동으로 해당 조종사가 처벌받는 것을 면하게 해주었다. 유사한 오류가 충분히 수집되면, NASA는 그것들을 분석하여 보고서와 권고안을 항공사들과 FAA에 발송하곤 했다. 이러한 보고서는 또한 조종사들로 하여금 그들의 오류 보고서가 안전을 높이는 데 유용한 도구였다는 것을 깨닫게 하는 데 도움을 주었다.

D1
해설 민항 산업에서의 안전을 위해 오류를 발견하고 보고하는 시스템의 형태로 이루어져야 하는데, 이를 익명으로 보고하도록 하여 효과를 봤다고 했으므로 ① '무기명 보고서로 세워진 항공 안전'이 제목으로 적절하다.

오답 풀이

선택률	보기 해석
② 6%	유연성이 높은 매뉴얼은 무시된 안전을 의미한다.
③ 13%	예상치 못한 실수에서 나온 위대한 발명품들
④ 7%	새로운 안전 규정에 대한 논쟁들
⑤ 3%	누가 항공 기술을 혁신하고 있는가?

D2
해설 반익명의 형태로 사고를 자발적으로 보고하고 제출하게 했다는 설명만 나올 뿐, 보고서를 누가 '거절했는지'에 대한 언급은 없다. 따라서 ④가 흐름상 가장 어색하며, 이는 submitted로 대체되어야 한다.

오답 풀이

선택률	보기 해석
① 7%	admitting(인정하기)
② 13%	voluntary(자발적인)
③ 22%	detach(떼어내다)
⑤ 5%	valuable(유용한, 가치 있는)

구문 풀이 11행

This meant that NASA no longer knew who had reported the error, which **made it impossible** for the airline companies or the FAA (which enforced penalties against errors) **to find out** who had submitted the report.
→ 관계대명사 which절에 <make+가목적어(it)+목적격 보어(impossible)+진목적어(to find out ~)>의 5형식이 쓰였다. 가목적어 it에 진목적어는 to

find out ~이다.

구문 플러스' 가목적어 it (2)

5형식 문장의 진목적어인 to부정사 앞에 의미상 주어가 끼어들면 <동사+it+목적격보어(명/형)+for 목적격+to부정사> 형태가 된다.

His strong accent made **it** hard **for us to understand him**.

E 정답 1. ③ 65% 2. ④ 78% *2019 6월 학평*

해석 (A) 6개월 전에 55세의 Billy Ray Harris는 노숙자였다. 그는 Kansas City의 길모퉁이에서 컵을 내밀어 지나가는 사람들에게 잔돈을 구걸하며 살았다. 그러나 그러던 어느 날 그의 인생이 바뀌었다. 2월에 Sarah Darling이 항상 그 자리에 있던 Harris를 지나갔고 약간의 잔돈을 그의 컵에 떨어뜨렸다. 그러나 그녀는 또한 우연히도 그녀의 약혼반지까지 떨어뜨렸다. 비록 Harris가 그 반지를 팔까 생각했지만(그는 그것을 4,000달러로 감정받았다), 며칠 후 그는 그 반지를 Darling에게 돌려주었다. "나는 내가 성자라고 말하려는 것은 아니지만, 나는 악마도 아닙니다."라고 그 때 그는 말했다.
(C) 감사를 표할 한 가지 방법으로 Darling은 Harris에게 그녀가 지니고 있던 현금 전부를 주었다. 그러고 나서 그녀의 남편 Bill Krejci가 Harris를 위한 돈을 모금하기 위해 Give Forward 페이지를 시작하였다. 화요일 오전 중간쯤에 거의 152,000달러가 기부되었다. 주말 동안, 그는 Harris와 그 기부금을 가지고 무엇을 하고자 계획하는지에 대해 이야기를 나누었고 그가 그것을 실현시킬 매우 확고한 계획을 가지고 있다는 것을 알게 되었다.
(D) 기금 관리 조직은 그들 중 누가 예상했던 것보다 훨씬 더 많은 기금을 모았고 단 3개월 만에 사람들이 190,000달러 이상을 기부하였다. Harris는 변호사와 이야기하였는데 그 변호사는 그가 그 돈을 신탁에 넣도록 도와주었다. 그 때 이후로, 그는 차를 살 수 있게 되었고, 집에 돈(보증금)을 걸어 그 집을 그가 직접 고치고 있다. 그리고 그것이 전부가 아니다. 그가 TV에 출연하고 난 후 16년 동안 그를 찾고 있었던 가족들이 그를 찾을 수 있었다.
(B) 그들은 행복하게 재결합하였고 Harris는 이제 그들과의 관계를 위해 애쓰고 있다. 그리고 Kansas City 지역 사회는 Harris와 그의 선행에 대해 잊지 않았다. 그는 "나는 여전히 똑같은 사람 중 몇몇을 봅니다."라며, "하지만 단지 지금은 그들이 다가와서 나에게 잔돈을 주는 대신에, 다가와 악수를 하고 '이봐, 참 훌륭한 일을 했어'라고 말합니다."라고 말한다. Darling의 반지가 그의 컵에 떨어졌던 그 운명의 날 이후로 Harris의 인생은 완전히 달라졌다. "나는 나를 도와주었던 모든 사람에게 감사하고 싶습니다."라고 그는 말한다.

E1
해설 Darling이 잃어버린 반지를 노숙자였던 Harris가 찾아주었다는 (A) 뒤로, Darling 부부가 그를 도우려는 모금을 시작했다는 (C), 모금 활동의 결과와 더불어 Harris가 가족까지 찾게 되었다는 (D)가 차례로 연결되고, (B)는 Harris의 인생이 송두리째 달라졌다는 결말을 제시한다. 따라서 글의 순서로 가장 적절한 것은 ③ '(C)-(D)-(B)'이다.

오답 풀이

선택률	오답 풀이
① 5%	(B)는 이 모든 사건 이후의 삶이므로 맨 마지막에 나온다.
② 14%	①과 동일
④ 7%	①과 동일
⑤ 6%	기금 전에 후원 단체 조직이 먼저이다.

E2

해설 (D)에서 빠른 시간 내에 모금액이 많이 모였다고 하므로, 내용과 일치하지 않는 것은 ④이다.

오답 풀이

선택률	오답 풀이
① 4%	(A) But she also accidentally dropped in her engagement ring.
② 4%	(B) And the Kansas City community hasn't forgotten about Harris and his good deed.
③ 7%	(C) As a way to say thank you, Darling gave Harris all the cash she had with her.
⑤ 4%	(D) After he appeared on TV, his family members who had been searching for him for 16 years were able to find him.

구문 풀이 20행

Harris talked to a lawyer, **who** helped him put the money in a trust.
→ 콤마 다음에 쓰인 관계대명사는 계속적 용법으로, 해석은 and he/she(=a lawyer) ~으로 한다.

구문 플러스 계속적 용법의 who

계속적 용법의 who(m)는 사람 선행사를 보충 설명한다. 선행사는 who(m) 앞에 바로 붙어 나오지 않아도 된다.

The actor gave an inspiring speech, **who** is known for his charity efforts.
→ 문장을 완결지어 놓고 주어에 대해 보충 설명하는 구조

F 정답 1. ① 62% 2. ④ 44%   *2018 9월 학평*

해석 2000년에 Illinois 대학의 James Kuklinski가 1,000명이 넘는 Illinois의 거주자들에게 복지에 대해 질문한 영향력 있는 실험을 이끌었다. 절반이 넘는 응답자들이 그들의 답이 맞다고 확신한다고 말했지만 사실은 오직 그 사람들의 3퍼센트만이 질문의 답을 절반 넘게 맞혔다. 아마도 더 충격적인 것은, 그들이 맞았다고 가장 확신했던 사람들이 대체로 그 주제에 대해 가장 적게 알았던 사람들이었다. Kuklinski는 이러한 종류의 응답을 "내가 맞았다는 것을 나는 안다"는 신드롬이라 불렀다. "이것은 대부분의 사람들이 그들의 사실적 믿음을 고치는 것에 저항할 뿐만 아니라 또한 그것들(자기가 믿고 있는 사실들)을 가장 고쳐야 할 필요가 있는 바로 그 사람들이 그렇게 할(고칠) 가능성이 가장 적다는 것을 의미한다."라고 그가 말했다. 어떻게 우리는 그렇게 틀리고도, 우리가 맞다고 그렇게 확신할 수 있을까? 정답의 일부는 우리의 뇌가 구성된 방식에 있다. 일반적으로, 사람들은 <u>일관성</u>을 추구하는 경향이 있다. 사람

들이 그들의 기존의 견해들을 강화하는 쪽으로의 시각을 가지고 정보를 해석하는 경향이 있다는 것을 보여주는 상당한 양의 심리학적인 연구조사가 있다. 만약에 우리가 세상에 대해 무언가를 믿는다면, 우리는 우리의 믿음을 확인해주는 어떠한 정보라도 수동적으로 사실이라고 받아들이고, 그렇지 않은 정보는 적극적으로 멀리하는 경향이 더 있다. 이것은 "의도적 합리화"라고 알려져 있다. 일관성이 있는 정보가 정확하든 아니든 간에, 우리는 그것을 사실로, 우리의 믿음에 대한 확인으로 받아들일 것이다. 이것은 우리가 (말로) 서술한 믿음에 더 확신을 갖게 만들고, 그리고 심지어 그것들에 모순되는 사실을 받아들일 가능성을 더 낮게 만든다.

F1

해설 사람들은 일관성을 갖고 싶어하기 때문에 자신의 믿음을 쉽게 바꾸지 않는다는 내용이므로, 제목으로 가장 적절한 것은 ① '믿음이 사실을 이긴다'이다.

오답 풀이

선택률	보기 해석
② 7%	여전히 외모로 판단하는가?
③ 10%	당신에게 필요한 모든 것은 동기부여이다
④ 7%	합리적 추론을 촉진하라
⑤ 11%	오류를 제때 고쳐라

F2

해설 사람들이 쉽게 견해를 바꾸지 않는다는 내용의 글이므로 그들이 ④ '일관성'을 추구하는 경향이 있다고 해야 적절하다.

오답 풀이

선택률	보기 해석
① 9%	diversity(다양성)
② 27%	accuracy(정확성)
③ 11%	popularity(인기)
⑤ 6%	collaboration(협동)

구문 풀이 16행

This **is known as** "motivated reasoning."
→ <be known as>는 '~라고 알려지다'라는 의미이다.

구문 플러스 be known + 전치사

'알려져 있다'는 의미의 수동태 be known은 다양한 전치사와 결합한다. be known as(~라고 알려지다), be known to(~에게 알려지다), be known for(~로 알려지다) 등이 있다.

• That woman **is known as** a famous singer.
• That woman **is known to** the police.
• That woman **is known for** the quickness of her wit.

해석　(A) 1990년대 후반에, 내가 청각장애인을 가르치는 공립 초등학교로 한 가족이 방문하였다. 그들은 이 지역으로 이사 와서 청각장애인 딸을 1학년으로 입학시킬 것이라고 말했다. 딸의 유치원 선생님이 그들에게 딸에 대하여 학업적으로 큰 희망을 갖지 말라고 주의를 주어서 부모들은 언짢아했다. 그 선생님은 평가 결과에 근거하여 그들의 어린 딸의 미래에 대하여 희망 없는 그림(전망)을 그렸다. 부모 뒤에는 빛나는 긴 갈색 머리와 반짝이는 짙은색 눈을 한 예쁜 다섯 살 난 아이 Kathy가 서 있었다. 부모가 있는 내내, 그녀는 심지어 부모가 시켜도, 소리를 내거나 수화를 사용하거나 하지 않았다.

(C) Kathy와 함께한 몇 주가 지난 후, 나는 매우 영리하고 의지력이 강한 아이를 맡고 있다는 것을 발견하였다. 나는 그녀를 다양한 학습 활동에 참여하게 할 수 있었지만, 글쓰기는 계속 힘든 일이었다. 나는 그녀가 작문 시간에 흥미를 갖도록 모든 것을 시도했지만 그녀는 어떤 것도 쓰는 것을 거부하곤 했다.

(D) 어느 날, Kathy는 버스에서 내린 후 학교 앞에서 울며 서 있었다. 거기에 있던 학교 직원은 그녀가 왜 울고 있는지 물어볼 만큼 충분한 수화를 알지 못했다. 마침내, 그 직원은 Kathy를 사무실로 데려와서 펜과 메모장을 건네주었다. Kathy는 "PAC BAK"이라고 썼다. 그녀는 즉시 아이가 버스에 책가방을 놓고 왔다는 것을 알아차렸다. 그녀는 버스를 다시 학교로 불렀고, 곧 Kathy는 자신의 책가방과 다시 만날 수 있었다.

(B) 그 날 Kathy는 펜의 힘을 발견하였다. 그때부터, 그녀는 글쓰기에 대해 새롭게 인식하게 되었다. 그녀는 지금은 젊은 여성이고, 뛰어난 작가, 연설가, 학생 리더이다. 그녀의 고등학교 졸업반 때, Kathy는 Douglas County Rodeo Queen이 되었고, 다음 해에 교사가 되려고 University of Northern Colorado에 입학하였다. Kathy는 계속 연락을 해오고 있으며, 나는 특히 학기말 과제가 첨부된 그녀의 이메일을 소중하게 여긴다. 이 젊은 여성은 매우 뛰어난 필력을 발휘한다!

G1

해설　Kathy 가족이 이사를 온 뒤, (C) Kathy가 원래는 글쓰기를 거부하였지만, (D) 가방을 잃어버렸다가 다시 찾은 후에 (B) 글쓰기에 매진하게 되었다는 흐름이 적합하다. 따라서 순서로는 ③ '(C)-(D)-(B)'가 적절하다.

오답 풀이

선택률	오답 풀이
① 6%	(B)는 가방 사건(D)의 결과이므로 (D)보다 뒤에 나와야 한다.
② 5%	①과 동일
④ 9%	(C)는 가방 사건(D) 이전의 이야기이므로 (C)가 (D)보다 먼저 나와야 한다.
⑤ 11%	④와 동일

G2

해설　(D)에서 'Kathy가 자신의 책가방과 다시 만날 수 있었다'고 했으므로 ⑤는 적절하지 않다.

오답 풀이

선택률	오답 풀이
① 5%	(A) They said ~ their deaf daughter as a first grader.
② 5%	(A) Standing behind them was Kathy, a beautiful five-year-old ~
③ 5%	(B) ~ she enrolled at the University ~ to become a teacher.
④ 7%	(C) ~ but she would refuse to write anything.

구문 풀이　3행

They **were upset** that their child's kindergarten teacher cautioned them not to have high hopes for her academically.

→ upset 뒤의 that은 '언짢은' 이유를 설명하는 부사절을 이끈다.

구문　플러스⁺　부사절 접속사 that

① 감정형용사 뒤에서 감정의 이유를 설명
② <so ~ that …> 구문에서 주절의 결과를 설명

I'm **happy that** you got the job. → '기쁜' 이유
He was **so** disappointed at the result **that** he couldn't even eat anything. → '실망'의 결과

유형　플러스⁺　장문의 이해

장문의 지문을 읽고 해당 지문과 관련된 여러 유형의 문제를 동시에 풀어야 한다. 주로 다음과 같은 조합으로 하나씩 출제된다.

① 주제or제목 + 빈칸or어휘 → 최근에는 주로 어휘만 나옴
　- 소재를 둘러싼 논리와 맥락을 올바르게 파악하여야 한다.
② 순서 + 지칭 + 내용불일치
　- 스토리의 흐름과 구체적인 내용을 빠르게 파악하여야 한다.